PROPERTY

By

Steven L. Emanuel

Harvard Law School, J.D. 1976

Property, 4th Edition (1993-94)
Emanuel Publishing Corp. • 1865 Palmer Avenue • Larchmont, NY 10538

for my mother

Abbreviations Used in Text

CASEBOOKS

B,C&S — Browder, Cunningham, et. al., *Basic Property Law*
(5th Ed. 1989)

C&J — Cribbet, Johnson, et. al., *Cases and Materials on Property*
(6th Ed. 1990)

C&L — Casner and Leach, *Cases and Text on Property*
(3rd Ed. 1984, with 1989 Supplement)

D&K — Dukeminier and Krier, *Property* (3rd Ed. 1993)

R&K — Rabin and Kwall, *Fundamentals of Modern Real Property Law*
(3rd Ed. 1992)

HORNBOOKS AND TREATISES

A.L.P. — A.J. Casner, Ed., *American Law of Property*,
(1952, with 1976 Supplement)

Brown — Ray Brown, *The Law of Personal Property* (3d Ed. 1975)

Burby — William Burby, *Handbook of the Law of Real Property* (3d Ed. 1965)

Cribbet — John Cribbet, *Principles of the Law of Property* (3d Ed. 1989)

C,S&W — Cunningham, Stoebuck & Whitman, *The Law of Property*
(2nd Ed. 1993)

Land Use Nutshell — Wright and Webber, *Land Use in a Nutshell*
(2d Ed. 1985)

Moynihan — Cornelius Moynihan, *Introduction to the Law of Real
Property* (1962)

Nutshell — Roger Bernhardt, *Real Property in a Nutshell* (2d Ed. 1981)

Powell — Powell and Rohan, *Powell on Real Property* (Abridged Ed., 1968)

Williams — Norman Williams, *American Planning Law: Land Use
and the Police Power* (1974, with 1985 Supplement)

RESTATEMENTS

Rest. — *Restatement of the Law of Property* (1936)

Rest.2d — *Restatement of the Law Second, Property (Landlord & Tenant;
Donative Transfers)* (1977-79; 1983, 1986)

(This page intentionally left blank)

CASEBOOK CORRELATION CHART

(**Note:** general sections of the outline are omitted from this chart. **NC** = not directly covered by this casebook.)
Updates to this chart can be found at our web site — **http://www.emanuel.com**

Emanuel's Property Outline *(by chapter and section heading)*	Dukeminier & Krier **Property** (4th ed. 1998)	Cribbet, Johnson, Findley, & Smith **Cases and Materials on Property** (7th Ed. 1996)	Browder, Cunningham, Nelson, Stoebuck, & Whitman **Basic Property Law** (5th ed. 1989)	Donahue, Kauper & Martin **Property** (3rd Ed. 1993)	Casner & Leach **Cases and Text on Property** (3rd ed. 1984)
CHAPTER 2 **POSSESSION AND REAL TRANSFER OF PROPERTY**					
I. Rights of Possessors	3-59, 99-116	65-76, 97-125, 145-66	24-43	2-42, 45-63, 261-71	9-28, 29, 65-88
II. Accession	15-16	167-75	NC	NC	23, 178
III. *Bona Fide* Purchasers	157, 160, 165-67	135-44	814, 819-31	44	137-181
IV. Bailments	101-02	126-133	97-111	42-43	29-49
V. Gifts	168-84	176-98	701-48	319-46	89-125
CHAPTER 3 **ADVERSE POSSESSION**	117-68, 573-76, 862-63, 867	162-66, 1320-40	44-97	63-106	49-64, 878-80
CHAPTER 4 **FREEHOLD ESTATES**					
I. Introduction	185-99	199-215	202-07	384-87	185-207
II. Fee Simple	199-206, 229, 259-60, 272	215-26, 239-59	207-18	387-89, 391-97	208-212
III. Fee Tail	205-10	259-64	218-22	389-91	213-218
IV. Life Estates	210-28, 253-55, 275-76	226-39	222-23	397-402	218-219
CHAPTER 5 **FUTURE INTERESTS**					
I. Possibility of Reverter and Right of Entry	230-39, 246-43, 257, 259-60, 297-300	244-45, 255-59	225-27	499-505 407-18	212, 290, 291-93
II. Reversions	210, 257-59	265	225	407-18	290-91
III. Remainders	210, 257, 261-66	265-74	227-39	430	293-302
IV. Rule in Shelley's Case	284-86	274-78	242-44	431	302-10
V. Doctrine of Worthier Title	286-87	278-84	244-45	418-28	310-16
VI. Statute of Uses and Executory Interests	266-75	284-315	239-42		317-335
VII. Waste	224-25, 532-534	234-39	253-66	402-06	72, 413
VIII. Rule Against Perpetuities	291-319	295-97, 308-15	246-49	428-29, 471-99	335-51
IX. Restraints Upon Alienation	204205, 210-17, 245-46, 253-55	297	249-53	431-33, 449-71	351-52
CHAPTER 6 **MARITAL ESTATES**					
I. Rights During Marraige	360-76	321-24	276, 280-82, 324-27	435-37, 530-34, 564-71	219-21
II. Effect of Divorce	376-93, 396-97	NC	NC	553-64	NC
III. Death of a Spouse (Dower and Curtesy)	393-97	324-25	266-76	436-37, 505-09, 542-53	221-28
IV. Community Property	397-404	326-28	276, 324-27	442, 557-64 539-40, 546	238-43

CASEBOOK CORRELATION CHART (Continued)

Emanuel's Property Outline *(by chapter and section heading)*	Dukeminier & Krier **Property** (4th ed. 1998)	Cribbet, Johnson, Findley, & Smith **Cases and Materials on Property** (7th Ed. 1996)	Browder, Cunningham, Nelson, Stoebuck, & Whitman **Basic Property Law** (5th ed. 1989)	Donahue, Kauper & Martin **Property** (3rd Ed. 1993)	Casner & Leach **Cases and Text on Property** (3rd ed. 1984)
CHAPTER 7 **CONCURRENT OWNERSHIP**					
I. **Joint Tenancy**	321-40	317-21, 328-32, 349-78, 389-98	277-80, 283-302	438-39, 510-16	254, 255-59
II. **Tenancy in Common**	322-23	316-17	282-83	439, 516-20	254, 257-59
III. **Tenancy by the Entirety**	323-24, 363-70	321-23, 378-89	280-82	439, 530-39	254, 257, 260-67, 281
IV. **Relations between Co-tenants**	340-60	332-49	300-04, 310-14	516-30	268-81
V. **Tax Consequences**	359	397	304-10	540-42	1255, 1269-70
CHAPTER 8 **LANDLORD AND TENANT**	(419-546)	(409-522)	(328-513)	(663-850)	(353-661)
I. **Various Tenancies and Their Creation**					
Estate for (Term of) Years	229, 419-20	434	342-43	434-35, 705	243-44
Periodic Tenancies	229, 420-27	434-35	343, 370-74	435, 706	244-45
Tenancy at Will	421-25, 517	434	343-44	435, 706	246-47
Tenancy at Sufferance	425-31	433-42	344, 346-55	435, 676-80	245, 587-605
II. **Tenant's Right of Possession and Enjoyment**	508-18. 1123-24	409-14, 423-33	384-91, 402-07, 503-13	694-95, 725-33, 741-49	359-63, 459-65, 470-80
III. **Condition of the Premises**	519-29	447-61, 495-501	407-09, 415-34, 436-64	706-15, 749-91	363-75, 465-70, 492-538
IV. **Tort Liability of Landlord and Tenant**	516, 530-31, 533-34	482-89	478-503	737-39, 791-802	375-96
V. **Tenant's Duties**	432, 470-72, 532-34	473-82	409-15	719-25, 741-49	396-422, 607-26 423-43, 480-92
VI. **Landlord's Remdies**	425-31, 484-92, 494-504, 504-07	489-95, 501-09	374-84, 391-402, 434-36	681-91, 695-705, 741-49	
VII. **Transfer and Sale by Lessor; Assignment and Subletting by Lessee**	465-84	510-22	355-70	691-94	553-585
VIII. **Fair Housing / Rent Control Laws**	434-59, 538-40	414-23, 442-47, 462-73	464-78	189-91, 715-19, 802-50	956-61
CHAPTER 9 **EASEMENTS AND PROMISES CONCERNING LAND**					
I. **Easements Generally**	780-83, 854-57	523-25	514-17	889-92	1056-58
II. **Creation of Easements**	783-89, 795-823	525-38, 546-76, 715-26	542-68	294-317, 892-95, 935-50	1058-83
III. **Scope of Easements**	832-42	576-85	568-88	904-12	1089-98
IV. **Transfer and Subdivision of Easements**	823-32	585-90	517-37	912-16, 927-35	1098-1101
V. **Termination of Easments**	842-53	590-95	588-95	951-54	1083-89, 1101-05
VI. **Licenses**	790-95	538-46	537-42	917-27	1106-14
VII. **Covenants Running with the Land**	857-940	595-613	596-628, 631-45, 654-58, 675-83	954-59, 962-81	987-1013
VIII. **Equitable Servitudes**	863-64, 868-72, 873-85, 907-19, 921-40	613-63	629-31, 645-54, 658-75, 683-87	896-904, 959-62, 981-1012	1013-1039

CASEBOOK CORRELATION CHART (Continued)

Emanuel's Property Outline *(by chapter and section heading)*	Dukeminier & Krier **Property** (4th ed. 1998)	Cribbet, Johnson, Findley, & Smith **Cases and Materials on Property** (7th Ed. 1996)	Browder, Cunningham, Nelson, Stoebuck, & Whitman **Basic Property Law** (5th ed. 1989)	Donahue, Kauper & Martin **Property** (3rd Ed. 1993)	Casner & Leach **Cases and Text on Property** (3rd ed. 1984)
CHAPTER 10 **ZONING AND OTHER PUBLIC LAND-USE CONTROLS**					
I. Takings Clause	1123-1216	815-19, 835-900	1000-10, 1040-1108	1082-84, 1096-1173	1166-73
II. Zoning Generally	941-60	759-67	1010-21, 1123-32, 1148-70	1027-28, 1033-40	1116-31
III. Legal Limits of Zoning	949-60, 1012-61	767-71, 907-914, 931-43	1132-48	1040-54, 1077-80	1138-45
IV. Zoning Administration	975-1010	776-82, 790-808	1112-23, 1170-1231	1028-33	1154-66
V. Exclusionary Zoning	1061-88	808-14, 901-07, 914-31	1232-1302	1054-82	1131-37
VI. Regulation of Subdivision and Growth	1010-11, 1088-89	772-76	1303-76	NC	1151-54
VII. Historical and Environmental Preservation	1019, 1159-67	819-35, 931-46	1021-40	1084-96	1145-51
VIII. Eminent Domain	1101-23	782-89	994-1000	862, 903-04, 1097	1166-92
CHAPTER 11 **LAND SALE CONTRACTS, MORTGAGES, AND DEEDS**					
I. Land Sale Contracts	561-600	947-97, 1023-1105	915-32, 947-84	572-90, 647-62	663-706, 716-37
II. Mortgage and Installment Contracts	632-49	997-1023	933-36	590-605	739-54
III. Deeds	600-32, 665-69, 934-40	1106-68	749-809	347-83	755-99
CHAPTER 12 **RECORDING SYSTEM AND TITLE ASSURANCE**					
I. Recording Statutes	651-717	1169-1228	810-47	372-83, 606-15	801-67
II. Title Registration (Torrens System)	717-22	1286-97	908-14	641-46	901-17
III. Method of Title Insurance	722-37	1229-86, 1297-1361	848-90	605-06, 615-41	919-36
CHAPTER 13 **RIGHTS INCIDENT TO LAND**					
I. Nuisance	741-78, 995-97, 1091	663-81	112-31	855-89	1144-45
II. Lateral and Subjacent Support	752-53	681-88	189-201	NC	1195-1204
III. Water Rights	38-39	688-726	148-89	245-60	1205-26
IV. Air Rights	1138-39	735-56	139-46	271-94	1227-42

TABLE OF CONTENTS

ADVERSE POSSESSION

FREEHOLD ESTATES

FUTURE INTERESTS

MARITAL ESTATES

CONCURRENT OWNERSHIP

LANDLORD AND TENANT

EASEMENTS AND PROMISES CONCERNING LAND

ZONING AND OTHER PUBLIC LAND-USE CONTROLS

LAND SALE CONTRACTS, MORTGAGES AND DEEDS

THE RECORDING SYSTEM AND TITLE ASSURANCE

RIGHTS INCIDENT TO LAND

CAPSULE SUMMARY

This Capsule Summary is intended for review at the end of the semester.
Reading it is not a substitute for mastering the material in the main
outline. Numbers in brackets refer to the pages in the main outline
where the topic is discussed.

POSSESSION AND TRANSFER OF PERSONAL PROPERTY

I. RIGHTS OF POSSESSORS:

A. Wild animals: Once a person has gained possession of a *wild animal*, he has rights in that animal superior to those of the rest of the world. [3]

B. Finders of lost articles: The finder of *lost property* holds it *in trust for the benefit of the true owner,* as a bailee. But the finder has rights *superior* to those of everyone except the true owner. (*Example*: P finds logs floating in bay. He takes them and moors them with rope. The logs break loose, and are found by D, who takes them and refuses to return them to P. P may recover the value of the logs from D. P's possession is the equivalent of ownership as against anyone but the true owner.) [4-7]

   1. Statutes of limitations: Although the possessor of goods holds them in trust for the true owner, all states have *statutes of limitations*, at the end of which the true owner can no longer recover the good from the possessor. Usually, the statute of limitations does not start to run until the true owner knows or with reasonable diligence should know the possessor's identity. [8-9]

II. *BONA FIDE* PURCHASERS

A. *Bona fide* purchasers: The problem of the *"bona fide purchaser"* arises when one who is in *wrongful possession of goods* (e.g., a thief, defrauder, finder, etc.) sells them to one who *buys for value* and *without knowledge* that the seller has no title. (This buyer is the "bona fide purchaser" or *b.f.p.*)

   1. General rule: The general rule is that *a seller cannot convey better title than that which he holds* (but subject to exceptions summarized below).

      a. Stolen goods: This general rule is always applied when the seller (or his predecessor in title) has *stolen* the property. (*Example:* X steals a car from P and sells it to Y, who ultimately sells it for fair value to D, who does not know it is stolen. P may recover the car from D, because a possessor of stolen goods can never convey good title, even to a b.f.p.) [10]

   2. Exceptions: But where the goods are acquired from the original owner not by outright theft, but by less blatant forms of dishonesty and/or crime, the b.f.p. may be protected. [11]

      a. "Voidable" title: First, a b.f.p. who takes from one who has a *"voidable"* title (as opposed to the "void" title that a thief has) will be protected. Thus if B obtains goods from A by *fraud* (e.g., B pays with counterfeit money or a bad check), B gets a voidable title, and if he immediately re-sells the goods to C, a b.f.p., A cannot get them back from C.

      b. Estoppel: Also, the owner may lose to the b.f.p. by the principle of **estoppel**. If A expressly or impliedly represents that B is the owner of goods or has the authority to sell them, A cannot recover if C buys the goods in good faith from B. Today, one who entrusts goods to a **merchant** who deals in goods of that type gives the merchant power to transfer full ownership rights to a b.f.p. See UCC §2-402(2). (*Example:* Consumer leaves his watch with Jeweler for repairs. Jeweler is in the business of selling used watches as well as repairing them. Jeweler sells the watch to Purchaser, who pays fair market value and does not suspect that Jeweler does not own the watch. Consumer may not recover from Purchaser.)

III. BAILMENTS

A. Bailments: A **bailment** is the **rightful possession** of goods by one who is **not their owner**. [12]

B. Duty during custody: During the time that the bailee (the person holding the goods) has the object in his possession, he is **not an insurer** of it. He is liable only for **lack of care**, but the precise standard depends on who is benefitted:

    1. Mutual benefit: If the bailment is beneficial to **both parties**, the bailee must use **ordinary diligence** to protect the bailed object from damage or loss. (*Example:* A hotel which takes guests' possessions and keeps them in its safe is liable for lack of ordinary care, such as where it fails to use reasonable anti-theft measures.) [14]

    2. Sole benefit of bailor: If the benefit is solely for the bailor's benefit, the bailee is liable only for **gross negligence**. [14]

    3. Sole benefit of bailee: If the bailment is solely for the benefit of the **bailee** (i.e., the bailor lends the object to the bailee for the latter's use), the bailee is required to use **extraordinary care** in protecting the goods from loss or damage (but he is still not an insurer, and is liable only if some degree of fault is shown). [14]

    4. Contractual limitation: The modern trend is that the parties may change these rules by **contractual** provisions. But even by contract, the bailee generally may not relieve himself from liability for **gross** negligence. [14-15].

      a. Acceptance: Also, for such a provision to be binding, the bailee must know of it and **"accept"** it. [15] (*Example:* P puts his car into a commercial garage run by D. The claim check asserts that D has no liability for negligence. The provision will be binding only if D can prove that P knew of and accepted this provision — D probably cannot make this showing, since P can argue that he regarded the claim check as merely a receipt.)

IV. GIFTS

A. Definition: A gift is a **present transfer** of property by one person to another **without any consideration** or compensation. [16]

B. Not revocable: A gift is generally **not revocable** once made; that is, the donor cannot "take back" the gift. (But gifts "causa mortis," i.e., made in contemplation of death, are revocable if the donor escapes from the peril of death which prompted the gift.)

C. Three requirements: There are three requirements for the making of a valid gift: (1) there must be a **delivery** from the donor to the donee; (2) the donor must possess an **intent** to make a present gift; and (3) the donee must **accept** the gift.

    1. Delivery: For the **delivery** requirement to be met, **control** of the subject matter of the gift must pass from donor to donee. Thus a mere oral statement that a gift is being made will not suffice. [16] (*Example:* O says orally to P, "I'm hereby giving you ownership of my valuable painting," but O does not give P the painting or any written instrument referring to the painting. There is no gift, and O still owns the painting.)

    a. Symbolic and constructive delivery: *"Symbolic"* or *"constructive"* delivery will suffice in the case of property which cannot be physically delivered (e.g., *intangibles*, such as the right to collect a debt from another person), or which would be very inconvenient to deliver (e.g., heavy furniture). That is, delivery of something *representing* the gift, or of something that gives the donee a *means of obtaining* the gift, will suffice. [17-18] (*Example*: O is bedridden and cannot get to his locked bank safe-deposit box in another city. O gives P the key to the box, and tells P that the contents of the box now belong to P. Probably the transfer of the key will meet the delivery requirement as a "constructive delivery" of the box.) [17]

    b. Written instrument: Most courts today hold that a *written instrument* (even if it is not under seal) is a valid substitute for physical delivery of the subject matter of the gift. [18-19] (*Example*: O writes a letter to P saying, "I am hereby giving you my 500 shares of ABC stock as a present." Most courts today will hold that this letter is a written instrument the delivery of which to P meets the delivery requirement, so that physical transfer of the shares themselves is not necessary to make a gift of the shares. But a minority of courts would disagree.)

    c. Gifts *causa mortis*: Courts are generally hostile to gifts *causa mortis* (in contemplation of death). Therefore, they frequently impose *stricter requirements* for delivery in such cases than where the gift is made *inter vivos* with no expectation of death. For instance, courts are less likely to accept symbolic and constructive delivery in lieu of actual physical transfer of the subject matter of the gift.

        i. Revocation: Also, gifts *causa mortis* may be *revoked* if the donor does not die of the contemplated peril (and most courts hold that revocation is *automatic* if the donor recovers). [20-21]

  2. Intent: In addition to delivery, there must be an *intent* on the part of the donor to make a gift. The intent must be to make a *present* transfer, not a transfer to take effect in the future. (A promise to make a *future* gift is not enforceable because of lack of consideration.) [21]

    a. Present gift of future enjoyment: However, a gift will be enforced if the court finds that it is a present gift of the *right* to the subject matter, even though the *enjoyment* of the subject matter is postponed to a later date. [21] (*Example*: O writes to P, "I am now giving you title to my valuable painting, but I want to keep possession for the rest of my life." Most courts would hold that the gift is enforceable, because it was a present gift of ownership, even though enjoyment was postponed to the future.) [22]

  3. Acceptance: The requirement that the gift be *accepted* by the donee has little practical importance. Even if the donee does not know of the gift (because delivery is made to a third person to hold for the benefit of the donee), the acceptance requirement is usually found to be met. However, if the donee *repudiates* the gift, then there is no gift. [22]

D. Bank accounts: One common kind of gift arises out of the creation of a *joint bank account*. For instance, A may deposit in an account called "A and B jointly, with right of survivorship," or "A in trust for B." (The form "A in trust for B" is called a *"Totten Trust"*).

  1. Survivorship rights: Then, if B survives A, B will generally be entitled to *take the balance* of the account unless there is clear evidence that A did not intend this result. Also, the modern rule is that the fact that A reserved the right to *withdraw* funds during his lifetime does not change the fact that B gets the funds on A's death. [22-23]

  2. Rights of parties *inter vivos*: While both parties to the bank account are still *alive*, ownership of the funds depends on the type of account.

a. **Totten trust:** If the account is a ***Totten Trust*** ("A in trust for B"), or the account is in A's name, but with a clause stating "payable on death to B," the courts generally presume that during A's life he has the right to withdraw all funds (but subject to rebuttal by B's showing that A intended an immediate gift). In the case of a ***joint*** account, the modern trend seems to be that during the lifetime of both, the funds belong to the parties in proportion to the net contributions of each, in the absence of a contrary intent. See Uniform Probate Code. [23-24]

ADVERSE POSSESSION

I. ADVERSE POSSESSION GENERALLY

A. Function: All states have ***statutes of limitation*** that eventually bar the owner of property from suing to ***recover possession*** from one who has wrongfully entered the property. (Suits to recover property are called ***"ejectment"*** suits.) Once the limitations period has passed, the wrongful possessor effectively gets ***title*** to the land. This title is said to have been gained by ***"adverse possession."*** [26]

1. **Clears title:** The doctrine of adverse possession also furnishes the additional benefit of ***clearing titles to land***.

   Example: A state has a 20-year statute of limitations on ejectment actions. X claims that he holds title to Blackacre, and wants to sell it to Y. Y will only have to check the land records going back 20 years — plus perhaps some additional period to cover the possibility that the running of the statute of limitations might have been "tolled" for some reason — in order to check X's claim of ownership. The fact that, say, 100 years ago X's alleged "predecessor in title" took the property by wrongfully entering on it, is irrelevant, since the right of the rightful possessor to regain possession has long since been barred by the statute of limitations.

B. Requirements generally: To obtain title by adverse possession, the possessor must satisfy four main requirements: (1) he must actually ***possess*** the property, and this possession must be ***"open, notorious and visible"***; (2) the possession must be ***"hostile,"*** i.e., without the owner's consent; (3) the possession must be ***continuous***; and (4) the possession must be for at least the length of the ***statutory period*** (perhaps longer if the owner was under a disability). [27]

II. OPEN, NOTORIOUS AND VISIBLE

A. "Open, notorious and visible" requirement: The adverse possessor's use of the land must be ***"open, notorious and visible."*** Usually, this means that the possessor's use of the property must be similar to that which a typical owner of ***similar property*** would make. [27] (*Example:* Blackacre is undeveloped wild land suitable only for hunting and fishing. If D builds a small hunting cabin on the land, and enters several times per year to hunt and fish, this will meet the "open, notorious and visible" requirement if a typical owner of similar property would make such limited use. But it would not qualify if a typical owner would use the property more extensively, build a much bigger dwelling, etc.)

III. "HOSTILE" POSSESSION

A. "Hostile" possession: The adverse possession must be ***"hostile."*** This merely means that possession must be ***without the owner's consent***. [29]

   Example: T occupies Blackacre under a lease from O, the record owner. T's possession of the premises is not "hostile" since it is with O's consent, so even if T resides for more than the statutory period, he does not become the owner by adverse possession.

B. Bad faith possessor: A *minority* of courts impose the additional requirement that the possessor must have a *bona fide belief* that he has *title* to the property. Thus in these minority states, a mere *"squatter"* never gets title. [30]

C. Boundary disputes: Adverse possession is most frequently used to resolve mistakes about the location of *boundary lines*. Most courts hold that one who possesses an adjoining landowner's land, under the mistaken belief that he has only possessed up to the boundary of his own land, meets the requirement of "hostile" possession and can become an owner by adverse possession. (*Example*: O is the true owner of Blackacre, and A is the true owner of the adjoining parcel, Whiteacre. When A moves onto Whiteacre, he mistakenly believes that his land goes all the way up to a creek, but the creek is in fact 15 yards into Blackacre. Accordingly, A builds a fence up to the creek, and uses the enclosed portion of Blackacre for farming. At the end of the statutory period, most courts would hold that A becomes the owner of the 15-yard portion by adverse possession.) [31-32]

IV. CONTINUITY OF POSSESSION

A. Continuity of possession: The adverse possession must be *"continuous"* throughout the statutory period, as a general rule. [33]

   1. Interruption by owner: Thus if the owner *re-enters the property* in order to regain possession, this will be an interruption of the adverse possession. When this happens, the adverse possessor must start his occupancy *from scratch*. [33-34]

B. Tacking: Possession by two adverse possessors, one after the other, may be *"tacked"* if the two are in *"privity"* with each other. That is, their periods of ownership can be *added together* for purposes of meeting the statutory period. [34-35]

     Example: A, who owns Whiteacre, adversely possesses a small strip of the adjacent Blackacre, due to confusion about boundaries. A adversely possesses that piece of Blackacre for 15 years; he then sells Whiteacre to P, who holds for another seven years (and who adversely possesses the same strip). A's 15 years of possession can be "tacked" to P's seven years, so that P meets a 20-year limitations period. (In most courts, this is true whether A's deed to P recited the false boundary lines that A and B believe to be correct, or recited the true boundary lines that do not include part of Blackacre.) [35]

   1. No privity: But if the two successive adverse possessors are not in *"privity,"* i.e., do not have some continuity of interest, then *tacking will not be allowed*. [35] (*Example*: A adversely possesses Blackacre for 15 years. He then abandons the property. B then enters for another seven years. B cannot "tack" his holding period to A's holding period, since they had no continuity of interest. But if A had purported to give B his interest by oral gift, deed, bequest or inheritance, then B could tack.)

V. MISCELLANEOUS

A. Length of time: The length of the holding period for adverse possession varies from state to state. It is usually 15 years or longer.

   1. Disabilities: If the true owner of property is under a *disability*, in nearly all states he is given *extra time* within which to bring an ejectment action. (*Example*: Statutes often hold that the running of the limitations period is suspended until the true owner becomes 21. Usually, the person is given an additional time, say 10 years, to sue after he reaches 21.) [36]

**C
A
P
S
U
L
E**

2. **Tacking on owner's side:** There is effectively "tacking" on the **owner's** as well as the possessor's side. (*Example*: O is the owner of Blackacre in 1950, when A enters and begins to adversely possess. In 1960, O conveys to X. Under a 21-year statute, A will gain adverse possession in 1971, even though he has not held for 21 years against either O or X separately.) [37-38]

B. **Rights of adverse possessor:** Once the statutory period expires, the adverse possessor effectively gets **title**. However, the possessor usually cannot **record** title (since he has no deed). But he can apply for a judicial determination of adverse possession, and if he gets it, that determination can be recorded as if it were a deed. [39]

1. **Need to inspect:** Since a title gained by adverse possession usually cannot be recorded, a buyer of property cannot be sure that the record owner still owns it (and that the record owner can therefore convey a good deed) unless the buyer **physically inspects** the property. [39]

2. **Scope of property obtained:** Normally, the possessor acquires title only to the portion of the property **"actually"** occupied. [40]

a. **Constructive adverse possession:** But there is one important exception: by the doctrine of **"constructive"** adverse possession, one who enters property under **"color of title"** (i.e., a written instrument that is defective for some reason) will gain title to the **entire area described in the instrument**, even if he "actually" possesses only a portion. [41]

C. **Conflicts:** If there is a conflict between two person's whose interests are solely possessory, the general rule is that the **first possessor has priority over the subsequent one**. [42]

FREEHOLD ESTATES

I. INTRODUCTION

A. **Estates generally:** One does not really "own" Blackacre. Instead, one owns an "estate in Blackacre." Traditionally, there are two types of estates: **freehold** and **non-freehold**.

1. **Freehold estates:** The three freehold estates are: (1) the **fee simple** (which may be either absolute or defeasible); (2) the **fee tail**; and (3) the **life estate**. [46]

2. **Non-freehold:** The non-freehold estates are: (1) the estate for **years**; (2) the **periodic estate**; and (3) the **estate at will**. [46]

II. THE FEE SIMPLE

A. **Fee simple absolute:** The **fee simple absolute** is the most unrestricted and longest estate. [47]

1. **Inheritable:** The fee simple absolute is **inheritable** under intestacy statutes. Thus if the owner of a fee simple absolute dies, the property passes to the people deemed to be his "heirs" under the intestacy statute of the state where the land is located.

2. **Words to create:** Generally, a fee simple absolute is created by using the words **"and his heirs."** Thus at common law, the only way for O to convey a fee simple absolute to A is for O to convey "to A and his heirs." [47]

a. **Abolished:** But most states have **abolished** the requirement that the phrase "and his heirs" be used. Thus in most states, if O conveys "to A," this will give A a fee simple absolute. [48]

B. Fee simple defeasible: The holder of a fee simple *defeasible* may hold or convey the property, but he and those who take from him must use the property *subject to a restriction*. [48-53]

    1. Three types: There are three types: (1) the fee simple *determinable*; (2) the fee simple *subject to a condition subsequent*; and (3) the fee simple *subject to an executory limitation*.

    2. Determinable: A fee simple *determinable* is a fee simple which *automatically* comes to an end when a stated event occurs (or, perhaps, fails to occur). [48-49]

        a. Restriction on uses: Most often, the fee simple determinable is used to *prevent the property from being put to a certain use* which the grantor opposes. The limitation controls even after the property changes hands numerous times. (*Example*: O owns Blackacre in fee simple. He sells the property "to A and his heirs so long as the premises are not used for the sale of alcoholic beverages." A then purports to convey a fee simple absolute to B, who builds a bar. When the first alcoholic beverage is sold, B's interest *automatically* ends, and the property reverts to O (or his heirs).)

        b. Possibility of reverter: The creator of a fee simple determinable is always left with a *"possibility of reverter,"* i.e., the possibility that title will revert to him if the stated event occurs. (*Example*: In the above example, O, following the conveyance, is left with a possibility of reverter if alcohol is sold.)

        c. Statute of limitations: Many states have enacted *statutes of limitation* which bar a possibility of reverter after a certain period. Some statutes begin to run after the fee simple determinable is created, others don't start to run until the stated event occurs.

        d. Words creating: A fee simple determinable is usually created by words that make it clear that the estate is to end *automatically* upon the occurrence of the stated event. Such words include "so long as . . . ," or "until . . . ," or "during. . . ." Also, if the conveyance says that the property is to *"revert"* to the grantor, that's a sign of a fee simple determinable.

    3. Fee simple subject to condition subsequent: The fee simple *subject to a condition subsequent* is also geared to the happening of a particular event, but unlike the fee simple determinable, the fee simple subject to a condition subsequent *does not automatically end* when the event occurs. Instead, the grantor has a *right of entry*, i.e., a right to *take back* the property — but nothing happens until he *affirmatively exercises that right*. [50]

        a. Words creating: The words that create a fee simple subject to condition subsequent usually have a "conditional" flavor, such as *"upon express condition that . . . ,"* or *"provided that. . . ."* Also, most courts require that there also be a statement that the grantor may *enter the property* to terminate the estate if the stated event occurs. (*Example*: O conveys Blackacre to A and his heirs "but upon condition that no alcohol is ever served; if alcohol is served, Grantor or his heirs may re-enter the property and terminate the estate." A has a fee simple subject to condition subsequent.)

        b. Distinguishing from fee simple determinable: A key difference between the fee simple subject to condition subsequent and the fee simple determinable relates to the *statute of limitations*. When an f.s. determinable is involved, the holders of the possibility of reverter often have a long or unlimited time to sue (see above). But in the case of an f.s. subject to condition subsequent, the statute of limitations usually starts to run upon the occurrence of the stated event, and usually is for a very *short* period — so if the holder of the right of entry does not promptly re-enter or sue, he will lose the right. [51]

    4. **Fee simple subject to executory limitation:** A fee simple *subject to an executory limitation* provides for the estate to pass to a *third person* (one other than the grantor) upon the happening of the stated event. (*Example*: O conveys "to A and his heirs, but if A dies without children surviving him, then to B and his heirs." A has a fee simple subject to an executory limitation.) [52-53]

III. THE FEE TAIL

A. Fee tail generally: The *fee tail* allows the owner of land to ensure that the property *remains within his family* indefinitely. If O conveys a fee tail to his son, A, and the fee tail is enforced, then upon A's death the property will go to A's heir, then to that heir's heir, etc. — A and his decedents can never convey the property outside the family line. (If they try to do so, then the property reverts to O's heirs.) [53]

    1. Words to create: The most common way of creating a fee tail is by a grant "to A and the *heirs of his body*." [53-54]

        a. Death without issue: Also, a *minority* of states recognize a fee tail where the conveyance is by O "to A and his heirs, but if A dies without issue, then to O's heirs." But *most* states hold that this means that O gets back the property only if A *himself* dies without children or grandchildren, not that O's line gets it whenever A's *line* dies out.

B. Modern treatment: Today, in most states a grant or bequest that would be a fee tail at common law is simply *converted* by statute to a *fee simple absolute*. (But a minority of states follow various approaches, including life estate to the grantee, with a remainder in fee simple to his issue.) No states today fully enforce the fee tail as a method of ensuring that property will descend along bloodlines and will not be conveyed outside the family tree. [54-55]

IV. THE LIFE ESTATE

A. Life estate generally: A *life estate* is an interest which lasts for the lifetime of a person. Ordinarily, the lifetime by which the life estate is "measured" is that of the holder of the life estate. (*Example*: O conveys "to A for his lifetime, then to B in fee simple.") [55]

    1. Phrase creating: A life estate is usually created by the words "to A during his life" or "to A for life."

    2. Defeasible: A life estate may be *defeasible*, just as a fee simple may be. [56] (*Example*: O conveys "to A, for so long as she shall remain my widow, then to my son B." A has a life estate determinable.)

    3. Life estate per autre vie: There can be a life estate that is measured by the life of someone other than the grantee. This is called a life estate *"per autre vie"* ("by another life"). [57] (*Example*: O conveys "to A for the life of B, then to C and his heirs." A has a life estate per autre vie.)

        a. Grantee dies before end of measuring life: Today, if the grantee of a life estate per autre vie dies before the end of the measuring life, the balance of the estate is treated as personal property, which passes by will or by intestacy. Thus in the above example, if A died before B, A's interest would pass as provided in A's will or under the intestacy statute.

B. Duties and powers of life tenant:

    1. Duties: The life tenant has a number of duties vis a vis the future interest. Most importantly, he may not commit *waste*, i.e., he may not unreasonably impair the value which the property will have when the holder of the future interest takes possession. Thus he must make reasonable repairs, not demolish the structure, pay all property taxes, etc. [58]

2. **Powers:** The life tenant ***cannot convey a fee simple***, or any other estate greater than the life estate he holds. But he may convey the interest which he does hold, or a lesser one. (*Example*: If A holds a life estate, he may convey to B either for the life of A, or for a term of years.) [58-59]

FUTURE INTERESTS

I. FUTURE INTERESTS GENERALLY

A. **Five future interests:** There are five future estates: (1) the possibility of reverter; (2) the right of entry; (3) the reversion; (4) the remainder; and (5) the executory interest.

II. POSSIBILITY OF REVERTER; RIGHT OF ENTRY

A. **Possibility of reverter and right of entry:** The ***possibility of reverter*** and the ***right of entry*** follow the fee simple determinable and the fee simple subject to a condition subsequent, respectively. [60-62]

1. **Possibility of reverter:** When the owner of a fee simple absolute transfers a fee simple ***determinable***, the grantor automatically retains a ***possibility of reverter***. All states allow this possibility of reverter to be ***inherited***, or to be devised by will; most but not all states also allow it to be conveyed *inter vivos*. [60-61]

2. **Right of entry:** If the holder of an interest in land (e.g., a fee simple absolute) conveys his interest but attaches a ***condition subsequent***, the transferor has a ***"right of entry."*** Most commonly, one who holds a fee simple absolute and who then conveys a fee simple subject to condition subsequent has a right of entry. (*Example*: O owns Blackacre in fee simple absolute. He conveys "to A and his heirs, on condition that liquor never be sold on the premises; if liquor is sold thereon, O or his heirs may re-enter the premises." The conveyance to A is a fee simple subject to condition subsequent, and O therefore reserves a right of entry.) [61]

   a. **Incident to reversion:** Often, a transferor who holds a right of entry also holds a ***reversion***. Thus the typical lease contains various right of entry clauses (e.g., the right to re-enter if the tenant does not pay rent), as well as a reversion at the end of the lease term. [61]

   b. **Alienability:** If the right of entry is incident to a reversion (as in the prior paragraph), it ***passes with the reversion***. (Thus if a landlord sells his property, he will be deemed to have also sold his right of entry to the buyer.) If the right of entry is ***not*** incident to a reversion, in most states the right of entry may be left by will and passes under the intestacy statute, but may not be conveyed *inter vivos*. (But some states allow even the *inter vivos* conveyance). [61]

III. REVERSIONS

A. **Reversions generally:** A ***reversion*** is created when the holder of a vested estate transfers to another a ***smaller estate***; the reversion is the interest which ***remains in the grantor***. (*Example*: A holds a fee simple absolute in Blackacre. He conveys "to B for life." A is deemed to have retained a "reversion," which will become possessory in A (or his heirs) upon B's death.) [62]

1. **Distinguishing from possibility of reverter:** Distinguish between a reversion and a possibility of reverter. If the grantor has given away a fee simple determinable, he retains only a possibility of reverter. If he has given away something ***less*** than a fee simple, he retains a reversion. [63]

2. **Alienability:** Reversions are completely alienable: they may pass by will, by intestacy or by *inter vivos* conveyance. [63]

IV. REMAINDERS

A. **Remainders generally:** A *remainder* is a future interest which can become possessory only upon the *expiration* of a *prior possessory interest*, created by the *same instrument*. [63]

1. **Requirements:** So there are three requirements: (1) the grantor must convey a present *possessory* estate to one transferee; (2) he must create a non-possessory estate in *another* transferee by the *same instrument*; and (3) the second, non-possessory, estate (the remainder) must be capable of becoming possessory only on the *"natural"* expiration (as opposed to the cutting short) of the prior estate. [63]

   Example: O conveys "to A for life, remainder to B and his heirs." B has a remainder because: (1) a present interest was created in A; (2) a future interest was created in someone other than A, by the same instrument; and (3) the second interest (the remainder) will become possessory only after the natural expiration of the first one (i.e., after A's death).

2. **Following a term of years:** Today, we refer to an estate *following a term of years* as a remainder. (*Example*: O conveys "to A for 10 years, then to B and his heirs." Today, B is said to have a remainder, even though this would not have been called a remainder at common law.) [63]

3. **Distinguished from reversion:** Distinguish between the remainder and the reversion. Most importantly, the remainder is created in someone *other than the transferor*, whereas the reversion is an interest left in the transferor after he has conveyed an interest to someone else. [63-64]

4. **No remainder after fee simple determinable:** There cannot be a remainder after any kind of fee simple, including after a *fee simple determinable*. If an interest is created in a third person to follow a fee simple determinable, that interest is called an "executory interest," not a remainder. [64]

B. **Vested remainders:** A remainder is *"vested"* (as opposed to "contingent") if: (1) no *condition precedent* is attached to it; and (2) the person holding it has already been *born*, and his identity is *ascertained*. [65]

   Example: O conveys Blackacre "to A for life, remainder to B and his heirs." B has a vested remainder, since his identity is ascertained, and there is no condition precedent which must be satisfied in order for his interest to become possessory.

1. **Meaning of "condition precedent":** No condition precedent is deemed to exist so long as the remainder will become possessory *"whenever and however the prior estate terminates."* Thus in the above example, no matter how and when A's life estate ends, B's estate will immediately become possessory; therefore, B's remainder is vested. [68]

C. **Contingent remainders:** All remainders that are not vested are *contingent*. A remainder will be contingent rather than vested if: (1) it is subject to a *condition precedent*; *or* (2) it is created in favor of a person who is either *unborn* or *unascertained* at the time of creation. [67-69]

1. **Condition precedent:** The "condition precedent" branch of "contingent" means that if some condition must be met before the remainder could *possibly become possessory*, the remainder is contingent. (*Example:* O conveys "to A for life, then, if B is living at A's death, to B in fee simple." B must meet the condition precedent of surviving A, before his remainder can possibly become possessory. Therefore, B's remainder is contingent.) [68-69]

   a. **Distinguish from condition subsequent:** Distinguish between condition precedent (making the remainder contingent) and condition subsequent (making the remainder vested). If the condition is incorporated into the clause which gives the gift to the remainderman, then the remainder is contingent. But if one clause creates the remainder and a separate *subsequent* clause takes the remainder away, the remainder is vested (subject to divestment by the condition subsequent). [69]

> **Example:** O conveys "to A for life, remainder to B and his heirs, but if B dies before A, to C and his heirs." B's remainder is vested, not contingent, because the condition is not part of the clause giving B his interest, but is instead part of a second added clause. But if the conveyance was "to A for life, then if B survives A, to B and his heirs; otherwise to C and his heirs", B's remainder would be contingent because the condition is incorporated into the very gift to B, making it a condition precedent.

> **Note:** The key phrase *"but if"* indicates a condition subsequent rather than a condition precedent, so it's a clue to a vested rather than a contingent remainder.

2. **Unborn or unascertained:** A remainder is also contingent rather than vested if it is held by a person who, at the time the remainder is created, is either (1) *unborn* or (2) *not yet ascertained*. [69-70]

> **Example of unborn:** O conveys "to A for life, then to the children of B." At the time of the conveyance, B has no children. Therefore, the remainder in the unborn children is contingent. (But a remainder in favor of unborn children, like any other contingent remainder, may *become vested* due to later events. Thus if prior to A's death, B has a child, X, X will now have a vested remainder "subject to open" (in favor of any other children of B born before A's death).)

> **Example of unascertained:** O conveys "to A for life, then to A's heirs." Assuming that the Rule in Shelley's Case (discussed below) is not in force, the heirs have a remainder, and it is contingent. That's because until A dies, it is impossible to say who his heirs are. (At A's death, the remainder will both vest and become possessory.)

3. **Destructibility of contingent remainders:** At common law, a contingent remainder is deemed *"destroyed"* unless it *vests at or before the termination of the preceding freehold estates*. This is the doctrine of *"destructibility of contingent remainders"*. (*Example:* O conveys "to A for life, remainder to the first son of A who reaches 21." At A's death, he has one son, B, age 16. Since B did not meet the contingency (becoming 21) by the time the prior estate (A's life estate) expired, B's contingent remainder is destroyed. Therefore, O's reversion becomes possessory.) [70-74]

   a. **Normal expiration:** One way the contingent remainder can be destroyed is if the preceding freehold estates *naturally terminate* before the condition precedent is satisfied. This is the case in the above example. [71]

   b. **Destruction by merger:** A contingent remainder can also be destroyed because the estate preceding it (usually a life estate) is *merged into* another, larger, estate. The doctrine of merger says that whenever *successive vested estates* are owned by the *same person*, the smaller of the two estates is *absorbed* by the larger. [72]

   > **Example:** O conveys "to A for life, remainder to A's first son for life if he reaches 21, remainder to B and his heirs." When A has a 19-year-old son, A conveys his life estate to B. Since B now has two successive vested estates (the life estate and B's own vested remainder in fee simple), the smaller estate — the life estate — is merged into the fee simple and disappears. Since the son's remainder has not yet vested when A's life estate disappears, the son's contingent remainder is destroyed. [72]

   c. **Destructibility rule today:** About half the states have passed statutes *abolishing the destructibility of contingent remainders*. Some additional states reach this result by case law. [73]

D. Why it makes a difference: Here are the main consequences of the vested/contingent distinction:

1. Rule Against Perpetuities: The consequence that most significantly lives on today relates to the *Rule Against Perpetuities*. Contingent remainders are subject to the Rule Against Perpetuities, but vested remainders are not.

2. Transferability: At common law, the two types of remainders differed sharply with respect to *transferability*. Vested remainders have always been transferable *inter vivos*. Contingent remainders, on the other hand, were basically not transferable *inter vivos*. But today, in most states, contingent remainders, too, are transferable *inter vivos*.

3. Destruction: At common law a contingent remainder was *destroyed* if it did not vest upon termination of the proceeding life estate (the doctrine of "destruction of contingent remainders discussed above.") There was no comparable doctrine destroying vested remainders. But this distinction is not as significant today, because as noted above most states have abolished the doctrine of destruction of contingent remainders.

V. RULE IN SHELLEY'S CASE

A. Rule generally: The *Rule in Shelley's Case* provides: *if a will or conveyance creates a freehold in A, and purports to create a remainder in A's heirs* (or in the heirs of A's body), and the estates are *both legal or both equitable, the remainder becomes a remainder in A*. Usually, the result is that A ends up getting a fee simple. [74]

> **Example:** O conveys "to A for life, remainder to A's heirs." If there were no Rule in Shelley's Case, the state of the title would be: life estate in A, contingent remainder in A's heirs, reversion in O. But by operation of the Rule in Shelley's Case, the state of the title becomes: life estate in A, remainder in A (not A's heirs). Then, by the doctrine of merger, A's life estate will merge into his remainder in fee simple, and A simply holds a present fee simple.

1. Freehold in ancestor: For the Rule to apply, there must be a *freehold estate* given to the ancestor. Basically, this means that the ancestor must have a *life estate*. [75]

2. Remainder in heirs or heirs of the body: There must be a *remainder*, and it must be in the *heirs of the ancestor*, or in the *heirs of the ancestor's body*. [76]

    a. Can't be executory interest: This means that the heirs (or heirs of the body) cannot have an *executory interest* (as opposed to a remainder).

3. Life estate and remainder separated by other estate: The Rule applies even if there is *another estate* between the life estate and the remainder. Thus the Rule may apply even though there is no *subsequent merger* of the life estate and the remainder. (*Example*: O conveys "to A for life, remainder to B for life, remainder to A's heirs." Since there is both a life estate in A and a remainder in his heirs, the Rule in Shelley's Case applies, to transform the remainder into one in A. But there is no merger, because of the vested life estate in B separating the two. Thus the title is: life estate in A, vested remainder for life in B, vested remainder in fee simple in A.) [77]

B. Modern treatment: About two-thirds of the states have enacted statutes *abolishing the Rule*. But the remaining states still apply the common-law version. Also, some of the statutory abolitions apply only to wills, not to *inter-vivos* deeds. [78]

VI. DOCTRINE OF WORTHIER TITLE

A. Doctrine generally: The Doctrine of Worthier Title provides that *one cannot, either by conveyance or will, give a remainder to one's own heirs*. [78] (We are interested only in the "conveyance," or *"inter vivos,"* aspect of the Doctrine, since that is the only aspect that remains important today.)

     1. Consequence: The consequence of the Doctrine of Worthier Title is that if the owner of a fee simple attempts to create a life estate or fee tail estate, with a remainder to his own heirs, the remainder is *void*. Thus the grantor *keeps a reversion*. (This is why the Doctrine is sometimes called the *"rule forbidding remainders to grantors' heirs."*) [79]

         Example: O conveys "to A for life, remainder to O's heirs." The Doctrine of Worthier Title makes the remainder void. Consequently, O is left with a reversion. He is thus free to convey the reversion to a third party; if he does so, his heirs will get nothing when he dies, even if he dies intestate.

B. Rule of construction: In most states, the Doctrine has been transformed into a *rule of construction*. That is, the Doctrine only applies where the grantor's language, and the surrounding circumstances, indicate that he *intended to keep a reversion*. So in most states, the Doctrine today just establishes a presumption that a reversion rather than a remainder in the grantor's heirs is really intended. [79]

VII. EXECUTORY INTERESTS AND THE STATUTE OF USES

A. Statute of Uses: The Statute of Uses provides that any *equitable estate* is *converted into the corresponding legal estate*. [83]

     1. Equitable estates: An equitable estate is similar to a trust: if O conveys "to T and his heirs, to the use of A and his heirs," then T's estate is "legal" and A's estate is "equitable." (So look for the phrase "to the use of," which means that the person named following the phrase gets an equitable interest.)

     2. Operation of Statute: The Statute of Uses converts any equitable estate into the corresponding legal estate. (*Example:* O conveys Blackacre "to T and his heirs, to the use of A and his heirs." The Statute of Uses transforms A's equitable fee simple into a legal fee simple. T's legal estate is nullified. So the state of title is simply: legal fee simple in A.)

B. Modern executory interests: The Statute of Uses makes possible modern "shifting" *executory interests*. [84-85]

     1. Shifting executory interests: A *"shifting* executory interest" is a legal estate in someone other than the grantor, that *cuts short* a prior legal interest. [84]

         Example: O, who owns Blackacre, "bargains and sells" it — i.e., he creates an equitable estate in it — "to A and his heirs, but if the premises are ever used for other than residential purposes, then to B and his heirs." The bargain and sale raises a use in A in fee simple subject to condition subsequent, and a use in B. The Statute of Uses executes both of these uses, so title becomes: fee simple in A subject to an executory limitation, and a shifting executory interest in fee simple in B. If A or his heirs fail to use the property for residential purposes, the gift over to B will take effect.

     2. Distinguish equitable interest from remainder: Distinguish between an executory interest and a remainder. The difference is that a remainder *never cuts off* a prior interest, but merely awaits the prior interest's *natural termination*. An executory interest, by contrast, *divests* or *cuts off* a prior interest before the latter's natural termination. (*Example 1*: O bargains and sells "to A for life, then to B and his heirs if B survives A, otherwise to C and his heirs." B and C each have contingent remainders. *Example 2*: O bargains and sells "to A for life, then to B and his heirs, but if B should die before A, to C and his heirs." Here B's interest is vested subject to divestment because the "but if . . . " divesting language comes in a separate clause, and C's interest is therefore an executory interest.) [86]

3. **Statute of Uses today:** The Statute of Uses is still in force. Thus a "bargain and sale" deed will generally create a legal estate. Even where the Statute is not in force, the modern deed can be used to produce the same result (e.g., shifting executory interests, which will cut off prior interests). [88]

VIII. THE RULE AGAINST PERPETUITIES

A. Rule Against Perpetuities generally:

1. **Statement of Rule:** The Rule Against Perpetuities can be summarized as follows: *"No interest is good unless it must vest, if at all, not later than 21 years after some life in being at the creation of the interest."* Try to memorize this phrase. [92]

2. **Paraphrase:** Paraphrasing, an interest is invalid unless it can be said, with absolute certainty, that it will either *vest or fail to vest*, before the end of a period equal to: (1) a life in existence (and specified in the document creating the interest) at the time the interest is created plus (2) an additional 21 years.

> **Example:** O conveys Blackacre "to A for life, remainder to the first son of A whenever born who becomes a clergyman." At the date of the conveyance, A has no son who is presently a clergyman. Viewing the matter from the date of the conveyance, it is possible to imagine a situation in which the remainder to the son could vest later than lives in being plus 21 years. Thus A's son could be born to A after the date of the conveyance, and this son could become a clergyman more than 21 years after the death of A, and more than 21 years after the death of all of A's sons living at the time of the conveyance. (A and A's sons living at the time of the conveyance are the "measuring lives," since they're living people specifically mentioned in the conveyance.) Since this remote vesting is possible — even though unlikely — the contingent remainder is *invalid*. This is so even though it *actually turns out* that A has a son alive before the date of the conveyance who ultimately becomes a clergyman.

3. **Judged in advance:** As the above example shows, the common-law version of the Rule requires that the validity of the interest be judged *at the time it is created*, not at the time the interest actually vests. So if it is *theoretically possible* (even though very unlikely) that the interest will vest later than 21 years after the expiration of lives in being, the interest is invalid. This is true even if it actually turns out that the interest vests before the end of lives in being plus 21 years. (But see the discussion of "wait and see" statutes below.) [93]

B. Applicability of Rule to various estates:

1. **Contingent remainders:** The Rule applies to *contingent remainders*. [93]

> **Example:** O conveys "to A for life, remainder to the first son of A to reach the age of 25 and his heirs." At the time of the conveyance, A does not have a son who has reached the age of 25. The remainder in the unborn son is contingent, rather than vested, since it is not yet known which son if any will reach the age of 25. Since there is a possibility of remote vesting, the gift to the oldest son violates the Rule and is invalid.

2. **Vested remainder:** A *vested* remainder, by contrast, can *never* violate the Rule, because a vested remainder *vests at the moment it is created*. [93]

> **Example:** O conveys "to A for life, remainder to A's children for life, remainder to B and his heirs." The gift to B and his heirs does not violate the Rule, because that gift

is a vested remainder, which vested in interest (though not in possession) on the date of the conveyance. Therefore, even though the remainder to B and his heirs might not become possessory until later than lives in being plus 21 years (as where A's last surviving child is one who was not born on the date of conveyance, and who dies after age 21), the gift to B is valid. [93]

3. Reversion: The Rule does **not** apply to **reversionary interests** (reversions, possibilities of reverter, and rights of entry). These are deemed to vest as soon as they are created. [93-94]

4. Executory interests: The Rule applies to **executory interests**, because such interests are **not vested** at their creation. [94]

> **Example**: O conveys "to the City of Klamath Falls, so long as the city maintains a library on the property, then to A and his heirs." The executory interest in A violates the Rule, because it might vest beyond lives in being plus 21 years — the city might maintain a library on the property longer than any life in being at the time of the gift plus 21 years. Therefore, instead of the executory interest in A being valid, O and his heirs have a possibility of reverter which will become possessory if the city ever stops using the library.

5. Options to purchase land: An **option** to **purchase land** will often be subject to the Rule. [94-95]

> **a. Option as part of lease:** If an option to purchase property is part of a **lease** of that property and is exercisable only during the lease term, then the option is **not** subject to the Rule.

> **b. Option "in gross":** But if the option is **not** part of a lease or other property interest, most states hold that the Rule **does** apply. Such an unattached option is called an option **"in gross."** (*Example:* O sells Blackacre to A, with the condition that if at any time the property is used for the sale of alcohol, O or his heirs may repurchase the property for the amount originally paid by A. Since there is no time limit to this option, and since the option is not attached to any lease or continuing interest by O, the option is void as a violation of the Rule.)

C. "Lives in being": Normally, "lives in being" means one or more persons who are **actually mentioned** in the conveyance or bequest. These are sometimes called **"measuring lives."** [95] (*Example:* O conveys "to my daughter D for life, then to her first child to reach the age of 21." D is childless at the date of the conveyance. D is the "life in being" or "measuring life." The contingent remainder to D's oldest child is valid, because we know that any child D may eventually have will reach 21 within 21 years after D's death.)

D. Special situations: At common law, there are some remote possibilities that nonetheless count for the purposes of the Rule:

1. Fertile octogenarian: There is a conclusive presumption that any person, regardless of age or physical condition, is capable of **having children**. This is the **"fertile octogenarian"** rule, which will sometimes make a reasonable gift invalid. [96]

> **Example**: T conveys "to A for life, then to A's surviving children for life, then to the surviving children of B." At the time of T's death, B has three children, and B herself is 80 years old. But it is conceivable that B could now have another child, and that that child would take after lives in being plus 21 years — for instance, all of A's children might be born after T's death, and might die more than 21 years after T's death. Therefore, B's three now-living children will not take anything since their interest violates the Rule. It doesn't matter that B could not possibly have any further children as a medical matter.

2. **Unborn widow:** Similarly, if a conveyance or bequest is made to the "widow" of X, at common law this is held not to refer to the person who is now married to X, and may refer to a person who is not yet even a life-in-being. This is the ***"unborn widow"*** rule. [96] (*Example:* In 1975, T bequeaths Blackacre "to A for life, then to A's widow." At the time of T's death, A is married to B. It is possible that B will either predecease or divorce A, and that A will then marry someone born after 1975. This other person would be a life not yet in being, so the bequest to "A's widow" is invalid, under the strict common law approach.) (But a modern court might accept evidence that T intended "A's widow" to refer to B in particular, in which case the gift will be valid.)

3. **Class gifts:** If a gift is made to all members of a ***class***, the entire gift fails unless it can be said that ***each member of the class*** must have his interest vest or fail within lives in being plus 21 years. This rule will be triggered if the class could ***obtain new members*** following a testator's death. [97]

> **Example:** T bequeaths property "to A, then to A's surviving children who attain the age of 25." At the time of the bequest, A has two children, B and C. It is possible that another child (called hypothetically "D"), will be born after T's death. Since A, B and C might all die prior to D's fourth birthday, D's interest would then vest too remotely (more than 21 years after the deaths of A, B and C, the measuring lives). Therefore, not only is the gift invalid as to children born after T's death, but it is also invalid as to B and C, according to the strict common-law approach.

E. **"Wait and see" statutes:** Many states reject the common-law principle that if a scenario could be imagined whereby the interest might vest too remotely, it is invalid regardless of how things actually turn out. These states have adopted ***"wait and see"*** statutes, by which if the interest actually vests within lives in being at the time of creation plus 21 years, the fact that things might have worked out differently is irrelevant. [97-98]

> **Example:** O conveys Blackacre "to A and his heirs, but if A or his heirs ever uses Blackacre for other than residential purposes, to B and his heirs." At common law, the executory interest in B is void, since the premises might stop being used for residential purposes more than lives in being plus 21 years. But under the wait-and-see test, if the property ceases to be used for residential purposes within 21 years after the death of the survivor of O, A and B, the gift over to B and his heirs is valid.

1. **Effect on fertile octogenarian and unborn widow cases:** The wait-and-see approach virtually knocks out the fertile octogenarian and unborn widow cases. So long as the octogenarian does not in fact have a child, or the widow referred to in the instrument in fact turns out to be someone born prior to the instrument, the Rule Against Perpetuities is not violated.

IX. RESTRAINTS ON ALIENATION

A. **Restraints generally void:** A ***restraint on the alienation*** of a ***fee simple*** is generally ***void***. (*Example:* O conveys Blackacre "to A and his heirs, but no conveyance by A to any third party shall be valid." Since this restricts the alienation of a fee simple, the restriction will be void, and A may convey to whomever he wishes.) [98]

1. **Life estates:** But a ***life estate*** may be subjected to restraints on alienation. (*Example:* O conveys "to A for life, but A shall have no right to convey his interest; then to B and his heirs." The restraint upon A's life estate will generally be upheld.) [98]

2. **Use restrictions:** ***Use restrictions*** will generally be ***upheld***. (*Example:* O conveys "to A and his heirs, provided that the property not be used for non-residential purposes." This use restriction will be upheld, and will not be struck down as a restraint upon alienation.)

3. **Defeasible estates:** The defeasible estates (e.g., fee simple determinable) are also enforced, even though they are in a sense restraints on alienation. (*Example*: O conveys "to A and his heirs, but if the property is ever used for the purposes of sale of alcohol, Grantor or his heirs may re-enter." This will be enforced even though it to some extent restrains alienability.) [99]

MARITAL ESTATES

A. **The common-law system generally:** All but eight states govern marital property in a way that is derived from traditional common-law principles. [101]

B. **The feudal system:** The feudal system gave the husband extreme dominion over his wife's property, by means of the doctrines of coverture and *jure uxoris*. [101]

1. **Personal property (coverture):** Under the doctrine of *"coverture"*, all personal property owned by the wife at the time of the marriage became the property of the husband.

2. **Real property (*jure uxoris*):** Under the doctrine of *"jure uxoris"*, the husband had the right to **possess** all his wife's lands during the marriage, and to spend the rents and profits of the land as he wished.

C. **Married Women's Property Acts:** All states have enacted Married Women's Property Acts, which undo couverture and *jure uxoris*, give the woman equality, and protect her assets from her husband's creditors. [102]

II. THE COMMON-LAW SYSTEM — EFFECT OF DIVORCE

A. **Traditional "title" view:** Under traditional common-law principles, if the parties were **divorced**, the division of their property depended heavily on who held formal legal *"title"* to the property. [102]

1. **Title in husband's name:** Most significantly, if the legal title to property was held by one spouse alone, that spouse **retained title upon divorce**. This was usually to the husband's advantage.

B. **Modern "equitable distribution":** Today, every common-law property state has **abolished** the "title" approach to property division at divorce. Instead, all have substituted by statute a doctrine called *"equitable distribution,"* by which property is divided by the court according to the demands of fairness, not based on who has title. [103]

1. **What property is covered:** Most states allow the court to divide only *"marital property"* under equitable distribution principles. Usually, marital property is defined to include only property **acquired during the marriage from the earnings of the parties**. (So property acquired **before marriage**, or acquired by one spouse through a **gift or bequest** to that spouse, is not included in the assets to be distributed.) [103-04]

III. THE COMMON-LAW SYSTEM — DEATH OF A SPOUSE

A. **Dower and curtesy:** At common law, the surviving spouse was provided for by the doctrines of "dower" and "curtesy".

1. **Dower:** A widow (W) received *"dower."* This was defined as a **life estate** in **one-third** of the **lands** of which H was seised at any time during the marriage, provided that H's interest was **inheritable by the issue** of the marriage (if any). So any land owned in **fee simple** by H alone, or by H and a third person as tenants in common, qualified for dower.

(But there was no dower in a life estate held by H, even a life estate per autre vie.) [105]

a. **Dower inchoate:** While H was alive, W got a right of ***dower inchoate*** as soon as H became seized. This meant that any conveyance of the freehold by H to a third party did not affect the right of dower inchoate, so after H died W could still demand her dower rights from the person who bought from H. [105]

2. **Curtesy:** A widower (H) was entitled to ***"curtesy."*** This was a life estate in ***each piece*** of real estate in which W held a freehold interest during their marriage, provided the freehold was inheritable by issue born alive of the marriage. (So if H and W were childless, and W predeceased H, H had no right of curtesy). [105]

3. **Abolished in most jurisdictions:** In all but six American jurisdictions, dower and curtesy have been ***abolished***. [105]

4. **Practical importance:** Where dower and curtesy still exist, the main consequence is that ***both husband and wife*** must ***sign any deed*** if the recipient is to take free and clear of the right, even if only one spouse holds title. [106]

a. **Elective share available:** In the six remaining dower and/or curtesy states, the survivor may take an "elective share" (see below) instead, which is almost always more generous.

CAPSULE

B. **Modern "elective share" statutes:** The modern substitute for dower and curtesy is the ***"elective share."*** The surviving spouse has the right to ***renounce the will***, and instead receive a designated portion of the estate. [106]

1. **Effect:** The effect of an elective share statute (which all common-law property states but Georgia have) is that ***one spouse cannot "disinherit" the other.***

2. **Size of share:** Most commonly, the elective share is ***one-half*** or ***one-third***. Both personal and real property are covered.

3. **Length of marriage irrelevant:** Most elective share statutes treat the ***length of marriage*** as ***irrelevant*** — a woman widowed after one day of marriage gets the same share of her husband's estate as one married for 50 years.

III. COMMUNITY PROPERTY

A. **Community property generally:** In eight states, the rights of husband and wife in property is governed by the ***civil-law*** concept of ***"community property"***. These states are Arizona, California, Idaho, Louisiana, New Mexico, Nevada, Texas and Washington. [107]

1. **General approach:** The key tenet of community property is that property acquired during the marriage (with exceptions) belongs ***jointly*** to husband and wife from the moment it is acquired. Thus upon ***divorce*** or ***death***, the property is treated as belonging ***half to each spouse***.

B. **What is "community property":** All property acquired during the marriage is ***presumed*** to be community property (though this presumption may be rebutted by showing it falls within one of the classes of "separate property" described below). [107-08]

1. **Before marriage:** Property acquired by either spouse ***before marriage*** is separate, not community, property.

2. **Gift or inheritance:** Property acquired by ***gift, inheritance or bequest***, even ***after marriage***, is separate property.

3. **Earnings:** Income produced by either spouse's ***labor*** is community property. (*Example*: H is an employee. His salary is community property. Also, if he gets stock in his employer, pension rights, or insurance as part of his job, these probably also are fruits of his labor and

therefore community property.)

C. **Divorce:** Generally, if *divorce* occurs, the community property is *evenly divided*. [110]

D. **Death:** Upon the *death* of one of the parties, the community property is treated as having belonged half to the deceased spouse and half to the surviving spouse. A deceased spouse's half is thus subject to his right to devise it by will to whomever he wishes. [110] (*Example:* H and W hold Blackacre as community property. H dies, and his will gives whatever interest he has to S, his son by a prior marriage. S and W will hold the property as tenants in common, each with an undivided one-half interest.)

IV. HOMESTEAD EXEMPTION

A. **Homestead exemptions:** Most states have enacted *"homestead exemptions."* Exempted property may not be seized and sold by *creditors*. Usually, the family's *residence* is exempt from seizure, but only up to a certain dollar limit. Also, homestead exemptions do not bar a *mortgagee* from foreclosing — the exemption only protects against seizure by "general" or "unsecured" creditors. [111]

CONCURRENT OWNERSHIP

I. CONCURRENT OWNERSHIP GENERALLY

A. **Three types:** There are three ways in which two or more people may own present possessory interests in the same property: (1) joint tenancy (which includes the right of survivorship); (2) tenancy in common (which does not have the right of survivorship); and (3) tenancy by the entirety (which exists only between husband and wife, and which includes not only survivorship but "indestructibility.") [113]

II. JOINT TENANCY

A. **Joint tenancy generally:** In a *joint tenancy*, two or more people own a *single, unified* interest in real or personal property. [113]

  1. **General attributes:** Here are the most important attributes of a joint tenancy:

    a. **Survivorship:** Each joint tenant has a *right of survivorship*. That is, if there are two joint tenants, and one dies, the other becomes *sole owner* of the interest that the two of them had previously held jointly.

    b. **Possession:** Each joint tenant is entitled to *occupy* the *entire* premises, subject only to the same right of occupancy by the other tenant(s).

    c. **Equal shares:** Since the joint tenants have identical interests, they must have "equal shares." Thus one joint tenant cannot have a one-fourth interest, say, with the other having a three-fourths interest.

B. **Creation:** A joint tenancy must be created by a *single instrument* (deed or will), and must be created in both or all joint tenants at the *same time*. [114]

  1. **Language used:** Usually, a joint tenancy is created by specific language: "To A and B as joint tenants with right of survivorship."

  2. **Conveyance by A to A and B:** At common law, A (owner of a fee simple) *cannot* create a joint tenancy between himself and another by conveying "to A and B as joint tenants." But many states, by statute or case law, now permit this result. [115]

C. Severance: There are a number of ways in which a joint tenancy may be *severed*, i.e., *destroyed*. Severance normally results in the creation of a *tenancy in common*. [116]

1. **Conveyance by one joint tenant:** A joint tenant may *convey* his interest to a *third party*. Such a conveyance has the effect of destroying the joint tenancy. [116] (*Example*: A and B hold Blackacre as joint tenants. A conveys his interest to C. This conveyance destroys the joint tenancy, so that B and C now become tenants in common, not joint tenants.)

   a. **Three or more joint tenants:** If there are *three* or more original joint tenants, a conveyance by one of them to a stranger will produce a tenancy in common as between the stranger and the remaining original joint tenants, but the joint tenancy will continue as between the original members. (*Example*: A, B and C hold Blackacre as joint tenants. A conveys his interest to X. Now, X will hold an undivided one-third interest in the property as a tenant in common with B and C. B and C hold a two-thirds interest, but they hold this interest as joint tenants with each other, not as tenants in common. Thus if X dies, his interest goes to his heirs or devisees. But if B dies, his interest goes to C.)

2. **Granting of mortgage:** Courts are split as to whether the *granting of a mortgage* by one joint tenant severs the joint tenancy. In so-called "title theory" states, the mortgage is treated as a conveyance, and thus severs the joint tenancy (so that the mortgagee can foreclose on the undivided one-half interest of the mortgagor, but the interest of the other party is not affected). In "lien theory" states, the mortgage does not sever the joint tenancy; in some but not all lien theory states, if the mortgagee dies first, the other joint tenant takes the whole property free and clear of the mortgage. [118]

3. **Lease:** Most courts seem to hold that a *lease* issued by one joint tenant does not act as a severance. [118-19]

III. TENANCY IN COMMON

A. Tenancy in common: Whereas in a joint tenancy each party has an equal interest in the whole, in a "tenancy in common" each tenant has a *separate "undivided"* interest. [120]

1. **No right of survivorship:** The most important difference between the tenancy in common and the joint tenancy is that there is *no right of survivorship* between tenants in common. Thus each tenant in common can make a *testamentary transfer* of his interest; if he dies intestate, his interest will pass under the statute of descent. (*Example*: A and B take title to Blackacre as tenants in common. They have equal shares. A dies, without a will, leaving only one relative, a son, S. Title to Blackacre is now: a one-half undivided interest in S, and a one-half undivided interest in B.) [120-21]

2. **Unequal shares:** Tenants in common may have *unequal shares* (unlike joint tenants). (*Example*: A and B may hold as tenants in common, with A holding an "undivided one-quarter interest" and B an "undivided three-quarters interest.") [120]

   a. **Rebuttable presumption of equality:** If the conveyance does not specify the size of the interests, there is a *rebuttable presumption* that *equal* shares were intended.

3. **Presumption favoring:** Most states have a *presumption* in *favor* of tenancies in common, rather than joint tenancies, so long as the co-tenants are not husband and wife. But this can be rebutted by clear evidence showing that the parties intended to create a joint tenancy. [121]

4. **Heirs:** Apart from a conveyance directly creating a tenancy in common, a tenancy in common can result from operation of law, including the *intestacy* statute: if the intestacy statute specifies that two persons are to take an equal interest as co-heirs, they take as tenants in common. (*Example*: A, fee simple owner of Blackacre, dies without a will. His sole surviving relatives are a son, S, and a daughter, D. The intestacy statute says that heirs who

are children take "equally." S and D will take title to Blackacre as tenants in common, each holding an undivided one-half interest.) [121]

IV. TENANCY BY THE ENTIRETY

A. Tenancy by the entirety generally: At common law, any conveyance to two persons who were ***husband and wife*** resulted automatically in a ***"tenancy by the entirety."*** [121]

    1. Usually abolished: Only 22 states retain the tenancy by the entirety. Even in these states, it is no longer the case (as it was at common law) that a conveyance to husband and wife necessarily creates a tenancy by the entirety — instead, there is usually just a rebuttable ***presumption*** that a conveyance to a husband and wife is intended to create a tenancy by the entirety. [121]

    2. No severance: The key feature of the tenancy by the entirety is that it is ***not subject to severance***. So long as both parties are alive, and remain husband and wife, neither one can break the tenancy. Most significantly, each spouse knows that if he or she survives the other, he/she will get a ***complete interest***. [122]

        Example: H and W hold Blackacre as tenants by the entirety. H conveys his interest to X. In all states, if W survives H, W will get the property outright and X will get nothing. (But in some states, the conveyance will be effective to the limited extent that if H survives W, X, not H, will get the property.)

    3. Divorce: If the parties are ***divorced***, the tenancy by the entirety ***ends***. The parties are then treated as owning equal shares (usually as tenants in common). [124]

V. RELATIONS BETWEEN CO-TENANTS

A. Possession: Regardless of the form of co-tenancy, each co-tenant has the ***right to occupy the entire premises***, subject only to a similar right in the other co-tenants. (But the parties may make an ***agreement*** to the contrary.) [125]

    1. No duty to account: If the property is solely occupied by one of the co-tenants, he normally has ***no duty to account*** for the value of his exclusive possession (e.g., he has no duty to pay the non-occupying co-tenant one-half of what a normal rent would be). But there are two main exceptions: [125]

        a. Ouster: If the occupying tenant ***refuses to permit*** the other tenant equal occupancy, then he is said to have ***"ousted"*** the other tenant, and must ***account*** to the ousted co-tenant for the latter's share of the ***fair rental value*** of the premises. [126]

        b. Depletion: Also, the occupying tenant will have a duty to account if he ***depletes the land***. (*Example*: A and B are co-tenants of Blackacre; A mines coal from the property. A must split the profits with B.) [126]

B. Payments made by one tenant: If one tenant makes ***payments*** on behalf of the property (e.g., property tax, mortgage payments, repairs, etc.), that tenant does ***not*** have an automatic right to ***collect*** the share from the other tenants. However, the tenant making the payment may ***deduct*** the payment from rents he collects from third parties; also, he will be reimbursed for these payments "off the top" before any proceeds from a ***sale*** are distributed. [127-28]

C. Partition: Any tenant in common or joint tenant (but not a tenant by the entirety) may bring an equitable action for ***partition***. By this means, the court will either ***divide*** the property, or order it ***sold*** and the proceeds distributed. [129-30]

LANDLORD AND TENANT

I. INTRODUCTION

A. **Various types:** There are four estates that involve a landlord-tenant relationship: (1) the tenancy for *years*; (2) the *periodic* tenancy; (3) the tenancy *at will*; and (4) the tenancy at *sufference*. [133]

B. **Statute of Frauds:** Under the original English Statute of Frauds, any lease for *more than three years* must be *in writing*. (Otherwise, it merely creates an "estate at will.") In the U.S., most statutes now require a writing for all leases for *more than one year*. [134]

   1. **Option to renew:** In calculating whether a lease is for more than one year (so that it probably has to be in writing), most courts add together the fixed term and any period for which the tenant has the *option* to *renew*. [134]

C. **The estate for years:** Most leases are *estates for years*. An estate for years is any estate which is for a *fixed period of time*. (So even a six-month lease is an "estate for years.") [135]

   1. **Certain term:** For a lease to be an estate for years, the beginning date and end date must be *fixed*.

   2. **Automatic termination:** Because an estate for years contains its own termination date, *no additional notice of termination* need be given by either party — on the last day, the tenancy simply ends, and the tenant must leave the premises.

D. **Periodic tenancy:** The *periodic tenancy* is one which *continues* from one period to the next *automatically*, unless either party terminates it at the end of a period by notice. Thus a year-to-year tenancy, or a month-to-month one, would be periodic. [136-37]

   1. **Creation by implication:** Normally a periodic tenancy is created by *implication*. Thus a lease with no stated duration (e.g., T agrees to pay L "$200 per month," but with no end period) creates a periodic tenancy. Also, if a tenant *holds over*, and the landlord accepts rent, probably a periodic tenancy is created. [136]

   2. **Termination:** A periodic tenancy will automatically be *renewed* for a further period unless one party gives a valid *notice of termination*. [136-37]

      a. **Common law:** At common law, six months' notice was needed to terminate a year-to-year tenancy, and a full period's notice was necessary when the period was less than a year (e.g., 30 days notice for a month-to-month tenancy). Also, at common law, the notice had to set the *end of a period* as the termination date.

      b. **Modern:** Most states today require only 30 days notice for any tenancy, even year-to-year. Notice today must still generally be effective as of the end of a period, but if the notice is not sufficiently in advance of one period, it is automatically applicable to the following period. (*Example*: L and T have a month-to-tenancy; if one gives the other notice of termination on January 4, this will be effective as of February 28.)

E. **At-will tenancy:** A *tenancy at will* is a tenancy which has *no stated duration* and which may be *terminated at any time* by either party. [137-38]

   1. **Implication:** Usually a tenancy at will, like a periodic tenancy, is created by *implication*. For instance, if T takes possession with L's permission, with no term stated and no period for paying rent defined (so that the lease is not even a periodic one), it will probably be at will. Also, a few courts hold that if one party has the option to terminate at will, the other party has a similar option so that the tenancy is at will.

F. Tenancy at sufferance: There is only one situation in which the "tenancy at sufferance" exists: where a tenant *holds over* at the end of a valid lease. Here, the landlord has a *right of election*, between: (1) *evicting* the tenant; and (2) holding him to *another term* as tenant. (If L elects to hold T to another term, most courts hold that a periodic tenancy is then created, and the length of the period is determined by the way rent was computed under the lease which terminated.) [139-41]

II. TENANT'S RIGHT OF POSSESSION AND ENJOYMENT

A. Tenant's right of possession: Courts are split about whether L impliedly warrants to T that he will deliver *actual possession* at the start of the lease term. The question usually arises when a prior tenant *holds over*.

 1. **"American" view:** The so-called *"American"* view is that the landlord has a duty to deliver *only* legal possession, *not actual possession*. Despite the name, at most a slight majority of American courts follow this rule. [141]

 2. **"English" rule:** Other courts follow the so-called *"English"* rule, by which L *does* have a duty to deliver actual possession. In courts following this rule, T has the right to *terminate the lease* and recover damages for the breach if the prior tenant holds over and L does not oust him. Alternatively, T may continue the lease and get damages for the period until the prior tenant is removed. [141-42]

B. Quiet enjoyment: T has the right of *"quiet enjoyment"* of the leased premises. This right can be violated in two main ways: (1) by claims of *"paramount title"*; and (2) by acts of L, or persons claiming under him, which interfere with T's *possession or use* of the premises. [142]

 1. **Claims of paramount title:** L, by making the lease, impliedly warrants that he has *legal power* to give possession to T for the term of the lease. If someone else successfully asserts a claim to the property which is superior to T's claim under the lease (a claim of *"paramount title"*), L has breached this warranty. Thus suppose that X shows that L does not have title to the premises at all (because X has title), or that X shows that L has previously leased the premises to X, or that X shows that X holds a mortgage on the premises, and is entitled to foreclose because L has not made mortgage payments — in all of these instances, X's claim of paramount title constitutes a breach by L of his implied warranty. [142]

  a. **Before T takes possession:** If T discovers the paramount title *before* he takes possession, he may *terminate the lease*.

  b. **After T takes possession:** Once T takes possession, he may *not* terminate the lease (or refuse to pay rent) merely on the grounds that a third person *holds* a paramount title. (It is sometimes said that T is *"estopped to deny L's title"* to the leased property.) On the other hand, if the third person then *asserts* his paramount title in such a way that T is *evicted*, T may terminate the lease and recover damages.

 2. **Interference by landlord or third person:** If L himself, or someone claiming under L, *interferes* with T's *use* of the premises, this will be a breach of the covenant of quiet enjoyment. [143]

  a. **Conduct by other tenants:** If the conduct of *other tenants* makes the premises uninhabitable for T, the traditional view is that L is *not* responsible (unless the other tenants use their portion for immoral or lewd purposes, or conduct their acts in the *common areas*). But the *modern trend* is to impute the acts of other tenants to L where these acts are *in violation of the other leases*, and L could have prevented the conduct by eviction or otherwise. (*Example:* Suppose that other tenants make a great deal of noise in violation of their leases, so that L could evict them, but does not. The modern trend, but not the traditional rule, is that T may terminate the lease.)

    b. Constructive eviction: If T's claim is merely that his *use* or *enjoyment* of the property has been substantially impaired (e.g., excessive noise, terrible odors) the eviction is *"constructive"*. When T is constructively evicted, even if this is L's fault, T is not entitled to terminate or stop paying rent unless he *abandons the premises*. (*Example:* Other tenants make so much noise that T's use is severely impaired. If T remains in the premises, he may not reduce the rent payments to L; he must leave and terminate the lease, or else pay the full lease amount.) [144]

C. Condemnation: If the government uses its right of eminent domain to *condemn* all or part of the leased premises, T may have a remedy. [145]

    1. Total taking: If the *entire* premises are taken, the *lease terminates*, and T does not have to pay the rent.

    2. Partial: But if only a *portion* of the premises is taken (even a major part), at common law the lease is *not terminated*. Also, T must *continue paying the full rent* (though he gets an appropriate portion of any condemnation award which L collects from the government). However, the modern trend is to let T terminate if the condemnation *"significantly interferes"* with his use, and to give him a reduction in rent even for a small interference.

D. Illegality: If T intends to use the property for *illegal purposes*, and L knows this fact, the court will probably treat the lease as *unenforceable*, especially if the illegality would be a serious one (e.g., crack distribution). [146-47]

    1. Variance or permit: If the use intended by T requires a *variance* or *permit*, and T is unable to get the variance or permit after the lease is signed, most courts hold that the lease *remains valid*.

III. CONDITION OF THE PREMISES

A. Common-law view: At common law, T takes the premises *as is*. L is *not* deemed to have made any implied warranty that the premises are *fit* or *habitable*. Nor does L have any *duty to repair* defects arising during the course of the lease (unless the parties explicitly provide that he does). [149]

    1. Independence of covenants: Also, the common law applies the doctrine of *"independence of covenants"* in leases. Thus even if L does expressly promise to repair (or warrants that the premises are habitable), if he breaches this promise T must still pay rent. T may sue for damages, but he is stuck in the uninhabitable living conditions. [150]

    2. Constructive eviction: However, even at common law, T can raise the defense of *"constructive eviction"* — he can terminate the lease if he can show that the premises are virtually uninhabitable. But he can only assert constructive eviction if he first *leaves the premises*, something which a poor tenant in uninhabitable residential space can rarely afford to do. [150]

B. Modern implied warranty of habitability: But today, the vast majority of states (either by statute or case law) impose some kind of *implied warranty of habitability*. That is, if L leases residential premises to T, he impliedly warrants that the premises are in at least *good enough condition to be lived in*. If L breaches this warranty, T may (among other remedies) withhold rent, and use the withheld rent to make the repairs himself. [151]

    1. Waiver of known pre-existing defects: Some (but by no means all) courts hold that if T *knows* of the defect *before he moves in*, he will be held to have *waived* the defect, so that the implied warranty of habitability does not apply to that defect. (If the defect is one which T neither discovered nor reasonably could have discovered before moving in, then all courts agree that an otherwise-applicable implied warranty of habitability protects T against the defect.) [152-53]

2. **Standards for determining "habitability"**: All courts agree that the existence of a *building code violation* is at least *evidence* of uninhabitability. However, most courts require that to prove uninhabitability, T must show that the conditions not only violate the building code, but are also a *substantial threat to T's health or safety*. (Conversely, most courts hold that if conditions *are* a substantial threat to T's health or safety, the warranty is breached even if there is no building code violation.) [154]

   a. **Relevance of nature of building**: Some (but not all) courts hold that the *age of the building* and the *amount of rent charged* may be considered in determining whether there has been a breach. Thus a given condition might be a breach of the warranty as to a new luxury highrise, but not as to an old low-rent structure.

3. **Kinds of leases**:

   a. **Residential**: Most *statutes* imposing an implied warranty of habitability apply to *all residential* leases (though some apply merely to units in multiple dwellings, so that a single-family house would not be covered). [154]

   b. **Commercial leases**: Most statutes and cases do *not* impose an implied warranty of habitability as to *commercial* leases. [154-55]

4. **Waiver in lease**: Generally, a clause in the lease expressly stating that there is no implied warranty is usually *not effective*. (But some statutes, such as the URLTA, will enforce a deal in which T promises, in a *separate writing*, and for adequate consideration such as a lower rent, to *make repairs himself*.) [155]

5. **Remedies**: If T shows a breach of the implied warranty of habitability, he may have a number of *remedies*:

   a. **Terminate lease**: T may usually *vacate the premises* and *terminate* the lease (after he puts L on notice and L still refuses to make the repairs). [156]

   b. **Withhold rent**: T may also *withhold rent* until the defects have been cured. (But most statutes, and some cases, require T to *deposit* the rent in some sort of escrow account.) [157]

   c. **Use rent for repairs**: Many cases and statutes allow T to *make the repairs* and then to *deduct the reasonable costs* of those repairs from the rent. T must usually give L advance notice of his intent to make the repairs and to deduct (so that L can make the repairs himself to avoid the loss of rent). [158]

6. **Retaliatory eviction barred**: By the doctrine of *"retaliatory eviction,"* L usually may not terminate a periodic lease, or deny T's request for a new lease at the conclusion of a tenancy for years, on account of T's assertion of the right to habitable premises. The doctrine is most likely to be applied where L tries to terminate the tenancy in retaliation for T's complaints made to a housing authority about *code violations*. Also, some courts apply the doctrine where the non-renewal or termination is in retaliation for T's withholding of rent or his joining in a tenants' organization. [160-62]

C. **Destruction of premises**: If the premises are suddenly *destroyed* or *damaged* (by fire, flood, lightning or other natural elements), at common law T must *keep paying rent*, and may not terminate the lease. [162]

   1. **Modern view**: But most states have now passed *statutes* changing this common-law rule — if the premises are destroyed or damaged so that they are no longer habitable, T may now usually *terminate the lease* and stop paying rent. Also, some courts have reached this result by case law. (But T usually cannot recover damages, so termination of the lease is his only remedy.)

IV. TORT LIABILITY OF LANDLORD AND TENANT

A. Tenant's tort liability: T, during the time he is in possession of the premises, is treated *like an owner*, for purposes of his *tort liability* to others who come onto the property. (*Example*: Since L would have a duty to warn a social guest, or licensee, of known dangers, T has a similar duty to warn of dangers that he is aware of.) [164]

B. Landlord's liability:

1. **Common law:** At common law, L is generally *not liable* for physical injury to T, or to persons who are on the leased property with T's consent. That is, L has no general duty to use reasonable care to make or keep the premises safe. [164] However, there are a number of *exceptions* (including some developed by courts recently), including the following:

   a. **Concealment:** L is liable if he *conceals*, or *fails to disclose*, a dangerous defect existing at the start of the lease of which he is *aware*. [164]

      i. **L should know but does not:** Most courts also hold that if L does not have actual knowledge but *should know* about the danger, based on facts that he does know, he will be liable for failing to warn.

      ii. **No duty of inspection:** But L has *no duty of inspection*, i.e., no obligation to inspect the property to find out whether there are hidden defects.

   b. **Liability to persons other than T:** Nearly all courts hold that if L would be liable to T, he is also liable to *persons on the premises with T's consent*. (But if L has told T about the defect, L will not be liable to T's guests even if T did not pass on the warning.) [165]

   c. **Areas under L's control:** L has a duty to use *reasonable care* to keep the *common areas* safe (e.g., lobbies, elevator, corridor, etc.). [165]

      i. **Security against criminals:** Most courts now require L to use reasonable care to prevent *unauthorized access* to the building. (*Example*: L, the owner of an apartment building, fails to repair the building's outer lock after being told that it is broken. X enters, and mugs T. Most courts would hold L liable for not using reasonable care to secure the building.)

   d. **Repairs negligently performed:** If L *attempts* to make a repair, he will be liable if the repair is done negligently, and L has made the condition more dangerous or lulled T into a false feeling of security. (But if L's negligent repair does not make the condition worse or lull T, the courts are split as to whether L is liable if T is injured.) [166]

   e. **L contracts to repair:** If a *clause in the lease* requires L to make *repairs* or otherwise keep the premises safe, L will be liable in tort if he fails to use reasonable care and T is injured. Also, L is probably liable to *third persons* on the premises with T's consent in this situation. [167]

   f. **L's legal duties:** If *building codes* or other laws impose a duty on L to keep the premises safe, L will generally be liable in tort if he fails in this duty. Probably L will also be liable if he breaches an implied warranty of habitability, and the uninhabitable condition causes injury to T or T's guest. [167-68]

   g. **Admission of public:** If L has reason to believe that T will *hold the premises open to the public*, and L has reason to know that a dangerous condition exists, L will be liable for resulting physical harm to the public. (L usually has an affirmative *duty to inspect* in this situation.) [168-69]

2. **General "reasonable care" theory:** Some recent cases have simply *rejected* the common law view that L has no general duty to use reasonable care. Under these cases, P does not

have to fit within one of the above exceptions, and merely has to show that: (1) L failed to use reasonable care and (2) the lack of reasonable care proximately caused P's injury. [169-70]

3. **Exculpatory clauses:** At least in the case of a *residential* lease, most courts today *refuse* to enforce an *"exculpatory clause"* in a lease, that is, a clause purporting to relieve L of tort liability for his negligence. About half the states accomplish this by statute, and some others by case law. [170]

V. TENANT'S DUTIES

A. **Duty to pay rent:** T of course has a duty to *pay rent.*

1. **Breach of L's duties:** Most courts today hold that if L *materially breaches* his implied or express obligations (e.g., the implied warranty of habitability), T is temporarily *relieved* from continuing to pay rent. [170-71]

B. **Duty to repair:** At common law, T had an implied duty to make *minor repairs.* [171]

1. **Modern rule:** However, most courts today do not impose this duty on T (and indeed, most impose it on L under the doctrine of implied warranty of habitability, at least for residential leases).

C. **Fixtures:** A *fixture* is an item of personal property which is *attached* to the land (e.g., lighting, built-in bookcases, etc.). [172]

1. **Right to affix:** T is usually allowed to *attach* fixtures if this would not unfairly damage the value of L's reversion.

2. **Right to remove:** Similarly, most courts today say that T may *remove* a fixture installed by him if this removal will not damage L's interests (so that T must normally *restore* the premises to the way they were before the fixture was attached).

D. **Duty to behave reasonably:** T has the implied duty to *behave reasonably* in his use of the premises. (*Examples*: T must not unreasonably disturb other tenants, and must obey reasonable regulations posted by the landlord.) [173]

VI. LANDLORD'S REMEDIES

A. **Security deposits:**

1. **Interest:** In many states, L is required by statute to pay *interest* on the security deposit. [174]

2. **Right to keep:** Once the lease terminates, L must *return* the deposit to T, after subtracting any damages. If T abandons the lease before the end of the lease term and L re-lets, L must *immediately* return the deposit (after subtracting damages).

3. **Commingle:** L may normally *commingle* the security deposit with his own funds.

4. **Purchaser's obligation:** Courts are split as to whether one who *purchases* L's interest in the property must account to T for the end of the deposit at the end of the lease term. [174]

B. **Acceleration clause:** Most leases contain an *acceleration of rent* clause, by which if T fails to pay rent promptly or otherwise breaches the lease, L may require that all of the rent for the rest of the lease term is payable at once. [175]

1. **Generally valid:** Most courts *enforce* such acceleration clauses. (But if L decides to sue for enforcement of the acceleration clause, he may not also demand possession of the premises.)

C. Eviction:

    1. Express forfeiture clause: Most leases explicitly give L the right to **terminate the lease** if T fails to pay rent or violates any other lease provision. Such clauses will be enforced, but only if T's breach is **material**. (*Example*: If T is merely a couple days late with the rent on one or two occasions, the court will probably not allow L to terminate the lease.) [175]

    2. Summary proceedings: In most states, if L is entitled to terminate the lease and regain possession (or if T holds over at the end of the lease term and L wants to get him out), L may do so by **"summary proceedings,"** which provide for a **speedy trial** of L's right to immediate possession. Summary proceedings usually work by **limiting the defenses** which T may assert. (*Example*: Some summary proceeding statutes prevent T from asserting the breach of the implied warranty of habitability as a defense in L's action to regain possession for non-payment of rent.) [176-77]

D. Damages for holdover: If T **holds over** after the lease terminates, L is entitled to **damages** as well as eviction. [178]

E. Abandonment: If T **abandons** the premises (and defaults on the rent) before the scheduled end of the lease term, L has three basic choices: (1) to **accept a surrender** of the premises, thus terminating the lease; (2) to **re-let** on T's behalf; and (3) to leave the premises **vacant** and sue for rent as it comes due. [178-81]

    1. Accept surrender: L may treat T's abandonment as a **surrender**, and accept it. This has the effect of **terminating** the lease, so that **no further rent becomes due from T**. (If T takes possession and/or leases to someone else, and does not notify T that he is acting on T's behalf, then this will probably be held to be an acceptance of surrender, causing T's rent obligation to end.) [179]

    2. Re-letting on T's account: L may **re-let on T's behalf**, if he notifies T that he is doing so. This has two advantages to L: (1) T remains liable for all rents coming due, if no new tenant is found; and (2) if a new tenant is found who pays a lesser rent, T is still liable for the difference between this and the original rent due under the L-T lease. (Courts are split on whether L must give the surplus to T if L relets for a **higher** amount.) [179-80]

    3. Leave vacant: Courts are split on whether L has the right to **leave the premises vacant**, and hold L to the lease. Usually, the question is phrased, "Does L have the duty to mitigate?"

        a. Traditional view: The traditional view is that L has **no duty to mitigate**, i.e., no duty to try to find a new tenant. [180-81]

        b. Duty to mitigate: But an increasing minority of courts now hold that L **does have a duty to mitigate**, by attempting to find a suitable replacement tenant. In these courts, if L does not make such an effort, T is off the hook. [181]

VII. TRANSFER AND SALE BY LESSOR; ASSIGNMENT AND SUBLETTING BY LESSEE

A. Generally allowed: Unless the parties to a lease agree otherwise, either may **transfer** his interest. Thus L may sell his reversion in the property, and T may either **assign** or **sublease** his right to occupy. [182]

    1. Distinguish assignment from sublease: Be sure to distinguish **sublease** from **assignment**. An assignment is the transfer by T of his **entire interest** in the leased premises. Thus he must transfer the **entire remaining length** of the term of his lease. A **sublease** is the transfer by T of **less** than his entire interest. (*Example*: T's lease has one year to go. T transfers the first 11.5 months of this interest to T1. In most states, this is a sublease, not an assignment.) [183]

    a. Significance: The main significance of this distinction is that if T assigns to T1, T1 is ***personally liable*** to ***pay rent*** to L, even if he makes no express promise to L or T that he will do so. If T merely subleases to T1, T1 is not personally liable to L for the rent (absent an explicit promise). [184]

B. Running of benefit and burden: Determine whether a particular promise ***runs with the land***, either as to benefit or burden. If the ***benefit runs***, then an assignee of the promisee can sue to enforce; if the ***burden runs***, an assignee of the promisor will be liable. If neither the burden nor benefit runs, then the promisor's assignee is not liable, and promisee's assignee cannot sue. [184]

    Example 1 (benefit runs): In the L-T lease, T promises to make repairs. This promise "touches and concerns the land" both as to benefit and burden, so benefit and burden run. Thus if T assigns to T1, T1 is personally liable for making the repairs. Conversely, if L assigns to L1, L1 can sue T (and T1 if T has assigned to T1) to enforce this promise.

    Example 2 (burdens runs, but benefit does not): In the L-T lease, T promises not to compete with L's use of certain other property. If T assigns to T1, T1 is liable not to compete. But if L assigns to L1, in most states L1 cannot enforce the promise against either T or T1.

  1. "Touch and concern" test: The burden runs if the promise ***"touches and concerns"*** the promisor's assignee's interest in the land. Similarly, the benefit runs if the promise "touches and concerns" the promisee's assignee's interest in the property. [185]

  2. Normally both or neither: Normally, either the benefit and burden will both run, or neither will run. (The non-competition situation described in Example 2 above is one of the few examples where this is not true.) [184-85]

C. Rights after T assigns: Here are the rights of the parties after T assigns to T1 his rights under the L-T lease:

  1. T's liability to L: After the assignment, T ***remains liable*** to L (whether T's promise to L does or does not "touch and concern" the land). (*Example*: T remains liable for the rent after assignment to T1. This is true even if L consents to the assignment, and even if L accepts some rent payments from T1.) [187]

  2. T's rights against T1: After the assignment, T1 becomes ***primarily liable***, and T is only secondarily liable. Therefore, if L sues T when T1 does not make the rent payments, T can then sue T1 for the amount that T has had to pay (even if T1 never expressly assumed the lease duties at the time of the assignment). [187]

  3. L's rights against T1: Assuming that T1 does not make any specific promises of performance when he takes the assignment, T1 is liable only for those promises made by T whose burden ***runs with the land***. [188]

    Example 1: T1 is liable to L for ***rent***, since the burden of T's original rent promise ran with the land. Thus T1 must make the rent payments even if he did not expressly promise either T or L that he would make these payments.

    Example 2: In the original L-T lease, T promises to keep the premises insured. Assume that the burden of this promise does not run with the land (the majority rule). If T assigns to T1 and T1 does not make any promise of insurance, T1 is not liable for failing to insure the property (though L can terminate the lease for breach if T1 does not do so).

  a. Assignment by assignee: But T1 remains liable (even on promises whose burdens run with the land) only for the period when he is in ***actual possession***. If he ***reassigns***, he is ***not liable*** for breaches by the subsequent assignee. [188] (*Example*: T assigns to T1. T1 remains in possession for six months, then assigns to T2. T1 is liable for the rent that accrued during the six months he was in possession, but not for any rents accruing after he left possession and T2 took possession.)

> **b. Assumption:** However, if T1 *assumes* the lease (i.e., expressly promises T that T1 will obey all terms of the L-T lease), then T1 is liable both to T and L for all T's obligations, including those accruing after T1 re-assigns to T2. [189]

D. Assignment by L: Now, assume that L assigns his rights to L1. Here, the same rule applies: L1 has the burden of covenants whose burden runs with the land, and has the benefit of covenants whose benefit runs with the land. [190-91]

> **1. Repair obligation:** Thus if L promised T that he would keep the premises in repair, L1 is liable for making the repairs after the sale. (Also, the implied warranty of habitability, if it applies at all, probably binds L1 just as it bound L.)

E. Agreement by the parties about transfer: All of the above assumes that the lease itself contains no provisions restricting transfer. Most leases, however, contain a promise by T that he will *not assign or sublease his interest without L's consent.* [191-92]

> **1. Generally enforced:** Most states *enforce* such a clause, even if L is completely *unreasonable* in refusing to consent to the transfer.

> > **a. Strict construction and waiver:** However, courts construe such anti-transfer clauses strictly, and are quick to hold that L *waived* the benefit of the clause. (*Example:* If L knowingly accepts rents from T1 he will probably be held to have waived his right to refuse to consent to the transfer.)

> > **b. Consent to second transfer:** Also, if L consents (or waives his objection to) a particular transfer, he is usually held to have also waived his right to a *subsequent* transfer, under the rule of *Dumpor's Case.* (*Example*: L consents to T's assignment to T1. In most states, L is also held to consent to T1's further assignment to T2.) [192]

> **2. Modern trend:** An increasing minority of states hold (often by statute) that even if the lease says that L has an *unconditional* right to refuse to consent to a transfer by T, the *consent may not be unreasonably withheld.* (In such a state, L should get a lease provision giving him the right to *make his own deal* directly with T1 — this way, if T1 is willing to pay more than the original lease amount, L, not T, gets the benefit.) [193]

EASEMENTS AND PROMISES CONCERNING LAND

I. EASEMENTS GENERALLY

A. Definition: An *easement* is a privilege to *use the land of another*. [201]

> **1. Affirmative easement:** An *affirmative* easement is one entitling its holder to *do a physical act* on another's land. (*Example*: A, who owns Blackacre, gives B a *right of way* over Blackacre, so that B can pass from his own property to a street which adjoins Blackacre. B holds an affirmative easement.)

> **2. Negative easement:** A *negative* easement is one which enables its holder to *prevent* the owner of land from making certain uses of that land. These are rare. (*Example*: A owns Whiteacre, which is next to the ocean; B owns Blackacre, which is separated from the ocean by Whiteacre. A gives B an easement of "light and air," which assures B that A will not

build anything on Whiteacre which would block B's view of the ocean. B holds a negative easement.)

B. Appurtenant vs. in gross: Distinguish between easements that are *appurtenant* to a particular piece of land, and those that are *"in gross."* [201]

    1. Appurtenant: An easement *appurtenant* is one which benefits its holder in the use of a *certain piece of land*. The land for whose benefit the appurtenant easement is created is called the *"dominant tenement."* The land that is burdened or used is called the *"servient tenement."* (*Example*: Blackacre, owned by S, stands between Whiteacre, owned by D, and the public road. S gives D the right to pass over a defined part of Blackacre to get from Whiteacre to the road. This right of way is an easement that is appurtenant to Whiteacre — Blackacre is the servient tenement, and Whiteacre is the dominant tenement.)

        a. Test for: For an easement to be appurtenant, its benefit must be intimately *tied to a particular piece of land* (the dominant tenement).

    2. Easement in gross: An easement *in gross* is one whose benefit is *not tied* to any particular parcel. (*Example*: O, who owns Blackacre, gives E, who lives across town, the right to come onto Blackacre anytime he wants, and use O's swimming pool. Since the grant is not given because of E's ownership of nearby land, the easement is in gross.) [202]

    3. Profit: Related to easements is something called the *"profit a prendre."* A profit is the right to go onto the land of another and *remove the soil or a product of it*. Thus the right to mine *minerals*, drill *oil*, or capture wild game or fish, are all profits. (In the U.S., profits are functionally identical to easements.)

II. CREATION OF EASEMENTS

A. Four ways to create: There are four ways to create an easement: (1) by an *express* grant; (2) by *implication*; (3) by strict *necessity*; and (4) by *prescription*.

B. Express creation: If a easement is created by a *deed* or a *will*, it is *"express."* [203]

    1. Statute of Frauds: An express easement *must be in writing*. This is required by the Statute of Frauds.

    2. Reservation in grantor: Often, an express easement is created when the owner of land conveys the land to someone else, and *reserves for himself* an easement in it. This is called an "easement by reservation." (*Example*: A deeds Blackacre to B, with a statement in the deed that "A hereby retains a right of way over the eastern eight feet of the property.") [203-04]

    3. Creation in stranger to deed: At common law, it was *not* possible for an owner to convey land to one person, and to establish by the same deed an easement in a *third person*. (Thus an easement could not be created in a *"stranger to the deed."*) But most modern courts have *abandoned* this rule. (*Example*: O owns two parcels, 1 and 2. O sells parcel 1 to P, without recording any easement over parcel 2 in favor of parcel 1. O then deeds parcel 2 to D, with a statement in the deed, "Easement reserved in favor of P or his successors to parcel 1." Today, this easement will be enforced even though P was not a party to the O-D deed.) [204]

C. Creation by implication: An easement by *implication* may sometimes be created. If so, it does *not have to satisfy the statute of frauds.* [204-05]

    1. Requirements: There are three requirements for an easement by implication: (1) land must be *divided up* (or "severed"), so that the owner of a parcel is either selling part and retaining part, or subdividing the property and selling pieces to different grantees; (2) the use for which the implied easement is claimed must have *existed prior to the severance*; and (3) the easement must be at least *reasonably necessary* to the enjoyment of the dominant tenement.

2. **Severance:** An easement will only be implied where the owner of a parcel *sells part and retains part*, or *sells pieces simultaneously* to more than one grantee. This is the requirement of *"severance."* (*Example*: A and B are neighboring landowners. A new street is built adjoining B's property, and A can only get to this street by crossing B's property. A crosses B's property at a particular spot for several years, then sells to C. C has no easement by implication across B's property, because there was never any conveyance between A and B, required for the creation of an easement by implication.) [205]

3. **Prior use:** The use for which the easement is claimed must have existed *prior* to the severance of ownership. [206]

4. **Necessity:** According to most courts, the easement must be *reasonably necessary* to the enjoyment of what is claimed to be the dominant tenement. Courts are stricter in imposing this requirement where the easement is created by *grant* (i.e., in favor of the grantee), than where the easement is *reserved* (i.e., in favor of the grantor). [207-08]

> **Example of easement by implication:** O owns two houses side by side on one parcel. To give the garage behind house no. 1 access to the street, he builds a driveway which runs between the two houses. O then conveys house no. 2, including part of the land and the driveway, to A. An implied easement in favor of house no. 1, and against the land on which house no. 2 is located, will be reserved with respect to the driveway. Also, if O conveys house no. 1, an implied easement in favor of that house will be created against the land of house no. 2. This is because: (1) O was the owner of both tenements just before the easement came into being; (2) the use existed prior to the severance of the two tenements; and (3) the easement is reasonably necessary to the enjoyment of house no. 1's garage.

5. **Easement of light and air:** An easement of *"light and air"* (the right to have one's view remain unobstructed) *cannot* be created by implication, in most states. [208-09]

D. **Easement by necessity:** The courts will find an "easement by *necessity*" if two parcels are so situated that an easement over one is *"strictly necessary"* to the enjoyment of the other. [209]

1. **Common grantor:** The courts require that *at one time*, both the alleged dominant tenement and the alleged servient tenement were owned by the same person. [209]

2. **No prior use:** But unlike the easement by implication, there does not have to have been a *"prior use,"* that is, the easement does not have to have been used prior to the time the two parcels were split up. (*Example*: O owns parcel 1 and parcel 2, which adjoin each other. In 1950, he sells parcel 1 to P and parcel 2 to D. In 1960, an old road serving parcel 1 is closed, and a new one is built so that the only way to get from parcel 1 to the road is by crossing parcel 2. Because both parcels were owned originally by the same owner, O, the courts will grant parcel 1 an easement over parcel 2 to get to the road, even though no such easement was in use at the time O split up the ownership of the parcels.)

3. **Landlocked parcels:** The most common example of an easement by necessity is where a parcel is *landlocked*, so that access to a public road can only be gained via a right of way over adjoining property (as in the above example). [209]

E. **Easement by prescription:** An easement by *"prescription"* is one that is gained under principles of *adverse possession*. If a person uses another's land for more than the statute of limitations period governing ejectment actions, he gains an easement by prescription. [210]

> **Example:** In state X, the statute of limitations on actions to recover possession of real estate (ejectment actions) is 21 years. A, the owner of lot 1, uses a path over lot 2, owned by B, for 21 years. Assuming that the use meets the requirements discussed below (e.g., use must be "adverse," not "permissive"), after the 21 years A gains an

C
A
P
S
U
L
E

S
U
M
M
A
R
Y

easement by prescription, and may use the path as a right of way forever afterwards.

1. **When statute starts to run:** The statutory period does not begin to run until the owner of the servient tenement *gains a cause of action* against the owner of the dominant tenement. Therefore, an easement of *"light and air"* cannot be acquired by prescription (since the owner of the servient tenement never can sue the owner of the dominant tenement, because the latter merely looks out over the former's property, rather than trespassing upon it). [210]

2. **Adverse use:** The use must be *adverse* to the rights of the holder of the servient tenement, and without the latter's *permission*. (*Example*: P and D are next-door neighbors. Solely out of friendship, D agrees that P may use D's driveway to get to P's garage. P thanks D for this, and does not say that he is asserting an actual legal right to use the driveway. P's use is therefore not adverse, so even if the usage continues longer than the statute of limitations, no easement by prescription will be gained. Instead, the use is merely a *license*, which is revocable at will by D.) [210-11]

3. **Continuous and uninterrupted:** The use must be *continuous and uninterrupted* throughout the statutory period. Thus if the use is so *infrequent* that a reasonable landowner would not be likely to protest, the continuity requirement is not satisfied. [212]

4. **Tacking:** There can be *tacking* on the dominant side of the prescriptive easement. (*Example*: In a state with a 21-year statute of limitations on ejectment actions, A, the owner of Blackacre, uses a path across Whiteacre for 12 years. He then sells Blackacre to B, who uses the same path for an additional 9 years. At the end of this 9 years, B will have an easement by prescription, because he is in privity of estate with A and therefore can tack his use onto A's use.) [213]

III. SCOPE OF EASEMENTS

A. **Prescriptive easement:** If the easement is created by *prescription*, the *scope* of the allowable use is determined by looking at the use that took place during the statutory period. Therefore, a use that is substantially *broader* (or more burdensome to the servient tenement) than existed during the time when the statute of limitations was running, will *not* be allowed. [215]

B. **Development of dominant estate:** Regardless of how the easement was created (e.g., whether by implication, prescription, etc.), the court will allow a use that increases dues to the *normal, foreseeable development* of the dominant estate, so long as this does not impose an *unreasonable burden* on the servient estate. (*Example*: A right-of-way easement is created by prescription in favor of the sole house then located on a dominant tenement. After the easement is created, two more houses are built on the dominant property. The residents of all three houses may use the right of way, since the basic use — as a pedestrian right of way — remains unchanged, the increased use is a function of normal development, and the increase in the burden is slight.) [216]

C. **Use for benefit of additional property:** The holder of the dominant estate is normally *not* allowed to *extend his use* of the easement so that *additional property* owned by him (or by others) is benefitted. (*Example*: W, the owner of Whiteacre, gives B, the owner of Blackacre, an express easement by which B may cross W's property to get from the road to a house on Blackacre. B then buys an adjoining parcel, Greenacre, tears down the house on Whiteacre, builds a new house on Greenacre, and extends the path represented by the easement through Blackacre (which he still owns) to get to the new house on Greenacre. W will be able to enjoin this extended use, since the easement is now being used to benefit additional property beyond Blackacre, the originally-contemplated dominant estate.) [217]

IV. TRANSFER AND SUBDIVISION OF EASEMENTS

A. Transfer of burden: When the title to the *servient estate* is *transferred*, the burden of the easement *remains* with the property. (*Example*: O, the owner of Blackacre, gives A, a neighboring landowner, an express right of way over Blackacre. O then sells Blackacre to B. After the sale, A's easement remains valid against Blackacre.) [218]

B. Transfer of benefit: Whether the *benefit* of an easement "runs with the land" (i.e., is *enforceable by an assignee*) depends on whether the easement is appurtenant or in gross.

    1. Transfer of easements appurtenant: An easement *appurtenant* (one where the benefit applies to particular land only) normally *passes with the transfer of the dominant estate*. (Thus in the above example, if A sells his land to X, X may enforce the easement against either O or one who bought from O.) [218]

        a. Subdivision: Also, if the dominant estate is *sub-divided* into smaller lots sold to different people, and the geography is such that each of the smaller lots can benefit from the easement, then each will generally be permitted to do so. (But this will not happen if this would result in an extreme *increase* in the burden to the servient estate.)

    2. Easements in gross: But easements *in gross* are different. [220]

        a. Common law: At common law, easements in gross are *not transferable*. (*Example*: O owns Blackacre, which adjoins a public beach. O gives A, a friend of his who lives in a different city, the right to park in O's driveway and walk across A's land to the beach. Since this easement is "in gross" — it is not intimately tied to particular land held by A — at common law it is not transferable by A to anyone else.)

        b. Modern view: Today, courts continue to apply this rule of non-transferability to easements that are *"personal"* (as in the above example). But courts will often find that a *commercial* easement was intended to be transferable and will therefore hold it to be so. (*Example*: O gives the telephone company the right to string wires over his land. Today, because of the commercial nature of this easement in gross, most courts would hold that the phone company can assign this right to some other outfit that takes over the phone operations.)

V. TERMINATION OF EASEMENTS

A. Abandonment: Unlike estates in land, an easement may be *terminated* by *abandonment* in some circumstances. [224]

    1. Words alone insufficient: The easement holder's *words alone* will *never* be sufficient to constitute an abandonment. [224]

    2. Intent plus conduct: But if the easement holder *intends* to abandon an easement, and takes *actions* manifesting that intent, he will be held to have abandoned the easement, and it will be extinguished. [224]

        a. Non-use: For instance, *non-use* may on particular facts be action which manifests the easement holder's intent to abandon, in which case the abandonment will be effective. (*Example*: A owns a summer cottage, which holds an appurtenant easement to use a driveway on B's next-door property. If A uses the cottage each year for three years, and fails to ever use the driveway, he may be held to have intended to abandon the easement. But if A's non-use for three years is because he doesn't even use the cottage, then no intent to abandon will be found, and therefore there will be no abandonment.)

C
A
P
S
U
L
E

VI. LICENSES

A. Definition: A *license* is a right to use the licensor's land that is *revocable* at the will of the licensor. This revocability is the main thing that distinguishes licenses from easements. (But there are a couple of exceptions to the revocability of licenses, described below.) [225-27]

    1. No Statute of Frauds: A license is *not* required to satisfy the *Statute of Frauds*, so it may be created *orally*.

    2. Illustrations: Some licenses are much like easements, except for revocability (e.g., O orally gives A the right to use O's driveway to get from A's land to the public highway; this would be an easement if it were in writing, but is a license because it is oral). Other licenses are much more transitory. For instance, a *ticket* to a sports event or concert is a license; similarly, the right to use a *parking lot* is generally only a license.

B. Exceptions to revocability: There are a couple of exceptions to the general rule that licenses are revocable at the grantor's will.

    1. Oral license acted upon: Most important, a license is *irrevocable* if its use would have been an easement except for failure to meet the Statute of Frauds, and the licensee makes *substantial expenditures* on the land in *reliance* on the licensor's promise that the license will be permanent or of long duration. (*Example*: P orally gives D permission to build a roadway across P's land so that D can get from his land to the public highway. D expends substantial money digging and paving the road. P attempts to revoke, and sues D for trespass. A court would probably hold that the license, though oral, was irrevocable because of D's substantial reliance expenditures.) [227-28]

VII. COVENANTS RUNNING WITH THE LAND

A. Definition: Like easements, *"covenants"* may under some circumstances run with the land. A covenant running with the land is simply a contract between two parties which, because it meets certain technical requirements, has the additional quality that it is *binding against one who later buys the promisor's land*, and/or *enforceable by one who later buys the promisee's land*. [228]

    1. Legal relief: When we use the term "covenant," we are talking about a promise that is subject to *legal* rather than equitable relief. That is, when a covenant is breached the relief granted is *money damages*, not an injunction or decree of specific performance. (An injunction or specific performance may be granted for breach of what is called an "equitable servitude," discussed below.) [228]

B. Statute of Frauds: For a covenant to run with the land, it must be *in writing*. [229]

C. Running with the land: The only interesting question about covenants is, When do they *run with the land*?

    1. Running of burden and benefit: More specifically, we want to know: (1) When does the *burden* run (so that the promisor's assignee is bound)? and (2) When does the *benefit* run (so that the promisee's assignee can sue for damages if the covenant is breached)? We have to worry about: (1) the "touch and concern" requirement; and (2) the privity requirements.

        a. "Touch and concern": For the burden to run, the burden must *"touch and concern"* the promisor's land. Similarly, for the benefit to run, the benefit must "touch and concern" the promisee's land.

        b. Privity: Also, for the burden to run, there must be *"privity of estate,"* which usually means both a land transfer between the promisor and promisee ("horizontal" privity) plus a succession of estate from promisor to promisor's assignee ("vertical" privity). For the benefit to run, horizontal privity is sometimes required, but vertical privity is generally not. (See further discussion immediately below).

2. Privity between promisor and promisee ("horizontal" privity): Where a court requires *"horizontal" privity*, it means that there must be some land transfer between the original promisor and the original promisee. [231]

a. Running of burden: In America, *horizontal privity is required in order for the burden to run*. This mainly means that if the original parties are "strangers to title," the burden will not run. Thus two *neighboring landowners* cannot get together and agree that neither will use his property for a certain purpose, and have this restriction be binding on a subsequent purchaser from either of them. (*Example*: A and B, neighboring landowners, agree in writing that neither will tear down his house to erect a new structure. B sells his property to X, who tears down that house. A cannot sue X for damages, because the burden of the covenant does not run with the land. This is so because there was never any land transfer between A and B, and thus no horizontal privity between them.)

i. Requirement satisfied: But the horizontal requirement is satisfied if the original promisor and promisee have some land-transfer relationship. (*Example*: A owns two parcels, each with a house on it. He sells one of the parcels to B. In the transfer agreement, A and B each promises the other that he will not tear down the house to build a new structure. B then re-conveys his parcel to X, who tears down the house. Now, A can sue X for damages, because there was horizontal privity between A and B, in the sense of a land transfer between them.)

b. Running of benefit: Most courts hold that there must also be horizontal privity for the *benefit* to run. (Nearly all courts hold that the same privity rule that applies to running of burden applies to running of benefit; since most courts require horizontal privity for running of burden, they also require it for running of benefit.) (*Example*: A and B own adjacent parcels. They each agree not to tear down their house and rebuild. A conveys to X; B tears down and rebuilds. Assuming that the state, like most, requires horizontal privity for the burden to run, it will apply the same rule for running of benefit. In that case, X will not be able to sue B for damages, because the benefit does not run due to lack of horizontal privity between A and B.)

3. Privity between litigants ("vertical" privity): When a court requires *"vertical"* privity, this refers to the relationship between the promisor and his successor in interest, or the relation between the promisee and his successor. [233]

a. Running of burden: For the burden to run, the party against whom it is to be enforced must succeed to the *entire estate* of the original promisor, in the durational sense. (*Example*: A and B, owners in fee simple of neighboring parcels, each agree to maintain half of a hedge between the properties. B gives a long term lease to X. X fails to maintain his part of the hedge. A cannot sue X for damages, because there is no vertical privity between B and X — when X took a long term lease, he took only part, not all, of B's fee simple.)

b. Running of burden: But the vertical privity requirement has much less bite on the *benefit* side. The benefit may be enforced by anyone who has taken *possession* of the promisee's property with the promisee's permission. (*Example*: On the facts of the above example, if A gave a long-term lease to Y, Y could sue B if B failed to maintain his part of the hedge.)

i. Homeowners association: If P is a homeowners' association set up by a developer to collect annual fees from homeowners in a subdivision (used to maintain any common areas), the association may sue non-payers even though the association owns no property in the development. Thus the requirement of vertical privity is almost completely relieved in this instance.

4. **"Touch and concern" requirement:** [234-38]

    a. **Running of benefit:** For the *benefit* to run, that benefit must *touch and concern* the promisee's land. But this requirement does not have too much practical bite — most kinds of covenants that have anything to do with real estate (e.g., promises to make repairs, promises not to demolish, promises to pay money to a homeowners association, etc.) are found to "touch and concern" the promisee's land (as well as the promisor's land).

        i. **Burden in gross:** If the benefit touches and concerns the promisee's land, the benefit will run *even though the burden does not*. That is, *the benefit can run even if the burden is "in gross,"* i.e., personal to the promisor. [235]

        Example: D sells land containing a restaurant to P; as part of the transaction, D promises not to operate a competing restaurant within a two mile radius. (Assume that the state holds that a non-compete promise "touches and concerns" the promisee's land.) P then conveys the property to X. X can sue D for breach of the promise — since the benefit touches and concerns the P/X land, the benefit can run even though the burden is "in gross," i.e., personal to D.)

    b. **Running of burden:** For the *burden* to run, that burden must "touch and concern" the promisor's land. But about half of the courts impose an additional significant requirement: these courts hold that the burden will not run if the *benefit* does not touch and concern the promisee's land. (That is, half the courts say that *the burden may not run when the benefit is in gross.*) [235]

    Example: A, the owner of Blackacre, sells it to B. B promises not to operate a liquor store on the property so as not to compete with a similar store owned by A on different property. Assume that the state is one which holds that a non-compete promise does not touch and concern the promisee's land. B then sells Blackacre to C. About half of the courts would hold that A cannot sue C for breach, because the burden will not run where the benefit is in gross, i.e., personal to A.

VIII. EQUITABLE SERVITUDES

A. **Generally:** The above rules apply where a promise concerning land is sought to be enforced at law, i.e., by the award of damages. But a promise may also be enforced *at equity*, by the award of an *injunction* (ordering the defendant not to do something) or a decree of *specific performance* (ordering the defendant to do something). When a court not only gives equitable relief, but applies it against an *assignee* of the original promisor, the promise is referred to as an *"equitable servitude"* against the burdened land. [238-39]

    1. **Less rigid requirements:** In general, the technical requirements for establishing an equitable servitude that burdens the land are *less difficult* to meet than the requirements for covenants at law. Therefore, the law of equitable servitudes is generally more important today than the law of covenants at law.

    2. **Affirmative vs. negative:** Most agreements for which equitable enforcement is sought are *negative* in nature — they are usually agreements not to violate certain *building restrictions*. But occasionally, an equitable servitude may involve an *affirmative* promise (e.g., the promise to pay dues to a homeowners' association, or the promise to make certain repairs), at least in American courts. [240-41]

B. **Privity not required:** The requirements of *privity* are virtually *non-existent* in connection with equitable servitudes. For instance, two *neighboring landowners* that never had any land-transfer relationship between them can, by agreement, impose land-use restrictions that will be binding on assignees. (*Example*: A and B, who own adjacent parcels, agree that neither will tear down his house without the other's consent. A and B sell their properties to X and Y, respectively. Assuming requirements of notice are met, X can get an injunction against Y to stop a threatened demolition in violation of the restriction, even though Y may not have expressly agreed to honor the restrictions. By contrast, X could not sue Y for damages under a covenant-at-law theory, because of the lack of horizontal privity between A and B.) [241-42]

C. "Touch and concern" still required: Neither the benefit nor the burden of a restrictive covenant will run unless it can be said to *"touch and concern"* the promisor's land (in the case of a running burden) or the promisee's land (in the case of a running benefit). But this requirement has little bite — courts are extremely loose in determining what kind of benefit or burden "touches and concerns" land. [242]

    1. Running of burden or benefit is in gross: Courts are in dispute about whether equity will enforce a burden where the benefit is in gross, just as they are in dispute about whether a suit at law for money damages may be awarded in this situation. [243]

D. Notice to subsequent purchaser: The most important thing to remember about equitable servitudes is that equity will not enforce an agreement against a subsequent purchaser unless he had *notice* of the restriction. Notice may be either *"actual"* or *"constructive."* [244-45]

    1. Actual notice: Thus if the subsequent purchaser of the burdened land happens to know about the restriction, it is irrelevant that the restriction is not recorded anywhere. (*Example*: A and B each agree in writing not to use their properties for anything but residential premises. Neither records this promise in the land records. B assigns to X, and orally tells X, "You should know that I have promised A that I'll never use the property for non-residential purposes." A will be able to enjoin X from making non-residential use of the property, because X was on actual notice of the restriction at the time he bought.)

    2. Recording: Also, the subsequent purchaser will be deemed to be on notice if he has *"constructive"* knowledge of the restriction. Most importantly, if the restriction is properly *recorded* in the land records, the purchaser is bound even if he does not discover the restriction by the time he buys.

E. Developer's building plan: A general *building plan* formulated by a developer will often bind all parcels in the development. The developer records the plan in the form of a subdivision "plat" or map. To see how the burden and benefit can run to all parcels, assume that Developer (who has recorded a subdivision plat) conveys one parcel to B1 and, subsequently, another parcel to B2. Assume that the deed from Developer to each imposes the requirement that the buyer use the property in accordance with the recorded building plan (e.g., that he not use the property for non-residential uses if the building plan prohibits this). [245-51]

    1. Enforcement by subsequent purchaser: First, consider a suit by B2 against B1. Here, B2 can enjoin B1 against violating the use restrictions. This would probably be true even if the deed from Developer to B1 did *not* expressly mention the plan or the restrictions — the fact that the plan had been publicly filed would probably be enough to put B1 on notice.

    2. Enforcement by prior purchaser against subsequent one: Now consider a suit by B1 against B2. This is trickier, because by hypothesis B1 received his property before the restriction against B2 even existed. Nonetheless, B1 can probably get an injunction against any violation by B2. Courts often do this by the doctrine of *"implied reciprocal servitude"* — when B1 acquired his land in expectation that he would get the benefit of subsequently-created servitudes, there was immediately created in him an implied reciprocal servitude against Developer's remaining land (even if Developer did *not* put the restriction in later deeds, including the deed to B2!)

F. Selection of neighbors: Equitable restrictions (as well as covenants at law) may be used to facilitate the *selection of neighbors*. Such agreements will generally be enforced as long as they are *reasonable* in scope (so that they do not constitute an unreasonable "restraint on alienation") and are not in violation of any anti-discrimination law. [251-53]

Example: Each deed executed by a developer provides that the purchaser must become a member of the homeowners' association, and that the purchaser may not sell his land to anyone who is not a member of the association. It also provides that the association has the right of first refusal to buy any property offered by a member. Such a restriction will generally be enforced, and will give the association's other members (providing that the association has enough money) the practical ability to keep property out of the hands of anyone deemed undesirable. Such a provision is often used by *condominiums* and *co-ops*.

ZONING AND OTHER PUBLIC LAND-USE CONTROLS

I. THE "TAKING" CLAUSE, AND LAND-USE CONTROLS AS IMPLICIT TAKINGS

A. The "Taking" Clause generally: State and federal governments may take private property for public use — this is the power of "eminent domain." However, the Fifth Amendment to the U.S. Constitution provides that "private property [shall not] be taken for public use, without just compensation." This is the so-called "Taking" Clause, made binding on the states by means of the Fourteenth Amendment. [261]

    1. Land-use control as taking: Normally, land-use controls will *not* constitute a taking for which the government must pay compensation. But very occasionally, a regulation may so drastically interfere with the private owner's use of his property, or with the value of that property, that the court will conclude that there has been an *implicit* "taking."

    2. Damages vs. injunction: If the court does find an implicit "taking," it will award one or both of the following remedies: (1) it will strike down the regulation, i.e., *enjoin* the government from enforcing it any more; or (2) it will award *damages* to the owner for his lost use or value.

B. Taking/regulation distinction: If the state merely *regulates* property use in a manner consistent with the state's *"police power,"* then no compensation needs to be paid, even though the owner's use of his property or even its value has been substantially diminished. Thus zoning regulations, environmental protection rules, landmark preservation schemes, etc., will usually not constitute a compensable "taking." But if the regulation goes too far, it will become a "taking" even though the state calls it a regulation. Here are some of the principles the courts look to to decide whether a regulation has become a compensable "taking": [262]

    1. Substantial advancement of legitimate state interests: The land regulation will be a taking unless it *"substantially advances legitimate state interests."*

        a. Broad range of legitimate interests: A *broad range* of governmental purposes constitute "legitimate state interests." These include maintaining residential uses (often done by zoning), preserving landmarks, protecting the environment, etc.

        b. Tight means-end fit: There must be a fairly *tight fit* between the state interest being promoted and the regulation chosen (more than a mere "rational relation" between means and end).

    2. Deprivation of all use: If a regulation is found to deny the landowner of *all economically viable use* of his land, this will make the regulation a "taking." (*Example:* Regulations prevent a particular owner of vacant land from building any structure on the property. This will probably deprive him of all economically viable use, and will thus be a compensable taking unless necessary to serve some overriding governmental interest, such as prevention of flooding or erosion.)

3. **Physical use:** If the government makes or authorizes a permanent ***physical occupation*** of the property, this will automatically be found to constitute a taking. (*Example:* The state orders O to give the public a permanent ***easement*** across his property so that the public can get to a beach — this would be a permanent physical occupation, automatically amounting to a compensable taking.)

4. **Diminution in value:** The more drastic the ***reduction in value*** of the owner's property, the more likely a taking is to be found. This ***"diminution in value"*** standard is probably the single most important factor. (*Example:* Particular land is valuable mostly for the coal to be found under it. The state bars the owner of the mineral rights from doing any coal mining under the land. *Held*, the value of the mining rights was so completely impaired as to amount to a taking.)

5. **Prevention of harm:** A taking will probably ***not*** be found where the property use being prevented is one that is ***harmful*** or ***"noxious"*** to others. (*Example:* A zoning ordinance may properly prevent the operation of a steel mill in the middle of a residential neighborhood.)

C. **Damages for temporary taking:** If a land-use regulation is so broad that it constitutes a taking, the owner may bring an ***"inverse condemnation"*** suit. Under such a suit, he may receive ***damages*** for the ***temporary*** taking (temporary because the regulation is struck down by the court). See *First English Evangelical Lutheran Church v. L.A. County*. [267-68]

II. ZONING

A. **Generally:** The main type of public land-use regulation is ***zoning***. Zoning is generally done on the local, municipal, level. The municipality's power to zone comes from the state "police power," or power to act for the general welfare, which is delegated by state statute to the municipality.

1. **Use zoning:** Most zoning is ***"use zoning,"*** by which the municipality is divided into districts, in each of which only certain uses of land are permitted (e.g., a residential-only district, a commercial district, etc.) [268]

2. **Density controls:** Other zoning laws govern the ***density*** of population or construction. Thus a town might establish a ***minimum lot size*** for single-family homes, minimum ***setback*** requirements (requiring a certain amount of unbuilt land on some or all sides of the structure), ***minimum square footage*** for residences, and ***height*** limits. [269]

B. **Legal limits on zoning:**

1. **Constitutional limits:** Several different federal constitutional provisions may limit a city's ability to zone in a particular manner:

a. **Taking Clause:** First, the Fifth Amendment's "Taking" Clause means that if a zoning regulation is so overreaching that it deprives the owner of all economically viable use of his land, or is not substantially related to some legitimate public purpose, the zoning will be treated as a taking for which compensation must be paid. (See the discussion of the Taking Clause above.)

b. **Procedural due process:** The Fourteenth Amendment's Due Process Clause imposes certain ***procedural requirements*** on the zoning process. For a zoning action that is ***administrative*** rather than legislative (e.g., the granting of a variance or special-use permit for a particular property), an owner is entitled to a ***hearing***, an impartial tribunal, and an explanation of the government's decision. [269]

c. **Substantive due process:** If the zoning law fails to bear a ***rational relation*** to a ***permissible state objective***, it may violate the ***substantive*** aspect of the Due Process

Clause. (*Example*: A zoning law that limits a district to single-family occupancy, and defines "family" so as to exclude most extended families, violates substantive due process. See *Moore v. City of East Cleveland*.) [271-73]

    d. Equal protection: A zoning law that is adopted for the purpose of excluding racial minorities will trigger strict judicial scrutiny, and will probably be found to be a violation of the *Equal Protection* Clause of the Fourteenth Amendment. [273]

2. Aesthetic zoning: Most courts hold today that *aesthetic* considerations may constitute *one factor* in a municipality's zoning decision. But aesthetics may not be the *sole* factor. (*Example*: A city provides that only Georgian Colonial-style houses may be built, because these structures are the most beautiful. A court would probably strike down this regulation on the grounds that although aesthetics may be one factor, they may not be the sole factor.) [274-75]

C. Administration of zoning:

1. Bodies involved in: Several governmental bodies generally get involved in zoning: [275]

    a. Town council: The *zoning code* is enacted by the *municipal legislature*. Usually this is the *town council*.

    b. Board of zoning appeals: A "board of adjustment" or "board of zoning appeals" usually exists to award or deny *variances*, and to hear appeals from the building department's enforcement of the zoning laws.

    c. Planning or zoning commission: The town council generally appoints a *planning commission* or zoning commission. The commission generally *advises* the town council on (but does not independently determine) the contents of the zoning code.

2. Variances: Virtually all zoning ordinances have a provision for the granting of *variances*, i.e., relief in a particular case from the enforcement of an ordinance. [278-80]

    a. Requirements for: Most states impose these requirements for a variance: (1) denial would result in *"unnecessary hardship"* to the owner; (2) the need for the variance is caused by a problem *unique to the owner's lot* (not one shared by many lots in the area); and (3) the variance would not be *inconsistent* with the overall purpose of the ordinance, or inconsistent with the general welfare of the area.

3. Special uses: Zoning ordinances also usually provide for *"special use"* permits. Typically, a special use permit must be obtained for such things as private schools, hospitals and churches. Generally, an applicant is not entitled to a special use permit "as of right," but only in the discretion of the zoning board; however, usually no showing of "special hardship" has to be made (as is the case for a variance). [280]

4. Conditional zoning: Many ordinances provide for *"conditional"* zoning. Under this device, the rezoning of a particular parcel is made subject to the developer's promise to comply with certain conditions, which will protect neighbors. (*Example*: O owns a parcel in an area zoned residential-only. If the ordinance allows for conditional zoning, the town might rezone O's parcel for light industry, but only if O agrees to large set-backs, a low floor-space-to-land-area ratio, or other condition.) [283]

5. Non-conforming uses: When a zoning ordinance is enacted or made more stringent, the pre-existing uses that are now banned by the ordinance are called *"non-conforming uses."* Virtually all ordinances either: (1) grant a non-conforming user a *substantial period* within which he may continue his use; or (2) let him continue that use *indefinitely*. [284-86]

    a. Constitutional issue: Probably it would be a violation of an owner's due process or other constitutional rights for him not to be given at least a substantial period within which to phase out the non-conforming use.

    b. Amortization: If the ordinance does give an owner a substantial period to phase out his use (called an *"amortization"* provision), most courts hold that no violation of the owner's constitutional rights results from the fact that he must eventually cease the non-conforming use.

D. Exclusionary zoning: *"Exclusionary* zoning" is the use of zoning laws to exclude certain types of persons and uses, particularly *racial and ethnic minorities* and *low-income* persons. [287]

    1. Examples of exclusion: A town might exclude certain types of people by putting tight restrictions on the kinds of allowable *residential uses*. Thus a high minimum-acreage requirement, a ban on multiple dwellings, a ban on mobile homes, or a ban on publicly-subsidized housing are all ways a town could try to keep out poor people (and, to the extent that blacks, say, are on average poorer than whites, a way to keep out black people).

    2. Equal Protection law: Exclusionary zoning may be attacked as a violation of the *Equal Protection* Clause of the U.S. Constitution. An equal protection argument has the best chance of success when it argues that a town is discriminating on the basis *race* or *national origin*, since these are "suspect classes"; an attack based on the claim that the town is discriminating against the *poor* will probably not succeed (because poverty is not a suspect class).

        a. Effect vs. purpose: Also, the plaintiff in an equal protection case will probably only win if the court applies *"strict scrutiny"* to the ordinance. This, in turn, will happen only if the court believes that the town acted with the *purpose* of discriminating on racial or ethnic grounds, not if the ordinance merely has the *effect* of making it harder for minorities to live there. [288]

        b. Standing: The *standing* requirements for an equal protection attack in federal court are very difficult. In most instances, P will have to prove that: (1) the zoning rules have prevented a particular project from being built on particular land; and (2) P would probably become a resident of the housing if the zoning limit were overturned and the project built. [291]

    3. Federal statutory suits: Zoning may also be attacked in federal court suits based on federal statutory law, especially the Fair Housing Act. Zoning enacted for the purpose of limiting access by racial or ethnic minorities violates the Act. [292]

        a. Effect vs. purpose: In a Fair Housing Act suit, P does not have to show a discriminatory purpose behind the zoning enactment. Instead, he merely has to show a discriminatory effect; then, the burden shifts to the defendant town to show that its enactment serves legitimate governmental interests rather than discriminatory ones.

    4. State case law: A number of *states*, by case law, have held that zoning may not be used to *exclude the poor*.

        a. Mt. Laurel cases: The most important such cases are the two *Mt. Laurel* cases, in which the New Jersey Supreme Court held that a town must allow its *"fair share"* of the region's demand for low and middle-income housing. According to the *Mt. Laurel* principle, not only may zoning not be used to keep out the poor, but affirmative measures must be taken by a town to cause such housing to be built (e.g., density bonuses given to developers who build some low income housing; cooperation with developers seeking federally-subsidized housing; allowing of mobile homes, etc.) Also, builders must be allowed to seek *site-specific relief* (in which the court orders the builder's parcel to be rezoned to allow the particular project, if the court finds for the developer). [294-98]

III. REGULATION OF SUBDIVISION AND GROWTH

   A. Subdivision regulation: Towns often extensively regulate the process of **subdivision**. This is the process of dividing a parcel into two or more smaller ones, for resale to different purchasers. [298]

   1. Sewers and water mains: For instance, towns usually have detailed requirements that the developer put in water mains, sewers, gutters, and other drainage facilities.

   2. Street design: Similarly, towns regulate **street design**, and require the developer not only to furnish the land for streets, but to build the streets himself.

   B. Growth control: Towns and regions also sometimes attempt to regulate their rate of **growth** (or the **sequence** in which the various parcels of land are developed). [300]

   1. Generally upheld: Generally, growth-control regulations are **upheld** so long as they are reasonable. For instance, a town would probably be entitled to prevent premature subdivision and "urban sprawl" by prohibiting residential construction unless various public facilities (e.g., schools, parks, roads, firehouses, sewers, etc.) were in place first.

   a. Moratoria and limits: In fact, a town ordinance will probably be upheld if it tries to place an absolute **limit** on the number of new units that will be constructed during a particular time period. Even a complete **moratorium** on new residential or commercial construction might be upheld if this was a reasonable way of achieving an important local government goal (e.g., avoiding strain on roads or other public facilities).

IV. HISTORICAL AND ENVIRONMENTAL PRESERVATION

   A. Historical preservation: Municipalities often try to protect buildings or districts of great **historical** or **architectural** interest. [302]

   1. Districts and landmarks: Sometimes, an entire **historical district** is protected. (For instance, the French Quarter in New Orleans is protected because of its great age, uniformity and architectural significance.) Alternatively, sometimes a particular **structure** will be protected because of its historical or architectural significance. In either event, historical preservation schemes generally prohibit the owner from **altering** or **demolishing** the building without a special **permit**.

   2. Generally upheld: A historic preservation ordinance will generally be **upheld** so long as: (1) it gives reasonably precise **standards** to the board charged with enforcement, so that the board does not behave in an **arbitrary** or **discriminatory** manner; and (2) it does not constitute a "taking" without compensation, in violation of the Fifth Amendment. [302]

   a. Taking: The owner's best chance of attacking a scheme is by arguing that it deprives him of all economically viable use of his land, without compensation, in violation of the Fifth Amendment's Taking Clause. But even such arguments are hard to win. For instance, in the **Penn Central** case, the Supreme Court held that a New York City ordinance preventing major changes to Grand Central Terminal, but allowing the owners to continue their present use of the property (as a terminal with office space above it) did not amount to a taking. (But a prohibition on *all* development of a building beyond the current use might be found to deny the owner all economically viable use of the property, in which case the preservation scheme would be a taking for which compensation must be paid.) [303-05]

   b. Transferable Development Rights (TDRs): Some ordinances avoid "taking" problems by giving the owner "Transferable Development Rights" or "TDRs," by which he may transfer his development rights from the preserved building to other nearby parcels. If in the particular real estate market the TDRs have substantial economic value, this may turn what would otherwise be a "taking" (because the owner is deprived of all economically viable use of his land) into a non-taking. [303-04]

B. Environmental preservation: Towns and regions also frequently attempt to protect the *environment*. Of special interest are regulations that attempt to maintain *open areas* by limiting or prohibiting certain kinds of development. [305]

    1. Urban park land: Occasionally, a city may prohibit the development of privately-owned urban *park land*. But prohibiting all development of otherwise-valuable vacant land in the middle of a downtown area is likely to constitute a compensable "taking," because the owner is being deprived of all economically viable use of his land. (But the problems might be eased by allowing TDRs, as discussed above.)

    2. Wetlands and coastlands: More frequently, towns and regions try to limit or prohibit development on *wetlands* and *coastland*. By and large, such preservation schemes have been *upheld*, on the grounds that preservation of these areas is a goal of great social importance, outweighing the landowner's interest in land development. (But a permanent ban on development might be a compensable "taking," unless the government shows that construction would be dangerous, as in the case of a coastal area subject to heavy flooding and erosion.)

V. EMINENT DOMAIN

A. Generally: State and federal governments have the power of *eminent domain*, i.e., the power to take private property for public use. Usually this is done through *condemnation proceedings*, in which the government brings a judicial proceeding to obtain title to land that it needs for some public use. Alternatively, the government occasionally simply makes *use* of a landowner's property without bringing formal condemnation proceedings; here, the landowner may bring an *"inverse condemnation"* action, in which he seeks a court declaration that his property has been taken by the government and must be paid for. The two requirements for the government to use its eminent domain power are: (1) the property must be put to a *"public use"*; and (2) *"just compensation"* must be paid. [308]

B. "Public use": The requirement of *"public use"* (imposed by the Taking Clause of the Fifth Amendment) is very *loosely* interpreted. So long as the state's use of its eminent domain power is "rationally related" to a "conceivable public purpose," the public-use requirement is satisfied. (*Example*: Hawaii condemns lots owned by large landowners, and transfers them to the tenants living on them. *Held*, because there was tremendous inequality in land ownership in Hawaii, this scheme was a rational attempt to remedy a social and economic evil, and therefore satisfied the "public use" requirement. *Hawaii Housing Authority v. Midkiff.*) [308-09]

    1. Urban renewal: Thus as part of an *urban renewal* project, a city may condemn private land, then turn it back to a *private developer* for private use. (The renewal program meets the "public use" requirement even if the particular parcel condemned is not a slum.)

C. "Just compensation": In general, the requirement of *"just compensation"* means that the government must pay the *fair market value* of the property at the time of the taking. [309]

    1. Highest and best use: This fair market value is usually based on the *"highest and best use"* that may be made of the property (at least under current zoning regulations). Thus if a vacant parcel is zoned for subdivision, the value that must be paid is the value the land would have to a subdivider, not the value based on the current rental value of vacant land.

LAND SALE CONTRACTS, MORTGAGES AND DEEDS

I. LAND SALE CONTRACTS

A. Statute of Frauds: The *Statute of Frauds* is applicable in all states to any contract for the sale of land, or for the sale of any interest in land. Therefore, either the contract itself, or a memorandum of it, must be *in writing*. [312]

    1. Memorandum satisfying: A *memorandum* of the parties' agreement, summarizing some terms but not the entire oral agreement, will satisfy the Statute if it specifies the following: (1) the *names* of the parties; (2) the *land* to be conveyed; (3) normally, the *purchase price*; and (4) the *signature* of the party to be charged (i.e., the party against whom enforcement is sought). (*Example*: Seller writes a letter to Buyer, confirming the provisions of their oral contract for the sale of Blackacre. This letter will constitute a sufficient memorandum if Buyer seeks to enforce the contract against Seller, but not if Seller seeks to enforce it against Buyer.) [312-13]

    2. Part performance exception: There is one major exception to the Statute of Frauds for land sale contracts: under the doctrine of *part performance*, a party (either buyer or seller) who has taken action in *reliance* on the contract may be able to gain at least limited enforcement of it. [313-15]

        a. Acts by vendor: If the vendor *makes a conveyance* under the contract, he will then be able to sue for the agreed-upon price, even if the agreement to pay that price was only oral.

        b. Acts by purchaser: Courts are split as to what acts by the *purchaser* constitute part performance entitling him to specific performance.

            i. Possession plus payment: Many states hold that if the buyer takes *possession*, and also *makes payments*, this will be sufficient part performance that the seller will be required to convey the property.

            ii. Improvements: Also, in many states, a buyer who takes possession and then either makes permanent *improvements*, or changes his position in *reliance*, can require the seller to convey.

            iii. "Unequivocally referable" requirement: Most courts say that the buyer's part performance must be *"unequivocally referable"* to the alleged contract. Thus the buyer must show that the part performance was clearly *in response* to the oral contract, and not explainable by some other aspect of the parties' relationship. (*Example*: D orally promises to convey Blackacre to P if P will move in with D and care for D in his old age. P does so. P is distantly related to D. D dies without ever having made the conveyance. If P sues D's estate to enforce the alleged oral agreement, P will probably lose because P's part performance (moving in and caring for P) is not "unequivocally referable" to the oral contract, since P may have been doing it out of affection for a relative.)

B. Time for performance: In a suit for damages, the *time* stated in the contract will be deemed to be *of the essence*, unless the parties are shown to have intended otherwise. (*Example*: Seller refuses to close on the date specified in the contract. Buyer may bring a suit for damages for the delay, even if it is only a few days.) [316-17]

1. **Equity:** But in a suit in *equity* (i.e., a suit for *specific performance*), the general rule is that time is *not* of the essence. Therefore, even if the contract specifies a particular closing date, either party may obtain specific performance though he is unable to close on the appointed day (so long as he is ready to perform within a reasonable time after the scheduled day). (*Example:* The sale contract specifies a November 1 closing date. Buyer has trouble lining up his financing, so he can't close on November 1. The contract is silent about whether time is of the essence. By November 15, Buyer has his financing lined up, and asks Seller to close. Seller now refuses. In the absence of strong evidence that the parties intended time to be of the essence, Buyer will probably get a court to order Seller to convey even though Buyer missed the November 1 closing date.)

C. **Marketable title:** Nearly all land sale contracts require the vendor to convey a *marketable* title. (Even if the contract is silent on this issue, an obligation to convey a marketable title will be *implied* by the court.) [317]

   1. **Definition of "marketable title":** A marketable title is one that is *free from reasonable doubt* about whether the seller can convey the rights he purports to convey. Thus it is *not* sufficient that a court would probably hold the title good in a *litigation*. Instead, the title must be *free from reasonable doubt* so that the buyer will be able to resell in the future. The purchaser is not required to *"buy a lawsuit"*. [318]

   2. **Defects making title unmarketable:** Here are some of the defects that might make title unmarketable: [319]

      a. **Record chain:** First, anything in the prior chain of title indicating that the vendor does not have the *full interest* which he purports to convey, may be a defect. (*Examples:* A substantial variation between the *name* of the grantee of record in one link and the name of the grantor in the following link is a defect. Similarly, a substantial variation in the *description of the land* between one deed and the next may be a defect.)

      b. **Encumbrances:** Second, even if the vendor has valid title to the property, an *encumbrance* on the property will normally constitute a defect. [319-21]

         i. **Mortgage or lien:** Thus an outstanding *mortgage* would be an encumbrance making the title unmarketable. (However, the vendor has the right to *pay off the mortgage at the closing*, out of the sale proceeds.) Similarly, *liens* (e.g., a lien for unpaid taxes, or a lien gotten by a judgment creditor) are defects.

         ii. **Easement:** An *easement* will be a defect if it reduces the *"full enjoyment"* of the premises.

         iii. **Use restrictions:** Similarly, privately-negotiated *use* restrictions (e.g., a covenant whose burden runs with the land, to the effect that only residential structures will be built) can be a defect.

         iv. **Land-use and zoning violations:** Most courts hold that violations of *building codes* are *not* encumbrances on title. But a violation of a *zoning ordinance* usually *is* treated as an encumbrance.

   3. **Agreement and notice:** But the parties may *agree* that certain kinds of defects will *not* constitute unmarketable title. This agreement will normally take place in the contract of sale. (*Example*: Buyer and Seller agree that a particular easement held by X across the property will not render title unmarketable. The court will enforce this agreement.) Also, the buyer may be held to be on *notice* of certain defects, and therefore held to have implicitly agreed to take subject to them (e.g., where a right of way across the property is very visible to anyone who looks even casually at the property).

   4. **Time for measuring marketability:** Unless the contract specifies otherwise, the vendor's title is not required to be marketable *until the date set for the closing*. Thus the vendor

may sign a contract to sell property which he does not yet own (or on which there are several defects in title), and the purchaser cannot cancel the contract prior to the closing date because of this fact. [321]

D. Remedies for failure to perform: Where one party fails to perform a land sale contract, the other party may have two remedies: (1) a suit for *damages*; and (2) a suit for *specific performance*. [323-25]

    1. Damages: If one party breaches a land sale contract, the other may almost always sue for *money damages*. Generally, P recovers the *difference between the market price and the contract price* (the "benefit of the bargain" rule).

    2. Specific performance: Usually, an action for *specific performance* may be brought against the defaulting party, whether the defaulter is buyer or seller. Most commonly, the seller changes his mind, and buyer is able to get a decree of specific performance ordering seller to convey the property. (Each parcel of land is deemed unique, so the court presumes that money damages would not be adequate to compensate the buyer.)

    3. Deposit: If buyer is unable to close on the appointed date, most courts do *not* allow him to recover his *deposit* (on the theory that a suit to recover a deposit is in effect an action at law, and time will be deemed to be of the essence in a suit at law).

E. Equitable conversion: For many purposes, the courts treat the *signing of the contract* as vesting in the purchaser *equitable ownership* of the land. (Conversely, the vendor is treated as becoming the equitable owner of the purchase price.) [325]

    1. Risk of loss: Most courts hold that since the vendee acquires equitable ownership of the land as soon as the contract is signed, the *risk of loss* immediately *shifts to him*. This is true even if the vendee never takes *possession* prior to the casualty. (*Example:* S contracts to sell land to B. Prior to the closing, while S is still in possession, a hurricane destroys the house located on the land. Most courts hold that the loss falls upon B — B must still pay the agreed-upon purchase price, and does not receive any abatement of price, nor does he get his deposit back.) [327-28]

        a. Exceptions: But courts following this majority rule have a couple of key *exceptions* to it: (1) the vendor bears any loss resulting from his own *negligence*; and (2) the vendor bears the loss if at the time it occurred, he could not have conveyed title (e.g., because his title was *unmarketable*).

        b. Insurance: But very importantly, courts who place the risk of loss on the purchaser give him the *benefit of the vendor's insurance*. [328]

II. MORTGAGES AND INSTALLMENT CONTRACTS

A. Nature of mortgage: A *mortgage* is a financing arrangement, in which the person buying property (or one who already owns property) receives a loan, and the property is pledged as security to guarantee repayment of the loan. [330]

    1. Two documents: There are two documents associated with every mortgage: (1) the *"note"* (or "bond"); and (2) the *mortgage* itself.

        a. The note: The *note* is the buyer's personal *promise to make the repayments*. If there is a foreclosure against the property and the foreclosure sale does not yield enough to cover the outstanding mortgage debt, the note serves as the basis for a *deficiency judgment* against the borrower for the balance still due.

        b. Mortgage: The *mortgage itself* is a document which gives the lender the right to *have the property sold* to repay the loan if the borrower defaults. Since the mortgage in effect gives the mortgagee an interest in the land, the mortgage is *recorded*.

2. **Sale of mortgaged property:** Usually, when mortgaged property is sold the mortgage is paid off at the closing. But property can be sold without paying off the mortgage, either by: (1) having the purchaser take "subject to" the mortgage; or (2) having the purchaser "assume" the mortgage. [331]

 a. **Sale "subject to" mortgage:** If the purchaser merely takes *"subject to"* the mortgage, he is *not personally liable* for payment of the mortgage debt. True, the mortgagee can foreclose if the buyer does not make the payments. But the mortgagee may not sue the buyer for any balance still remaining on the loan after foreclosure; that is, the mortgagee may not get a deficiency judgment against the purchaser. (But the mortgagee may in this instance sue the original mortgagor for this balance.)

 b. **Assumption:** If the new buyer *assumes* payment of the mortgage, he is liable, both to the original mortgagor and to the mortgagee, for re-payment of the mortgage loan. Thus the mortgagee can get a deficiency judgment against the assuming purchaser.

3. **Foreclosure:** *Foreclosure* is the process by which the mortgagee may reach the land to satisfy the mortgage debt, if the mortgagor defaults. [333]

 a. **Judicial foreclosure:** Usually, foreclosure is *judicially supervised* — the foreclosing mortgagee must institute a lawsuit, and the actual foreclosure sale takes place under supervision of a government official (usually a sheriff).

 b. **Private foreclosure sale:** Some states allow the mortgage lender to use a document called a *"deed of trust"* rather than a "mortgage." The deed of trust allows the lender (or a third person) to hold the property as *"trustee,"* and to sell it in a *private sale* if the borrower defaults. However, the private sale must be held in a *commercially reasonable manner* so as to bring the highest price possible — if the lender does not do this, he will owe damages to the borrower in the amount that the borrower might have gotten back (representing the borrower's equity above the mortgage amount) had the sale been a commercially reasonable one.

B. **Installment contracts:** Land can be bought under an *installment contract*. The buyer makes a down payment, and pays the rest of the purchase price in installments (usually monthly). Here, the buyer does *not receive his deed* until after he has paid all (or, sometimes, a substantial portion) of the purchase price. [335-36]

1. **Forfeiture:** If the installment buyer defaults, the seller does not need to go through complex foreclosure proceedings — he can just exercise his contractual right to declare the contract *forefeited* (in which case the seller theoretically gets to keep whatever has been paid on account). But modern courts often hold that if the buyer has paid a *substantial portion* of the purchase price, and the seller would be unjustly enriched by a complete forfeiture, ordinary *foreclosure proceedings* (applicable to mortgages) must be used.

III. DEEDS

A. **Nature of deed:** The *deed* is the document which acts to *pass title* from the grantor to the grantee. [336]

1. **Merger:** Under the doctrine of *merger*, most obligations imposed by the contract of sale are *discharged* unless they are repeated in the deed. (*Example:* The contract calls for merchantable title, in the form of a warranty deed. Buyer carelessly accepts a "quitclaim" deed which makes no warranties. Buyer will not be able to sue Seller on the contractual provision if the title turns out to be defective — the contractual provisions are extinguished and replaced by whatever provisions are contained in the deed, under the merger doctrine.) [336]

2. **Two main types of deeds:** There are two basic types of deeds: (1) the *quitclaim* deed, in which the grantor makes no covenant that his title is good (he merely passes on to the

grantee whatever title he in fact has); and (2) the *warranty deed*, in which the grantor makes one or more promises about the state of the title.

B. Description of the property:

1. **Types of description:** There are three main ways of *describing* land in a deed. Their use varies by region and type of land: [337-41]

   a. **Metes and bounds:** A *"metes and bounds"* description begins by establishing a starting point (usually based on a visible landmark or "monument"). Then a series of "calls and distances" is given, each of which represents a line going in a certain direction for a certain distance. (*Example*: "From the southwest corner of East and Main Street, then running north 50 degrees 26 minutes for 273 feet, then west 59 degrees 8 minutes for 100 feet," etc.) [337]

   b. **Government survey:** In many rural areas, especially west of the Mississippi, the description method uses the U.S. *government survey*. Land is divided into six-mile-square tracts called "townships"; each township is divided into 36 one-mile-square tracts called "sections"; each section contains 640 acres, each of which can be directly referred to. [337]

   c. **Plat:** The *"plat"* method relies on the recording of a map or "plat" of property by a developer, in which the plat shows the location of individual lots. [338] (*Example*: "Lot 2 in Block 5 in Highwood, a subdivision platted on a map filed in the Register's Office of the County of Westchester on June 13, 1910.") [338]

2. **Interpretation:** In interpreting the description of the land conveyed, the court attempts to ascertain the *intent* of the parties.

   a. **Construction in grantee's favor:** Courts tend to interpret the deed in a way which is *most favorable to the grantee* (i.e., the document is construed against the grantor, since the grantor usually drafts the deed). [340]

C. Formalities: Deeds must meet certain *formalities*, which vary from state to state. [341]

1. **Signature:** The grantor must place his *signature* on the deed. The signature of the *grantee* is generally *not* necessary.

2. **Attestation or acknowledgment:** In most states, statutes require the deed either to be *"attested"* to (i.e., *witnessed* by one or more persons not parties to the transaction) or to be *notarized*.

D. Delivery of deed: For a deed to be valid, it must not only be executed, but also *"delivered."* But this "delivery" requirement does not necessarily refer to physical delivery; what is required is that the grantor use words or conduct evidencing his intention to make the deed *presently operative* to vest title in the grantee. [342-47]

1. **Not revocable:** If the delivery occurs, title passes immediately to the *grantee*. Thereafter, return of the deed to the grantor has *no effect* either to *cancel* the prior delivery or to reconvey the title to him. The only way the title can get back to the grantor is if a new, formally satisfactory, conveyance takes place.

E. Covenants for title in warranty deed: If the deed is a *"warranty"* deed (as opposed to a "quitclaim" deed, which merely conveys whatever interest the grantor has without making any promises), the grantor is held to be making various promises about the state of his ownership. These promises are called *"covenants for title."* [347]

1. **The covenants:** The covenants fall into three basic groups: [347-48]

   a. **Seisin and conveyance:** The covenants of *"seisin"* and of *"right to convey"* mean that the grantor has an *indefeasible estate* in the quality and quantity which he purports to convey. (*Example*: These covenants might be breached if the grantor purported to convey a fee simple absolute, but actually only owned and conveyed a fee simple subject to condition subsequent or a fee simple subject to an executory limitation.)

b. Against encumbrances: The covenant *"against encumbrances"* is a promise that there are no encumbrances against the property, that is, no impediments to title which do not affect the fee simple but which diminish the value of the land. (*Examples*: *Mortgages*, *liens*, *easements* and *use restrictions* are all encumbrances, so if the grantor gives a deed containing a covenant against encumbrances, the existence of any of these will constitute a breach of that covenant.)

c. Quiet enjoyment and warranty: The covenants of *"quiet enjoyment"* and *"warranty"* represent a *continuing contract* by the grantor that the grantee will be entitled to *continued possession* of the land in the future. (*Example*: These covenants would be breached if a third person not only asserted that he had paramount title, but commenced proceedings to *eject* the grantee.)

2. Present vs. future covenants: Be sure to distinguish between: (1) *present* covenants; and (2) *future* covenants. [349]

a. Present covenants: The covenants of *seisin*, *right to convey*, and *against encumbrances* are *present covenants*. They are breached, if at all, at the *moment the conveyance is made*. Thus a breach can occur *even though there is no eviction* — all the grantee needs to do to recover on the claim is to show that title was in fact defective on the date of the conveyance.

b. Future covenants: By contrast, the covenants of *quiet enjoyment* and *warranty* are *future covenants*. They are breached *only when an eviction occurs*. (*Example*: Grantor conveys Blackacre to Grantee under a warranty deed. Ten years later, Grantee discovers that X has a paramount title to that held by Grantor. This is a breach of the present covenants (seisin, right to convey and against encumbrances), even though there is no eviction. But it is not a breach of the future covenants (quiet enjoyment and warranty), because X has not tried to evict Grantee.)

3. Statute of limitations: The main reason for distinguishing between present and future covenants involves the *statute of limitations*. The statute starts to run on a *present* covenant *at the time the conveyance is made*. It starts to run on a *future* covenant only *when an eviction occurs*. Therefore, if many years pass from the time of the conveyance, and the grantee discovers that someone has paramount title, the grantee is likely to be out of luck: the time for suing on the present covenants is likely to have passed (since that clock started running at the time of the conveyance), yet there will be no breach of the future covenants if the holder of the paramount title has not attempted to eject the grantee. (Thus on the facts of the above example, Grantee is likely to be out of luck, with his present covenants time-barred and his future covenants not yet breached due to the absence of any ejectment action by X.) [349]

4. Enforcement by future grantee (running of covenants): A second reason for distinguishing between the present and future covenants concerns whether the covenant *runs with the land*, i.e., whether it is *enforceable by subsequent grantees*. [350]

a. Present covenants: The present covenants usually *do not run with the land*.

b. Future covenants: But the future covenants *do run with the land*.

Example: O conveys to G1 under a warranty deed. G1 conveys to G2. G2 discovers that X has always held a paramount title superior to O's. G2 cannot sue O on the present covenants (seisin, right to convey and against encumbrances), because these do not run with the land. But he may sue O for breach of the future covenants (warranty and quiet enjoyment). (But remember that these future covenants will not be breached unless X actually sues to eject G2.)

5. **Measure of damages:** If the grantor breaches any of these warranties, the grantee's recovery is generally limited to the ***purchase price paid*** — the grantee may ***not*** recover for any ***appreciation*** in the value of the land since the conveyance. [351]

F. **Warranty of habitability:** Most courts today recognize an ***implied warranty of habitability*** on behalf of the purchaser of a ***new residence*** against a ***professional builder*** who built the house. (*Example*: Developer, who is in the business of building homes, sells a home to P. Shortly after P moves in, he discovers that the foundation is cracked and the roof is structurally unsound. In most states, P may sue Developer for breach of the implied warranty of habitability.) [352]

1. **Used homes:** The buyer of a ***used home cannot*** sue the prior "amateur" owner. But the second buyer may, in most states, sue the ***original builder*** for breach of the implied warranty of habitability, provided that: (1) the defect was ***not obvious*** at the time of the second purchase, and (2) the defect occurred within a ***reasonable time*** after construction of the house. (*Example*: On the facts of the above example, if P sold the house to P1, P1 could sue Developer if the foundation and roof problems were not obvious at the time of the P-P1 sale, and occurred within a reasonable time after Developer built the house.) [353]

G. **Co-ops and condos:**

1. **Co-ops:** The term ***"co-operative"*** or ***"co-op"*** usually refers to a means of owning an apartment house. The building is owned by a co-operative ***corporation***. What the lay-person thinks of as an "owner" of an individual apartment unit is really a ***shareholder*** in the corporation. Each shareholder is entitled to enter into a ***"proprietary lease,"*** in which the corporation is lessor and the shareholder is lessee. The lessee is generally required to pay his portion of the building's ***mortgage*** interest and principal, and various ***"carrying charges"*** used to defray the maintenance and operating costs of the building. [355]

2. **Condominium:** The ***condominium*** or ***"condo"*** is a form of ownership in which each individual resident holds a ***fee simple*** in a certain physical space or parcel, but all the residents collectively own certain ***"common areas."*** In the typical "horizontal" condo structure (e.g., two-story townhouses spread over a large parcel), each individual resident might own the soil upon which his townhouse stands, but he would not own the surrounding lawns, swimming pool, etc. — these would be held by the condominium association. [355]

THE RECORDING SYSTEM AND TITLE ASSURANCE

I. RECORDING STATUTES

A. **General function of:** The main function of ***recording acts***, which are in force in every jurisdiction, is to give a purchaser of land a way to check whether there has been an ***earlier transaction*** in the property inconsistent with his own. Even if there has been an earlier transaction, if it is not recorded the later purchaser will generally gain priority — thus the recording acts give a buyer a way to be sure that he is getting good title. [360]

1. **Relations between original parties:** Recording acts only govern the relationship between a grantee and a subsequent purchaser of the same property. They do ***not*** govern the relation between the ***grantor and the grantee under a particular conveyance***.

> **Example**: D conveys Blackacre to P. D then conveys it again to X, who doesn't know about the D-P conveyance. X records his deed before P can record his. Because of the

recording act, X's deed takes priority over P's. P sues D for his double-dealing. P will be able to recover against D, because the recording act has no effect upon the relations between both parties to a particular deed (i.e., P and D), only the relationship between two grantees under different deeds (i.e., P and X).

B. Different types of acts: There are three basic types of recording acts: (1) *"pure race"* statutes; (2) *"pure notice"* statutes; and (3) *"race-notice"* statutes. [360]

    1. Pure race statutes: A *race* statute places a premium on the *race to the recorder's office*. The subsequent purchaser must *record before the earlier purchaser*, but he is protected *regardless of whether he has notice* of the earlier conveyance. Very few pure race statutes remain on the books.

    2. Pure notice statute: A pure *notice* statute provides that an unrecorded instrument is invalid against *any* subsequent purchaser without notice, *regardless of whether the subsequent purchaser records prior to the first purchaser*.

    3. Race-notice statute: A *race-notice* statute protects the subsequent purchaser only if he meets *two* requirements: (1) he *records before* the earlier purchaser records; and (2) he takes *without notice* of the earlier conveyance.

        Illustration: In 1985, O conveys Blackacre to A. In 1986, O conveys to B. In 1987, B records. In 1988, A records. Here is how the rights of A and B to Blackacre would be resolved under various types of recording acts:

        Race: Under a pure race statute, B wins automatically, without regard to whether he had actual notice of the earlier conveyance to A — B recorded his deed before A did, so that is the end of the matter. (Had A recorded in 1987 and B in 1988, A would have won, even though at the time B took, he had no way to find out about the earlier conveyance to A.)

        Notice: Under a pure notice statute, B wins. In fact, B would have won even if he never recorded at all, or recorded after A — the mere fact that B took after A, and without notice of A's interest, would be enough to give him the victory.

        Race-notice: Under a race-notice statute, B will win only if he took without actual notice of A's interest. Furthermore, if B had recorded after A (instead of before A, as really happened), B would have lost due to his late recording even if he took without actual notice of A's interest. So under the race-notice statute (probably the most common kind of statute), the subsequent purchaser (here, B) has two obstacles to overcome: (1) he must record first; and (2) he must take without actual notice of the earlier interest.

C. Mechanics: Here is a summary of the mechanics of recording: [362-63]

    1. Deposit: The grantee (or the grantee's title insurance company) brings the deed to the recording office (usually located in the county where the land lies). The recorder stamps the date and time of deposit, and then places a photocopy of the deed in a chronological book containing all recorded deeds.

    2. Indexing: Then, the deeds are *indexed*. Usually there is both a *grantor* index (enabling a searcher to find all conveyances made by a particular grantor) and a *grantee* index (permitting the searcher to find all conveyances made *to* a particular grantee).

D. What instruments must be recorded: Recording acts generally allow (and in effect require) the recording of *every instrument by which an interest in land*, whether legal or equitable, is *created* or *modified*. Thus not only fee simple conveyances, but also *life estates*, *mortgages*, *restrictive covenants*, and *tax liens*, are all required to be recorded. [363-64]

    1. Not recordable: Some types of interests are usually *not recordable*:

a. Adverse possession: Thus titles based upon *adverse possession* are usually not recordable (since there is no instrument to record).

b. Some easements: Similarly, an *easement* by *implication or necessity* usually does not have to be recorded (since it does not give rise to a recordable document). (But in some instances, a conveyance of the property to a bona fide purchaser who takes without notice of the easement may cut the easement off.) On the other hand, an *express* easement is recordable.

c. Short leases: In many states, a *short term lease* (e.g., less than three years) may not be recorded. If so, that lease will be valid against a subsequent bona fide purchaser.

d. Contracts: Similarly, some states do not allow executory *contracts of sale* to be recorded. (But the vendee's rights will be subordinate to that of a subsequent claimant who actually buys the property.)

E. Parties protected: The subsequent grantee, to get the protection of the recording act against a prior grantee, must either be: (1) a *"purchaser for value"* or (2) a *creditor* meeting certain standards. [364-66]

1. Purchaser for value: In most states, a grantee gets the benefit of the recording act (i.e., he takes priority over an earlier unrecorded conveyance) only if he *gives value* for his interest. [364]

a. Donee: Thus a *donee* is usually *not protected* by the recording act. (*Example*: O conveys to A. O then purports to give the property, for no consideration, to B. B records, A never does. Under most statutes, B still loses to A, because B — although he is a subsequent grantee who recorded first — did not give valuable consideration.)

b. Less than market value: Although consideration is required, it does *not* have to be an amount *equal to the market value of the property* (but it must be more than *nominal* consideration). (*Example*: On the facts of the above example, if B had paid half the market value of the property, he would probably have prevailed against A; but if he only paid $1, he would not.)

c. Purchase from or through grantee: One who purchases for valuable consideration from the record owner is of course protected. But also, one who buys from the *heirs or devisees* of the record owner will also be protected. (*Example*: O conveys to A. O then conveys to B for value. B records, A does not. B then bequeaths the property to C. C conveys to D. D will prevail against A — even though B in one sense took "nothing," his right to prevail under the recording act against a prior unrecorded deed is itself devisable.)

2. Creditors: A landowner's *creditors* may also receive the protection of the recording act. [365-66]

a. Mortgage: If a creditor receives a *mortgage* from the landowner, he is treated as a "purchaser," and he must generally meet the consideration requirement. This means that if he is giving something of *new value* (e.g., cancelling part of the debt in return for the mortgage, or extending the owner's time to pay), he will probably be deemed to have given consideration, and will thus be protected against a prior unrecorded conveyance. But if he merely retains the same rights he always had (to be paid the full amount of his debt, at the time promised), then he is not giving new value, and his mortgage will not be protected against a prior unrecorded conveyance.

b. Judgment and execution creditors: A creditor who obtains a *judgment*, or who is allowed to *attach* his debtor's property at the beginning of the lawsuit, gets a *lien* against the debtor's property. This lien may or may not be protected under the recording act against a prior unrecorded purchase, depending on how the statute is drafted.

(If the statute only protects "purchasers," the lien creditor probably does not get protection against the prior unrecorded deed.)

3. Eligible to be recorded: The subsequent purchaser who wants the protection of the recording act must record his own deed, and that deed must be one which is in fact *eligible to be recorded*. If it is not, the purchaser will not be protected even if the recording clerk makes a mistake and accepts the document. [368]

   a. Must record whole chain: Also, the subsequent grantee must see to it that his *entire chain of title* is recorded. (Thus if one of the subsequent grantee's predecessors in interest submitted, say, an improperly-notarized document that was therefore not eligible for recording, the subsequent grantee would lose.)

F. Notice to subsequent claimants: In virtually all jurisdictions (that is, jurisdictions having notice or race-notice statutes, but not those very few having pure race statutes) the subsequent purchaser will lose if he was on *notice* of the earlier deed. A purchaser can be on notice in three ways: (1) *actual notice*; (2) *record notice*; and (3) *"inquiry"* notice. [368]

1. Actual notice: If the subsequent purchaser is shown to have had *actual* notice of the existence of the prior unrecorded interest, he will not gain the protection of the recording act in a notice or notice-race jurisdiction.

2. Record notice: The subsequent grantee is deemed to have *"record"* notice if the prior interest is *adequately recorded*. However, the mere fact that a deed is recorded somewhere in the public records does not mean that the recording is "adequate" — the document must be recorded in a way that a reasonable searcher would *find* it. [369-76]

   a. Defective document: A document which is *not entitled to be recorded* will not give record notice, even if it is mistakenly accepted for recording. (*Example*: If the jurisdiction requires the deed to be *notarized*, and it is not, it will not give record notice. However, states often treat certain formal defects in deeds as being "cured" after the passage of a certain amount of time.)

   b. Imputed knowledge: If proper recording of the earlier document took place, subsequent purchasers are on "record notice" even if they *never actually see* the document that has been filed. That is, the court *imputes* to the subsequent purchaser the knowledge which he *would have obtained* had he conducted a diligent title search.

   c. "Chain of title": Therefore, the recording of an instrument gives record notice to a subsequent searcher only if that searcher *would have found the document* using generally-accepted searching principles (use of the grantor and grantee indexes). A recorded instrument which would not be found by these principles is said to be outside the searcher's "chain of title," and prevents the giving of record notice. [371-76]

   Example: O conveys to A; A never records. A then conveys to B; B records. O conveys the same property to C; C records. Assume that C has no knowledge of the O-to-A or A-to-B conveyances. C will have priority over B, even though B's interest is recorded. This is because C, when searching title, has no way to know of the A-to-B deed — C would never find the original O-to-A conveyance, and thus cannot know to look under A's name in the grantor index to discover whether he ever conveyed to anyone else. (Nor would C have any way to know to look for B's name in the grantee index.) The A-to-B deed is said to be "outside C's chain of title"; C is therefore not on record notice of the A-to-B deed, and will take priority over B.

3. Inquiry notice: Even if a purchaser has neither record notice nor actual notice of a prior unrecorded conveyance, he may be found to have been on *"inquiry" notice* of it. Inquiry notice exists where a purchaser is in *possession of facts which would lead a reasonable person in his position* to make an *investigation*, which would in turn advise him of the existence of the prior unrecorded right. Such a person is on inquiry notice even if he does not in fact make the investigation. (But the purchaser is responsible only for those facts which the investigation would have disclosed.) [376-80]

    a. Possession: Thus if the parcel is *possessed* by a person who is *not the record owner*, this will place a subsequent purchaser on inquiry notice. That is, the purchaser must: (1) *view* the property, to see whether it is in the possession of someone other than the record owner; and (2) if there is such a possessor, he must inquire as to the source of the possessor's rights in the property. (*Example:* Same facts as above example. C had a duty to inspect the property — if inspection would have disclosed that B (or someone claiming under B) was in possession of the property, C would be held to be on "inquiry notice" of B's interest. Since C could then have learned B's name, he could have checked back in the records to find the A-to-B deed, and perhaps might have discovered the O-to-A unrecorded deed. If a judge decided that this investigation would have enabled C to trace B's interest all the way back to O, C would lose in a contest with B because of the inquiry notice principle.)

4. Timing of notice: In order for a subsequent purchaser to be protected by the recording act, she must have made *substantial payments* before being on notice of the prior conveyance. [380-81]

    a. Installment contract: Where the subsequent purchaser is buying under an *installment contract*, if she receives *record notice* (but not actual notice), she is protected as to payments she makes. (*Example:* O conveys to A, who does not record. O conveys to B under an installment contract. After B has started making payments, A records. B doesn't learn of the recording, and keeps making payments. Most courts hold that B is protected as a b.f.p. as to payments made before and after A's recording, as long as the payments are made before B received *actual* notice of the prior conveyance to A.)

5. Purchaser from one without notice: If a purchaser who takes without notice of a prior unrecorded instrument *resells* the property, the *new* purchaser is treated as one who may claim the benefit of the recording act, even if *he* buys *with* actual notice. This is done to protect the earlier (innocent) purchaser's market for the property. [381]

II. TITLE REGISTRATION (THE TORRENS SYSTEM)

A. How the system works: In some parts of the U.S., the *"title registration"* system or *"Torrens"* system is available as an *option*. This system enables the owner of a parcel to obtain a *certificate of title*, similar to an automobile certificate of title. When the holder of the certificate wishes to sell, his prospective purchaser merely has to inspect the certificate itself (on which nearly all encumbrances must be noted) — a lengthy title examination is unnecessary. [381-82]

    1. How it works: The registration process begins with an *application* by a person claiming ownership of a parcel to have it registered. Notice is given to anyone shown on the ordinary land records as having an interest in the property. Then, a court hears any claims regarding the property, and if satisfied that the applicant indeed has good title, orders a certificate of title to be issued. [382-83]

B. Where used: The Torrens system is never required, but is available as an option in 11 states. In only a few areas does the system account for a significant portion of the land area (e.g., Hawaii, Boston, parts of Minnesota and parts of Ohio.) [382]

III. TITLE ASSURANCE

A. Examination by lawyer: One way the purchaser sometimes assures himself that he is getting valid title is to have a title examination performed by his *lawyer*. Usually, the lawyer does not directly search the records; instead, he orders an *"abstract"* of title from an abstract company and reviews that abstract. The lawyer then gives his client a written opinion as to the state of the title. The lawyer is liable for his own negligence in rendering an opinion on the title as presented in the abstract (but not liable for any mistake in the abstract itself — here, the abstract company might be liable). [385]

B. Title insurance: The leading means by which a buyer of property can assure himself of a good title is *title insurance*. [385-89]

    1. Covers matters not shown in title search: Title insurance will protect the buyer against many risks that would *not* be disclosed even by the most careful title search. For instance, the buyer would be covered if title turns out to be bad because of forgery of an instrument in the chain, fraudulent misrepresentation of marital status by a grantor (so that the spouse's inchoate right of dower persevered), defects in a prior grant due to lack of delivery, etc. Also, the policy usually covers the insured's *litigation costs* in defending his title even if the defense is successful.

    2. Scope: But title policies usually contain a number of *exceptions*, including the following: [386-87]

        a. Facts which survey would show: Policies usually exclude facts which an *accurate survey* of the property would disclose. Thus *encroachments* (either by the insured onto adjacent property or vice versa) and violations of set-back rules are generally not covered.

        b. Adverse possession: Also, the title policy does not protect against a claim of *adverse possession*, at least if the physical possession exists at the time the policy is written. Therefore, the buyer must still *inspect* the property.

RIGHTS INCIDENT TO LAND

I. NUISANCE

A. Defined: A landowner may sue another person for *"private nuisance."* Private nuisance is an interference with a landowner's *use and enjoyment of his land*. [394]

    1. Substantial interference: The interference with the plaintiff's use and enjoyment must be *substantial*. Thus if P's damage consists of his being *inconvenienced* or subjected to unpleasant smells, noises, etc., this will be "substantial" damage only if a person of *normal sensitivity* would be seriously bothered.

    2. Defendant's mental state: There is *no* rule of *"strict liability"* in nuisance. P must show that D's conduct was *negligent*, *intentional* or *abnormally dangerous*.

        a. Intentional: If P wants to show that D's conduct was "intentional," P does not have to show that D *desired* to interfere with P's use and enjoyment of his land. P merely has to show that D *knew with substantial certainty* that such interference would occur. (*Example:* D, a factory owner, knows that his plant is spewing pollutants and smoke into the air over P's property. P can sue D for "intentional" nuisance so long as P can show that D was on notice of what was happening, even if D did not "desire" this result to occur.)

    3. Unreasonableness: Even if D's conduct is intentional, P will not win in nuisance unless he shows that D's actions were *"unreasonable."* In determining what is reasonable, the *nature of the neighborhood* is likely to be quite significant. (*Example:* A steel mill located in an otherwise completely residential area is much more likely to be found an "unreasonable" interference than is a steel mill in the middle of an industrial park.)

CAPSULE

B. Remedies: P has a chance at either or both of the following remedies: [396]

    1. Damages: If the harm has already occurred, P can recover ***compensatory damages***.

    2. Injunction: If P can show that damages would not be a sufficient remedy, he may be entitled to an ***injunction*** against continuation of the nuisance. To get an injunction, P must show that the harm to him actually ***outweighs*** the social utility of D's conduct. (*Example*: D operates a large cement plant employing hundreds of people. The Ps sue D for nuisance because of dirt, smoke and vibrations, which interfere with their nearby property. A court might not issue an injunction even though nuisance occurred, because the harm to the Ps may be found not to outweigh the job-creation and other economic utility of D's plant. But in that event, D would still have to pay money damages for the harm, no matter how socially useful D's conduct.)

II. LATERAL AND SUBJACENT SUPPORT

A. Generally: Every landowner is entitled to have his land receive the necessary ***physical support*** from adjacent and underlying soil. The right to support from adjoining soil is called the right of ***"lateral"*** support. The right to support from underneath the surface is known as the right to ***"subjacent"*** support. [396]

B. Lateral support: The right to ***lateral*** support is ***absolute***. That is, once support has been withdrawn and injury occurs, the responsible person is liable ***even if he used utmost care*** in his operation. (*Example*: A and B are adjoining landowners. A very carefully constructs a large excavation extending almost to the edge of his property. This causes B's soil to run into A's excavation, impairing the surface of B's property. B's right to lateral support has been violated, and he may recover damages.) [397]

    1. Building: But the absolute right to lateral support exists only with respect to land in its ***natural state***. If the owner has constructed a ***building***, and the soil under the building subsides in part due to the adjacent owner's acts, but also in part because of the weight of the building itself, the adjacent owner is ***not liable*** unless he has been ***negligent***. (If P's building is damaged, and he can show that his land would have been damaged even with no building on it, courts are split as to whether D is liable in the absence of negligence.)

C. Subjacent support: The right to ***subjacent*** support arises only where sub-surface rights (i.e., ***mineral rights***) are ***severed*** from the surface rights. When such a severance has taken place, the owner of the surface interest has the right not to have the surface subside or otherwise be damaged by the carrying out of the mining. [397-98]

    1. Structures existing: The surface owner has the absolute right to support, not only of the unimproved land, but also support of ***all structures existing*** on the date when the severance took place.

III. WATER RIGHTS

A. Drainage: Courts are split as to the rights of an owner to ***drain surface water*** from his property onto the property of others. In general, courts seem to be moving to a rule that an owner may do this only if his conduct is ***"reasonable"*** under all the circumstances. [398]

B. Streams and lakes: States are sharply split as to when and how a landowner may make use of waterfront ***streams and lakes*** that abut his property. [399-401]

    1. Common law approach: In all parts of the country except for about 17 western states, courts apply the common-law ***"riparian rights"*** theory. Under this theory, ***no advantage is gained by priority of use***. Instead, each riparian owner is entitled to only so much of the water as he can put to ***beneficial use*** upon his land, with due regard for the equal rights of the other riparian owners, and without regard to how long the owner has been using the water. (*Example*: A and B each own property that abuts a river. A is upstream from B. Under the common-law "riparian rights" theory, A may make "reasonable use" of the water — for instance, to irrigate his crops — but reasonableness will be determined by reference to B's reasonable needs as well as A's. The fact that A has been using the river for a particular use longer than B, or vice versa, is irrelevant.)

    a. Riparian only: *Only riparian owners* are entitled to make use of the water, under this doctrine. That is, the owner's land must *abut* the stream or lake, at least in part. So one whose land is not contiguous with the water may not carry the water by pipe or ditch to his property.

  2. Prior appropriation doctrine: Seventeen *arid* states (all west of the Mississippi) adopt a completely different theory, called the *prior appropriation* doctrine. In many of these states (e.g., California), an owner must apply for a *permit* to use the water; if the application is accepted by the government, the user's priority dates from the time of the application.

    a. Riparian ownership not required: Under the prior appropriation system, water may be appropriated by a *non-riparian owner*.

C. Ground water: In most American states, an owner may make only *"reasonable use"* of *ground water* drawn from under his property. For instance, he may generally use as much of the water as he wishes for applications on the parcel which sits on top of the pool, but he may *not divert* the water to other properties which he may own. [401-02]

IV. AIR RIGHTS

A. Airplane flights: [402]

  1. Direct overflights: If an airport permits flights to occur *directly over* an owner's property, and within the *"immediate reaches"* of his land, the landowner may sue in *trespass*. But flights beyond a certain height are not deemed to be in the "immediate reaches," so no trespass suit may be brought.

  2. Adjacent areas: If flights occur at low altitude on property *adjacent* to P's property, some states may permit him to bring a suit for *nuisance* if the flights are low enough, frequent enough and noisy enough to substantially interfere with his use and enjoyment of his land. Also, a court may let such an owner bring a suit in "inverse condemnation," to establish that the interference is so great that it amounts to a "taking" for which compensation must be given under the U.S. Constitution.

B. Other air-rights issues: [403-04]

  1. Tall buildings: An owner generally has the right to build as *high a building as he wishes* (assuming that it satisfies all applicable zoning requirements and building restrictions). Thus if two owners are adjacent to each other, one cannot object to the other's tall building on the grounds, say, that it ruins the quality of radio and television signals.

  2. Right to sunlight: Generally, a landowner has *no right to sunlight*. For instance, an owner almost never acquires an easement of "light and air" by implication or even by necessity. So if A and B are adjoining owners, B can, without liability, build in such a way that A's sunlight is blocked. (But if A uses sunlight as a source of *solar energy*, it is possible that he might have a claim — perhaps in nuisance — against B for blocking that energy source by a tall building.)

INTRODUCTION

I. "PROPERTY" GENERALLY

A. General definition: A person may be said to hold a property interest, in the broadest sense, if he has any **right** which the **law will protect** against **infringement by others**. In addition to **tangible** property (land and chattels), courts have increasingly recognized broad categories of **intangible** property interests. For instance, a teacher with tenure in a public school system may be found to have a constitutionally-protected property interest in continued employment.

    1. Real and personal property: In this book, we are concerned almost exclusively with rights in tangible property, i.e., all **real** property and tangible **personal** property. "Real" property includes land and any structures built upon it. "Personal" property includes all other kinds of property; while our discussion of personal property concentrates on tangible property (e.g., an automobile), a few types of intangible property (e.g., bank accounts) are considered. The bulk of the treatment of personal property is in the following chapter, so that the remainder of the book concentrates heavily on real property.

B. Possession vs. title: Perhaps the most important distinction which will appear throughout the course of this outline is the distinction between **possession** and **title**.

    1. Possession: There is no precise definition of the term "possession", and its use varies according to the context. However, a person may generally be said to have possession of land or personal property if he has **dominion and control** over it.

    2. Title: Title, on the other hand, is roughly synonymous with what the layman thinks of as "ownership." Thus a tenant in a residential apartment building has possession of the apartment, but the landlord has title to it.

        a. Divided title: A unique feature of Anglo-American property law is that title to a parcel of real estate can be spread among numerous owners and in several different ways. The chapters on future interests, marital estates and concurrent interests are all illustrations of this fact.

C. Law and equity: Another frequently-drawn distinction is between **law** and **equity**. The difference between courts of law and courts of equity is discussed more fully *infra*, p. 82. The basic idea is that a law court awards **money damages**, and an equity court awards other sorts of relief, usually **injunctions**.

D. Bundle of rights: The non-lawyer thinks of property as a single right: one either "owns" personal or real property, or one does not. But in fact, ownership consists of a number of different rights, often called a **"bundle"**: the right to **possess** the object; the right to **use** it; the right to **exclude** others from possessing or using it, and the right to **transfer** it. Even the right of transfer has two distinct aspects, the right to make a **gift**, and the right to **sell**. See D&K, p. 86.

    1. Splitting up: Frequently, an "owner" of real or personal property will be found to have some but not all of these rights. For instance, one who "owns" a vacant downtown acre in "fee simple" (the broadest form of ownership known to American law — see *infra*, p. 47) does not have the right to erect a 150 story building on the site, if buildings of that height are forbidden by the local zoning code. Similarly, a person "owns" his kidneys in the sense that government cannot remove a kidney without his consent, yet one may not make a for-profit sale of one's kidney to be transplanted into another. (See *infra*, p. 7.)

2. **The right to exclude others:** Even the right to *exclude* others, which goes to the core of what it means to "own" property, is subject to limits imposed by society. Most obviously, a property owner must allow fire and police officials on his property in certain circumstances. Some courts have cut back even further on the owner's right to exclude. For instance, one court has held that the owner of a farm may not use trespass statutes to keep out private citizens who are trying to furnish medical or legal services to migrant workers living on the farm. See *State v. Shack*, 277 A.2d 369 (N.J. 1971). As the court said in *Shack*, "title to real property cannot include dominion over the destiny of persons the owner permits to come upon the premises."

II. SOURCES OF PROPERTY LAW

A. **Cases:** The principal source of property law is *case law*, i.e., opinions by judges. Property case law is largely the product of decisions by the appellate courts of the individual *states*. In contrast to many other areas of the law (e.g., constitutional law), the state courts are more or less free to develop their own property case law without interference by the U.S. Supreme Court. (However, in a few situations, e.g., zoning, constitutional issues will arise, and as to these the U.S. Supreme Court has the final word.)

B. **Statutes:** Another large body of law is *state statutes*. The law of property has been heavily subjected to statutory modification of the old common-law principles and there are few property questions that can be answered wholly without reference to any statute.

C. **Restatements and model acts:** A third source of authority consists of secondary materials prepared by law professors and other experts. Foremost among these is the *Restatement of Property* (published in 1936), and the *Second Restatement of Property* (which is in progress, and which, so far, deals only with landlord-tenant law and selected topics under the general title of "Donative Transfers.")

1. **Model acts:** Also, a number of *model statutes* have been drafted (e.g., the Uniform Residential Landlord-Tenant Act.) These have been enacted in some states, and are sometimes looked to (on a non-binding basis) by the courts of other states.

POSSESSION AND TRANSFER
OF PERSONAL PROPERTY

Introductory note: This chapter considers several aspects of the possession and transfer of personal property. It represents the main discussion of personal property in this book. The principal areas considered are: (1) the rights of finders of lost chattels; (2) the rights of *bona fide* purchasers of goods; (3) bailments; and (4) gifts.

I. RIGHTS OF POSSESSORS

A. Rights from possession generally: Normally, one obtains title to goods by acquiring them from, and with the consent of, their prior owners (e.g., a purchase or gift transaction). There are a few situations, however, in which one may obtain title, or its rough equivalent, by the mere fact of *possessing* the article. The best examples of title from possession are: (1) *wild animals* ; (2) the *finding* of *lost articles*; and (3) *adverse possession*.

B. Wild Animals (ferae naturae): Wild animals (often referred to in court decisions by their Latin name, *ferae naturae*) are normally not owned by anyone, of course. Therefore, it is not surprising that the courts have held that once a person has *gained possession* of such an animal, he has rights in that animal superior to those of the rest of the world.

   1. What constitutes "possession": However, it is not always easy to tell when a person has obtained "possession" of a wild animal. Obviously, the *capture* of such an animal is sufficient. But where less than outright capture has occurred, the line between possession and non-possession becomes blurry.

   a. Chasing: The mere fact that one has *spotted* and *chased* an animal is not sufficient to constitute possession. Thus in the classic case of *Pierson v. Post*, 3 Cai. R 175 (Sup. Ct. N.Y. 1805), P found and chased a fox as part of a hunt; D then stepped in, killed the fox, and carried it away. The court held that "mere pursuit" gave P no legal right to the fox, and that D thus had the right to interfere.

   b. Trapping or wounding: One who *mortally wounds* an animal or fish, so that capture is almost certain, is deemed to have possession. Brown, pp. 15-16. Similarly, the catching of an animal or fish in a *trap* is sufficient. But the capture of the quarry must be *virtually complete* before possession will be found. See *Young v. Hichens*, 6 Q.B. 606 (Eng. 1844).

   c. Business competition: The courts are more likely to be sympathetic to the interfering defendant if he acts out of *business competition* with the plaintiff, rather than out of spite or malice. For instance in *Keeble v. Hickeringill*, 103 Eng. Rep. 1127 (K.B. 1707), P claimed that he had set some decoys on his own pond to lure ducks in order to hunt them, and that D fired guns nearby to drive the ducks away. The court held that P was entitled to recovery, because D's act was a violent and malicious interference with P's livelihood; but the court noted that if the ducks had been lured away from P's pond by D's use of the same type of decoys for his own business, P would not have been entitled to recover.

d. Custom: In a close case, the court may look to the *"customs"* or *"usages"* prevailing in the activity or trade involved. For instance, the custom among American *whalers* was that the ship or company which lanced the whale and thereby killed it was the owner, even though the whale immediately sank, floated to the surface several days later, and was found by another. In *Ghen v. Rich*, 8 F. 159 (D.Mass. 1881), the court applied this usage, and thus granted the company which killed the whale recovery against D, who had bought the whale at an auction from the person who found it on a beach. (The court ignored the fact that D had already paid the fair value for the whale, and was thus required to pay twice; it is possible that a modern court would recognize a defense by D that he was a *"bona fide* purchaser". See *infra*, p. 10.)

2. Return to natural state: If a wild animal is captured, and then escapes to **return to its natural state**, the courts have generally held that the finder's ownership is **extinguished**. The animal then becomes the property of whoever recaptures him. Brown, p. 18.

C. Finders of lost articles: The saying "finders keepers, losers weepers" is **not accurate**. The finder of lost property holds it, at least for a certain time, **in trust** for the benefit of the true owner; thus he is a custodian, or "bailee" (see *infra*, p. 13) for the true owner. What is important for our purposes here, however, is that the finder has rights **superior to those of everyone except the true owner**. Brown, p. 24.

> **Example:** P, a chimney sweep, finds a jewel, and carries it to the shop of D, a goldsmith. He asks D's apprentice to examine it and tell him what it is. The apprentice takes out the stones, and refuses to return them. P sues for the value of the stones. *Held*, for P. The finder of an object, although he does not by finding acquire absolute ownership, is entitled to possess it as against anyone but the true owner. *Armory v. Delamirie*, 1 Strange 505 (K.B. 1722).

1. Possession derived from trespass: The rights of finders are an example of the broader principle that a possessor of personal property has rights superior to those of anyone except the true owner. Thus even if the possessor has obtained his possession **wrongfully**, he will be entitled to recover from a third person who interferes with that possession. See, e.g., *Anderson v. Gouldberg*, 53 N.W. 636 (Minn. 1892), where P cut logs without the consent of the owner of the real estate, and D took them from him. Notwithstanding the fact that P obtained the logs by trespass, he was held to be entitled to recover them from D, a complete stranger to the property. The court observed that "Any other rule would lead to an endless series of unlawful seizures and reprisals in every case where property had once passed out of the possession of the rightful owner."

2. Measure of damages: Most courts allow the possessor the right to recover the **full value** of the object from the third party who has taken it. That is, the old common-law action of **trover** (which entitles the plaintiff to the object's value, and lets the defendant keep the object) is allowed. But a few courts (particularly North Carolina) hold that an action in trover is only allowed if the plaintiff shows either that he had title or that his possession was rightful; see e.g. *Russell v. Hill*, 34 S.E. 640 (N.C. 1900).

3. Article lost by possessor: As a corollary of the rule that a possessor has rights superior to those of everyone except the true owner, the courts hold that a possessor who **loses** the property after finding it or otherwise acquiring it may nonetheless recover it from the third person who subsequently finds or takes it.

4. **What constitutes acquisition:** For the finder to gain these special rights, he must do more than merely discover the property, he must take it into his **possession**. Just as in the case of wild animals, the existence of "possession" is sometimes hard to determine. The finder must have: (1) **physical control** over the goods; and (2) an **intent** to assume **dominion** over them. Brown, p. 24.

> **Example:** P discovers a shipwreck at the bottom of the Mississippi River. He attaches a temporary buoy to the wreck, and intends to begin salvaging the next day. However, he does not return, and eight months later D salvages the ship's contents. *Held*, P never took possession of the ship and its contents. His placing of a temporary buoy did not constitute a physical taking, but was merely an expression of his intent to appropriate the property. (But the commencement of actual salvage operations would have been sufficient.) Therefore, D had the right to take the property. *Eads v. Brazelton*, 22 Ark. 499 (1861).

5. **Conflict with the owner of real estate:** When the person who finds the item is not the owner of the real estate on which it is found, a conflict between the **finder** and the **real-estate owner** is likely to develop. The courts have not devised very clear rules for resolving such conflicts.

   a. **Trespasser:** If the finder is a **trespasser**, the owner of the real estate where the object is found will be preferred. Brown, p. 26.

   b. **Other cases:** But if the finder is on the property with the owner's implied or express **consent**, the cases are divided and confused. In general, the English courts tend to award possession to the property owner, and the American courts tend to grant possession to the finder. But these are by no means hard-and-fast rules, and the presence of other factors will often be dispositive.

   c. **Affixed to soil:** Where the object is **embedded in the soil** (rather than lying on the surface), courts have tended to give possession to the owner of the **real estate**. See, e.g., *Goddard v. Winchell*, 52 N.W. 1124 (Iowa 1892), giving the landowner superior rights in a **meteorite**, which the court described as "one of nature's deposits, with nothing in its material composition to make it foreign or unnatural to the soil." (But where money or other valuables are intentionally buried below the surface, the court may treat them as falling into the separate category of "treasure trove", discussed *infra*, p. 6.)

   d. **"Lost" vs. "mislaid" property:** Courts have frequently distinguished between **"lost"** and **"mislaid"** property. An object has been "mislaid" rather than lost when it was **intentionally put in a certain place**, and then forgotten by its owner. Such mislaid objects are usually held to have been, in effect, placed in the "custody" of the landowner; therefore, the finder does not obtain the right to possession. See e.g., *McAvoy v. Medina*, 11 Allen 548 (Mass. 1866), where P, a customer in D's barbershop, found a pocketbook that had been left there by some other customer; the court, in awarding possession to D, stressed that the owner had intentionally placed the pocketbook on D's table, and had thus entrusted it to D's care.

      i. **"Lost property":** Conversely, property which has clearly not been intentionally deposited by the owner (i.e., "lost" rather than "mislaid" property) is likely to be awarded to the finder. The classic illustration is *Bridges v. Hawkesworth*, 21 L.J.N.S. 75 (Q.B. 1851), where P found a parcel of bank notes on the floor of D's shop. The court awarded possession to P, on the grounds that the notes had apparently not been intentionally deposited in the shop, and therefore never came into D's custody or protection.

e. Public vs. private portion of premises: Courts have frequently distinguished between objects found in a *private* portion of the landowner's premises, and objects found in a portion of the premises *open to the public*. The landowner has a better chance of prevailing against the finder if the object is found in a private area, usually on the rationale that the owner of the premises not open to the public has an intent to possess the place and whatever may be located within it. Brown, p. 26.

i. Private portion: The classic example of an object found upon the *private* portion of premises is *South Staffordshire Water Co. v. Sharman*, 2 Q.B. 44 (Eng. 1896). The Ps, landowners, hired D and a number of other workmen to clean out a pool on their property. While doing so, D found two gold rings at the bottom of the pool. The court awarded possession to the Ps on the grounds that: (1) they had the right to "say that their pool should be cleaned out in any way that they thought fit, and to direct what should be done with anything found in the pool . . . ."; and (2) the possessor of a house or land should be presumed to have an intent to exercise control over any object found in or on it.

ii. Public place: Conversely, the finder, rather than the landowner, is more likely to prevail if the object is found in the portion of the premises which is held *open to the public*.

f. Underlying equities: However, a court's decision on whether the goods are "lost" or merely "mislaid", or whether they have been found upon "private" as opposed to "public" premises, is likely to be heavily influenced by the court's perhaps unconscious sense of the *equities*. For instance, in *Hannah v. Peel*, 1 K.B. 509 (Eng. 1945), P was a soldier who was billeted during the war in a house owned by D. P discovered a brooch on the windowsill of his room, which the court found him to be entitled to in preference to D. The court relied on the fact that D had never actually lived in the house, and that he has therefore never been "physically in possession" of the premises. The court attempted to distinguish *South Staffordshire Water Co., supra*, but not very successfully (since the house was indisputably not open to the public.) Probably the decision can best be explained on the grounds that it simply seemed *fairer* to the court to award possession to the soldier than to the homeowner who had never lived in the house.

g. Statutory solutions: Many states have enacted *statutes* governing the disposition of lost and mislaid property. These statutes, sometimes called "estray" statutes, typically require the finder of lost or mislaid property to notify a designated government official who enters a description of the item in a registry. These statutes have often rendered less significant the distinction between property found in a "public" place and that found in a "private" place.

6. Treasure trove: English courts have established a separate category, called *"treasure trove"*, for valuables which have intentionally been buried beneath the surface and then never reclaimed by their owner. Under English law, such property *belongs to the state*. Brown, p. 28.

a. Rejected in America: American courts have generally *declined* to establish a separate category for treasure trove. See, e.g., *Schley v. Couch*, 284 S.W.2d 333 (Tex. 1955), holding that currency buried beneath D's garage, and dug up by P, his employee, was "mislaid" property, custody of which should be given to the landowner. (A concurring opinion rejected the majority's strained idea that the goods had been "mislaid", and stated that it should fall within the general principle that anything embedded in the soil, whether naturally there or not, should be given into the landowner's custodianship.

D. Ownership of bodily tissues: Does a person "own" her own organs, blood and other ***bodily tissues***? To the extent that by "ownership" we mean the right to ***sell*** the object, the answer under present American law is mixed — some bodily tissues may be sold, for some purposes, but for the most part a person is not permitted to sell her organs or other tissues.

    1. Transplant: The question arises most commonly in the case of ***organ transplants***. Here, American law is clear: a person may ***not*** sell his organ to be used in a transplant. A federal statute, 42 U.S.C. §274(e), makes it "unlawful for any person to knowingly acquire, receive, or otherwise transfer any human organ for valuable consideration for use in human transplantation if the transfer affects interstate commerce" (as virtually any organ transfer would be found to do). This ban applies even to direct donor-donee deals, so you commit a federal crime if you sell, say, your kidney directly to a donee who desperately needs it.

        a. Policy determination: In essence, Congress has made a policy determination that a person should not have the right to sell her organs for transplantation.

        b. Other sales allowed: But other types of tissue sales are implicitly allowed, both by the federal statute and by most states. For instance, most states allow a person to sell his ***blood*** to a ***blood bank***.

    2. Use of cells in research: The other "hot topic" relating to ownership of bodily tissues is this: When a person's tissues are extracted as part of a medical procedure, does the patient continue to "own" the extracted materials, so as to control how they are used for ***scientific and commercial purposes***? The main case to have considered the issue so far, ***Moore v. Regents of the University of California***, 793 P.2d 479 (Cal. 1990), has answered ***"no"*** to this question.

        a. Facts: The plaintiff in *Moore* was John Moore, who had been a leukemia patient at the UCLA Medical Center. The defendants were the Center, and UCLA, which owns the Center. The defendants, in the course of treating P, removed his spleen with his consent. They then used cells from P's spleen to establish a "cell line," which they patented. The cell line turned out to have great medical and commercial value — products derived from the cell line are expected to have sales in the billions of dollars, and at the time of suit, UCLA had already earned hundreds of thousands of dollars in royalties. P sued the Ds on a number of theories, including conversion — he asserted that by taking his spleen, without telling him that his cells had commercial value or that they would be used for commercial purposes, the Ds had converted P's "property."

        b. Claim rejected: A majority of the California Supreme Court ***rejected*** P's conversion claim. The court held that once P's cells had been removed from his body, he simply ***did not retain any ownership interest in them***. Under existing law, the majority wrote, human biological materials are not viewed as "belonging" to the person from whom they have been taken. Furthermore, to extend conversion liability to bodily tissues that have been removed from a patient would "threaten with disabling civil liability innocent parties who are engaged in socially useful activities, such as researchers who have no reason to believe that their use of a particular cell sample is, or may be, against a donor's wishes." (Even a "bona fide purchaser" who buys from a thief or other wrongful taker of property does not get good title, as is discussed *infra*, p. 10, so an innocent researcher who bought a product derived from P's cells without knowledge of P's ownership interest would nonetheless face civil liability if P's conversion claim had been upheld by the court.)

   i. Breach of fiduciary duty claim upheld: The majority did, however, hold that P could sue the attending physician who removed his spleen, for breach of fiduciary duty or lack of informed consent, if P could show that the physician did not tell him that his cells had commercial value that the physician intended to exploit. However, this was a Pyrrhic victory for P, since this claim would be good only against the physician, not against richer defendants such as UCLA.

c. Dissents: Two members of the court dissented from the majority's conclusion that P did not "own" his cells and thus could not recover in conversion. One of them argued that P should be found to have had, at the time his spleen was removed, "at least . . . the right to do with his own tissue whatever the defendants did with it" (i.e., contract with researchers and drug companies to exploit its commercial potential), even if society properly prevents the sale of, say, organs for transplantation. The majority's ruling simply unjustly enriched UCLA at P's expense.

d. Relevance of the "bundle of rights": Recall (see *supra*, pp. 1-2), that "ownership" of property is not really an all-or-nothing concept, but rather a "bundle of rights," including the right to possess, the right to use, the right to exclude and the right to transfer. D&K, p. 86. The court in *Moore* could have reached much the same result by holding that P had certain ownership rights in his spleen at the moment of removal, such as the right to exclude the defendants from commercially exploiting his cells. The court could then have held that P did not have the right to transfer his organ by sale (just as one may not sell an organ for transplantation). That way, P could have received some compensation from UCLA for what the court found was the wrongful act done to him (the physician's taking without adequate disclosure), while the court could have avoided allowing the naked sale of body parts to researchers. D&K, p. 87.

E. Adverse possession: In every jurisdiction, there exist *statutes of limitations*, which place limits upon the time within which the owner of real or personal property must bring a suit to recover possession, or for damages for the loss of possession. After the statutory period (and any extensions of it) have passed, the actual possessor of the goods or real estate is immune from any suit by the rightful owner. He is said to have gained title by *adverse possession*. The rules of adverse possession are discussed extensively in the next chapter, in a real estate context; here we touch briefly upon several elements relating to adverse possession of personalty.

   1. Same rules traditionally applied: Traditionally, the *same rules* have been applied to adverse possession of personalty as to the adverse possession of real property. Most importantly, the possession has been required to be *adverse* or "*hostile*" to the rights of the true owner, rather than being in subordination to his rights. (See *infra*, p. 29.)

   Example: Suppose that a painting is stolen from Owner, and the thief sells it to an art dealer, who sells it to Possessor. Possessor and his heirs hold the painting for 100 years, during which time none of them has the slightest reason to believe that the painting is stolen. However, Possessor and his heirs keep the painting in the family vault during the entire time.

   Under the traditional rule, Owner or his heirs could come along, even at the end of the 100-year period, and recover the painting, because the statute of limitations would never have run. (Possessor would never have been an "adverse possessor," since his possession was not "open" or "hostile" due to the fact that the painting was never displayed.) This would be true even if Owner and his heirs never made reasonable efforts to find out what had become of the painting.

2. **Modern trend:** But recently, some courts have rejected this traditional rule, in favor of a *"discovery"* rule. By this rule, the true owner's cause of action accrues "when she first knew, or reasonably should have known through the exercise of due diligence, of the cause of action, *including the identity of the possessor* . . . ." *O'Keeffe v. Snyder*, 416 A.2d 862 (N.J. 1980).

   a. **Distinction:** Under the discovery rule, if the true owner, immediately after the loss, fails to use reasonable diligence to find the possessor, and the use of such diligence would have identified the possessor, *the statute of limitations will begin to run immediately*, even if the possessor keeps the property hidden. Conversely, even if the possessor displays the property openly, if the owners fails to learn that the possessor has it (and this failure is not due to the owner's lack of diligence), the statute of limitations will *never* start to run.

   b. **Rationale:** The principal reason for the modern use of the "discovery" rule for personal property is that, in contrast to the possession of real estate, "open and visible possession of personal property . . . may not be sufficient to put the original owner on actual or constructive notice of the identity of the possessor." *O'Keeffe, supra.* "For instance, if jewelry is stolen from a municipality in one county in New Jersey, it is unlikely that the owner would learn that someone is openly wearing that jewelry in another county or even in the same municipality." *Id.*

   c. **Tacking:** What if the first possessor transfers the property to a second, thence to third, etc.? Courts applying the discovery rule have generally held that the statute of limitations does *not* begin anew with each change of possession. Therefore, if an owner knows or should know the identity of the first possessor, and the statutory period passes during the first possession, the owner does not get another bite at the apple if the first possessor transfers to a second possessor, whose identity remains unknowable to the owner.

      i. **Criticism:** This rule has been criticized as making it "relatively more easy for the receiver or possessor of an art work with a 'checkered background' to gain security and title than for the artist or true owner to reacquire it." *O'Keeffe, supra*, (dissent).

3. **Nature of title acquired:** Once the statutory period has passed, the possessor becomes, for all practical purposes, the *owner* of the property. Thus not only can the true owner no longer sue to regain possession, but he is not entitled to use *self-help* to recover possession; see *Chapin v. Freeland*, 8 N.E. 128 (Mass. 1886) to this effect.

II. ACCESSION

A. **Concept of accession generally:** It may happen that a person *improves the property of another* by mistake. This is known as *accession*. Most situations of accession involve the use of *labor* to improve another's property, and it is on this sort of accession that we focus.

   1. **Traditional rule:** The traditional rule was that the owner of the original materials had title to the finished product, unless that product was so different from the original materials that essentially a *new species* of object had been created. If a wholly new

product were created (e.g., wine made from another's grapes), the maker, not the owner of the materials, had title.

2. **"Disproportionate value" test:** But most modern decisions have abandoned the "different species" test, and instead look at the extent to which the maker has **added value** to the other person's materials. If the value added is **wholly disproportionate** to the value of the original materials, the maker gains title; otherwise, the owner of the original materials has title to the finished product.

   a. **Found disproportionate:** Thus in *Wetherbee v. Green*, 22 Mich. 311 (1871), D made hoops from wood cut from the Ps' land. The court rejected the Ps' replevin action, on the grounds that the extreme disproportion between the value of the completed hoops and the value of the raw timber (estimated at a 28:1 ratio of values) justified giving equitable protection. (The court held, however, that D would be entitled to this protection only if he was shown to have believed in **good faith**, though mistakenly, that he was entitled to cut the trees.)

   b. **Good Faith requirement:** Virtually all of the cases which have granted title to the person who improved another's property have imposed a requirement of **good faith**. A **willful trespasser** upon another's property will probably not be entitled to recover, no matter how much he has increased the value of the materials by his labor.

3. **Right to compensation:** Suppose the original owner of the materials has **recaptured them**, either by a legal action in replevin, or by self-help. Is the person who mistakenly added to their value entitled to any compensation? In an action for damages, at law, most courts have said "no". Brown, p. 60. However, courts of **equity** (see *infra*, p. 82) have sometimes granted relief on general principles of fairness. See, e.g., *Hardy v. Burroughs*, 232 N.W. 200 (Mich. 1930), where the Ps mistakenly built a house on land belonging to the Ds and the Ds then occupied the house. The court noted that had the Ds brought an equitable action against the Ps, the Ds would have been required to give the Ps fair compensation on the grounds that "he who seeks equity must do equity". There was no reason, the court held, for refusing to allow compensation merely because the suit happened to be brought by the Ps.

III. *BONA FIDE* PURCHASERS

A. **Nature of problem:** Suppose that one who is in wrongful possession of goods (e.g., a thief, a defrauder, a finder, etc.) **sells them** to a **"bona fide purchaser"**, i.e., one who buys for value and without knowledge that the seller is without title. It might be thought that the seller cannot convey better title than he himself holds; courts frequently so state, and sometimes this statement is true. But there are a number of situations in which the holder of a less-than-good title can indeed convey better title than he holds.

   1. **General rule:** As noted, the general rule is that a seller cannot convey better title than that which he holds. This rule is universally applied, for instance, where the seller has **stolen** the property.

      Example: A car is stolen from P, a car rental agency. The car is ultimately purchased by Consumer from a car dealer in another state. Consumer pays fair value for the car, and has no idea that the car is stolen. *Held*, P may recover the car: "But a possessor of stolen goods, no matter how innocently acquired, can never convey good title . . . For a sale of such merchandise, though to a *bona fide* purchaser for value, does not divest the person from whom stolen, of title." *Schrier v. Home Indem. Co.*, 273 A.2d 248 (App. Ct. D.C. 1971).

2. **Exceptions:** But where the goods are acquired from the original owner not by outright theft, but by less blatant forms of dishonesty and/or crime, a *bona fide* purchase may be **protected**. The two principal areas where the *bona fide* purchaser receives better title than his seller are: (1) where the seller has a **"voidable"** rather than a "void" title; and (2) where the true owner has been **estopped** from denying that the possessor/seller has good title (e.g., the owner **entrusts** the goods to a **merchant**).

3. **"Voidable" title:** Whereas the thief, and anyone holding under him, has an absolutely "void" title, courts have recognized something called a "voidable" title. If goods pass from the owner to one with a voidable title, the owner may recover the goods as long as they are still in the hands of the person with the voidable title; but once the voidable-titleholder transfers them to a *bona fide* purchaser, the true owner's right are **extinguished**. The voidable title thus becomes "firm" in the hands of the *bona fide* purchaser. This principle of voidable title is incorporated in § 2-403(1) of the *Uniform Commercial Code*, which is binding in all states on sales of goods and in certain other transactions; § 2-403(1) states that "A person with voidable title has power to transfer a good title to a good faith purchaser for value."

   a. **Fraud:** One who takes from the true owner gains a voidable title even if the taking was **fraudulent**. Thus if A sells goods to B and B pays in counterfeit money, or a bad check, B has nonetheless obtained voidable title, and if he immediately re-sells the goods to C, A cannot get them back from C.

   b. **Identity:** Similarly, if A is **deceived about B's identity**, B nonetheless gains voidable title under UCC § 2-403(1)(a). At common law, this rule was followed where the deception as to the buyer's identity occurred in a **face-to-face transaction**. See *Phelps v. McQuade*, 115 N.E. 441 (N.Y. 1917).

      i. **Letter transaction:** But where the sale transaction took place via **letter**, the common law rule was that a deception as to the buyer's identity blocked even voidable title from passing. UCC § 2-403(1)(a) makes voidable title pass even in a letter transaction.

4. **Estoppel:** A second way in which the true owner of a chattel may lose his right to recover it from a *bona fide* purchaser who took it from a person with less-than-good title, is through the principle of **estoppel**. If the owner, by his words or conduct, has expressly or impliedly represented that the possessor of the goods is the owner of them, or that he has the authority to sell them, the owner is "estopped" (i.e., precluded) from denying the truth of these representations to one who buys in good-faith reliance on the representation. Brown, p. 202.

   a. **Entrusting to merchant:** Estoppel usually arises in cases where the true owner **entrusts the goods** to a **merchant**, who then (in violation of his agreement with the true owner) sells them to a good-faith purchaser. At common law, the mere fact that the true owner entrusted the goods to a merchant was never enough to estop him from recovering them from the good-faith purchaser; some **additional conduct** by the true owner inducing reliance on the part of the good-faith purchaser had to be shown.

   b. **UCC expands doctrine:** The **UCC** goes further in protecting the good-faith purchaser against an owner who has entrusted good to a merchant. Under UCC §2-

403(2), "**Any entrusting** of possession of goods to a merchant who deals in goods of that kind gives him power to transfer all rights of the entruster to a buyer in ordinary course of business." Thus in contrast to the common-law rule, the mere act of entrusting the goods is sufficient to estop the true owner from recovering them, once they have passed to a good-faith purchaser.

> **Example:** Consumer leaves his watch with Jeweler for repairs. Jeweler is in the business of not only repairing watches, but of selling used and new watches. Jeweler sells the watch to Purchaser, who pays fair market value, and who has no suspicion that the watch belongs to Consumer. Under UCC § 2-403(2), Consumer may not recover from Purchaser! See Quinn, UCC Commentary and Law Digest (1978), p. 2-260.

   c. Rationale: The result in the above example seems harsh, and one may wonder why the UCC expanded the common-law doctrine of estoppel so substantially. One commentator has explained that "the need to expedite sales of inventory by protecting buyers in the ordinary course of business is a widely felt commercial reality, while the risk to original owners such as those who bring watches to a retail jeweler for repair is more theoretical than real." Brown, p. 205.

IV. BAILMENTS

   A. What constitutes a bailment: A **bailment** can be defined as the **rightful possession** of goods by one who is **not their owner**. Brown, p. 209. The bailee (the person holding the goods), by virtue of his possession, owes a duty of care to the bailor (the owner). This duty, which varies depending on the circumstances, is discussed *infra*, p. 13.

   B. Creation of bailment: Some cases state that a bailment only arises where the parties make a valid **contract** for it to exist. However, most courts agree that no formal contract is actually necessary; for instance, **consideration** is not a requirement. Brown, p. 210. Nonetheless, there are two requirements which must be met before a bailment arises: (1) the bailee must have actual **physical control** over the object; and (2) he must **intend** to assume custody and control over it. *Id.* at 213-23.

    1. Physical control: The bailee must come into **actual physical control** of the bailed property.

     a. Parking lot cases: The issue of actual control arises frequently in **parking lot cases**. If the parking is done by the parking-lot attendant, and the car owner turns over the key, actual control will almost always be found. But in a **"park-and-lock"** lot, where the car owner parks himself and keeps his own key, most courts have found that the lot never obtains actual control of the car. See, e.g., *Wall v. Airport Parking Co. of Chicago*, 244 N.E.2d 190 (Ill. 1969).

      i. Presence of attendants: But even in the park-and-lock case, if the lot provides substantial **attendant presence**, and makes implied or express **assurances** that security will be maintained, the court may conclude that control has passed to the lot; this occurred, for instance, in *Parking Management, Inc. v. Gilder*, 343 A.2d 51 (Ct. App. D.C. 1975).

    2. Intent to possess: The bailee must also have an **intent** to possess the bailed goods, i.e., to assume custody and control over them. The issue usually arises where the person alleged to be a bailee has not expressly consented to assume custody, but has by words or action arguably induced the owner of the item to place it under the former's control.

a. **Presence of attendant:** Where the owner merely *puts down* a coat or other item in a commercial establishment, and does not entrust it directly to an attendant, the courts have frequently found that no bailment was created.

  i. **Contrary intent:** But by conduct or words, one may impliedly represent to another that objects will be cared for. If so, presence of an attendant, or any other kind of knowledge on the part of the bailee, may not be necessary. For instance, if a store contained a sign saying "coat rack for customers' use," there might be a bailment even if the store's employees never learned that O was actually using the rack.

b. **Underestimate of value:** If the person alleged to be a bailee is completely *mistaken* as to the *nature* of the object being entrusted, the court may find that the intent necessary to bailment was lacking. But a mistake that is merely as to the *value* of the object will probably not prevent a bailment from arising. For instance, in *Peet v. Roth Hotel Co*, 253 N.W. 546 (Minn. 1934), P deposited a ring with the cashier of the D hotel. The cashier realized that what had been deposited was a ring, but did not realize how valuable it was (over $2,000); the court held that P's failure to divulge the unusual value of the ring did not prevent a bailment from arising, and that D was therefore liable for its negligence in allowing the ring to be stolen.

c. **"Constructive" or "involuntary" bailment:** There are situations in which the "bailee" does not affirmatively desire to control the object, but has it *thrust upon him*. This might happen, for instance, if A lost or mislaid his property on B's premises. Or, a letter or package addressed to A might be misdelivered to B. Similarly, if T is L's tenant, and moves out, L may find himself in possession of property left behind by T. In all these cases, the intent to assert dominion on the "bailee's" part is lacking. Nonetheless, the courts have been unwilling to scrap the idea of bailment entirely in these cases. They have therefore adopted the notion of *"constructive"* or *"involuntary"* bailment. The two terms are used to cover much the same circumstances, but the bailee's duty of care is likely to be somewhat higher if the court uses the label "constructive" rather than "involuntary". (See *infra*.)

  Example: The Ps are staying as guests at the D hotel. After eating dinner in the hotel restaurant, they leave a purse behind. The busboy gives the purse to the cashier. She mistakenly delivers it to a third person who claims it. The purse turns out to have contained jewelry worth over $13,000. *Held*, for the Ps. There was a "constructive bailment" of the purse. The fact that the Ps were not aware of the misplacement did not prevent a bailment from arising, since had they known the facts, they would have desired the person finding the article to keep it safely for them. (Consequently, D owed a duty of reasonable care, which it violated.) *Shamrock Hilton Hotel v. Caranas*, 488 S.W.2d 151 (Civ. App. Tex. 1972).

C. **Rights and duties of bailee:** The precise duties owed by the bailee depend upon a number of factors, including who is benefited by the bailment, how the damage to the bailed property arises, and the presence of any contractual limitations.

  1. **Duty during custody:** During the time that the bailee has the object in his possession, he is *not an insurer* of it. He is liable for loss or damage occurring to the object only if he is shown to have exercised some *lack of care*. The precise degree of carelessness which will be required before the bailee is liable, however, traditionally has turned upon *who is benefited* by the bailment.

a. Mutual benefit: If the bailment is *mutually beneficial to both parties*, the bailee must use *ordinary diligence* to protect the bailed object from damage or loss. Brown, p. 258.

　i. What is "mutual benefit": There is usually not much question about whether the bailment is for the bailor's benefit. As to the benefit to the bailee, such benefit of course exists when the bailee makes a *charge* for the bailment itself. But even beyond this, courts have been quick to find benefit to the bailee if the bailment is done as part of *other services* being rendered to the bailor, for which the bailor is paying. Thus in *Peet v. Roth Hotel Co., supra*, p. 13, the deposit of a ring with a hotel cashier was held to be for the hotel's benefit, since the ring was accepted "in the ordinary course of business . . . in rendering a usual service for a guest . . . ."

　ii. Potential customer: Where the bailment is performed for one who is merely a *potential* customer, the cases are *split* as to whether the bailee is benefited. See Brown, pp. 260-61.

b. Sole benefit of bailor: If the benefit is found to be *solely for the bailor's benefit*, the bailee is generally held to be liable *only for gross negligence*. Brown, p. 265.

c. Sole benefit of bailee: Conversely, if the bailment is *solely for the benefit of the bailee* (i.e., The bailor lends the object to the bailee for the latter's use), the bailee is required to use *extraordinary care* in protecting the goods from loss or damage. *Id.*, at 264-65. (But even in this situation, the bailee is not an insurer, and some degree of fault must be shown before he will be liable.)

d. Involuntary bailment: Where the bailment is found to be "involuntary" (see *supra*, p. 13), the cases are in confusion. Since the bailee has had the goods thrust upon him, the courts have sometimes held that he owes *no duty to take affirmative steps to protect the property*. *Id.* at 322. However, if he does take action concerning the goods, he is usually held to at least a standard of slight care; for instance, if a landlord finds a former tenant's possessions in the vacated premises, he may not have to use special precautions to protect the goods, but he probably cannot dump them out into the street in such a way that they are almost sure to be stolen. (At the least, he is probably required to attempt to contact the tenant before removing the goods.)

2. Duty to redeliver: The discussion above concerns the loss or damage to the goods while they are still in the bailee's possession. A different problem arises when the bailee *turns them over* to a third person, perhaps one who claims to be the true owner. As to misdelivery, most courts hold that the bailee is *strictly liable*. That is, even if he uses reasonable care, but nonetheless delivers the goods to a clever imposter, the bailee is liable to the bailor for the true value of the goods. Brown, pp. 282-83. Similarly, if the bailee simply *keeps the goods*, he will be liable for their full value, under the tort doctrine of conversion.

a. Involuntary bailee: One exception to the rule of strict liability for misdelivery is applied to cases of *involuntary bailment*. The involuntary bailee is generally liable for misdelivery only if it arises from his *negligence*. *Id.* at 327.

3. Contractual limitations on liability: Bailees, particularly those operating in a commercial context, frequently attempt to modify their duty of care, or the extent of their liability, by **contractual provision**.

a. **Modification of duty of care:** Many courts have refused to allow a bailee to contract to **exempt** himself from liability for his own negligence. Brown, p. 273. But other courts, and the Restatement 2d of Contracts §195, allow such agreements as long as they do not relieve the bailee from liability for "**gross** negligence" or "**willful** and wanton" carelessness. *Id*. at 273.

b. **Limitation of liability:** Virtually all courts allow the parties to place a **contractual limit** on the **extent** of the bailee's financial liability if he does violate the relevant standard of care. However the limitation must be reasonable under the circumstances, and, again, it must not protect the bailee from liability for his willful or gross negligence. *Id*. at 273.

c. **What constitutes a contract:** Both modification of the standard of care and limitation of liability can only be accomplished by a **contract**, which of course requires the mutual assent of bailor and bailee. This means that the bailee cannot accomplish either of these goals merely by **posting a sign** limiting his liability; he must show that the bailor **saw and accepted** the terms of the sign. Brown, p. 270.

   i. **Ticket or claim check:** Frequently, the bailee prints terms limiting his liability on the **claim check**, **receipt** or **ticket** which is given to the bailor. If the bailee can show that the bailor either was, or reasonably should have been, **aware** of the terms on the document, the printed terms will be binding. However, it is generally difficult for the bailee to show actual knowledge on the bailor's part, and most American courts have held that one in the bailor's position might reasonably have regarded the document as a **mere token for identification purposes**, not as a contract. *Id*., 272-73. In that event, the terms are not binding, and usual principles of liability apply.

4. **Burden of proof:** In many cases where the bailed goods are lost or damaged, neither party will be able to offer clear and convincing proof of how or why the casualty occurred. Therefore, the allocation of the **burden of proof** is likely to have an extremely important impact upon the outcome of the case. There are really two different questions involved: (1) on whom does the **burden of going forward with evidence** rest? and (2) on whom does the **"burden of persuasion"** rest? (For a discussion of the difference between these two concepts, see Emanuel on *Civil Procedure*.)

a. **Burden of going forward:** Most courts hold that once the bailor shows that he entrusted the goods to the bailee, and that they were lost or damaged, the burden of going forward with evidence about what happened **shifts to the bailee**. Then, if the bailee does not introduce evidence showing what happened to the goods, he loses. To put it another way, proof of creation of a bailment and of loss or damage establishes the bailor's **prima facie case**.

   i. **Rebuttal by bailee:** There is dispute about whether the bailee can rebut the bailor's *prima facie* case simply by showing the loss or damage resulted from a fire or other specific casualty. Most recent cases hold that this is not enough, and that the bailee must also show that the casualty was not connected to any negligence on his part. B,C,&S, p. 104, note 10.

b. **Burden of persuasion:** A different question is "who bears the **burden of persuasion**"? That is, if the jury believes that it is equally likely that the bailee was negligent or was not, who wins? The usual view is that the presumption of negligence on the part of the bailee (which arises when the bailor makes his *prima facie* case) **disappears** when the bailee produces rebuttal evidence. Under this view, the burden of persuading the jury by a preponderance of the evidence that the bailee was negligent rests with the **bailor**. Brown, p. 295. There are some cases to the contrary, however. *Id.*

V. GIFTS

A. Definition of gift: A **gift** is the voluntary transfer of property by one person to another **without any consideration** or compensation.

   1. Present transfer: A gift is a **present transfer** of property. If the gift is to take effect only in the future, it is a mere **promise** to make a gift, and is unenforceable as a contract because of its lack of consideration. (However as noted *infra*, p. 21, the courts have striven to find a present, rather than future, gift where the situation is ambiguous.)

   2. *Inter vivos* vs. *causa mortis* gift: We do not discuss gifts of property **by will** in this chapter. The gifts that we consider here fall into two categories: (1) gifts "*inter vivos*" and (2) gifts "*causa mortis*". An **inter vivos** gift is an ordinary one in which the donor is not responding to any threat of death. A gift **causa mortis** is one made in contemplation of immediate approaching death. Brown p. 77. Most of the rules governing the two classes of gifts are the same, but where there are differences, these are noted below. The principal difference is that an ordinary gift *inter vivos* is **not revocable** once made (i.e., the donor cannot "take back" the gift, as a matter of law) but the gift *causa mortis* is automatically revoked if the donor escapes from the peril of death which prompted the gift.

   3. Requirements: There are three requirements for the making of a valid gift (whether *inter vivos* or *causa mortis*): (1) there must be a **delivery** from the donor to the donee either of the subject matter of the gift, or of a written instrument embodying the terms of the gift; (2) the donor must possess an **intent** to make a gift; and (3) the donee must **accept** the gift. Brown, pp. 77-78.

B. Delivery: The essence of the requirement of delivery is that **control** of the subject matter of the gift must pass from the donor to the donee.

   1. Rationale: The main rationale for the requirement of delivery is that without such a requirement, gifts would be enforceable even if the only evidence showing they had been made was an **oral statement** on the part of the alleged donor. This would leave people open to ill-founded and fraudulent claims of gift. Therefore, courts require delivery as additional proof that a gift was really intended and made. Brown, p. 78.

   2. Manual transfer not necessarily required: However, the requirement of delivery does **not** mean that **manual transfer** of the subject matter of the gift, must necessarily take place. It is sufficient if the grantor deprives himself of **control** or **dominion** of the subject matter of the gift, and in some situations this may occur without a manual transfer to the donee. See, e.g., *Ferrell v. Stinson*, 11 N.W.2d 701 (Iowa 1953) (O puts deed to real property in a metal box kept in O's house, and gives instructions to her nurse to mail the deed to D after O dies; because O was physically unable to return to the box during her lifetime because of her illness, she parted with dominion and control and a delivery occurred.)

3. **Delivery through third person:** Suppose the donor puts the property into the hands of a ***third person*** rather than giving it directly to the donee. If the third person re-transfers the property to the donee, no difficulty of delivery arises. But if this re-delivery from third person to donee does not occur (or occurs only after the donor's death) the transfer to the third person is ***not necessarily adequate delivery***.

    a. **Agency test:** The general rule is that transfer to a third person will constitute valid delivery only if the third party is acting as an ***independent*** agent, or as the agent of the ***donee***. If the third party is the ***donor's agent***, no delivery has occurred. The rationale for this is that if transfer has merely been made to the donor's agent, the donor has not parted with dominion and control, the basic test for delivery. Brown, p. 87.

4. **Symbolic and constructive delivery:** There are some types of personal property which because of their nature cannot be physically delivered (e.g. certain intangibles, such as the right to collect a debt from another person). There are other types of personal property which, while theoretically capable of manual delivery, would be highly inconvenient to deliver (e.g. heavy furniture.) Yet to dispense with the requirement of delivery altogether in such cases would leave alleged donors open to false claims that a gift had been made. Accordingly, the courts have adopted a middle position in such cases, and permit *"symbolic"* or *"constructive"* delivery. (A delivery is symbolic if, instead of the thing itself, some other object is handed over in its place. A delivery is constructive if the donor delivers the means of obtaining possession and control of the subject matter, rather than making a manual transfer of the subject matter itself. Brown, p. 92.)

    a. **Difficult or impossible to make manual transfer:** Constructive or symbolic delivery will not be allowed unless delivery of the actual subject matter would be ***impossible*** or ***impractical***. *Id.* at 93.

    b. **Dominion must be surrendered:** Also, a symbolic or constructive delivery will not be effective unless the donor has ***parted with dominion*** and ***control*** of the property.

    c. **Use of key:** The delivery of a ***key*** to a locked receptacle will often constitute adequate constructive delivery of the receptacle's contents. Use of the key will be upheld whenever the manual transfer of the contents would be impractical or inconvenient.

        Example: O is paralyzed and confined to his bed. O gives various keys to P (his housekeeper), telling her that everything in the house is hers. The keys unlock several items of heavy furniture, including a bureau in which a life insurance policy on O's life is found. *Held,* the delivery of the keys constituted constructive delivery of the items of furniture themselves, since the weight and bulk of these items made actual manual delivery nearly impossible. But the keys did not constitute constructive delivery of the insurance policy, because the policy could have been manually delivered (e.g., by O's telling his nurse to hand the policy to O, who could have then handed it to P). *Newman v. Bost,* 29 S.E. 848 (N.C. 1898).

    d. **Intangibles:** Often the subject matter of a gift is an ***intangible***, i.e., a claim of some sort against another person. Since the claim itself cannot be physically transferred, the courts are compelled to recognize constructive or symbolic delivery.

i. Document as embodiment of claim: Some types of intangibles have a *document* so closely associated with them that the document is treated as the *embodiment* of the claim. The business custom is to assign the obligation by transferring the document, and by surrendering the document to the obligor when the obligation has been satisfied. Any *negotiable* instrument falls within this class (e.g., promissory notes, bonds, bills of lading, etc.). Also usually considered within this class are *stock certificates*, insurance policies and savings bank account passbooks (discussed *infra*, p. 22). Therefore, as to all these items, courts hold that *delivery of the document* is sufficient to constitute delivery of the intangible claim represented by it. Brown, pp. 156, 162.

ii. Issuance of new shares: Usually, delivery of the document will be the *only* way of making delivery of the underlying obligation. But in the case of *stock certificates*, the courts have generally held that if the owner of the shares has the corporation *issue* new shares in the donee's name, this issuance will constitute delivery even if physical possession of the new shares is never turned over to the donee. See, e.g., *Owens v. Sun Oil Co.*, 482 F.2d 564 (10th Cir. 1973) (transfer of the stock certificate from donor to donee, even though only made on the books of the corporation, sufficient to establish donee's *prima facie* case of a gift.)

iii. Savings accounts: In some situations, a gift of the contents of a savings account may be made even without delivery of physical possession of the savings passbook to the donee; the issue of bank accounts is discussed further *infra*, p. 22.

5. Property already in donee's possession: Suppose the subject matter of the gift is *already* in the donee's possession. Where the transaction is an ordinary *inter vivos* gift, nearly all courts hold that no further act of delivery is necessary. Brown, p. 101.

Example: A lends a book to his friend B. While B still has the book, A says to him, "I've discovered I've got a second copy, so you may keep that one." No additional act of delivery is necessary, and the gift is complete. *Id.* at 101.

a. *Causa Mortis* gifts: But where the gift is made in *causa mortis* (in contemplation of death), the courts are sharply *split* as to whether pre-existing possession of the subject matter by the donee is sufficient delivery. Courts holding that the pre-existing possession is not sufficient stress that the oral gift is in effect fulfilling the function of an invalid oral will, and that the possibilities of fraud are greater than where the purported donor is alive to offer evidence that no gift was intended. *Id.* at 102.

6. Written instrument: Virtually all courts hold that delivery to the donee of a *written instrument under seal* stating the particulars of the gift constitutes sufficient delivery. See *Cochrane v. Moore*, 25 Q.B. Div. 57 (Eng. 1890.) (However, a few courts have indicated that a sealed writing will not be sufficient to constitute delivery where the gift is made in *causa mortis*. Brown, p. 107.)

a. Unsealed instrument: Where a written instrument is given to the donee, but it is *not under seal*, the courts are split. Because of the lessened importance of seals today, most courts hold that even an unsealed instrument is a valid substitute for physical delivery of the subject matter of the gift.

Example 1: On the birthday of P, O, her husband, gives her a paper stating that he is giving her 500 shares of American Sumatra Tobacco Company stock as a present. O explains to P and the other members of the family that he doesn't yet have possession of the stock, but that he will give it to her as soon as he gets it. Two days later, he orders his lawyers to take certain action to expedite the physical transfer of the certificates. Four days after that, he dies. O's estate refuses to give P the shares.

Held, for P. Delivery of the "instrument of gift" was sufficient, even though the shares themselves were never physically transferred. The instrument was a "symbol which represented the donee's right of possession."

But a dissent argued that for the use of a written instrument to constitute delivery, the writing must: (1) divest the donor of title, dominion and right of possession; and (2) be the best delivery that can be made under the circumstances. Here, the dissent said, neither of these requirements was met. *In re Cohn*, 176 N.Y.S. 225 (App. Div. 1919).

Note: It is not clear whether the majority in *Cohn* meant to hold that delivery of a written instrument of gift to the donee will suffice in all circumstances, or that the written instrument in this particular case sufficed because it met the requirements for "symbolic" delivery (e.g., impracticality of making a physical transfer). In any event, most modern courts would hold that even without impracticality of making physical transfer of the certificates, use of the instrument of gift would be sufficient.

Example 2: O writes to his son, P, that O wishes to give P his valuable Klimt painting, but that O wishes to retain possession of the painting for his lifetime. *Held*, this letter (together with other correspondence between O and P) sufficed to meet the delivery requirement, and physical delivery of the painting itself was therefore not required. *Gruen v. Gruen*, 496 N.E.2d 869 (N.Y. 1986), discussed more extensively *infra*, p. 22.

b. **Minority view:** A minority of courts, however, are unwilling to recognize unsealed instruments as being a substitute for physical delivery of the subject matter of the gift. Such a holding is particularly likely to result where the writing is not only unsealed, but quite *informal*. For instance, in *Foster v. Reiss*, 112 A.2d 553 (N.J. 1955), O, before undergoing major surgery, wrote a note to her husband D, telling him to take possession of various items of O's personal property, which would now belong to D. O left the note in a drawer, and D did not learn about it until after O was under anesthesia (from which she never recovered). The court held that an "informal writing" such as the note was not sufficient to meet the delivery requirement. The court relied in part on the fact that the gift was clearly one in *causa mortis*, and that if the writing was held sufficient, "we should, in effect, be enabling persons to drive a coach and four through the Wills Act."

i. **Possession not authorized:** The court also held that the fact that D took physical possession of the items before O's death was insufficient, on the grounds that D's authority to act as O's agent for purposes of obtaining possession was revoked as soon as she was anesthetized and thereby became incapacitated.

ii. **Dissent:** But a three-judge dissent in *Foster* (including Justice Brennan, later of the Supreme Court) argued that, regardless of the sufficiency of the note standing by itself, the note authorized D to take possession and when he did, delivery was complete. The dissent noted that the majority's rule (that lack of capacity revokes the agency granted by the note) would invalidate all powers of attorney once incapacity occurred, rendering such instruments nearly worthless.

7. **Gifts *causa mortis*:** As the majority opinion in *Foster* indicates, courts are generally hostile to gifts *causa mortis* (in contemplation of death), and frequently impose stricter requirements for delivery in such cases than where the gift is made *inter vivos* with no expectation of death. Brown, pp. 132-33. Courts have been more likely to require actual physical delivery in such cases.

   a. **Contemplation of death:** The gift *causa mortis*, as noted, is one made in contemplation of death. Sometimes the donor himself will make it clear that the gift falls in this category, as where he says "I fear that I may not recover from my operation tomorrow, and if I don't, I want you to have my diamond ring." But in **any case** where the donor dies shortly after making the gift, the court will **presume** that the gift is *causa mortis*, unless the donee comes forward with evidence that the donor was **not** acting in contemplation of death. The key element of the gift *causa mortis* is that the donor does not intend it to take effect **until he dies**; thus the donee must show that the transfer was intended as a present and irrevocable one in order for it to qualify as an *inter vivos* gift.

      i. **Suicide:** Some courts have held that where the gift is followed by the donor's **suicide**, the gift should virtually **never** be regarded as a present (and therefore binding) transfer unless there was actual physical delivery. The rationale for these decisions is that where the death being contemplated is suicide, the donor knows that he can change his mind about the suicide at any moment; therefore the gift should not be regarded as intended to be final. However, the modern trend seems to regard a gift in contemplation of suicide as being no different from a gift in contemplation of any other form of death — "the notion that one in a state of mental depression serious enough to lead to suicide is somehow 'freer' to renounce this depression and thus the danger than one suffering from a physical illness . . . has long since been replaced by more enlightened views of human psychology." *Scherer v. Hyland* 380 A.2d 698 (N.J. 1977).

   b. **Condition precedent or subsequent:** Courts are sensitive to the danger that the gift *causa mortis* will be used as a **substitute for a will**. Therefore, many courts have stated the requirements that the gift must be phrased as a **condition subsequent**, rather than as a condition precedent. That is, the gift must be **effective immediately**, with the donor's **failure to die** acting as a condition subsequent **revoking** the previous donation. *Id.* at 133.

      i. **Modern trend:** However, the modern trend in America has been not to insist too strictly that the gift be phrased so as to create a condition subsequent. Some courts simply find a condition subsequent even where by any reasonable interpretation, a condition precedent was intended (e.g., "This ring is yours if I die from my operation tomorrow.") Other courts have flatly rejected the requirement that there be a condition subsequent for a valid gift *causa mortis*. See, e.g., *In re Nols' Estate*, 28 N.W.2d 360 (Wis. 1947).

   c. **Revocation:** As noted, the essential feature of the gift *causa mortis* is that if the donor **does not die of the contemplated peril**, the gift may be revoked. In fact, most courts hold that the failure of the donor to die from the contemplated peril **automatically** revokes the gift, even if the donor indicates a desire that the gift remain valid.

    i. Exact cause feared: The courts have also held that the gift will be revoked if the donor dies from a ***different cause*** than the one feared.

  d. Delivery: A gift *causa mortis*, like any other gift, requires ***delivery*** to be effective. In fact, because the death seals the lips of the donor, courts are frequently even stricter in construing the delivery requirement in such cases than in cases not involving death.

    i. Constructive delivery possible: Nonetheless, constructive delivery may sometimes be found in *causa mortis* situations. See e.g., *Scherer v. Hyland*, 380 A.2d 698 (N.J. 1977), in which the donor endorsed a check over to P and left it in an apartment they shared, with a note saying that the check was for P. The donor then left the apartment, locked the door (to which only she and P had keys), and committed suicide. The court held that these facts were sufficient to amount to constructive delivery, and that the gift was therefore valid even though it was *causa mortis*.

8. Declaration of trust: One situation in which delivery is not really required is where the owner of the property ***declares a trust*** for the benefit of another, with ***himself as trustee***. While a discussion of the law of trusts is beyond the scope of this outline, a few principles may be stated:

  a. Unless a statute so requires, the declaration of trust does ***not*** have to be in ***writing*** (Brown, p. 147).

  b. Proof that the trust was indeed created must be "complete, certain, and unequivocal." *Id.*

  c. In most courts, the declaration of trust is valid even though the settlor (the owner of the property) has ***reserved the power to revoke***. *Id.* at 149.

  d. If the owner attempts to make an ordinary gift by delivery, and fails, the court will not sustain it as a trust. *Id.* at 149.

C. Donor's intent to give: In addition to a delivery, there must be an ***intent*** on the part of the donor to make a gift. Obviously, if A hands B A's diamond ring and says "Take care of this for me until I ask for it back," there has been no gift even though there has been a delivery.

  1. Intent to make present gift: Furthermore, the intent must be to make a ***present*** transfer, not one to take effect in the future. (As noted *supra*, p. 16, a promise to make a future gift is not enforceable because of lack of consideration.)

  2. Present gift of future enjoyment: However, courts generally go out of their way to find that there has been a present gift of the ***right*** to the subject matter, with only the ***enjoyment*** postponed to a later date. In the case of personal property (as with real property; see *infra*, p. 60), there may be a present transfer of title, with the right of enjoyment postponed until a future date. See, e.g., *Innes v. Potter*, 153 N.W. 604 (Minn. 1915).

    a. Gift subject to life estate: For instance, most courts hold that a donor may make a valid gift of a ***future interest*** in personal property, subject to the donor's ***life estate***. In this situation, even though the donor does not immediately deliver the subject matter of the gift to the donee, the intent to make a present gift will usually be found to have been satisfied.

Example: In 1963, O writes a letter to his son, P, saying that O is giving P his valuable Gustav Klimt painting for P's birthday. The letter says, however, that O wishes to retain possession of the painting for O's lifetime. A subsequent letter by O to P similarly refers to O's intent to make a present gift of the painting to P, subject to O's right to lifetime possession. The painting remains in O's possession until his death in 1980, at which time D, P's stepmother, refuses to turn the painting over to P. D contends that: (1) O never intended to make an ownership transfer in 1963, but only expressed the intent that P would get the painting on O's death; and (2) if physical delivery of the subject of the gift is possible, such delivery (rather than delivery of a written instrument) must take place for the gift to be valid.

Held, for P. As to argument (1), it is true that the donor must intend a present gift (not a future gift), but here there was clear evidence of O's intent to make a present transfer of a remainder interest in the painting (subject to O's life interest). As to argument (2), the very purpose of the remainder-subject-to-a-life-interest structure used by O was to permit O to keep possession of the painting during his lifetime, so it would be illogical (and therefore not required) for O to deliver the painting to P; therefore, a written instrument was enough to meet the delivery requirement. *Gruen v. Gruen*, 496 N.E.2d 869 (N.Y. 1986).

D. Acceptance: It is usually held that the giving of a gift is a **bilateral** transaction requiring an **acceptance** of the gift on the part of the donee. Brown, p. 127. However, at least if the gift is a beneficial one, the court will **presume** that the donee intended to accept.

   1. Donee unaware: The issue usually arises where the donor gives the property to a **third person** to be held until it is given to the donee; if the donor dies before the donee ever learns of the gift, it can be argued that the gift was invalid for lack of acceptance (since the gift could obviously not have been made after the donor died.) However, the courts have usually held that the gift took effect **immediately** upon its execution by the donor, subject to the donee's right to repudiate it subsequently. So long as no repudiation occurs after the donor's death, the gift is valid. *Id*, at 128.

E. Special problems of bank accounts: A common and troublesome class of gifts is that involving **bank accounts**, particularly savings accounts. Where the depositor of funds wishes to give another person either present or future rights in the funds, he may set up the account in any of four basic ways: (1) by opening the account in the **other person's name** (e.g., A deposits the funds in an account bearing B's name); (2) by acting as **trustee** for the other person (e.g., A deposits funds in an account bearing the designation "A in trust for B" — this is the so-called "Totten Trust"); (3) by having the account **jointly** in his own name and that of the other, subject to withdrawal by either (e.g., A deposits funds in an account denominated "A and B jointly, with right of survivorship" — this is the usual form for a joint savings or checking account); and (4) by depositing in his own name, but with a clause stating *"payable on death"* to the other person — this is the so-called "P.O.D. account").

   1. Right of survivor: Most litigation arises when the depositor **dies** before the other person. In most states, so-called "bank protection" statutes exist which permit the bank to pay over the funds to the survivor; the bank is assured by the statute that it will not be liable to the decedent's estate if it does so. However, the existence of such a statute does not necessarily establish, as between the decedent's estate and the survivor, who is entitled to the money.

      a. Right of withdrawal: The person depositing the funds frequently maintains (either as a practical or legal matter) the right to control and **withdraw** the funds during his lifetime. Prior to the last several decades, courts frequently held that: (1) this right of withdrawal prevented any gift from taking place when the funds were deposited; and (2) no gift could arise on the depositor's death, because this would constitute an invalid testamentary substitute. As a result, the survivor *lost* the right to the funds.

i. Modern view: Recently, however, courts have tended to hold that the depositor's right to withdraw or control the funds during his lifetime does *not* prevent a valid gift from arising as to the balance remaining at the depositor's death. In fact, the so-called "Totten Trust" (A deposits in a account denominated "A in trust for B") derives its name from the case of *In re Totten*, 71 N.E. 748 (N.Y. 1904), holding that the depositor's right to withdraw the funds and thereby revoke the arrangement does not invalidate the gift of the balance remaining at death. For a more recent case, see *In re Estate of Michaels*, 132 N.W.2d 557 (Wis. 1965), holding that where the depositor created a joint bank account with an implicit right of survivorship, the fact that the depositor held sole control and right of withdrawal during her lifetime did not invalidate the survivorship feature or make it an ineffective testamentary disposition. The court alluded to the fact that such joint accounts are often called *"the poor man's will"*, and indicated its sympathy for the device.

b. Donative intent required: Even if the jurisdiction is one which recognizes the survivorship features of the various types of two-party accounts, the survivor in a particular case is not *necessarily* entitled to the balance. Rather, he is entitled to the balance only where a *donative intent* on the part of the depositor existed. For instance, suppose that A deposits funds in the name of A and B jointly, and that the signatory arrangements with the bank are such that either party has the right to make withdrawals. If it is shown that A put B's name on the account merely as a *convenience*, so that B could pay A's bills, etc., and that A had no intent to make a gift to B either during A's life or of the balance existing at A's death, B will *not have any survivorship rights*. (Or, the court may hold that B has legal title as survivor, but that he holds in trust for the benefit of A's estate.) Brown, pp. 175-78.

i. Presumption: However, most states have established, either by case law or statute, a *presumption* that the survivor is entitled to the funds in some or all of the four types of accounts mentioned. Although this presumption is rebuttable, the effect is that if neither the estate nor the survivor presents evidence as to the depositor's intent, the survivor gets the funds. See e.g., *Dyste v. Farmers' & Mechanics' Savings Bank of Minneapolis*, 229 N.W. 865 (Minn. 1930), applying a presumption in favor of the survivor both as to a joint account and as to a Totten Trust. See also *In re Estate of Michaels, supra*, where the court held that a presumption in favor of the surviving joint tenant could only be rebutted by *"clear and convincing evidence"* that the survivor's name had been added for convenience rather than with an intent to make a gift; the court found that such rebuttal evidence had not been presented.

ii. Uniform Probate Code: The *Uniform Probate Code* follows the modern view, by making the survivor of a joint bank account, and the beneficiary of a trust account following the death of the trustee, entitled to the remaining balance unless there is clear and convincing evidence of a contrary intent. Where the account is a P.O.D. account, the P.O.D. payee has conclusive rights to the property. U.P.C. §6-104.

    c. Revocation by will: As long as the depositor held the exclusive right to control and withdraw the funds during his lifetime, the courts uniformly hold that no gift occurs until the moment of death. Going one step further, at least one court has held that the depositor's *will* may *revoke* the survivor's right to the balance in the account at death; *Bauer v. Crummy*, 267 A.2d 16 (N.J. 1970).

2. Rights of parties *inter vivos*: Disputes between two parties to a bank account may also arise while *both* are still *alive*.

    a. Totten and P.O.D. accounts: In the case of a Totten trust or P.O.D. account, the courts generally *presume* that during the depositor's lifetime, he has the right to withdraw all funds. (However, a contrary showing may be made, at least in the case of the Totten Trust, by the beneficiary, to the effect that an immediate gift was intended by the depositor.)

    b. Joint account: But in the case of a *joint account*, the courts frequently presume that a joint tenancy was intended to be created. Therefore, there is a presumption that all sums withdrawn (regardless of by whom) are owned one-half by each joint tenant. If the presumption is not rebutted, the person who withdraws sums must pay over half to the other person.

        i. Uniform Probate Code: But the *Uniform Probate Code*, by contrast, provides that a joint account, during the lifetime of the parties, belongs to the parties *in proportion to the net contributions of each*, unless there is clear and convincing evidence of a different intent. See B,C&S, pp. 745-46, note 9.

3. Application to other devices: The principles discussed above have occasionally been applied to *other types* of joint property. For instance, in *Blanchette v. Blanchette*, 287 N.E.2d 459 (Mass. 1972), H and W held *stock certificates* as joint tenants. The court held that the situation should be treated in the same way as a joint bank account. Accordingly, the husband (who had bought the certificates out of his own funds) was held to have a right to revoke the joint tenancy, since he had no donative intent to give his wife a present interest. The court indicated that if the husband died without having made such a revocation, the wife would have a right of survivorship, and that this right of survivorship was not an invalid will-substitute.

Chapter Review Questions

(Answers are at back of book)

    1. Oscar was the owner of a very valuable painting, "Rosewood." In 1970, Rosewood was stolen from Oscar's home. Oscar reported the theft to the police, collected insurance proceeds, and made no further efforts to locate the painting. (For example, he did not report the theft to a national information bank that lists stolen paintings, nor did he notify local art dealers.) In 1973, unbeknownst to Oscar, Anita, an art collector, "bought" Rosewood from a private gallery for $10,000. (This price was approximately the fair market value of the painting at the time, on the assumption that there was clear title.) The galley showed Anita documents indicating that the gallery had the right to sell the painting, and Anita had no reason to believe the painting to be stolen.

    Anita proudly displayed the painting at her house for the next 17 years. Even though Anita and Oscar lived in the same town, Oscar did not learn of Anita's possession of the painting until 1990, when a friend happened to mention it to him. The local statute of limitations on actions to recover personal property is 10 years. Assuming that the state follows the "modern" rule regarding when the statute of limitations on stolen personal property begins to run, if Oscar sues Anita in 1990, may he recover the painting from her?

2. Olivia's 1989 Suburu was stolen one day while parked on the street in front of her house. Six months later, Arnold purchased from Dealer a used 1989 Suburu to which Dealer appeared to have good title. Arnold paid the full fair market value for the car. In fact, the car was the one which had been stolen from Olivia, though there was no way Arnold could reasonably have known that the car was stolen property. Through a random check of Vehicle Identification Numbers by local police, the police discovered that the car being driven by Arnold was stolen property, and so notified Olivia. Olivia has now sued Arnold in 1990 for return of the car. Arnold defends on the grounds that he is a bona fide purchaser for fair value. Assume that there are no relevant statutes. May Olivia recover the car?

3. In 1980, Sidney, a wealthy industrialist, said to his son Norman, "I am hereby giving you my valuable Monet painting, 'Ballerinas.'" Sidney did not, however, at any time give Norman possession of the painting, nor did he give him any document indicating any transfer. The painting continued to hang on Sidney's wall for the next 10 years. In 1990, Sidney died. His will bequeathed all of his personal property to his daughter, Denise. Who owns the painting, Norman or Denise?

4. Albert, an elderly widower, placed $100,000 in a bank savings account bearing the designation, "Albert in trust for Bertha." Bertha was Albert's girlfriend. During the next two years, Albert made no withdrawals, nor did Bertha. Albert then died, leaving all of his personal property by will to his son Steven. Steven and Bertha each now claim the proceeds of the bank account. Neither produces any evidence of Albert's intent in creating the bank account. What part, if any, of the proceeds should be awarded to Bertha?

ADVERSE POSSESSION

I. INTRODUCTION

A. Purpose of Doctrine: Just as there are Statutes of Limitation that bar the bringing of criminal prosecutions or suits for breach of contract after a certain period of time, so there are Statutes of Limitations that eventually bar the owner of property from suing to *recover possession* from one who has wrongfully entered the property. A property owner's cause of action against a wrongful possessor of it is known as the action of *ejectment*. In virtually all states, the owner must bring his ejectment action within 20 years of the time the wrongdoer enters the land; some states allow only a shorter period, e.g. 10 years. (See *infra*, p. 36.)

    1. Barring of stale claims: One reason, of course, for the existence of a time limit on the bringing of an ejectment action is to *bar stale claims*. With the passage of time, witnesses' memories grow dim and unreliable, and the reliance interest of the defendant (the wrongful possessor) in not having to face a lawsuit becomes stronger. Therefore, it is not unfair to have a cut-off point after which no further ejectment action may be brought.

B. Gaining title by adverse possession: But a Statute of Limitations on actions to recover real property has an additional major effect, not shared by other Statutes of Limitations: once the limitations period has passed, the wrongful possessor now in reality has *title to the land*, since the original owner can no longer recover it from him. This title is said to have been gained by *adverse possession*.

    1. Clearing titles to land: The doctrine of adverse possession thus furnishes the additional benefit of *clearing titles to land*. Suppose, for instance, that D, the present possessor of Blackacre, holds a deed to that land from C, who held one from B, who held from A. Suppose further that A's conveyance to B took place 70 years ago, but that there is no evidence of how A received the land in the first place. It is possible that A never really owned the land in the first place; it may really have been owned at that point by X, who conveyed it to someone else, who reconveyed it to a third person, etc. Given the grantor-grantee method by which most recording systems are set up (see *infra*, p. 369), there would be no way that D could prove that he had valid title to the property, since there would be no way of negating the possibility that someone held better title to the land through a chain going back to the hypothetical X.

        a. Effect of adverse possession doctrine on record searches: If, on the other hand, there is, say, a 20-year Statute of Limitations on ejectment actions, D's title probably only has to be traced back for 20 years, plus perhaps an additional 20- or 30-year period to negate the possibility that a disability stopped the running of the Statute at one point (see *infra*, p. 36) or the possibility that there is an easement, possibility of reverter (*infra*, p. 60), or some other impediment to title. See the discussion of the mechanics of searching title (*infra*, p. 369). See also C&L, pp. 878-80.

C. Scope of this chapter: Most of this chapter is devoted to a discussion of how one becomes the owner of property by adverse possession. A final section at the end of the chapter (*infra*, p. 39) discusses the kind of title which one gets by adverse possession, including the boundaries of the property acquired.

D. Components of adverse possession: Gaining title by adverse possession involves four principal aspects:

1. **Physical requirements:** *Physical requirements* relating to the possession (principally the requirement that the possession be "open, notorious, and visible";

2. **Mental requirements:** *Mental requirements*, principally the requirement that the possession be "hostile", i.e., without the owner's consent;

3. **Continuity of possession:** The requirement that the possession be *continuous*, rather than interrupted; and

4. **Statutory period:** The requirement that the possession be for at least the length of the *statutory period*, and perhaps longer if the owner was under a disability.

II. PHYSICAL REQUIREMENTS

A. Summary: The concept of gaining title by adverse possession requires, of course, that the person entering the land actually *"possess"* it. However, the concept of possession is a vague one. Accordingly, courts have developed a number of catch-words by which to determine whether the requisite possession exists. The precise wording varies from state to state, but typically the possession must meet the following requirements:

1. It must be *open, notorious*, and *visible*;

2. It must be *exclusive*;

3. It must be *actual*; and

4. It must be *continuous* (discussed under a separate heading, *infra*, p. 33).

B. "Open, notorious, and visible": One of the functions of a Statute of Limitations is to penalize a claimant who "sleeps on his rights". The owner of real property who fails to bring an action for ejectment should be penalized (by the drastic step of taking his title away from him) only if he could reasonably be *expected to know* that another person has entered the property, and was asserting a claim to it. Therefore, nearly all courts require that the adverse possessor's use of the land be *"open, notorious, and visible"*.

1. **Effect of actual notice by owner:** If the possessor can show that the owner had *actual* notice that the former was in possession of the land and asserting a claim to it, the "open, notorious, and visible" requirement is met. Powell, Par. 1013, p. 1089.

2. **Measured against typical owner's conduct:** Where actual knowledge by the true owner cannot be shown, the "open, notorious, and visible" test is met if the adverse possessor's use of the property is similar to that which a *typical owner* of *similar property* would make of it.

   a. **Nature of land taken into account:** Thus the *nature of the land* is taken into account. A more noticeable possession would be required for land within a city or town (e.g., the building of a structure) than for land in a sparsely settled area or wilderness.

   Example: Blackacre is a wild and undeveloped parcel of land, suitable only for hunting and fishing. The Ds build a hunting cabin, and use the cabin about six times a year as a base for hunting and fishing. They pay the taxes virtually every year, throughout the statutory period. P, the record owner, then seeks to recover the property, arguing that the Ds never improved the land, fenced it, posted it, attempted to keep off others or lived on it.

> *Held*, the Ds gained title by adverse possession. Acts of possession and ownership are sufficient if they openly and publicly indicate a degree of control "consistent with the character of the premises in question." Since the land was not suitable for cultivation or permanent habitation, the building of the cabin, the use for hunting and the payment of taxes were sufficient. *Monroe v. Rawlings*, 49 N.W.2d 55 (Mich. 1951).

b. **Effect of fence or other enclosure:** The necessary possession will often be shown by the fact that the possessor has put up a *fence* or otherwise enclosed the land. The existence of such an enclosure is not likely to be sufficient in a densely populated and built-up area, but in rural areas this will often be dispositive. A few states have statutes *requiring* enclosure for adverse possession. See Burby, p. 271, fn. 31.

c. **Acts toward outside world:** The possessor's *conduct* towards persons *other than the true owner* may also help establish the required open and notorious possession.

> **Example:** D claims adverse possession of an unfenced, unimproved lot, whose principal value is as a source of sand and gravel. During the statutory period, he allows some persons to remove sand and gravel, and denies permission to others. He brings trespass actions against those who do so without permission. (He also pays taxes on the land.) P, the record owner, then sues to eject D, following the statutory period.
>
> *Held*, D owns the lot by adverse possession. His possession met the "open and notorious" requirement even though the land was not enclosed or built up. D's conduct towards persons who wanted to take the sand and gravel constituted "public acts of ownership", particularly since the kind of possession required "depends on the nature and situation of the property [and] the uses to which it can be applied." *Ewing v. Burnet*, 36 U.S. 41 (1837).

C. **Exclusive possession:** The adverse possessor must be in *exclusive* control of the property. This really only means that he must not be sharing control of the property with the true owner, and the property must not be available to the public generally. However, it is possible for two persons (neither of them the record owner) to be in joint possession of property, in which case they would eventually gain joint title to the property by adverse possession. Burby, p. 273.

D. **Actual possession:** Courts often say that the possession must be *"actual"*. This term, however, overlaps largely with the requirement that possession be "open, notorious and visible".

1. **Percentage of land used:** At least a *reasonable percentage* of the land claimed by the adverse possessor must be actually used. Again, however, the precise percentage of use required will vary depending upon the nature and utility of the property. As one case noted, if a mine or quarry were located on a one-acre plot, use of the mine without use of any other land might constitute sufficient possession; use of a similar mine on a tract of 1,000 acres, on the other hand, would not be enough for possession of the entire plot. *Brumagim v. Bradshaw*, 39 Cal. 24 (1870) (holding that the enclosure of a 1,000-acre peninsula, and its use for cattle pasturing, could be found by a jury to constitute sufficient possession).

2. **Occupation by tenant of adverse possessor:** The adverse possessor does not necessarily have to be in possession of the property *personally*. For instance, if he leases his possessory interest to a *tenant*, the tenant's possession may suffice for meeting the "actual possession" requirement. Burby, p. 272.

3. **Possession of sub-surface minerals:** If a possessor can show adequate dominion over the surface of the land, his claim will usually extend *below the surface*, and thus will include *minerals*.

   a. **Pre-adverse possession severance of mineral rights:** However, if the record owner has *severed* the mineral rights from the surface rights, and has conveyed the former to someone other than the adverse possessor (e.g., by a lease of the mineral rights), then subsequent adverse possession of the surface will not give rights to the minerals.

      Example: P and her husband live on Blackacre for 40 years (and also hold a valid deed to the surface). D, a mining company, holds a valid lease on the mineral rights (granted before P took occupancy). P asserts that her continuous possession of the surface is sufficient to give her title by adverse possession of the mineral rights as well.

      Held, for D. Where the mineral interest has been severed from the surface interest, which is the case here, possession of the surface does not equal possession of the minerals. For P to have gained title to the minerals by adverse possession, she would have had to actually removed minerals from the ground, or otherwise put the public on notice that she was specifically claiming the minerals. She did not do this. *Failoni v. Chicago & North Western Railway Co.*, 195 N.E.2d 619 (Ill. 1964).

4. **Distinguished from constructive possession:** The concept of "actual" possession should be distinguished from that of *"constructive"* possession. The latter, discussed *infra*, p. 41, applies where one holds a defective, but written, title to a described parcel of land, and takes actual possession of only a small portion of it; by doing so, he may be held to have "constructive" possession of the entire parcel. But except in this defective-instrument situation (often called holding "color of title"), actual possession of the entire parcel is necessary for obtaining title by adverse possession to it.

E. **Payment of taxes:** In most states, it is not necessary that the adverse possessor pay the *taxes* on the property during his possession. However, in these states, the fact that he has done so is usually admissible as evidence of the requisite dominion and notice to the outside world. Burby, p. 280.

1. **Statutory provisions:** In a few states, however, statutes provide that payment of taxes is a *prerequisite* to an adverse possession claim. Such statutes allow the record owner of the property to verify, by looking at the tax rolls, whether any claims to his property are being asserted. Burby, p. 280.

III. MENTAL REQUIREMENTS

A. **"Hostile" possession:** Most courts require that the adverse possession be *"hostile"*. However, this does not mean that the possession must be characterized by ill-will towards the true owner. Rather, it refers to the fact that the possession must be inconsistent with the true owner's rights and *without the owner's consent*.

1. **Possession by tenant:** A prime example of a possession that is **not** "hostile" is possession by a **tenant** under a valid lease. The tenant's possession is obviously with the landlord's permission, so the tenant does not become the owner of the property by adverse possession merely because he has been there under a lease for more than the statutory period. (However, if the tenant repudiates the lease, or in some states if the lease term ends and the tenant stays in possession, his possession may be transformed into a "hostile" possession; see *infra*, pp. 32-33 and 139.)

2. **Measured by objective evidence:** In determining whether the necessary hostility exists, courts generally do not attempt to delve deeply into the subjective thoughts of the adverse possessor. Instead hostility is determined by looking at the possessor's **actions**, and his **statements** to the owner and to others.

   a. **Offer to buy property:** An **offer** by the possessor to **buy** the property from the owner may sometimes indicate that the possessor acknowledges that he has no lawful claim to the property. But such an offer may merely represent the possessor's attempt to avoid litigation in such a matter where he believes that he has a valid claim to the property.

B. **"Claim of right":** Many cases insist that the possession must be pursuant to a **"claim of right"** by the possessor. However, courts may vary radically in the meaning they attach to the phrase "claim of right".

   1. **Majority usage is synonymous with "hostile":** Most courts hold that the requirement that the possessor have a "claim of right" merely means that his possession must be hostile, i.e., not with the owner's permission.

   2. **Minority rules out bad faith possessor:** But a minority of courts hold that the possessor must have a **bona fide belief** that he has **title to the property**. Thus under this view, a mere **"squatter"**, one who possesses the property but who is well aware that another person owns it, would never gain title by adverse possession, no matter how long his occupancy of the land was undisturbed. As one court following this minority position put it, "This idea of acquiring title by larceny does not go in this country. A man must have a *bona fide* claim, or believe in his own mind that he has got a right as owner, when he goes upon land that does not belong to him, in order to acquire title by occupation and possession." *Jasperson v. Scharnikow*, 150 F. 571 (9th Cir. 1907).

      a. **Majority allows squatters:** But the majority view, as noted, does not require a *bona fide* belief that one has title. Thus in most jurisdictions, the squatter who takes possession of land without making any bones about his lack of ownership, may gain title by adverse possession.

      b. **Owner induced not to bring action:** But the squatter may, by his words, lull the true owner into not bringing an action; if so, the requisite hostility is probably absent. Thus if the squatter tells the true owner, "I'll leave the property as soon as you want me off," title by adverse possession probably would never have been obtained. 3 A.L.P. 776. In this situation, the possession would be more or less with the owner's consent.

   3. **Minority rules out non-hostile mistake:** Another minority of courts holds that if the possessor **mistakenly believes** that he holds title to the property, and it is shown that he would not have held possession of it if he knew that it did not belong to him, the possession is not sufficiently hostile. This view is treated more fully in the discussion of boundary disputes, *infra*.

4. Color of title: One may possess property under a ***written instrument*** purporting to give him title to that property. If the instrument is invalid for some reason (e.g., because the property described in the deed does not match the property occupied), the possession is said to be under "color of title". Such "color of title" is virtually always sufficient to meet the hostility requirement. Also it meets the "claim of right" requirement in states which do not allow a bad-faith "squatter's" claim (*supra*, p. 30).

    a. Usually not required: While existence of an instrument giving color of title will be compelling evidence of "hostility", only a few jurisdictions make such an instrument a ***prerequisite*** for adverse possession. Thus one possessing property under an oral gift (invalid under the Statute of Frauds; see *infra*, p. 312) will usually be held to meet the hostility requirement, even though there is no written instrument.

        i. Relation to "constructive possession" doctrine: The other significance of an instrument giving "color of tile" is in connection with the doctrine of "constructive possession", discussed *infra*, p. 41.

C. Boundary disputes and other mistakes: The layman's notion of the utility of adverse possession is that it validates claims by squatters. But in the vast majority of cases where the doctrine applies, the possessor is operating under the ***mistaken, but honest belief***, that he has title to the property in question. Such a situation most commonly involves a mistake as to the location of a ***boundary line***.

    1. Majority view: The majority view is that one who possesses an adjoining landowner's land, under the mistaken belief that he has only possessed up to the boundary of his own land, ***meets the requirement of "hostile" possession***, and will become an owner by adverse possession.

        Example: O is the true owner of Blackacre. A is the true owner of Whiteacre. When A moves onto Whiteacre, he mistakenly believes his land goes all the way up to a creek, which is in fact 15 yards into Blackacre. Accordingly, he builds a fence up to the creek, and uses the enclosed portion of Blackacre for farming. At the end of the statutory period, according to most courts, A becomes the owner of that portion by adverse possession, even though he would not have used it had he known the true boundaries.

    a. Minority view: But a minority of courts holds that the possessor in this kind of "mistaken boundary" situation does ***not*** hold "hostilely", if it can be shown that he would not have held the land had he known that he lacked title to it.

        i. Criticism: This minority rule has frequently been criticized. As one authority put it, "Why a man without title who as an honest man admits that he wanted only what was his, and occupied in the belief that the land was his, should be worse off than the wilful wrongdoer who enters, and occupies in order to get title by adverse possession is not explained in these cases." 3 A.L.P. 789. Furthermore, the minority rule requires the court to make a deep examination of the possessor's state of mind, rendering the result in any particular case hard to predict. *Id.*

    2. Agreement on boundaries: It often happens that the two adjoining landowners realize that there is some uncertainty about where the true boundary lies, and therefore make an ***agreement*** fixing the boundary. If this agreement turns out to be wrong, when measured against the true state of title, can the party who has gotten the better end of the agreement gain title up to the agreed boundary by adverse possession?

    a. Majority view allows adverse possession: Most courts would hold that in this situation, a claim of adverse possession may be made. 3 A.L.P. 790. This is not really a situation in which the encroached-upon landowner "consents" that the other party occupy his land. Rather, it is a case of mistake, and under the majority view would presumably be dealt with like any other mistaken possession (so that the requisite "hostility" is present).

    b. Tentative agreement: But if the parties agree merely on a *tentative* boundary, with the understanding that they will readjust it if a later survey shows that their line is wrong, possession up to this line is probably not sufficiently hostile to constitute adverse possession. 3 A.L.P. 790, fn. 7.

D. Oral grants of land: Another common adverse possession situation arises when the owner of land makes an *oral gift* or other oral grant of the land to A, who takes possession of it. Because the Statute of Frauds in all states requires that land transfers be in writing, the oral gift is ineffective. However, if the possessor occupies the land for the statutory period, his possession will meet the hostility requirement even though it is technically with the owner's consent.

    1. Continued occupancy by grantor: It might even be held that continued occupancy by the *true owner* following his ineffective oral conveyance is attributable to the grantee, so that the grantee becomes owner by adverse possession. This is likely to happen principally in cases where the original owner makes an invalid oral gift to his son or daughter, and then continues to live on the property.

E. Co-tenants: Suppose that A and B hold title to Blackacre as *co-tenants*. If A has sole possession of the property for the statutory period, does he thereby take title by adverse possession to B's one-half interest (thereby becoming sole owner)?

    1. Other co-tenant must be on notice: The answer is, "not necessarily". In a co-tenancy, each party is entitled to occupy the premises, and one cannot exclude the other. Thus unless A has *actively blocked* B from taking joint possession, or has otherwise put B on notice that he is repudiating B's one-half interest, the requisite hostility as to B does not exist.

        Example: The Ps and Ds are all co-tenants of Blackacre. The Ps (or their predecessors in interest) occupy and farm the property for the statutory period, pay the taxes, and execute leases and mortgages concerning the land. The Ds never occupy the premises. *Held*, these facts are not enough to give the Ps full possession by adverse possession. There must be a showing that the Ds were actually put on notice that the Ps claimed the full property, which could have been done by refusing to allow the Ds to enter. The payment of taxes, execution of leases and mortgages, etc., were not inconsistent with joint ownership, since a co-tenant can take these actions on behalf of the other co-tenants. *Mercer v. Wayman*, 137 N.E.2d 815 (Ill. 1956).

    2. Conveyance of fee simple by one tenant: If one co-tenant purports to *make a conveyance in fee simple* to a third person, and the other co-tenant knows of the conveyance, the conveyance will be held to represent the necessary declaration of hostility. (Then, possession by the third party purchaser would also be adverse to the non-conveying co-tenant. Burby, p. 278.)

F. Tenant's hostility to landlord: Where one occupies property as a *tenant* of the true owner, this possession is not hostile, since it is with the owner's (the landlord's) permission.

But there are at least two situations in which possession begun as a tenant can turn into the sort of hostile possession required for the adverse possession doctrine.

1. **Repudiation or disclaimer:** First, if the tenant *repudiates or disclaims* the lease, hostile possession will begin. For instance, if Tenant tells Landlord that in Tenant's opinion the lease is invalid because it fails to meet the Statute of Frauds, this would be sufficient to make his possession thereafter hostile. If he then kept the property for the statutory period following the disclaimer, he would be the owner by adverse possession. Similarly, if Tenant purported to convey a fee simple interest to a third person, the latter's possession would be hostile, at least assuming that Landlord knew or should have known that a purported fee simple had been conveyed. 3 A.L.P. 792-3.

2. **Holdover tenant:** Secondly, the tenant may become an adverse possessor if he *holds over* at the end of the lease term. In most states, the landlord faced with a holdover tenant may *elect* either to eject the tenant, or to treat him as a "tenant at sufferance" (one who is allowed to remain only as long as the landlord wishes.) If ejectment proceedings are started, this is sufficient to make the tenant's further possession adverse. But if the landlord does nothing, thus creating a tenancy at sufferance, this would probably be treated as "permissive" possession, and therefore the adverse possession doctrine does not apply.

   a. **Statutory solution:** A number of states have enacted *statutes* providing that for a stated period following the end of the lease, the tenant's possession is not adverse, but that after this additional period, the adverse-possession statutory period begins. See, e.g., N.Y. Real Prop. Acts. Law §711, deeming the first ten years following the end of a lease to be possession with the landlord's permission; after that, the tenant's occupancy may be hostile.

IV. CONTINUITY OF POSSESSION

A. **The continuity requirement generally:** The adverse possession must be "continuous" throughout the statutory period. However, this requirement does not mean that the possessor must occupy the property every day throughout the statutory period, or else begin all over again. A number of special rules, discussed below, may permit him to use even time when he is not in actual occupancy towards the statutory period, or at least prevent him from having to start all over again following an interruption.

   1. **Abandonment:** However, it is clear that if the possessor *abandons* the property, his possession is deemed to end. Then, if he returns, the statutory period starts all over again.

B. **Seasonal possession:** Suppose the possessor occupies the property only *seasonally* (e.g., during the summers, or during a one-month-per-year hunting season). If the property is such that this kind of seasonal use is all that most owners of similar property would make, the possession is deemed to be continuous, and the entire twelve months of the year will be counted towards the Statute of Limitations. See, e.g., *Howard v. Kunto*, 477 P.2d 210 (Ct. App. Wash. 1970), in which summer occupancy of a beach home not reasonably designed for round-the-year living was held sufficient. (Another aspect of this case is discussed *infra*, p. 35.)

C. **Interruption by owner:** An attempt by the true owner to reestablish his entitlement to the property may constitute an interruption.

1. **Bringing of lawsuit:** The fact that the owner brings an *ejectment* action, or any other lawsuit to regain possession, merely *suspends* the running of the Statute of Limitations. If the owner wins the action, the possession is deemed interrupted, and the adverse possessor must start again for the full statutory period if he is to gain title.

   a. **Action abandoned or lost by owner:** But if the owner, after beginning the action, *abandons it*, or loses it, then there is no interruption. The Statute of Limitations is deemed to have run, even during the period in which the action was pending. 3 A.L.P. 808.

2. **Entry by owner:** If the owner *enters* the property, in order to regain possession, this will be an interruption of the adverse possession. However, the retaking of the property must meet the same requirements as the original adverse possession; i.e., it must be hostile, open, notorious, etc. 3 A.L.P. 809.

   a. **Need not be exclusive:** But the retaking by the owner need *not* be *exclusive* That is, even if the true owner and the adverse possessor occupy the land simultaneously, this will be an interruption of the adverse possession. 3 A.L.P. 809.

   b. **Statutes requiring lawsuits:** Some states have statutes which provide that even where the owner retakes the property, the adverse possessor will not be deemed to have been interrupted unless the owner follows up with an ejectment action within, say, a year. 3 A.L.P. 810.

   c. **Brief interruption :** Even a brief re-entry by the owner, not made for the purpose of permanently regaining title, may be sufficient to interrupt the adverse possessor's path to title.

      Example: P owns Whiteacre and D owns Blackacre; the two parcels are adjoining. D puts up a fence on his own land, failing to enclose a twenty-five-foot wide strip, which is then occupied by P. P's occupancy of the strip is continuous throughout the statutory period, except that during a three-week period, a contractor working for D stores some building material on the strip. *Held*, this three-week use of the strip by D was sufficient to interrupt P's possession, and P does not become owner of the strip by adverse possession. *Mendonca v. Cities Service Oil Co.*, 237 N.E.2d 16 (Mass. 1968).

D. **Interruption by non-owner:** An entry onto the property by one *other than the true owner* may similarly interrupt the adverse possessor's possession.

   1. **Ouster by second adverse possessor:** For instance, suppose A adversely possesses property owned by O, and is then ousted by B, who starts his own adverse possession of the property. If B in this situation continues to hold the property, A's possession has obviously been interrupted. Nor will B be allowed to "tack" A's time of possession onto his own possession (see *infra*, p. 36).

      a. **Recapture by original adverse possessor:** But if A then *regains* the property by throwing B out, most courts hold that his leaving the premises was involuntary, and that he may therefore join together his first period of possession with his new time of possession. Powell, Par. 1014, p. 1090. Some courts might even allow him to count the time B was in possession; but this result is rejected in 3 A.L.P. 817.

E. **Tacking:** One who has adversely possessed property for less than the statutory period may not yet have title to it, but he nonetheless has a possessory interest. That interest is capable of being *transferred* to another, by oral transfer, written deed, bequest, or even inheritance.

When such a transfer occurs, the question arises, may the original possessor's time of possession be added to the time of possession of the recipient, so as to meet the statutory requirement?

1. **Tacking allowed where privity exists:** This adding together of periods of possession is called *"tacking"*. It is allowed wherever the transferor and transferee can be said to be in a relation of *"privity"* with each other. While "privity" does not have a precise definition in this context, it means in general that the two parties must have some continuity of interest, that the recipient must have a direct relationship (usually either familial or economic) with the transferor. In cases of an oral gift, deed, bequest, or passage by inheritance, this requirement will almost always be held to have been met.

   a. **Life tenant and remainderman:** Suppose that O, the record owner of a certain parcel, attempts to bequeath a life interest in the property to L, remainder to R. If the will is void (so that record title to the property passes to A's heir, X), L becomes an adverse possessor. When L dies, if R takes over the property, some courts would even allow R to tack his possession to that of L, on the theory that the necessary legal relationship, and therefore privity, is present. See Burby, p. 274.

2. **Parol description not agreeing with deed:** Recall that most adverse possession cases arise out of a mistake as to the location of boundaries (*supra*, p. 31). Consequently, it often happens that a landowner, A, who has adversely possessed a strip of his neighbor's property sells his interest to a buyer, P. If the deed from A to P recites boundaries that include the adversely-possessed strip, then the general principles of tacking just discussed would permit P to add A's time of possession of the strip to his own possession. But suppose that A's deed merely recites the true boundaries of A's land; can P still tack his holding of the strip to A's possession of that strip?

   a. **Tacking allowed:** Tacking is usually allowed in this situation, if the purchaser can show that his seller intended to turn over the adversely-possessed property, and orally referred to this property. See, e.g., *Brand v. Prince*, 324 N.E.2d 314 (N.Y. 1974).

   b. **Different land than in deed:** An even more extreme situation is presented where the land possession of which is turned over, is *completely different* from the land described in the deed. At least one court has held that there may be tacking even in this situation. In *Howard v. Kunto*, 477 P.2d 210 (Ct. App. Wash. 1970), an entire series of beachfront property owners each occupied a fifty-foot lot directly west of that described in his deed. The court allowed one of these owners, D, to tack to his actual possession of the incorrect lot the possession of A, who had purported to convey that lot to him (but who had really deeded to him the next lot over). The court held that adequate privity was established between D and A, since privity is "no more than judicial recognition of the need for some reasonable connection between successive occupants of real property so as to raise their claim of right above the status of the wrongdoer or the trespasser." (See *supra*, p. 33.)

3. **Ouster or abandonment:** Where the only connection between the first adverse possessor and the second is that the latter has *ousted* the former from the land, the latter may *not tack* to the former's possession. Similarly, if the first possessor has *abandoned* the land, the second may not tack. In these two situations, there is no community of interest linking the two possessors.

4. **Tacking on owner's side:** An "inverse" tacking problem is presented where the true owner of the property conveys it during the time an adverse possessor holds it. This problem is discussed *infra*, p. 38.

V. LENGTH OF TIME REQUIRED

A. Statutory period: The basic length of time for which the property must be adversely possessed varies from state to state. Two-thirds of the states require fifteen years or longer. Powell, Par. 1019, p. 1098. In some states, the period becomes shorter if one pays taxes, or if one has "color of title" (i.e., a defective written instrument purporting to give title).

B. Disabilities: If the true owner of property is under a *disability*, in nearly all states he is given *extra time* within which to bring an ejectment action, and the adverse possession period is correspondingly lengthened.

    1. **Disability must exist at time adverse possession began:** Most disability statutes apply only to *disabilities existing at the time the adverse possession began.*

        a. **No tacking:** Thus there can be no "tacking of disabilities", either in the case of successive disabilities in the same owner, or disabilities in each of two successive owners. Burby, p. 277.

        b. **Two disabilities existing when possession begins:** However, if at the time adverse possession begins the true owner suffers from *two disabilities*, whichever disability lasts the longest will control. Burby, *ibid*.

    2. **Types of disability:** Disability statutes typically cover *infancy* (i.e., anything less than the age of majority), insanity, imprisonment, and occasionally, being outside the jurisdiction. Powell, Par. 1022, p. 1102.

    3. **Statutes giving grace period:** One common kind of statute provides that where a disability exists at the time adverse possession begins, the true owner may bring his action anytime within ten years after the lifting of the disability. Thus the Ohio statute (Ohio Rev. Code Ann. §2305.04) provides for a basic 21-year period for suits to recover possession of real estate, but then states that "if a person entitled to bring such action, at the time the cause thereof accrues, is within the age of minority, of unsound mind, or imprisoned, such person, after the expiration of twenty-one years from the time the cause of action accrues, may bring such action within ten years after such disability is removed."

        Examples of disability: The following examples are based upon the above-quoted Ohio statute. All the examples assume the following fact pattern: Owner owns Blackacre before and during 1940. Able enters adversely in the middle of 1940, and continues in adverse possession. In each of the following situations, we are interested in the date on which Able acquires title by adverse possession.

        Example 1: Owner is insane in 1940. He dies without a will in 1950. Howard is his heir, and has no disability in 1950 or thereafter.

        Able acquires title in 1961. By that year, the regular 21-year statute has expired. Since the disability was terminated in 1950 (by Owner's death), ten years following that termination of disability had passed by 1960. Therefore, the ten-year disability provision does not change the outcome of the problem.

        Example 2: Owner is insane in 1940 and he dies without a will in 1960. Howard is his heir, and has no disability in 1960 or thereafter.

Able acquires title in 1970. The regular 21-year statute would expire in 1961, as in the previous example. However, the disability is not eliminated until 1960 (by Owner's death). The real issue is whether Howard, as heir, has the right to use the ten-year period. Although it might be argued that the ten-year period is personal to Owner, and the benefit of it terminates with his death, a court would probably hold that the statutory scheme is best served by allowing an heir to bring suit. If so, ten years from the date of Owner's death equals 1970.

Example 3: Owner has no disability in 1940. He dies without a will in 1960. Howard is his heir and, in 1960, is six years old.

Able acquires title in 1961. Howard's disability is irrelevant. The statute, like most other disability statutes, refers only to a disability possessed by "a person entitled to bring such action at the time the cause thereof accrues . . . ;" Owner is the only person who had the right to bring an ejectment action when that action accrued, and he had no disability then. Therefore, the usual 21-year period applies.

Example 4: Owner is insane in 1940. He dies without a will in 1960. Howard is his heir, and in 1960 is six years old. Able acquires title in 1970. Again, Howard's disability is irrelevant; it cannot be "tacked" to Owner's disability, anymore than it could serve as a disability in the previous problem. Therefore, Owner's disability is the only relevant one and the problem is resolved the same way as Example 2.

Example 5: Owner is ten years old in 1940. In 1950, he is convicted of a felony offense, and is jailed until 1965.

Able acquires title in 1961. The only disability to be considered is Owner's youth, not his imprisonment. This is because the imprisonment did not exist at the time the adverse possession began, and the statute applies only to disabilities existing at that time. (But if he had been in prison from 1940 through 1965, he would have been entitled to sue anytime up to 10 years after the termination of the longer-lasting of the two disabilities, or 1975). Owner's minority ended in 1951, and the ten-year period expires in 1961; this is the same date produced by the regular 21-year statute.

4. **Criticism of disability statutes:** Observe that a disability statute such as the Ohio one might prolong the running of the Statute of Limitations indefinitely. For instance, if Owner in Example 5 above had been in jail in 1940, and had remained there for the next 50 years, the statute would not have expired until 2000. This result has been criticized, on the grounds that a disabled person's friends and relatives would normally sue to protect his rights, and that such a long extension unnecessarily interferes with the clearing of land titles. (For instance, a title searcher would not know how far back to go, since the possible existence of a long-term disability somewhere back in the chain of title could not be negated.)

    a. **Solution:** Accordingly, some states set a maximum length on the disability exemption; see Burby, p. 278.

C. **Successors in interest:** Suppose that after an adverse possession has begun, the true owner conveys his record title to another, either by deed, will, or inheritance. Does the time of possession against the first owner get added to the time against the subsequent owner? The answer is "yes". This might be termed "tacking" on the *owner's side*. See Cribbet, pp. 335-36.

Example: O is the owner of Blackacre in 1950, when A enters and begins to adversely possess. In 1960, O conveys the property to X. Under a 21-year Statute of Limitations, A will gain title by adverse possession in 1971, even though he has not held for 21 years against either O or X separately.

1. **Tacking on both sides:** There can be "tacking" on both the owner's side **and** the possessor's side simultaneously.

    Example: Owner is the record owner of Blackacre. In 1950, Able enters into adverse possession against him. In 1960, Owner conveys his interest in the property to Owner-2. In 1965, Able, after being continuously in adverse possession, conveys his entire interest to Alfred. If Alfred continues in adverse possession, he will gain title in 1971, assuming a 21-year statute. First, Alfred may tack Able's time of possession onto his own. Secondly, the time that the statute ran against Owner is "charged" to Owner-2. Therefore, 21 years from the date of original entry by Able is all that is required.

2. **Some states don't allow conveyances:** A few states follow the even more drastic rule that where property is adversely possessed, any conveyance by the true owner is **null and void**. See Burby, p. 269. In this situation, the statute continues to run against the true owner after the void conveyance, and the question of "tacking" does not even arise.

D. **Effect on future interests:** Where the record ownership of property is held not by one person, but is split between a **present** and a **future interest**, the length of time needed for adverse possession may be affected.

   1. **Future interest created after entry of possessor:** Where the future interest is not created until **after** the adverse possession has begun, the future interest is charged with the prior possession, and the Statute of Limitations continues to run against that future interest. That is, the future interest takes subject to whatever claims exist against the property, and the adverse possession is such a claim. See 3 A.L.P. 803.

       Example: O is the owner of Blackacre. A begins to adversely possess the land in 1940. In 1950, O dies, bequeathing the land to Life Tenant for life, remainder to Remainderman in fee. Life Tenant dies in 1965. That same year, Remainderman brings an ejectment action against A. Under a 21-year statute, Remainderman will lose. The adverse possession began while O was still owner of the land. Therefore, when Remainderman's future interest was created in 1950, it was already subject to A's claim, and that claim matured in 1961 (21 years after possession started). The fact that Remainderman was not in possession of the property until 1965 is irrelevant.

   2. **Interest already existing at time of entry:** But if the future interest **already exists** at the time the adverse possessor enters, the Statute of Limitations does not begin to run against the future interest **until it becomes possessory**. The theory behind this is that the Statute of Limitations is running against an ejectment action, and the ejectment action does not exist except by a present possessory interest. 3 A.L.P. 802-803.

       Example: In 1949, Testator dies, bequeathing Blackacre to Life Tenant for life, remainder to Remainderman in fee. In 1950, A enters adversely. Life Tenant dies in 1965. A will not become owner by adverse possession until 1986 (21 years after Remainderman's interest becomes possessory).

VI. RIGHTS OF ADVERSE POSSESSOR

A. Rights before end of statutory period: Prior to the end of the statutory period, the adverse possessor has, of course, not yet obtained title to the property. But he does have some rights, at least against persons other than the true owner.

    1. Suit against third person: Thus the adverse possessor is entitled to bring a *trespass* action against one who enters the land; this is because trespass is an action that vindicates possessory, rather than ownership, interest in the land. (To put it another way, the trespasser may not raise the defense that the plaintiff lacks title). Burby, p. 270. However, the measure of damages is likely to be reduced to take into account the fact that the adverse possessor does not yet have a permanent interest in the land.

    2. Relations with owner: The adverse possessor does not, however, yet have any meaningful rights as against the *true owner* of the land. In fact, if the owner brings suit before expiration of the statutory period, he can recover *mesne profits*, an amount equal to the reasonable rental value of the land for the period that the adverse possessor has held it. Burby, p. 270.

B. Rights after expiration of statutory period: Once the statutory period has expired, so that the adverse possessor gains title, his position is of course improved.

    1. Possessor gains good title: In fact, a title gained by adverse possession is almost as good, as a legal matter, as one obtained by a deed from the record owner.

        a. Owner loses right to profits: Once the statutory period is over, the true owner loses not only his right to recover the property via an ejectment action, but he also loses his right to recover the *reasonable rental value* (the *mesne profits*) of the land during the period of adverse possession. Similarly, he loses the right to recover for the value of minerals or timber taken from it. The doctrine of *relation back* is said to apply, so that the adverse possessor's title in effect dates back to the time he first took possession.

        Example: O is the owner of Blackacre. A begins adverse possession of the property in 1945. He remains in adverse possession until 1965. The Statute of Limitations in ejectment suits is 20 years; in actions for trespass and recovery for mesne profits the period is six years. In 1966, O sues A for damage to Blackacre inflicted between 1960 and 1965 and for profits taken from the land by A in the same 1960-65 period. O cannot recover on either claim. Since the ejectment claim is time-barred, A's title "relates back" to 1945, and he is not liable for trespass or mesne profits for any period after that.

    2. Easements may not be extinguished: If an adjoining landowner has an *easement* against the adversely-possessed property, this easement will probably not be extinguished by the passage of the statutory period. This is because the holder of an easement normally does not have a right of action against a mere possessor, so there is nothing for the Statute of Limitations to run against. 3 A.L.P. 825-26.

    3. Not valid against interest of government: Generally, it is not possible to gain title by adverse possession to land owned by the *federal government*, or by a *state* or a political subdivision thereof. 3 A.L.P. 827.

    4. Not recordable: It is usually not possible to *record* a title gained by adverse possession, since there is no deed. However, if a judicial determination is made that title by adverse possession has vested, then the decision can be recorded. 3 A.L.P. 830.

     a. No need to record: As a corollary, there is no penalty for failing to record a title gained by adverse possession. This means that one who wishes to purchase property from its record owner *cannot be sure* that title has not passed to someone else by adverse possession, unless he makes a *physical inspection* of the property. In fact, even if he finds that the record owner is currently in possession, he cannot negate the possibility that title by adverse possession vested in someone else, and that the record owner is himself now an adverse possessor who has not yet held long enough to re-acquire title! However, such a sequence of events is so unlikely that it is, for practical purposes, disregarded by title examiners.

  5. Hard to prove marketability: Although one who holds title by adverse possession theoretically holds a title as good as record ownership, he will find it difficult to sell the property. His contract of sale will usually require him to convey *"marketable"* title (*infra*, p. 317). It will often be impossible to prove that there is no person who could assert a valid claim, since a claimant's time to sue may have been extended, under many statutes, due to disabilities, the non-possessory status of the remainder interests, etc.

     a. Modern view: However, modern courts will generally find a title to be "marketable" once the statutory period and another ten or so years have passed, even though there is some remote possibility that the record owner's claim may still be alive. See *Rehoboth Heights Devel. Co. v. Marshall*, 137 A. 83 (Del. Ch. 1927).

  6. Transferred like any other title: A title gained by adverse possession is transferred in the same way as any other title. The transfer must thus be *in writing*, in accordance with the Statute of Frauds. This means that an oral transfer, or a disclaimer of interest in the property, or an abandonment of it, will not by itself suffice to strip the adverse possessor of his title.

     Example: A School District owns a school and the land it sits on. Officials construct an additional building on land which they believe belongs to the District, but which actually belongs to X. The additional building remains on X's land for the statutory period. After that, X discovers the error, and complains to District officials; they apologize and remove the building. A new set of officials, however, decides to erect a new building on the land in question, and brings an ejectment suit against X. *Held*, for the School District. Once the District acquired title by adverse possession, that title could not be divested by an apology or by removal of the building, just as these actions would not be sufficient to transfer a title gained by any other means. *Inhabitants of School District No. 4 v. Benson*, 31 Me. 381 (1850). See also 3 A.L.P. 829.

     a. Compare with transfer made before title passes: Contrast this with a transfer made before the statutory period has expired. Before the end of the statutory period, the adverse possessor may convey his possessory interest orally, since the Statute of Frauds does not cover such a transfer. Similarly, he may lose his interest by abandoning it, or by permitting the true owner to enter.

C. Scope of property obtained: By hypothesis, there will never be a valid, enforceable deed describing the property obtained by adverse possession. (If there were, the adverse possession doctrine would not be necessary). Consequently, there will often be a serious question about exactly what land the adverse possessor acquires.

1. **Property actually occupied:** Normally, he acquires title only to that property *"actually"* occupied. The amount of property so occupied by a particular act of dominion will vary with the nature of the property. Thus where property is not suitable for cultivation, fencing in a large area, and hunting over a portion of it, may suffice to occupy the whole enclosed area. Conversely, in more densely populated areas, direct use and occupancy of each portion of land may be necessary. See the discussion of the "actual possession" requirement *supra*, p. 28.

2. **Constructive adverse possession:** There is, however, one important exception to this rule requiring "actual" possession. By the doctrine of *"constructive"* adverse possession, one who enters property under *"color of title"* (i.e., a written instrument that is defective for some reason) will gain title to the **entire area described in the instrument**, even if he "actually" possesses only a portion of it.

   Example: P holds a deed of questionable validity to the "Townsend Tract." The tract is accurately described by metes and bounds in the deed, and has 6,918 acres. P has tenants and agents living on part, but not all, of the land. D enters a portion not actually occupied by P's agents or tenants, and P sues for forcible entry, defined by statute as entry without the consent of the person having "actual possession".

   Held, for P. Because the entire tract was included within P's deed (even though it may have been an invalid one), he is deemed in possession of the entire tract, even though he and his agents are occupying only part of it. *New York-Kentucky Oil & Gas Co. v. Miller*, 220 S.W. 535 (Ky. 1920).

   a. **Must be recognized as unit:** The parcel of land claimed to be constructively possessed must be one which is recognized in the community as a *single parcel* likely to be owned by a single owner. In a farming area where most farms are small, for example, it would be difficult to establish constructive possession of a huge tract of woodlands. 3 A.L.P. 820.

      i. **Must be contiguous:** This means that, at the very least, the part actually occupied and the part constructively claimed must be *contiguous*.

      Example: O is the record owner of lot X in Boston and lot Y in Chicago. A executes a deed of both lots to B. B takes actual occupancy of lot X, and holds it for the statutory period. He has not gained title to lot Y by constructive adverse possession, since the two lots are not contiguous, or recognized in the community as being a single parcel.

   b. **Conflicting possessions:** A claim of constructive adverse possession can be partly or totally destroyed by *actual occupancy* by someone else.

      i. **Actual occupancy by owner:** If *any part* of the area constructively claimed by the adverse possessor is actually occupied by the *true owner*, the entire constructive claim is destroyed.

      ii. **Actual possession by third party:** Where part of the land constructively claimed by an adverse possessor is actually occupied by a *third person* (i.e., one other than the true owner), the constructive claim is vitiated only to the extent of the land actually occupied by that third person.

VII. CONFLICTS BETWEEN POSSESSORS

A. Nature of problem: Up to now, we have been concerned with conflicts between the adverse possessor and the "true" owner. Now we consider conflicts between two persons whose interests are solely possessory, where one has ousted the other from possession.

B. "First in time, first in right": The general rule is that the *first possessor has priority over the subsequent one*.

> **Example:** O owns Blackacre. P moves on to the land, claiming he is the rightful owner. Before expiration of the statutory period, D forces him off the land, and occupies it himself. P can successfully sue to regain possession of the land (by use of an action called "ejectment," discussed immediately below). See *Tapscott v. Cobbs*, 52 Va. 172 (1854). See also Boyer, pp. 235-36.

1. Passage by gift or will: The prior possessor can also pass along his possessory interest by gift or will, so that the person who takes by that gift or will can recover the property from the dispossessor.

C. Remedy of ejectment: As the above example indicates, a person who has the right to possess land and who is ousted from that possession by another, may bring the action of *ejectment* to regain possession.

1. The defense of *jus tertii*: Generally, the plaintiff in an ejectment must "recover on the strength of his own title and not on the weakness of the defendant's." Boyer, p. 235. That is, he must make an affirmative showing that he holds title, not merely show that there is some third person whose title is superior to that of the defendant. As a corollary, the defendant may normally defend by doing what the plaintiff may not do — showing that the title is in a third person. *Id.* As the rule is sometimes put, in an ejectment action *jus tertii* (Latin for "right of another") is a defense.

2. Conflict between possessors: If the rule allowing assertion of *jus tertii* were applicable in controversies between two persons whose interest was solely possessory, the result in the above example would be reversed. That is, the most recent possessor would always be able to defeat any claim by the person he had ousted. Since such a rule would put a premium on violent self-help, courts have not applied it in cases where both parties assert solely a possessory interest. *Tapscott v. Cobbs, supra.*

a. Suit to establish right to possession: The different result in cases involving two adverse possessors can also be explained by the fact that the purpose of the ejectment suit is different from that in the usual ejectment case. In the usual case, the ejectment suit includes an attempt by the plaintiff to establish that he has title, so it makes sense to let the defendant defend by showing that some third person has title. But where the two adverse possessors are in conflict, all the suit is about is who has the right to possess, not who has title; therefore, it makes sense to deny the defendant the right to defend by showing that title is in some third person.

Chapter Review Questions

(Answers are at back of book)

5. In 1960, Beck purchased valid title to Blackacre, located in Ames. That same year, Warren purchased valid title to Whiteacre, the adjoining parcel. Both parties reasonably but mistakenly believed that the boundary line between Blackacre and Whiteacre was a large oak tree, so in

1961 both fenced their property accordingly. In reality, the proper boundary between the two parcels is 30 yards to the south of the oak tree, so that the existing fencing has been depriving Warren of the use of land which belongs to him. In 1990, Warren discovered the error, and has brought an action to recover the 30-yard strip. May Warren recover the strip?

6. In 1950, Osmond, the owner of Blackacre, left the property "to my son Steve and my daughter Deborah in equal shares." Steve moved onto the property and lived there for the next 40 years. Deborah never liked the property, and made no attempt to live there at any time. In 1989, Deborah died, leaving all of her personal and real property to her son Frank. If Frank now seeks a judicial declaration that he is the owner of a one-half interest in Blackacre, will he succeed?

7. Orlando acquired Blackacre in 1950. In 1960, Alice acquired Whiteacre, the adjacent parcel. Alice built a fence on what she thought was the border between the two properties. In fact, her fence encroached 40 yards into Orlando's property. Alice actively, openly and continuously occupied this 40-yard strip for the next 25 years. In 1985, Orlando discovered the error, and informed Alice that she had been using his property. Alice said, "O.K., I now recognize that this strip is your property." She also moved the fence. Shortly thereafter, Alice died, leaving Whiteacre to her son Stokes. Who owns the strip, Stokes or Orlando?

FREEHOLD ESTATES

I. INTRODUCTION

A. Feudalism in brief: American property law is in large part derived from English land law. English land law, in turn, is in important part a product of English society as it existed during the Middle Ages. In particular, it is helpful to understand a little bit about *feudalism*, which was the economic structure of England during at least the 13th through the 15th Centuries.

    1. Nature of feudalism: In feudal times, all land was treated as owned, in the first instance, *by the king*. He then in turn gave possession (but not what we would consider untrammeled ownership) of various parcels to his lords and barons, who had a corresponding obligation to provide the king with a certain number of soldiers (knights).

        a. Subinfeudation: Each lord then had the right to give possession of a parcel to an underling, in return for either production of a certain number of soldiers, or for other services (e.g., farming of the parcel). The party receiving possession was said to be a *vassal*. His holding of the land was said to be in *tenure*. He could in turn give possession of this land to someone else, creating a new tenure. This process of tenures within tenures was called subinfeudation.

        b. No substitution: The key aspect of subinfeudation was that each person in the chain who at one point held possession *kept his place* in the chain. Thus if A held Blackacre "of the king" (i.e., the grant of the land by the king was directly to A), and A wished to give possession to B, he made sure that B held in tenure from him, not from the king. That is, B had to render his services (e.g., production of knights) directly to A, not to the king.

    2. The Statute *Quia Emptores*: The Statute *Quia Emptores* gave tenants (i.e., persons who held in tenure from another) the right to convey their interest in the property without penalty. However, the statute *forbade "subinfeudation."*

        Example: Suppose that A held Blackacre "of the king". Then suppose that prior to 1290, he granted tenure to B. After 1290, B could convey his interest in the property to C without penalty. However, C would not then hold his tenure from B, but rather, from A. C was simply substituted for B in the chain of ownership.

        a. Gradual abandonment of tenure: *Quia Emptores* thus prevented new tenures from being created. Other aspects of the feudal system also gave way through the centuries, until the last vestiges of the tenurial system that were of any practical importance were abolished in England in 1925.

    3. Tenure in the United States: The system of tenure existed in many of the thirteen colonies. Moynihan, p. 25. Furthermore, since the king had the right to waive the effect of the Statute *Quia Emptores*, persons receiving colonial lands from him were free to subinfeudate (as did the family of William Penn in Pennsylvania). Again, however, as in England, statutory reforms have removed the present-day importance of tenure in the U.S.

        a. Shaped historical events: However, many of the rules and statutes which are discussed elsewhere in this book represent responses to the system of tenure. This is true, for instance, of the all-important Statutes of Uses (*infra*, p. 83).

b. Inheritance taxes: Also, occasionally modern-day questions of *inheritance taxes* may involve the concept of tenure. This is so because statutes in many states base the right of the state or county to collect such taxes upon the passing of property by will or inheritance. The statutes do not typically apply to the mere passage of possession of property pursuant to a reversion or remainder. (Thus if O leaves Blackacre "to A for life, remainder to B", the state may collect a tax on O's death, but may not collect a second tax when A dies.) When a person dies totally without heirs, the property typically *escheats* to the state.

i. Importance of tenure questions: In most cases of escheat, if all land is viewed as being held tenurially (i.e., in tenure from the state), then the escheat is simply a type of reversion, and no inheritance tax should be due. If, on the other hand, the land is viewed as being held "allodially" (outright, or non-tenurially), then passage of the property by escheat would be comparable to any other kind of intestate succession, and therefore taxable.

Example: X dies without heirs. His property therefore escheats to D, the state of Nebraska. P, the county where X lived, asserts that the state must pay the county an inheritance tax. The County argues that the right of escheat is given as part of the state's general intestate descent statute; therefore, it claims, the property passing by escheat is property passing by inheritance, and is thus taxable. *Held*, for D. The state's right of escheat is a reversion, because all land is held in tenure from the state. No inheritance tax is payable when property reverts to a reversioner. *In re O'Connor's Estate*, 252 N.W. 826 (Neb. 1934).

B. The concept of "estate": The system of tenure has contributed to our modern-day Anglo-American notion of an *"estate"* in land. As we shall see, it is never really correct to say that X "owns" Blackacre. Instead, one owns an "estate in Blackacre", which may either be an extensive one (e.g., a fee simple absolute) or a more limited one (e.g., a term of years).

1. "Estate" defined: An estate is an interest in land which has two characteristics: (a) it is or may become "possessory"; and (b) it is measured in "terms of *duration*". Restatement, §9.

a. Distinguished from easements and restrictive covenants: Requirement (a) means that neither an *easement* (*infra*, p. 201) nor a *covenant running with the land* (*infra*, p. 228) is an "estate", since these cannot become possessory. Powell, Par. 172, p. 12.

b. Meaning of duration: The key aspect of our concept of estates is that of *duration*. Ownership of a given parcel of land may be split into two or more time periods. For instance, suppose that O, the outright owner (the owner in "fee simple") of Blackacre bequeaths it "to A for life, remainder to B, but if B dies without issue, then to C." As soon as O dies, A, B, and C all acquire estates; A's is present, and B's and C's are future in the sense that they are not now possessory. Thus the ownership of Blackacre is divided into three temporal portions.

2. Freehold and non-freehold estates: Estates in land are traditionally divided into *freehold* and *non-freehold*. The distinction is essentially historical; to understand the distinction, one must first understand a little about the mysterious feudal concept of *seisin*.

    a. Meaning of "seisin": We will discuss the concept of seisin more thoroughly *infra*, p. 80, in connection with the treatment of springing and shifting future interests. For the moment, it suffices to say that a person had seisin of Blackacre (or, in the terminology of the Middle Ages, was "seized of Blackacre") if he had: (1) possession and (2) one of certain types of claims to what might roughly be termed "ownership" of the property.

        i. Seisin and freehold estates: In particular, the requisite claim of "ownership" was that associated with several estates, called the *freehold estates*. Thus one who had both a freehold estate, and possession, had seisin of the land; one who had a non-freehold estate could not have seisin.

3. The freehold estates: Three freehold estates have been recognized since the Middle Ages:

    a. Fee simple: The *fee simple* (which may be either absolute or defeasible);

    b. Fee tail: The *fee tail*; and

    c. Life estate: The *life estate*.

4. Non-freehold estates: The non-freehold estates (i.e., those to which seisin does not attach) are:

    a. Estate for years: The *estate for years* (e.g., a 20-year lease);

    b. Periodic estate: The *periodic estate* (e.g., a month-to-month tenancy);

    c. Estate at will: The *estate at will*; and

    d. Estate at sufferance: The *estate at sufferance*.

    The non-freehold estates are discussed *infra*, p. 133.

5. Example of seisin: To see the relationship between seisin and the freehold estates, consider the following example: O has a fee simple absolute interest in Blackacre. Since the fee simple is a freehold estate, O has seisin of Blackacre. Suppose O now grants A a life interest in Blackacre, and keeps a reversion (i.e., the right to regain possession of Blackacre after A's death) in himself. Since a life estate is a freehold estate, A gains seisin as soon as he enters the property. But now, suppose that A gives B a 20-year lease on Blackacre. Even if B enters, he does not obtain seisin, since his lease is an estate for years, which is a non-freehold estate. The seisin remains in A; he is also treated as being constructively in possession of the land.

6. No new estates creatable: Apart form the recognized freehold and non-freehold estates listed above, *no new estate may be created*. That is, one who wishes to convey property either by deed or will may convey only one (or more) of these estates; he may not make up a new kind of estate. If he tries to do so, the courts will generally treat the conveyance as establishing one of the conventional estates. This is one of several ways in which courts have attempted to prevent undue restraints on the alienation of the land. Moynihan, p. 34.

    Example: O bequeaths Blackacre to "my grand-daughter Sarah and her heirs on her father's side." Sarah then conveys Blackacre to "Albin Johnson and his heirs." *Held*, O's bequest to Sarah, since it attempts to restrict intestate descent of the property to her paternal side, is not one of the traditional estates and is therefore invalid. Accordingly, Sarah will be deemed to have received a fee simple absolute, which she has conveyed to Johnson. *Johnson v. Whiton*, 34 N.E. 542 (Mass. 1893).

C. Chain of title: One of the central concepts in property law is **"chain of title."** Chain of title refers to the sequential links between the various owners of a parcel: A conveys to B, who conveys to C, etc. As we examine the freehold estates in this chapter (and the future estates in the next chapter), we will be tracing a parcel's chain of title from one grantor to the next. Chain of title problems are discussed in more detail in our treatment of the recording system, beginning *infra*, p. 371.

  1. Grant from U.S. Government: For most parcels in America, the chain of title traces back to a grant by the **U.S. Government.** D&K, p. 11. (Actually, when the U.S. Government conveys public lands to a private person, the grant is referred to by the special term **"patent."**) The federal government in turn traces its title back to the original "discovery" (and conquest) of America by white European explorers. *Id.*

    a. Effect of Indian titles: Obviously, Native Americans were here before the white man arrived. However, American courts have held that although Indians had "possession" of the land on which they lived, they did not have "title" to it, and could thus not convey title. Therefore, a title derived from the federal government, or from one of the states or colonies, has priority over an earlier purported "grant" from an Indian tribe. See *Johnson v. M'Intosh*, 21 U.S. (8 Wheat) 543 (1823).

II. FEE SIMPLE

A. Fee simple absolute: The *fee simple absolute* is the most unrestricted estate, and that of longest duration, known to Anglo-American law.

  1. Restrictions on use: Even a fee simple absolute, however, is subject to certain limitations. For instance, the holder of such a fee cannot use the property in violation of valid zoning rules (*infra*, p. 261). Similarly, he cannot use the property in a way constituting a nuisance to an adjoining landowner (*infra*, p. 394). But the fee simple absolute, unlike all the other estates (both freehold and non-freehold) is of *infinite duration*.

  2. Inheritability: One important attribute of the fee simple is that it is *inheritable*, under intestacy statutes. In fact, under the statutes of nearly all states, if the owner of a fee simple absolute dies without any direct descendants (i.e., children or grandchildren), and without a will, then his *collateral relatives* (e.g. brothers and sisters) will inherit the property.

    Example: O, a New York resident, holds a fee simple absolute in Blackacre. He dies without a will, and without issue (i.e., without children, grandchildren or great-grandchildren). He also has no surviving spouse or parent. However, he is survived by a brother and a sister. Under N.Y. Est., Powers and Trusts Law 4-1.1(a) (7), the brother and sister will each take a one-half interest in Blackacre by intestate succession.

  3. Words needed to create: The common law was extremely restrictive with respect to the words needed to create a fee simple absolute. Such an interest could be *conveyed* (i.e., transferred *"inter vivos"*, or between living persons) only by use of the magic words **"and his heirs"**. Thus a conveyance "to A and his heirs" gave A a fee simple absolute, but a conveyance "to A" or "to A forever or "to A and his assigns or even "to A in fee simple" merely gave A a life estate! Moynihan, p. 32. However, a grant "to A *or* his heirs" was acceptable; see Powell, Par. 180, p. 21

a. Meaning of "and his heirs": The common-law requirement that the conveyance be to A "and his heirs" does not mean that A's heirs obtain any interest from the conveyance. For once the conveyance is made, A could turn around and transfer the property to B, and upon A's death, his heirs would get nothing.

    i. Distinction between words of limitation and purchase: Rather, the words "and his heirs" are *words of limitation*, not *words of purchase*. Words of limitation are those which *describe* the estate being transferred. Words of purchase, on the other hand, indicate *who* is getting the estate.

b. Not required for bequest: The common-law rule requiring use of the phrase "and his heirs" applied only to *conveyances*, i.e., *inter vivos* transfers. In the case of a *devise* (i.e., a bequest in a will), a grant made simply "to A" sufficed to give A a fee simple. Moynihan, p. 32. Also, where the recipient was a corporation (even if the interest was transferred by conveyance rather than by will), the words " and his heirs" were considered unnecessary, since a corporation has no heirs. Moynihan, p. 32.

c. Modern states abolish requirement: In the substantial majority of states, statutes now *abolish* the requirements that the phrase "and his heirs" be used. Some other states have reached a similar result by case law. But there are a few states (e.g., Maine and South Carolina) where these magic words appear still to be required. Powell, Par. 180, p. 21. And in one or two other states, the matter is enough in doubt that one who holds land received under a conveyance without these words may have trouble selling it as a fee simple.

    Example: D receives Blackacre under a conveyance made to D "and [his] assigns forever". D contracts to sell the property to P, and also contracts to convey "marketable title". P refuses to go through with the sale on the grounds that the title is not marketable, and sues D for return of a deposit. *Held*, for P. In a lawsuit between D and his grantor, a court might well find that a fee simple was created. But since the grantor is not a party to the present proceeding, the matter is uncertain, and this uncertainty is enough to render D's title unmarketable. *Cole v. Steinlauf*, 136 A.2d 744 (Conn. 1957).

d. Meaning of "heirs": Incidentally, the word *"heirs"* has a particular meaning when used in its technical sense. The term applies only to persons taking under the *intestate descent statute*. One who receives a bequest under a will is not an heir, but is rather a "devisee" if the property is real estate, or a "legatee" if the property is personalty. C&J, p. 227.

B. Fee simple defeasible: In contrast to the fee simple absolute, the fee simple *defeasible* has "strings attached". That is, although one who holds a fee simple defeasible may use and hold the property forever, or convey it, or have it be inherited by his heirs, he must use it *subject to a restriction*. Fees simple defeasible fall into three categories: (1) the fee simple *determinable*, which lapses automatically if an impermissible event occurs; (2) the fee simple *subject to a condition subsequent*, which gives the grantor a right to reenter the property and terminate the estate if the impermissible event occurs; and (3) the fee simple *subject to an executory limitation*, which provides for the transfer of the property to a third person (one other than the grantor) if the impermissible event occurs.

1. Fee simple determinable: A fee simple *determinable* is a fee simple which *automatically* comes to an end when a stated event occurs (or, perhaps, fails to occur).

a. **Restriction on uses:** The most common function of the fee simple determinable is to *prevent the property from being put to a certain use* which the grantor opposes. The limitation gives the grantor control over the use of the property, even after it has changed hands several times.

Example: O holds a fee simple absolute in Blackacre. He is a staunch teetotaler, and is determined that Blackacre will never be used for the sale of liquor. He therefore sells the property "to A and his heirs as long as the premises are not used for the sale of alcoholic beverages, and if they are so used, then the premises shall revert to O." A then purports to convey a fee simple absolute to B, who builds a bar on the premises. When the first alcoholic beverage is sold, B's interest automatically ends, and the property reverts to O.

i. **Possibility of reverter:** By definition, the creator of a fee simple determinable is left with an interest, i.e., the right to regain title if the stated event occurs. This right is called a *possibility of reverter*. Thus in the above example, O, following the conveyance, is left with a possibility of reverter if alcohol is sold. The possibility of reverter is discussed more extensively *infra*, p. 60.

b. **Not subject to Rule against Perpetuities:** In order to prevent undue restraints on alienation of land, the Rule against Perpetuities prevents most estates from taking effect after a certain period following their creation. (*Infra*, p. 92.) However, the Rule has been held not to apply to a possibility of reverter following a fee simple determinable. Thus in the above example, suppose that B had not built a bar, and had sold his interest to C, who sold to D. Theoretically, even 100 years after the grant from O, the sale of alcohol by D would cause D's interest to come to an end, and O's heirs would regain title. D, could, of course, attempt to locate all the heirs and purchase their interests, but since the possibility of reverter is now distributed among a large number of heirs (some of whom may not even be traceable) this is likely to be difficult or impossible. Cribbet, p. 45.

i. **Statute of Limitations:** Accordingly, many states have enacted *Statutes of Limitations* which bar a possibility of reverter after a certain period. Many of these statutes bar the possibility of reverter after a certain period (e.g., 40 years) following the *creation* of the fee simple determinable. Thus in the above example, 40 years after O conveyed to A, the limitation would in effect disappear and the then owner of the fee simple determinable would have a fee simple absolute. Other statutes, however, do not start to run until the stated event occurs (i.e., in the above example, the sale of alcohol); such statutes are obviously much less effective at clearing title, since the statute might not start to run until 100 years following the conveyance of by O to A. In the meantime, the utility and marketability of the land will have been much impaired, since even a prospective purchaser who does not intend to sell alcohol on the premises will be reluctant to buy for fear that he will have trouble selling a less-than-fee-simple-absolute interest.

c. **Words needed for creating:** The words used to create a fee simple determinable are generally ones which make it clear the estate is to end *automatically* upon the occurrence of the stated event. Thus a conveyance made *"so long as . . . "*, or *"until . . . "*, or *"during . . . "* probably creates such an estate. Also, a provision that upon the occurrence of the stated event, the property is to *"revert"* to the grantor is a sign of the fee simple determinable. It is not always easy to distinguish a fee simple determinable form a fee simple subject to a condition subsequent; this issue is discussed further *infra*, p. 51.

d. Widowhood: A fee simple determinable might be used to give land to a testator's surviving spouse during her **widowhood**. For instance, a bequest might be made "to A, my beloved wife, in fee simple for so long as she shall remain my widow, and if she remarries, to revert to my estate." (Alternately, this might be viewed as a **life estate** determinable; see *infra*, p. 56.)

2. Fee simple subject to condition subsequent: A close relative of the fee simple determinable is the fee simple **subject to a condition subsequent**. The latter is also geared to the happening of a particular event, but unlike the fee simple determinable, the fee simple subject to a condition subsequent **does not automatically end** when the event occurs. Instead the grantor has a **right** to take back the property, but nothing happens until he **affirmatively exercises that right**.

   a. Words used: In most jurisdictions, the language of the grant must meet two requirements before it will be found to establish a fee simple subject to a condition subsequent:

   i. Words of condition: First, it must indicate that the grant is **subject to a condition** by such phrases as "upon express condition that", "upon condition that", or "provided that", etc. Restatement, §45;

   ii. Right of re-entry: Also, there must generally be a provision that if the stated event occurs, the grantor may **re-enter the property**, and terminate the estate. *Id*.

   Example: O conveys Blackacre to A in fee simple, "but upon condition that no alcohol is ever served upon the premises. If alcohol is served, grantor or his heirs may re-enter the property and terminate the estate." A then sells the property to B, who builds a tavern. The mere sale of alcohol by B will not bring the estate to an end. Instead, O (or, if he is dead, one or more of his descendants) must re-enter the property or (under modern procedures) bring suit. Only when this happens will the estate terminate. Thus if O and his heirs do nothing, the condition is not enforced.

   b. Absence of re-entry clause: If the conveyance contains the appropriate phrase "upon condition that . . . ," but does **not** have a re-entry clause, most modern courts will not treat it as a condition subsequent. Powell, Par. 188, p. 32. Instead, the court is likely to treat the condition as simply establishing a **covenant** on the part of the grantee to obey the restriction. If he does not, all the grantor can get is **money damages**. (But Rest. §45, Comment 1, makes an exception to the requirement of a re-entry clause if the conveyance is made "upon **express** condition that . . . ").

   c. Terminology: Where a fee simple subject to a condition subsequent does exist, the grantor (the person creating the condition) is traditionally said to have a *"right of entry for condition broken."* The modern tendency is to call this a *"power of termination."* See 1 A.L.P. 418. The right of entry/power of termination is discussed more fully *infra*, p. 61.

   d. Perpetuities: Traditionally, the right of re-entry has not been subject to the Rule Against Perpetuities, so that it can theoretically go on forever. However, many states have set a time limit on the use of the right, just as with possibilities of reverter. (*Supra*, p. 49.) Cribbet, pp. 45-46.

3. **Condition subsequent distinguished from fee simple determinable:** In a few cases, it may make a great deal of difference whether something is a fee simple determinable or a fee simple subject to condition subsequent. In the case of the former, as noted, the estate ends *automatically* on the happening of the stated event; in the case of the latter, a grantor or his heirs must *actually re-enter or bring suit*, which in a particular case they may not bother to do. In the first example below, the conveyance was held to be a fee simple subject to a condition subsequent; in the second, a fee simple determinable was found.

> **Example 1 (subject to a condition subsequent):** The city of Ocean City conveys undeveloped land to D, under a deed providing that D will place land-fill on the property within one year. The deed also states that "a failure to comply with the covenants and conditions [regarding land-fill] will automatically cause title to all lands to revert to the city of Ocean City. . . ." The day before the one-year period expires, the City passes a resolution giving D at least another four years to do the land-fill. The Ps, residents of the City, sue to have the extension of time ruled invalid, and to have the property forfeited back to the city.
>
> *Held*, for D. Despite the reference to "automatic reversion" of title, the conveyance was a fee subject to a condition subsequent, not a fee simple determinable. This is indicated by the reference in the conveyance to "covenants and conditions", and by the reservation by the City of the right to make subsequent changes or modifications of these conditions. Also, the City's purpose was to make sure that the land-fill was done, not to automatically gain back the property if there were any delay. Accordingly, the City has the power to waive the condition, and the land does not revert. *Oldfield v. Stoeco Homes, Inc.*, 139 A.2d 291 (N.J. 1958).

> **Example 2 (fee simple determinable):** The Os convey property (later known as the Hutton School grounds) to the Ds, a school district. The deed provides that "this land to be used for school purpose only; *otherwise to revert to Grantors herein.*" The Os die intestate, leaving S as their only heir. The Ds stop holding classes on the property in 1973, and begin using it for storage purposes only. In 1977, S, without having taken any legal steps to re-enter the land, conveys to the Ps all of his interest in the Hutton School grounds. The Ps bring suit to acquire title to the property. They argue that the deed from the Os to the Ds created a fee simple determinable, that title therefore reverted to S (as the Ds' heir) automatically when the Ds stopped using the property for school purposes, and that S's conveyance of his interest in the property to the Ps was therefore effective to give the Ps a fee simple absolute.
>
> *Held*, for the Ps. The original deed from the Os to the Ds created a fee simple determinable in the Ds, leaving a possibility of a reverter in the Os and their heirs. The use of the word "only" immediately following the grant demonstrates that the Os wanted to give the land to the school district only as long as it was needed and no longer (thus suggesting a limited grant, rather than a full grant subject to a condition). Also, the phrase "otherwise to revert to grantors herein" suggests a mandatory return rather than a permissive return. Therefore, if there came a time when the property was no longer used for school purposes, it reverted to S without any formal action on his part. *Mahrenholz v. County Board of School Trustees*, 417 N.E.2d 138 (Ill. 1981).

a. Statute of Limitations: Another difference between a fee simple subject to conditions subsequent and a fee simple determinable involves the **Statute of Limitations**. Where a fee simple determinable is involved, the holders of the possibility of reverter (the grantor or his heirs) in some states have an unlimited time in which to sue; in other states, a very long Statute of Limitations exists (e.g., 40 years from the grant). In the case of a condition subsequent, however, the statute usually starts to run **upon the occurrence of the stated event**, and is usually for a relatively **short period**. See, e.g., *Johnson v. City of Wheat Ridge*, 532 P.2d 985 (Col. Ct. App. 1975), in which a deed of land to be used for park purposes was found to be a fee simple subject to a condition subsequent, not a fee simple determinable. Therefore, the one-year Statute of Limitations started to run when certain facilities were not installed promptly in the park, and the grantor's claim was time-barred.

b. Courts prefer condition subsequent: Courts **dislike forfeitures**, particularly **automatic** ones such as those involved in fees simple determinable. Therefore, when there is some doubt about whether a conveyance establishes a fee simple determinable or a fee simple subject to a condition subsequent, the court will interpret it as the **latter**. It may do this even though the words used in the conveyance are those traditionally associated with a fee simple determinable.

i. Other ways of avoiding forfeiture: Before allowing a forfeiture, courts also require the occurrence of the terminating event to be **clearly established**, whether the interest is found to be a fee simple determinable or one subject to a condition subsequent. Thus a **minor deviation** from the use specified in the deed will **not** result in a foreeiture. C,S&W, p. 49, n. 23. Similarly, if a grantor fails to terminate a fee simple subject to a condition subsequent **within a reasonable time** after breach, he will often be held to have **waived** his right to do so. C,S&W, pp. 49-50, and p. 47, n. 9.

4. Fee simple subject to executory limitation: A third kind of defeasible fee simple is called a fee simple **subject to an executory limitation**. The fee simple determinable, and the fee simple subject to a condition subsequent, exist by definition only when the estate will return to the **grantor** (or his heirs) when the stated event occurs. An executory limitation, by contrast, provides for the estate to pass to a **third person** (one other than the grantor) upon the happening of the stated event.

Example: O conveys Blackacre "to A and his heirs, but if the property is used for other than residential purposes, then to B and his heirs." A holds a fee simple subject to an executory limitation in favor of B. If either A, or one who receives the property from him, uses the property for commercial purposes, then title automatically passes to B or (if B is dead) his heirs.

a. Death without issue: One common kind of fee simple subject to executory limitation centers around the **death without issue** of the original grantee. Thus O might convey "to A and his heirs, but if A dies without children surviving him then to B and his heirs".

i. Must refer to definite failure of issue: However, the reference to death, without survivors, issue, etc., must refer to what is called a **"definite" failure of issue**, rather than to an indefinite failure of issue, for the estate to be a fee simple subject to executory limitation. That is, the stated event that will cause the fee simple to shift to someone else must be the death of the grantee without **survivors**, not the running out of the grantee's line of descent at some date following his death. In the latter case, the estate is a fee tail (discussed *infra*, below).

   ii. Illustration: Thus if O conveyed "to A and his heirs, but if A dies without issue, then to B and his heirs", and the court interpreted this to mean that the estate shifts to B whenever A's line of descent ends completely (e.g., A dies leaving a surviving son S, and S dies without surviving children), then the estate is a fee tail, not a fee simple subject to an executory limitation. However, most courts today construe the phrase "to die without issue" to refer to a *definite* failure of issue, i.e., A's death without surviving children, making the estate a fee simple subject to executory limitations.

b. Not allowed at early common law: At early common law, the only estates that could follow a fee simple were the possibility of reverter (which follows a fee simple determinable) and the right of entry for condition broken (which follows a fee simple subject to a condition subsequent). Both of these, as noted, are for the benefit of the grantor or his heirs. The fee simple subject to an executory limitation, insofar as it would cause seisin to shift to a *third person*, was an *illegal "shifting" interest*.

   i. Statute of Uses: However, the Statute of Uses (enacted in 1535) made such shifting interest feasible. Therefore, executory limitations are analyzed further *infra*, p. 84, in connection with the discussion of the Statute of Uses. See Cribbet, p. 46.

5. Defeasible estates other than fee simple: The fee simple is not the only estate that may be defeasible. For instance, it is possible to have a *defeasible life estate*. Defeasible life estates are discussed *infra*, p. 56.

III. THE FEE TAIL

A. Keeping property in the family: Suppose that O, the owner of a fee simple in Blackacre, wished to ensure that the property would *remain within his family* indefinitely. If O had a son, A, he would attempt to reach his objective by making a conveyance or bequest "to A *and the heirs of his body*". If this bequest were given effect as intended, then upon A's death the property would go to A's heirs (who under the English system of primogeniture would be limited to A's oldest surviving son), then to the heirs of that person, and so on through the centuries. It could not be conveyed to someone outside of the family.

1. The "fee tail": This form of bequest — "to A and the heirs of his body" — is known as the *"fee tail"*. (The term probably derives from the French "tailler", which means to "cut down" or carve, indicating an estate cut down to the grantor's liking.)

B. Words creating fee tail: The words needed to create a fee tail are ones which indicate the property is to pass *only to the issue* of each tenant in tail (not to collateral heirs, such as brothers and sisters, nephews, uncles, etc.), and that the property is to *revert* to the grantor if the line of descent runs out. The most common way of doing this, as noted, is by a grant "to A and the *heirs of his body*."

1. Grant to A "and his children": There is one other kind of bequest which, traditionally at least, can create a fee tail. Suppose O bequeaths Blackacre "to A *and his children*". By a dictum known as "the *first rule in Wild's Case*", A would take a fee tail. That is, the words "and his children" are treated as words of limitation (describing the estate given to A) rather than as words of purchase (giving the children an estate of their own).

    a. Rule generally repudiated today: Most modern American courts have **repudiated** the first rule in Wild's Case. The general rule is now that A takes a **life estate**, and any children ultimately born receive a **remainder** in fee simple. 5 A.L.P. 296. This is sensible, since the fee tail itself exists hardly anywhere in its original form (*infra*).

    b. Children alive before bequest: If A has children **alive** prior to the testator's death, the first rule of Wild's Case, does not apply. However, there was a **second** rule in Wild's Case to deal with this situation: A and his children took **concurrent interests** as **joint tenants for life**. Today, most states apply a similar, but not identical, rule: A and his children would hold as tenants in common (rather than as joints tenants; see *infra*, p. 114), and they would hold a fee simple, rather than a mere life estate. 5 A.L.P. 300-01.

C. Modern U.S. treatment of the fee tail: The fee tail, as a method for insuring that property will descend along blood lines and will not be conveyed outside the family tree, is completely **dead** in the U.S. (as it is in England). A few states still recognize the fee tail, but permit a "disentailing conveyance" to be made. Other states have a variety of ways of treating a conveyance which at common law would have created a fee tail. The various treatments (usually by statute) are as follows:

    1. Fee simple conditional: A few states (most significantly South Carolina) treat a conveyance "to A and the heirs of his body" as creating a **fee simple conditional**. This means that A, once he has a child, may convey the property in fee simple to a third person. If he does die with issue, and has not conveyed the property, the survivors who take the property probably also take a fee simple conditional, rather than a fee simple absolute. Powell, Par. 195, p. 46.

    2. Disentailable fee tail: Four states, Delaware, Maine, Massachusetts, and Rhode Island (as to deeds only) continue to recognize the common-law fee tail. However, each of these states permits a simple **"disentailing conveyance"** to a third party, so that the latter may receive a fee simple.

    3. Fee tail for one generation: A few other states (e.g., Connecticut and Ohio) have statutes providing that **only the grantee** gets a fee tail, and his issue get the property in **fee simple absolute**. In Connecticut and Ohio, that first generation which holds in fee tail may **not** make a **disentailing conveyance**. Powell, Par. 198, p. 49.

    4. Life estate in grantee, followed by fee simple: Eight states (e.g., Florida, Illinois, Missouri, and in some cases Georgia) give the grantee or devisee a **life estate**, with a remainder in fee simple to his issue. This result is functionally quite similar to the kind of provision described in paragraph (3) *supra*.

    5. Fee simple absolute: In 27 states, a grant or bequest that would be a fee tail at common law is simply **converted by statute to a fee simple absolute**. Thus a grant "to A and the heirs of his body" gives A a fee simple absolute. Moynihan, pp. 41-2. Thus in a majority of states, the fee tail is completely without consequence, at least in the case of a present-day conveyance.

        a. Remainder following fee tail: If the conveyance or devise was intended so that there would be a **remainder** to follow the fee tail, about half of these states treat the grantee's interest as being a fee simple **subject to an executory limitation**.

For instance, suppose O leaves Blackacre "to A and the heirs of his body, remainder to B and his heirs". In roughly 13 states A gets a fee simple, but if he dies without surviving issue, the property passes to B in fee simple. Powell, Par. 198, p. 52.

IV. LIFE ESTATES

A. General meaning of "life estate": The *life estate*, unlike the fee tail, retains tremendous practical significance today. As the term indicates, the estate is one which lasts for the lifetime of a person.

   1. Ordinary life estate and estate *per autre vie*: Ordinarily, the lifetime by which the life estate is "measured" is that of the holder of the life estate (e.g., O grants a life estate "to A for his lifetime, then to B in fee simple.") Occasionally, however, the measuring life is that of someone other than the holder of the life estate (e.g., O grants "to A for the life of B, then to C in fee simple".) This latter type of life estate is called an estate *"per autre vie"*. The estate *per autre vie* is discussed further *infra*, p. 57.

   2. Life estate by operation of law: Ordinarily, a life estate is created at the wishes of the grantor or testator. Occasionally, however, a life estate may be created **by operation of law**.

      a. Fee tail with possibility of issue extinct: For instance, we have already discussed the *fee tail with possibility of issue extinct* (*supra*, p. 54), which amounts to a life estate.

      b. Dower and curtesy: Similarly, a surviving spouse at common law gained the right of dower (for a widow) or curtesy (for a widower). Dower and curtesy are in essence life estates, and are discussed *infra*, p. 105.

B. Creation of the ordinary life estate: The most common phrase used for creating a life estate is "to B during his life" or "to B for life".

   1. Other phrases used to create: However, there are a number of other phrases which may create a life estate.

      a. Until death: For instance, "to B until he dies" would create a life estate. See Moynihan, p. 48.

      b. Gift over upon death: Also, a life estate may be inferred from the fact that following the grantor's death, there is a gift over to another. For instance, "to B and then at his death to B's children in fee simple" would give B a life estate. Moynihan, p. 48.

      c. Common-law conveyance to "B": Furthermore, recall that at common-law, a conveyance "to B", without reference to "his heirs", created a life estate. (*Supra*, pp. 47-48.) However, in virtually all American states today, a conveyance "to B" without reference to his heirs would create a fee simple.

   2. Right to sell or mortgage property: Normally, the life tenant does **not** have the power to **sell**, or even **mortgage**, the property. (*Infra*, p. 58.) Therefore, if a transfer reads "to B with the right to sell or mortgage the property", this will be interpreted to grant B a fee simple, not a life estate. Moynihan, p. 49.

      a. Restriction to life estate: But if the words used indicate that the estate will terminate at B's death, the fact that he is given the right to sell or mortgage the property will not prevent the estate from being a life estate. Thus "to B and upon his death to B's children but B may dispose of the property if he finds it necessary" creates a life estate with an additional power to sell or mortgage. Moynihan, *id.* Observe that this is different from a fee simple, since B cannot make a bequest of the property, and if he dies without surviving children, the property may not be inherited by his collateral heirs under the intestacy statute.

C. Life estate defeasible: Just as a fee simple may be *defeasible* rather than absolute, so a life estate may be defeasible. For instance, suppose that A devises Blackacre "to B, for so long as she shall remain my widow, then to my son C." This would create a life estate determinable, by analogy to the fee simple determinable. Moynihan, p. 50.

   1. Difficulty of construction: If there is no gift over upon the recipient's death (i.e., in the above example, the bequest read simply "to B for so long as she remains my widow"), it may not be clear whether there is a fee simple determinable or a life estate determinable. This issue can be important, since if B dies without having remarried, the property can be taken by will or intestacy if it is a fee simple determinable, but will revert to A's heirs if it is a life estate determinable. The modern trend is probably towards treating this as a *fee simple determinable.* Moynihan, p. 51.

   Example: X bequeaths real estate "to my niece, P, so long as she remains single and unmarried. In the event that P shall marry, then the property shall be divided equally as follows: to my niece P, an undivided one-third, to my niece Y, an undivided one-third, and to my nephew C an undivided one-third." Forty-three years later, P has still not married, and brings suit to gain an adjudication that she holds a fee simple determinable. The suit is opposed by the Ds, the sons of now-deceased C, who argue that P has only a life estate determinable. (Apparently, they hope that when P dies, the property will revert to X's heirs, including themselves.)

   Held, for P. There are several indications that a fee simple determinable, not a life estate determinable, was intended. First, if P did marry, she gained a one-third fee simple interest; this indicates that X was thinking in terms of fee estates rather than life estates. Secondly, since X's will had no residuary clause, if P died, a construction favoring a life estate would lead to a partial intestacy (the property reverting to X's estate), and a construction avoiding intestacy is preferred. Thirdly, the will expressly provided for a gift over following P's marriage, and did not so provide following P's death. Finally, a state statute establishes a presumption in favor of the creation of a fee simple rather than a life estate. *Lewis v. Searles*, 452 S.W.2d 153 (Mo. 1970).

D. Estate now of limited utility: A life state in real property is very *inflexible*, and is therefore of limited utility. For instance, suppose that A leaves Blackacre to his widow, B, for life, then to their surviving children. As long as B is willing to live on the property for the rest of her life, the arrangement works out all right. But suppose that she finds the property too large and expensive to keep up, and wants to move to a Florida condominium. She cannot convey a fee simple interest in the property unless she gets the written consent of the remaindermen (in this case, the children of her marriage with A). If even one of the children objects, she is locked in.

   1. Unascertained remaindermen: Even worse, there can be situations where the *identity of the remaindermen* cannot be ascertained until the life estate ends. For instance, suppose A devised the property "to my wife B for life, then to her surviving issue." No matter how old B is, it is always possible that she could have another child (perhaps by adoption). Since it is not possible to obtain the consent of the hypothetical, unborn child, who could take an interest in the property as a surviving issue, the property is effectively unsalable.

2. **Additional power of disposition:** One way around this problem is for the grantor to give the life tenant the power to sell, rent, or mortgage the property. There is still a life estate, since upon the life tenant's death, the property cannot pass by devise or intestacy.

3. **Equitable life estate:** The problem of inflexibility is also avoided by the use of an *equitable* life estate (as distinguished from the "legal" life estate that we have been discussing). An equitable life estate is one in which the legal ownership of the property is given to a *trustee*, and the *use* of the property is the only thing given to the life tenant. The trustee is given the right to sell, rent, mortgage or otherwise administer the property as he deems fit. Following the death of the life tenant, the property can either continue under the trustee's administration, for the benefit of other persons (e.g., the surviving issue of the testator and his widow) or the trust can end with legal title vesting directly in a third person. See the discussion of equitable estates, and modern trusts, *infra*, p. 80.

E. **Life estate *per autre vie*:** Usually, a life estate is measured in terms of the life of the grantee. However, it is possible to create a life estate that is measured by the life of *someone other than the grantee*. Such a life estate is called an estate *per autre vie* ("by another's life", *supra*, p. 55).

1. **Death of the life tenant:** The estate *per autre vie* is identical to the ordinary life estate in most respects. However, there is one important difference: where the measuring life is that of the grantee, upon the grantee's death the estate automatically comes to an end, and possession passes to the grantor or to some third person. But in the case of an estate *per autre vie*, upon the death of the life tenant, the estate can *continue*, since the measuring life may still exist. Who gets the estate next has been the subject of great confusion and controversy.

   a. **Common-law approach:** At common law, it was held that *no one* had the right to the balance of the life estate. Thus suppose that O conveyed Blackacre "to A for the life of B, then to C and his heirs". If A died while B was still alive, C did not yet have any right to the property, since the life estate measured by B's life continued. Nor could the interest pass to A's heirs, since the life estate was not an estate of inheritance. Accordingly, the common rule was that *whoever entered* the property first had the right to keep possession until the measuring life terminated; this first possessor was called a *common occupant*.

   b. **Modern-day statutes change rule:** This common-law scheme has been modified by statutes both in England and in most American states. Generally, upon the life tenant's death, the balance of the life estate is treated as *personal property*, which passes by will or by intestacy. (Some states have intestacy statutes making a distinction between real and personal property so that heirs who would receive real estate will not necessarily be the ones to receive the personalty.

F. **Duties and powers of life tenant:** Since a life tenancy is by definition to be followed by another interest (either a reversion to the grantor or a remainder to a third person), a life tenant does not have the same freedom in his use or disposition of the land as the holder of, say, a fee simple absolute.

1. **Duties:** The life tenant therefore has a number of *duties vis a vis* the future interest. These include the following:

   a. **No waste:** He may not commit *waste*, i.e., an unreasonable impairment of the value which the property will have when the holder of the future interest takes possession. Since the rule against waste applies to landlord-tenant relations, and to relations between all other present and future interests, the topic is discussed more extensively *infra*, p. 89.

   b. **Duty to make repairs:** A corollary of the rule against waste is that the life tenant must make *reasonable repairs* on the property, if it includes a structure. However, he is not required to *rebuild* a structure if it is damaged by fire, flood, etc. 1 A.L.P. 147.

   c. **Payment of taxes:** The life tenant must pay all *property taxes* which come due while he holds possession of the property. (However, he is liable for these taxes, in a suit by the holder of the future interest, only to the extent of rents received from the property, or its fair rental value if the life tenant himself occupies it. 1 A.L.P. 148.)

   d. **Payment of mortgage interest:** Similarly, the life tenant must make *current interest payments* on any mortgage, although this obligation is also limited to the rents he receives from the property (or to its fair market value if he occupies it himself).

   e. **Mortgage principal:** The life tenant does *not* have the duty to make payments of the *principal* of the mortgage, even if these come due while he is in possession. But the holder of the future interest then has the right to make such payments; if he does so, the life tenant can be forced to choose between giving up the life estate or making a contribution to the principal payments. Rest. §132. (If he decides to make a contribution, the proportion required is determined by comparing the value of his estate with that of the future interest; this is done by use of the mortality tables, since the value of the life tenancy is tied to the tenant's life expectancy.)

2. **Life tenant's right to dispose of the property:** The life tenant *cannot convey a fee simple*, or any other estate greater than the life estate he holds. (At common law, if he tried to do so, the holder of the future interest could sue to terminate the life estate.)

   a. **Conveyance of life estate:** But the life tenant may, in all jurisdictions, *convey the interest which he does hold*, or a lesser one. Thus if A holds a life estate, he may convey to B either for the life of A, or for a term of years (which would obviously be cut short if A died). Observe that if A conveys his full interest to B, he has created an estate *per autre vie*.

   b. **Restriction on alienation:** If the instrument which created the life estate contains a prohibition on alienation, it will usually be held to be *void*. Thus if O conveys "to A for life, without power to convey", A may nonetheless usually transfer his life estate to B.

      i. **Indirect prohibition:** But this same result may usually be accomplished by less direct language. For instance, suppose O conveys "to A for life, but if he ceases to live on the land, to B". This limitation will probably be judicially enforced. See Moynihan, p. 59.

c. Extra power to convey fee simple: It is possible for the creator of a life estate to grant the additional power to **dispose** of the property (i.e., to convey a fee simple absolute). See *supra*, p. 57.

Chapter Review Questions

(Answers are at back of book)

8. O'Malley was the owner in fee simple of Blackacre. As a gift, O'Malley delivered to Abel a deed to Blackacre; the deed read, "to Abel and his heirs." Abel recorded the deed as required by local statutes. Abel then delivered a deed to Blackacre to Barbara, who recorded it. Abel then died, leaving as his sole heir his son, Callaway. Who owns Blackacre?

9. In the State of Ames, there is a one-year statute of limitations on actions to enforce a right of entry for condition broken. Ames also has a statute barring any possibility of reverter 50 years following the creation of a fee simple determinable. In Ames, O held a fee simple absolute in Blackacre. Because O had watched his daughter's marital prospects be ruined by her early involvement as a pornography star, O sold Blackacre to A, a nightclub operator, under a conveyance, "To A and his heirs so long as the premises are not used for topless or erotic dancing, and if they are so used, then the premises shall revert to O." This conveyance took place in 1960. A complied with this restriction. In 1968, O died, leaving all his real and personal property to his son S. In 1970, A conveyed, "To B and his heirs, in fee simple absolute." That same year, B began to use the premises as a topless bar, and continued doing so for the next 10 years. In 1980, S asks the court for a determination that the property now belongs to him because of B's operation of the topless club. Should the court grant S's request?

10. Same facts as the prior question. Now, however, assume that the deed from O to A stated, "To A and his heirs, provided that no topless or other obscene dancing ever takes place on the premises. If such dancing does take place, Grantor or his heirs may re-enter the property." All other facts remain the same, except that in 1980, S files suit for a decree authorizing him to re-enter the property. Should the court grant S's request?

11. O conveyed Blackacre "to A for life, remainder to B." One year later, A quitclaimed all of his interest in Blackacre to C. After this quitclaim deed, what is the state of title?

FUTURE INTERESTS

I. INTRODUCTION

A. Five future interests: The estates discussed in the previous chapter are ones which are **possessory**, or present. The common law also recognizes, however, a number of estates that are non-possessory. Since these estates may or will become possessory in the future, they are commonly referred to as **future estates**.

1. **Estate exists in present even though not now possessory:** These future estates, even though they are not possessory, nonetheless exist in the present. For instance, suppose A conveys Blackacre "to B for life, remainder in fee simple to C and his heirs". At the time of conveyance, C has a remainder in fee simple; it is only the aspect of possession that is future.

B. Five estates: There are five kinds of future estates, each of which will be discussed in this chapter:

1. **The possibility of reverter**, which follows the fee simple determinable (*infra*);

2. **The right of entry**, which follows an interest (fee simple or other) subject to a condition subsequent (*infra*, p. 61);

3. **The reversion**, which is left in a grantor after he makes a conveyance of a lesser estate (*infra*, p. 62);

4. **The remainder**, which is a future interest in one other than the grantor, and which takes effect after the termination of an earlier estate (*infra*, p. 63); and

5. **The executory interest**, which like the remainder is a future interest in one other than the grantor, but which generally takes effect by cutting short a prior interest.

II. THE POSSIBILITY OF REVERTER AND THE RIGHT OF ENTRY

A. Reversionary interests: We have seen that under the Anglo-American system of estates, ownership of a given parcel of land may be split among a present interest and one or more future interests. One way such a split can occur is if the owner of a present estate (either a possessory fee simple absolute or some lesser present interest, such as a life estate) transfers possession, but not the full interest he owns. Where this happens, the grantor is left with one of several kinds of **reversionary interests**: (1) the **possibility of reverter**; (2) the **right of entry**; and (3) the **reversion**.

B. Possibility of reverter: Suppose the owner of a fee simple absolute transfers a **fee simple determinable** (*supra*, pp. 48-50). The grantor is said to retain a **possibility of reverter**. That is, if the fee simple determinable comes to an end, possession reverts to the grantor; since it is not certain that this will ever occur, the word "possibility" is used.

> **Example:** O owns a fee simple absolute in Blackacre. He conveys "to A and his heirs, so long as no liquor is sold on the premises, and if liquor is sold thereon, title to revert to O and his heirs". After the transfer, O has a possibility of reverter; he will automatically regain possession if A or anyone holding under him sells liquor.

1. **Distinguish from reversion:** The possibility of reverter should be distinguished from the *reversion* (discussed *infra*, p. 62), which is a non-contingent prospect of getting the property back, Thus, if in the above example, O's conveyance had been "to A for life," with nothing more, O would have a reversion, not a possibility of reverter, since A's life is sure to come to an end.

2. **Alienability of possibility of reverter:** All states agree that a possibility of reverter is *inheritable* under the intestacy statute, and devisable by will. However, the states are in dispute about whether such a possibility of reverter may be *conveyed inter vivos*; the modern trend is to *allow* such conveyances. B,C&S, p. 226.

C. **Right of entry:** If the holder of an interest in land conveys all or part of his interest and attaches a *condition subsequent* to the transferee's interest, the transferor is said to have a *right of entry* (or as it is sometimes called, a right of entry for condition broken). This right gives the transferor ability to take back the estate if the condition subsequent occurs.

> **Example:** O owns Blackacre in fee simple. He conveys "to A and his heirs, on condition that liquor never be sold on the premises; if liquor is sold thereon, O or his heirs may re-enter the premises." The conveyance to A has been made subject to a condition subsequent, and O therefore reserves a right of entry.

1. **Not incident to reversion:** Sometimes, the *only* interest retained by a grantor is this right of entry for condition broken. This is the case in the above example, since O conveyed all his other interest in the land (his fee simple).

   a. **Incident to reversion:** Much more commonly, however, a transferor who holds a right of entry *also holds a reversion*. For instance, nearly every *lease* contains several right of entry clauses, by which the landlord may re-enter if the tenant breaches a covenant (e.g., the covenant to pay rent). Such a right of entry is incident to the landlord's reversion at the end of the lease term.

2. **Alienability:** The distinction between a right of entry incident to a reversion and one that is not so incident is important with respect to *alienability*.

   a. **Incident to reversion:** Where the right of entry is incident to a reversion the general rule today is that it *passes with the reversion*. Thus if a landlord sells his interest in property, and assigns the leases he holds, the assignee may retake the premises in situations where the original landlord could have done so. Moynihan, p. 108.

   b. **Not incident to reversion:** Where a right of entry is not incident to any reversion, however, alienability may be somewhat more restricted.

      i. *Inter vivos* **transfer:** At common law, such a right of entry could *not be conveyed inter vivos*. Furthermore, some American courts have even held that where an *attempted conveyance* of a right of entry is made, this act *destroys the right of entry*. See *Rice v. Boston & Worcester R.R.Corp.*, 12 Allen 141 (Mass. 1866) (It is doubtful whether a court would follow the *Rice* rule today.)

      ii. **Present-day split:** Today, most states continue to treat a right of entry unaccompanied by a reversion as *not transferable inter vivos*. A minority, however, have enacted statutes permitting such a transfer, either in all cases or at least where a breach of the condition has already occurred. Powell, Par. 282, pp. 249-52.

    iii. Devise and descent: On the other hand, in most states a right of entry without a reversion is *devisable* and *descendible*. Moynihan, p. 109. See Rest., §164, Comment a; §165. A minority of states maintain the traditional rule that the right of entry is neither descendible nor devisable.

D. Executory interests: The possibility of reverter and the right of entry are both defined as to belong to the *grantor*, rather than a third person. However, under modern law, an interest similar to a fee simple determinable, or to a fee simple subject to a condition subsequent, can be created that gives a third person an interest comparable to a possibility of reverter or to a right of entry. In such a case, the present interest is called a "fee simple subject to an executory interest," and the third party has an *executory interest*. See the further discussion of this topic *infra*, p. 84.

III. REVERSIONS

A. Reversions generally: A *reversion* is created when the holder of a vested estate transfers to another a *smaller estate*; the reversion is the interest which *remains in the grantor*. See Rest. 2d (Donative Transfers) §1.4, Comment c.

> **Example:** A holds a fee simple absolute in Blackacre. He conveys "to B for life." A has retained a reversion, which will become possessory in A (or his heirs) upon B's death.

    1. No reservation needed: It is not necessary that the grantor specifically reserve a reversion in himself. As long as the estate conveyed is legally smaller than the grantor's original estate, he retains a reversion. Thus in the above example, A retained a reversion even though nothing to this effect was stated in the grant, since a life estate is smaller than a fee simple.

    2. Holder of less-than-fee-simple: Even when A holds a *less-than-fee-simple interest*, he can create a reversion in himself by transferring a still smaller estate. Thus if A held a fee tail, and conveyed "to B for life", A would have a reversion in fee tail.

        a. Two life estates: Similarly, under the modern view, if A owns a life estate, and conveys to B for B's life, A has a reversion. In this situation, although it can be argued that one life estate can't be smaller than another, the fact is that B's life estate can terminate before A's, whereas A's cannot terminate before B's. See Moynihan, p. 94, n. 2.

    3. Transfer of term of years: At common law, if an owner of a freehold estate created a *leasehold interest* (i.e., a term of years) in another, the grantor was not said to retain a reversion. Instead, he was regarded as continuing to hold the seisin in the land, and his freehold was merely subject to the terms of years. But in modern parlance, the landlord is said to have a reversion subject to the lease term. C&L, p. 290.

B. Will not necessarily become possessory: A reversion will *not necessarily ever become possessory*. If events occur in such a way that it becomes certain that the reversion can never become possessory, it is said to have been *divested*.

> **Example:** O conveys Blackacre "to A for life, and then to B and his heirs if B survives A." O has a reversion which will become possessory when A dies, if B has predeceased A. But if A dies before B, the reversion is divested, since B now holds a fee simple absolute.

C. Distinguishing from possibility of reverter: It will sometimes be important to distinguish between a reversion and a possibility of reverter (particularly in the context of the doctrine of merger, *infra*, p. 72). To do this, one must examine the interest given away by the grantor; if he has given away a fee simple determinable, he retains only a possibility of reverter. If he has given away something less than a fee simple, he retains a reversion.

D. Alienability: Reversions have always been viewed as *alienable inter vivos*. Moynihan, p. 95. Furthermore, they are *devisable* and *descendible*.

    1. Possibility of divestment: However, remember that a reversion may be subject to divestment. Thus suppose that A, who holds a fee simple, conveys to B for life, than to C and his heirs if C survives B. A is free to transfer or devise his reversion to X. But if, following such a transfer or bequest, B dies while C is still living, X takes nothing.

IV. REMAINDERS

A. Definition: A *remainder* is a future interest which can become possessory only upon the *expiration* of a *prior possessory interest*, created by the *same instrument*. That is, for a remainder to exist, the following requirements must be met:

    1. A grantor must convey a present possessory estate (called the "particular" estate) to one transferee;

    2. He must create a non-possessory estate in *another* transferee, by the *same instrument*; and

    3. The second, non-possessory, estate (the remainder) must be capable of becoming possessory only on the "*natural*" expiration (as opposed to the cutting short) of the prior estate.

        Example: O conveys "to A for life, remainder to B and his heirs." B has a remainder because: (1) a present interest has been created; (2) a future interest has been created in a different person by the same instrument; and (3) the second interest will become possessory only after the natural expiration of the first one (i.e., after A's death).

B. Following a term of years: In modern parlance, one can refer to an estate following a *term of years* as a remainder. Thus if O conveys "to A for 10 years, then to B and his heirs", B would today be said to have a remainder.

    1. Common-law view: But at common law, B would be said to have not a remainder, but a *present freehold*, subject to A's less-than-freehold term of years. C&L, p. 294. That is, at the time of the conveyance the seisin was deemed to pass from O directly B (since by definition the holder of a non-freehold estate could not hold seisin).

C. Remainders distinguished from reversions: It is usually not difficult to distinguish a remainder from a reversion.

    1. Created in one other than the grantor: First, and most important, the remainder is by definition created in *someone other than the transferor*. The reversion, by contrast, is an interest left in the transferor after he has conveyed an interest to someone else.

        a. Reversion may be transferred: However, keep in mind that a reversion may be transferred from the transferor to a third person. What determines whether something is a remainder is its *original* status.

Example: O conveys "to A for life, then to B and his heirs." B then conveys his interest back to O. O holds a remainder, not a reversion, since the interest was originally created in a third party (B), not the transferor (O).

2. **Operation of law:** Secondly, a remainder arises only by an express or implied grant by the transferor, whereas a reversion arises independently of the grantor's wishes (by operation of law). Moynihan, p. 111.

D. **Successive remainders:** It is possible to have *successive remainders*, with no limit.

> **Example:** O conveys "to A for life, then to B for life, then to C for life, then to D and his heirs." B, C, and D all have remainders. See Moynihan, p. 110.

E. **No remainder following fee simple:** At common law, a fee simple is regarded as the maximum estate that may be created. Furthermore, all types of fee simple (absolute, determinable, and subject to condition subsequent) are regarded as being of equal size. The result is that, under the common-law view, there can be *no remainder after any kind of fee simple*.

1. **No remainder after fee simple determinable** Most significantly, this means that there cannot be a remainder following a *fee simple determinable*. At early common law, the only thing that could follow a fee simple determinable was a possibility of reverter (*supra*, p. 49); this was a consequence of the fact that the only future interest in a stranger allowed by common law was the remainder. (However, after the enactment in 1536 of the Statute of Uses, it became possible to create an executory interest in a third person following a fee simple determinable; see *infra*, p. 83. C&L, p. 294.)

> **Example:** In 1500, Owner conveys "to Able for life, and then to Baker and his heirs, but if Baker marries Carr before Able's estate ends, then to Davis, and his heirs." Baker's interest would probably be viewed as a vested remainder in fee simple determinable (a kind of vested remainder subject to divestment; see *infra*, p. 67). Therefore, Davis' interest cannot be a remainder, for the reasons stated in Par. 1. above. Accordingly, Davis takes nothing, since a shifting executory interest will not be permissible until 1536. The state of the title is thus life estate in Able, vested remainder in fee simple determinable in Baker, and the possibility of reverter in Owner.

F. **Two kinds of remainders:** Remainders are usually divided into two main classes: *vested* and *contingent*.

1. **Why it makes a difference:** Why do we have to worry about distinguishing between vested and contingent remainders? At common law, there were three main consequences to the distinction, though only one of these has major practical importance today.

a. **Rule Against Perpetuities:** The consequence that most significantly lives on today relates to the *Rule Against Perpetuities* (*infra*, p. 92). ***Contingent remainders are subject to the Rule Against Perpetuities, but vested remainders are not.*** See D&K, pp. 272-73. Thus a particular bequest or conveyance creating a remainder may turn out to be completely enforceable or completely unenforceable, depending solely on whether the remainder is contingent or vested. See *infra*, p. 93.

b. **Transferability:** At common law, the two types of remainders differed sharply with respect to *transferability*. Vested remainders have always been transferable *inter vivos*. Contingent remainders, on the other hand, were basically not transferable *inter vivos* (though there were major exceptions). Today, in most states, contingent remainders are transferable *inter vivos*, so the vested/contingent distinction is not important with respect to transferability. *Id.* See *infra*, p. 78.

c. Destruction: Finally, at common law a contingent remainder was **destroyed** if it did not vest upon termination of the proceeding life estate. This is the doctrine of "destruction of contingent remainders", discussed *infra*, p. 70. There was no comparable doctrine destroying vested remainders. But again, this distinction is not very significant today, because most states have abolished the doctrine of destruction of contingent remainders. *Id.* See *infra*, pp. 73, and 87.

d. Federal estate tax: A fourth key distinction did not exist at common law, but exists today: this is a distinction relating to the **federal estate tax** consequences of a remainder. Suppose that B has a remainder contingent upon B's surviving A (e.g., "to A for life, then to B if he survives A"); if B dies before A, there will be no estate tax on the value of the remainder, since it is extinguished at B's death. Now, assume that B has a remainder which is vested, even though it does not become possessory until A's death (e.g., "to A for life, then to B and his heirs"). Here, even if B dies before A, the value of B's remainder will be taxable as part of B's estate (since there is something of value going to B's heirs, namely the right to take possession once A dies). See D&K, p. 273.

G. Vested remainders: There is no agreement as to the exact definition of a vested remainder. In general, however, it is safe to say that a remainder is vested if the following two conditions are met: (1) *No condition precedent* is attached to it; and (2) the person holding it has already been *born*, and his identity is *ascertained*.

> **Example:** O conveys Blackacre "to A for life, remainder to B and his heirs." B has a vested remainder, since his identity is ascertained, and there is no condition precedent which must be satisfied in order for his interest to become possessory. (It is true A must die in order for B to take possession, but this is not the fulfillment of a condition precedent; it is simply the natural expiration of the prior estate.)

> **Note:** Our discussion of exactly what constitutes a condition precedent is postponed until the treatment of contingent remainders, *infra*, p. 67. For the moment, it suffices to state that as long as the remainder will become possessory *whenever and however the prior estate terminates*, no condition precedent exists. Thus in the above example, no matter however and whenever A's life estate ends, B's estate will immediately become possessory; therefore B's remainder is vested.

1. Three types: Within the class of vested remainders, there are three sub-classes: (1) remainders indefeasibly vested; (2) remainders vested subject to open; and (3) remainders vested subject to complete defeasance.

2. Remainder indefeasibly vested: A remainder *indefeasibly vested* is one which is *certain to become possessory* at some future time.

> **a. Possession in heirs or devisees:** For the remainder to be indefeasibly vested, it is not necessary that the remainderman himself is certain to come into possession in the future; it will suffice that either the remainderman or his successors in interest (e.g., his devisees or grantees) will someday take possession. Thus suppose O conveys Blackacre "to A for life, remainder to B and his heirs." It is not certain that B himself will ever take possession since he may die before A. But it is certain

that either B or someone who acquires B's interest through conveyance, bequest, etc., will someday take possession.

b. Successive life estates: Suppose O conveys "to A for life, then to B for life." B's interest is sometimes viewed as an indefeasibly vested remainder. See Moynihan, p. 118. However, the more correct view seems to be that B's remainder is vested subject to defeasance (*infra*), since if B dies before A neither B nor his successors will get anything. See Rest. §157, Comment p, and Illustration 11.

c. Conditional form but unconditional substance: If a remainder is sure to become possessory when the prior estate ends, the remainder is indefeasibly vested even though the conveyance states that it will take effect "upon" or "after" a certain event. Powell, Par. 275, p. 236.

> **Example:** O conveys "to A, then upon A's death to B and his heirs." Although it could be argued that a condition has been imposed that A die, this conveyance is simply another way of stating that A has a life estate, following which B's remainder is sure to become possessory. Therefore, B's remainder is indefeasibly vested.

3. Vested remainder subject to open: The vested remainder *subject to open* exists when it is possible to point to one or more persons and say that they (or their successors) are certain to have a possessory interest someday, but there remains a chance that *others will share this interest*. That is, a remainder is subject to open when, in addition to the persons now vested, others may also gain a vested portion.

a. After-born children: The principal situation in which a remainder vested subject to open is likely to exist is where a gift is made to the *"children"* of someone, and the possibility exists that *additional children will be born* subsequently.

> **Example:** O conveys "to A for life, remainder to B's children and their heirs." At the time of conveyance, B has only one child, X. Immediately following the conveyance, X is said to have a vested remainder subject to open; if another child, Y, is then born to B, X's remainder "opens up" to give Y a half interest in it. (The remainder stays open until either A dies, in which case only the then-living children of B will take anything, or B dies, in which case he can have no further children. See Moynihan, p. 119, footnote 3).

4. Vested remainder subject to complete defeasance: Suppose the remainderman exists, his identity is ascertained, and his interest is not subject to a condition precedent. Suppose further, however, that although his interest will become possessory if all prior interests were to end today, it cannot be said with certainty that his interest will ever in fact become possessory. In this situation, the remainder is said to be *vested subject to complete defeasance*. See Rest. §157(c), and Comment o thereto. This defeasance may occur either through natural termination or through "divestment" (i.e., a cutting short of the remainder).

a. Possibility of expiring before becoming possessory: A vested remainder may fail to become possessory because it naturally *expires* before all prior interests end. For instance, suppose O conveys "to A for life, then to B for life." B's interest is a vested remainder subject to complete defeasance through expiration, since if B dies before A, his remainder will never become possessory. See Rest. §157, Illustration 11.

i. Possibility of reverter: Similarly, if a remainder is in fee simple ***determinable***, it can be viewed as vested subject to defeasance by natural expiration. Thus suppose O conveys "to A for life, then to B and his heirs so long as the premises are used for residential purposes." B could be said to have a vested remainder subject to defeasance by natural expiration, since use of the property for non-residential purposes would cause a natural termination. O has a corresponding possibility of reverter. See Rest. §157, Illustration 21.

b. Divestment: The other way in which a remainder subject to defeasance can fail to become possessory is if it is ***divested***, i.e., ***cut off*** prior to its natural termination. There are several ways this can happen:

i. Executory interest: The remainder may be subject to divestment by what is called an ***executory interest*** (described more fully *infra*, p. 84). Such an interest cuts off the remainder (either before or after it becomes possessory) and gives it to someone other than the grantor.

Example: O conveys "to A for life, then to B and his heirs, but if B dies without issue, then to C and his heirs." B has a remainder vested subject to divestment. If A died immediately, B's interest would become possessory. But if B died without issue (either before or after A's death), B's interest would be completely defeated or "divested." C's interest, which cuts short B's vested interest, is called an executory interest. See Moynihan, p. 120.

ii. Right of entry: Similarly, if the grantor retains a ***right of entry*** if the remainderman does not meet a certain condition, the remainder is vested subject to divestment.

Example: O conveys "to A for life, then to B and his heirs, upon condition that the premises always be used for a church; if the premises are not so used, O or his heirs shall have the right to re-enter the premises." B's interest is vested, but the cessation of church activities, plus the re-entry by O or his heirs, would cause the title to return to O. Therefore, B's interest is subject to divestment.

iii. Power of appointment: A ***power of appointment*** in the prior estate may also suffice to make the following remainder subject to divestment.

Example: O conveys "to A for life, remainder as A shall appoint, and if A does not exercise this power, to B and his heirs." A's power of appointment gives him the right to specify who gets the property on his death; an exercise of this right would divest B of his remainder. See Moynihan, p. 120.

c. Distinguished from contingent remainders: The principal difficulty in dealing with vested remainders subject to divestment is that they are often hard to distinguish from ***contingent*** remainders that are subject to a condition precedent. This matter is more fully discussed *infra*.

H. Contingent remainders: All remainders that are not vested are ***contingent***. The remainder will be contingent rather than vested if: (1) it is subject to a ***condition precedent***; or (2) it is created in favor of a person who is either ***unborn*** or ***unascertained***.

1. Contingent can become vested: The fact that a remainder is contingent at the time of its creation does not mean that it can never become vested. On the contrary, we will see frequent examples below of remainders which become vested either through the satisfaction of a condition precedent, through the birth of a child, or through the eventual determination of the identity of a person or class.

> **Example:** O conveys "to A for life, then to the children of B who survive B." At the time of the conveyance, the remainder in B's children is contingent, since there is no way to know which children will survive B. But if B dies while A is still alive, the remainder becomes vested in those children who have survived B.

2. **Condition precedent:** Where a remainder is *subject to a condition precedent*, it is contingent. That is, the fact that some condition must be met before the remainder could possibly become possessory is by itself enough to make it contingent. See Rest. 2d (Donative Transfers) §1.4, Comment b.

> **Example;** O conveys "to A for life, then, if B is living at A's death, to B in fee simple." B must meet the condition precedent of surviving A, before his remainder can become possessory. Therefore, his remainder is contingent.

    a. Distinguishing from condition subsequent: Recall that where a remainder is subject to a condition *subsequent*, it is termed a vested remainder subject to divestment (*supra*, p. 67). It is thus important to be able to distinguish between a condition precedent and a condition subsequent. This is not always an easy thing to do.

    b. Traditional test: The difference between the two is really one of *words alone*, not of substance. The traditional test is as follows: if the condition is incorporated into the clause which gives the gift to the remainderman, then the remainder is contingent. If, on the other hand, one clause creates the remainder, and a *subsequent clause* takes the remainder away, the remainder is vested (subject to divestment). See Moynihan, p. 121.

> **Example:** Suppose O conveys "to A for life, remainder to B and his heirs, but if B dies before A, to C and his heirs." Although for B's interest ever to become possessory, B must live longer than A, B's remainder is not contingent under the traditional test. This is because no condition was attached in the clause giving B his interest ("then to B and his heirs . . . "), and a second clause was added to take the interest away from B if he fails to survive. (The second clause is thus a condition subsequent). Suppose, on the other hand, that the conveyance read "to A for life, then if B survives A, to B and his heirs; otherwise to C and his heirs." Here, B has a contingent remainder. This is because the condition of survivorship is incorporated into the very gift to B, making it a condition precedent. See C&L, p. 295, examples 2 and 6.

    c. Use of the word "but": One key phrase that the student should look for is *"but if"*. Where the condition occurs following this phrase, it will almost always be an indication that the remainder is being taken away, and is therefore subject to a condition subsequent rather than to a condition precedent. This was true, for instance, in the first conveyance quoted in the above example. By contrast, where the condition follows the phrase "then if . . . ", the condition is probably precedent. This is true of the second conveyance quoted in the above example.

    d. Requirement of survivorship: One frequent situation in which a condition precedent occurs is where the remainderman must *survive* the holder of the prior interest.

i. Still necessary to distinguish from condition subsequent: But always remember that a condition of survivorship can be a condition subsequent just as easily as a condition precedent.

Example: The Os convey "to [our] son Ross for life, at his death to his lawful children, the lawful child or children of any deceased lawful child of Ross to have and receive its or their deceased parent's share. . . ." Prior to Ross' death, one of his children, Oscar, goes bankrupt, and his trustee in bankruptcy deeds Oscar's interest in the property to D, a third party. When Ross dies, the Ps, Ross' surviving children (including Oscar) sue D, claiming that the trustee's deed under which he took an interest in the property was void. Under local law, a contingent remainder does not pass to a trustee in bankruptcy, whereas a vested remainder does. The Ps therefore claim that Oscar's interest was only contingent prior to Ross' death.

Held, for D. Ross' children had vested remainders prior to their father's death, since the grant to them was not subject to a condition precedent. Rather, each of the plaintiff's remainders was subject to divestment by his own children, if that plaintiff had died before Ross. The grammatical structure of the conveyance controls; here the gift to each child of Ross occurs in one clause, and the taking away of that gift (and transfer to that child's children) occurs in a different, subsequent, clause. It is true that, since the remainders were vested, a plaintiff's children would have taken had that plaintiff died before Ross, even without the divesting clause in the conveyance; but the fact that this clause was surplusage is irrelevant. *Kost v. Foster*, 94 N.E.2d 302 (Ill. 1950).

Note: Today, most states allow not only vested remainders, but also contingent ones, to be ***transferred by deed or will***, and to be attached by creditors. See C&J, p. 277, note 1. Thus in most jurisdictions, a litigation like that in *Kost* would not arise, since it would make no difference whether the remainder was vested or contingent; in either case, the trustee's deed would be valid. The question of alienability of remainders is discussed further *infra*, p. 74.

e. Preference for vested construction: Where it is not clear whether the remainder is contingent or vested, most courts show a ***preference for the vested construction***.

f. Alternative contingent remainders: A conveyance may create what are usually called ***alternative contingent remainders***. These are particularly likely to occur where a condition precedent involves survivorship.

Example: O conveys "to A for life, then to B and his heirs if B survives A, otherwise to C and his heirs." B's remainder is contingent upon surviving A; C's remainder is contingent upon B's not surviving A. Therefore, B and C have alternative contingent remainders. (But suppose the conveyance read "to A for life, then to B and his heirs; but if B dies before A, to C and his heirs." B would have a vested remainder subject to divestment, and C would have an executory interest, cutting off B's remainder. This is another illustration of the fact that the form, rather than the substance, of the words of the conveyance frequently controls.)

3. Unascertained remaindermen: A remainder is also contingent, rather than vested, if it is held by a person who is either: (1) ***unborn*** or (2) ***not yet ascertained***.

   a. Unborn: A contingent remainder in favor of an unborn person can arise as follows: O conveys "to A for life, then to the children of B." At the time of the conveyance, B has no children. Therefore, the remainder is contingent in the unborn children. (At common law, if A died before B had any children, the contingent remainder would be destroyed, and O's reversion would become possessory. See *infra*.)

   i. May later vest: But a remainder in favor of unborn children, like any other contingent remainder, may **become vested** due to later events. Thus if, prior to A's death, B had a child, X, X would have a vested remainder subject to open (in favor of any other children of B born before A's death).

   b. Unascertained persons: Similarly, a remainder may be contingent because it is in favor of a person of class whose identity **cannot yet be ascertained**.

   i. Heirs of living person: The most common example of this is a remainder in favor of the **heirs of a living person**.

   Example: O devises Blackacre "to A for life, then to A's heirs." Assuming that the Rule in Shelley's Case is not enforced in the jurisdiction (see *infra*, p. 74), the heirs have a remainder, and it is contingent. The reason for this is, of course, that until A dies, it is impossible to say who his heirs are. At A's death, the remainder will both vest and become possessory.

   ii. Widow: Similarly, a conveyance in favor of the **widow** of a living person might be held to be contingent. Thus O conveys "to A for life, then to his widow." At the time of the conveyance, A is married to B. If the term "widow" is held to have been used in its literal sense of a surviving spouse, the remainder in the widow is contingent, since there is no way to know whether B will survive A or will still be married to him when A dies. See Moynihan, p. 126.

I. Destructibility of contingent remainders: The common law treated contingent remainders differently from vested ones in several respects, one of which was crucially important: a contingent remainder was deemed "**destroyed**" unless it **vested at or before the termination of the preceding freehold estates**. This rule was usually called the "**destructibility of contingent remainders**".

   Example: O conveys "to A for life, remainder to the first son of A who reaches twenty-one." At A's death, he has one son, B, age sixteen. Since B did not meet the contingency (becoming twenty-one) by the time the prior estate (A's life estate) expired, B's contingent remainder is destroyed. Therefore, O's reversion becomes possessory.

   1. Reason for rule of destructibility: The basis for the common-law destructibility rule stems from the concept of seisin. One of the common-law rules regarding seisin was that a freehold interest could not "spring" out of the estate of the grantor at some future time. This rule against freeholds commencing *in futuro* is usually called the rule against springing interests; see *infra*, p. 80.

   a. Illustration: Now, consider the remainder of B, in the above example. At A's death, B has not yet met the conveyance. Since another of the rules concerning seisin is that it can never be in "abeyance" (i.e., it must always be "in" someone) it must return to O. Then, when B becomes twenty-one, for him to obtain seisin would require that the seisin "spring" out of O's estate. Since this springing would be taking place at a time other than the time when the original conveyance was made, it would seem to violate the rule against springing interests. Since there was no way in which B's interest could legitimately become possessory, it was deemed destroyed. See C&L, p. 299.

2. **Ways of destroying a contingent remainder:** We will consider two of the common law that a contingent remainder could be destroyed: (1) *normal expiration* of the supporting freeholds; and (2) *merger* of the supporting freeholds.

3. **Normal expiration:** One way the contingent remainder could be destroyed is if the preceding freehold estates had a *natural termination* before the condition precedent was satisfied. This is the case in the above example, where B has failed to reach the age of twenty-one by the time A's life estate terminates.

   a. **Remainder vests at the same time:** But if the contingent remainder vests at precisely the *same moment* that the supporting prior freehold terminates, the remainder is *not destroyed*.

      Example: O conveys "to A for life, remainder to his surviving children." A dies, survived by a son, B. During A's life estate, B's remainder was contingent, since it was subject to the condition that he survive A. Since that remainder vested at precisely the moment of A's death, the remainder was not destroyed. B therefore takes title.

   b. **Existence of a second supporting freehold:** Even if the freehold immediately preceding the contingent remainder terminates, there will be no destruction if there is *another supporting freehold* which still exists. See 1 A.L.P. 514.

      Example: O conveys "to A for life, remainder to B for life, remainder to B's first son who shall reach 21 and his heirs." B dies, leaving a 19-year-old son. Although the freehold immediately preceding the son's contingent remainder (B's life estate) has terminated, there remains another preceding freehold, A's life estate. Since the seisin remains in A, the destructibility doctrine does not apply. B's son retains his contingent interest, and when and if he reaches 21, that interest will vest (assuming that A has not yet died).

   c. **Equitable remainder:** Also, a contingent remainder that is *equitable* will not be destroyed by termination of the prior freehold.

      Example: O conveys "to T and his heirs in trust to pay the income from the land to A for life, then in trust to convey the land to A's first son to reach the age of 21." A dies, leaving an 18-year-old son. Three years later, when the son reaches 21, he should get the land. is contingent remainder was an equitable one, legal title to the land remained in T. See 1 A.L.P. 514.

   d. **Where remainder is leasehold:** Similarly, if the remainder is a *leasehold interest*, it is not subject to destruction.

      Example: O conveys "to A for 999 years." A dies, devising the term "to B for life, remainder to the first son of B who reaches the age of 21." B dies, leaving a 19-year-old son. Although the son has a contingent remainder, this remainder was not destroyed by its failure to vest at A's death. When the son reaches 21, he will hold an interest in the land for the remainder of the 999 year term. See 1 A.L.P. 514.

4. Merger: Secondly, a contingent remainder could be destroyed because the estate preceding it (usually a life estate) was *merged into* another, larger, estate. The smaller estate thus disappears, and the contingent remainder dependent upon it is destroyed.

   a. Basic doctrine of merger: The basic rule of merger is that whenever *successive vested estates* are owned by the *same person*, the smaller of the two estates is *absorbed* by the larger. See Moynihan, p. 131.

      Example: O conveys "to A for life, remainder to A's first son for life if he reaches 21, remainder to B and his heirs." When A has a 19-year-old son, A conveys his life estate to B. Since B now has two successive vested estates (the life estate and B's own vested remainder in fee simple), the smaller estate, the life estate, is merged into the fee simple and disappears. Since the son's remainder has not yet vested at the time A's life estate disappears, the contingent remainder is destroyed. See C&L, p. 300.

   b. Must not be intermediate vested estate: For the merger doctrine to apply, the two vested estates in question must not be *separated* by a third vested estate in someone else.

      Example: O conveys "to A for life, then to B for life, then to C and his heirs." A conveys his life estate to C. A's life estate will not merge into C's remainder in fee simple, because another vested estate (belonging to B) separates the two.

      Note: But a *contingent* remainder that falls between two vested estates will *not* prevent the two from merging. Thus if the conveyance in the above example had read "to A for life, then to B for life if he marries X, then to C and his heirs", and at the time of conveyance B had not married X, a conveyance by A of his life estate to C would result in a merger, and would destroy B's contingent remainder.

   c. Fee tail does not merge into fee simple: The general rule, as noted, is that the smaller estate merges into the larger. Thus a life estate will merge into a fee simple, or into a fee tail. But there is an important exception: a *fee tail will not merge into a fee simple*.

      Example: O conveys "to A and the heirs of his body." O then dies intestate, and A is his sole heir. A now holds both a fee tail and a remainder in fee simple. But these two estates do not merge. Thus the rights of A's issue are not cut off, and if he dies, his issue (if any) will take the property. (However, A may cut off the rights of his issue by certain types of disentailing procedures. See *supra*, p. 54.)

   d. Two vested estates created simultaneously: Another exception to the merger rule is that if a life estate and the next vested estate are created in the same person *simultaneously*, the two estates do not merge so as to destroy contingent remainders.

      Example: O dies, devising Blackacre "to A for life, remainder to A's first son and his heirs." (At the time of O's death, A has no son). A is also O's heir. A therefore holds both a life estate and the reversion (which he gets by descent). No merger between the life estate and the reversion takes place, because the two were created simultaneously in the same person. See C&L, p. 301.

      i. Rationale: The reason for this rule is that otherwise, the estate of a grantor or testator would frequently be completely frustrated. For instance, a conveyance "to A for life, remainder to A's first son to become 21, remainder to A and his heirs" would, if A had no son 21 or over at the time, become simply a fee simple in A.

ii. Transfer of two vested estates to a third person: But if the person in whom the two vested estates were simultaneously created then *transfers them* to a third person, merger will now take place. Thus suppose that, in the above example, before A had a son he transferred his life estate and his reversion to B. In the hands of B, the life estate and the reversion would merge, destroying the contingent remainder in the unborn son. (B could then convey back to A, who would then acquire a fee simple; this would furnish an easy way for A to disinherit his unborn child.) *Id.*

5. **Trustees to preserve contingent remainders:** The destructibility of contingent remainders gave an unscrupulous life tenant a chance to manipulate interests in such a way that contingent remainders following his life estate would be destroyed; Paragraph d(ii) above contains an example of this. Such manipulations threatened the entire English system of intra-family land transfers, which was based upon the concept of life estates followed by contingent remainders in fee simple. To thwart this danger, conveyancers adopted the device of *"trustees to preserve contingent remainders"*; this device worked in the manner described in the following example.

   Example: O, the owner of the family estate, desires to make sure that it stays in the family for at least two more generations. His eldest son, S, to whom the estate will pass, has no children yet. O conveys "to S for life, remainders to Trustees for the life of S to preserve contingent remainders, remainder to S's first son and the male heirs of his body"; successive remainders to the other sons of S in fee tail male are also given. If S should become the holder of the reversion in O (which might happen if O died and S was his only heir), S's life estate would not merge with the reversion, because the trustees to preserve contingent remainders have a vested estate between the life estate and the reversion. Therefore, the contingent remainder in S's unborn son is not destroyed. Similarly, if S commits a forfeiture of his life estate, the contingent remainder in the unborn son will not be destroyed, because the trustee's estate will become possessory, and will suffice to support the contingent remainder. It is thus certain that if S ever has a son, that son will get a vested remainder, which will become possessory on S's death. See C&L, p. 327.

6. **The destructibility rule today:** The destructibility rule obviously defeats the intention of the grantor most of the time. Also, the doctrine depends on the illegality of springing interests, which is no longer much of a factor following the Statute of Uses (*infra*, p. 83). Therefore, about half the states have passed statutes *abolishing destructibility of contingent remainders*. Several additional states have reached this result by case law. The Restatement of Property (§240) also rejects destructibility. See Moynihan, pp. 134-35.

   Review examples on remainders

   Example 1: Owner conveys "to Able for life, remainder to Able's widow for her life, remainder to Baker and his heirs." Able is living and is married to Wanda. Baker is living.

   The remainder to Able's widow is contingent, since it is not known whether Wanda will survive Able and still be married to him at Able's death. The remainder to Baker is vested. The contingent remainder to Able's widow will vest, if at all, upon Able's death, since at that time his widow can be ascertained.

Example 2: Owner conveys "to Able for life, remainder to Able's children and their heirs." Able is living, and has one child, C1. Later, another child, C2 is born. Then, C1 dies. One year after that, Able dies.

At the time of conveyance, C1 obtained a vested remainder subject to open. This remainder opened up to admit C2 at the latter's birth. Therefore, each held a one-half interest. When C1 died, his half interest passed to his heirs. C2 maintains the other half interest. Both half interests became possessory on Able's death.

Example 3: Owner conveys "to Able for life, remainder to Able's first son and the heirs of his body, remainder to Baker and his heirs." While Able is still childless, Owner dies without a will, leaving Able as his heir.

Able has a life estate. His unborn first son has a contingent remainder in fee tail. Baker has a vested remainder in fee simple. Owner had no interest left following the conveyance, so Able inherits nothing from him.

J. Alienability of remainders: Historically, one of the principal differences between vested and contingent remainders was that vested ones were more freely *alienable*.

   1. Vested remainders: Vested remainders have always been alienable *inter vivos* (i.e., by deed), devisable, and descendible.

   a. Subject to divestment: This is true even if the vested remainder is subject to partial or total divestment or defeasance. However, the remainder is subject to the same possibility of divestment in the hands of the person who acquires it.

   Example: O conveys "to A for life, then to B and his heirs, but if alcohol should ever be sold upon the premises, O or his heirs may re-enter the property." B is free to transfer his vested remainder (in fee simple subject to condition subsequent) to X. But if, after the transfer to X, alcohol is sold on the premises, O or his heirs still has the right to re-enter.

   2. Contingent remainders: Contingent remainders, on the other hand, were largely *inalienable* at *common law*. Thus there could be no *inter vivos* conveyance, nor any involuntary transfer (e.g., in bankruptcy, or by attachment of creditors).

   a. Modern American view: But in most American states, the present view is that a contingent remainder is *alienable, devisable,* and *descendible*, just as a vested remainder is. See Moynihan, pp. 136-7. In a few states, there are some limits on *inter vivos* transfers, but contingent remainders are apparently devisable and descendible in every jurisdiction. See 1 A.L.P. 533, 535.

V. THE RULE IN SHELLEY'S CASE

A. The rule summarized: Feudal property law produced several strange rules. One of the most bizarre of these is known as the Rule in Shelley's Case. The Rule provides as follows: *if a will or conveyance creates a freehold in A, and purports to create a remainder in A's heirs* (or in the heirs of A's body) and the estates are *both legal or both equitable, the remainder becomes a fee simple* (or fee tail) *in A.* C&L, p. 302.

   Example: O conveys "to A for life, remainder to A's heirs." If there were no Rule in Shelley's Case, the state of the title would be: life estate in A, contingent remainder in A's heirs, reversion in O. But by operation of the Rule in Shelley's

Case, the state of the title is this: life estate in A, remainder in A (not A's heirs). Then, by the doctrine of merger, A's life estate will merge into his remainder in fee simple, and A simply holds a present fee simple.

B. Reasons for the Rule: Observe that application of the Rule in Shelley's Case makes it more likely that land will pass by descent, rather than by will or conveyance.

    1. Illustration: Suppose, for instance, that A in the above example had a son, B, who turns out to be A's sole heir. At A's death, B would be certain to take the property by descent at least prior to the enactment of the Statute of Wills in 1540). If there were no Rule, on the other hand, B would take the land as a remainderman, under the original conveyance. Since the passage of land by descent gave great benefits to the lord of the manor, the Rule was instrumental in maintaining the feudal order. C&L, pp. 302-33. The Rule was, in effect, a crude device for preventing the avoidance of feudal tax-like obligations.

C. Requirements of the Rule: The Rule in Shelley's Case applies where there are: (1) a *freehold* in the ancestor; (2) a *remainder* created by the same instrument in the ancestor's *heirs*, or the *heirs of the ancestor's body*, and (3) the same "quality" in both freehold and remainder, i.e., *both legal* or *both equitable*. These requirements are discussed one at a time below.

    1. Freehold in ancestor: There must be a *freehold estate* given to the ancestor.

        a. Life estate required in U.S.: In England, the Rule could apply where the ancestor was a *fee tail*. But in America, it seems to be the case that only a *life estate* in the ancestor will suffice. See 1 A.L.P. 482.

        b. Future freehold: It is *not* required that the freehold be a *present possessory one*. That is, the life estate may *itself* be a *remainder*.

        Example: O conveys "to A for life, remainder to B for life, remainder to B's heirs." The Rule in Shelley's Case applies to this situation, even though the estate in the ancestor (B) is a remainder. Thus B has both a life estate and a remainder in fee simple, which merge to give him a remainder in fee simple. When A dies, B will then have a present, possessory, fee simple. (If B died before A, his remainder in fee simple would go to his heirs or devisees.)

        c. Cannot be personalty or term of years: The requirement that the interest in the ancestor be a freehold means that a *term of years* will not suffice. Nor will an interest in *personal property*, as opposed to real estate.

        Example: Owner conveys land "to Tom as trustee, to be sold and the proceeds to be held in trust and income paid to Able for life. Upon Able's death, the principal to be paid to Able's heirs."

        The trustee is to sell the property, and to receive money in return. Since the trust principal will then not be real estate, the Rule will not apply. The state of title will therefore be: legal fee simple in personalty to Tom, equitable life estate in personalty to Able, and equitable contingent remainder in fee simple to Able's heirs.

        d. Co-tenancy: If the life estate is held by both the ancestor and a third party as co-tenants the Rule may apply. See the discussion of co-tenancy *infra*, p. 113.

2. Remainder in heirs or heirs of the body: There must be a *remainder*, and it must be in the *heirs of the ancestor*, or in the *heirs of the ancestor's body*.

    a. Can't be executory interest: The requirement of a remainder means that the heirs (or heirs of the body) cannot have an *executory interest* (as opposed to a remainder). Such an interest, usually called either a "springing" or "shifting" interest, became possible after the Statute of Uses; see *infra*, p. 84.

        Example: Owner devises "to Able for life, remainder to Baker and his heirs, but if Baker dies without issue surviving him, to Carr for life, and then to Carr's heirs." We will examine the state of the title following the devise, and then following the death of Baker without issue.

        The life estate in Carr, and the subsequent interest in Carr's heirs, are executory interests rather than remainders. This is so because the remainder to Baker and his heirs is not a contingent remainder, but rather, a vested remainder subject to divestment. (See *supra*, p. 67.) Therefore, at the time of the devise, the state of title is: life estate in Able; vested remainder in fee simple in Baker, subject to divestment; executory life estate in Carr; and executory fee simple in Carr's heirs. The Rule in Shelley's Case therefore does not apply immediately.

        But if Baker than dies without issue (while Able is still living), Carr's interest will be transformed into a vested remainder for life, with a contingent remainder to his heirs. The Rule will then operate, together with the doctrine of merger, to give Carr a remainder in fee simple.

    b. Must be heirs of ancestors: Keep in mind that the remainder must be to the heirs of *the ancestor*, i.e., the one to whom the prior freehold was given. Thus if O conveys "to A for life, remainder to the heirs of B", the Rule does not apply. (A would simply have a life estate, with a remainder to B's heirs that is either contingent, if B is still living, or vested, if B is dead.)

    c. Remainder must be to "heirs": There has been a lot of dispute about exactly what constitutes a remainder to the "heirs" of the ancestor.

        i. Remainder to "children" insufficient: A remainder to "the *children*" of the ancestor is *not* sufficient to make the Rule applicable. The reason for this is that under the usual intestacy statute, "children" are not the same thing as "heirs". For instance, if one is survived by a widow and two children, all three are heirs under the usual intestacy statute, not just the children.

        ii. Problem of construction: The problem is really one of construction: did the grantor intend to give the remainder to all persons who would take under the intestacy statute (in which case it is to his "heirs" for purposes of the Rule), or was it his intent to limit the remainder to a narrower class?

    d. Remainder in fee tail: At common law, the remainder could be to "the heirs of the body", as well as to the "heirs." However, nearly all states have statutorily abolished the fee tail in one way or another (*supra*, p. 54). The effect of such a statute upon the Rule is unclear. At least if the way the statute works is to convert the fee tail into fee simple, the Rule probably can still apply. See 1 A.L.P. 495.

        Example: O conveys "to A for life, remainder to the heirs of A's body". The jurisdiction in question has a statute transforming the fee tail into a fee simple. Probably a court would first apply the Rule, giving A a present fee tail, and would then apply the statute, transforming A's present fee tail into a fee simple.

3. **Both equitable or both legal:** The life estate in the ancestor and the remainder to the heirs or heirs of the body must either be **both legal** or **both equitable**.

> **Example:** O conveys land "to T for life of A, in trust to collect the rents and pay them to A, remainder to the heirs of A."
>
> The trust applies only during A's lifetime; the remainder to the heirs of A is, presumably, intended to be legal. Since the life estate and the remainder are not both legal, or both equitable, the Rule in Shelley's Case does not apply. Therefore, the state of the title is: legal life estate in T, equitable life estate in A, contingent legal remainder in fee simple in A's heirs, and reversion in O.

4. **Life estate and remainder separated by other estate:** The Rule in Shelley's Case will apply even though there is **another estate** (either vested or contingent) **between the life estate and the remainder**. As the idea is often put, the remainder may follow the life estate either "mediately or immediately."

   a. **No merger necessary:** Consequently, the Rule may apply **even though there is no subsequent merger** of the life estate and the remainder.

   > **Example:** O conveys "to A for life, remainder to B for life, remainder to A's heirs." Since there is both a life estate in A and a remainder in his heirs, the Rule in Shelley's Case applies, to transform the remainder into one in A. But there is no merger, because of the vested life estate in B separating the two. (Also, the simultaneous creation exception would prevent merger; see *supra*, p. 72.) The state of the title is therefore: life estate in A, vested remainder for life in B, vested remainder in fee simple in A.

5. **Co-tenancy:** Suppose that the life estate, the remainder, or both, are held in **co-tenancy**. The Rule may nonetheless apply in this situation, although the precise way it applies is not always clear.

   a. **Both estates held in co-tenancy:** If **both** the life estate and the remainder are held in co-tenancy, the Rule applies to the entire joint interest. Thus if O conveys "to A and B for their lives, remainder to the heirs of A and B", the Rule will give A and B a remainder in fee simple as co-tenants. (This would either be a tenancy in common, a joint tenancy or a tenancy by the entirety, depending on the relation between A and B and the presumptions existing in the jurisdiction; see *infra*, p. 113.) See 1 A.L.P. 492-93.

   b. **Only remainder in co-tenancy:** The Rule may also apply where only the remainder is held in co-tenancy. Thus suppose O conveys "to A for life, remainder to be held in equal shares by B and the heirs of A". The Rule will give A a remainder in an undivided one-half interest, as co-tenant with B. The merger doctrine will then make an undivided one-half of A's life interest merge with his one-half interest in the remainder, giving A an undivided one-half interest in fee simple, plus an undivided one-half interest for life. See 1 A.L.P. 493.

   c. **Only life estate held in common:** But if it is only the **life estate** that is held in common, the situation is more difficult. Most courts hold that the Rule makes the entire remainder one in fee simple.

   > **Example:** Nye conveys Blackacre "to Joseph and Mora as tenants in common for their respective lives, remainder to the heirs of Joseph." Most cases hold that the Rule makes the entire remainder a remainder in fee simple in Joseph. After

merger, Joseph thus gets a present fee simple subject to an undivided one-half interest for life in Mora.

D. Rule of law, not construction: The Rule in Shelley's Case is a *rule of law*, not merely a rule of construction. Thus even if the grantor makes it clear that he wants the remainder to be in the ancestor's heirs (and not in the ancestor himself), his intent will be irrelevant.

> **Example:** O conveys "to A for life, remainder to A's heirs. The deed includes the following statement: "It is my intention that A shall take no more than a life estate and that his heirs shall take a remainder as purchasers." The Rule will nonetheless apply, so that the state of title will be: life estate in A, remainder in A, merging to give A a present fee simple. See Moynihan, p. 141.

E. The Rule under modern law: The Rule in Shelley's Case serves no useful purpose today. It is often a trap for the unwary, and virtually always thwarts the will of the grantor. For these reasons, at least thirty-seven states (plus the District of Columbia) have enacted *statutes abolishing the Rule*. Two more states have reached this result by case law. See Powell, Par. 380, p. 464.

   1. States still in force: The common-law version of the Rule is still in force, however, in at least the following states: Arkansas, Colorado, Delaware, Indiana, and North Carolina. See C,S&W, p. 123, n. 7. Other states maintain the common-law version of the Rule for inter vivos transfers (but not for transfers by will): Alabama, Alaska, New Hampshire and Oregon. *Id.*

   2. Some statutes are incomplete: Also, in some of the states which have statutes purporting to abolish the Rule, only an *incomplete* eradication has occurred. For instance, some of the statutes apply only to wills, and not to *inter-vivos* deeds. See Powell, Par. 380, p. 465. Furthermore, the statutes generally do not apply to conveyances made prior to the enactment date of the statute. Therefore, for title examination purposes it may still be necessary to evaluate the impact of the Rule on an older transfer.

   3. Means of avoiding Rule: In those states where the Rule is still in effect, either in part or in full, a skilled draftsman will always be able to avoid it. For instance, A could convey "to B for 100 years if he so long lives, then to the heirs of B." The Rule would not apply because B holds a term of years rather than a freehold. Or, A could convey "to B for life, and one day after B's death to the heirs of B." The interest in the heirs is not a remainder, but is rather an executory interest of the "springing" variety (*infra*, p. 84); therefore, the Rule does not apply. See Moynihan, p. 148.

VI. DOCTRINE OF WORTHIER TITLE

A. General statement of rule: Just as the Rule in Shelley's Case tends to make property pass by descent rather than by purchase (*supra*, p. 74), so another common-law rule, the *"Doctrine of Worthier Title"*, has this effect. The Doctrine provides that *one cannot, either by conveyance or will, give a remainder to his own heirs*. See Moynihan, p. 149. Actually, the "Doctrine" is really two fairly distinct rules having a common origin, one involving wills, and the other involving *inter vivos* conveyances. Only the *inter vivos* rule is of importance today, so we concentrate our treatment on that.

B. The *inter vivos* branch: The *inter vivos* branch of the Doctrine of Worthier Title is still very much alive in many jurisdictions, and when it applies it can have important practical consequences.

1. **Common-law statement of rule:** The *inter vivos* branch of the Worthier Title Doctrine, in its common-law form, provides that if the owner of a fee simple attempts to create a life estate or fee tail estate, with a **remainder to his own heirs**, the **remainder is void**. Thus the grantor **keeps a reversion**. C&L, pp. 310-11. (The *inter vivos* branch is sometimes called the **rule forbidding remainders to grantors' heirs**.)

   Example: O conveys "to A for life, remainder to O's heirs." The Doctrine of Worthier Title makes the remainder void. Consequently, O is left with a reversion. He is thus free to convey the reversion to a third party; if he does so, his heirs will get nothing when he dies, even if he dies intestate.

2. **Practical effect of rule:** The *inter vivos* branch of the Doctrine often has an important practical impact. If the Doctrine did not exist, the grantor's heirs would have a contingent remainder, which would not be affected by any conveyance made by O or any devise made in O's will. But when the Doctrine applies, the remainder is completely nullified, and an *inter vivos* conveyance by O of his reversion, or a devise of it in his will, will prevent the heirs from taking anything.

   a. **Termination of trust:** The Doctrine frequently applies to allow a settlor to **terminate a trust** which he has created.

      Example: O conveys Blackacre "to T as trustee, to pay the income therefrom to O for life, then to convey the premises to O's heirs." The Doctrine will invalidate the equitable remainder in O's heirs, leaving an equitable reversion in O. Later, if O wishes to terminate the trust, he will probably be able to do so; only the consent of persons having a beneficial interest in the trust is required, and because of the Doctrine, O is the only such person. See C&L, p. 311.

3. **Rule of law, not construction:** In its common-law form, the Doctrine of Worthier Title is a **rule of law, not of construction**. Thus even if, in the above example, the trust document makes it clear that O intends to give a remainder to his heirs, the Doctrine will apply.

4. **Now generally rule of construction:** The common-law version of the Doctrine, in its *inter vivos* branch, is still in force in a few states. But in most states, the rule has been **transformed into one of construction**. That is, the Doctrine applies only where the grantor's language, and the surrounding circumstances, indicate that he **intended to keep a reversion**; in a sense, the Doctrine merely establishes a **presumption that a reversion rather than a remainder is really intended**.

   Example: O is the fee simple owner of Blackacre. He conveys to his son, Nathaniel, "during his natural life and to his lawful heirs at his death." The conveyance adds that if Nathaniel dies without issue, "then the land herein shall revert back to [O] or to his lawful heirs." O dies intestate, leaving his three sons (Nathaniel and the two Ds) as his equal heirs. Nathaniel then dies without issue, bequeathing all his real property to P. P sues the Ds for a one-third interest in Blackacre, arguing that the Doctrine of Worthier Title cancels the remainder in O's heirs, giving O a reversion, one-third of which passed first to Nathaniel and then to P. The Ds argue that the Doctrine does not apply.

   Held, for P. The Doctrine is no longer a rule of law; instead there is "a presumption in favor of reversions, which presumption may be rebutted by a contrary intent gathered from the instrument as a whole." Here, however, there is no evidence sufficient to rebut the presumption in favor of a reversion. To the contrary, O's statement that upon Nathaniel's death without issue, the property should "revert back" to O or O's heirs, indicates an intent that there be a reversion. Accordingly, a one-third interest in the reversion passed to P. *Braswell v. Braswell*, 81 S.E.2d 560 (Va. 1954).

a. Often applies to personal property: The common-law Doctrine applies only to realty, not to personalty. But of the states that have transformed the Doctrine into a rule of construction, many have also made the rule applicable to conveyances of **personal property**. For the Doctrine to be applicable to personalty, the gift probably must be to the class of persons who would take the grantor's personalty if he died intestate; this is usually, but not always, the same as the class who would take his real estate. This extension of the Doctrine, even as a rule of construction, is quite significant, because it affects many trusts composed of stocks and bonds.

Example: O sets up a trust for himself consisting of stocks and bonds. The trustees are to pay the income to O for life, and then to convey the corpus of the trust to O's heirs. In many states the Doctrine of Worthier Title will apply as a rule of construction, so that there will be a presumption that O really intended a reversion in himself, not a remainder in his heirs. Therefore, O will have the right to terminate the trust during his lifetime, and do whatever he wishes with the funds. Even if he does not do this, the funds will pass under the residuary clause of his will, rather than to his heirs. See C&L, p. 312.

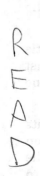

VII. THE STATUTE OF USES AND EXECUTORY INTERESTS

A. Concept of "seisin": Before we explore the mysteries of the "Statute of Uses," you must first understand a little bit about the concept of **"seisin"**. A person was said to have seisin of a parcel of land (or to be "seised of it") if he had **possession of it under a claim of freehold**. That is, he had to meet two requirements: (1) he had to be in **possession** (though this could be done for him by a tenant); and (2) he had to own a **freehold estate** in the property, i.e., either a **fee simple**, a **fee tail** or a **life estate**.

1. Transfer of present freehold: The deed as we know it today did not exist at common law (at least where the estate being transferred was a present, possessory, freehold). Instead, a freehold was generally transferred by the **"livery of seisin"** (sometimes called a **"feoffment"**). This was accomplished by having the transferor and the transferee **go onto the land**, at which point the transferor handed the transferee a twig, stating that he was transferring seisin. It was required that the transferee **immediately take possession** after the livery of seisin (so that O could not enfeoff A today, the feoffment to take effect on, say, A's death or the passage of one year).

B. Common-law restrictions: The common law imposed several very important **restrictions** on the types of estates that could be created:

1. No springing interests: A freehold estate could not be created to **commence in futuro**. This was a direct consequence of the requirement that seisin be delivered by a present transfer of possession. Such an estate was known as an illegal **"springing interest"**, because the estate would take effect in the future by springing out of its present owner.

Example: O is the owner of Blackacre. His daughter, D, is engaged to marry A. O wishes to ensure A that A will receive a fee simple in Blackacre when he marries D. But the rule against "springing" interests, or interests to begin *in futuro*, means that O cannot convey "to A and his heirs from and after A's marriage to

D."

    a. Freehold following lease term: But the owner of a freehold estate could create a freehold to commence after a term of years. Thus O could convey "to A for 10 years, then to B and his heirs."

2. No "shifting" interests: A grantor could not give to any grantee an estate which would *cut another estate short*. This prohibition is frequently referred to as the ban on *"shifting" interests*. Like the rule against springing interests, the ban on shifting interests seems to derive from the requirement that a livery of seisin take effect immediately rather than in the future.

    a. Interest in stranger can't follow fee simple determinable: One consequence of the ban on shifting interests is that a *fee simple determinable* could be followed only by a possibility of reverter in the grantor, and *not by a shifting interest to a third person*.

        i. Common-law view: Recall that the common-law took the view that a fee simple (even a determinable one) could not be followed by a remainder. (See *supra*, p. 64.) Since the remainder was the only type of estate in a third person recognized by the common law, any interest in one other than the grantor purporting to follow a fee simple determinable was treated as void.

        Example: O conveys "to A and his heirs as long as the property is used during the next twenty years for agricultural purposes, and then to B and his heirs." The gift to A and his heirs is probably a fee simple determinable (to last forever, unless the land is used for non-agricultural purposes at some point during the first twenty years). Therefore the interest in B and his heirs cannot be a remainder. The only way to construe the gift to B is as a shifting interest (which cuts off A's interest) and such an interest is not valid. Consequently, there is a possibility of reverter in O.

    b. No gift in stranger following fee simple subject to condition subsequent: The ban on shifting interests also meant that there could be no interest in a third party after a fee simple *subject to a condition subsequent*.

    Example: O conveys "to A for life, then to B and his heirs, but if B marries C before A's estate ends, then to D and his heirs." B has a remainder in fee simple subject to divestment if the condition subsequent is met. Since D's interest can become possessory only by cutting short B's interest, D's interest is not a remainder, but a shifting interest that is invalid.

    c. Not applicable to leasehold estates: But the rule against shifting interests was not applicable to *leasehold interests*, since these did not involve seisin. For instance, suppose O conveys "to A for life, then to B for ten years, but if B uses the land for non-residential purposes, then to C for the balance of the term." B and C each have a leasehold, not a freehold. Therefore, C's interest, although it is a shifting one in the sense that it cuts off B's interest, is a valid one.

3. No gap between estates: There could be no *gap* between the *end* of an estate and the *start* of a succeeding remainder. If there was such a gap, the remainder was void.

    Example: O conveys "to A for life, then one day after A's death, to B and his heirs." The interest in B is not a valid remainder, since it does not follow immediately upon the expiration of the preceding estate. Therefore, the interest in B is void.

a. Relation to destructibility doctrine: This rule against gaps may be viewed as the basis for the doctrine of *destructibility of contingent remainders* (*supra*, p. 70). For if a contingent remainder has not vested by the time the preceding freehold terminates, the remainder could vest at a later date only if a gap were allowed. Thus if O conveyed "to A for life, then to B when he reaches the age of 21, and at A's death B was 19, it would violate the rule against gaps for B's interest to be allowed to vest and become possessory two years after A's death.

4. No contingent remainder supported by a term of years: *A freehold contingent remainder could not be supported by a term of years.* Moynihan, p. 169.

> **Example:** O, who owns Blackacre in fee simple, conveys "to A for 100 years if he so long live, remainder to A's children who shall survive him and his heirs." Since A takes only a leasehold term, the contingent remainder in the children is void, and the state of the title is: fee simple in O, subject to a term of years in A. (Nor can the interest in the children become possessory upon A's death, because this would amount to an illegal springing interest.)

a. Not applicable where remainder is in leasehold: But again, remember that this rule did not apply where the remainder was itself a part of a term of years. Thus if O owned a term of 999 years in Blackacre, and conveyed "to A for 100 years if he so long live, remainder to A's children who shall survive him", the remainder in the children would be valid. They would have a valid contingent remainder in the 999-year lease term.

> **Note:** Each of these common-law rules was largely emasculated by the Statute of Uses, enacted in 1536. The Statute made possible the creation of legal springing and shifting interests, for example. Therefore, before concluding that the common-law prohibitions apply in a particular case, make sure that the Statute is not applicable. The workings of the Statute are described extensively *infra*, p. 83.

C. Uses before the Statute of Uses: Until now, everything we have said about estates in land has referred to *legal* title, i.e., title that would be enforced by a court of law. But the law courts were not the only source of judicial relief in England; a separate court, called the Court of Chancery, gave relief if: (1) the rigid rules of the common law did not provide it and (2) fairness required. The relief given by the chancellor was known as *equitable* relief, and the court system that grew up around the chancellor was known as *equity*.

1. Equity enforces the use: In the case of land law, the jurisdiction of the equity courts applied to cases where a *use* was established. Thus O, the owner of a legal fee simple in Blackacre, might transfer legal title to T as Trustee, for the use of O. If T failed to use the property for O's benefit (e.g., he failed to pay over the rents, or he sold the property), the court of equity could intercede, to force T to use the property for O's benefit. The court had no power to affect the legal title, which would remain in T.

a. Cestui que use: The person in whose favor a use is created is commonly called the *cestui que use* (i.e., beneficiary).

2. Flexibility: Prior to 1536, landowners found that the system of uses gave them much flexibility in dealing with their lands, which would not be available if only legal estates were considered.

a. **Springing and shifting interests:** Most importantly, uses could be employed to create *shifting* and *springing* interests, which were not available at common law. Thus O could convey "to T and his heirs for life, for the use of A and his heirs, but if A or his heirs should fail to live on the property, then to the use of B and his heirs." If A or his heirs failed to live on the property, the equitable title would "shift" to B, whereas such a shifting estate was not valid with respect to the legal title.

3. **Bargain and sale:** There were several ways in which a use could be created. Most important was the *bargain and sale*. A bargain and sale was an *agreement* by which the owner of land promised in writing to sell the land to another, or to hold it for the other's use. The existence of the bargain and sale deed gave the beneficiary equitable title to the property, just as, under modern law, the vendee under a land sale contract may obtain specific performance of the contract (an equitable remedy).

D. **Enactment of the Statute of Uses:** In addition to the ability of uses to allow shifting and springing interests, uses had another virtue (from the landowner's point of view): uses could be employed to *escape the feudal incidents of tenure* (*supra*, p. 44). Since these incidents passed directly or indirectly to the king, the rise of uses meant the fall of the public treasury. Therefore, in 1536, Parliament enacted the *Statute of Uses*, generally considered to be the most important statute ever passed dealing with English land law.

1. **Meaning of Statute:** The Statute of Uses provided that *where one person is seised of land to the use of another person, the latter shall be seised of the same size estate as he had in use*. That is, the *equitable estate is converted into the corresponding legal estate*.

Example: O conveys Blackacre "to T and his heirs, to the use of A and his heirs." The requirement for application of the Statute of Uses are met, since T stands seised of a fee simple estate, to the use of A. Therefore, the Statute transforms A's equitable fee simple into a legal fee simple. T's legal estate is, consequently, nullified. The state of the title is simply: legal fee simple in A. (The Statute of Uses is said to "*execute*" the use in A, i.e., transform it into the corresponding legal estate.)

2. **Holder of legal title must be seised:** The Statute does not apply if the person who is holding to the use of another is not himself *seised* in the first instance. Thus if O conveys "to T and his heirs for 999 years, to the use of A for life, then to the use of B and his heirs", the Statute does not apply. This is because T, as the holder of a non-freehold term of years, does not have seisin.

E. **Conveyancing after the Statute:** The Statute of Uses completely changed the patterns of land conveyancing. As noted, prior to the Statute, uses were much more flexible than legal estates; enactment of the Statute gave the conveyancer the ability to obtain the same flexibility in a legal estate.

1. **Other kinds of conveyancing:** The principal effect of the Statute was to allow the types of conveyancing that had previously been employed to create uses, to be utilized now for the purpose of creating legal estates.

a. **Bargain and sale:** For instance, recall that the *bargain and sale* could be used, before the Statute of Uses, to raise a use in another. After the Statute was enacted, the bargain and sale became a very powerful way of transferring a legal estate.

i. No livery of seisin necessary: The key feature of the bargain and sale was that it *did not require any livery of seisin*. It did not require the parties to visit the land, nor did it require an immediate change in possession. The entire transaction could be done in secret, far from the property.

Example: O, the fee simple owner of Blackacre, wishes to transfer legal title to A; he wants to do this secretly, in his lawyer's office. O executes a bargain and sale deed which states that O "bargains and sells Blackacre to A and his heirs." The deed raises a use in A, which is immediately executed by the Statute of Uses, transforming A's interest from an equitable into a legal fee simple.

F. Future interests after the Statute: The Statute of Uses virtually nullified the impact of the common-law restrictions on future interests (summarized *supra*, p. 80). Although these restrictions still applied to a conveyance that was strictly common-law (e.g., a formal livery of seisin), these restrictions *did not apply to a use which was transformed by the Statute into a legal estate*.

1. Springing executory interest: Recall that a use could be of the *"springing"* variety, i.e., one that is to take effect at some point after the date of the conveyance. Such a springing use could now be executed, i.e., transformed into the corresponding legal estate. This type of interest, created by action of the Statute upon a springing use, became known as a *springing executory interest*.

Example: O is the fee simple owner of Blackacre. He wishes to convey title to his prospective son-in-law A, but only from the time that A actually marries O's daughter B, yet he also wishes to convince A right now that A will definitely get the land if he goes through with the marriage. O therefore bargains and sells the property "to A and his heirs from and after the date of A's marriage to B." The bargain and sale raises a use in A, which is executed under the Statute, becoming a fee simple in A to commence upon the marriage date. A's interest is a springing executory interest.

2. Shifting executory interest: Prior to the Statute, a *shifting* use could be created, i.e., one which cut short a prior equitable interest that had not yet naturally terminated. After the Statute, this shifting use would be executed, becoming a *shifting executory interest*.

Example: O, who owns Blackacre in fee simple, bargains and sells it "to A and his heirs, but if the premises are ever used for other than residential purposes, then to B and his heirs." The bargain and sale raises a use in A in fee simple subject to condition subsequent, and a use in B. The Statute executes both of these uses, so that the state of title becomes: fee simple in A subject to an executory limitation, and shifting executory interest in fee simple in B. If A or his heirs fail to use the property for residential purposes, the gift over to B will take effect.

Note: Observe that the legal fee simple created in A in the above example is not called a fee simple subject to condition subsequent, but rather, a fee simple *subject to an executory limitation*. Similarly, what would be a fee simple determinable if it were followed by a reversion in the grantor, is called a fee simple subject to an executory limitation where the gift over is to a third person. (See *infra*, p. 85.)

3. Gap in seisin: The Statute of Uses also made it possible to create legal interests in such a way that there could be a "gap" between two interests. The interest following the gap can be thought of as another type of springing executory interest.

> **Example:** O bargains and sells Blackacre "to A for life, and one day after A's death, to B and his heirs." The bargain and sale raises an equitable life estate in A, an equitable reversion for one day in O, and an equitable fee simple in B. The Statute executes the uses, so that the title is: legal life estate in A, legal reversion in O, springing executory interest in B in fee simple.

4. **Contingent remainder following term of years:** Prior to the Statute, an equitable contingent remainder could be created following a term of years. After the Statute, it became possible to create a *legal contingent remainder after a term of years*.

> **Example:** O bargains and sells Blackacre "to A for ten years, then to A's oldest son then living." The bargain and sale deed creates an equitable leasehold interest in A, and an equitable contingent fee simple in A's oldest son. The Statute executes these uses, so that the state of title is: legal leasehold in A, contingent remainder in fee simple in A's oldest son.

5. **Interest in stranger after fee simple determinable:** Recall that prior to 1536, the only interest that could be created following a *fee simple determinable* was a possibility of reverter. (*Supra*, p. 81.) But by means of the Statute, an *executory interest* could be created in a *third person* following a fee simple determinable (or, more properly, a fee simple subject to an executory limitation.)

> **Example:** O bargains and sells Blackacre "to A and his heirs, for as long as no alcohol is sold on the premises; then to B and his heirs." The bargain and sale deed raises a use in fee simple determinable in A and his heirs, and a remaining use in fee simple in B and his heirs. The Statute executes these uses, so that the state of title is: legal fee simple in A subject to an executory limitation, executory interest in B.

6. **Outwitting the Rule in Shelley's Case:** The Statute of Uses provided a convenient way of avoiding the *Rule in Shelley's Case*.

> **Example:** In the year 1600, O bargains and sells "to A for life and one day after A's death to A's heirs." The bargain and sale raises a use in A for life and a springing use in A's heirs. The Statute of Uses executes these uses, so that the legal title becomes: life estate in A, springing executory interest in A's heirs. The Rule in Shelley's Case does not apply, because the heirs take by executory interest rather than by remainder. (See *supra*, p. 76.)

G. Identifying executory interests: The following rules will assist in identifying executory interests:

1. **Use required:** An executory interest, by definition, can be created only by a conveyance that raises a use (usually, a bargain and sale deed). Thus where a conveyance is accomplished by means of a common-law feoffment (i.e., livery of seisin), there can be no executory interest created.

   a. **Common-law interest may be created under Statute of Uses:** The converse, however, is not true. That is, the traditional common-law interests (reversions, remainders, etc.) may be created by action of the Statute of Uses, just as executory interests can be so created. Thus although one can say that a conveyance not involving a use cannot produce an executory interest, one cannot deduce anything at all about the nature of interests created from the mere fact that a bargain and sale deed, or covenant to stand seised, was used.

> **Example:** O bargains and sells his fee simple interest in Blackacre "to A for life, then to B and his heirs." The bargain and sale deed raises a use in A for life, and a remaining use in fee simple in B. The Statute of Uses then executes these uses, making the state of title: legal life estate in A, legal remainder in fee simple in B.

2. **Cannot be created in grantor:** By definition, an executory interest cannot be created in the original grantor; executory interests are always created in *third persons*. Thus there should be no difficulty in distinguishing between an executory interest on the one hand, and a reversion, possibility of reverter and right of entry on the other.

3. **Distinguishing between executory interest and remainder:** But it is not always so easy to distinguish between an executory interest and a *remainder*, since both are created in persons other than the grantor. The difference is essentially that a remainder *never cuts off* a prior interest, but merely awaits the prior interests's *natural termination*. An executory interest, on the other hand, is generally one which *divests*, or *cuts off*, a prior interest before that prior interest's natural termination.

   a. **Test:** To determine whether the second interest is cutting short the first, or merely awaiting the natural termination of the first, use the test described *supra*, p. 68, in connection with conditions precedent and subsequent.

   > **Example:** O is the fee simple owner of Blackacre. He bargains and sells "to A for life, then to B and his heirs if B survives A, otherwise to C and his heirs." Because the limitation on B's interest is stated in the same clause as the gift to B, B and C each have equitable contingent remainders that are executed by the Statute of Uses into alternate legal contingent remainders. But suppose that the bargain and sale had been "to A for life, then to B and his heirs, but if B should die before A, to C and his heirs." Now B's interest would be vested subject to divestment, because the divesting language ("but if . . . ") comes in a separate clause following the clause giving the gift to B. C's interest would then be an executory interest, divesting B's interest. See Moynihan, p. 198.

4. **Executory interest following fee simple determinable:** There is one *exception* to the rule that an executory interest always takes effect by cutting short a prior interest. Recall that the common law took the view that there could not be a remainder following a *fee simple determinable* (*supra*, p. 64). Accordingly, if an interest following a fee simple determinable is in a stranger (rather than in the grantor, which would make it a possibility of reverter), that interest is called an executory interest. Yet it does not cut short the fee simple determinable; by definition, the fee simple determinable ends naturally when the limiting event takes place. Thus if O bargains and sells "to A and his heirs for as long as the property is used for residential purposes, then to B and his heirs," the interest in B is an executory interest even though it follows upon the natural expiration of A's fee simple determinable.

H. **Destructibility of contingent remainders:** If the courts had been logical, they would have *abolished* the doctrine of *destructibility of contingent remainders* as soon as the Statute of Uses was enacted. The principal reason for the destructibility doctrine was that without it, seisin would revert to the grantor, and then spring out once the contingent remainder vested. Since the Statute of Uses established that springing interests were acceptable, this should have been enough to abolish destructibility. For instance, suppose that O bargained and sold "to A for life, then to A's first son to become 21." If A died leaving a son age 19, the courts could have held that seisin reverted to O upon A's death, and sprang out into the son by an executory interest two years later. See C&L, p. 325. But the courts did no such thing.

1. **Doctrine of *Purefoy v. Rogers*:** Instead, they established the rule that *no limitation* capable of taking effect as a *contingent remainder* shall, if created *inter vivos*, be construed as a springing use under the Statute of Uses. Also, no limitation created by will capable of taking effect as a contingent remainder would be construed to be an executory devise under the Statute of Wills. C&L, p. 326. These two related rules were known as the *Rule of Purefoy v. Rogers*, after the case in which the rules were articulated.

2. **Effect of *Purefoy*:** The effect of the rule of *Purefoy v. Rogers* was to maintain the destructibility doctrine in full force.

   > **Example:** O owns Blackacre in fee simple. He bargains and sells "to A for life, then to A's oldest son who reaches the age of 21." At the time of the bargain and sale deed, A does not have a son who has reached the age of 21. Viewed as of the day of the bargain and sale deed, the gift to A's son can be construed as a contingent remainder. Therefore, if A dies when his oldest son is 19, the interest in the son will be regarded as a contingent remainder, and will be held to be destroyed. Under *Purefoy v. Rogers*, the court will not take the view that title reverts to O, and then jumps out to the son as a springing executory interest when the son becomes 21.

3. **Modern status of destructibility:** Recall that the doctrine of destructibility of contingent remainders has been abolished in most jurisdictions (*supra*, pp. 70, 73). Therefore, in these jurisdictions there is not likely to be much practical difference between an executory interest and a contingent remainder, and the rule of *Purefoy v. Rogers* is not of great importance. In a jurisdiction where destructibility has not yet been abolished, however, the distinction between contingent remainders and executory interests continues to be an important one.

I. **Unexecuted uses:** There are some types of uses as to which the Statute of Uses is *not applicable*. These uses, since they are not transformed by the Statute into legal interests, are usually called *unexecuted uses*. They fall into two main categories: (1) the use on a use; and (2) the active use (or active trust).

1. **Use on a use:** A *use on a use* does not fall within the Statute. Thus suppose O bargains and sells Blackacre "to T and his heirs as trustees for the use of A and his heirs." The bargain and sale creates a use in T; the use in A, since it is a use piled on top of the prior use in T, is not executed by the Statute (so it remains an equitable interest, i.e., T must run the property for A's benefit).

   a. **Statute works only once:** That is, the Statute works only once as to a particular estate. You might think of the Statute as "getting tired" after the first use, so that it cannot execute the second use. See C&L, p. 330.

2. **Active trust:** The Statute of Uses was directed at the situation where the legal title was a sham, and actual possession of the property was in the hands of the equitable owner. Thus where the holder of the legal title took a more *active* interest in the property, the Statute has always been held not to apply. For instance, if the legal titleholder occupies the premises and pays rent to the equitable owner, or actively rents out the premises and pays the rents over to the equitable owner, this will be considered an *active trust* to which the Statute is inapplicable.

Example 1: Owner, the fee simple owner of Blackacre, devises "to Trustee and his heirs to the use of Able for life and then to the use of Able's heirs." The will states that Trustee is to collect the income during Able's life and pay it over to Able quarterly.

    The use during Able's life is an active one, since Trustee is required to collect the income and pay it over to Able. Therefore, the Statute does not execute Able's equitable life estate. But the use in Able's heirs is not active, since no management duties are imposed on Trustee. This use is therefore executed. Thus the state of the title is: legal life estate *per autre vie* in Trustee, equitable life estate in Able, legal contingent remainder in fee simple in Able's heirs. (The Rule in Shelley's Case cannot apply, since the estate in the ancestor is equitable and the estate in the heirs is legal; see *supra*, p. 77.)

Example 2: Owner, the fee simple owner of Blackacre, devises "to Trustee and his heirs to the use of Able for life and then to the use of Able's heirs." Trustee is then to collect the income during Able's life and pay it over to Able quarterly, and on Able's death is too convey the premises to Able's heirs.

    The analysis is the same as in the preceding example, except that here, Trustee has active duties with respect to the heirs as well as with respect to Able, by virtue of the duty to convey the premises. This means that neither use is executed. Thus Trustee has a legal fee simple, Able has an equitable life estate and Able's heirs have an equitable contingent remainder in fee simple; the Rule in Shelley's Case then applies, so that the remainder in the heirs becomes an equitable remainder in Able. Able's equitable life estate then merges into this remainder, giving Able a present equitable fee simple.

  a. **Foundation of modern trust:** The recognition that the Statute of Uses does not apply to an active use was the foundation of the ***modern trust***. The trust as we now know it is an active one, with substantial duties of management given to the trustee. Thus even where the Statute of Uses is still in force (see *infra*), the modern trust is not affected.

J. The Statute of Uses today: In many states, the Statute of Uses is considered to be part of the common law, and is thus in force unless repealed. Only a few states (e.g., New York) have expressly repealed the Statute, so that in many states it is ***still in force***. In other states (e.g., Illinois), statutes have been explicitly enacted containing provisions similar to those of the Statutes of Uses. C&L, p. 334.

  1. **Common-law deeds:** Even in those states where the Statute of Uses is not in effect, it is possible to accomplish the two basic objectives that the Statute permitted: (1) the transfer of title without an immediate change in possession; and (2) the creation of shifting and springing interests. These results are made possible by statutes allowing the ***modern deed*** to transfer title without a change in possession to take effect at a future time, to provide for a cut-off of a prior interest, etc. Moynihan, p. 206. The modern deed may thus be considered a common-law conveyance without the common-law restrictions.

  2. **Bargain and sale still possible:** But it is still possible in most states to make a ***bargain and sale***. Since, as noted, most states continue to apply the Statute of Uses, this bargain and sale deed will usually have the same effect as a modern legal deed.

  3. **Alienability:** In nearly all jurisdictions, executory interests are ***completely alienable***. That is, they may be transferred *inter vivos*, devised by will, and passed under the intestacy statutes. Moynihan, p. 206-07. Thus they are no different from remainders (either

contingent or vested) with respect to transfer.

VIII. WASTE

A. The concept of waste generally: Whenever ownership of property is divided between a present and future interest, there is the possibility that the acts of the present holder will be to the detriment of the future interest. The doctrine of *waste* provides that if the present interest's acts: (1) substantially *reduce the value* of the future interest; and (2) are *unreasonable* under the circumstances, the holder of the future interest has a cause of action.

B. Life tenant and tenant for years: A claim of waste can arise against any holder of a present interest that amounts to less than a fee simple absolute. Most commonly, waste is committed by a *life tenant*, or a tenant for a *term of years*.

  1. Fee simple determinable: But waste can also be committed by one who holds a fee simple *determinable*, or a fee simple subject to a condition subsequent or to an executory interest. However, since usually it is far from certain that these interests will ever end, the courts are much more reluctant to find that a given act constitutes waste. In general, the less likely the future interest is to become possessory, or the further away the date of likely possession, the stronger a showing will be required to establish a case of waste.

  2. Tenants in common and joint tenants: The common-law concept of waste, as noted, requires damage to the holder of a future interest. In a few states, however, the doctrine is also applied where one holder of a present interest interferes with the rights of *another present interest*. Thus one tenant in common might be liable to another tenant in common for acts which diminish the value of the latter's interests. See Burby, pp. 33-34.

C. Types of waste: Waste is usually divided into three general categories: (1) voluntary waste; (2) permissive waste; and (3) equitable waste.

  1. Voluntary waste: *Voluntary waste* exists where an *affirmative act* causes unreasonable, permanent damage to the holder of a future interest.

    Example: T has a 20-year lease on Blackacre, owned by O. The premises include a residential structure. T demolishes the structure to use the property as a parking lot. Assuming that T's action was unreasonable, he has committed voluntary waste (even though the value of the property may actually have been increased by his action; see *infra*, p. 91).

    a. Act by third person: If the damage is committed not by the holder of the present interest, but by a *third person*, the present holder will not be liable for waste, if he was without fault. Burby, p. 34.

      i. Negligence: If, however, the third person's act was facilitated by the *negligence* of the present holder, the latter is liable for waste.

    b. Act of God: If the premises are damaged by an *act of God* (e.g., a fire or a hurricane), the present holder will not be liable, again assuming that his negligence did not contribute to the damage. Nor will he have the duty to rebuild.

    c. Ameliorative: Voluntary waste may exist even where the value of the property *increases* as a result. See *infra*, p. 91. Such waste is sometimes called *ameliorative* waste.

2. **Permissive waste:** *Permissive waste* results not from an affirmative act, but from *omission* by the present holder to *care for the property adequately*. The present holder has an obligation to keep the land and buildings in a *reasonable state of repair*. Thus a failure to keep a building *painted* so that the wood does not deteriorate, or to fix small *leaks*, is waste.

   a. **Act of God:** But, as noted, there is no duty to repair major damage done by force of nature or by the acts of a third person. Thus if a roof is severely damaged by a hurricane, it is probably not waste to fail to repair it. See Rest. §146.

3. **Equitable waste:** The holder of a *legal fee simple* (even one that is subject to an executory interest) is immune from legal liability for waste. But a court of *equity* will grant relief if his conduct will damage the prospects of the holder of an executory interest, possibility of reverter, etc. The equity court may enjoin this conduct under the doctrine of *equitable waste*.

D. Acts constituting waste: Decisions about what constitutes waste are necessarily on mostly a case-by-case basis, since no two fact patterns are exactly the same. However, the courts have evolved fairly specific rules dealing with several common types of cases.

1. **Cutting up timber:** As a general rule, a life tenant or a tenant for a term of years commits waste if he *cuts timber* on the land. There are, however, a number of exceptions:

   a. **Estovers:** Under the common-law doctrine of *estovers*, the tenant may cut timber needed for repairs, fencing, and fuel, so long as the wood is used on the property in question.

   b. **Commercial use:** If the only *commercially-feasible* use of the property is for commercial timber-cutting, the tenant may use it for this purpose.

   c. **Prior use:** Similarly, if the property was used for commercial harvesting of timber *prior* to the life estate of term of years, the tenant may continue this use.

   d. **Agricultural purposes:** Finally, if the land is clearly of an *agricultural* nature, the tenant may clear the timber so as to be able to farm. Burby, p. 38.

2. **Earth and minerals:** The tenant may normally not remove *earth and minerals* from the property. Again, however, there are exceptions:

   a. **"Open mines" doctrine:** First, if the property was used for mining *prior* to the commencement of the life estate or term of years, the tenant may *continue* this use.

   b. **Accomplishing purpose of tenancy:** Secondly, the tenant may mine if this is the only way of accomplishing the purpose of the lease or life estate. This would be the case where mining is the only use for which the property is suitable. Similarly, if removal of earth and stones was necessary to permit the agricultural use that the grantor or landlord intended, this could be done. Burby, p. 38.

3. **Structural changes:** Traditionally, *any structural change*, even one that improved the value of the property, was deemed waste. Thus *removal of a building*, or major *alterations* to one, were automatically considered waste. But present-day courts generally do not hold that any structural alteration is automatically waste. The following rules seem to be generally applicable:

a. **Diminution in value:** If the alteration *lessens the market value* of the future interest, the alteration automatically constitutes waste, regardless of the economic needs motivating the holder of the present interest. See Rest. §138.

b. **Change in neighborhood:** If the alteration would not reduce the value of the future interest, and a *change in the conditions of the neighborhood* in which the land is located deprives the land of usefulness in its present form, the change will not be waste. See Rest. §140, Comment f.

   i. **Increase in value not sufficient:** But an *increase in value* will *not*, by itself, necessarily be enough to mean that the tenant has not committed waste by an alteration. It will often be necessary to convince the court that the neighborhood has so completely changed that maintenance of the prior use is completely *impractical*, not just uneconomical.

c. **Effect of option:** If the holder of the present interest holds an *option* to acquire the fee simple, this may permit him to do things which would otherwise be waste, or at least lessen the damages if his acts are found to be waste.

   Example: Landlord and Tenant make a written lease for Blackacre, for 99 years. The lease gives Tenant an option to buy the property for $10,000 at any time during the lease term, if Landlord is given 60 days advance notice. In the middle of the lease term, Tenant tears down a building on the property in order to build a parking lot, although the building could have been used profitably had it not been demolished. Landlord sues Tenant to recover for waste.

   Since Tenant had the right to buy the property at any time (even at the very end of the lease) for $10,000, that option should be exercisable even following the demolition. Therefore, Tenant can make a strong argument that his liability should at the very most be limited to $10,0000. Furthermore, it can be argued that the court should not award damages until it is known whether Tenant will exercise the option; many courts have held that upon exercise of such an option, the exercise "relates back" to the date when the option was created (here, the date the lease was signed). In that event, Tenant would have no liability once he exercised the option. See 1 A.L.P. 363.

E. **Remedies for waste:** There are several possible remedies for waste:

   1. **Damages:** If the future interest is *sure to become possessory* (e.g., a landlord's interest, or a reversion or remainder vested absolutely), the court will generally award *damages*. The damages will be based upon the *diminution in value* of the future interest stemming from the waste.

   2. **Injunction:** An *injunction* issued by a court of equity is also frequently available. If the future interest is *not certain* to become possessory (e.g., a contingent remainder, or an executory interest following a fee simple determinable), an injunction may be the only relief that the court may award (since damages for an interest not sure to become possessory are highly speculative). The acts being enjoined are referred to as "*equitable waste*".

      a. **Injunction with damages:** Occasionally, the court will award an injunction together with money damages, even though the usual rule is that equitable relief is not available where money damages will suffice.

3. **Forfeiture:** Two Thirteenth Century statutes, the Statute of Marlbridge and the Statute of Gloucester, gave the courts power to hold that a tenant who committed waste *forfeited* his estate. Today, only a few states allow the remedy of forfeiture under any circumstances; many states, however, allow punitive measures (e.g., double or triple damages) for some kinds of waste. Burby, p. 35.

4. **Sale by judicial order:** Where a tenant wishes to alter the property substantially, and has not yet done so, another alternative is open to the court: it may, in some states, *order the property sold*. (But see *Baker v. Weedon*, 262 So.2d 641 (Miss. 1972), stressing that a sale should not be ordered no matter how much it would benefit the present tenant, if it would cause substantial loss of value to the holders of the future interest.)

IX. THE RULE AGAINST PERPETUITIES

A. **Historical development of Rule:** The rise of executory interests meant that it was possible to tie up the ownership of the land for long periods. For instance, it would be possible for O to convey by bargain and sale deed "to A for life, then to such of A's lineal descendants who are alive 100 years after A's death." See B,C&S, pp. 246-47. The interests in the descendants is not subject to destruction, since it is a springing executory interest, not a contingent remainder. This conveyance means that no disposition of the property can be made for A's life plus 100 years, during which time it may be highly desirable, from a social viewpoint, for the land to be transferred to someone else. It was in recognition of the undesirability of permitting title to be tied up for long periods that the courts developed the *Rule Against Perpetuities*.

> **Note:** A detailed treatment of the Rule, including its many exceptions and exceptions to exceptions, is beyond the scope of this outline. This subject is usually treated in detail in the course on wills and trusts or estate planning. (For a brief history of the Rule, see Rest. 2d (Donative Transfers), Part I, Introductory Note, pp. 5-11. Also, for a detailed discussion of the Rule, see Rest. 2d (Donative Transfers), Chapters 1 and 2).

B. **Statement of Rule:** The Rule Against Perpetuities is generally stated as follows: *"no interest is good unless it must vest, if at all, not later than 21 years after some life in being at the creation of the interest."* See B,C&S, p. 246.

1. **Paraphrase of Rule:** To paraphrase this statement, an interest is invalid unless it can be said, with absolute certainty, that it will either *vest or fail to vest*, before the end of the period equal to: (1) a life in existence at the time the interest is created plus (2) an additional 21 years.

   > **Example:** O conveys his fee simple interest in Blackacre "to A for life, remainder to the first son of A whenever born who becomes a clergyman." At the date of the conveyance, A has no son who is presently a clergyman. Viewing the matter from the date of the conveyance, it is possible to imagine a situation in which the remainder to the son could vest later than lives in being plus 21 years. Thus A's son could be born to A after the date of the conveyance, and this son could become a clergyman more than 21 years after the death of A and of any sons born before the conveyance. Since this remote vesting is possible (even though somewhat unlikely) the contingent remainder is invalid. This is so even though it *actually turns out* that A has a son alive before the date of the conveyance who ultimately becomes a clergyman. See B,C&S, p. 248.

2. **Judged in advance:** As the above example makes clear, the common-law version of the Rule Against Perpetuities requires that the validity of the interest be judged *at the time it is created*, not at the time the interest actually vests. If, at the time the interest is created, it is *theoretically possible* (even though very unlikely) that the interest will vest later than 21 years after the expiration of lives in being, the interest is invalid. This is so even if it actually turns out that the interest vests before the end of lives in being plus 21 years. (But the Restatement 2d and a number of states have adopted "wait and see" statutes changing this common-law rule; see *infra*, p. 97.)

C. **Interests to which the Rule applies:** For the Rule to have any force, the interest must be one that is *contingent*, i.e., not automatically vested at the time it is created.

1. **Contingent remainders:** The Rule applies to *contingent remainders*. In fact, one of the principal reasons why it is still necessary to be able to distinguish between vested and contingent remainders is precisely because a vested remainder is vested from the moment of its creation, whereas a contingent remainder violates the Rule if it might not vest or fail before the end of lives in being plus 21 years.

   Example: O conveys "to A for life, remainder to the first son of A to reach the age of 25 and his heirs." At the time of the conveyance, A does not have a son who has reached the age of 25. The remainder in the son is contingent, rather than vested, since it is not known which son, if any, will reach the age of 25. It is possible that the first son to reach 25 will be one who has not yet been born as of the date of the conveyance; such a son's interest would vest later than lives in being plus 21 years, if A has no other sons, or if all his sons die within four years of the conveyance. Since there is a possibility of remote vesting, the gift to the oldest son violates the Rule Against Perpetuities and is invalid. See B,C&S, p. 248.

2. **Vested remainders:** A *vested* remainder, by contrast, can *never* violate the Rule Against Perpetuities. A vested remainder, by definition, vests at the moment it is created. This is true even if *possession* is not to occur until the future; the important thing is that the remainder vests "in interest'", not possession, immediately.

   Example: O conveys "to A for life, remainder to A's children for life, remainder to B and his heirs." It is possible that A's last surviving child will be one who has not been born as of the date of the conveyance, and who will live more than 21 years longer than any of A's other children born before the date of the conveyance. It is also possible that, following the last child's death, possession will go not to B (who may already be dead) but to an heir or devisee of B not yet living at the time of the conveyance. Nonetheless, the gift to B and his heirs does not violate the Rule Against Perpetuities, because that gift is a vested remainder, which vested in interest (though not in possession) on the date of the conveyance. Burby, p. 419.

3. **Reversionary interests not within Rule:** The Rule does *not* apply to *reversionary interests* (i.e., reversions, possibilities of reverter and rights of entry; see pp. 62, 60, and 61 *supra*). This is because these interests, like vested remainders, are deemed to vest as soon as they are created.

   a. **Criticism:** However, there is no logical reason why these reversionary interests should be treated as vested at their creation; they are not at all certain to take effect. For instance, if O conveys "to A and his heirs for as long as liquor is not sold on the premises", liquor may never be sold on the premises, in which case O's possibility of reverter would never become possessory. Or, it might become possessory 300 years from now, surely a severe restraint on alienation. Nonetheless, the common-law rule view has always been that the Rule does not apply. But some states have enacted special statutes of limitation requiring either that such reversionary interests be recorded within a length of time, or that they become possessory within a certain period of time (e.g., thirty years after creation). See *supra*, p. 49.

4. **Executory interests:** An *executory interest* is *not vested at its creation*. Thus such an interest may violate the Rule.

> **Example:** O conveys certain property to the city of Klamath Falls, "so long as it complies with [certain] conditions", including the building and maintenance of a library on the property. The deed provides that after the property is no longer used for a library, title is to pass to A and B and their heirs. Some years later, the city stops using the library, and sues the Ds (who are the heirs of A and B) too gain an adjudication of the rights of the parties.
>
> *Held*, the gift over to A and B was an executory interest, and was thus subject to the Rule Against Perpetuities. Since there was a possibility, at the time of the gift, that the city might continue to maintain a library on the property indefinitely, it was possible that the gift over to A and B would not vest (and become possessory) until after lives in being plus 21 years. Therefore, the gift to A and B was void, and their heirs take nothing. However, this does not mean that the city gets a fee simple absolute. Instead, the possibility of reverter in O (a corporation) becomes possessory, and goes to the corporation's successors in interest. *City of Klamath Falls v. Bell*, 490 P.2d 515 (Ore. Ct. App. 1971).

5. **Options to purchase land:** An *option* to *purchase land* will often be subject to the Rule Against Perpetuities.

   a. **Option as part of lease:** If an option to purchase property is part of a *lease* of that property and is exercisable only during the lease term, then the option is (at least in the United States) *not* treated as being subject to the Rule. The theory behind this exclusion is that the option gives the lessee an incentive to improve the property, and does not really restrict alienability very much. See C,S&W, p. 132.

   > **Example:** Tenant leases Blackacre from Landlord. The lease runs for 50 years. The lease provides that at any time until the end of the lease, Tenant may purchase the property for $200,000. Since the purchase option is part of a lease, it need not satisfy the Rule Against Perpetuities. Therefore, even though no measuring life is listed and the option is exercisable more than 21 years after its creation (so that the option would be a violation of the Rule if the Rule applied), the option is valid.

   b. **Options "in gross":** But if the option is *not* part of a lease or other property interest, most states hold that the Rule *does* apply. (Such unattached options are called options *"in gross"*.) Thus an option in gross will be unenforceable if it could be exercised beyond the end of the Perpetuities period, even though the optionee paid real money for it the belief that it would be exercisable. *Id.* See, e.g., *Certified Corp. v. GTE Products Corp.* 467 N.E.2d 1336 (Mass. 1984).

   > **Example:** In 1941, Greyhound Corp. sells a parcel to a government body, the Central Delaware County Authority ("Authority"). The deed conveys the property in fee simple, but states that the property "shall be kept available for and shall be used only for public purposes. . . . In the event that at any time hereafter said use shall be abandoned . . . then [seller], its successors and assigns, shall have

the right to repurchase, retake and reacquire the same" upon payment of an amount equal to the original purchase price. In 1980, the Authority ceases to use the property for public purposes, but continues to maintain the land. In 1983, the Authority brings an action to quiet title to the land, contending that the deed's public use restriction violates the Rule Against Perpetuities.

Held, for the Authority. The restriction in the deed here was an option to purchase, not an interest subject to a condition subsequent. An option to purchase (unlike an interest subject to a condition subsequent) is subject to the Rule Against Perpetuities. Since the option was not exercised within 21 years after the 1941 grant, the option was void as against the Rule Against Perpetuities. *Central Delaware County Authority v. Greyhound Corp.*, 588 A.2d 485 (Pa. 1991).

Note: Pennsylvania, the state that decided *Central Delaware*, has a "wait and see" statute, by which a grant that might or might not vest within the lives in being plus 21 years can be "saved" by the fact that it does in fact vest within that period. (See *infra*, p. 97 for a discussion of the "wait and see" approach.) Therefore, if the Authority had in fact stopped using the property for public purposes prior to 1962, and Greyhound had attempted to exercise its repurchase option before that year, the option probably would have been enforceable despite the Perpetuities problem. But, as the court noted, what in fact happened was that more than 21 years passed from the 1941 grant without any abandonment or attempted exercise, so at that moment the purchase option was extinguished even under the wait-and-see approach.

6. **Preference for Rule to apply in ambiguous cases:** Where two interpretations of a grant are possible, the court will normally prefer the interpretation under which the Rule Against Perpetuities would ***apply***. This is because courts attach great importance to the public policy behind the Rule — the encouragement of property transferability. Thus in *Central Delaware County Authority*, *supra*, the grant could have been construed either as a fee simple subject to a condition subsequent (in which case the resulting right of entry would not have had to satisfy the Rule; see *supra*, pp. 50-51) or as an option to re-purchase (in which case the Rule would have to be satisfied); the court applied the preference in favor of finding an option, so that the Rule applied.

D. **Meaning of "lives in being":** Normally a conveyance or bequest will mention a person (probably a beneficiary) as to whom it can be said that all interests will vest within 21 years after that person's death. For instance, O conveys "to my daughter D for life, then to her first child to reach the age of 21." We know that D is alive at the date of the conveyance; we also know that any child she has will have to reach 21 within 21 years after D's death. Therefore, D would be the measuring life in this conveyance, and the contingent remainder to D's children is valid.

1. **Measuring lives too numerous:** The measuring lives named in the conveyance must ***not be so numerous*** that it will be impractical to determine whether any is still alive many years later. For instance, suppose T puts a clause in his will stating that "any interest hereunder shall fail if it has not vested as of the date of death of the last surviving member of the First Unitarian Church of New York City now alive"; if the Church now has 200 members, these are too numerous to constitute measuring lives. Unless another measuring life can be inferred from the instrument, some of the gifts may be void under the Rule.

E. **Special situations:** The common-law Rule requires, as noted, that there be ***no possibility*** that the interest in question might vest after lives in being plus 21 years. There are a number of special sub-rules that have evolved to deal with certain possibilities.

1. **Fertile octogenarian:** There is a *conclusive presumption* that *any person, regardless of age* or physical condition, is capable of *having children*. This presumption is often referred to as the *"fertile octogenarian"* rule. When coupled with the rule that a gift to a class is invalid if the gift to any member of the class is invalid (*infra*, p. 97), the fertile octogenarian rule can have a devastating effect.

   Example: T devises property "to A for life, then to A's surviving children for life, then to the surviving children of B." At the time of T's death, B has three children, and B herself is 80 years old. It is conceivable that B could now have another child, and that that child would take after lives in being plus 21 years (for instance, if all of A's children were born after T's death, and died more than 21 years after T's death). Therefore, B's three now-living children will not take anything, since their interest violates the Rule. It is irrelevant that, as a medical matter, B could not possibly have any further children. Burby, p. 415. See also *Jee v. Audley*, 1 Cox 324 (Ch. 1787).

2. **Unborn widow:** Similarly, if an interest is created which will flow through the *"widow"* of X (by naming and relying on her in determining when the interest will vest), the common-law view is that the interest *must fail*. The "widow" is not necessarily the person who is married to X when the interest is created; X could later marry someone born after the interest was created, who would not be a relevant life-in-being for the purposes of the vesting of the interest in question. Since the "unborn widow" might live longer than 21 years after the death of X, the only life in being, the interest *might* not vest within 21 years of X's death and is therefore invalid under the Rule Against Perpetuities. This is often called the *"unborn widow"* rule. (The rule developed in a less gender-equal time; it would, of course, apply equally to widowers.)

   Example: In 1995, T bequeaths Blackacre "to A for life, then to A's widow, then to the issue of A and A's widow who survive them." At the time of T's death, A is married to B. It is possible that B will either predecease or divorce A, and A will then marry someone born after 1995 (we'll call her C.) C would be not be a life-in-being in 1995, the time of the bequest. Since the contingent remainder to the issue can't vest without referring to the life of C, it is not certain to vest within 21 years of the relevant lives that were in being *at the time the remainder was created* (C might live longer than 21 years after the death of A). Therefore, the contingent remainder to the issue of A and "A's widow" must fail.

   a. **Problem solved by "wait and see" statutes:** The "unborn widow" rule only applies where the validity of the interests is judged at the time the conveyance was created. In those states that have adopted "wait and see" statutes (see *infra*, p. 97), the conveyance will be valid so long as the "widow" turns out to be a person born before the conveyance or bequest.

   b. **Existing spouse intended:** Also, most courts will accept evidence that by the term "widow," the grantor intended to refer to an existing spouse (in the above example, A's spouse in 1995, B). If this evidence is accepted, then the existing spouse will be a relevant life in being, and the remainder will be valid (since it will vest immediately after the existing spouse's death.)

3. **Happening of event: :** A gift is sometimes drafted in such a way that vesting will only occur after a certain event, e.g., the probating of a will, the payment of certain debts and taxes, etc. Some courts (though fortunately not most) have held that the event might take *more than 21 years*, and that the gift which is to vest after that event is therefore invalid.

Example: T bequeaths property "to A for life, then following the probating of A's estate and the payment of all taxes due thereon, the balance to B and his heirs." A court could conclude that the probating of the estate and the payment of taxes might take more than 21 years, in which case a descendant of B (not born at the time of the bequest) would take too remotely. Therefore, the gift to B could be struck down.

Note: However, most courts have assumed that such an administrative event will occur within a "reasonable time", i.e., less than 21 years. Powell, Par. 764, p. 892. (See also Rest. 2d (Donative Transfers) §1.4, Comment n.

4. **Gifts switched from one charity to another::** One who makes a charitable gift or bequest will often provide that if the charity receiving the gift ceases to exist, the gift shall go to a different charity. Thus S might set up a trust, the income from which is to go "to the Red Cross, but if the Red Cross should cease to exist, to the World Health Organization." It is possible that the Red Cross might cease to exist more than lives in being plus 21 years from the creation of the trust. Nonetheless, such a shift in interest, provided that it is from one charity to another, does **not violate** the Rule. Burby, p. 241. See also Rest. 2d (Donative Transfers) §1.6.

5. **Gestation::** The **period of gestation** may be added to the lives in being plus 21 years. Thus suppose O bequeaths property "to A for life, then to A's first son to reach the age of 21." A is a man. It is possible that A might die without any living children, but with a pregnant widow. Without an exception for the period of gestation, it would take the unborn child 21 years plus up to nine months to reach the age of 21, making his interest invalid. The "period of gestation" exception renders the child's interest valid. Powell, Par. 766, p. 900. See also Rest. 2d (Donative Transfers) §1.3(2) and Comment h thereto.

6. **Class gift::** If a gift is made to all members of a **class**, the entire gift fails unless it can be said that **each member of the class** must have his interest vest or fail within the lives in being plus 21 year period. The problem usually arises where the class obtains new members following a testator's death.

   Example: T bequeaths property "to A, then to A's surviving children who attain the age of 25." At the time of the bequest, A has two children, B and C. It is possible that another child (whom we shall hypothetically call "D"), will be born after T's death; since A, B, and C might all die prior to D's fourth birthday, D's interest would then vest too remotely (more than 21 years after the deaths of A, B and C, the measuring lives). Because of this theoretical possibility, not only is the gift invalid as to children born after T's death, but it is also invalid as to the rest of the class of children, i.e., B and C. See Burby, p. 422.

   Note: But a court might avoid the result in the above example by construing the class refer only to those members who could take without violating the Rule Against Perpetuities. Alternately, the court might view the class as closing at the time of T's death. Finally, if the bequest referred not to "the children" but specifically to "B", "C", etc., then each gift would be evaluated on its own, and would be valid. See Burby, pp. 423-24.

7. **"Wait and see" approach::** Under the common-law Rule as noted, the validity of an interest is to be measured as of the time it is created; if a scenario could be imagined whereby the interest might vest too remotely, it is invalid regardless of how things actually turn out. But the Restatement 2d and a number of jurisdictions have now adopted the **"wait and see"** rule (see generally Rest. 2d (Donative Transfers) Chapters 1&2), by which the validity of an instrument is determined **at the time it vests**. Rest. 2d (Donative Transfers) §1.4. (In other words, under the "wait and see"

approach the interest fails if it "does not vest" with the period of the Rule; the approach rejects the common-law view that the interest fails "if it 'might not vest', if it ever vests, within the period of the rule." Rest. 2d (Donative Transfers) §1.4, Comment a. ***If the interest actually vests within lives in being at the time of creation plus 21 years, the fact that things might have worked out differently is irrelevant*** — the interest is valid. Some of the states which have enacted such statutes include: Connecticut, Florida, Kentucky, Maryland, Massachusetts, Ohio, Pennsylvania and Washington. See Rest. 2d (Donative Transfers) §1.1, Statutory Note.

> **Example:** O, who owns Blackacre in fee simple, conveys "to A and his heirs, but if A or his heirs ever use Blackacre for other than residential purposes, to B and his heirs." Under the traditional what-might-happen view, the gift over to B is void, since the premises might stop being used for residential purposes more than lives in being plus 21 years following the conveyance. But under the wait-and-see test, if the property ceases to be used for residential purposes within 21 years after the death of the survivor of O, A and B, the gift over to B and his heirs is valid. That is, the interest in B has actually vested within the required period, so it is valid even though things might have worked out in such a way that vesting was too remote. See Rest. 2d (Donative Transfers) §1.4, Illustr. 17.

> **a. Effect on fertile octogenarian and unborn widow cases::** Observe that the "wait-and-see" rule renders the "fertile octogenarian" and "unborn widow" cases almost impossible to occur. So long as the octogenarian does not in fact have a child, or the widow referred to in the instrument in fact turns out to be someone born prior to the instrument, the Rule Against Perpetuities cannot be violated. See Rest. 2d (Donative Transfers) §1.4, Comments h and i, Illustr. 8 and 9.

> **b. Effect on class gifts::** The "wait-and-see" approach provides that in most cases involving transfers to a class of persons, "the interest of each class member will in fact vest in time," thereby allowing those members of the class whose interests have not yet vested to have a valid interest under the Rule. Rest. 2d (Donative Transfers) §1.4, Comment k.

8. **Uniform Rule::** The Uniform Statutory Rule Against Perpetuities, drafted in 1986, has been adopted in 20 states. It uses a special kind of "wait-and-see" approach: No interest may be held void on account of the Rule until **90 years** have passed from its creation; at that time, the court looks to see whether the interest actually vested beyond the Perpetuities period. If so, the court invalidates it. D&K, pp. 321-22. This Uniform approach makes the Rule even less likely to result in the invalidation of an interest than does the typical wait-and-see statute (by which an interest that vests beyond the period of the Rule can be *immediately* invalidated).

X. RESTRAINTS UPON ALIENATION

A. **General problem:** There is another respect to which one who conveys land might attempt to tie it up for future generations. He might explicitly provide that the grantee ***may not alienate*** (i.e., transfer) the property. Thus O might convey "to A and his heirs, but no conveyance by A to any third party shall be valid." Such a restriction is known as a ***restraint on alienation***.

1. **Generally void:** A detailed discussion of restraints on alienation is beyond the scope of this outline. However, the general principle is that restraints upon the alienation of a ***fee simple*** are ***void***. Burby, p. 427. See generally Rest. 2d (Donative Transfers), Part II. Thus the restriction imposed by O in the above paragraph would certainly not be upheld; A would be entitled to covey to whomever he wished. Direct

restraints upon the grantee's right to dispose of the property **by will** or **by intestacy** also come within the ban upon restraints upon alienation.

2. **Life estate:** A life estate, however, may be subjected to restraints. Thus O might convey "to A for life, but A shall have no right to convey his interest; then to B and his heirs." The restraint upon A is justified by the need to protect B's future claim interest. Burby, p. 428.

3. **Indirect restraint:** Certain types of **indirect** restraints on the use or disposition of property are upheld by the courts. (See also Rest. 2d (Donative Transfers) §3.4 which does not consider "use" restrictions as restraints on alienation.) **Use restrictions** fall within this category. For instance, O might convey "to A and his heirs, provided that the property not be used for non-residential purposes." Such restrictions are discussed in the chapter on land-use controls, beginning *infra*, p. 261.

   a. **Defeasible estates:** Also, the defeasible estates (e.g., the fee simple determinable) can be viewed as permissible restraints on alienation. See *supra*, p. 48. For instance, O may convey to A and his heirs, but if the property shall ever be used for purposes of the sale of alcohol, grantor or his heirs may re-enter." .sp 2l

Chapter Review Questions
(Answers are at back of book)

12. O held a fee simple absolute in Blackacre. He conveyed "to A for life." After this conveyance, what interest, if any, does O hold in Blackacre?

13. O conveyed Blackacre "to A for life, then to B and his heirs." Immediately after the conveyance, what interest, if any, does B have in Blackacre?

14. O conveyed Blackacre "to A for life, then to B's children and their heirs." At the time of this conveyance, B had one child, C. Immediately following the conveyance, what interest, if any, does C have in Blackacre?

15. O conveyed Blackacre "to A for life, then to B and his heirs. However, if B dies without issue, then to C and his heirs." Immediately following this conveyance, what interest, if any, does B have in Blackacre?

16. O conveyed Blackacre "to A for life, then, if B is living at A's death, to B in fee simple." Immediately after this conveyance, what interest, if any, does B have in Blackacre?

17. O conveyed Blackacre "to A for life, then to B and his heirs, but if B dies before A, to O and his heirs." Immediately after this conveyance, what interest, if any, does B have in Blackacre?

18. O conveyed Blackacre "to A for life, remainder to the first daughter of A who produces a child while married." A then died. At A's death, he has one daughter, D, who has not yet married or had a child. O is still alive. Immediately after A's death, what is the state of title to Blackacre? Assume that all common-law doctrines are in force without statutory modification.

19. O conveyed Blackacre "to A for life, remainder to A's oldest daughter for life if she has a child while married, remainder to B and his heirs." At a time when A's oldest daughter, D, had not yet married, A conveyed his life estate to B. After that conveyance, what is the state of title? Assume that all common-law doctrines are in force without statutory modification.

20. O, in his will, left Blackacre "to A for life, remainder to A's heirs." A then issued a quitclaim deed (giving whatever interest A had, without specifying or warranting what that interest was) to B. Two years later, A died, leaving as his sole heir at law S, a son. What is the state of title to Blackacre?

21. In a state with no statutes modifying the relevant common-law rules, O conveyed Blackacre "to A for life, remainder to O's heirs." Shortly thereafter, O quitclaimed any interest he might have in Blackacre to B. O then died, leaving as his sole heir a son, S. A then died. What is the state of title?

22. The same facts as the prior question. Now, however, assume that all transactions occurred in the late 20th century, in a state that follows the usual 20th-century approach to conveyances of the ones described in the question. Assume further that in O's initial conveyance to A, he added the sentence, "I mean for this gift to take effect in exactly the manner that I have expressed." What is the probable state of title?

23. O owned Blackacre in fee simple. He bargained and sold it "to A and his heirs, but if liquor is ever served on the premises, then to B and his heirs." Immediately after this conveyance, what is the state of title?

24. O conveyed Blackacre "to A for life." At the time of the conveyance, Blackacre had always been used as farm land, and O knew that A was a farmer. However, the parties made no agreement concerning the use to which A would put the property. A took possession, and began farming. Shortly thereafter, oil was discovered on an adjacent parcel. A immediately drilled an oil well on the property, and struck a gusher. A sold the resulting oil and put the proceeds of the sale in his bank account. Has A's conduct violated O's rights?

For questions 25-30, assume that the common-law Rule Against Perpetuities is in effect.

25. O conveys "to A for life, remainder to A's oldest son who survives A for life, remainder to B and his heirs." A and B are alive at the time of the conveyance, but A does not yet have a son. Is the remainder to B and his heirs valid?

26. In 1960, O conveys "to A for life, remainder in fee simple to the first son of A who has a child while married." At the time of this conveyance, A has no son who has had a child while married, but does have an unmarried childless son, B. In 1965, B has a child while married. In 1970, A dies. Is the remainder to B valid?

27. In 1960, O, the owner of Greenacre, gave to A Corporation (in return for a payment of $20,000) the following document: "I, O, hereby grant to A Corp. an option to purchase Greenacre at any time during the next 30 years for a price equal to $100,000 plus an additional sum equal to the compounded interest, at 10%, on $100,000 from the date of this option." O died in 1970, leaving all his real and personal property to B. In 1988, A Corp. seeks to exercise its option. Does it have a right to do so?

28. In 1980, O bequeathed Blackacre "to A for life, then to A's widow." At the time of this bequest, A was not yet married. In 1982, A married B, a 30-year-old woman. A died in 1988. Does B get Blackacre?

29. In 1960, O bequeathed Whiteacre "to A for life, then in equal shares to those of A's children who survive him, but only when each attains the age of 30. I want to be sure that children born to A after my death are included in this bequest." In 1960, A had one child, B, who was 10. In 1985, A died, without ever having had any other children, and with B still alive. Does B take the property?

30. Same facts as prior question. In a state following the most common statutory modification to the Rule Against Perpetuities, would the gift to B be valid?

MARITAL ESTATES

Introductory Note: In this chapter, we examine the special property problems raised by the fact that two people having an interest in property are married. Any discussion of property rights during marriage must be divided into the common-law system (followed in most states) on the one hand, and the system of community property (followed in eight states) on the other hand. Therefore, our first three sections treat three different aspects of the common-law system: property rights during marriage, property rights upon divorce, and property rights on death of one spouse. Then, we treat the community property system. Finally, we discuss briefly homestead laws, which protect the family residence from seizure by creditors.

I. THE COMMON-LAW SYSTEM — RIGHTS DURING MARRIAGE

A. Introduction: All but eight states govern marital property in a way that is derived from traditional common-law principles. The common-law system of marital estates, as it existed in, say, the England of the 1500s, has been so changed by modern statutes that it is almost unrecognizeable. However, because a few vestiges of the traditional system survive, you must have some sense of how the common-law approach to marital property worked.

B. The feudal system: The feudal era granted the husband extreme dominion over his wife's property — the husband received virtually unfettered ownership of his wife's property during their joint lives.

    1. Coverture and jure uxoris: This complete dominance was carried out in part by two doctrines, coverture and *jure uxoris*.

        a. Personal property (coverture): At the moment of marriage, the wife ceased to be a separate person for legal purposes — "husband and wife were regarded as one, and that one was the husband." D&K, p. 367. Under the doctrine of *"coverture,"* *all personal property owned by the wife at the time of the marriage became the property of the husband.*

        b. Real property (*jure uxoris*): The husband's dominion over his wife's *real estate* was almost as complete. The husband did not gain formal legal title to lands owned by his wife at the moment of marriage. But under the doctrine of *"jure uxoris"*, the husband had the right to *possess* all his wife's lands during marriage, including land acquired by the wife after the marriage. D&K, p. 368. Two practical consequences of the *jure uxoris* were that the husband could *spend* the rents and profits of the land as he wished, even if the wife protested, and he could *sell* his right (e.g., assign to another person the right to rents and profits).

        c. Abolished today: The doctrines of coverture and *jure uxoris* do not exist anywhere at present, due to the enactment of Married Women's Property Acts, discussed below.

C. Tenancy by the entirety: A second doctrine which was of great importance during the feudal era was the *"tenancy by the entirety."* Since husband and wife were viewed as one person in the eyes of the law, any *conveyance* to two people who were in fact married created a tenancy by the entirety. We will discuss the tenancy by the entirety in much greater detail beginning *infra*, p. 121. For now, understand two main things about the tenancy by the entirety, as it stood under the feudal-era common law: (1) it was the only way that two people who were in fact married could receive a conveyance of property (so that even if a conveyance stated that H and W were to take as "joint tenants" or as "tenants in common," the tenancy by the entirety was created); and (2) neither spouse, acting alone, could **terminate** the tenancy by the entirety (unlike the "tenancy in common," which could be "severed" by either party's unilateral action).

D. Married Women's Property Acts: Beginning in 1839, all states enacted Married Women's Property Acts, designed to give the woman legal equality, and to protect her property from her husband's creditors. D&K, p. 368.

   1. Effect on coverture and *jure uxoris*: These Married Women's Acts have almost completely abolished the doctrines of coverture and *jure uxoris*. For instance, if a woman holds title to real estate at the moment of her marriage, or receives sole title by gift or bequest after marriage, she **controls the management** of that property herself. Similarly, any property held by a married woman in her own name is **immune from the claims of her husband's creditors**.

   2. Effect on tenancy by the entirety: The effect of Married Women's Acts on the tenancy by the entirety is less clear. Many of these Acts have had the effect of abolishing the tenancy by the entirety, which now exists in only about half of the common-law states (see *infra*, p. 121). All states hold that the husband's creditors today cannot get at the wife's interest in the tenancy by the entirety, and most seem to hold that while the marriage and the tenancy by the entirety exist, one spouse's creditors cannot even separately attach or sell that spouse's interest. The topic is discussed more fully *infra*, p. 123.

II. THE COMMON-LAW SYSTEM — EFFECT OF DIVORCE

A. The traditional "title" view: Under traditional common law principles, if the parties were *divorced*, the division of their property depended heavily on who held formal legal *"title"* to the property.

   1. Title in husband's name: Most significantly, if the legal title to property was held by one spouse alone, that spouse **retained title upon divorce**. Since the husband was usually the sole wage earner, property was far more often in his sole name than in the wife's sole name, so this principle benefitted husbands.

   2. Co-tenancy: If the property was held in one of the three forms of co-tenancy, this arrangement generally persisted after the divorce. Thus property held by the spouses as tenants in common (see *infra*, p. 120) continued as such after the divorce, so each could sell or keep his or her undivided one-half interest. If the spouses held the property as joint tenants (a form that gives full ownership to whichever spouse survives; see *infra*, p. 113), the joint tenancy continued after divorce. If the property was held in a tenancy by the entirety (see *infra*, p. 124), the divorce acted as a "severance," converting ownership into a tenancy in common. D&K, p. 382.

   3. Alimony: Since the wife was not entitled to any share of property as to which the husband held sole legal title, the common law needed some way to make sure that the wife would not be left destitute. The answer was to require the husband to continue **supporting** the wife, by payment of *"alimony."*

B. The modern doctrine of "equitable distribution": Today, every state that follows the common-law (rather than community property) approach to property has **abolished** the doctrine that legal title controls the division of property upon divorce. Instead, all of the common-law states have substituted, by statute, a doctrine called **"equitable distribution."** Under the equitable distribution approach, property is divided by the court according to principles of "equity" or "fairness," not according to legal title.

1. **Move towards equality of split:** When the court divides the property according to equitable principles, the modern trend is towards an **equality** of division. Some states *require* an equal division, others institute a *presumption* of equality, and others merely use equality as a *starting point* at which individual factors are then considered. D&K, p. 384. In all states, the equitable distribution principles reflect the view that marriage should be looked upon as an **economic partnership**, and that a wife who has served as a homemaker rather than wage earner should be regarded as having contributed to that partnership just as heavily as the wage earning husband did.

2. **Factors governing split:** In those states that allow the judge to consider individual circumstances of the marriage in deciding how the property should be split, a number of factors are usually considered. Here are some of the common ones:

   a. The **duration** of the marriage (so that the longer the marriage, the more likely the court is to award an equal distribution);

   b. The **age, health, occupation, income sources** and **employability** of each spouse. (Thus a wife who is elderly and without job skills is likely to be awarded a higher percentage of the marital assets than a young wife who has already established a career.)

   c. The contribution of each party to the **acquisition** or **appreciation in value** of the marital property. (Thus a husband who mismanages the marital property would get a lesser division than a husband who, through great effort and skill, caused the marital assets to appreciate.)

   d. The contribution of a spouse as a **homemaker** or to the family unit. (Thus a wife who has stayed home and reared children might get a larger portion than the wife in a childless marriage, all other factors being equal.)

   Most of these factors, as well as several others, are listed in §307 (alternative A) of the Uniform Marriage and Divorce Act, which is representative of the equitable distribution principles applied by most states.

3. **What property is covered:** Most states allow the court to divide only **"marital property"** under equitable distribution principles. Usually, marital property is defined to include only property **acquired during the marriage from the earnings of the parties**. So property acquired by a spouse **before marriage**, or acquired by one spouse through a **gift or bequest** to that spouse, is not included in the pile of assets that may be distributed. The most frequently-litigated question is whether the value of a **professional degree** earned by one spouse during the marriage may be counted as marital property, and thus subject to equitable distribution.

   a. **Majority view:** Most courts have concluded that a professional degree should **not** be treated as marital property, and thus should not be subject to equitable distribution. See, e.g., *In re Marriage of Graham*, 574 P.2d 75 (Col. 1978), holding that H's MBA was not marital property, because it did not have an exchange value, could not be assigned or sold, could not be acquired by the mere expenditure of money, would terminate on the death of the holder, and thus had none of the attributes usually associated with the concept of "property." (A dissent in *Graham* argued that W's earnings were "invested" in H's education so that H would have the time and funds needed to obtain his degree, and that equity demanded treating H's increased earning power from the degree as a distributable asset.)

   i. Reimbursement theory: Although most courts, as noted, refuse to find a professional degree to be marital property, some states, most notably New Jersey, allow the other spouse to obtain *reimbursement* for that spouse's contribution to the acquisition of the degree. Under this reimbursement theory, if H's medical or other professional degree had a "cost" of, say, $40,000 (measured by both the cost of tuition and the earnings that the couple forewent by having H study rather than earn), the non-degreed spouse could receive a reimbursement of half this amount (on the assumption that H and W each contributed half the cost or "sacrifice" for the acquisition of the degree). See D&K, pp. 391-92. The leading case allowing reimbursement is *Mahoney v. Mahoney*, 453 A.2d 527 (N.J. 1982).

b. Minority (New York view): One of the very few states that recognizes a professional degree as marital property is New York. See *O'Brien v. O'Brien*, 489 N.E.2d 712 (N.Y. 1985), holding that H's medical license was marital property for equitable distribution purposes, and refusing to allow mere reimbursement of expenses as a remedy. The result in New York seems to be due mostly to that state's unusual language in its equitable distribution statute, by which the court is directed to consider each party's "direct or indirect contribution . . . *to the career or career potential* of the other party. . . ." N.Y. Dom. Rel. L. §236.

   i. Celebrity status: In fact, the New York courts have treated as marital property not just professional degrees but also one spouse's *celebrity status* or other enhanced earning power. Most strikingly, in *Elkus v. Elkus*, 572 N.Y.S.2d 901 (1st Dept. 1991), an intermediate trial court held that the career and celebrity status of W (opera star Frederica von Stade) were a marital asset, which she could be required to share with H, who had served as W's vocal coach and travelling companion during their marriage, while W rose from unknown to star.

c. Professional good will: Even in the majority of courts that do not treat a professional degree as a marital asset, *"professional good will" is* a marital asset that may be equitably distributed. By "professional good will," the courts mean the enhanced earning capacity that comes from a professional's *reputation* and *client or customer list*. For instance, whereas a newly-graduated neurosurgeon in most states has no career-related prospects that are to be treated as marital property, a neurosurgeon who has built up a practice and reputation and who has been earning large sums from that practice will usually be found to hold an asset — the practice — that can be valued and subject to distribution. See, e.g., *Dugan v. Dugan*, 457 A.2d 1 (N.J. 1983).

III. THE COMMON-LAW SYSTEM — DEATH OF A SPOUSE

A. The traditional common-law approach (dower and curtesy): At common law during the feudal era, a wife who survived her husband did not normally inherit his property, nor did a husband who survived his wife. Instead, the surviving spouse was provided for by the doctrines of "dower" and "curtesy."

1. **Dower:** At common law, a widow was not the heir of her deceased husband; that is, if he died without a will, she took nothing. Instead, under the doctrine of primogeniture, all property went to the oldest son. Therefore, to provide for the widow (as well as to provide for her younger sons and all of her daughters, who similarly got nothing), the estate of *dower* was established.

    a. **What constitutes dower:** The estate of dower entitled a widow, on her husband's death, to a *life estate* in *one-third* of the lands of which he was seised at any time during their marriage, provided that the husband's interest was *inheritable by the issue* of the marriage (if any). So any land owned in *fee simple* by the husband alone, or in fee simple by the husband and a third person as tenants in common, qualified for dower.

        i. **No dower in life estate:** The requirement that the husband's interest had to be one which would be inheritable by the issue fo the marriage meant that there could be no dower in a *life estate* held by the husband, even one *per autre vie.*

    b. **Dower inchoate:** While the husband was still alive, the wife got a right of *dower inchoate* as soon as the husband became seised of any eligible freehold. One of the key features of common-law dower was that a conveyance of the freehold by the husband to a third party did *not affect the right of dower inchoate*. So the husband could not, by conveying property during his life, defeat the right of dower. If he purported to make such a conveyance, and then died, his widow could subsequently make her claim for dower against the holder of the property. Similarly, creditors of the husband's estate were subordinate to the dower rights — if the husband owned land, but died deeply in debt, dower rights were the widow's only chance of receiving anything. (However, the wife could, during the marriage, consent to release her inchoate dower interest in property so that the husband could transfer it free and clear.)

2. **Curtesy:** At common law, a *widower* was entitled to a *life estate* in *each piece of real property* in which the wife held a freehold interest during their marriage, provided the freehold was inheritable by the issue of the husband and the wife. This was known as the right of *"curtesy."*

    a. **Issue born alive:** Curtesy was similar to dower in most respects. The biggest difference was that the right of curtesy attached only where *issue of the marriage* were *born alive*. So if H and W were childless, and W predeceased H, H would have no right of curtesy.

    b. **Applies to all land, not one-third:** Also, whereas dower entitled the widow to a life interest in only one-third of her husband's inheritable freeholds, curtesy gave a life estate in *all* the wife's inheritable freeholds.

3. **Abolished in most jurisdictions:** As of 1991, dower and curtesy have both been *abolished* in all but *six* American jurisdictions (Arkansas, D.C., Kentucky, Ohio, Michigan and Iowa). See D&K, p. 401. Of these states, four have abolished curtesy and extended dower to husbands. *Id.* Also, Virginia abolished dower and curtesy in 1990 but preserves any dower or curtesy rights vested before then. *Id.*

4. **Practical importance:** In those states where dower or curtesy still exist, the main practical consequence is that *both husband and wife* must *sign any deed* if the recipient is to take free and clear of the right, even though only one spouse holds title. *Id.*

   a. **Elective share available:** The six states in which dower and/or curtesy still exist also give the surviving spouse the right to an "elective share" (see *infra* this page). The elective share is usually more generous than dower or curtesy. Therefore, the survivor almost always takes the elective share rather instead.

B. **Modern "elective share" statutes:** The modern substitute for dower and curtesy is the *"elective share"*. Under an elective share statute, the surviving spouse has the right to *renounce (or "take against") the will*, and instead receive a portion (set by statute) of the estate. All states following the common-law approach to property have a forced elective share statute, except for Georgia. D&K, 402.

   1. **Effect:** Since in community property states the surviving spouse is deemed to own half the marital property (see *infra*, p. 107), and since all common-law property states except Georgia now have forced elective shares, it is now virtually everywhere the case that *one spouse cannot "disinherit" the other*.

   2. **Personal as well as real property:** Forced elective share statutes virtually always apply to *personal property* as well as *real property*. (Contrast this with dower and curtesy, which apply only to real property.)

   3. **Size of share:** The elective share is usually expressed as a *fraction* of the property owned by the decedent at his or her death, not as a dollar amount. Most commonly, the fraction is *one-half* or *one-third*. D&K, 402. Usually, the elective share is somewhat less generous than the intestate share, giving the decedent some ability to disfavor the surviving spouse.

   4. **Property to which share applies:** The elective share generally applies only to property owned by the decedent *at death*. This is quite different from dower and curtesy, which attach to property owned at any time during the marriage.

      a. **Non-probate assets not included:** Only *probate assets* are typically included in the elective share. Thus assets passing outside of probate are generally *not* covered, including:

         i. *life insurance proceeds*; and

         ii. property held by the decedent and a third person as *joint tenants*.

      b. **Right to set aside certain transfers:** However, many states "call back" into the elective share certain assets that were transferred by the decedent before his death. For instance, many states count in the elective share gifts made by the decedent to third persons during the last few years of life (or gifts made with the apparent intent to defeat the elective share).

         i. **Assets controlled but not owned:** Similarly, many states count assets that the decedent didn't "own" at death, but that he or she *controlled*. For instance, assets in a revocable trust set up by the decedent are frequently treated as part of the elective share. D&K, 402.

   5. **Length of marriage irrelevant:** Most elective share statutes treat the *length of the marriage* as *irrelevant* — a woman widowed after one day of marriage gets the same fraction of her husband's estate as one married for 50 years.

    a. Contrast with community property: Contrast this with a community-property system (see *infra*, below), in which there is no elective share but property acquired by either party during the marriage, and wages earned by either party, are deemed owned 50/50 — under such a system, the longer the marriage, usually the larger the amount of marital property.

    b. Uniform Probate Code's sliding scale: Some jurisdictions are starting to believe that the community-property approach is better in this respect, and that the elective share should get larger the longer the marriage lasts. Thus the Uniform Probate Code was amended in 1990 to incorporate a *"sliding scale"* for the elective share — the longer the marriage, the larger the fractional share. The scale ranges from 3% for marriages of less than a year to 50% for marriages of 15 years or more. See UPC § 2-201.

IV. COMMUNITY PROPERTY

A. Introduction: In eight states, the system of marital property rights is completely different from the common-law system derived from dower and curtesy. The system of *community property* is in force in Arizona, California, Idaho, Louisiana, Nevada, New Mexico, Texas, and Washington. The system derives from European *civil-law* jurisprudence, not from the Anglo-American common law.

B. Basic theory: The basic premise of the community property system is that property acquired during a marriage results from the joint efforts of husband and wife. Implicitly, the system recognizes that a wife, even one who stays at home and does only housework and childbearing, contributes as much to the economic well-being of the marriage as does the husband who is the actual wage earner.

    1. Consequence: Consequently, the property acquired during the marriage (with certain exceptions discussed briefly below) belongs *jointly* to husband and wife from the moment it is acquired. This joint ownership has its most significant consequences when property is disposed of, or when the marriage terminates by divorce or death.

    2. Enactment, then repeal, in other states: During the 1940's, a number of states that had not previously had community property laws discovered that the community property system offered great tax benefits, since the husband and wife each claimed half of the family income, generally minimizing taxes. Therefore, five additional states (plus the then-territory of Hawaii) enacted community property laws. In 1948, however, the Internal Revenue Code was amended to allow couples in non-community property states to file a joint return, thus removing the community-property advantage. In response, five of the "new" community property states or territories repealed their laws, and in the sixth (Pennsylvania), the law was found unconstitutional.

    3. Not a detailed treatment: Community property is an extremely complex subject, which is often treated as a separate course in schools located in community property states. Furthermore, since community property systems are almost completely statutory, they vary substantially among the eight community property states. Therefore, our discussion below treats only a few major issues, and then only in an extremely general fashion.

C. What is community property: The biggest single issue in most community property disputes is whether the property at issue constitutes *community* property, or *separate* property. There is a *presumption* that all property acquired during the course of the marriage is *community* property, but this may be rebutted by a showing that the property is part of a class treated as separate property.

1. **Acquired before marriage:** All property acquired by either spouse *before marriage* is separate, not community, property.

2. **Acquired by gift or inheritance:** Property acquired by *gift, inheritance* or *bequest*, even after marriage, is separate property.

3. **Income from separate property:** *Income from separate property* is, in most states, separate property itself. Thus if H owns a bond before marrying W, not only is the bond separate, but any interest received on the bond after marriage is also, in most states, separate property. (But Idaho, Louisiana, and Texas treat income from separate property as being, in most circumstances, community property. C&L, p. 239.)

4. **Income and proceeds from community property:** *Income* that is earned from *community* property is itself community property. Furthermore, if community property is sold, and new assets are purchased with the sale proceeds, the assets are community property.

   a. **Title irrelevant:** Keep in mind that the *title* recited on a deed, stock certificate or other form of property is *irrelevant*. If H sells a bond that is community property, and uses the cash proceeds to buy a car, the car is community property even if the bill of sale and certificate of title are in his name alone.

5. **Earnings:** A key feature of the system is that income produced by either spouse's *labor* is *community property*. Thus if H is an employee, his salary is community property. Furthermore, if he receives stock in his employer, pension rights or insurance, these would be treated as fruits of his labor, and therefore community property.

   a. **Closely-held business started before marriage:** One of the most difficult problems arises when H starts a business prior to the marriage, and continues to run it thereafter. If the business increases in value, H can argue that the increase was a return on his premarital (and therefore separate) investment. W can argue that the increase is due to H's labor and skill, and is therefore community property.

      i. **Two views:** There are two different methods typically used by the courts in resolving this kind of issue. One is to estimate the capital investment in the business (which is separate property), allow a reasonable rate of interest on that investment (making the interest separate property), and treat the rest as community earnings attributable to the husband's labor. This is known in California as the *Pereira* approach). The other is the reverse: first, the reasonable value of the husband's services in running the business is measured, and treated as community property. The balance is treated as separate property attributable to the return on the initial investment. (This is referred to in California as the *Van Camp* approach).

6. **Purchases made on credit:** When property is bought on *credit*, it will frequently not be clear whether the property is community or separate property. If the note or obligation is signed by only one spouse, and is secured by separate property belonging to that spouse, the asset is separate property. But in most other situations (e.g., note signed by the husband, but no security given), courts are likely to find that the asset is a community one. See 2 A.L.P. 151-55.

a. **Down payment made before marriage:** A similar problem arises when a down payment is made out of separate property (e.g., H supplies the down payment to buy a house, and then marries W), and community funds are then used to finish paying for the purchase. There are at least three ways of handling this; perhaps the most reasonable is to treat the property as part separate and part community, in proportion to the separate and community funds used to pay for it. See B,C&S, p. 326.

7. **Conflict of laws:** Complications arise when the parties live in one state and acquire property located in another. Similarly, the effect of a *change of domicile* from one state to another is sometimes complicated.

   a. **Domicile in community property state at time of acquisition:** If the parties live in a community property state at the time they acquire property, the property's status depends on whether it is realty or personalty.

      i. **Realty:** If *real estate* is acquired, the law of the state *where the land is situated* determines whether the land is community or separate property. Thus if H and W are residents of California (a community property state), and they use money saved from the husband's salary to buy land in New York (not a community property state), the law of New York applies. The property is therefore separate property, belonging to either H or W or both, depending on how the deed is drafted. B,C&S, p. 327.

      ii. **Personalty:** But any *personal property* the couple acquire is measured by the law of the *state of domicile*. Thus if H and W live in California, and buy a car in New York while on vacation, California law applies. If the car is purchased with savings from the husband's salary, it is community property.

      iii. **Move to non-community state:** If the parties *then* move to a non-community property state, the property keeps whatever status it had as of the time of its acquisition. Thus community assets acquired in California remain such if the parties move to New York. C&L, p. 240-44.

   b. **Property acquired before move to community state:** But if the parties live first in a non-community property state, buy assets, and then move to a community property state, the law is less clear. Certainly *real estate* is evaluated by the laws of the state *where the land is located*, just as if the parties had lived in a community property state when they bought the land.

      i. **Personal property:** Where personal property is concerned, most states apply the law of the *domicile* at the time of acquisition. Thus a car bought while the parties reside in New York would remain the separate property of whomever held formal title to it, even if the parties moved to, say, Texas.

      ii. **California "quasi-community property" rule:** But California has made such personal property "*quasi*-community property". The property is separate property in the sense that the non-owner spouse has no testamentary rights in it, and has no right of control, management or disposition. But when a divorce occurs, or the owner dies, the property is treated as if it were community property; thus the divorce court may assign one-half (or in certain cases even more) to the non-owner, and the non-owner gets a one-half interest as survivor. Burby, p. 242.

8. **Transformation of status:** Property which starts out as being separate property can be *transformed* into community property by act of the owning spouse. Thus if H owns a house when he marries W, he may be found to have made either a written or oral agreement to treat the house as belonging jointly to H and W.

D. **Management:** The right to *manage and control* community property has been subject to great change in recent years.

  1. **Traditional view:** Traditionally, the right to manage and control the property was given exclusively to the husband; his role was that of a fiduciary, who was required to act with due regard to his wife's interests as well as his own.

    a. **Personal property:** This meant that the husband could convey personal property to a third person, even without adequate consideration, and the third person would take free and clear of the wife's interest. (However, the husband, as fiduciary, would be liable to the wife if he misused his authority by giving the property away or receiving too little money for it.)

    b. **Real property:** But a *conveyance or mortgage of real property*, or a lease for more than a year, have generally not been allowable unless the *wife joins*.

  2. **Greater role for women:** Most of the community property states have changed their statutes in the last ten years, to give the spouses roughly *equal management and control rights*. For instance, the California Code is now sexually neutral with respect to control; either spouse may manage and control any item of community property, but most conveyances of personal as well as real property require the written consent of both spouses. See Cal. Civil Code §§ 5125, 5127.

E. **Divorce:** In most states, and in most circumstances, when *divorce* occurs the community property is *evenly divided*. However, some states allow the court to divide the community property as it sees fit, if the divorce is granted on grounds of adultery or extreme cruelty; the court may thus award more than half to the innocent spouse. Burby, p. 261. If the divorce is given to *both* parties, an even division of community property is always required.

F. **Death:** Upon the *death* of one of the parties, the community property is treated as having belonged half to the deceased spouse and half to the surviving spouse. The half belonging to the deceased spouse is thus subject to his right to devise it by will to whomever he wishes. If no testamentary disposition is made, the property passes in some states to the surviving spouse (who now owns the entire interest), and in other states to the issue or heirs. Burby, p. 263.

G. **Uniform Marital Property Act:** Many of the concepts of community property are embodied in the 1983 *Uniform Marital Property Act*. For instance, property acquired during the marriage is treated by the Act as "marital property", in which each spouse has an undivided one-half interest. Each spouse can then *bequeath* that one-half interest however he or she wishes. See Cribbet, pp. 97-100.

  1. **Divorce:** Under the Uniform Act, in the event of *divorce* the property is distributed under the state's divorce-based system, not as provided in the Act. In nearly all non-community-property states, the system for dividing property upon divorce is "equitable distribution", a concept that looks to fairness rather than to who holds legal title.

  2. **Wisconsin adopts:** So far only one state, Wisconsin, has adopted the Uniform Marital Property Act. D&K, p. 404.

V. HOMESTEAD EXEMPTIONS

A. Purpose of homestead exemptions: Most states have enacted so-called *"homestead exemptions"*. The purpose of these homestead laws is to ensure that general creditors of a homeowner cannot have the property sold to satisfy a money judgement; thus the ability of the homeowner and his family to keep the residence is maintained.

1. **Usually limited dollar amount:** The homestead statutes almost never provide that the homestead is immune from creditors regardless of its size or cost. Instead, most states establish a dollar limit (e.g., $10,000 in New York); if the home is worth more than that, it may be sold at the behest of creditors, but the homeowner gets to keep the statutory dollar amount. Other states place a limit on the acreage of the real estate.

2. **Subject to purchase-money mortgages:** In all states, the exemption does *not apply* to a *purchase-money mortgage*, i.e., a mortgage given as security for a loan used to buy the property in the first place. Powell, Par. 263, p. 193.

3. **Right of surviving spouse:** Where title to homestead property is held by one spouse, if that spouse dies first the *surviving spouse* usually continues to have some degree of protection against creditors of the other's estate. Also, some states limit the extent to which the spouse who has title may *devise* the property. See generally B,C&S, p. 277 and C&J, pp. 336.

B. Bankruptcy Law: The Federal Bankruptcy Act (which went into effect in 1979) grants a homestead exemption of its own, in *bankruptcy cases*. The bankrupt's property used as a residence is exempt up to a value of $7,500. (If an exemption in a residence is not claimed up to this amount, the amount not claimed may be applied to any other assets, such as bank accounts, stocks and bonds, etc.; the intent is to avoid discriminating against non-homeowners.) See §522(d)(1), (5).

1. **State alternative:** Alternatively, the bankrupt may take advantage of the *state exemption* given by the state of his domicile, if he feels this is more advantageous. §522(b)(2).

2. **State may forbid federal exemption:** But the Act gives each state the right to enact a statute *preventing* its citizens from claiming the federal exemption. In that case, the bankrupt is forced to use the state exemption. §522(b)(1).

   Note: In addition to the real property homestead exemption discussed above, nearly all states, and the federal Bankruptcy Act, also provide certain exemptions for various items of personal property (e.g., prescription drugs, farm implements, the family Bible, etc.).

Chapter Review Questions

(Answers are at back of book)

31. In 1960, O conveyed Blueacre, a 900-acre farm, to H. In 1965, H married W. In 1970, H, in return for reasonable consideration, delivered to A a deed in fee simple for Blueacre. In 1980, H died. What is the state of title in Blueacre? (Assume that the common law is in force in all relevant particulars.)

32. H and W live in a community property state. If H and W are divorced, which of the following items will be community property? (Assume that H and W's divorce is no-fault.)

(a) Blackacre, which W bought before the marriage, and which has remained in her name before the divorce.

(b) Whiteacre, which W inherited from her father after the marriage, and which has remained in her name until the divorce.

(c) $20,000 in a bank account entitled "H and W jointly," representing net rental proceeds paid by a tenant of Whiteacre; all of these payments were made after W inherited the property as described in (b) above.

(d) $100,000 in a bank account in H's name alone; this represents money earned by H from his salary during the years following the marriage, while working for ABC Corp., a large company.

(e) Stock in ABC Corp. held in H's name, which he received as part of ABC Corp.'s stock ownership plan.

(f) A summer home purchased by H, in his own name, from which the down payment and all subsequent mortgage payments have been made out of H's earnings.

CONCURRENT OWNERSHIP

Introductory note: This chapter examines various ways in which two or more persons may own present possessory interests in the same property. The three varieties of co-tenancy are: (1) joint tenancy (which includes the right of survivorship; (2) tenancy in common (which does not have the right of survivorship); and (3) tenancy by the entirety; which exists only between husband and wife, and which includes not only survivorship but indestructibility, in the sense that neither party can convey his interest or otherwise destroy the right of survivorship. After these three types of co-ownership are discussed, various issues involving the relation between parties (e.g., the right to possession of the premises, the duty to account for rents received from third persons, etc.) are treated.

I. JOINT TENANCY

A. Each tenant owns whole interest: In a *joint tenancy*, two or more people own a *single, unified*, interest in real or personal property. Each joint tenant has exactly the same rights in the property; thus one cannot have a greater interest than the other.

    1. Right of survivorship: Perhaps the most significant feature of the joint tenancy is that each joint tenant has a *right of survivorship*. That is, if there are two joint tenants, and one dies, the other becomes sole survivor of the interest that the two of them had previously held jointly. Survivorship is discussed more fully *infra*, p. 116.

    2. Right of possession: In a sense, each of the joint tenants owns the "entire" interest, subject only to the rights of the other(s). While this may sound somewhat metaphysical, it has one clear consequence: each joint tenant is entitled to *occupy* the *entire* premises, subject only to the same right of occupancy by the other tenants. Thus the parties are not required to divide up the premises for occupancy, though they are free to do this if all agree. Relations between joint tenants (and between other types of co-tenants, including tenants in common and tenants by the entirety) are discussed *infra*, p. 125.

B. Four unities: Under the traditional common-law view, a joint tenancy exists only where the so-called *"four unities"* exist: (1) the unity of "interest", (2) the unity of "title", (3) the unity of "time" and (4) the unity of "possession". See Moynihan, p. 217.

    1. Unity of interest: Unity of *interest* means that the joint tenants must have *identical interests*, both as to their share, and as to the *duration* of their interest. Thus one joint tenant *cannot* have a *one-fourth* interest and the other a *three-fourths* interest. Similarly, if one person has a one-half interest for life, and the other has a one-half interest in fee simple, the two are not joint tenants because the durations are not identical. See 2 A.L.P. 6.

    2. Unity of title: Unity of *title* means that the joint tenants must each acquire title by the *same deed or will*.

    3. Unity of time: The unity of *time* means that each joint tenant's interest must *vest at the same time*.

        a. Conveyance by A to A and B: One consequence of the requirement of unity of time is that, at common law, the owner of a fee simple cannot directly create a joint tenancy in himself and another. Thus if A owns a fee simple, he cannot convey "to

A and B as joint tenants"; since one cannot convey to oneself, it follows that B's interest vests at a later time than A's (which has already vested). Modern statutes frequently change this rule; see *infra*, p. 115.

4. **Unity of possession:** Unity of *possession* means that all the joint tenants have a right to possess and enjoy the entire property. (This unity, unlike the other three, also exists as to tenants in common.)

C. Creation of joint tenancies: At common law, there was a *presumption* that any co-tenancy was a joint tenancy, unless a clear intention to create a tenancy in common was shown. (The presumption did not apply where the co-tenants were husband and wife; here there was a presumption that a tenancy by the entirety was intended; see *infra*, p. 122.)

1. **Source of presumption:** This presumption arose from the fact that the joint tenancy included a right of survivorship; if one of two joint tenants died, the entire interest in the property would be in the surviving joint tenant. This is turn meant that all feudal obligations would be owed by one person; this was more desirable to the feudal lord than was a tenancy in common, where upon the tenant's death his interest passed not to the surviving tenant but to the deceased tenant's own heirs, thus dividing the feudal obligations. See Moynihan, p. 217.

2. **Modern statutes reverse presumption:** Feudal obligations are obviously of no significance today. Therefore, all states have *reversed* the common-law presumption, and now presume a co-tenancy is a *tenancy in common* unless there is a clear intent to establish a joint tenancy. Most states have done this by statute; some have done it by case law.

   a. **Exception for fiduciaries and executors:** However, the modern presumption in favor of the tenancy in common generally does *not apply* to *fiduciaries and executors*. For instance, if Blackacre is conveyed to A and B as trustees for the benefit of C, it is desirable that B take sole title to the property if A dies, so that the fiduciary duties will not be split among B and A's heirs. 2 A.L.P. 12.

3. **Ambiguous language:** The usual (and clearest) phrasing used to create a joint tenancy is "*to A and B as joint tenants with right of survivorship, and not as tenants in common*." There are some formulations, however, which hint that a joint tenancy may be desired, but which are sufficiently ambiguous that the modern presumption in favor of tenancies in common might nonetheless be applicable. Two of these formulations are as follows:

   a. **To A and B "jointly":** Suppose property is conveyed "to A and B *jointly*." A few courts have held that the use of the word "jointly" is enough to make the ownership a joint tenancy. But most courts have held that the term "jointly" is ambiguous, and that the usual presumption in favor of a tenancy in common applies. 2 A.L.P. 13.

   b. **"To A and B and the survivor and his heirs":** Sometimes a conveyance is made "to A and B and to the *survivor*, and to the survivor's heirs." The courts are divided as to the interpretation of such a conveyance. Some hold that it creates a joint tenancy in fee simple. But others interpret it as creating a *joint life estate*, with a *contingent remainder in fee simple* to the survivor. If so, the right of survivorship cannot be *destroyed*, as it can in the case of the conventional joint tenancy in fee simple; see *infra*, p. 116.

Example: O conveys Blackacre "to Nathan Palmer and Alice Palmer as joint tenants, and not as tenants in common, to them and their assigns and to the survivor, and the heirs and assigns of the survivor forever." Alice and Nathan are divorced, and Alice gives Nathan a quitclaim deed. Nathan then (by use of a "straw man"; see *infra*) puts the property in the name of himself and his sister, Roxa, as joint tenants. Nathan then dies. Alice sues Roxa, claiming that the original conveyance to Alice and Nathan established a joint life estate with a contingent remainder in fee to the survivor, and that Alice's quitclaim deed to Nathan did not transfer her contingent remainder (under a probably now obsolete law restricting transfers of contingent remainders; see *supra*, p. 74).

Held, the original conveyance created a joint tenancy in fee simple, not a joint life estate with a contingent remainder to the survivor. Although the phrasing of the conveyance is not standard, the parties intended a conventional joint tenancy (which is subject to severance), not an unseverable remainder in fee simple in the survivor. Therefore, Alice's quitclaim deed to Nathan conveyed all her interest, and Roxa is now the owner in fee simple. *Palmer v. Flint*, 161 A.2d 837 (Me. 1960).

4. **Conveyance by A to A and B:** Frequently the holder of a fee simple interest will wish to establish a joint tenancy between ***himself and another***. The most direct way to do this, of course, would be to convey to himself and that other person as joint tenants; thus A would convey his fee simple "to A and B as joint tenants."

   a. **Common law view prohibits:** But this could not be done at common law. Recall that two of the "four unities" were those of ***time*** and ***title***. (*Supra*, p. 113.) Because of the common-law rule that no person could convey to himself, a conveyance that purported to be from A to "A and B as joint tenants" really conveyed only a one-half interest to B. Both the unity of time and the unity of title were therefore broken, and A and B took as tenants in common.

      i. **Conveyance to "straw man":** Therefore, if A wished to create a joint tenancy in himself and B, he had to convey to a *"straw man"*. He would thus convey to C and C would in turn convey to A and B as joint tenants.

   b. **Modern view allows direct creation:** But many states have enacted ***statutes*** explicitly authorizing the holder of a fee simple to create a joint tenancy in himself and another. Other states have reached this result by ***case law***.

Example: Mrs. Wagar, an elderly woman, has two nieces, P and D. She lives with D, and sets up a joint checking account and joint safe deposit box, both in the names of herself and D. She also takes half of her stock certificates and has the ownership changed to be "Mrs. Wagar and [D], as joint tenants with right of survivorship and not as tenants in common." Mrs. Wagar and D agree that Mrs. Wagar will have full rights to the dividends for her life. The stocks, and all dividends, are kept in the safe deposit box. Mrs. Wagar dies. D concedes that all property in the box belongs to the estate (of which P and D are both beneficiaries), except that she claims that the stock is also part of the estate, on the grounds that the joint tenancy was simply for the convenience of Mrs. Wagar.

Held, for D. Even though the other contents of the box were admittedly part of the estate, Mrs. Wagar manifested a clear intention that D would take the stock if she were to survive Mrs. Wagar. Testimony as to Mrs. Wagar's intention was admissible; her accountant testified that her intent was to treat the stock as being in joint tenancy with D. Also, the creation of the joint tenancy does not fail because of destruction of the "four unities". Since Mrs. Wagar could have created the tenancy by conveying to a straw man and having it reconveyed to her and D as joint tenants, there is no sound reason to prevent this result from being accomplished directly, as a majority of states now permit. Finally, the fact that the dividends from the stock were to go solely to Mrs. Wagar does not mean that the stock itself was not in joint tenancy; joint tenants are always free to make any agreement they wish regarding use of the property, including its income. *Miller v. Riegler*, 419 S.W.2d 599 (Ark. 1967).

5. **Personal property:** Joint tenancies may also be created in ***personal property***. The statutes establishing a presumption in favor of tenancies in common apply to personal property as well as real property.

   a. **Bank accounts:** One common example of a joint tenancy in personal property is the ***joint bank account***, either checking, savings, or safe deposit. Typically, the depositor signs bank documents stating that either party may remove all or part of the contents at any time, and that upon the death of one, the other shall have sole title. In a sense, therefore, these documents provide for a joint tenancy. Joint bank accounts are discussed more fully *supra*, p. 22.

D. **Right of survivorship:** As noted, the principal distinguishing feature of the joint tenancy is that the ***surviving*** tenant has the ***entire interest*** in the property. The deceased tenant does not have the ability to ***leave his interest by will***, nor is there anything to pass by intestacy to his heirs. Strictly speaking, what happens is that there are two joint tenants each of whom owns a complete interest, and when one of them dies, the other has an interest that is no longer subject to the former's rights. But, loosely speaking, the survivor is said to receive the other's interest under a "***right of survivorship***".

   1. **Dower and curtesy do not attach:** Because a joint tenancy is not an estate of inheritance, ***no rights of dower and curtesy*** attach. 2 A.L.P. 11.

   2. **Creditors:** A ***creditor*** of one joint tenant does not have rights against the interest of the other joint tenant. Therefore, if the debtor joint tenant dies first, the surviving joint tenant usually takes the property ***free and clear*** of the deceased tenant's creditor. Moynihan, p. 220. However, in some states there are statutes preserving an attachment, mortgage, or other lien on a joint tenant's interest after his death. Moynihan, p. 220, n. 2. See the discussion of mortgages *infra*, p. 118.

E. **Severance:** There are a number of ways in which a joint tenancy may be ***severed***; severance will normally result in the creation of a ***tenancy in common***.

   1. **Conveyance by one joint tenant:** A joint tenant may ***convey*** his interest to a ***third party***. Since this third party does not have unity of time or title (*supra*, p. 113) with the remaining original joint tenant, the joint tenancy relationship has been destroyed.

      a. **Joint tenancy between two persons:** Thus if there are two original joint tenants, A and B, and A conveys his interest to C, B and C become ***tenants in common***, not joint tenants.

      b. **Where three or more joint tenants:** Suppose, however, that there are ***three*** or more original joint tenants. A conveyance by one of them to a stranger will produce a ***tenancy in common*** as between the ***stranger and the remaining original joint tenants***, but the ***joint tenancy will continue*** as between the ***original members***.

Example: A, B, and C hold Blackacre as joint tenants. A conveys his interest to X. The conveyance by A severs the joint tenancy as between A and the other two. Thus X holds an undivided one-third interest in the property as a tenant in common with B and C. B and C holds a two-thirds interest, but they hold this interest as joint tenants with each other, not as tenants in common. Thus if X dies, his interest goes to his heirs or devisees. But if B dies, his interest goes to C.

c. **Conveyance between joint tenants:** Essentially the same analysis applies if there are three joint tenants, and one conveys to *another of the joint tenants*. As to the interest conveyed, the grantee becomes a tenant in common. But as to the interest not conveyed, the joint tenancy survives.

Example: O devises Blackacre to his sisters, Nellie, Anna, and Katherine, as joint tenants. Nellie then conveys all her interest in the property to Anna. Anna then dies, bequeathing her interest in the property to her four nieces, the Ps. The Ps sue Katherine, claiming that the conveyance by Nellie severed the entire joint tenancy, and that Anna thereby gained a two-thirds interest in the property held as tenants in common with Katherine's one-third interest. The four Ps thus claim to each have a one-sixth interest.

Held, for Katherine. Nellie's conveyance of her interest severed the joint tenancy, but *only as to that share*; Anna then held this share as a tenant in common with Katherine. But as to the remaining interest in the property, Anna and Katherine continued to hold this interest (representing two-thirds) as joint tenants. Katherine gained sole title to this two-thirds interest upon Anna's death, so that the four Ps each hold only one-fourth of one-third, or one-twelfth. *Jackson v. O'Connell*, 177 N.E.2d 194 (Ill. 1961).

d. **Conveyance to one's self:** Suppose a joint tenant tries to terminate the joint tenant's fee by conveying his interest to *himself*. Since the joint tenant could terminate the joint tenancy by conveying to third person, and that third person could then re-convey to the original joint tenant (thus leaving the original joint tenant with a tenancy in common), why shouldn't the joint tenant be able to accomplish the same objective without all the hocus-pocus of a "straw man"? At least one court (in the case set forth in the following example) has held that a conveyance by a joint tenant to himself, made for the purpose of terminating the joint tenancy, does indeed have that effect.

Example: T learns that certain property is held by herself and P (her husband) as joint tenants. She wants to be able to bequeath the property to someone other than P. She therefore executes a deed in which she grants to herself an undivided one-half interest in the property; the deed states that its purpose is to terminate the joint tenancy. Simultaneously, she executes a will leaving her one-half interest in the property to someone else. She then dies.

Held, the deed by T to herself was effective to terminate the joint tenancy. A transfer by T to X, followed by a re-transfer by X to T, would have sufficed to terminate the joint tenancy. Therefore, there is no reason that T could not accomplish the same result without use of a straw-man intermediary. Since T always had the power to sever the tenancy, allowing her to do this by grant to herself does not enlarge her powers. Therefore, T's undivided one-half interest in the property passes by her will, not by right of survivorship to P. *Riddle v. Harmon*, 162 Cal. Rptr. 530 (Cal. Ct. App. 1980).

Note: Observe that P, in *Riddle*, would not necessarily ever have learned about the termination until T died and her will was read — P could have gone for years thinking that he held a joint tenancy when he did not. Allowing T to terminate the joint tenancy without giving notice to P can therefore be criticized as unfairly violating P's reliance interest. Also, allowing the joint tenant to break the tenancy by transferring to herself can be criticized as an invitation to *fraud* — for instance, the deed executed by T to herself in *Riddle* was never recorded and did not have to meet any sort of formalities, so it could have been forged after T's death by a beneficiary under her will. See D&K, pp. 335-36.

2. **Granting of mortgage:** Jurisdictions are not in agreement as to whether the ***granting of a mortgage*** by one joint tenant severs the joint tenancy. The answer in a particular state depends principally upon whether the state treats a mortgage as representing a transfer of title, or as merely being a lien to secure repayment.

     a. **Title theory states:** In some states, the mortgagor, by granting the mortgage, is deemed to transfer title to the property to the mortgagee. In such a state, called a "title theory" state, the mortgage is, not surprisingly, a severance since it is a conveyance. Moynihan, p. 222. If the mortgage is defaulted upon, the mortgagee can foreclose on the undivided one-half interest of the mortgagor, and have this auctioned at the foreclosure sale. The interest of the other party is not affected.

     b. **Lien theory state:** Most states, however, follow the *"lien theory"* of mortgages, by which a mortgage is deemed to be merely a security for repayment, and not a transfer of title. In such states, the mortgage does not act as a severance, at least in the sense that the right of survivorship is not destroyed. However, in lien theory states, the key issue becomes: Is the mortgage enforceable if the mortgagor *dies* before the other tenant? Courts in lien theory states are split on this issue.

         i. **Mortgage remains effective:** Some states, either by case-law or statute, hold that the mortgage can be ***enforced*** against the decedent's interest (so that the case is treated basically as if the state were a title theory state — the foreclosing mortgagee auctions off the decedent's one-half interest, with the survivor given the right to pay off the mortgage if he chooses). C,S&W, pp. 201-02.

         ii. **Mortgage not effective:** But other states take the view that the mortgage is ***not effective*** if the mortgagor dies before the other tenant.

     Example: P and his brother, B, own property as joint tenants. Without P's knowledge, B and his friend D1 sign a note in favor of D2, and B gives a mortgage on the joint property to secure this note. B dies before the note is paid. B bequeaths all his property to D1. P brings suit to have the court declare that P takes the entire property by right of survivorship, and that D2's mortgage was extinguished on B's death.

     Held, for P. Illinois is a lien theory state, so P's execution of a mortgage did not sever the joint tenancy. Upon B's death, P therefore became the sole owner of the property. Furthermore, the mortgage was merely a lien on B's interest in the joint tenancy; since B's interest ceased to exist the moment he died, so did the lien on his interest. Therefore, P holds sole title to the property, and D2's lien is extinguished. *Harms v. Sprague*, 473 N.E.2d 930 (Ill. 1984).

3. **Lease:** If one joint tenant executes a ***lease***, the courts are also in dispute about whether the joint tenancy is severed. Most courts probably hold that such a lease (which applies only to the lessor's interest in the property) is ***not*** a severance. See, e.g., *Swartzbaugh v.*

Sampson, 54 P.2d 73 (D.C. App. Cal. 1936), holding that where the lessee was in sole possession of the premises, the non-lessor joint tenant could not have the lease judicially rescinded.

   a. Where non-lessor survives: If the granting of a lease by one joint tenant is not a severance, the issue then arises as to the lease's status if the lessor *predeceases* the other joint tenant. Most courts hold that the lease is *invalid* against the non-lessor joint tenant. See, e.g., *Tenhet v. Boswell*, 554 P.2d 330 (Cal. 1976).

4. Partition: The joint tenancy can be severed by *partition*, i.e., the dividing up and distribution of the land (partition "in kind") or the sale of the land and distribution of the proceeds. This can be done either by agreement of the parties, or by court order at the request of one party. See *infra*, p. 129.

   a. Contract to sever: Similarly, the parties may make an *agreement* to sever the joint tenancy, even without partitioning the property.

   i. Separation agreement: For instance, this can be done as part of a *separation agreement* between a husband and wife. Thus in *Mann v. Bradley*, 535 P.2d 213 (Colo. 1975), H and W owned the family residence as joint tenants. Their separation agreement, incorporated into their subsequent divorce, provided that the family residence should be sold and the proceeds divided if W remarried, if the couple's youngest child reached 21, or if the parties mutually agreed to sell. The court held that, notwithstanding a provision in the agreement that the property "shall remain in the joint names of the parties," the separation agreement constituted an agreement that the right of survivorship would no longer apply. Therefore, H and W became tenants in common, and W's undivided one-half interest in the property passed upon her death to her children, not by right of survivorship to H.

5. Contract to sell: A few courts have held that a *contract to sell* the property, when executed by all of the joint tenants, severs the joint tenancy even before title is actually transferred. Moynihan, p. 223. If the sale goes through, the courts are in dispute about whether the purchase money is held as joint tenants or as tenants in common. *Id.*

6. Wrongful act: A *wrongful act* by one joint tenant to the other may cause a severance. For instance, in *Duncan v. Vassaur*, 550 P.2d 929 (Ok. 1976), W shot and killed H; the court held that the homicide was "inconsistent with the continued existence of the joint tenancy" between W and H. Therefore, the court treated the property as going one-half to H's heirs and the other half to W, as tenants in common.

   Note: Observe that the doctrine of severance, insofar as it results in a termination of the right of survivorship, applies only to joint tenancies, and not to joint *life estates* with a contingent *remainder* in fee to the survivor. In the latter case, the right of survivorship is more or less indestructible. See *Holbrook v. Holbrook*, 403 P.2d 12 (Or. 1965), discussed *infra*.

F. Abolition in a few states: In at least two states, Georgia and Oregon, joint tenancies have been completely *abolished*. In a number of other states, joint tenancies continue to exist, but the *right of survivorship* has been either abolished or required to be expressly provided for in the creating instrument. Arizona, Illinois, Kentucky, North Carolina, Tennessee, Texas, and Washington are among the states that have done this. See 2 A.L.P. 14, n. 12, and A.L.P., 1976 Supp., p. 163, n. 12. Insofar as such a statute has the effect, in a particular case, of eliminating the right of survivorship, the joint tenancy is for practical purposes transformed into a tenancy in common, even though it may still be called a joint tenancy.

1. **Joint life estates with contingent remainders:** In a state where joint tenancies have been completely abolished, or where the right of survivorship in a joint tenancy has been abolished, courts will sometimes be faced with a conveyance expressly providing for the right of survivorship. One solution is to treat the language as establishing *concurrent life estates*, with a *remainder* in fee simple in the survivor. See e.g., *Holbrook v. Holbrook*, 403 P.2d 12 (Or. 1965).

II. TENANCY IN COMMON

A. Nature of tenancy in common: The tenancy in common, like the joint tenancy, is an estate shared by two or more people in the same property at the same time. But whereas in a joint tenancy each party has an equal interest in the whole, each tenant in common has a *separate* "undivided" interest. The most important practical difference between the tenancy in common and the joint tenancy is that there is *no right of survivorship* between tenants in common.

1. **Only one unity required:** Recall that a joint tenancy must have four "unities"; see *supra*, p. 113. The tenancy in common, by contrast, requires only *one unity*, the unity of *possession*. That is, each tenant in common is entitled to possession of the *whole property*, subject to the same rights in the other tenants. But since the unities of time, title, and interest are not required, the tenants may receive their interests at *different times* and by *different conveyances*.

     a. **May have unequal shares:** Even more importantly, the tenants in common may have *unequal shares*. Thus A and B may hold as tenants in common, with A holding an "undivided one-quarter interest" and B an "undivided three-quarters interest". Similarly, A may hold an undivided one-half life estate, and B an undivided one-half fee simple; the two could still be tenants in common with respect to each other. See Moynihan, p. 224.

         i. **Presumption as to size of interest:** If the conveyance does not state the size of the interest of each tenant in common, there is a *presumption* that the shares are *equal*. But this presumption may be *rebutted* by evidence, drawn from surrounding circumstances, that unequal shares were intended. For instance, suppose that A and B (not husband and wife) take title to Blackacre as tenants in common, and that A puts up one-third of the money and B two-thirds; if B can show that there was no intent by him to make a gift to A, he will be held to have a two-thirds interest. See 2 A.L.P. 20.

B. No right of survivorship: Each tenant in common takes his share as an individual; this is in contrast to the joint tenancy, where the joint tenants take as a single "unit". As a consequence, each tenant in common has the right to make a *testamentary transfer* of his interest, and if he dies intestate, his interest will *pass under the statutes of descent*. In other words, there is *no right of survivorship*.

     Example: A and B take title to Blackacre as tenants in common. They have equal shares. A dies, without a will, leaving only one relative, a son S. Title to Blackacre is now: a one-half undivided interest in S, and a one-half undivided interest in B.

1. **Right to convey or lease:** Similarly, the tenant in common may convey his undivided interest, or lease it to a third party. If he leases it, he may have the duty to share the

rents with his co-tenants; see *infra*, p. 127.

C. Presumption favoring tenancy in common: As noted, most states now have either a statutory or case law *presumption* in favor of tenancies in common rather than joint tenancies, as long as the co-tenants are not husband and wife. See *supra*, p. 114.

D. Heirs: A tenancy in common can, of course, be created by action of the parties (e.g., O conveys "to A and B as tenants in common.") But such a tenancy can also result from *operation of law*; one common way is through *intestacy*. Where the intestacy statute specifies that two persons are to take an equal interest as co-heirs, they take as tenants in common.

> **Example:** A, the fee simple owner of Blackacre, dies without a will. His sole surviving relatives are a son, S, and a daughter, D. Under the local intestacy statute, where a person is survived by two or more children and not by a spouse, the children share equally. S and D will therefore take title to Blackacre as tenants in common, each holding an undivided one-half interest.

1. Coparceny: At common law, heirs who took as co-tenants had a special estate, called *coparceny*. However, today the rights of heirs who take as co-tenants are identical to the rights of tenants in common, so that the separate category of coparceny has disappeared.

III. TENANCY BY THE ENTIRETY

A. Common-law concept of entirety: At common law, the husband and wife were regarded as *one person*. (See *supra*, p. 101.) As a consequence, there was a special form of co-ownership between husband and wife, the *tenancy by the entirety*.

1. Four unities required: The same four unities required in the case of joint tenancy (*supra*, p. 113) must be met for a common-law tenancy by the entirety.

2. Right of survivorship: Similarly, the surviving spouse has a *right of survivorship*.

3. No severance: The critical difference between the tenancy by the entirety and the joint tenancy is that as to the former, there is *no doctrine of severance*, i.e., no way to terminate the tenancy while husband and wife are both still alive and still married. The indestructibility of the tenancy by the entirety is discussed further *infra*, p. 122.

B. Creation of estate: At common law, *any conveyance* to two persons who were in fact husband and wife *necessarily* resulted in a tenancy by the entirety. 2 A.L.P. 24. Even if the conveyance stated that H and W were to take "as joint tenants" or "as tenants in common", a tenancy by the entirety was created, since the husband and wife were one person for legal purposes.

1. No creation by one spouse: Because of the strict requirement of the four unities, a man or a woman who owned a fee simple could not create a tenancy by the entirety by conveying a partial interest to his spouse. Instead, as with a joint tenancy, title had to be conveyed to a "straw man", and reconveyed to the husband and wife.

2. Modern view: The modern view universally treats husband and wife as two individuals. Consequently, *only twenty-two states* retain the tenancy by the entirety at all. (The eight community property states never had it in the first place, and twenty states have abolished it). See Moynihan, p. 231.

3. Presumption favoring entirety: In those states where the tenancy by the entirety survives, there is usually a *presumption* that a conveyance to persons who are actually husband and wife is intended to create a tenancy by the entirety. 2 A.L.P. 25. However, in most of these states the presumption is a **rebuttable** one, so that if there is outside evidence that a tenancy in common or a joint tenancy was intended, or if the deed itself contains the words "joint tenants" or "tenants in common", the grantor's intention will be respected.

    a. Exception in few states: But in a few states, the presumption in favor of the tenancy by the entirety remains so strong that even the use of the words "joint tenancy" or "tenancy in common" in the deed will **not** be sufficient to rebut it.

    b. Presumption favoring tenancy in common: In those minority states that still recognize the tenancy by the entirety, but do not presume that a conveyance to a husband and wife creates such an estate, the presumption is generally that a **tenancy in common** is created. See Moynihan, p. 231, n. 3. This is in keeping with the modern tendency to presume a tenancy in common in preference to a joint tenancy (*supra*, p. 114).

4. Conveyance to husband, wife and third person: Occasionally, a conveyance is made to H, W and a **third person**. Unless otherwise specified, H and W will take a one-half interest, and the third person will take the other one-half interest. The two units will hold as tenants in common to each other. But H and W will hold their one-half interest as tenants by the entirety with respect to each other, so that if H dies, W will take the entire one-half interest.

5. Personal property: At common law, there could not be a tenancy by the entirety in **personal property**. But most states that now allow such tenancies at all allow them in personal as well as real property.

    a. Minority forbids tenancy in personalty: But a few states, including Michigan, New Jersey and New York, do not allow a tenancy by the entirety in personal property.

6. Invalid marriage: It is necessary that there be a **valid marriage** between the parties, for there to be a tenancy by the entirety. For instance, suppose that mistakenly A believes that he has procured a valid divorce from his first wife, B, and then purports to marry C; a conveyance "to A and C as tenants by the entirety" will not create a tenancy by the entirety, even if the invalidity of the divorce is not discovered until many years later.

    a. Tenancy in common results: The courts are split as to whether, in the case of such an invalid marriage, the parties hold as tenants in common or joint tenants. See *Fuss v. Fuss*, 368 N.E.2d 276 (Mass. 1977), holding that a tenancy in common results.

C. Indestructibility: As noted, the key feature of the tenancy by the entirety is that it is **not subject to severance**. So long as both parties are alive, and remain husband and wife, neither one can break the tenancy.

1. Right of survivorship: This means that if H and W take property as tenants by the entirety, they know that the survivor of them is assured of a complete interest in the property.

2. No partition: Thus neither party may obtain a **judicial partition** of the property.

a.   **Termination by agreement:** However, if *both spouses* are so inclined, they may agree to terminate the tenancy by the entirety, replacing it by a tenancy in common or joint tenancy.

3. **Conveyance:** In some (but not all) states one spouse may *convey* his interest in the tenancy. But this conveyance cannot affect the other spouse's right to the entire estate if the latter survives. Thus even if a state permits, say, H to convey his interest to X, if H predeceases W, W will own the property outright and X will get nothing. (But conversely, if W dies before H, X will own the property outright). See Moynihan, p. 234. Thus a buyer in a state where tenancies by the entirety exist must be sure to have his deed signed by both H and W; otherwise, he may not even end up with a one-half interest.

4. **Rights of creditors:** Courts are in dispute about whether a *creditor* of one of the spouses may attach or levy on that spouse's interest in the tenancy by the entirety.

   a.   **Minority view:** A *minority* of states allow the creditor to attach the debtor's interest in the entirety.

   i.   **If debtor survives:** Under this minority approach, if the debtor is the *surviving spouse*, the creditor has a lien on the entire estate, which can be sold at auction.

   ii.   **Divorce:** If the parties get *divorced* (see below for a discussion of the effect of divorce), under this view the creditor of one spouse receives a lien on the resulting one-half tenancy-in-common interest, which the creditor can arrange to have sold at auction.

   iii.   **Debtor dies first:** But if the *debtor dies first* while the parties are still married, under this minority approach the creditor's lien is probably *extinguished*.

   b.   **Majority view does not allow claim:** But most states do *not allow* a creditor to attach or force a sale of the debtor's interest in the entirety while the other spouse is still alive. See, *e.g.*, *Sawada v. Endo*, 561 P.2d 1291 (Hawaii 1977), holding that this result follows from the indivisibility of tenancies by the entirety.

   c.   **Forfeiture proceedings by federal government:** In one special situation, one spouse's interest may be taken by a type of "creditor" under federal law, even if local state law follows the majority view that a creditor may not attach or force a sale of the debtor's interest while the other party is still alive. This is the situation of *forfeiture* proceedings against property that is used for the illegal sale or distribution of *drugs*.

   i.   **Illustration:** Thus in *U.S. v. 1500 Lincoln Avenue*, 949 F.2d 73 (3d Cir. 1991), the court held that where H and W were tenants by the entirety of a pharmacy, and H (without W's knowledge) used the pharmacy to illegally distribute prescription drugs, the government could take over H's interest in the property notwithstanding the tenancy by the entirety. This would permit the government to obtain sole interest in the pharmacy if W should die before H, or to receive equal proceeds in partition if H and W should be divorced. But, the court held, as long as W was alive and the parties were still married, W would have exclusive use and possession of the property (and if she outlived H, the government would take nothing).

5. Divorce: If the parties are *divorced*, the tenancy by the entirety *ends*. In some states, the property is then deemed to be held in joint tenancy. But in most states, the property is held as tenants in common, so that if one tenant dies before there has been a sale of the property, there is no right of survivorship in the ex-spouse.

   a. Equal shares: Where the property is deemed to be held in joint tenancy following a divorce, the shares are by hypothesis equal, since that is the nature of a joint tenancy. (*Supra*, p. 113.) Where the property is held in a tenancy in common, most courts *presume* that the shares are also equal. See, e.g., *Sebold v. Sebold*, 444 F.2d 864 (D.C. Cir. 1971), holding that a tenancy by the entirety was transformed into a tenancy in common following the divorce, and that even if H paid more than W to acquire the property in the first place, W's faithful performance of her marriage vows entitled her to a one-half interest under local D.C. law.

6. Simultaneous death: Suppose the spouses die *simultaneously*. Neither spouse can be said to have survived the other, so it is difficult to know what to do with the property. The Uniform Simultaneous Death Law, adopted in a number of states, provides that the property is to be distributed one-half as if the husband survived, and one-half as if the wife survived. The effect is thus the same as if they had held the property as tenants in common at the moment of their death. (The Uniform Law also applies to joint tenants, similarly providing that the property should be evenly divided between or among the estates.)

D. Management of the property: Recall that at common law, the husband had the exclusive right to use and manage the property in which his wife had an interest. (*Supra*, p. 101.) This was, not surprisingly, as true of property held as tenants by the entirety as it was of property to which title was solely in the wife. The husband could convey a fee simple without the wife's consent, and his creditors could attach and sell the entire estate if the wife died first. 2 A.L.P. 28.

1. Married Women's Acts: The enactment of Married Women's Acts has changed this result in all states except Massachusetts. In some states, the Act has been held to give the wife the same rights as a husband at common law; thus either spouse can convey his interest in the property, and a creditor of either spouse may attach that spouse's interest. (See the more full discussion of the rights of creditors *supra*, p. 123.) Most states, however, have taken the opposite tack; that is, they hold that *neither spouse* may convey his interest in the property or have it attached or levied on by his creditor. 2 A.L.P. 29.

E. Future of tenancy by the entirety: As noted, only 22 jurisdictions now permit the tenancy by the entirety. Even in these states, the numerous statutory presumptions favoring other tenancies, or allowing a conveyance of a one-half interest, have lessened the practical significance of the tenancy by the entirety.

1. Estate criticized: Many commentators have argued that the estate is socially undesirable, since it gives one spouse the ability to frustrate the rights of the other. For instance, if the marriage turns sour but has not yet ended in divorce, one spouse has a veto power over partition or severance; in some states he may even block the other party from conveying a one-half interest to a third person. See Moynihan, p. 235; 2 A.L.P. 32.

2. Advantage: However, the estate does have the advantage that it prevents one spouse from dissipating the family wealth held in such manner. For instance, if H and W own the family residence as tenants by the entirety, and H runs up huge gambling debts, in most states recognizing the tenancy by the entirety H's creditors cannot attach even his interest in the property, and H cannot convey that interest to a third person to raise additional funds. Furthermore, W has the assurance that if she is the survivor, she will have the estate free and clear of any of H's obligations.

3. **Not sex discrimination:** The tenancy by the entirety has survived at least one *sex discrimination attack*. Recall that Massachusetts is the sole state where the tenancy in its strict common-law form still exists (*supra*, p. 124); thus the husband has sole right to manage, encumber and convey the property. In *D'Ercole v. D'Ercole*, 407 F.Supp. 1377 (D. Mass. 1976), W argued that this right of management in the husband violated her due process and equal protection rights, since it gave H the right to sole occupancy of the premises and the right to refuse to sell it as W requested.

     a. **Holding:** The federal court acknowledged that this was the tenancy's effect, but noted that the parties could, at the time they took the property, have elected to take it as joint tenants or tenants in common rather than as tenants by the entirety. By selecting the tenancy by the entirety, W gained the security of indefeasible survivorship. W's rights had not been violated merely because she turned out to have made a bad bargain, the court held. This is true even though "there is no equivalent female-biased tenancy, nor is there a 'neutral' married persons' tenancy providing for indefeasible survivorship but not vesting paramount lifetime rights in the male."

IV. RELATIONS BETWEEN CO-TENANTS

A. **Few distinctions among tenancies:** The rights and duties of each co-tenant during the co-tenancy are more or less the same regardless of whether a joint tenancy, tenancy in common or tenancy by the entirety is involved. Therefore, the following discussion is applicable to all types unless otherwise noted.

1. **Some differences:** Some differences among types have been discussed above; for instance, under the common-law view the husband has sole right of management and use in a tenancy by the entirety, whereas each party to a joint tenancy or tenancy in common has an equal right of management and use. However, the following discussion assumes that where tenancy by the entirety is involved, the modern view (equal rights of management for both spouses) is in force.

B. **Possession by one tenant:** Each co-tenant has the *right to occupy the entire premises*, subject only to a similar right in the other co-tenants. Moynihan, p. 225.

1. **Agreement regarding possession:** The parties are always free to change this equal right by *agreement*. For instance, in *Miller v. Riegler, supra*, pp. 115-16, the parties agreed that although certain stocks were held as joint tenants, full use of the income (dividends) therefrom would belong to one tenant.

2. **Normally no duty to account:** Suppose property held in co-tenancy is solely occupied by *one tenant*. With certain exceptions, that occupying tenant has *no duty to account* for the value of his exclusive possession. That is, he has no duty to calculate the reasonable rental value of his sole possession, and pay one-half of it to the other tenant. See, e.g., *Pico v. Columbet*, 12 Cal. 414 (Cal. 1859). Nor is he normally liable for any profits he makes from his use of the land.

     a. **Rationale:** This rule follows from the notion that each tenant is entitled to occupy the entire premises subject to the same right in the other. If the sole occupant were required to account for the reasonable value of his occupancy, then the non-occupying co-owner would be able, merely by refusing to exercise *his* right to possession, to "convert the status of the occupying tenant from that of co-owner to rent-paying tenant." Moynihan, p. 226.

3. **Ouster:** But if the occupying tenant *refuses to permit* the other tenant equal occupancy, then he must account to his co-tenant for the latter's share of the fair rental value of the premises. In this situation, there is said to be an *ouster* of the tenant who has been refused occupancy.

   a. **What constitutes ouster:** What constitutes "ouster" for these purposes? Most courts holds that ouster occurs only when the out-of-possession tenant *physically attempts* to occupy the premises, and the occupying tenant refuses to allow this access. Most courts hold that ouster does *not* occur where the out-of-possession tenant merely demands that the occupying tenant either *pay rent or vacate*. So in the common situation where one co-tenant has a use for the property and the other does not, the former can effectively occupy the premises without paying rent, a situation that many commentators think is unfair.

      Example: Spiller, Mackereth and others own a building as tenants in common. The lessee of the building vacates. Spiller then enters and begins using the building as a warehouse. Mackereth writes to Spiller demanding that Spiller either vacate half the building or pay rent. Spiller does neither. Mackereth brings suit for half the fair rental value of the premises.

      Held, Spiller owes nothing. To start with, "in [the] absence of an agreement to pay rent or an ouster of a co-tenant, a co-tenant in possession is not liable to his co-tenants for his use and occupation of the property." Ouster will be deemed to occur only when the occupying co-tenant refuses a demand by the other co-tenants that the latter be allowed in to use and enjoy the land. Mackereth's demand letter, and Spiller's refusal to agree to pay rent or move out, was not enough to oust Mackereth, because Mackereth was not demanding equal use/enjoyment of the premises, merely rent. Nor did Spiller's placement of locks on the building act as an ouster of Mackereth, since the evidence was that Spiller was trying to protect goods he was storing in the building, not trying to keep Mackereth or the other co-tenants out. *Spiller v. Mackereth*, 334 So.2d 859 (Ala. 1976).

4. **Depletion:** A second situation in which the occupying tenant will have a duty to account is if he *depletes the land*, or otherwise lessens its value. For instance, if he takes away and sells its mineral resources, such as oil, gas or coal, he will be liable to his co-tenants for their share of the profits he has made. Moynihan, p. 227.

   Example: D owns a one-ninth interest in certain land, and in the rock-asphalt content of other land. He informs the other co-tenants that he intends to remove up to one-ninth of the rock-asphalt from the lands, and that they may likewise remove their share. He then goes ahead and removes many tons of rock, which he sells for a profit (after expenses) of approximately $250,000. The Ps, the other co-tenants, sue him for eight-ninths of this profit.

   Held, for the Ps. If the property had been capable of being partitioned in kind (*infra*, p. 129), so that D could receive a one-ninth parcel equivalent to all the other parcels, then he would have no liability. But since the composition of the land is not uniform, such partition is impossible. Accordingly, D is subject to the general rule that a co-tenant who removes minerals must account to the other tenants for their share of the profits. Furthermore, D is liable not merely for the value of the rock as if it were still *in place* (i.e., in the ground); this would be a relatively small sum. Rather, he must account for the profit he made selling the rock after its removal; he is entitled to a deduction for his actual expenses, including the value of his machinery and services. Although the rock was not sold until after it had received certain chemical treatments, the treatment was part of the mining procedure and all profits from it must be shared among the landowners. If D were liable only for the value of the rock in place, the other tenants would lose their rights to benefit from the fact that this particular quarry was very rich, and was easily (and cheaply) accessible.

A dissent argued that D should be liable only for the value of the rock in place; otherwise, the Ps are receiving a windfall from D's own risk-taking and investment, with no risk on their part. *White v. Smyth*, 214 S.W.2d 967 (Tex. 1948).

C. Premises rented to third party: Although a co-tenant is normally entitled to occupy the premises himself without accounting for their reasonable rental value, the same is not true if he *leases the premises* to a third person. Once he does this, and collects rents, he is required to *share* these rents with his co-tenants.

1. **Statute of Anne:** This duty to account for rents received derives from an English statute, the Statute of 4 and 5 Anne. A majority of states have enacted similar statutes, and nearly all the remainder hold as a matter of case law that there is a duty to account for such rents. Moynihan, p. 226. But these statutes and decisions generally apply only to rent received from third persons, not to the rental value of occupancy by a co-tenant himself.

D. Payments made by one tenant: Sometimes, one co-tenant will make certain payments, and then wish to recover from the other co-tenants their share of the expenditures. Or, he may wish to deduct such expenditures before paying his co-tenants their share of rents he has collected from a third person. Finally, he may wish to have the expenditures credited to him before the proceeds are distributed in a partition proceeding (*infra*, p. 129).

1. **Taxes and mortgage payments:** One tenant may make *property tax* or *mortgage* payments on the property. Generally, such payments are viewed as being made for the benefit of all the co-tenants, since their interest in the property is protected. Therefore, the tenant making the payment will be allowed to *deduct* the payment from the rents he has collected from third persons, and he will be reimbursed for the payments "off the top" before any proceeds from a partition sale are distributed. If the other co-tenants are personally liable for the indebtedness (e.g., if they have assumed the mortgage), in some states the tenant who has made the payment may bring a *direct suit* against them for contribution. 2 A.L.P. 73-75.

   a. **Mortgage completely paid off:** If a mortgage is completely paid off by one co-tenant, he becomes "subrogated" to the mortgagee's interest, and thus holds an "equitable lien" against the property. He can therefore usually have the property sold and recover his overpayment from the proceeds.

2. **Repairs:** The cost of *repairs* is handled in a similar way. If one tenant pays these costs, and the others have not agreed to help him, most courts do not allow him to make a direct recovery against his co-tenants for their share. But he may deduct their portion of the repairs before turning over any rents received from third persons, and he may receive credit for his expenditures before any partition proceeds are distributed.

a. Right of contribution where possession shared: Where *possession is shared* between the tenant who makes the payment for repairs and another tenant, a number of courts will allow a direct action for contribution. Moynihan, p. 228.

3. Improvements: If one tenant pays for *improvements* to the property, which the other tenants have not agreed to, the former is *never* permitted to recover contribution in a direct suit. And he is not normally permitted to deduct the cost of improvements from rents that he collects from a third person. However, if the rents he collects are *increased* as a result of the improvements, he may collect just the increase, up to the cost of the improvement.

    a. Rationale: The reason for these rules is that it would be unfair to allow the non-paying tenant to be "improved out of his estate"; for instance, if an automatic deduction from third-party rents were allowed, a tenant who counted on receiving his share of the rents would be deprived of them. 2 A.L.P. 81. Yet where a tenant, by paying for improvements, has increased the cash flow of the property, it is fair to allow him to recoup his payment from the increase.

    b. Partition: The party who pays for an improvement is always free to seek *partition* from the court, and except in the case of a tenancy by the entirety, he will get it. (*Infra,* p. 129.) If the property can be divided "in kind" in such a way that the parcel containing the improvement can be given to the person who paid for it, the court will do so. Otherwise, it will order the property sold and the person who paid for the improvement will get, off the top, any increase in value from the improvement up to its cost.

4. Acquisition of outstanding interest: Co-tenants are required to act towards each other in *good faith*. If they receive their interests at the same time (e.g., from the same will, or by the same conveyance), they will usually be held to be in a *fiduciary relationship*. One important consequence is that if one of them *buys an outstanding interest*, he holds that interest on behalf of all of them.

    a. Buying at foreclosure or tax sale: The same principle generally applies to a co-tenant who buys the property at a *foreclosure sale* or *tax sale*. The foreclosure or tax title is not automatically held for the benefit of the other tenants, but they have a *right to elect to contribute* within a reasonable time after the sale; if they do so, they maintain their ownership interest. The courts have been fairly lenient in determining what constitutes a "reasonable time" for making contribution.

    Example: P owns a three-fourths, and D a one-fourth, interest in Fireside Lodge. The property is subject to a mortgage, and both parties learn in July, 1971, that there will be a foreclosure if the mortgage is not paid. In April, 1972, the day before the scheduled foreclosure sale, P pays off the mortgage in order to save the property. Meanwhile, D has learned that the property has substantially increased in value as the result of development of an adjoining parcel. D waits until January, 1973, and then when P sues to quiet title in himself, D offers to pay his share of the mortgage.

    Held, for D. When P paid off the mortgage, he did so for the benefit of his co-tenant. D was required to elect whether to contribute within a reasonable time; his nine-month delay was not, however, unreasonable. Therefore, he maintains his one-fourth interest, but P has a lien on the property to ensure that D actually makes payment. *Laura v. Christian,* 537 P.2d 1389 (N.M. 1975).

E. Partition: Any tenant in common or joint tenant (but not a tenant by the entirety) may bring an equitable action for ***partition***. By this means, the court will either divide the property, or order it sold and the proceeds distributed. Normally, each tenant has an absolute right to partition.

   1. Partition in kind: In some cases, there is a fair way to divide the property, so that each tenant can be given a parcel proportional to his interest. For instance, a large farm, all of whose acreage is roughly comparable, might be subdivided. This is known as partition "***in kind***". Even if a precise apportionment is impossible, the court may order partition to another, to reflect the disparities in the physical division.

   2. Partition by sale: Where partition in kind is not possible, or would be unfair to one party, the court will order the property sold, and the proceeds divided. This is a partition "***by sale.***"

      a. Preference for partition in kind: Most courts state a preference for partitioning the property in kind rather than by sale, and say that they will approve a partition by sale only if the ***physical characteristics*** of the property prevent division of the property in kind, or if division in kind would be ***extremely unfair*** to one party. Where the party who is resisting partition by sale lives on the property or uses it for a business, courts are especially reluctant to in effect evict that party by requiring that the entire parcel be sold.

         Example: The Ps own 99/144ths of a 20-acre parcel, and D owns the remaining 45/144ths. D lives in a house at one edge of the property, and operates a rubbish and garbage removal business from part of the property. The remainder of the property is unused, and the Ps are not in possession of any part. The Ps want to convert the entire parcel into a residential development (and do not want the property partitioned in kind, since the residential parcel would be less valuable per acre with D's older house and garbage business adjacent to it than if the whole parcel became a development). D resists partition by sale, because she does not want to move her home or relocate her garbage business.

         Held, D wins, and the property will be partitioned in kind, not by sale. Under Connecticut law, partition by sale will only be ordered if the physical attributes of the land are such that partition in kind would be impractical or inequitable, and the interests of the owners would be better promoted by partition by sale. The burden is on the party requesting partition by sale to demonstrate that these requirements are met. Here, the Ps have failed to meet either requirement. The property could certainly be partitioned in kind, with the Ps left to convert their roughly 2/3 portion to residential use. Furthermore, it is the interests of *all* the tenants in common, not merely the economic gain of one tenant or group of tenants, that the court must consider. Here, the lower court failed to give adequate weight to the fact that D would lose both her home and her livelihood if she were forced to participate in a sale of the entire property. *Delfino v. Vealencis*, 436 A.2d 27 (Conn. 1980).

         Note: Courts continue to say that partition in kind is preferred over partition by sale. But in most cases where the parties disagree about which type of partition should be used, the court ends up decreeing partition by sale. D&K, p. 352. One reason is that courts usually conclude that a sale is the fairest for all parties (though a case in which only one party lives or works on the property, such as in *Delfino*, the fairness of a sale is harder to see). Probably economic efficiency will be better served in most instances by a sale; for instance, the plaintiffs in *Delfino* were probably right in arguing that any gain to D in being able to continue to live and operate her business on the property would be outweighed by the loss of the ability to develop the whole parcel as residential real estate — in any event, if D's use of the property was really more valuable than the lost residential development use, D should in theory be able to be the highest bidder for the property at the partition sale.

    b. Accounting for rents and profits: As noted above, before the proceeds from a partition sale are distributed, a tenant who has paid more than his share for repairs, mortgages, taxes, or improvements, will be repaid from the proceeds. Conversely, if one co-tenant has received more than his share of third-party rents, the other tenants will receive a matching share of the partition proceeds off the top; thus an accounting for rents and profits is often part of a partition proceeding.

3. Statute of Limitations on adjustment: As long as the Statute of Limitations for bringing a partition action is met, the court may make adjustments for overpayments or unshared rents *regardless of how long ago these occurred*, according to most courts. Thus in *Goergen v. Maar*, 153 N.Y.S.2d 826 (App. Div. 1956), one co-tenant had received rents ranging back 11 years before a partition suit was brought. The court held that since the partition suit itself was not time-barred, the trial court could go back the full 11 years to figure out how much of a credit out of first partition proceeds was due the other tenant.

4. Agreement not to partition: The parties are always free to *agree* that they will *not partition* the property in the future. However, since partition is an equitable action, the court may disregard the agreement, and order partition, if the agreement is for an unreasonably long period of time, or if circumstances have changed. For instance, in *Michalski v. Michalski*, 142 A.2d 645 (Super. Ct. App. Div. N.J. 1958), H and W, tenants in common of various properties, signed an agreement that neither would "do or permit anything . . . to defeat the common tenancy of said properties. . . ." The court noted that since both H and W were elderly when they signed the agreement, and it applied only to their own lifetimes, the restraint on partition was not for an unreasonable period. But in view of the fact that the parties had separated, and H had become disabled so that he was in need of his share of the proceeds from a sale, the court disregarded the agreement and ordered partition.

V. TAX CONSEQUENCES

  A. Tax consequences generally: A full treatment of the tax consequences of concurrent interests is beyond the scope of this outline. However, a few highlights are as follows:

    1. Income taxes: Where property held in co-tenancy produces *income*, the income is taxed to each co-owner on the proportion that he is entitled to receive. What portion a co-owner is entitled to receive is governed by local law; state law might, for instance, provide that real estate, and the income from it, is presumed to be owned equally among co-tenants unless shown to have been allocated otherwise.

      a. Bank accounts: Income from *joint bank accounts* is allocable in proportion to the contribution to the account made by each co-tenant, since each has the right to remove his contribution at any time. C&L, p. 1255.

    2. Gift taxes: If one person puts up all the money to buy real property, and the property is acquired as joint tenant or tenant in common with another, a *gift tax* on one-half the value of the property will be owed by the person putting up the money. (But an annual $10,000 exemption per donee and a unified lifetime credit may prevent any actual tax from being owed.)

    a. Tenancy by the entirety: But where a *husband and wife* buy real property as tenants by the entirety or joint tenants, no taxable gift is deemed made. However, because the entire property will remain in the gross estate of the donor for estate taxes (see *infra*), the donor may *elect* to treat the property as a gift. Then, there will be gift tax liability for one-half the value of the property, but that half will no longer be part of the donor's estate.

3. Estate tax: Federal estate taxes are imposed upon the *"gross estate"* of a decedent. Where the decedent owned property under a *tenancy in common*, only the value of his interest (e.g., an undivided one-half interest) is includable in his gross estate. But where the tenancy includes a right of survivorship (i.e., the joint tenancy or tenancy by the entirety), the *"consideration-paid"* test is applied. That is, there is includable in the estate of the first to die a proportion of the value of the property corresponding to the proportion of the *consideration furnished* by the decedent for that property.

    Example: H furnishes two-thirds of the acquisition price for Blackacre, and W one-third. H dies before W. Two-thirds of the market value of Blackacre at the time of H's death will be includable in his estate.

    a. Exception where gift tax declared: The one exception to the "consideration paid" test is that if, at the time property was acquired by a husband and wife as joint tenants or tenants by the entirety, the *election* to make a *gift* was used (see *supra*, p. 130), only one-half of the value of the property is included in the decedent's gross estate, even if he furnished all or most of the consideration, C&L, p. 1269.

Chapter Review Questions

(Answers are at back of book)

33. O conveyed Blackacre "to A and B as co-tenants." A then died, bequeathing all of his real and personal property to his son, S. B is still alive. What is the state of title to Blackacre?

34. O conveyed Blackacre "to A and B as joint tenants." B then conveyed to C, by a quitclaim deed (conveying whatever interest B had in the property). Subsequently, A died, bequeathing all of his real and personal property to his son, S. What is the state of title?

35. O, the fee simple owner of Whiteacre, died, leaving the property by will to his three children, A, B, and C, "as tenants in common." A purchased C's interest. The property is a single-family home. A moved in, and used the property as his principal residence. B, a bachelor, has now demanded to live in the home as well. If A refuses, will a judge order A to share the house with B?

36. Henry and Wanda were husband and wife. Using funds supplied entirely by Henry, the two purchased Blackacre from Oscar. (The deed from Oscar to Henry and Wanda read, "To Henry and Wanda in fee simple," without further elaboration.) Shortly thereafter, Henry became infatuated with a younger woman, Georgia. To celebrate the six-month anniversary of their affair, Henry conveyed to Georgia his interest in Blackacre. (Assume that the land is located in a state that permits such a conveyance.) For the next five years, Henry continued to be married to Wanda, but carried on his affair with Georgia. Then, Wanda died, leaving all of her real and personal property to her and Henry's daughter, Denise. Shortly thereafter, Henry died. What is the state of title? (Assume that the common-law approach to all relevant matters is in force, unmodified by statute or case law.)

37. Herb and Wendy, husband and wife, were the owners of Blackacre, which they held by tenancy of the entirety. In 1989, Herb and Wendy were divorced. They intended to sell the property, but before they could do so, Herb died suddenly. Herb's will leaves all his real and personal property to his son by a prior marriage, Stan. What is the state of the title to Blackacre?

38. Arthur and Bertha, after inheriting Blackacre from their father, held it as tenants in common. Originally, Arthur lived in the premises, and Bertha had no interest in doing so. After a few years, Arthur moved out, and sent Bertha the following letter: "I am moving out of Blackacre. You have the right to live on the property. If you do not do so, I will rent it out." Bertha made no response. Arthur, after advertising for a tenant, rented the property to Xavier, who responded to the ad. Xavier paid $20,000 of rent during the first year. (Xavier paid all operating costs, such as utilities.) At the end of the first year of this rental, Bertha learned of the arrangement and sent Arthur a letter stating, "You owe me one-half of the rents paid by Xavier." Is Bertha correct?

39. Omar, the owner of Whiteacre, left the property to his daughter Carol and his son Dan, in equal parts. The will said nothing about who should occupy the property. The property was a single-family home. Dan already had a home of his own, suitable for his family. Carol did not. Therefore, Carol moved into the house, and has since occupied it. The estimated fair market rental value of the house is $18,000 per year. Dan has demanded that Carol pay him one-half of this amount, to compensate for her use of the premises. Carol has responded, "You are free to live here with me, but I'm not paying you any money for my use of the premises." If Dan sues for one-half of the fair market rent represented by Carol's occupancy of the premises, will Dan prevail?

40. Edward and Felicia, brother and sister, received Whiteacre as a bequest in their mother's will. Edward, who had been living on the property while his mother was still alive, continued to do so after her death. Felicia has never had any interest in living on the property. The property is presently worth approximately $800,000, and has a rental value of $50,000 per year. However, Edward has rejected all suggestions by Felicia that the property be sold or rented out to third parties (though Edward has always indicated that Felicia is welcome to live on the property with him). What sort of action, if any, may Felicia bring to accomplish her goals?

LANDLORD AND TENANT

I. INTRODUCTION

A. Non-freehold estates: This chapter is about the ***non-freehold estates***. (See *supra*, p. 46.) The estates that are non-freehold are: (1) the tenancy for ***years***; (2) the ***periodic*** tenancy; (3) the tenancy at ***will***; and (4) the tenancy at ***sufferance***. These estates are discussed one at a time beginning *infra*, p. 135.

    1. Landlord-tenant relationship: These non-freehold estates have one particularly important characteristic: each normally includes a duty, on the tenant's part, to ***pay rent***. Thus they involve the ***landlord-tenant*** relationship.

    2. Distinguished from freehold estates: We have seen at least one important respect in which the non-freehold estates were treated differently from the freehold estates: the tenant of a non-freehold ***does not hold the seisin***. (*Supra*, p. 46.) Another difference is that a leasehold (as a non-freehold is often called) is ***personal***, not real, property. At one time, this meant that the leasehold was treated differently for purposes of intestate succession, but most states today treat leaseholds and freeholds identically for this purpose. Moynihan, p. 64, and n. 3.

B. Conveyance aspects: Despite these differences, the leasehold and the freehold at common law had a key feature in common: they were both ***estates in land***, typically created by a ***conveyance***. Until about the last few decades, the law of landlord-tenant was dominated by these estate, conveyancing, aspects.

    1. Independent covenants: For instance, since a tenant was deemed to receive an estate in land, his rights and duties were treated as ***independent*** of the landlord's rights and duties. Thus if the landlord promised to keep the property in repair (a promise which landlords seldom make), a breach of this promise did not relieve the tenant from the duty of paying rent; the rent was owed as payment for the estate, and the promise to do repairs was merely a collateral promise which could be enforced only by a separate contractual suit brought by the tenant. This doctrine is generally referred to as the ***independence of covenants***.

    2. Destruction of premises: Similarly, if buildings upon the land were completely destroyed by fire or other act of nature, the tenant still had the duty to pay rent. Again, this stemmed from the idea that the tenant was paying rent for the land itself, not the buildings on it.

    3. Modern tendency: But during the last few decades, courts have shown an almost revolutionary tendency to move away from the doctrine of independence of covenants. See, e.g., Rest. 2d, Introduction to Landlord and Tenant, p. vii.

        a. Warranty of habitability: The most striking example is the present willingness of most courts to hold that, at least with respect to residential premises, the landlord makes an ***implied warranty of habitability***, the breach of which entitles the tenant to terminate the lease and move out, withhold rent, or use rent monies to make the repairs himself. See *infra*, p. 151.

        b. Destruction of premises: Similarly, in many states the tenant's duty to pay rent is dependent upon the continued existence of buildings on the property, so that fire or flood will relieve him. This result is often produced by statute, but sometimes by case law. See *infra*, p. 162.

C. Leaseholds distinguished from other interests: One characteristic of the leasehold is that the tenant, for the term of his lease, is entitled to ***exclusive possession***. This distinguishes the leasehold from several other types of property interests.

    1. Hotel guest: For instance, a ***guest in a hotel*** is usually held not to have a leasehold interest, but rather, a license. (Licenses are discussed *infra*, p. 225.) The same is true of a ***lodger*** in a boarding house. Consequently, statutes applicable to landlord-tenant relations may not apply; for instance, the hotel keeper may have the right to use self-help to evict a non-paying guest even though such self-help is forbidden by statute to a landlord. See Reporter's Note to Rest. 2d, § 1.2, Item 1.

    2. Parking lots, sign easements: Similarly, a spot in a ***parking lot*** is usually held to confer only a license, not a lease. And the right to put a sign upon another's building is generally merely an easement. 1 A.L.P. 184.

II. THE VARIOUS TENANCIES AND THEIR CREATION

A. Statute of Frauds: The original English Statute of Frauds (1677) provided that any lease for ***more than three years*** must be in writing (or else have the effect of creating merely an estate at will, discussed *infra*, p. 137). Powell, Par. 222, p. 84.

    1. American statutes: The need for a writing is similarly governed by statute in all American states. Most of these statutes, however, require a writing for all leases for ***more than one year***. 1 A.L.P. 215.

    2. Lease to commence in future: The Statute of Frauds in most states also has a separate ***contracts provision*** requiring a writing for any contract not to be performed within one year ***of the making of the contract***. Since a lease can be viewed as a contract, some courts have applied the contract provision, and have thus required a writing even for a one-year lease (or shorter) where, because of the gap between the making of the lease and its effective date, the end of the lease would be more than one year from its making.

        a. Majority view: But most courts hold that the contract section does ***not*** apply; thus a one-year lease does not have to be in writing, even if it is to begin in the future. 1 A.L.P. 215-16. This is also the position taken by Rest. 2d, § 2.1, Comment f.

    3. Option to renew: Where a lease provides for an initial fixed period, plus an ***option to renew*** by one or both parties, the courts are split as to how the Statute of Frauds applies.

        a. Majority rule: The majority of courts hold that the fixed term and the option period are ***added together***; if the total exceeds one year (or whatever the statutory period is), a writing is necessary. Rest. 2d, Reporter's Note to §2.1.

        b. Minority rule: But some courts hold that as long as the fixed period does not exceed one year, it is ***valid*** regardless of the existence of an option. Rest. 2d, §2.1, Comment c, takes this minority position. (But the Restatement suggests that, when the validity of the option itself is in question, a writing should be required if the option plus the original period exceed the statutory period; Rest. 2d, §2.5, Comment c.)

4. **Periodic tenancy:** A similar problem is posed by the ***periodic tenancy*** (discussed *infra*, p. 136), that is, a tenancy that is automatically renewed at the end of each period (e.g., each month) if neither party has decided to terminate it. So long as the basic period is not longer than a year (which it virtually never is), ***no writing is required***. See Rest. 2d, § 2.1, Comment d.

5. **Effect of non-compliance with Statute:** If the lease is one that is required to be in writing, and it is not, the lease is not necessarily void. If the tenant takes possession, this fact together with the fact that the invalid lease shows that entry is made with the landlord's permission will probably create a tenancy at will (*infra*, p. 137). If, in addition to taking possession, the tenant pays rent, a ***periodic tenancy*** is created in most states (*infra*, p. 136). 1 A.L.P. 218.

6. **Recording of lease:** Apart from the Statute of Frauds, nearly all states require that leases beyond a certain length be ***recorded*** in the public records. (See *infra*, p. 364.) 4 A.L.P. 551. In many cases, the cut-off is seven years. Generally, the effect of a failure to record where recordation is required is that the lease is not binding upon a ***subsequent purchaser*** from the landlord. Powell, Par. 222, p. 86.

B. The estate for years: The most common type of leasehold is the ***estate for years***. The estate for years is any estate which is for a ***fixed period of time***. Thus the lease does not have to be for one or more years; a six-month lease would qualify.

1. **Term must be certain:** The key feature distinguishing the estate for years from other tenancies is that both the beginning date and the ending date are ***fixed*** or ***"computable"***.

> **Example:** A lease between T and L is to last "so long as [T] continues to use it for sawmill purposes. . . ." *Held*, the term here was not certain, so the lease was not for a term of years. (Therefore, it created an estate from year to year, which L could terminate by giving proper notice of termination to T.) *F.H. Stoltze Land Co. v. Westberg*, 206 P. 407 (Mont. 1922).

   a. **Subject to earlier termination:** But a tenancy is not prevented from being an estate for years merely because it may be ***cut short*** by some event. For instance, nearly every term of years contains a provision that if the tenant fails to pay rent, the landlord may terminate and regain possession.

   b. **One party's option to terminate:** Where one party is given the right to terminate ***without cause*** at any time, the tenancy may still be an estate for years, according to most courts. See Rest. §1.6, Comment g. But if such a power of termination is given to ***both parties***, the tenancy is likely to be considered a ***tenancy at will*** (*infra*, p. 138).

2. **No notice needed to terminate:** An estate for years, by definition, contains its own termination date. Accordingly, ***no additional notice of termination*** is required to be given by either party; on the last day, the tenancy simply ends, and the tenant must leave the premises.

3. **Maximum duration:** Most states do not impose any ***outer limit*** on the length of a tenancy for years; thus a 2,000-year tenancy would be upheld in most states. But a few states have statutorily imposed length limits, at least with respect to certain kinds of leases, such as those for agricultural or mining properties. See 1 A.L.P. 211.

C. The periodic tenancy: The *periodic tenancy* is a tenancy which continues from one period to the next automatically, unless either party terminates it at the end of a period by notice. 1 A.L.P. 221-22. Examples are a tenancy from year-to-year, or month-to-month, or week-to-week.

  1. Distinguished from tenancy for years: Thus while a tenancy for years automatically expires when it reaches the end of its stated term, the periodic tenancy continues indefinitely, until terminated by one of the parties by proper notice.

  2. Creation of periodic tenancy: It is possible to create a periodic tenancy by *express agreement* (i.e., L and T explicitly agree that T will have a month-to-month tenancy of Blackacre.) Normally, however, a periodic tenancy is created by *inference*.

   a. Lease with no stated duration: For instance, the parties may make a lease without setting a duration, and also provide that the rent is to be, say, $400 per month. The fact that the rent is to be payable monthly will probably be enough to make the tenancy a month-to-month periodic one. See Rest. 2d §1.5, Comment d.

   b. Void lease: Similarly, the parties may make an *invalid lease*. This would probably be due to a failure to comply with the Statute of Frauds, but might be due to a state's requirement that the lease be notarized or in the form of a deed. When the tenant first enters, an at will tenancy is created (*infra*, p. 138), but as soon as the first *rent payment* is made, a periodic tenancy will generally be deemed to exist.

    i. Length of period: However, courts are not in agreement as to how the length of the period is to be determined. Most courts would probably hold that the period is the one that is *used in the void lease* for calculating rent. Thus if the rent in the lease is stated on an annual basis, the tenancy will be year-to-year, even though the rent is payable each month.

    ii. Minority based on actual rent payments: But a few courts hold that the period for a periodic tenancy is determined by the way the rent is *actually paid*, not the way it is calculated in the lease. 1 A.L.P. 228.

    iii. Restatement view: The Second Restatement has a unique, middle view. Initially, the period is determined by the interval between the rent payments specified in the invalid lease. But when successive rent payments add up to one of the longer traditional (month-to-month, quarter-to-quarter or year-to-year), the period becomes this longer total. Thus if the invalid written lease provided for weekly rental payments, there would be a week-to-week tenancy when T took possession and made the first couple of weekly payments. But once he had been in possession for a month, the tenancy would be treated as month-to-month. The maximum period provided for under this Restatement rule is a year-to-year tenancy. Rest. 2d, § 2.3, Comment d.

   c. Arising from holdover: Another way a periodic tenancy can arise is when a tenant *holds over* at the end of a lease. In the holdover situation, the landlord has the choice of either evicting the tenant or permitting him to stay; in the latter event, the tenancy is usually treated as a periodic one. This is discussed more fully *infra*, p. 140.

  3. Termination of tenancy: A periodic tenancy will automatically be renewed for a further period unless one party gives a valid *notice of termination*. At common law, *six months* notice was necessary to terminate a year-to-year tenancy, and a full period's notice was necessary where the period was less than a year (e.g., thirty days notice for a month-to-month tenancy). Rest. 2d § 1.5, Comment f. Today, most states have statutes modifying this rule; many of these statutes require only thirty days notice for any tenancy, even year-to-year. (But the parties are free to agree upon longer or shorter notice.)

　　a. Notice must specify end of period: At common law, the notice also had to set the *end of a period* as the termination date.

　　　　Example: T makes a written lease with L at a $700 annual rental, but the lease is invalid because it lacks a seal. A year-to-year tenancy on a calendar year basis is thus created. The property is destroyed by fire, and on October 31, 1898, T sends L a letter stating "we have vacated the premises . . . and hereby surrender possession of same."

　　　　Held, this letter was not sufficient to terminate the tenancy as of November 1, 1898, because there was no prior notice and the tenancy must terminate as of the end of a year. But furthermore, the notice was not effective to terminate the tenancy as of December 31, *1899*. This is because: (1) the notice is not of a future termination at the end of a year, but of a present abandonment; and (2) the notice fails to state a date to which the termination applies. Even the fact that in April, 1899, T defended an action for arrears in rent brought by L, giving L actual notice of its intent to quit, does not suffice to terminate the tenancy as of the end of 1899; a written notice stating a termination date is required. *Arbenz v. Exley, Watkins & Co.*, 50 S.E. 813 (W.Va. 1905).

　　　　i. Modern view relaxes rule: It is still the rule almost everywhere that a notice of termination may only be effective as of the end of a period. But where a notice is not sufficiently in advance of the end of the current period, most courts now allow it to be automatically effective as of the end of the *following period*. Thus although the October 31, 1898 notice in *Arbenz* would not be sufficient to terminate the lease as of the end of calendar year 1898 (assuming that six months notice was still required for a year-to-year tenancy), it would automatically be effective to terminate at the end of 1899. See Rest. 2d §1.5, Comment f. Thus in the case of a month-to-month tenancy, a notice of termination given on January 2 would be effective as of February 28.

　　b. Due process right: Although normally either party to a periodic tenancy has a right to terminate without cause (if the proper motive requirements are met), this may not be the case with *publicly financed or subsidized* housing. As to such housing, the tenant may have a due process right not to be evicted without cause. See *Joy v. Daniels*, discussed *infra*, p. 196.

D. Tenancy at will: A *tenancy at will* is a tenancy which has *no stated duration* and may be *terminated at any time* by either party.

　　1. No notice for termination: At common law, *no prior notice* of termination is required, as it is for periodic tenancies. (However, the tenant has a reasonable time within which to remove his goods if the landlord demands possession.) 1 A.L.P. 229.

　　　　a. Modern statutes: But modern statutes in many states give a tenant at will a right to prior notice, similar to that given to a short-term periodic tenant. This has tended to blur the dividing line between tenancies at will and periodic tenancies.

2. **How the at-will tenancy arises:** The parties could create a tenancy at will expressly, by agreeing that either may terminate at any time. But generally, such a tenancy is created by *implication*. For instance, T might take possession with L's permission, with no term stated and no period for paying rent defined. Or, T might take possession under a void lease; his possession would create a tenancy at will, but this would be transformed into a periodic tenancy as soon as he made the first rent payment (*supra*, p. 136). 1 A.L.P. 230-31.

3. **Lease terminable at the will of only one party:** Suppose that *only one party* has a right to terminate at any time. This generally does *not* make the tenancy one that is at will. Instead, the tenancy is usually analyzed by what it would be if the right of termination were not present. For instance, if it would otherwise be an estate for years, it becomes a determinable estate for years. Similarly, if it would be a periodic estate in the absence of the termination clause, becomes a determinable periodic estate. Rest. 2d § 1.6, Comment g.

> **Example:** L leases his house to T. The written lease agreement provides that the lease shall continue "for and during the term of quiet enjoyment from the first day of May, 1977," and lists no ending date. The lease also says that T "has the privilege of [terminating] this agreement at a date of his own choice." Four years later, L dies, and his heirs try to terminate the lease, claiming that the absence of a definite term, coupled with a right of termination on T's part, created an implied right of termination on L's part (making the lease an at-will tenancy).
>
> *Held*, for T. The lease created a determinable life tenancy on behalf of T, rather than a tenancy at will. The fact that T had the right to terminate the lease at some point earlier than his own death did not make the lease indeterminate or give L a similar option. To infer a termination option at L's will would violate the terms of the agreement and the express intent of the parties. *Garner v. Gerrish*, 473 N.E.2d 223 (N.Y. 1984).

   a. **Minority view:** A minority of courts, however, hold that where one party expressly retains an option to terminate at will, a similar option *in favor of the other party* also exists by implication. In the view of such courts, therefore, the tenancy is at will. See, e.g., *Foley v. Gamester*, 170 N.E. 799 (Mass. 1930). (In such a court, presumably *Garner, supra*, would have turned out the other way — in favor of recognizing a termination right on the part of L's heirs.)

4. **Events causing termination:** Apart from an affirmative notice of termination by either party, a tenancy at will will terminate automatically upon the *death* of either party, or upon a *conveyance* of the reversion by the landlord. An *assignment* by the tenant of his interest also terminates the tenancy, but most courts hold that a *sublease* does *not* terminate. Moynihan, p. 84.

   a. **Rent increase:** Suppose the landlord notifies the tenant that the at-will tenancy will be terminated unless the tenant consents to a *rent increase*. If the tenant pays the increased rent, or fails to object, a new at-will tenancy at the higher rent is created.

      i. **Tenant pays old rent:** But if the tenant objects, or simply continues paying the old, lower, rent, the result is unclear. In *Maguire v. Haddad*, 91 N.E.2d 769 (Mass. 1950), the court held that such a notice terminating the tenancy at will unless the tenant agreed to pay higher rent was *ineffective* either to terminate the old tenancy or to raise the rent, since the tenant continued to pay the old rent. Therefore, the old tenancy continued.

E. Tenancy at sufferance: The so-called *"tenancy at sufferance"* exists only in one limited situation: that in which a tenant *holds over* at the end of a valid lease. This "tenancy" is extremely insubstantial; it will end as soon as the landlord exercises his option either to evict the tenant or to hold him to another term. (See immediately below).

1. **Landlord's right of election:** When a tenant holds over after his lease has ended, the landlord has a *right of election*; he may choose between: (1) *evicting* the tenant, i.e., treating him as a trespasser; and (2) holding him to *another term* as tenant.

   a. **Right of eviction:** The landlord's right to evict a holdover tenant, and the means by which this is accomplished, are discussed *infra*, p. 175.

   b. **Right to elect new term:** The landlord may choose to *bind* the holdover tenant to a *new term*. In nearly all states, the landlord has this right even though the tenant has manifested no desire to remain for an entire additional term. 1 A.L.P. 237-38.

2. **Common law takes strict view:** The common law took an extremely strict view of holdovers; even a one day holdover, and even one that was virtually unavoidable, generally gave the landlord the right to bind the tenant for an additional term. See, e.g., *Mason v. Wierengo's Estate*, 71 N.W. 489 (Mich. 1897) (lease expires October 1; T starts to move out, but is taken sick on September 26, and dies on October 6. His clerks finish moving out on October 11. *Held*, L had the right to bind T and his estate to another term; the fact that T did not intend to hold over, and could not have avoided it, is irrelevant.)

   a. **Modern courts more lenient:** But modern courts are considerably more lenient towards the holdover tenant. Although the landlord's right to elect another term is not dependent upon the tenant's assent, the courts recognize *extenuating circumstances*, particularly where only a very short holdover period is involved.

      Example: L and T enter into a one-year written lease for an apartment. The lease provides that if T does not move out at the expiration of the lease, he will be liable for double rent for the holdover period. Two months before the end of the lease term, T notifies L that he will vacate at the end of the lease. He and his movers begin moving out his possessions three days before the end of the term. By midnight of the last day of the lease, everything has been moved out but some rugs and a few pieces of furniture. T and his family sleep in the apartment that night, and the next morning (October 1), promptly move everything out. That same October 1 morning, L notifies T that it has elected to hold T for an additional year.

      Held, for T. The evidence certainly does not show that the holdover was voluntary on T's part. Nor does justice require that L be given the right to bind T to a new term. Furthermore, the clause providing for double rent for any period of actual holdover was intended by the parties as L's sole protection against holdover, and no further relief was intended or would be fair. *Commonwealth Building Corp. v. Hirschfield*, 30 N.E.2d 790 (App. Ct. Ill. 1940).

      i. **Sickness:** Similarly, where T becomes *sick* and is unable to move out, most modern courts would not agree with the decision in *Mason, supra*, and would not permit L to elect a new term, if the holdover period was reasonably short. See, e.g., *Herter v. Mullen*, 53 N.E. 700 (N.Y. 1899).

　　b. Partial holdover: If the tenant retains possession of *any portion* of the premises, he will generally be considered to be holding over as to the entire premises. The landlord will thus obtain the right to hold him to a new term for the whole premises. See *David Properties, Inc. v. Selk*, 151 So. 2d 334 (Dist. Ct. App. Fla. 1963).

3. How landlord exercises option: Where the landlord does have the right to bind the tenant to another term, he may of course exercise this right by written notice. But an *oral notice* will also usually be sufficient. Furthermore, if the tenant *pays rent* for the premises for the time following termination, and the landlord accepts this rent, he will probably be deemed to have elected to hold the tenant for another term. See Rest. 2d § 14.4, Comment e and Illustr. 1.

　　a. Waiver: But the landlord may be found to have *waived* his right to treat the tenant as a holdover.

　　　　Example: L and T make a written lease for a one-year term. Just before this year is up, L and T begin negotiations for a new lease. They are still negotiating when the year is up, and T remains in possession. They finally fail to reach agreement, and T moves out as soon as the negotiations terminate. L may not treat T as a holdover, and bind him to another year. In this situation, L has implicitly consented to T's holding over for the duration of the negotiations. Therefore, he has no right to change this understanding and bind T to a one-year term. See 1 A.L.P. 214; see also *Lawson v. West Virginia Newspaper Publishing Co.*, 29 S.E.2d 3 (W. Va. 1944).

4. Length and nature of new tenancy: The courts are in dispute as to whether the new tenancy is a term of years or a periodic tenancy. They are also in dispute as to the *length* of the term or period.

　　a. Way rent calculated: Probably the majority view is that a *periodic* tenancy is created, and that the length of the period is determined by the *way rent was computed* under the lease which terminated. Thus if the original lease calculated rentals on an annual basis (even though the rentals may have been payable monthly), the tenancy produced by the landlord's election would be year-to-year. See, e.g., *Fetting Manufacturing Jewelry Co. v. Waltz*, 152 A. 434 (Md. 1930), to this effect. This is the position taken by Rest. 2d § 14.4, Comment f.

　　　　i. Minority view: But other courts hold that the length of the new tenancy is equal to the *term or period of the original lease*, up to a maximum of one year. Thus where the original lease was for a term of one or more years, the holdover term would be one year or from year to year regardless of how the rent was calculated. 1 A.L.P. 244.

　　b. Other provisions of holdover term: In all respects except length, the holdover term is governed by the *same provisions* as the original lease. Thus in the absence of an agreement otherwise, the rent remains the same, as does the allocation of duties between landlord and tenant (e.g., the duty of repair).

　　　　i. Landlord's right to raise rent: The landlord will sometimes not only elect to bind the tenant to a new term, but will also attempt to *raise the rent*. If the tenant pays the raised rent or otherwise manifests his consent, he will of course be bound to the higher rent. If he objects, the increase will probably not be binding. If he *remains silent*, the courts are in dispute about whether the higher rent applies to the new term; see *David Properties, Inc. v. Selk*, 151 So.

2d 334 (Dist. Ct. App. Fla. 1963), holding that the tenant's continued possession without protest constitutes an implied agreement to pay the increased rent.

5. **Election is binding:** Whichever route the landlord decides to take, termination or renewal, is binding upon him. Thus if he says that he is holding the tenant to another term, he cannot thereafter change his mind and evict; similarly, if he starts eviction proceedings, it is too late for him to change his tune and renew the lease. If he fails to take either action within a reasonable period of time, he may be held to have waived his right to elect a new term (though he is unlikely to be found to have waived the right to evict). See Rest. § 14.4, Comment c.

III. TENANT'S RIGHT OF POSSESSION AND ENJOYMENT

A. **Tenant's right of possession:** All courts agree that, unless the lease provides otherwise, the landlord is obligated to deliver *legal right* to possess the premises to the tenant at the commencement of the lease term. That is, the landlord impliedly warrants that he has legal right to give possession to the tenant; he would violate this warranty if, for instance, he had already given a lease for the same period to someone else. (See *infra*, p. 142.) But the courts are sharply split as to whether the landlord also impliedly warrants that he will deliver *actual* possession at the start of the lease term; the question usually arises when a *prior tenant holds over*.

1. **"American" view:** The so-called *"American" view* is that the landlord has a duty to deliver *only* legal possession, *not actual possession*. See, e.g., *Hannan v. Dusch*, 153 S.E. 824 (Va. 1930); *Teitelbaum v. Direct Realty Co.*, 13 N.Y.S.2d 886 (Sup. Ct. 1939). Despite the designation "American rule", probably at most a slight majority of American courts adhere to this view. See Rest. 2d § 6.2, Reporter's Note, Item 2.

   a. **Rationale:** Two principal arguments are given in support of the American rule.

      i. **Statutory proceedings:** First, in nearly all states, the incoming tenant has at least as effective a statutory right to have the holdover tenant evicted by summary proceedings as does the landlord. (*Infra*, p. 176.)

      ii. **Liability for third person's torts:** Secondly, imposing a duty on the landlord to oust the holdover tenant would amount to making the landlord liable for the torts of a third person, a highly unusual result and one that should not be produced by mere implication. Furthermore, all courts agree that once the tenant takes possession on the first day of the lease, the landlord has no duty to oust a trespasser who enters thereafter; as the court in *Hannan, supra*, noted, there is no compelling reason for treating a trespass which occurs before the incoming tenant takes possession any differently.

2. **"English" rule:** The contrary position, that the landlord does have a duty to deliver actual possession, is usually called the *"English" rule*, since it is followed by all English courts. But notwithstanding this label, almost half of American courts now follow this position. See, e.g., *Adrian v. Rabinowitz*, 186 A. 29 (N.J. 1936).

   a. **Rationale:** The English view is generally defended on the following grounds:

      i. the landlord is likely to have a better knowledge of whether the property is in someone else's possession prior to the start of the new lease, and whether that possession is proper or improper;

    ii. before the start of the lease, the landlord is generally the only one who has the right to evict a holdover tenant or trespasser; and

    iii. the parties generally intend that the landlord guarantees actual possession, and the tenant will be getting less than he bargained for if he has to make lease payments and fight a lawsuit simultaneously in order to get possession.

    See Rest. 2d § 6.2, Comment a. (§6.2 of the Second Restatement applies the English view.)

    b. Tenant's rights for breach: Where the English view is in effect, the lessee generally has the right to *terminate the lease* and recover the damages for the breach. Or, he may continue the lease, and recover damages accruing until either he or the landlord succeeds in getting the holdover tenant ousted. See *Adrian v. Rabinowitz, supra*, p. 141, holding that the lessee's measure of damages for the time he cannot occupy the premises is normally the difference between the rental value and the rent provided in the lease; the court refused to award the tenant the profits he would have made by selling merchandise, holding that the profits from a newly established business are too speculative.

B. Right of quiet enjoyment: The tenant has what is sometimes called the *"right of quiet enjoyment"* of the leased premises. Here are two principal ways in which this right can be interfered with: (1) by a third person's assertion of a title superior to that of the landlord, used to evict the tenant ("paramount title"); and (2) by acts of the landlord, or persons claiming under him, which interfere with the tenant's possession or use of the premises. (In addition, the landlord's failure to maintain the property in habitable condition, and the destruction of the premises by fire or other cause, are sometimes considered violations of the right of quiet enjoyment; however, for our purposes, these two subjects are treated separately, *infra*, pp. 151 and 162 respectively.)

C. Claims of paramount title: The landlord, by making the lease, impliedly warrants that he has *legal power* to give possession to the tenant for the term of the lease.

    1. Ways to violate: There are a number of ways in which this implied warranty might be violated, including the following:

    a. the landlord does not have title to the premises *at all*;

    b. the landlord has title to the premises, but has *already leased them* to someone else for a period overlapping that of the new lease;

    c. the landlord has only a *life estate* in the property, which might expire before the end of the lease term; and

    d. the landlord's title is subject to *termination* (e.g., if it is used for non-residential purposes, or if the landlord does not make the mortgage payments on a mortgage executed prior to the lease.)

    In all of these instances, there is said to be a *paramount title* which might be asserted by the third person.

    2. Remedies: The tenant's remedies depend upon whether or not he has taken possession.

    a. Before tenant takes possession: *Before the tenant takes possession*, he may upon discovering the paramount title *terminate the lease* (assuming that he did not know of the paramount title when he signed the lease). At least some courts seem to hold that he may do this even if the paramount title is unlikely to interfere with the tenant's possession. Thus Rest. 2d § 4.2, and Illustration 11 thereto, give T the right to terminate the lease before taking possession if he discovers a mortgage on the premises, even though L is not behind on the payments and there is little reason to believe that the mortgage will ever be foreclosed upon.

b. **After tenant takes possession:** But once the tenant takes possession, he may *not* terminate the lease, or refuse to pay rent, merely on the grounds that a third person holds a paramount title. However, if that third person then *asserts* his paramount title in such a way that the tenant is *evicted*, the tenant may terminate the lease and recover damages. Rest. 2d § 4.3. The rule that mere existence of a paramount title (without eviction) may not be used by the tenant as a defense in a rent action or eviction proceeding is sometimes stated as follows: the tenant is *estopped to deny his landlord's title to the leased property*. Rest. 2d § 4.3 Comment b.

D. **Interference by landlord or third person:** If the landlord himself interferes with the tenant's use of the premises, or aids someone else in doing so, this will be a breach of the covenant of quiet enjoyment.

1. **Acts by landlord:** The clearest breach exists when the landlord himself interferes with the tenant's use of the premises. If the landlord literally takes possession of all or *part* of the leased premises (e.g., he dumps his trash on it, or store his furniture), it is called *actual eviction*. If, by contrast, he merely interferes with the tenant's *use* or *enjoyment* of the property, there is a *constructive eviction*. (The distinction is discussed in more detail *infra*, p. 144.)

   Example: L leases a house to T. L also owns the property next door, and uses it to give constant loud parties that disturb T in his enjoyment of the house. L may be found to have constructively evicted T, if T moves out of the house because of the noise. Rest. 2d § 6.1, Illustr. 5.

   a. **Tenant's remedies:** The tenant's remedies depend in part upon whether the interference amounted to an actual, or just a constructive, eviction. Remedies are discussed *infra*, p. 150.

   b. **Landlord breaches non-competition clause:** A tenant who plans to use the leased property to run a particular trade or business sometimes obtains a promise from the landlord that the latter will not rent or use any of his nearby property for a purpose *competitive* with the tenant's proposed use. This is commonly called a *non-competition clause*. If the landlord breaches this promise, the tenant will be entitled to sue for damages, or to move out and terminate the lease. See, e.g., *Kulawitz v. Pacific Woodenware & Paper Co.*, 155 P.2d 24 (Cal. 1945).

2. **Persons holding under landlord:** Where T's use of the premises is interfered with by a person *holding under* L, L may be deemed to have breached the covenant of quiet enjoyment. For instance, if L's wife, while running the household she shares with L, throws garbage onto T's premises, this would probably constitute a breach by L.

   a. **Conduct of other tenants:** The most common issue is whether behavior by *other tenants* in the same building violates L's covenant of quiet enjoyment to T.

    i. No general duty: Most cases hold that there is *no general duty* imposed on the landlord to control the conduct of other residential tenants. See, e.g., *Stewart v. Lawson*, 165 N.W. 716 (Mich. 1917).

    ii. Exceptions: But there are two well-established situations where the conduct of other tenants *will* be attributable to the landlord: (1) the other tenants use their portion of the premises for *immoral or lewd purposes*; or (2) the objectionable conduct takes place in the *common areas* under the landlord's control.

    iii. Modern tendency where right of control exists: Also, some recent cases show a more general tendency to impute the acts of other tenants to L where these acts are *in violation of the relevant leases*, and L could have prevented the conduct by eviction or otherwise. This is the position of Rest. 2d, § 6.1, Comment d. This is particularly likely to be the case where L had reason to know, before making a lease with the misbehaving tenant, that a significant chance of inconvenience to others existed. Thus in *Blackett v. Olanoff*, 358 N.E.2d 817 (Mass. 1977), L rented an apartment to T, and rented the next-door premises to X to run a cocktail lounge. The lease with X explicitly provided that the noise level in the lounge could not disturb neighboring tenants. The court held that the particular potential for annoyance to the residential tenants, and L's contractual right to control the noise, justified holding L liable for constructive eviction of T.

3. Actual vs. constructive eviction: As noted, the courts have distinguished between *"actual"* and *"constructive"* eviction. If the tenant's possession of all or part of the premises is literally taken away from him, the eviction is actual. If it is merely his *use* or *enjoyment* of the property that has been substantially impaired (e.g., excessive noise, terrible odors, nearby premises used for immoral purposes, etc.) the eviction is *constructive*.

    a. Complete vs. partial actual eviction: Where the eviction is actual, it can be either *total* or *partial*. Partial eviction might, for instance, occur if the landlord ousted the tenant from a geographical portion of the premises (e.g., by knocking down one of several buildings on the leased property).

        i. Remedies: As one might expect, a tenant who has been totally evicted may regard the lease as *terminated*, and may refuse to pay any rent. Significantly, according to most courts a tenant who has suffered only *partial* actual eviction may also *refuse to pay rent, even though he remains in possession of the rest of the premises*. The courts following this majority view usually defend it by saying that "the landlord *cannot apportion his own wrong*". 1 A.L.P. 284. Rest. 2d § 6.1 changes this rule; if the tenant remains on the premises, he is entitled *only* to compensatory damages (though he may elect to terminate the lease and leave the premises, in which case he is relieved from making further rent payments). Reporter's Note to § 6.1, Item 6, argues that it is unjust to deprive the landlord of all rent when the tenant remains in possession of part of the premises; the Note analogizes to the right of a party in breach under a contract to recover restitution.

    b. Constructive eviction: But where the eviction is *constructive* rather than actual, the tenant is *not* entitled to terminate the lease, or to stop paying rent, unless he *abandons* the premises. If he stays on the premises, his only remedy is to sue for damages. Furthermore, the abandonment must occur within a *reasonable time* following the alleged constructive eviction.

    i. Little use in habitability cases: The defense of constructive eviction has also been used where the tenant claims that the premises were rendered *uninhabitable* due to the landlord's failure to keep them in repair. But the requirement that the tenant promptly leave the premises makes the defense unusable for many tenants, particularly residential slum-dwellers, who lack the funds to find alternative housing. The problems of habitability, including the use of the constructive eviction doctrine, are further discussed in a separate section beginning *infra*, p. 150.

4. Destruction of premises: If the premises are *destroyed* by an act of nature (e.g., fire), one might expect that the tenant would be allowed to claim that his right of quiet enjoyment had been disturbed, and that the lease was terminated. However, the common law had special rules, unfavorable to the tenant, governing destruction of the premises. These are discussed separately *infra*, p. 162.

E. Condemnation: The government may decide to take all or part of the leased premises by its right of *eminent domain*, or *condemnation*. Special common-law rules have evolved to deal with this situation.

    1. Total vs. partial taking: The government may *condemn* the entire leased premises or merely a portion.

    2. Total taking: If the entire premises are taken, the *lease terminates*, and the tenant does not have to pay any further rent.

    3. Partial taking: But where only a *portion* of the premises is taken (even a majority portion, or a portion necessary to the use that the tenant has been making of the property), the common-law rule is that the lease is *not terminated*. Furthermore, the tenant is required to *continue paying the full rent*. (But he may get part of the condemnation award, as discussed *infra*).

        a. Restatement view: Rest. 2d § 8.1(2) modifies this rule as to partial takings, in two respects. First, if the condemnation "significantly interferes" with the use contemplated by the parties, the lease terminates (and T is relieved from paying rent). Secondly, even if there is no significant interference, T may be entitled to a *reduction in rent* to reflect whatever small interference with his use has occurred.

    4. Damages: Under the state and federal constitutions, the government must pay the *fair value* of any property which it condemns. The common-law approach is to divide this award between the tenant and the landlord, in proportion to the damage each has sustained from the condemnation.

        a. No rent abatement for partial taking: As noted, whereas a total taking suspends the duty to pay rent entirely, under the common law a partial taking does not even reduce the tenant's duty to pay rent. Instead, the tenant is required to wait for the condemnation award, of which he will receive a portion. See, e.g., *Elliott v. Joseph*, 351 S.W.2d 879 (Tex. 1961).

        b. Majority rule criticized: A few courts have refused to follow the majority rule, on the grounds that it discriminates against the *landlord!* The reasoning for this is as follows: the tenant will obtain a piece of the condemnation award, presumably not too long after the taking has occurred. Since some or all of the tenant's portion of the award will reflect the fact that the tenant has to pay full rent even though he can no longer use part of the property, the net result is that the tenant gets a lump sum immediately, and gives part of this back to the landlord over the course of the lease in the form of full rent payments. This means that the landlord, rather than getting a check from the government large enough to compensate him for his loss, has to rely on the **tenant's solvency** for some of his money. It is for this reason that Rest. 2d § 8.1(2) provides (as noted *supra*, p. 145) for termination of the lease where the taking substantially interferes with the tenant's use, and for a reduction in rent even where it does not; the tenant's portion of the condemnation award is correspondingly less.

c. **Division of award:** In *dividing* the condemnation award between the landlord and tenant, courts have followed conflicting, and sometimes confused, approaches. All courts attempt to divide the award equitably, and nearly all follow at least one rule: the overall amount of the award should be the same as if there were no lease; only the division between the landlord and tenant, not the total given to the two interests, should depend upon the existence and terms of the lease. See *Kentucky Dept. of Highways v. Sherrod*, 367 S.W.2d 844 (Ky. 1963).

 i. **Tenant's loss of bargain:** The principal (and sometimes the sole) component of the tenant's portion of the award will be his **loss of bargain**. That is, he will get an amount equal to the difference between the total rent he would have to pay on the rest of the lease, and the **market value** of that lease, both sums discounted to their present value. Thus suppose the taking is total, the lease calls for ten remaining annual payments of $1,000 each, and the market value of the lease is $1,100 per year; T will get an amount equal to the present value of a $100 payment in each of the next ten years. (Conversely, if he made a bad bargain on the lease, so that he would have had to pay higher than fair market rentals, he will get no award). One important consequence is that the tenant normally does not get **special damages** (e.g., lost profits from the business run on the land), except insofar as these may be evidence of the fair market value of the lease.

 ii. **Award where taking is partial:** This approach is followed, in a general sense, whether the taking is total or partial. However, where the taking is partial, only the **reduction** in the fair market value of the lease, not the total value of that lease, is taken into account. Again, the emphasis is on **market value**, not on the actual use made by T; thus if only one-tenth of the property is taken, and this reduces the fair market value of the lease by 10%, T will not get a large award even though the one-tenth reduction proves fatal to his particular use (e.g., it takes away most of the parking area for his restaurant). See *Kentucky Dept. of Highways v. Sherrod*, 367 S.W.2d 844 (Ky. 1963).

 iii. **Effect of rent reduction:** Where the taking is total, the fact that the tenant no longer has to pay rent is factored into his share of the award. Similarly, in those jurisdictions where the tenant is entitled to a reduction in rent for a partial taking, most courts would presumably reduce his share of the condemnation award to reflect the fact that he has received this rent abatement. See Rest. 2d § 8.2, Comment e.

F. **Illegal use of premises:** At the time the lease is signed, it may happen that both parties intend that the tenant will use the premises in a way that is *illegal*. Or, the tenant's intended use may become illegal after the lease is signed. Similarly, his use may be illegal if done without a permit or variance, which he is ultimately unable to obtain. In some, but not all, of these situations, the court treat the lease as void, so that neither party has any obligation to the other.

1. **Both parties intend illegal use:** If both parties intend that the tenant will use the premises for a purpose which is *illegal under all circumstances*, all courts agree that the lease is unenforceable. Thus if L and T agree that T will run a gambling parlor, a drug-selling operation, or a house of prostitution, the court will not enforce the lease against either L or T. Rest. 2d §§ 9.1(1), 12.4(1).

2. **Landlord knows but does not intend:** If the landlord *knows* that the tenant will use the property for illegal purposes, but the landlord does *not actively assist* in the illegality, the result depends in part on the seriousness of the offense. Where the crime to be committed is "heinous" (e.g., heroin distribution), all courts will make the lease unenforceable. But where the use is not heinous (e.g., sale of obscene material, probably, in most jurisdictions), the courts are split as to whether the lease is enforceable. See Rest. 2d § 9.1, Reporter's Note, Item 2.

3. **Some but not all uses illegal:** If there are *several* proposed uses, and only one or some are illegal, the result depends on how significant a portion of the total use the illegal one(s) represents. Where the illegal use is *incidental* to the main use (e.g., lease calling for seven-day-a-week operation of store, in violation of Sunday Blue Law), the lease will be enforced. But if the illegality accounts for a substantial portion of the use (e.g., operation of a sizable numbers racket at the back of a small grocery store), the lease will generally not be enforced. Rest. § 9.1, Reporter's Note, Item 4.

4. **Violation of building codes:** An illegality theory has sometimes been used to invalidate a lease of residential premises where the property is in serious *violation of building codes* at the time the lease is executed.

   Example: L rents the basement of a house to T for residential purposes. At the time of the lease, numerous Housing Code violations exist in the basement (e.g., broken toilet, broken railing, and insufficient ceiling height); L is aware of the violations, and has promised the building inspector that the basement will not be occupied until the violations are corrected. T falls behind in her rent, and L sues for the arrears. T defends on the grounds that the lease was illegal.

   Held, for T. The local Housing Regulations explicitly provide that no residential property shall be rented unless it is in clean and safe condition; the Regulations also provide for penalties for violations. If the court were to uphold the lease, it would be thwarting the purposes of the housing laws. Therefore, the lease is invalid, and L may not recover any rent. (T has apparently left the premises, so that her right to continued occupancy is not at issue). *Brown v. Southall Realty Co.,* 237 A.2d 834 (Ct. App. D.C. 1968).

5. **Remedies:** Generally, neither party to an illegal contract is entitled to recover anything from the other; the court *leaves the parties as it finds them*. However, if the court concludes that one party is much more morally culpable than the other (i.e., that the parties are *not "in pari delicto"*), the court may award some kind of recovery to the less guilty party.

   a. **Restitution:** Also, even where the parties are in *pari delicto*, the court may simply decide as a matter of fairness that one is entitled to recover something from the other. Thus where a lease is held illegal for housing code violations, several courts have nonetheless awarded the landlord the *reasonable value* of the leased premises, for the period they were actually occupied by the tenant. See, e.g., *William J. Davis, Inc. v. Slade*, 271 A.2d 412 (Ct. App. D.C. 1970); *King v. Moorehead*, 495 S.W.2d 65 (Ct. App. Mo. 1973).

6. **Use subsequently becomes illegal:** The above discussion assumed that the proposed use was illegal at the time the lease was signed. It may happen, however, that the use becomes illegal only *after* the lease is signed.

 a. **Only one use allowed:** If the use which becomes illegal is the *only one allowed under the lease*, the tenant may terminate.

 b. **Other uses allowable:** But if the lease itself allows the tenant to make other uses of the property, and the problem is simply that the use desired by the tenant becomes illegal, most courts do *not* relieve the tenant. Rest. 2d § 9.2(2), however, relieves the tenant "if it would be unreasonable to place on the tenant the burdens of the lease after converting to the other use."

 c. **Variance or permit:** A related problem arises when the use intended by the tenant requires a *variance* or *permit*. If the tenant is ultimately unable to get the variance or permit, the courts are split.

  i. **Majority view:** The majority view is that the lease *remains valid* even if the tenant fails to get the variance, permit, or license. See, e.g., *Warshawsky v. American Automotive Products Co.*, 138 N.E.2d (Ct. App. Ill. 1956) (T deemed to have accepted risk that manufacturing of auto parts, the sole use permitted by the lease, might be in violation of local zoning ordinance).

  ii. **Minority view:** But a few courts hold that, at least where no other use is permitted under the lease, the tenant's inability to get the permit or license excuses him from liability for rent. Rest. 2d § 9.2, Reporter's Note, Item 3. Rest. 2d § 9.2(2) enlarges this minority view to excuse the tenant even where other uses are permitted, if requiring the tenant to convert would be "unreasonable" considering all the circumstances.

  iii. **Agreement otherwise:** Even where the facts are such that the court would not on its own relieve the tenant, there may be a *clause in the lease* which relieves him. For instance, the tenant might have an express right of termination in the event that he is unable to get a permit or license, or in the event that his proposed use subsequently becomes illegal. Or, the landlord may expressly warrant that the premises meet applicable zoning requirements for the proposed use; the tenant may sue for the breach of such a warranty. Rest. 2d § 9.2, Reporter's Note, Item 5. (But the converse is not true; an agreement that the tenant will continue to pay rent even though the sole use permitted in the lease is and has always been illegal, will not be enforced, as a matter of "public policy".)

G. **Frustration of purpose:** Events can sometimes occur which render it *economically impractical* for a tenant to go on with his planned use of the premises. Although the performance of the lease remains possible (in contrast to the illegality situation described above), the *purposes* of the lease have been thwarted. This situation is therefore usually termed *frustration of purpose*.

1. **Courts take strict view:** Courts have been somewhat less willing to discharge a tenant due to frustration of purpose than in the case of other, non-real estate, contracts.

The following requirements must generally be met:

a. Use known to landlord: The frustrated use must be the use for which the tenant signed the lease, and this use must have been **known to the landlord** at the time the lease was signed.

b. Total frustration: The purpose of the lease must be **nearly or totally frustrated**. The fact that the tenant's use is rendered somewhat less profitable is not sufficient.

c. Not reasonably foreseeable: The event which frustrates the lease must **not have been reasonably foreseeable** at the time the parties signed the lease.

d. Government restraints: Nearly all of the cases involving frustration of purpose have been ones where it is a **governmental restriction** which has thwarted the tenant. 1 A.L.P. 400, n. 1. Rest. 2d, § 9.3 limits the doctrine to cases of government interference, but there is no reason why, on principle, the doctrine could not apply to frustration from other, non-governmental sources.

H. Permitted uses: In the absence of an agreement otherwise, the tenant is permitted to use the property for **any purpose** that is not illegal. However, the parties are free to agree that the premises be used solely for a particular purpose, or that certain uses will not be permitted. For instance, if the property is designed for residential purposes, the lease will almost certainly restrict the use to non-commercial purposes. Similarly, many business leases set forth with some precision the uses the tenant may make.

1. Distinguish from mere description: But such restrictive clauses generally strictly construed against the landlord. Thus if the lease merely **describes** the tenant's use, and does not explicitly require the use, the tenant may usually do as he pleases. 1 A.L.P. 254. Similarly, the fact that both parties intended a particular use will not be dispositive, if the lease does not contain an express restriction.

2. Intent of the parties: But the courts will look to all the surrounding circumstances to determine the parties' intent, if there is ambiguity. For instance, in *Stroup v. Conant* 520 P.2d 337 (Ore. 1974), the lease provided that the property would be used "for the sale of gifts, novelties, etc." T told L that he planned to sell a few books as part of his operation, but he in fact opened an "adult" book store featuring pornographic materials. The court allowed L to rescind the lease, on the grounds that T had misrepresented his intended use "by half-truths and concealment. . . ."

IV. CONDITION OF THE PREMISES

A. Common-law view: The common law applied the principle of *caveat emptor* to the landlord-tenant relationship. Unless the parties explicitly agreed otherwise, the tenant took the premises **as is**. The landlord was **not** deemed to have made any **implied warranty** that the premises were fit or habitable, even in the case of residential property. Nor did the landlord have any **duty to repair** defects arising during the course of the lease, unless such a duty was explicitly provided for. See, e.g., *Anderson Drive-In Theatre v. Kirkpatrick*, 110 N.E.2d 506 (Ct. App. Ind. 1953) (no implied warranty of fitness for a particular purpose, so that where T leases land to build a drive-in theatre, L has no duty to communicate his knowledge to T that the land is too marshy for this use.)

1. Rationale: This *caveat emptor* approach dated back to an earlier agrarian economy, in which the tenant was interested principally in the land, not the structures on it. If any repairs were necessary, they were usually ones which he could do himself, since: (1) the structures were uncomplicated; and (2) as a farmer, the tenant presumably had some "jack of all trades" handyman abilities.

2. **No longer applicable:** This reasoning is no longer applicable, particularly in urban and suburban areas. Most residential leases are for units in apartment buildings. As one court noted, "in the case of the modern apartment dweller, the value of the lease is that it gives him a place to live. The city dweller who seeks to lease an apartment on the third floor of a tenement has little interest in the land 30 or 40 feet below, or even in the bare right to possession within the four walls of his apartment. When American city dwellers, both rich and poor, seek 'shelter' today, they seek a well known package of goods and services — a package which includes not merely walls and ceilings, but also adequate heat, light and ventilation, serviceable plumbing facilities, secure windows and doors, proper sanitation, and proper maintenance." *Javins v. First National Realty Corp.*, 428 F.2d 1071 (D.C. Cir. 1970) (discussed more extensively *infra*, pp. 151-52).

B. **Independent covenants:** The common law placed an additional obstacle in the path of any tenant who wished to hold his landlord accountable for the habitability of the premises. Recall that the common law followed the doctrine of ***independence of covenants*** in leases (*supra*, p. 133), so that the breach of a covenant by one party would not relieve the other party of his duties (though he could sue for damages for the breach). This meant that even where the tenant had the bargaining power to obtain a clause providing that the landlord would make repairs on the premises, and keep them habitable, a breach of this covenant by the landlord ***would not relieve the tenant of the duty to pay rent***. He could, it is true, sue for damages, but this was cold comfort in view of the legal expenses involved, and the fact that the tenant remained in uninhabitable living conditions.

C. **Constructive eviction:** The hardships of the common-law position were somewhat ameliorated by use of the ***constructive eviction*** doctrine (*supra*, p. 144). If the tenant could show that, due to the landlord's failure to make repairs, the premises were rendered virtually uninhabitable, he could claim that he had been constructively evicted; his duty to pay rent would then cease, and he might be able to get damages as well.

1. **Duty to vacate:** But the constructive eviction defense had one huge disadvantage: as noted *supra*, p. 144, it could only be asserted if the tenant ***left the premises***. To a tenant who because of lack of finances, a housing shortage, or whatever reason, could not feasibly find other shelter, this was a fatal obstacle.

2. **Constructive vs. actual eviction:** A tenant who did not leave the premises might try to argue that the eviction had been actual (although partial), not constructive. For instance, in *Barash v. Pennsylvania Terminal Real Estate Corp.*, 256 N.E.2d 707 (N.Y. 1970), T (a lawyer) leased office space from L, after being promised that the premises would be open and usable 24 hours a day. When he moved in, T found that the air conditioning system was shut off at six P.M., that the windows were sealed, and that the lack of ventilation made the premises unusable after hours. Since he did not vacate the premises, his only hope was to argue that there had been an actual, partial eviction. But this claim was denied by the court, on the grounds that there had been no actual physical expulsion; instead, the eviction was merely constructive, and T's failure to abandon the premises deprived him of that theory.

   a. **Waiver:** The requirement that T abandon the premises is even more burdensome when it is combined with the tendency of courts to find a ***waiver*** if the abandonment does not occur ***within a reasonable time*** after the premises deteriorate.

D. Illegality defense: Another defense has sometimes been available, at least where the premises were in violation of Building Code requirements at the time the lease was signed. This is the defense of *illegality*. The principal habitability case allowing the illegality defense is *Brown v. Southall Realty Co.*, 237 A.2d 834 (Ct. App. D.C. 1968), discussed *supra*, p. 147. Because of the modern-day general availability of the implied warranty of habitability in residential leases, discussed *infra*, the illegality defense, like the constructive eviction defense, is no longer frequently asserted.

E. Implied warranty of habitability generally: As noted, the traditional common-law view was that a landlord made no implied warranties that the premises were fit for habitation, or for any particular purpose.

   1. Exceptions: There were, however, several *exceptions*, in which a warranty as to the condition of the premises might be found:

   a. Furnished room: Where the leased premises are *furnished*, and the lease is for a *short period*, courts have generally been willing to find that the landlord made an implied warranty that the premises and furniture are fit for use. See, e.g., *Ingalls v. Hobbs*, 31 N.E. 286 (Mass. 1892). See also *Pines v. Perssion*, 111 N.W.2d 409 (Wisc. 1961).

   b. Uncompleted building: Similarly, if a lease is made for a building that has *not yet been completed*, there will be an implied warranty that it will be suitable for the tenant's intended use. Rest. 2d § 5.1, Reporter's Note, Item 2.

   c. Fraud: Finally, if the landlord *fraudulently conceals* defects from the tenant, the latter has always been able to get relief, either through rescission or damages.

   2. General warranty of habitability: Then, in the 1960's, there began an abrupt reversal of the general common-law *caveat emptor* position. State after state changed its position, either through case law or statute. Over forty states now impose some sort of *implied warranty of habitability*. C&J, p. 472, note 2.

   3. The *Javins* case: Perhaps the most important of the early cases imposing a common-law implied warranty of habitability was *Javins v. First National Realty Corp.*, 428 F.2d 1071 (D.C. Cir. 1970).

   a. Facts of *Javins*: In *Javins*, the Ts were residential tenants, whom L was seeking to dispossess on the grounds that they had defaulted in their rent. The Ts conceded the lack of payment, but asserted that the building contained hundreds of violations of the District of Columbia Housing Regulations.

   b. Implied warranty found: The court concluded that, at least in cases of *residential property*, the landlord makes an *implied warranty* that the premises are *habitable*. The court justified this holding with several arguments.

   i. Old assumptions unwarranted: First, the common-law, no-duty-to-repair rule was based on an agrarian society. Today, most lessees reside in apartment buildings, and have neither the know-how, the money nor the economic incentive to make repairs to their living quarters.

   ii. Consumer protection: Secondly, in other kinds of contractual situations (e.g., the purchase of a car), modern courts have given the consumer substantial protection. The tenant is an *amateur*, and the landlord is typically a businessman in the *business of selling housing*; the tenant must rely on the skill and good faith of the landlord just as much as a consumer must rely on the manufacturer of a product he buys. Therefore, the tenant is entitled to be protected by an implied promise that the landlord will keep the premises in the same condition they were in at the beginning of the lease term.

    iii. Housing shortage: There is a severe *shortage* of adequate housing. This, combined with the well-known inequality of *bargaining power* between landlord and tenant, means that the tenant has little ability to negotiate with the landlord for an express promise that the latter will keep the premises in repair.

    iv. Housing code: Finally, the District of Columbia has enacted *Housing Regulations*, which require that the landlord keep the premises in repair. Since official enforcement of the Housing Code has not always been effective, the legislative objective of requiring the landlord to keep the premises habitable can be fulfilled only if this duty is made contractually binding upon the landlord.

  c. Standard is Housing Regulations: The *Javins* court thus concluded that, as to any dwelling covered by the Housing Regulations, the landlord gives an implied warranty of habitability; this warranty can be fulfilled *only if the premises are maintained in such a way that the Regulations are not violated*. However, one or two "minor" violations would not, by themselves, constitute a breach.

  d. Suspension of rent: As a procedural matter, the court said, the trial court may (and probably should) order the Ts to pay rents coming due in the future into the court. If the Ts prove that violations existed during the period at issue, they will be entitled to a *reduction* or a complete *elimination* of *rent* for the relevant period. (The court did not specify how the amount of the reduction should be calculated, or whether any substantial breach entitled the tenant to be completely free of rent for the period in question.)

  e. Covenants no longer independent: Observe that the *Javins* decision makes two covenants, the tenant's duty to pay rent and the landlord's implied duty to make repairs, *dependent* rather than independent. That is, if the landlord fails to make repairs, the tenant is relieved of the duty to pay rent for the time in question. (Whether the converse is true, that a failure to pay rent then relieves the landlord of the duty to repair, is not stated by the court, though this would seem to follow logically.)

4. Conditions existing prior to entry: It may be important to distinguish between poor conditions existing *prior to entry* by the tenant, and those which arise thereafter. In analyzing conditions existing prior to entry, it may in turn by necessary to distinguish between so-called "*latent*" (unobvious) and "*patent*" (obvious) defects.

  a. Latent defects: Where the defect is a *latent* one, i.e., one which the tenant did not discover, and could not reasonably have discovered, prior to the signing of the lease, all courts hold that an otherwise applicable implied warranty of habitability protects the tenant against such a defect.

  b. Patent defect: But if the defect is a *patent* one, i.e., one which the tenant either knows about or should reasonably have discovered by inspecting the premises, the courts are *split*. Some hold that there is no implied warranty against such defects; this appears to be the case in New Hampshire, New Jersey and Iowa. (B,C&S, p. 440.) But other courts hold that an otherwise applicable implied warranty covers such defects. Since this is really a question of whether the tenant has *waived* the defect, a court's attitude is likely to be similar to its view on whether the tenant can waive the warranty by an express clause in the lease (as to which, see *infra*, p. 155). See, e.g., *Hilder v. St. Peter*, 478 A.2d 202 (Vt. 1984) (tenant entering into lease agreement with knowledge of defect in essential facilities cannot be said to assume risk; nor can implied warranty be waived orally or by written provision in lease).

c. Restatement approach: The Second Restatement starts from the general view that while there is an implied warranty of habitability for all residential units (§§ 5.1-5.5), a tenant who takes possession may sometimes be held to have waived pre-existing defects. Prior to the time he enters, the tenant may always terminate the lease, and collect damages. But once he takes possession, he will be held to have waived any pre-existing defects, unless: (1) it would be **unsafe or unhealthy** for him to use the property; (2) the parties have impliedly or expressly agreed that the landlord will have **more time** to correct the defect; or (3) the tenant neither knows nor should know about the defect at the time he enters.

    i. Practical effect: Since the implied warranty of habitability in residential dwellings is generally only triggered where the premises are unsafe or unhealthy, the tenant will rarely waive the warranty under this Restatement rule; waiver is likely only where the property is non-residential (and therefore not explicitly covered by the Restatement's implied warranty; see *infra*, p. 155) or where the landlord has made additional express or implied warranties as to fitness (e.g., in an expensive luxury building, that there will be a 24-hour doorman, even though absence of one would not necessarily be enough to make the premises "unsafe and unhealthy"; see *infra*, p. 154).

d. Illegality defense: Recall that the **illegality** defense may be applicable to building code violations existing prior to the signing of the lease; see *Brown v. Southall Realty Co., supra*, p. 147. This defense probably **remains** in most or all jurisdictions that recognize the implied warranty of habitability. See, e.g., *King v. Moorehead*, 495 S.W.2d 65 (Ct. App. Mo. 1973), recognizing both the implied warranty of habitability, and the illegality defense for building code violations, as being applicable to the same set of facts.

5. Conditions arising after tenant enters: Suppose that, at the time the tenant enters, the premises are in good condition, so that all implied warranties are met. If, **as the lease progresses**, the premises fall into disrepair, is the implied warranty of habitability violated? Certainly most, though perhaps not all, cases indicate that there is a **continuing duty** on the part of the landlord to keep the premises in habitable condition. Of course, if a defect was **caused by the tenant**, the court is not likely to hold that the landlord has a duty to correct it; but even in this situation, one can imagine cases where such a duty might nonetheless be found (e.g., T accidentally exposes wiring, and asks L to fix it).

    a. Restatement view: The Second Restatement imposes a general duty upon the landlord to keep residential premises in repair during the course of the lease. Rest. 2d, § 5.5(1). However, there is **no such duty** if the defect is: (1) the **fault of the tenant**; (2) caused by a **sudden non-man-made force** (in which case the tenant has the right to terminate but not the right to collect damages or withhold rent; see *infra*, p. 157); or (3) caused by the conduct of **third persons** (e.g., a robber who wrecks the apartment).

F. Standards for determining "habitability": There is a fair degree of controversy concerning the ***standards*** for determining whether premises are habitable.

1. **Building code violations:** All courts agree that the existence of ***building code violations*** is at least some evidence of uninhabitability. A few courts seem to hold that any non-trivial code violation ***automatically*** constitutes uninhabitability, even without a showing that conditions are unsafe or unhealthy. But most courts seem to require that the conditions not only violate the building code, but are also a ***substantial threat to the tenant's health or safety***. B,C&S, pp. 438-39, note 1.

2. **Absence of building code violations:** The big question is whether the converse is true, that is, whether the ***absence*** of building code violations automatically means that there is no violation of the warranty of habitability. Most courts indicate that presence of a code violation is ***merely one factor***; thus if T shows that there is a substantial danger to his health or safety, the warranty will be held to be breached even if there is no explicit housing code violation. See, e.g., *Hilder v. St. Peter*, 478 A.2d 202 (Vt. 1984).

   a. **Restatement view:** The Restatement provides that the test is whether conditions are unsafe or unhealthy for the tenant. Housing code violations are merely one way of showing this. But conversely, the mere fact that there is a housing code violation does not prove that conditions are unsafe or unhealthy, under the Restatement view. Rest. 2d, § 5.1 Comment e.

3. **Relevance of nature of building:** At least some cases indicate that the ***age of the building*** and the ***amount of rent charged*** may be considered in determining whether the implied warranty of habitability has been breached. This indicates that a condition which might constitute a breach of the warranty in the case of a new, luxury, high-rise, might not be a violation where the building is a 50-year-old low-rent structure occupied by low-rent tenants. See B,C&S, p. 439, note 1.

4. **Duty to provide security:** The amount of rent may also be relevant as to the extent of the landlord's duty to keep the premises ***secure*** against the criminal acts of others (e.g., robbers). This issue is discussed further *infra*, p. 165, in the context of the landlord's tort liability.

G. Kinds of leases to which implied warranty applies: The courts are split as to the types of leases to which the implied warranty applies.

1. **Residential leases:** With respect to ***residential*** leases, some courts hold that there is an implied warranty of habitability in ***all*** such leases. Others hold that there is such a warranty only where the lease is for a unit in a ***multiple dwelling*** (so that a single-family house, or, in many states, a two-family house would not be included). Still other states cover only ***urban*** residential property, or only property that is explicitly covered by ***housing codes***. B,C&S, p. 438, note 1.

   a. **Statutes:** Most ***statutes*** imposing implied warranties are based upon the Uniform Residential Landlord and Tenant Act (URLTA) and the Model Residential Landlord-Tenant Code (Model Code), which are relatively similar to each other. The URLTA applies to all residential leases, as does the Second Restatement (see Rest. 2d, § 5.1).

2. **Commercial leases:** Courts are ***split*** about whether the implied warranty of habitability should be applied to ***commercial*** leases. It is probably still the case that ***most*** courts do ***not*** apply the warranty in a commercial context. These courts reason that

commercial tenants are on average more sophisticated than residential ones, better able to make a pre-lease inspection, and better able to make repairs when needed.

a. Cases applying warranty: But the number of cases applying the warranty to commercial leases is clearly increasing. One of the most important cases is *Davidow v. Inwood North Professional Group — Phase I*, 747 S.W.2d 373 (Tex. 1988). There, the Texas Supreme Court held that "there is an implied warranty of suitability by the landlord in a commercial lease that the premises are *suitable for their intended commercial purpose*. This warranty means that at the inception of the lease there are *no latent defects* in the facilities that are vital to the use of the premises for their intended commercial purpose and that these essential facilities will *remain in a suitable condition*. If, however, the parties to a lease expressly agree that the tenant will repair certain defects, then the provisions of the lease will control."

   i. Facts of *Davidow*: The facts of *Davidow* establish how premises might be found to be commercially uninhabitable, in states imposing the warranty of habitability to commercial leases. D rented the premises to P as a doctor's office. Among the problems with the space were: The air conditioning did not work properly, sometimes resulting in temperatures above 85 degrees. The roof leaked whenever it rained. Pests and rodents infested the office. The hallways remained dark because the lights were unreplaced for months. Cleaning and maintenance was not provided; the parking lot was filled with trash; there was no hot water. In sum, the court held, a jury could properly find that this space was not fit for use as a medical office, so that P was justified in abandoning the premises and discontinuing his rent payments.

b. Restatement view: The Second Restatement takes no position on whether there is an implied warranty of habitability in commercial or industrial leases. See Rest. 2d, § 5.1, caveat. The Reporter for the Restatement, in Reporter's Note to § 5.1, Item 2, argues that the warranty should be extended to non-residential property, particularly to cases involving small commercial tenants.

c. Statutes: Most of the *statutes* imposing implied warranties of habitability apply *only to residential leases*. See Rest. 2d, Statutory Note to Chapter 5, Item 1.

H. Waiver of warranty by tenant: Where the implied warranty does apply, a crucial issue is whether and when the tenant may *waive* that warranty. In particular, will a clause in the lease *expressly stating that there is no implied warranty* be effective?

1. **"Boilerplate" clause:** At least where the waiver clause is a standard *"boilerplate"* clause contained in a standard printed lease, most courts have *not honored it*. The court in *Javins* (*supra*, p. 151), in dictum, indicated that it would not allow such a waiver: "We need not consider the provisions of the written lease governing repairs since this implied warranty of the landlord could not be excluded" (n. 49) and "Any private agreement to shift the duties would be illegal and unenforceable" (n. 58). This anti-waiver position would apply not only where the landlord expressly disclaims the warranty of habitability, but also where the contract purports to place the duty of repairs on the tenant rather than the landlord.

2. **Statutes:** Most statutes have more or less followed the approach of the URLTA. The URLTA provides, in §2.104(d), that a clause shifting the duty of repair onto the tenant is unenforceable. However, such a shifting will be allowed if it is "set forth in a *separate writing* signed by the parties and supported by *adequate consideration*",

and is made "in good faith and not for the purpose of evading the obligations of the landlord. . . ."

    a. Upgrading can't be required: Also, the separate agreement must not require the tenant to do work to bring premises that are now not in compliance with housing codes *into compliance*; thus L could not lease to T a run-down apartment and require him to fix it up to meet code standards. But the URLTA would permit L and T to make a separate agreement, not part of the lease, that T would keep the premises in repair, assuming that they already met code standards; it is not clear whether the requirement of "adequate consideration" could be satisfied by a reduction in the rent.

3. Restatement approach: The Restatement makes it somewhat easier for a landlord to disclaim the warranty of habitability or shift the burden of repairs to the tenant than does the URLTA. Rest. 2d, §5.6, makes a contractual modification of the landlord's duties binding unless it is *"unconscionable or significantly against public policy."* Comment e to §5.6 lists a number of factors which the court is to consider in determining the validity of the disclaimer or modification; some of these are:

    a. Public policy: The extent to which the agreement runs counter to the *"policy* underlying statutory or regulatory provisions", particularly those concerning public health and safety, and those relating to low- and middle-income tenants in multi-unit residences;

    b. Conscious negotiations: Whether the agreement serves a *"reasonable business purpose"*, and seems to have been the result of *"conscious negotiations* for the distribution of risks as part of the total bargain. . . .";

    c. Boilerplate lease: Whether the lease as a whole is an unduly harsh *"boilerplate"* lease;

    d. Bargaining power: Whether the lease "imposes unreasonable liabilities or burdens on persons who are *financially ill-equipped"*, and who have had "significant *inequality of bargaining power"*; and

    e. Lawyers: Whether the parties were each *represented by counsel*.

    f. Summary: At least with respect to a low- or middle-income tenant in a multi-unit apartment building, a waiver of the implied warranty would almost certainly not be enforceable under the Restatement test, if it is part of the standard lease and was not bargained for separately. As Reporter's Note to §5.6, Item 2, notes, "To impose a rule of implied warranty of fitness as this Chapter does, and to allow waiver by an imposed form lease is to reduce the rule to form, not substance."

I. Remedies for breach of implied warranty: Cases and statutes have recognized a variety of *remedies* for a breach by the landlord of his implied warranty of habitability.

1. Right to terminate lease: Where the breach of the warranty is a material one, and the landlord refuses to correct it after *reasonable notice*, the tenant generally has the right to *vacate the premises* and *terminate* the lease.

    a. Consequence: If he does so, he is, of course, relieved from the need to make future rent payments. Furthermore, he is entitled to collect *damages* for the breach, either as a set-off against rent which accrued before the termination and was not paid, or as an affirmative recovery from the landlord.

b. Measure of damages: Courts have not agreed upon the *measure of damages* to be used where the tenant terminates the lease. Putting aside the question of damages due for the period of actual occupancy by the tenant in sub-standard conditions (discussed in the context of rent abatement, *infra*, p. 159), the general approach seems to be to award the tenant who has terminated the *fair market value* of his lease, plus any special damages.

    i. Meaning of "fair market value": That is, the tenant is entitled to the difference between the fair rental value of the premises if they had been as warranted, and the promised rent for the remainder of the lease term. See *King v. Moorehead*, 495 S.W.2d 65 (Ct. App. Mo. 1973). Thus the tenant recovers only the *benefit of his bargain*, i.e., the extent to which the lease was worth more than other leases of similar (but habitable) property. To this, the tenant may also add his special damages, including the costs of relocation and any *business profits* that the tenant proves with reasonable certainty that he would have made, and which the landlord should reasonably have foreseen would be caused by the breach of warranty. See Rest. 2d §10.2.

c. Duty to vacate: It seems almost certain that the tenant will have the right to terminate the lease only if he has *vacated the premises*. But probably he is not required to vacate "within a reasonable time" after the breach, as he was in the older cases relying upon the constructive eviction defense (*supra*, p. 144). See B,C&S, p. 442. However, the tenant would presumably lose his right to terminate if he had not moved out by the time the landlord *cured* the defects.

d. Tenant in default before landlord breaches: If the *tenant* is in default before the premises become uninhabitable, it is not clear whether the tenant loses his right to vacate and terminate the lease.

2. Right to withhold rent: In those jurisdictions where an implied warranty of habitability is recognized, most courts and/or statutes allow the defendant the significant remedy of *rent withholding*. That is, once the premises fail to be in habitable condition, the tenant may *refuse to pay all or part of the rent to the landlord*, until the defects have been cured.

    a. Possible duty to deposit rent: A number of cases indicate that the tenant may simply *keep the rent* himself as it comes due, without paying it either to the landlord or anyone else. Many cases leave it to the trial court's *discretion* as to whether rents coming due once the suit starts should be required to be *deposited* with the court. Thus in *Javins, supra*, p. 151, the court stated that the jury could find that all or part of the tenant's rental obligations had been "suspended by the landlord's breach of warranty, but that the trial court "may" require the tenant to deposit rents with the court as they come due.

        i. Deposits required: A few cases, and nearly all statutes on the subject, *require*, in all cases, that the tenant immediately *deposit* the rent in some kind of *escrow account*, as it comes due each month, at least as long as the tenant remains on the premises. In favor of this requirement, it should be noted that the tenant is receiving *some* benefit from being able to remain on the premises, even if due to the landlord's breach of warranty the premises are worth less than they would be if they had been as warranted. Also, the landlord is entitled to protection in case it is finally determined judicially that some rent is due for the period in question; the landlord can recover this amount from the funds deposited, whereas otherwise he might end up merely with a worthless judgment against an impecunious tenant.

ii. **Where deposited:** The states are split with respect to whether the money must be deposited with a *public* account (e.g., the registry of a court), or may be deposited in a private escrow account. Rest. 2d §11.3, Comment e, provides that the tenant may use a private escrow account, the holder of which must be a person "selected by the tenant whom he in good faith believes to be responsible."

iii. **How much paid in:** Normally, the tenant has the right to withhold the *entire rent* for as long as the defect remains. But by the same token, if there is a duty to deposit the rent, the entire amount must be deposited. In most states, however, since the tenant has a right to obtain a rent reduction or abatement (see *infra*, p. 159), he may ask the court to declare a temporary abatement during the course of the litigation; probably only this lowered amount would have to be deposited.

b. **Rent strikes:** A few states have statutes which facilitate *rent strikes*, i.e., concerted rent withholding by a substantial group of tenants in a particular building. See, e.g, N.Y. Real Prop. Act. & Proc. Law, Art. 7A, §770, which provides that one-third or more of the tenants of a building may petition the court to authorize rent withholding where there are conditions dangerous to the life, health or safety of the occupants; the rent is to be deposited into the court.

c. **What happens to withheld money:** The rent withholding will usually be simultaneous with some court proceeding, either an attempt by the landlord to evict the tenant, a suit by the landlord for accrued rent if the tenant has vacated the building, or a damage suit by the tenant. At the conclusion of the litigation, when the court has decided what damages, if any, the tenant is entitled to, the rent withheld (and probably deposited) is apportioned between landlord and tenant to reflect the court's finding of liability. Thus all the money withheld might go to the landlord (if no breach was shown) or all to the tenant (if the tenant's damages were greater than the rent accruing, which might happen if violations existed for quite a while before the tenant started to withhold), or a division might be made.

i. **Tenant's right to pay balance:** Regardless of the court's finding, if more money is due the landlord than has been placed on deposit, the tenant will almost always be given a *reasonable time* within which to pay any balance due. If he does not do so, then he can be evicted.

3. **Application of rent for repairs:** A number of cases and statutes allow the tenant to *make the repairs* (either personally or by hiring someone to do them), and then to *deduct the reasonable costs* of those repairs from the rent. See, e.g., *Hilder v. St. Peter*, 478 A.2d 202 (Vt. 1984).

a. **Advance notice:** The tenant is generally required to give the landlord *advance notice* of his intent to make the repairs and deduct; the landlord then has a chance to make the repairs himself and avoid the loss of rent. Such a requirement of notice was imposed in *Hilder v. St. Peter, supra.*

b. **Amount of deduction:** Where the repair-and-deduct remedy is created by case law, the amount which may be spent and deducted by the tenant is generally limited only by the amount of rent to become *due during the rest of the lease*. Thus if T has one more year to run on his lease, at $300 a month, he could theoretically spend $3600 on repairs (assuming that this expenditure was reasonably needed to correct the defects), and deduct the full $300 due from the rent each month. This is the approach followed by Rest. 2d, §11.2, Comment c.

    i. Statutes place limit: But where the right to repair-and-deduct is *statutory*, there is often a lower limit on the dollar value of the repairs the tenant may make and deduct. Thus Cal. Civil Code §1942 limits the cost of the repairs to *one-month's rent*; also, the statute now provides that the repair-and-deduct remedy may be used only once in each twelve-month period.

  c. Not payable from arrears: Most statutes, and some cases, require the tenant to make the repairs *first*, and deduct only from rent thereafter coming due. This means that a tenant who is already in *arrears* cannot charge the cost of subsequent repairs against these arrears. (But he might be able to make the repairs out of the *current* rent, if he did not have other funds available and emergency repairs were involved.) Rest. 2d, §11.2, Comment b.

4. Abatement of rent: If the landlord breaches the implied warranty of habitability, the tenant is presumably entitled to some sort of compensation for the period he occupies the sub-standard premises. Typically, this issue will arise if the tenant goes into *arrears*, or withholds rent, and the landlord sues for possession and/or rent; the tenant then counterclaims for a reduction, or *abatement* in the rent. The courts are in sharp dispute about how the size of the rent reduction is to be calculated.

  a. Three approaches: There are three major approaches that have been used:

    i. the tenant is entitled to have the rent reduced from the amount agreed on to the *fair rental value* of the premises in their defective condition;

    ii. the tenant is entitled to deduct from the rent the difference between the rental value of the premises as it *would have been* if the lease had been complied with by the landlord (i.e., if the premises remained habitable) and its rental value in the condition it actually was; and

    iii. the tenant is entitled to a reduction in the rent in an amount equal to the *proportion* of the rent which the fair rental value of the premises in their actual condition bears to the fair rental value they would have had had they been as warranted. See Rest. 2d §11.1.

  b. "Proportional value" rule: The *"proportional value"* rule, damage measure number iii above, represents a middle-ground between the other two approaches. Typically, it enables the tenant to keep some of the benefit of his bargain (the amount by which the value of the premises as warranted exceeds the agreed-upon rent), yet it will always prevent the tenant from living rent-free.

    Example: T rents the premises for $200 per month. If they were as warranted, they would be worth $400 per month. In their run-down state, they are worth $150 per month. First, one calculates the value "as is" as a percentage of the value as warranted, i.e., $150 divided by $400, or 37.5%. T's rent is thus reduced to 37.5% of the stated rent, or $75. T has preserved some of his bargain (he is paying $75 for premises worth, even as is, $150), yet he is not living rent-free.

    i. Restatement approach: This "proportional value" rule is the approach taken by the Second Restatement. See Rest. 2d, §11.1, and Reporter's Note thereto,

Item 4.

5. Suit for damages: Some courts have also allowed the tenant to bring an *affirmative* suit for *damages* for the landlord's breach of the warranty of habitability (as opposed to using such a breach as a defense against the landlord's suit for rent). Any damages recovered by the plaintiff are in a sense a "return of rent" to him. See, *e.g.*, *Hilder v. St. Peter*, 478 A.2d 202 (Vt. 1984), in which the court allowed such a suit, and in fact awarded not only damages for the loss in the premises' market value stemming from the breach, but also damages for the tenant's *discomfort* and *annoyance*.

J. Retaliatory eviction: A landlord generally has the option to terminate a tenancy at will at any time (*supra*, p. 137), to give notice of the termination of a periodic tenancy (*supra*, p. 136), or to deny the tenant's request for a new lease at the conclusion of a tenancy for years (*supra*, p. 136). But if the landlord is permitted to exercise his right of termination in order to *retaliate* against a tenant who has asserted his right to habitable premises, the warranty of habitability loses much of its value. For this reason, the doctrine of *retaliatory eviction* has been developed, to *prevent the landlord from terminating* as a penalty for certain acts by the defendant.

1. Complaints about housing violations: The doctrine is most likely to be applied where the landlord attempts to terminate the tenancy in retaliation for *complaints* made by the tenant to a *housing authority* about *code violations* on the premises.

   a. *Edwards v. Habib*: The landmark case in this area is *Edwards v. Habib*, 397 F.2d 687 (D.C. Cir. 1968), written by Judge Wright, who also wrote *Javins*. In *Edwards*, T held under a month-to-month tenancy, which L purported to terminate after T had complained to authorities about sanitary code violations. The court held that L could terminate the tenancy for any legal reason, or for no reason at all, but *not for the purpose of retaliating for T's complaints*.

   i. Rationale: This conclusion was based principally on the theory that Congress, in authorizing the D.C. Housing Code impliedly prohibited landlords from using such retaliatory measures; a contrary holding, the court stated, would "clearly frustrate the effectiveness of the housing code as a means of upgrading the quality of housing in Washington." Not only would the tenant who complained be evicted, but *other tenants* would be *intimidated* into not making similar complaints.

   ii. Subsequent right to terminate: The court in *Edwards* acknowledged that T did not thereby gain a right to remain on the premises *perpetually*. She could be removed subsequently if the landlord could show that his illegal, retaliatory, purpose had been "dissipated". This issue is discussed further *infra*, p. 162.

   b. Actual existence of violation: *Edwards* did not address the issue of whether the violations complained of by the tenant must *actually exist* (since the housing authority there found that there were indeed violations). At least one case, *Dickhut v. Norton*, 173 N.W.2d 297 (Wisc. 1970), has held that the tenant must show by "clear and convincing" evidence that there *was in fact* a housing code violation. The court also required the tenant to show that the landlord knew that the tenant had reported the condition, and that retaliation was the "sole purpose" of the termination by the landlord.

   i. Restatement view: But the Restatement requires only that the tenant's complaint about violations be made in *good faith* and with "reasonable cause".

Rest. 2d, §14.8, Comment g, makes clear that reasonable cause may exist even where there is not actual violation, if the tenant actually investigated the property before complaining.

   c. **Burden of proof:** Most cases and statutes place the burden of proving a retaliatory motive **upon the tenant**. However, the URLTA, in §5.101(b), establishes a **presumption** that the landlord's conduct was retaliatory if it is shown that the tenant made a complaint to a government agency within one year prior to the attempted eviction. But the presumption does not arise if the tenant made the complaint after being notified of a proposed rent increase or diminution of services.

2. **Withholding of rent:** The retaliatory eviction defense may also be available where the defendant, rather than complaining to housing authorities, **withholds rent**, claims that the **lease is illegal** because of defects, or otherwise asserts his remedies for breach of the warranty of habitability. The principal case recognizing the retaliatory eviction defense in such circumstances is *Robinson v. Diamond Housing Corp.*, 463 F.2d 853 (D.C. Cir. 1972). In *Robinson*, T held under a month-to-month lease, entered into on the understanding that L would correct certain defects. When L failed to do so, T began withholding rent, and L sued to evict her. T raised a *Brown v. Southall Realty Co.* defense (*supra*, p. 147), i.e., that the lease was unenforceable because of the housing code violations. This defense was successful, so that she was not evicted. L then gave notice that it was terminating the tenancy at the end of the following month.

   a. **Holding:** The D.C. Circuit, again by Judge Wright, held that the rationale of *Edwards v. Habib* was applicable to this situation as well. Since T had the right to withhold rent, and the right to have the lease declared unenforceable under *Brown v. Southall*, she should not be penalized for asserting those rights by being evicted.

3. **Joining in tenants' organization:** The landlord might also seek to evict the tenant for having joined a **tenants' organization**. Even if this tenants' organization does not make a complaint to the authorities, and the eviction is simply because the tenant joined the organization, the retaliatory eviction defense has been allowed by a few courts. See Rest. 2d, §14.8, Reporter's Note, Item 4.

   a. **Constitutional association right:** An alternate ground for preventing the eviction in this situation is based upon **constitutional** freedom of association and due process concepts. If the tenant can show that the landlord's conduct was the equivalent of **state action** (e.g., the landlord is a public housing authority), the tenant may be able to resist eviction on the grounds that his First Amendment right to freedom of association and his Fourteenth Amendment due process rights have been violated. See, e.g., *McQueen v. Druker*, 438 F.2d 781 (1st Cir. 1971).

4. **Landlord raises rent:** It may happen that the landlord, rather than terminating the lease completely, **raises the rent substantially**, or otherwise makes the terms significantly less attractive to the tenant. Assuming that the other requirements for the retaliatory eviction doctrine are met, the court would probably allow the defense in this situation, even though there is not an "eviction," strictly speaking. See Rest. 2, §14.8, Comment b.

5. **Commercial leases:** Nearly all statutes dealing with retaliatory eviction restrict the defense to residential, as opposed to **commercial**, leases. Virtually all cases appear to do the same. See, e.g., *William C. Cornitius, Inc. v. Wheeler*, 556 P.2d 666 (Or. 1976). The Restatement does not take a position on whether the defense should apply to commercial leases; see Rest. 2d §14.8, Caveat.

6. **Dissipation of taint:** Assuming that the landlord is found to have attempted an illegal retaliatory eviction, is he stuck with the tenant forever? All court which have confronted the issue recognize that public policy should permit the landlord, at some point, to *remove the tenant*. The general approach is that the landlord may subsequently evict if he can show that his *retaliatory motive has been dissipated*, and that he now seeks to evict for other, legitimate, reasons. The question of whether the landlord's motive is no longer retaliatory is a question of fact for the jury. See *Edwards v. Habib*, 397 F.2d 687 (D.C. Cir. 1968) (discussed more extensively *supra*, p. 160).

K. **Merits of habitability warranty in general:** The implied warranty of habitability has, of course, been championed by those concerned with the housing problems of apartment dwellers, particularly low-income tenants.

   1. **Criticism:** But even among those concerned with the welfare of tenants, there are some who criticize the idea of a non-waivable implied warranty of habitability. See e.g., 27 Stan L. Rev. 879 (1975), arguing that such an implied warranty is likely to result in: (1) upgrading of some rental units, but only when accompanied by a *raising of rents* to cover the added costs (so that some tenants will be forced out); (2) the discouraging of construction of new low-rent housing, because of the additional costs that a landlord would have to bear; and (3) the *abandonment* of some rental stock, as to which rents cannot be raised enough to keep the building profitable in light of higher maintenance expenses. Also, the author argues that such a warranty, even if justified, should be enacted by the legislature, not by judicial fiat.

   2. **Rebuttal:** But there is at least some empirical evidence that public and private enforcement of housing standards does not cause a significant decrease in low-cost housing stock. See, e.g., 80 Yale, L.J. 1093 (1971), cited in *Robinson v. Diamond Housing Corp.*, 463 F.2d 853 (D.C. Cir. 1972). Furthermore, it is beyond dispute that at least some tenants will be benefitted in the short term by the implied warranty, since they will either get a reduction in rent or repairs of their premises. And where the implied warranty co-exists with a system of rent control (see *infra*, p. 196), the warranty will not result in a rise in rents which are already at the rent controlled level.

L. **Premises destroyed or suddenly damaged:** If the premises are *suddenly destroyed* or damaged by *fire*, flood, lightning, or other natural elements, the common-law view nonetheless requires the tenant to *keep paying rent*, and does *not* allow his to *terminate* the lease. The rationale for this position is that the tenant has purchased an estate in land, and assuming that the land itself is not destroyed, he has gotten what he bargained for.

   1. **Common-law exception:** Thus where the tenant leased only *certain rooms in a building*, or leased structures without leasing the land underneath, even under the common-law view he was relieved of rent liability if the premises were destroyed; in this case, the very subject matter of the lease was destroyed, unlike the case of a lease covering both structures and land. 1 A.L.P. 397-98.

   2. **Modern statutes relieve tenant:** The common-law rule, insofar as it required the tenant to keep paying rent for premises that were no longer usable, was obviously extremely harsh. Furthermore, the landlord, at least in cases of short-term leases, is much more likely to carry *insurance* against destruction of the building than is the tenant. Therefore, during the last century about half the states have passed *statutes* changing the common-law rule. These statutes typically provide that if the premises are destroyed or so damaged that they are no longer habitable, the tenant may *terminate the lease* and stop paying rent.

a. **Damage must be sudden:** The statutes typically apply only to *casualty-type* losses, i.e., ones that are *sudden* and unexpected. Thus if the premises *gradually deteriorate* because of the elements, the statute will not apply. See Rest. 2d, §5.4, Comment f.

Example: The roof of the premises develops a leak during the winter, which worsens until the premises become water-logged. T stops paying rent, and L sues. *Held*, for L. The relevant statute relieves the tenant where premises are "destroyed" or "injured" by the elements. This language does not apply to "gradual deterioration from the ordinary action of the elements . . . ," such as occurred here. *Suydam v. Jackson*, 54 N.Y. 450 (1873).

b. **Parties may agree otherwise:** Whether or not there is a statute relieving the defendant of liability, the parties are always free to make their *own agreement* governing the effects of sudden destruction. For instance, where such a statute does not exist, a clause in the lease may require the landlord to carry insurance, and also require him either to rebuild the premises within a stated period, or to release the tenant from rent liability.

c. **Case law in accord:** In state where there is no statute, courts have sometimes as a matter of case law relieved the tenant of the obligation to pay rent where the building has been destroyed. See, e.g, *Albert M. Greenfield & Co. v. Kolea*, 380 A.2d 758 (Pa. 1977), in which the court held that "if it is evident . . . that the parties bargained for the existence of a building, and no provision is made as to who bears the risk of loss if the building is destroyed, the court should relieve the parties of their respective obligations when the building no longer exists." See also, Rest. 2d §5.4, allowing the tenant to terminate the lease if "after the tenant's entry and without fault of the tenant, a change in the condition of the leased property . . . caused suddenly by a non-manmade force, makes the property unsuitable for the use contemplated by the parties. . . ."

   i. **Termination sole remedy:** Most courts would probably *not* allow the tenant to recover damages or abate the rent in this situation. The Restatement explicitly makes termination of the lease the tenant's *sole remedy* in the destruction situation; Rest. 2d, §5.4, Comment f.

3. **Damage caused by third persons:** It may happen that although the damage is directly caused by the elements, it is indirectly caused by the act of a *third person*; the courts are split as to whether the statute applies in this situation. See, e.g., *Polack v. Pioche*, 35 Cal. 416 (1868), holding that an exception from T's duty to repair for "damages by the elements or acts of Providence" does not include a flood caused by a third person's interference with a reservoir.

4. **Duty to repair:** Destruction or sudden damage to the property may also raise issues of whether either party is required to *repair* it. A statute which relieves the tenant of the duty to pay rent will almost certainly also relieve him of the duty to repair, at least where this duty of repair exists only by common-law implication and not by express promise. The duty of repair in general, and its application in cases of destruction, is discussed further *infra*, p. 172.

V. TORT LIABILITY OF LANDLORD AND TENANT

A. Tenant's tort liability: A tenant, during the time he is in possession of the premises, is treated *like an owner*, for purposes of his *tort liability* to others who come onto the property.

    1. Extent of duty: A full discussion of the tenant's tort liability to others is beyond the scope of this outline. However, a few general rules may be stated:

        a. Trespasser: The tenant has, generally speaking, no tort liability to a *trespasser* on the property (but there are exceptions).

        b. Licensee: One who comes on the premises as a *social guest*, but not for a business purpose, has the right to be *warned* by the tenant of dangers that the tenant is aware of. Such a guest is usually called a *licensee*.

        c. Invitee: One who comes on the premises for *business purposes*, called an *invitee*, is owed a full duty of *reasonable care* by the tenant. The latter is not only required to warn of dangers of which he is aware, but is also required to make *reasonable inspection* to discover defects, and to take reasonable steps to correct them. See, e.g, *King v. Cooney-Eckstein Co.*, 63 So. 659 (Fla. 1913), holding that T has a duty to keep the premises reasonably safe for invitees, even though L may have contracted to keep the premises in repair.

        d. Some courts abolish distinction: Some courts have abolished this three-part distinction, and hold that a tenant, or any other property owner, simply has a general duty to use *reasonable care* for the safety of anyone who comes on the premises. See *Sargent v. Ross*, discussed *infra*, p. 170 (decided in the context of the lessor's duty of care).

        For a more detailed discussion of the duties of landowners in general, and tenants in particular, see Emanuel on *Torts*.

B. Liability of landlord: At common law, the landlord is generally *not liable* for physical injury to the tenant, or to persons on the leased property with the tenant's consent. Like the absence of an implied warranty of habitability, the rule of no-tort-liability stems from the view that the tenant buys an estate in the land, and takes the premises as they are. See, e.g., *Bowles v. Mahoney*, 202 F.2d 320 (D.C. Cir. 1952).

    1. Exceptions: However, the common law has always recognized certain *exceptions* to the general rule that the landlord has no tort liability to his tenant, or to others on the premises with the tenant's consent. In recent years, additional exceptions have been recognized in many jurisdictions. Perhaps the most important development is that in those jurisdictions where there is an implied warranty of habitability (*supra*, p. 151), there is probably a corresponding tort liability imposed on the landlord if injury results from a failure to honor this warranty. The most important situations where the landlord is liable are as follows:

    2. Concealment or failure to disclose: The landlord will be liable if he *conceals*, or fails to disclose, a dangerous defect existing at the start of the lease.

        a. Landlord should know but does not: This rule applies, of course, where the landlord actually knows about the defect, and remains silent. Most courts also apply it where the landlord does not have actual knowledge, but *should know* about the danger, based on facts which he does know. See, e.g., *Johnson v. O'Brien*,

105 N.W.2d 244 (Minn. 1960) (L liable for injuries to T's daughter-in-law, where L should have known of defective condition of back stairway). See also Rest. 2d §17.1.

    i. No duty of inspection: But the rule making the landlord liable for concealment is *not* usually interpreted as requiring the lessor to *inspect* the property for hidden defects.

    ii. California case: However, a California case, *Becker v. IRM Corp.*, 698 P.2d 116 (1985), has interpreted the concealment doctrine as imposing on the lessor a duty to inspect rental property for dangerous conditions both when purchasing and when leasing out the premises. The lessor was charged with knowledge of those dangers that would have been disclosed by a reasonable inspection. (The *Becker* case is discussed further *infra*, p. 170.)

  b. Liability to persons other than tenant: Nearly all courts hold that if L would be liable to T, he is also liable to *persons on the premises with T's consent*. See Rest. 2d, §17.1(1). But if L has *told* T about the defect (so that it is not a concealed danger), L is not liable to T's guests even if T did not in turn tell them about the danger. Rest. 2d, §17.1, Reporter's Note, Item 7.

3. Areas kept under landlord's control: In a multi-unit dwelling or office building, certain areas will normally be *retained under the landlord's control*. These may be areas that the tenant is entitled to use (e.g., the *lobby*, *elevator* and *corridor*), or they may be areas to which the tenant normally does not have access (e.g., the *roof*). Regardless of whether the tenant has access, it is universally held that the landlord has a *duty to use reasonable care* to keep these *common areas* safe. See, e.g., *Pessagno v. Euclid Investment Co.*, 112 F.2d 577 (D.C. Cir. 1940).

  a. Defects existing at beginning of tenancy: All courts seem to agree that the landlord is required to use reasonable care in repairing defects in the common areas coming into existence *after the lease has begun*. Most courts also hold that he must use reasonable care to remedy dangers that existed *prior to the start of the lease*; but Massachusetts appears to hold that the landlord need only keep the common areas in as safe a condition as existed at the beginning of the lease (thus relieving him of the obligation to cure defects existing when the least starts). Rest. 2d, §17.3, Reporter's Note, Item 8.

    i. Restatement view: The Restatement requires the landlord to use reasonable care, regardless of whether the defect existed prior to the start of the lease, or developed subsequently. Rest. 2d, §17.3.

  b. Third persons protected: Anyone who is on the premises with the consent of the tenant may recover from the landlord for failure to keep the common areas safe. The fact that the tenant himself may have been aware of the danger, but has forgotten to warn the guest, will not prevent the guest from recovering from the landlord. (And in fact even if the guest knew of the danger, unless he was contributorily negligent, he will be able to recover.) Rest. 2d §17.3, Reporter's Note, Item 11.

  c. Security against criminal intrusion: Suppose the landlord fails to install adequate *security measures*, so that the criminals are able to enter the building, and rob and assault the tenants. Although courts traditionally have rejected liability in this situation, on the grounds that there is no duty to protect against the criminal acts of a third person, the tide has turned sharply in recent years. It is now probable that most courts will require the landlord to use reasonable care in preventing unauthorized access to the building (though what constitutes reasonable care may well depend on the rent level of the building, the nature of the neighborhood, and other factors). See Rest. 2d, §17.3, Comment 1.

i. Basis for duty: Of those decisions holding that the landlord may be liable, most seem to be based at least in part on the idea that entrances and lobbies are *retained within the landlord's control*. But the implied warranty of habitability has also been cited, as well as more general negligence principles.

Example: T is a tenant in a large apartment building owned by L. At the time she became a tenant, the building had a doorman, but L has thereafter ceased to furnish one, and has not adopted replacement security measures. T is assaulted and robbed in the hallway of the building one night, and sues L. There is evidence that there had been an increasing number of assaults and thefts in the building prior to the attack on T. *Held*, L had a duty to use reasonable care to protect its tenants from "foreseeable criminal acts committed by third parties". L was in a much better position to take such steps than its tenants; furthermore, it had notice of the dangers. And T was led to "expect that she could rely upon" protection, since there was a doorman when she moved into the building. L is not necessarily required to maintain a doorman, if other procedures (e.g, a tenant-controlled intercom latch system) could provide the same relative degree of security as that which T relied upon. *Kline v. 1500 Massachusetts Ave. Apartment Corp.*, 439 F.2d 477 (D.C. Cir. 1970).

4. **Repairs negligently performed:** If the landlord *attempts to make a repair*, he may incur liability if the repair is done *negligently*.

   a. **Condition made worse or concealed:** All courts agree that the landlord will be liable if his negligence makes the condition *more dangerous*, or lulls the tenant into a *false feeling of security*. This could occur, for instance, if L told T that the danger had been fixed, when in fact it had not.

      i. Condition not worsened or concealed: Where the landlord is negligent, but does *not* make the condition worse, or make it look deceptively safe, the courts are *split*. See the Caveat to Rest. 2d, §17.7, expressing no opinion as to whether there is liability for negligent repair if the risk has not been increased and no deceptive appearance of safety has been created.

   b. **Gratuitous repair:** This exception for negligent repair applies even where the landlord had *no legal duty to make the repair* at all, either by contract or by statute (discussed *infra*, p. 167).

   c. **Knowledge of tenant:** Most courts hold that L is liable only where T *does not know* that the repairs were negligent, or unfinished.

      i. Suits by third persons: Furthermore, although third persons who are on the premises with T's consent may sue, they will probably lose their right to do so if T knew the repairs had been negligently done or not finished, even if he did not pass on this knowledge.

      Example: P is a social guest in a house rented by T from L. Because of defects in the roofing, water continually drips on to the front steps and freezes in cold weather. L begins to repair the roof, but does not finish, and T is aware that the danger has not been corrected. He fails to warn P about the problem, and P slips.

P sues L. *Held*, for L. L "could reasonably assume that [T] would inform his guest about the icy condition on the front steps", and L is therefore not liable. *Borders v. Roseberry*, 532 P.2d 1366 (Kan. 1975)

5. **Landlord contracts to repair:** The landlord may sometimes be under a *contractual duty* to keep the premises safe; for instance, the lease might explicitly impose upon L the duty to make all or certain repairs on the property. If L has such a contractual duty, and fails to use reasonable care to perform it, about *half* the states now permit T to recover for personal injuries that result.

   a. **Only reasonable care required:** Even in these jurisdictions, L does not become liable in tort merely for having failed to perform his contract. Instead, T must show that L *failed to use reasonable care* to perform the contract. Thus L is entitled to *notice* of the danger, and a reasonable time within which to correct it, even though the contract may not explicitly give him this right.

   b. **Liability to third persons:** Most of the courts recognizing tort liability in this situation hold that a *third person* on the premises with T's consent may recover. Rest. 2d, §17.5 But a few courts hold that only the person in privity of contract with the landlord (i.e., the tenant) may recover based on the contractual duty. In view of the broad extension of tort liability deriving from contracts in other situations (e.g., products liability), the minority view will probably lose most of its present adherents eventually.

6. **Landlord under legal duty to repair:** Apart from an express provision in the lease itself, the landlord will today frequently have a *legal duty* to keep the premises in habitable, and safe, condition. Particularly in the case of *residential* leases, building codes are likely to impose such a duty upon him; furthermore, either case law or a statute may impose an *implied warranty of habitability*, whether based upon building codes or on some other standard. (*Supra*, p. 151.)

   a. **Express statutory duty:** When a statute expressly requires the landlord to perform a certain type of repair (e.g., maintenance of fire escapes or elevators) most courts agree that his violation of this duty can be relied upon by the tenant in a tort suit. Some of these courts hold that violation of the statutory duty is *negligence per se*. Others hold that the statutory violation is merely *evidence* of negligence, which the jury may or may not find is conclusive; see, e.g., *Whetzel v. Jess Fisher Management Co.*, 282 F.2d 943 (D.C. Cir. 1960), to this effect, but also holding that L need not be shown to have had actual knowledge of the dangerous condition needing repair, if he should have known of it.

      i. **Minority view:** But a minority of courts, probably dwindling in size, holds that a statutory violation cannot be relied upon at all by the tenant suing for personal injuries, unless the *statute itself* explicitly imposes tort liability. See, e.g., *Newman v. Sears, Roebuck & Co.*, 43 N.W.2d 411 (N.D. 1950).

   b. **Implied warranty of habitability:** Where the landlord's legal duty to repair is based not upon an explicit statutory violation, but merely upon a more general *implied warranty of habitability*, few cases have considered the landlord's tort liability. It seems probable, however, that most cases treating this issue will find that the implied warranty can give rise to tort liability; otherwise, the theory that private action by tenants will enforce the warranty loses much of its force. See *Old Town Development Co. v. Langford*, 349 N.E. 2d 744 (Ct. App. Ind. 1976), finding tort liability based upon the implied warranty of habitability. Rest. 2d, §17.6(1), explicitly allows tort liability based upon the implied warranty.

   c. Reasonable care standard: But as with liability based upon violation of a contractual duty to repair (*supra*, p. 167), any tort liability based upon the implied warranty of habitability is likely to require a showing of *negligence* on the landlord's part. That is, the mere fact that the premises were not maintained in safe and habitable condition will in most courts not be enough; there must be evidence that the landlord *knew*, or *should have known*, of the danger, and had *reasonable time to correct it*. Several courts have explicitly refused to allow tort liability to be based upon a *strict liability* theory (i.e., not requiring a showing of negligence), where a violation of the implied warranty of habitability was shown.

      i. New Jersey position: But one state, New Jersey, appears to have imposed something akin to *strict liability* for such a violation of the implied warranty of habitability. In *Trentacost v. Brussel*, 412 A.2d 436 (N.J. 1980), the court held that the implied warranty of habitability obliges a landlord to furnish "reasonable safeguards to protect tenants from *foreseeable criminal activity* on the premises." Although this sounds like a traditional negligence standard, the court went on to hold that "since landlord's implied undertaking to provide adequate security exists *independently of his knowledge of any risks*, there is no need to prove notice of such a defective and unsafe condition to establish the landlord's contractual duty. It is enough that the defendant did not take measures which were in fact reasonable for maintaining a habitable residence."

      ii. Significance: The principle express in *Trentacost* would apparently make the landlord liable for failure to install at least some security measures *even if there had not previously been criminal episodes* in the neighborhood (since, viewed after the fact, use of such measures would have been "in fact reasonable"). Nor would the court necessarily be permitted to take into account such considerations as the economic level of the dwelling, so that the same security might be required in a rent-controlled walk-up as in a luxury high-rise. No other state court seems to have come close to the *Trentacost* position; see B,C&S, p. 503, note 4.

   d. Third persons: Where liability to the tenant would exist, there will be similar liability to *third persons* on the premises with the landlord's consent. See Rest. 2d, §17.6, Reporter's Note, Item 6.

7. Admission of public: If the landlord has reason to believe that the tenant will *hold the premises open to the public*, and he also has reason to believe that this may occur before a condition which the landlord knows is dangerous has been repaired, the landlord will be liable. The rationale for this rule is that where the safety of the public at large is at stake, the landlord has a higher duty than where only casual visitors are expected; the landlord should not be allowed freely to transfer this responsibility onto the tenant.

   a. Duty of inspection: In most states, the landlord of such premises has an affirmative *duty to inspect* them to find and repair dangerous conditions. See Rest. 2d, §17.2(3).

   b. Defect must exist prior to lease: The landlord is only liable only for dangerous conditions existing *at the time the tenant takes possession*. Rest. 2d, §17.2. Thus if the premises are turned over in good condition, and due to the tenant's negligence the structure deteriorates to a dangerous point, the landlord has no liability even if he is aware of the condition.

c. **No requirement of paid admission:** Most courts do not require that the plaintiff be one who has *paid* to be admitted. For instance, one who has attended a free public meeting would normally be entitled to recover under this rule. Rest. 2d, §17.2, Reporter's Note, Item 5. But the plaintiff must be one who has entered for the very *purpose* for which the premises are held open to the public. Thus in the case of a restaurant, customers of the restaurant would be protected, but a *deliveryman* bringing in supplies would not be. Rest. 2d, §17.2, Comment e.

d. **Small number of persons expected at one time:** The public does not have to be expected to enter in *large numbers at one time*. It is enough that two or three members of the public will be on the premises at any one time, as in a doctor's office. See, e.g., *Spain v. Kelland*, 379 P.2d 149 (Ariz. 1963) (small tavern). See also Rest. 2d, §17.2, Comment d.

e. **Tenant's promise to repair:** The landlord is only liable if he has reason to believe that the tenant will admit the public prior to repair of the dangerous condition. But the landlord does not automatically escape liability merely because his lease contains a *promise by the tenant* to make the repairs. Nor will a clause in the lease exculpating the landlord be effective, particularly since a member of the public is, by hypothesis, not a party to that clause. Rest. 2d, §17.2, Comment j.

   i. **Promise about admitting public:** But if the lease contains an express promise by the tenant that he will *not admit the public* until he has made certain repairs, this will generally be enough to relieve the landlord of liability. Rest. 2d, §17.2, Comment i.

8. **General "reasonable care" theory:** Some courts have simply *rejected* the common-law view that a landlord has no general duty to use reasonable care. These courts have usually reached this result as part of an overall change in the common-law treatment of property owners (e.g., an abolition of the distinction between trespassers, licensees and invitees). In landlord-tenant cases, this change means that it is no longer necessary for the plaintiff to fit himself within one of the exceptions discussed above; instead, he need merely show that the landlord has failed to use reasonable care with respect to the property and that this lack of reasonable care has proximately caused the plaintiff's injury.

   Example: L owns a two-story apartment building, and lives on the ground floor. Her sons and daughter-in-law live on the second floor, and get to their quarters by an exterior stairway. The daughter-in-law is babysitting one day for P's four-year-old daughter, when the child falls off the stairway to her death. Evidence shows that the stairway was constructed in a dangerously steep way. P sues L.

   Held, L had a general duty to exercise reasonable care not to subject persons on the premises to an unreasonable risk of harm. This is so even though the stairway was not retained under L's control. To relieve L of liability because she no longer had control would leave P without a remedy, since the daughter-in-law testified that as tenant, she had no authority to rebuild the stairway. Henceforth, the issue of control will be irrelevant; landlords, like other people, will simply be required to *use reasonable care not to subject others to an unreasonable risk of harm*. This new rule flows naturally from the abolition of the *caveat emptor* doctrine in landlord-tenant relations and the establishment of the implied warranty of habitability in residential leases. Thus the jury could properly find that L was negligent in designing the staircase, or in not modifying it to reduce dangers. *Sargent v. Ross*, 308 A.2d 528 (N.H. 1973).

   a. Duty to provide security: Some of the cases requiring the landlord to follow *reasonable security measures* to protect his tenants from *criminal intrusion* may be seen as imposing a general duty of care on the landlord. See, e.g., *Kline v. 1500 Massachusetts Ave. Apartment Corp.*, 439 F.2d 477 (D.C. Cir. 1970), discussed *supra*, p. 166.

9. **Strict liability for latent defects:** One court has even imposed *strict liability* on a lessor, where a latent defect in the property resulted in personal injury. In *Becker v. IRM Corp.*, 698 P.2d 116 (Cal. 1985), the California Supreme Court held that P could recover for injuries he incurred when he broke a shower door in an apartment leased to him by D, even though the average person inspecting the glass would not have seen that it was of a dangerous "untempered" variety and even though the glass was already part of the premises when D acquired them. "A landlord engaged in the business of leasing dwellings *is strictly liable in tort for injuries resulting from a latent defect in the premises when the defect existed at the time the premises were let to the tenant.*" (The court relied on the fact that the landlord is in a better position to inspect for latent defects, and on the general rationale — derived from product liability cases — that the one who markets a product must bear the cost of injuries resulting therefrom.)

C. **Exculpatory clauses:** Courts are divided upon the effect of an *exculpatory clause* in a lease, which purports to relieve the landlord of any tort liability for his negligence. In keeping with the general broadening of landlords' tort liability, most courts today take a *hostile view* of such clauses, particularly in residential leases, and particularly where the clause is part of a standard "boilerplate" fine-print contract, and the clause is not separately bargained for. See, e.g., *McCutcheon v. United Homes Corp.*, 486 P.2d 1093 (Wash. 1971) (clause in a residential apartment lease, purporting to exonerate L from the consequence of his negligence in maintaining the common areas, is invalid).

   1. **Statutes:** Nearly half the states have *statutes* invalidating exculpatory clauses, in at least some situations. See Statutory Note to Rest. 2d, §17.3. California, Connecticut, Florida, Illinois, Massachusetts, New York and Ohio are among the states with such statutes.

      a. Residential limitation: Most of these statutes apply only to *residential leases*.

D. **Transfer of landlord's interest:** If the landlord *transfers his interest* in the property, this may have an impact upon his tort liability, at least for acts and conditions prior to this transfer. This subject is discussed further *infra*, p. 191.

VI. TENANT'S DUTIES

A. **Duty to pay rent:** The tenant normally has a duty, of course, to *pay rent*; this is one of the things that defines the landlord-tenant relationship.

   1. **Breach of landlord's duties:** At common law, as noted, covenants were independent, so that even a breach by the landlord of most of his duties did not entitle the tenant to stop paying rent. Most modern courts, particularly those that have recognized the implied warranty of habitability (*supra*, p. 151) have modified this rule, so that a *material breach* by the landlord of his implied or express obligations at least *temporarily relieves the tenant from continuing to pay rent*. Typically, the tenant has the right to withhold rent (which usually has to be paid into a private or public account

as it comes due), to make repairs himself and deduct the amount from the rent, or to gain a judicial abatement (i.e., reduction), of rent. These remedies are all discussed beginning *supra*, p. 156.

2. **Termination of lease:** The mere fact that the tenant has **abandoned the premises** will **not** relieve him from the duty to pay rent. But if the landlord has violated his express or implied duty to keep the property in repair, this may entitle the tenant to abandon the premises and also to **terminate the lease**, under the doctrine of constructive eviction. If he does so, no further rent is due. See *supra*, p. 156.

3. **Termination by landlord:** The landlord may be his own actions expressly or impliedly terminate the lease. For instance, if the tenant abandons the premises without cause, and the landlord takes possession for his own purposes, this will probably constitute an acceptance of surrender by the landlord, so that the tenant's further duty to pay rent is nullified. Termination of the lease is discussed more extensively *infra*, p. 175, in the treatment of landlords' remedies.

B. **Duty to repair:** The landlord, at common law, had no general duty to keep the premises in repair. (*Supra*, p. 149.) By contrast, the tenant had an implied duty to make **minor repairs**, an obligation arising from his duty not to commit waste (*supra*, p. 89). As the idea was sometimes put, the tenant was required to keep the buildings **"windtight and watertight"**. For instance, he was required to replace a broken window, or to repair a leaking roof. But he was not required to make **major** repairs, such as the reconstruction of a building severely damaged by fire or flood; nor was he required to correct defects existing at the beginning of his lease. 1 A.L.P. 347.

1. **Modern change in rule:** However, the widespread imposition of an implied warranty of habitability on the part of the landlord (*supra*, p. 151) has resulted in the shifting of the duty of repair from tenant to landlord. In any lease where the landlord is held to have made such a warranty, replacement of a broken window or repair of a leaky roof will probably be his obligation, not the tenant's.

2. **Express promise to repair:** The duty of repair may still be imposed on the tenant by means of an **express promise** to that effect in the lease. However, the courts sometimes refuse to enforce such clauses, particularly in residential leases (*supra*, pp. 155-56).

   a. **Ordinary wear and tear:** If the clause is simply a general promise to repair, the court will probably hold that there is no duty to overcome the effects of **ordinary wear and tear**. In any event, many repair clauses contain an explicit exception for such wear and tear.

   b. **Government regulations:** Repairs or modifications may be required by **government regulations**. If the lessee has promised to make repairs, he will have to make those required by the government if they would otherwise fall within his repair promise (e.g., fixing of a defective stairway), or if they result from his particular use of the premises. 1 A.L.P. 353.

      i. **Structural changes:** But if the government requires major, **structural** changes, the tenant will not normally be required to make them even under a general promise to repair. 1 A.L.P. 353-54.

3. **Destruction or sudden damage:** A duty to repair may also arise where the premises have been **destroyed** or substantially **damaged**, by fire, flood or other casualty.

a. Implied duty: Where the tenant's duty to repair is merely the implied common-law one (*supra*, p. 169), he will generally not be required to make the major repairs that are necessitated by such a casualty.

b. Promise to repair: But where the tenant has ***explicitly*** promised to make repairs, the courts are split; a decision is likely to turn in part upon the precise wording of the repair clause.

  i. General repair clause: If the repair clause simply states that T will keep the premises in repair, with no more specificity than that, most courts have traditionally held that the ***tenant must repair*** even damage caused by casualty. See, e.g. *Chambers v. The North River Line*, 102 S.E. 198 (N.C. 1920) (T promises to "maintain" a wharf in its "present condition"; T must rebuild wharf damaged by freeze so severe that there had been only three like it in 40 years.)

  ii. Minority view: But a minority of courts hold that a duty to "make repairs" does not contemplate major rebuilding, so that the tenant is required neither to build nor to continue paying rent. 1 A.L.P. 350-51. (For a fuller discussion of whether T must continue to pay rent, see *supra*, p. 162.)

  iii. "Major repairs": In any event, a promise to make ***"major repairs"*** will probably require rebuilding. See *Evco Corp. v. Ross*, 528 S.W.2d 20 (Tenn. 1975) (L required to rebuild where premises badly damaged by fire, because of its promise to make "all major repairs that may become necessary" and to carry fire insurance.)

c. Statutes: *Statutes* exist in some states relieving the tenant of the duty to repair in the casualty situation; this is sometimes done in conjunction with a statutory release of his duty to continue paying rent. 1 A.L.P. 351, n. 13.

C. Fixtures: The tenant may wish to take a ***chattel***, i.e., an item of personal property, and ***attach*** it to the land. When the attachment has occurred, the chattel is usually called a ***fixture***. There are two principal issues raised by fixtures in landlord-tenant cases: (1) does the tenant have the right to make the attachment? and (2) does he have the right to remove it, and if so, when?

  1. Right to affix: The tenant's right to affix a fixture is generally discussed in terms of the doctrine of ***waste*** (*supra*, p. 89). Thus the tenant is permitted to make the annexation, under the modern view, if this would ***not unfairly interfere with the value of the landlord's reversion***.

    a. Restatement test: The Restatement provides that the tenant may make annexations (or other changes) which are "reasonably necessary in order for the tenant to use the leased property in a manner that is reasonable under all the circumstances". Rest. 2d, §12.2(1). Thus it may be reasonable for a long-term tenant to build a garage in the back of a house that has none (Rest. 2d, §12.2, Illustration 9), and it may not be permissible for T to build a partition between two rooms of a house that he has rented for only one year (*Id*, Illustration 7).

    b. Duty to remove at end: Even if the annexation is permissible, the landlord always has the right to require the tenant to ***remove*** it at the end of the lease term. (But, as is discussed immediately below, the landlord may also have the right to ***prevent*** the tenant from removing the fixture.)

2. Removal: Courts are not in agreement as to the test for determining whether the tenant may *remove* the fixture at the end of the lease term. Older courts frequently said that the test was one of *intention*; if the tenant, at the time he annexed the chattel, intended for it to remain his personal property, he had the right to remove it. 5 A.L.P. 39. But the modern tendency seems to be to consider whether removal will *damage the landlord's interest*; if it will, the fixture may not be removed, even though the tenant may have intended to keep the property as personalty.

    a. Damage to landlord's interest: In courts following the "damage to the landlord's interest" test, the issue is not whether the landlord's reversion will be worth less if the fixture is removed. Rather, the issue is usually whether the premises may be *restored to their former condition* after the fixture is removed; if so, removal is generally permissible (proved that the tenant does the restoration). Rest. 2d, §12.2(4).

    b. Trade fixtures: Courts are particularly liberal in allowing tenants to remove so-called *trade fixtures*, i.e., fixtures used for the purpose of carrying on a trade or business. Courts reason that in order to encourage commercial activity, a tenant should be entitled to remove whatever trade fixtures he has placed on the premises, unless damage to the landlord's interest would clearly result. See, e.g, *Handler v. Horns*, 65 A.2d 523 (N.J. 1949), holding that where T transformed a building used largely for a warehouse into a meat packing plant, he could remove a refrigeration system, meat hangers, and any other trade fixtures that could be carried away without damaging the building.

    c. Time to remove: Where the lease is for a term of years, the tenant must, according to most courts, remove his fixtures *before he leaves the premises*. Otherwise they become the property of the landlord. 5 A.L.P. 43. In the case of a tenancy at will or periodic tenancy, the tenant is usually given a *reasonable time* following termination of the tenancy in which to remove. *Id.*

D. Duty to behave reasonably: The tenant has an implied duty to *behave reasonably* in his use of the premises.

    1. Disturbing of others: Thus he must not *unreasonably disturb other tenants*. However, the courts have made allowance for the fact that in modern apartment buildings, a certain degree of interference, particularly noise, is inevitable among tenants.

    2. Obey regulations: The tenant is also required to obey *reasonable regulations* promulgated by the landlord. For instance, a reasonable rule might prohibit ballplaying in the building parking lot.

    3. Health and building codes: Also, most *building and health codes* imposes certain duties directly upon tenants. For instance, the tenant will typically be required to dispose of his garbage in a certain way.

    4. Waste: The tenant has a duty *not to commit waste*. The common-law duty to make minor repairs, discussed *supra*, p. 171, in one facet of this duty. For a fuller discussion of waste, as it applies not only to the landlord-tenant relationship but in other situations as well, see *supra*, p. 89.

VII. LANDLORD'S REMEDIES

A. Security deposits: The lease will typically require the tenant to make a *security deposit* with the landlord, usually in an amount equal to one or two months rent. The purpose of the deposit is to secure the landlord against any damages which he may sustain as a consequence of a breach by the tenant. Typically, this security is left to defray damages caused by *abandonment* of the premises by the tenant, or by misuse by him (e.g, excessively large holes left in the walls from nails and tacks).

1. **Interest:** In may states, the landlord is required by statute to pay *interest* on the security deposit.

2. **Right to keep deposit:** Once the lease terminates, the landlord must return the security to the tenant, after subtracting any damages which he has suffered. Thus if the tenant abandons the premises prematurely, and the landlord relets on his own account (thus terminating the lease; see *infra*, p. 178), the landlord must immediately return the deposit after subtracting his damages; he is not entitled to keep the deposit until the scheduled end of the lease terms. Rest. 2d, §12.1, Reporter's Note, Item 11.

   a. **Regulating statutes:** Statutes passed in a number of states limit the landlord's right to retain residential security deposits. Such statutes often require the landlord to give the tenant an *itemized list* of claimed damages as well as *receipts* for alleged repairs. Also, the court may award the tenant double or treble damages and/or attorney's fees if the landlord wrongfully withholds a security deposit. C,S&W, pp. 378-79.

   b. **Advance rent:** Landlords frequently try to establish a right to keep the *entire* security deposit, regardless of the amount of damages actually sustained. To do this, they often call the security deposit by another name. If the lease labels the payment "liquidated damages" it will almost certainly be struck down, or limited to actual damages. But if the payment is termed *"advance rent"* or "prepaid rent", it may well be upheld, so that the landlord may keep the entire amount regardless of the amount of actual damages. Rest. 2d, §12.1, Reporter's Note, Item 11.

3. **Right to commingle:** In most states, the relation between landlord and tenant as to the security is merely a *debtor-creditor* relationship. Thus the landlord may *commingle* the money with his own funds, and if he goes bankrupt, the tenant is merely a general creditor.

   a. **Trust fund theory:** But several states treat the relationship either as one between a pledgor and pledgee (so that the tenant at least has a security interest in the deposit if the landlord goes bankrupt) or as creating a *"trust fund"* (in New York, by statute). Under the "trust fund" rule, the landlord must keep the deposit in a separate account, not commingled with his other funds. N.Y. Gen. Oblig. Law §7-103.

4. **Liability of purchaser from landlord:** The courts are split as to whether one who *purchases* the landlord's interest in the property must account to the tenant for the security deposit after the lease term.

   a. **Only if received by purchaser:** In some states, the purchaser is liable only if he has actually received the deposit from the prior landlord. See Rest. 2d, §16.1, Reporter's Note, Item 3.

b. Restatement position: The Restatement takes the position that the purchaser *must account* for the security deposit, even if he did not receive it from the prior landlord, on the grounds that this is an obligation which "touches and concerns the land" (see *infra*, p. 234). Rest. 2d, § 16.1, Illustration 13.

c. Statutes: A number of states have enacted *statutes* requiring the purchaser to account for the security deposit. See URLTA, §2.101(e).

B. Acceleration clause: The lease may contain an *acceleration of rent* clause. Such a clause provides that if the tenant fails to pay rent promptly, or otherwise materially breaches the lease, the landlord may require that *all of the rent for the rest of the lease term* is *payable at once*. This enables the landlord to bludgeon the tenant into making prompt payments, or to recover all his rent at once in court so that he doesn't have to worry thereafter about collecting month-by-month.

1. Generally valid: Most courts will *enforce* such acceleration clauses. See Rest. 2d, §12.1, Reporter's Note, Item 10.

2. Rules that must be followed: In those state enforcing acceleration clauses, courts impose two important restrictions:

a. Possession may not be demanded: If the landlord chooses to sue on the acceleration clause, *he may not demand possession* of the leased premises. Thus if he receives the entire rent that will come due, he must let the tenant remain on the premises. (Furthermore, the court may choose to allow L to receive only the *present value* of the remaining lease payments, particularly in times of high inflation, and where the lease has many years to run. Rest. 2d, §12.1, Comment k.)

b. Tenant abandons: If the tenant *abandons* the premises, the landlord may collect under the acceleration clause, provided that he does not take action that constitutes a termination of the lease (see *infra*, p. 178). However, if L subsequently *relets* the premises, he must then *return to the tenant* any amounts he gets from the new tenant. Rest. 2d, §12.1, Comment k.

C. Eviction: The landlord may desire to *remove the tenant from the premises*. This may happen either: (1) during the lease term, because the tenant has failed to pay rent or otherwise violated a term of the lease; or (2) after the lease has expired, and the tenant is improperly *holding over*.

1. Termination during the lease term: Prior to the scheduled expiration of the lease, the tenant may *fall behind in the rent*, or materially breach some other promise made by him in the lease (e.g., by making excessive noise and disturbing other tenants).

a. Express forfeiture clause: Most leases contain a special clause giving the landlord the right to *terminate the lease* if the tenant fails to pay rent or violates any other lease provision. Such clauses are often called *"forfeiture* clauses". These clauses are in principle enforceable in all courts (usually by means of summary proceedings, discussed *infra*, p. 176.

i. Breach must be material: However, because forfeiture of the right to remain on the premises is a drastic remedy, courts will generally allow it only where the tenant's breach has been *material*. Thus if T is merely a couple of days late with the rent on one or two occasions, the court will probably not allow L to oust him. See *Jamaica Builders Supply Corp. v. Buttelman*, 205 N.Y.S.2d 303 (Mun. Ct. N.Y. 1960) (refusing to allow forfeiture where notice of termination served nine days after rent was due).

    ii. Waiver: Furthermore, the courts will be quick to find that landlord has **waived** the benefit of the forfeiture clause as to a particular breach. For instance, even if T falls three months behind in his rent (enough so that a forfeiture clause would normally be enforced), if L then accepts T's payment of the past-due rent, L waives his right to rely on this default, at least if he remains silent. But L's right to forfeit is lost only as to this one breach; thus if T falls three months behind again, L can forfeit this time.

    iii. Tenant's right to rely: If a certain kind of breach by T is tolerated by L on several occasions, L may be required to give T some **advance notice** that he will no longer tolerate such breaches in the future, before L may invoke the forfeiture clause. Thus if T always pays his rent 30 days late, and L accepts it each time, L probably does not have the right to terminate when T is 25 days late with a particular payment, unless L has previously given notice that he will now strictly enforce the requirement of prompt payment.

  b. Forfeiture clause not used: If there is **no forfeiture clause** in the lease, and the tenant violates a lease term, the courts are split. The traditional **independence of covenants** doctrine prevented the landlord from terminating in this situation, since the landlord's duty to permit the tenant to remain on the premises was independent of the tenant's duty to pay rent or otherwise respect the lease.

    i. Dependent covenants: But in view of the recent tendency to hold that major covenants in a lease are **dependent**, some courts have permitted the landlord to terminate for a material breach by the tenant. See Rest. 2d, §13.1(1) (emphasizing, however, that termination is only permitted where the tenant's breach deprives the landlord of "a significant inducement to the making of the lease").

2. Hold-over tenant: If the tenant **holds over** after the lease term is over, the landlord is of course entitled to use legal proceedings to evict him. This is usually done by "summary" proceedings, discussed immediately below.

3. Summary proceedings: If the landlord is entitled to terminate the lease before its scheduled expiration, or the tenant is **holding over** after the scheduled expiration, the landlord may resort to judicial proceedings to oust the tenant. Traditionally, this was done by the common-law action of **ejectment**; but this was a terribly slow, cumbersome and expensive procedure. Accordingly, in all states, statutes have been enacted, usually called **summary proceedings** statutes, which provide for a **speedy trial** of the landlord's right to immediate possession.

  a. Defenses which must be raised: The speediness of the proceedings is accomplished partly by **restricting the defenses which may be raised**. Thus in many states, the tenant may not raise the defense of an **implied warranty of habitability** to justify his non-payment of rent. (But see *Jack Spring Inc. v. Little*, 280 N.E.2d 208 (Ill. 1972), allowing such a defense in a summary proceedings suit.)

  b. Constitutionality: A bar to raising the implied warranty of habitability in a summary procedure has been explicitly held **constitutional** by the Supreme Court. In *Lindsey v. Normet*, 405 U.S. 56 (1972), the Court held that such a bar was not a violation of due process, because T was free to sue in a separate, non-summary, action for any damages from breach of that warranty, and also for a return of any rent pre-paid.

i. **Rent during continuance:** The statute in *Lindsey* also provided that if the tenant wished a *continuance* before trial of more than two days, he must *post security* for the payment of any rent that might accrue during the continuance. The Supreme Court held that this provision, too, was constitutional.

ii. **Double bond on appeal:** But a third feature of the statute, requiring a tenant who wished to *appeal* from an adverse determination to post a bond in *twice the amount of the rent* expected to accrue during the appeal process, was struck down. The Court noted that virtually *all* appellants must post a bond during appeal; thus the tenant is required in any case to post a bond for the reasonable value of his use of the premises during the appeal. To tack a double-rent bond obligation on top of this, the Court held, constitutes a violation of the equal protection rights of tenants.

c. **Public housing evictions:** Additional constitutional protections may accrue to tenants in *public housing projects* whom the landlord seeks to evict. See *Joy v. Daniels*, discussed *infra*, p. 196.

4. **Self-help:** Despite the existence of judicial summary proceedings, the landlord will sometimes wish to use *self-help* to evict the tenant. That is, he may attempt to *physically oust* the tenant (e.g., by *changing the locks* when the tenant is out).

a. **Common law allows:** At common law, the landlord was *permitted* to use self-help, provided that he used no more force than was reasonably necessary to out the defendant. See, e.g., *Gower v. Waters*, 132 A.550 (Me. 1926) (L may use self-help, provided he uses no more force than is necessary to enter, and only mild force to oust T.)

b. **Modern courts split:** But at the present time, with summary proceedings available everywhere, the courts are *split* as to whether self-help may be used.

i. **Prohibition:** The modern trend is to entirely *prohibit* self-help, so that judicial proceedings are the only solution. This is the implicit position of Rest. 2d, §14.2

Example: L fears that T's continued remodeling of the leased premises without L's consent is damaging the premises and breaching the lease. L therefore retakes the premises, and changes the locks while T is absent. L then re-lets to someone else. T sues for damages.

Held, for T. From now on in Minnesota, if the tenant does not abandon or voluntarily surrender the premises, the landlord may regain possession (even if the tenant clearly breaches the lease) only by resort to judicial process. Public policy demands that the possibility of violence be kept to an absolute minimum, and the modern no-self-help rule best achieves this goal. Therefore, T may recover for lost profits. *Berg v. Wiley*, 264 N.W.2d 145 (Minn. 1978).

ii. **Other courts allow:** But other courts, probably still a slight majority, permit the landlord to use at least some degree of self-help to regain the premises. Rest. 2d, §14.2, Reporter's Note, Item 1. In some of these states, self-help may be used only if ouster may be accomplished *"peaceably"* (e.g., no touching of the tenant or his possessions is necessary, or the tenant is absent). Other courts continue to permit a *"reasonable"* degree of force.

   c. Tenant's remedies: If the landlord uses self-help when he is not permitted to, or uses more force than permitted, many states allow the tenant to sue in *tort* for damages. Also, the landlord may be *criminally liable*. But the tenant is never permitted to regain possession of the premises (assuming, of course, that the landlord would have had the right to possession by judicial means).

   d. Right to agree otherwise: Even if the jurisdiction does not permit self-help, the lease may contain a special clause whereby the tenant *consents* to such conduct by the landlord. Most states apparently *enforce* such a clause; see Rest. 2, §14.2, Reporter's Note, Item 5.

      i. Minority, but growing, view: But a growing minority of courts (and Rest. 2d, §14.2(2)) hold that where self-help is not otherwise permitted, an agreement to the contrary is *void* as against public policy. See, e.g., *Jordan v. Talbot*, 361 P.2d 20 (Cal. 1961); *Bass v. Boetel & Co.*, 217 N.W.2d 804 (Neb. 1974).

D. Damages for hold-over by tenant: If the tenant *holds over* after the lease terminates, the landlord is entitle to *damages* as well as eviction. This is true whether the tenancy has been terminated before its scheduled end because of a breach by the tenant, or the term has naturally expired and the tenant refuses to leave.

   1. Measure of damages: The landlord is entitled to the *reasonable value* of the tenant's use of the premises. Often, the amount set in the lease will be a good indication of the fair value; but the landlord may prove that the reasonable value was greater, and if he does, he may recover this larger amount. Rest. 2d, §14.5.

   2. Special damages: The landlord is also entitled to *special damages* caused by the hold-over, if the tenant could reasonably have foreseen that these would occur at the time he held over. Thus if T knows that L wishes to move a business from other premises to those now occupied by T, T will be liable for any damages suffered by L (e.g., loss of profits) that his hold-over causes. Rest., §14.6.

      a. Duty to mitigate: However, L may not recover for special damages which he *could have avoided* by taking reasonable measures. That is, L has a *"duty to mitigate"* his damages. Rest. 2d, §14.6.

         i. Exception for willful hold-overs: But in some (though not all) courts, this landlord's "duty to mitigate" may be found not to apply where the hold-over is "willful", i.e., the tenant could move out on time but chooses not to.

   3. "Double rent" provision: An English statute allows landlords to recover *double the rent* from a hold-over tenant in certain situations. See 1 A.L.P. 248. Several American states have similar statutes. However, these tend to be strictly construed; see, e.g. *Jones v. Taylor*, 123 S.W. 326 (Ky. 1909) (double rent statute does not apply where T has good faith belief that he has valid lease and is entitled to remain.)

E. Abandonment of premises by tenant: If the tenant *abandons* the premises (and defaults on the rent) before the scheduled end of the lease term, the landlord has three basic choices. Each has sharply different consequences, so that the landlord's choice is an important strategic decision which must be well thought-out. The three choices are: (1) to accept a surrender of the premises, thus terminating the lease; (2) to re-let on the tenant's behalf; and (3) to leave the premises vacant and sue for rent as it comes due (no longer an option in some jurisdictions).

1. **Accept surrender:** L may treat T's abandonment as a *surrender*, and accept it. This has the effect of *terminating* the lease, so that *no further rent becomes due from T*.

   a. **How manifested:** Such an acceptance of surrender will occur, of course, if L states that he regards the lease as terminated. But more probably, he will simply take possession of the premises himself, or lease them to someone else. If he does either of these things, and does *not notify T that he is acting on the latter's behalf*, then an acceptance of surrender will probably be found. In most states, the existence of an acceptance of surrender is a question of fact, to be resolved by gauging L's intent.

   b. **Prevention of vandalism:** If L reenters the premises merely to *secure them against vandalism*, or to inspect them for damage, this will not be an acceptance of surrender by itself. But if he performs *major alterations*, or *removes the tenant's remaining possessions*, this may be construed as being so directly against the tenant's interest in the leasehold as to amount to a termination (assuming that no notice was given to T that L was acting on T's account). Rest. 2d, §12.1, Reporter's Note, Item 8.

   c. **Lease provides for remaining rents:** The lease may contain a *provision* purporting to make T *liable for any rents accruing even after a termination* of the lease, or for any shortfall if L re-lets the premises. Assuming that a termination in fact occurs (under the test just described), such a clause will be *partially enforced* by most courts. L will be entitled only to the difference between the agreed-to rents and sums he receives from re-letting; also, he probably has a duty to mitigate his damages by making reasonable attempts to re-let. (This is in contrast to the majority rule applicable if no termination of the lease occurs; see *infra*.) For this reason, what the courts are really doing is giving L *damages* for the termination of the lease, not rents. See Rest. 2d, §12.1, Reporter's Note, Item 7.

   d. **Right to damages:** The kind of lease provision just described, making the tenant liable for "rent" even after termination, is as noted really just a way of measuring the landlord's damages following termination. If there is no such clause, the court will *not* generally award as damages an amount equal to the rent that would have been due.

      i. **Modern approach:** Instead, in most modern courts L will be awarded the *net value of the lease*, i.e., the present value of the amount by which the rentals that would have been due during the rest of the term exceed the rent that is (or could have been) received from a substitute tenant. Thus if the agreed-upon rent is exactly equal to the fair-market rental value of the property, L would get no damages (except perhaps special damages, such as for vandalism resulting from T's absence). Rest. 2d, §12.1, Comment i. This way of calculating damages in effect places on L a *duty to mitigate* if he accepts the surrender (i.e., terminates the lease).

      ii. **Minority view:** A minority of courts (but a substantial one), take the more traditional view that *once an acceptance of surrender occurs, even the right to damages for the period following the termination is lost*.

2. **Re-letting on tenant's account:** The landlord whose tenant has abandoned the premises will generally wish to *re-let*. If he does so without any notice to the tenant, his act is likely to be taken as an acceptance of surrender (just discussed), terminating the lease. But in most states, the landlord has the right to *inform* the tenant that he is

attempting to re-let *on the tenant's behalf*. This is generally a good idea (for the landlord), since there is no termination of the original lease, and the tenant will remain liable for: (1) all rents coming due, if no new tenant is found, assuming that L searches for one with reasonable diligence; or (2) the difference between the rent paid by the new tenant and the rent reserved in the original lease. See, e.g., *Liberty Plan Co. v. Adwan*, 370 P.2d 928 (Okla. 1962) (letter from L to T that it would "advertise the property and make every effort to mitigate . . . damages, but will definitely hold you liable for all costs of advertising [and] loss of rent . . .", held sufficient to make a re-letting done for T's account, so that L may recover the difference between old rent and new rent).

    a. No notice where duty to mitigate: In those minority jurisdictions which impose a *duty to mitigate* damages upon the landlord (*infra*, p. 181), it seems probable that no notice to the tenant is required before a re-letting for the tenant's account. Burby, p. 186.

        i. Lease provision: Also, if the *lease itself* contains a provision that the landlord may re-let for the tenant's account without notice, such a provision will probably be upheld.

        ii. Consent by tenant sometimes required: But by contrast, a few courts require not only notice to the tenant, but an express or implied *consent* by him that a re-letting be for his account. This is the case in New York; see, e.g., *Leo v. Santagada*, 256 N.Y.S.2d 511 (City Ct. Newburgh 1964).

    b. Re-letting produces excess: Suppose that L notifies T that he will try to re-let for the latter's account, and then re-lets for an amount in *excess* of the old rent. It would seem fair to require L to turn the surplus over to T, on the theory that if T has the burden of a continuing lease, he should also have the benefit. This is the position taken by Rest. 2d, §12.1, Comment i. But the little case law on the subject indicates a refusal to give the excess to the tenant, on the grounds that it would allow him to profit by his breach. See *Whitcomb v. Brant*, 100 A. 175 (Super Ct. N.J. 1917).

        i. Landlord's right to revoke: Suppose that L has told T that he will try to re-let on the latter's account, and L then discovers that a higher rent is available from the new tenant than is provided for in the old lease. In a jurisdiction that gives T the right to this excess, may L *revoke* his "agency" agreement, and sign the new lease on his own behalf? Rest. 2d, §12.1, Comment i, indicates that he may. However, if the new tenant then defaults, L has lost his recourse against T (which would not be the case if the new lease was signed for T's account).

    c. Summary of strategy: All things considered, if L plans to try to re-let, he is almost always better off telling T that he will do this for the latter's account. In most states, he is not liable to T for any excess rent received from the new tenant, and even where he does have this liability, he can probably revoke the agency agreement just before signing for the higher rent, as noted. By acting on T's behalf, he preserves the right to recover from T in the future if the new tenant defaults, or pays less than the rent provided in the original lease.

  3. Right to leave vacant: Perhaps the most important issue concerning landlord's rights in the event of an abandonment is *whether L must make reasonable attempts to re-let*.

a. Traditional view: The traditional view is that L has *no duty to try to find a new tenant*. He may simply let the property stay vacant, and recover rent from the tenant who has abandoned, even if a perfectly suitable tenant requests the right to lease the premises. See, e.g., *Heckel v. Griese*, 171 A. 148 (N.J. 1934) (fact that L refused to show the premises to prospective tenants or to rent it to them irrelevant).

　i. Rationale: The reasoning behind this position is that a lease of real property is not a contract, but a conveyance; T has bought the leasehold estate, and L has no obligation to, in effect, re-sell it for him. Also, as the Restatement notes, in imposing this traditional rule, "Abandonment of property is an *invitation to vandalism*, and the law should not encourage such conduct by putting a duty of mitigation of damages on the landlord." Rest. 2d, §12.1, Comment i.

b. Duty to mitigate: But an increasing minority of courts now hold that the landlord does have a *duty to mitigate*, by attempting to find a suitable replacement tenant.

　Example: The Ps contract with D for the Ps to build an office building, in which D (a dentist) will enter a lease for one of the offices. The Ps put up the building, and D refuses to enter a lease. D tells two doctor friends of his about the building, and each offers to lease the space that would have been taken by D under the same terms and conditions, but the Ps refuse this offer.

　Held, for D. The majority rule that no mitigation of damages is required in leases derives from the view that a lease is a conveyance. But a modern lease is an exchange of promises more than it is a conveyance; therefore, there is no reason why the usual contract principle of mitigation of damages should not be applied to it. No economic or social benefit is served by permitting the landlord to stand idly by while the premises remain vacant. This is particularly true where, as here, the tenant himself supplies prospective replacements (though the court's holding requiring mitigation of damages is not restricted to such a case). Finally, in this case, there was merely a *contract* to make a lease, not an actual lease; thus even if the court accepted the common-law rule that mitigation of damages is not necessary in leases, the rule would probably not be applicable here. *Wright v. Baumann*, 398 P.2d 119 (Ore. 1965).

　i. Limitation to residences: One court has implied that a duty to mitigate exists in *residential*, but not necessarily in commercial leases. *Sommer v. Kridel*, 378 A.2d 767 (N.J. 1977).

c. When suit may be brought: In a jurisdiction not imposing a duty to mitigate, if L wishes to keep the property vacant and recover the rent, he may only sue for rent installments that have *already come due*. Thus he must either bring multiple suits during the course of the term, or wait until the end and bring one suit for all past-due rents. *Jordan v. Nickell*, 253 S.W.2d 237 (Ky. 1952). (But L may instead regard the lease as terminated, and sue immediately for *damages*, under the doctrine of anticipatory breach. In such event, he does not recover the full amount of rent that would have come due during the rest of the term, but merely the value of his lost bargain; see *supra*, p. 179).

VIII. TRANSFER AND SALE BY LESSOR; ASSIGNMENT AND SUBLETTING BY LESSEE

A. Right to transfer generally: Unless the parties to a lease agree otherwise, either may *transfer* his interest. Thus a landlord may sell his reversion in the property, and the tenant may either *assign* or *sublease* his right to occupy. (The distinction between assignment and sublease is discussed *infra*, p. 183.) For purposes of simplicity, we shall refer to a sale by the landlord of his interest in the reversion as an assignment by him.

1. **Statute of Frauds:** There is no blanket requirement that an assignment or sublease be *in writing*. But if the duration of the assignment or sublease is such that an original lease of the same duration would have to be in writing, the transfer must be in writing. (See the general discussion of the Statute of Frauds for leases, *supra*, p. 134.) Where the term of the assignment or sublease is less than this, the states differ; a number of states have statutes requiring all transfers, or just all assignments, or just all transfers for longer than a certain period, to be in writing. See Rest. 2d, Statutory Note, to §15.1, Item 7.

2. **Privity of estate:** The principal significance of an assignment (whether made by landlord or tenant) is that it establishes a *new landlord-tenant-relationship* between the *assignee* and the original party who did not assign. These two people are now said to be in *privity of estate*. Thus if L assigns to L1, L1 and T are now landlord and tenant, and are in privity of estate. Similarly, if T assigns to T1, L and T1 are in privity of estate. And if both of these things happen, L1 and T1 are in privity of estate.

   a. **Significance of privity of estate:** The significance of privity of estate is this: since an assignee is in privity of estate with the non-assigning original party, the assignee *obtains the benefit*, and *bears the burden*, of any *covenants running with the land*. What covenants run with the land is discussed extensively *infra*, p. 184; the basic idea is that any promise made in the lease which *"touches and concerns"* the land runs with the land, and affects any assignee.

      Example: L and T make a lease, in which T promises to pay $200 per month rent, and L promises to keep the premises in repair. T then assigns to T1, and L assigns to L1. Both the promise to pay rent and the promise to make repairs run with the land, both as to benefit and burden. Therefore, L1 may sue T1 if he doesn't pay the rent, and T1 may sue L1 if he doesn't make the repairs.

   b. **Sublease distinguished:** But a *sublease* by a tenant does *not* establish privity of estate between sublessee and lessor. Consequently, the sublessee is *not liable* to the lessor on covenants running with the land. Instead, the *lessee* and the sublessees become in privity of estate; the sublessee is liable to the lessee on covenants running with the land.

      Example: L and T sign a lease, in which T promises to pay $200 per month rent. T then subleases to S, S promising to pay $150 per month rent to T. Since L and S are not in privity of estate, L may not sue S for the rent (though he may sue T, who remains liable for it). T may sue S, since they are in privity of estate (and also in privity of contract, discussed below).

3. **Privity of contract:** *Privity of contract* exists between two parties to a contract. Such privity can serve as a basis for a lawsuit, even where privity of estate is absent. Suppose, for instance, in the above example, that S made a separate contract with L to pay L $150 rent every month, but that no landlord-tenant relationship was created

between them. L and S would then be in privity of contract, so that L could sue S if he failed to pay the rent.

4. **Original parties to lease:** The original parties to a lease are both in privity of estate and privity of contract. If one of them assigns his interest, the privity of estate between them is ended, but not the privity of contract. Since either privity of estate or privity of contract can serve as the basis for a lawsuit, a party to the original lease will **not** normally be able to **escape liability** by assigning his interest.

> **Example:** L and T sign a lease, in which T agrees to pay monthly rent. T assigns his interest to T1. L may continue to collect the rent from T, because they remain in privity of contract. But he may also recover the rent from T1, since they are in privity of estate. (Of course, he may only recover from one, not both.)

B. Distinguishing sublease from assignment: Because of the difference described above between a sublease and an assignment, it is important to be able to tell whether a given transfer is one or the other.

1. **Assignment is transfer for balance:** An **assignment** is the transfer by the lessee of his **entire interest** in the leased premises. Therefore, he must transfer for the **entire remaining length** of the term of his lease with the lessor. If he transfers something less than that **(even one day less!)**, in nearly all courts he will be held to have made a **sublease**, not an assignment.

   a. **Right of re-entry:** Suppose the instrument of transfer gives the lessee the right to **re-enter the premises** if the transferee fails to pay rent. Is this right of re-entry a reversion, thus making the transfer a sublease rather than an assignment?

      i. **Majority view:** Most courts have held that such a right of re-entry is **not** a true reversion. (See the discussion *supra*, p. 61, in which reversions are distinguished from other "reversionary interests", including rights of re-entry.) Therefore, the transfer is an assignment, even though the lessee could regain possession if the default occurs. This is the position taken by Rest. 2d, §15.1, Comment i.

      ii. **Minority view:** But a fairly large minority holds that the right of re-entry is a "contingent reversionary interest", which is enough of a reversion to make the transfer into a sublease. See, e.g., *Davis v. Vidal*, 151 S.W. 293 (Tex. 1912), so holding, and concluding as a consequence that the lessor could not recover rent from the lessee's transferee.

   b. **Intent of parties:** A few courts have rejected the presence or absence of a reversion as the test entirely and instead look to the **intention of the parties** to the transfer.

   > **Example:** The lessee and his transferee execute a document called "contract and assignment". The contract permits the lessee to re-enter if the transferee does not make payments. *Held*, the intention of the lessee and transferee controls; since the contract used the word "assignment", and provided for payments directly to the lessor equal to the monthly rental reserved in the original lease, this intent was clearly for an assignment. The fact that a re-entry could be made by the lessee in case of default should not be in dispositive.
   >
   > The formalistic common-law rule can be highly unjust; for instance, suppose that L and T make a lease, and T then makes a transfer to A which both T and A

think is a sublease. Suppose also that T and A have ignorantly made the "sublease" for the entire remaining term. If A makes rent payments to T, and T is insolvent, A will have to make the payments a **second time** to L, since under the common-law rule this is an assignment. Looking to the intent of T and A avoids such unfairness. *Jaber v. Miller*, 239 S.W.2d 760 (Ark. 1951).

Note: In controversies between the **lessee** and the transferee, most courts are willing to look to the intention of the parties. It is only where the controversy is between the original lessor and one of the other two parties that most courts have declined to follow the *Jaber* intent-of-the-parties test.

    c. Transfer of part of premises: If the lessee transfers only **part** of the physical premises, but for the entire remaining term, this is generally considered to be a **partial assignment**. Moynihan, p. 76.

2. **Effect of sublease:** As noted, a sublease creates a new landlord-tenant relationship between lessee and sublessee. Therefore, there is **no privity of estate between lessor and sublessee**. Since there is also ordinarily no privity of contract between the two, **lessor cannot sue sublessee for rent**, or for any other covenant running with the land.

    a. Right to terminate: However, if the lessee does not pay the rent, or otherwise permit a breach of the lease (e.g., neither he nor the sublessee makes repairs that are required to be made by the original lease), the lessor may, or course, **terminate the lease**, and evict the sublessee. It is only the right to hold the sublessee personally liable for rent or breach of contract that the lessor loses.

        i. Special statutes: A few states have special **statutes**, allowing a lessor to recover rent directly from a sublessee. See 1 A.L.P. 300. Where such a statute exists, the distinction between assignment and sublease becomes much less important.

        ii. Lessee remains liable: The lessee continues to be liable to the lessor following a sublease, both under privity of contract and privity of estate, since the landlord-tenant relationship between him and the lessor remains.

    b. No suit by sublessee against lessor: Conversely, the **sublessee** may **not bring suit** directly against the **lessor** if the lessor breaches a term of the lease (e.g., failure to make required repairs). 1 A.L.P. 313.

3. **Effect of assignment:** Where the lessee assigns, rather than subleases, privity of estate is created between the lessor and the assignee. As noted (*supra*, p. 183), this means that the assignee will have the benefit and the burden of any covenants which were made by the original lessee and which run with the land.

C. Covenants running with the land: Any promise has, of course, two sides: a **burden** (someone must perform the promise) and a **benefit** (someone will gain from the performance by the other). The **burden** of a promise made in a lease will run with the land (i.e., be enforceable against an assignee of the promisor) if that promise **"touches and concerns"** the **promisor's assignee's interest** in the land. Similarly, the **benefit** of a promise will run with the land (i.e., be enforceable by an assignee of the promisee) if it "touches and concerns" the **promisee's assignee's interest** in the property.

1. **Not necessarily bilateral:** The vast majority of promises made in leases will either run with the land **both as to benefit and burden**, or as to **neither benefit nor burden**. However, there are a few situations in which a promise may run **just as to**

burden and not as to benefit, or vice versa.

> **Example:** L leases property to T for ten years. The parties contemplate that T will use the premises as a bakery. In a non-competition clause, L promises that he will not use any of the property he owns nearby as a bakery, to protect T. The benefit of this non-competition promise, since it protects T's use of the leased property, runs with the land. But the burden of the promise, since it affects L's use of other property, not the leased property, does not run with the land. Therefore, if L assigns his reversion to L1, T could not sue L1 for damages if L then used the nearby site as a bakery. But if L made no assignment and T assigned to T1, T1 would be able to sue L if L used the nearby site as a bakery. See Rest. 2d, §16.1, Illustration 5.

2. **Meaning of "touches and concerns":** There is no precise, mathematical, definition of "touches and concerns". Basically, the burden of a promise affects an interest in property if the burden relates specifically to that property, and *diminishes or limits* the promisor's (or his successor's) *use or enjoyment* of it. Conversely, the benefit of a promise touches and concerns the promisee's interest if it relates directly to the property, and increases his (or his successor's) use and enjoyment of it. The most practical way of getting a feel for this is to see how the courts have handled certain frequently-recurring types of promises.

3. **Promises to pay money:** If the lease contains a *promise to pay money*, one must first inquire why the money is to be paid; if the payment relates directly to the land, the promise probably runs with the land both as to benefit and burden.

   a. **Covenant to pay rent:** Thus a *promise to pay rent* is treated by *all courts* as *running with the land, both as to benefit and burden.*

   > **Example:** L leases premises to T at a rent of $400 per month. T assigns his interest to T1, and L assigns his reversion to L1. At least for the length of time that T1 is actually in possession of the premises, L1 may sue him for the $400 per month rent, since the benefit of the promise went along with L's assignment to L1, and the burden went along with T's assignment to T1. (The liability of T, and the liability of T1 after he assigns to someone else, are discussed *infra*, p. 187.)

   b. **Promise to pay taxes:** Similarly, a promise to pay *taxes* or other assessments on the property runs both as to benefit and burden. 2 A.L.P. 347.

   c. **Promise to keep property insured:** The lease may require the tenant to *insure the property*. The status of this promise depends on what is to be done with the insurance proceeds in the event of destruction.

      i. **"Bare" promise:** If there is merely a *"bare"* promise to insure, with no restriction on the landlord's use of the proceeds, so that he can simply pocket them, most courts hold that this promise is *personal*, both as to burden and benefit. Therefore, an assignee of the tenant cannot be forced to pay the premiums, and an assignee of the landlord cannot enforce the promise. See Rest. 2d, §16.1, Reporter's Note, Item 3. (But Rest. 2d, §16.1, Illustration 8, follows a minority position and treats the burden as running with the land.)

      ii. **Duty to rebuild:** If the lease requires the lessor to use the proceeds to *rebuild the property*, however, the promise *runs with the land* both as to benefit and burden. See, e.g., *Masury v. Southworth*, 9 Ohio St. 340 (1859) (T assigns to D, and L assigns to P; P may enforce the promise to insure against D because of the provision requiring rebuilding of the premises from the proceeds).

    iii. Pass through of premium increases: Similarly, if the lease requires the tenant merely to pay the *increase* in insurance premiums due to the particular hazardous use that the tenant makes of the premises, both the burden and benefit will run, since the clause is keyed directly to the way in which the property is used. A.L.P., 1976 Supp. at 262.

  d. Promise to buy improvements: A lease provision allowing or requiring the landlord to *purchase improvements* made by the tenant at the end of the lease term may or may not be found to touch and concern the land, depending on other lease terms and circumstances. See 2 A.L.P. 349-50.

  e. Security deposit: Where the landlord has collected a *security deposit*, there is either an express or an implied duty on his part to return it to the tenant at the end of the term, less any damages caused. The *benefit* of such a promise runs with the land, so that an assignee of the tenant will have the right to get the security back. But the courts are *split* as to whether the *burden* runs, so that only some courts require an assignee of a landlord who has not actually received the security deposit to account to the tenant. See 2 A.L.P. 350-51. See also *supra*, p. 174.

4. Promise to make repairs: A promise to *make repairs* on the property runs with the land both as to benefit and burden. Thus if T covenants to make repairs, this duty is binding upon an assignee from him, and enforceable by an assignee from L. (Similarly, if local law places an *implied warranty of habitability* upon the landlord, this will be *binding* upon subsequent assignees from the landlord.) See 2 A.L.P. 346.

5. Covenant not to compete: A promise by the tenant not to *compete* with the landlord's use of other property runs as to the burden (since it directly affects the tenant's use of the leased property), but does not run as to benefit (so that an assignee from the landlord cannot enforce it). Conversely, a promise by the landlord not to use other property to compete with the tenant's use of the leased premises usually runs as to benefit (since it helps the tenant's use of the leased property) but not as to burden. 2 A.L.P. 346-47. See also Rest. 2d, §16.1, Illustrations 5 and 6. As noted *supra*, p. 185, this is one of the comparatively rare situations where the benefit of a promise will run but not the burden, or vice versa.

6. Promises relating to duration of the lease: Promises relating to the *duration* of the lease will generally *run* with the land, both as to benefit and burden.

  a. Purchase option: For instance, a promise by the lessor to *sell the property* to the lessee at the latter's election for a stated sum, is held (by American courts, though not by English courts) to run both as to benefit and burden. 2 A.L.P. 352-53.

  b. Renewal clause: Similarly, a clause which gives the lessee the right to *renew* the lease for another term runs both as to benefit and burden. It is thus exercisable by the lessee's assignee and enforceable against the lessor's assignee. 2 A.L.P. 353.

D. Rights of parties after assignment: We are now in a position to examine in detail the right and liabilities of the *lessor*, the *lessee*, and the *lessee's assignee*, after an assignment has been made by the lessee. (Assignments by lessor are covered *infra*. p. 190.)

1. **Liability of tenant:** The *original tenant*, when he makes a promise in the lease that relates to the leased premises, is bound to keep that promise both by privity of estate and by privity of contract (*supra*, p. 182). If he assigns his interest, his privity of estate terminates. But *his privity of contract remains*; therefore, the *lessor may still sue him* if the promise is not kept. Rest. 2d, §16.1, Comment c.

   a. **Rent:** Thus where a lease sets forth a duty to pay rent (as does virtually every lease), the tenant may not escape his personal contractual liability for that rent by assigning. If L does not receive the rent after the assignment, he has a choice between suing T (on privity of contract) or T's assignee (on privity of estate).

      i. **Promise in lease to pay rent:** Of course, if T could show that he never made any contractual promise to pay the rent, and that any duty to pay rent depended on privity of estate, he would escape by making the assignment. But courts tend to find that virtually every contract includes at least an implied promise to pay rent. Thus in *Samuels v. Ottinger*, 146 P. 638 (Cal. 1915), the lease did not contain an explicit promise by T to pay rent, but stated that L agreed to lease to T at a given rental "payable" at stated times. The court held that this was the equivalent of an express promise by T to pay the rent, and that T therefore remained liable for the rent even after assigning to X.

   b. **Release:** The only way T can escape from his privity of contract with L is if, in conjunction with the assignment, he gets a *release* from L of his privity of contract liability. (If L releases T and get contractual rights against the assignee, all in one transaction, this substitution of parties is called a *novation*.)

      i. **Acceptance of rent:** The mere fact that L has consented to the assignment, and has *accepted rent payments* from the assignee, is *not* enough to release T from his contractual liability. See, e.g., *Cauble v. Hanson*, 249 S.W. 175 (Com. App. Tex. 1923).

2. **Tenant's rights against assignee:** Although the tenant remains with his privity of contract liability after an assignment, his relationship vis a vis the assignee becomes one of *suretyship*. That is, the assignee is *primarily liable* for the obligation, and the tenant is only *secondarily* liable. This means that if the landlord chooses to sue the tenant rather than the assignee, the tenant can *recover* whatever he has to pay *from the assignee*. This is true even if the assignee does *not expressly assume* the lease duties when the assignment is made.

   Example: L rents premises to T for $300 per month. T assigns his interest in the premises to A, but A does not make any promise, either to T or to L, that he will make rent payments. He fails to make payments, but remains on the property. L chooses to sue T rather than A (he could sue either). After T is forced to pay the past-due rent to L, he may recover that amount from A. This is because the primary liability is A's, based on privity of estate. T's liability, based on privity of contract, is a secondary one; T is simply a surety of A's performance to L. See 2 A.L.P. 355.

3. **Tenant's right to sue on landlord's promise:** Where the *landlord* has made a promise whose burden runs with the land, the tenant will lose the right to sue on this promise if he assigns to someone else, and the breach occurs after the assignment. That is, by assigning, T impliedly also assigns his privity-of-contract right to sue for breaches by the landlord occurring in the future. See 2 A.L.P. 354.

Example: L leases premises to T. The lease contains a promise by L to keep the premises in repair. T assigns his interest to T1. After the assignment, the premises need repairs. T will not be allowed to sue L for breach of the repair covenant, since he impliedly assigned the right of suit to T1, as to breaches occurring after the assignment. Thus T1 is the only one who may sue L on the promise. T1's suit would be based in part on privity of estate, since the benefit of the repair promise runs with the land, just as the burden does. (*Supra*, p. 187.) His suit would also probably be based on privity of contract, a status impliedly assigned to him via the transfer by T.

4. **Liability of assignee:** Assuming that the lessee's assignee does not make any specific promise of performance when he takes the assignment, his liability to the lessor is based upon *privity of estate*. During the time he is in *possession* of the premises, he is liable for performance of promises made by the lessee whose burden *runs with the land*.

Example: L leases premises to T, for $300 per month rent. T assigns to A. During the time A is in possession, he is liable to L for the rent, *even if he did not promise either T or L that he would make payments*. This is because the burden of a promise to pay rent runs with the land (*supra*, p. 184), and must therefore be honored by A as long as he is in privity of estate with L (i.e., as long as he is in possession of the leased premises).

a. **Rationale:** The rule that one who is in privity of estate must bear the burden of covenants running with the land is not a product of strict logic. Rather, it stems from the idea that one who is in possession of leased property should not be entitled to hold it free of the duties that the landlord bargained for. This rule is particularly reasonable where the promise concerns *acts to be done upon the land* (as opposed to promises to pay money), since only the assignee, and not the lessee who has parted with possession, can perform these. For instance, if T promises L that he will keep the property in repair, and T then assigns to A, it seems reasonable to require A to keep the premises in repair, and not to leave L with the possibly futile, and certainly time-consuming and expensive, resort of suing T for money damages.

b. **Assignment by assignee:** But since the assignee's liability is founded upon privity of estate, that liability applies only for the period when the assignee is *actually in possession*. He has no liability for breaches by the principal tenant or prior assignees, and he has no liability for breaches by *subsequent assignees*.

i. **Motivation irrelevant:** The termination of the assignee's liability upon a re-assignment occurs even if the assignee's motive is to *escape liability*, even if the new assignee is financially irresponsible, and even if there is no consideration for the transfer. (But if the re-assignment is collusive or a complete sham, so that the original assignee remains with *de facto* possession of the premises, then his liability under privity of estate will not be ended.)

Example: L leases premises to T. The property is assigned several times, until finally it comes into the hands of D. D assigns it to his own subsidiary, and the subsidiary then assigns it to X, an unrelated corporation. X makes one or two payments, and then defaults. P, an assignee of L's interest, sues D for rent due following the assignment to X. *Held*, for D. An assignee's liability, assuming that he has not made any assumption (discussed *infra*, p. 189), rests solely on privity of estate, and terminates as soon as the assignee's possession ends. This is true even though, as in the present case, X was financially irresponsible, and D sold its interest for a very low sum. Had there been collusion between D and X (e.g., an agreement that X would try to extract a lower rent for D's benefit, and that D would continue in possession), the assignment would not have ended D's liability. But such collusion was not shown here. *A.D. Juilliard & Co. v. American Woolen Co.*, 32 A.2d 800 (R.I. 1943).

5. **Assumption by assignee:** In the situations discussed thus far, we have assumed that there is an assignment, but that there is no express **assumption** by the assignee, i.e., no promise by him, either to the tenant or the landlord, that he will perform the promises made by the tenant in the lease. But if there *is* such an assumption by the assignee, the assignee is now bound by **privity of contract** as well as by privity of estate.

   a. **Promise made to tenant:** If the promise is made to the **tenant** (i.e., the assignee executes a contract with the tenant, in which he gains the tenant's right to the leasehold interest, and promises to fulfill the tenant's obligations), there is privity of contract between the tenant and the assignee. This has at least one, and probably two, important consequences:

      i. **Tenant may sue assignee:** First, the **tenant** may **sue the assignee** if the covenants are not performed. Even if the relationship rested solely upon privity of estate, the tenant would have the right to do this on suretyship principles for a breach occurring while the assignee remained in possession (*supra*, p. 187). But if the assignee has made an explicit promise, his privity of contract liability to the tenant remains **even after a further assignment**.

      Example: L rents premises to T for $300 per month. T assigns to A, and A assumes T's obligations, including the duty of rent payment. Two months later, A assigns to B. If B fails to make rent payments, T may sue A, not only for the two months that he was actually in possession (which he could do even without an assumption, based upon privity of estate), but for all subsequent rents during the occupation of B or any other person.

      ii. **Third-party beneficiary rights in landlord:** Secondly, in most states, the **landlord** is a **third-party beneficiary** of the assumption agreement between tenant and assignee. This means that the landlord and the assignee are now **in privity of contract**. So here too, just as in a suit brought by the tenant, the assignee will be liable not only for duties incurred during his actual possession, but also for duties incurred after a further assignment. Thus in the above example, A could be sued by L, just as by T, for the rent accruing after he reassigned to B. See 2 A.L.P. 358.

6. **Review illustrations:** The following hypotheticals review some of the principles applicable where the tenant assigns his interest.

   Hypothetical 1: L leases premises to T. The lease contains a promise by T to keep the premises in repair. T then assigns his interest to T1. After the assignment, the premises need repairs, and T1 does not make them. T sues T1 for the damage caused to the premises by T1's failure to make repairs.

   If T1 has not **assumed** T's obligations under the lease (and there is not evidence in the facts as stated that he has), the relationship between T and T1 is merely one of suretyship. (*Supra*, p. 187.) Thus until T is actually forced to pay damages to L, he is not entitled to recover anything against T1. See 2 A.L.P. 355.

L, however, may sue T1 on a privity of estate theory, since a covenant to repair certainly runs with the land as to burden (and also as to benefit).

Hypothetical 2: L makes a one-year lease with T, which contains an option to renew for a further term of five years at the expiration of the one year, and a second option for five years at the expiration of the first five-year option. During the initial year, T assigns his interest to T1. T1 wishes to exercise the renewal option; may he? Assume that T1 validly exercises the first renewal option, and then validly exercises the second renewal option as well. During the period covered by the second option, T1 defaults in the payment of rent and taxes, which the original lease between L and T required T to pay. T1 then vacates the premises. L sues T for the unpaid rent and taxes; T raises the defense that when T1 exercised his renewal options, a new contract was formed between L and T1, thus releasing T from liability. Should this defense succeed?

T1 probably had the right to exercise both renewal options. An option to renew, since it directly affects the lessee's interest, is almost always considered to be a covenant whose benefit runs with the land; therefore, T1, as an assignee, was entitled to the benefit of that option. (*Supra*, p. 186.) A court would probably view the renewal periods as being extensions of the original one-year lease, not as new leases; this was the conclusion of *Kornblum v. Henry E. Mangels Co.*, 167 So.2d 16 (Dist. Ct. App. Fla. 1964), on similar facts. However, T could argue that as to T1, he was merely a surety (*supra*, p. 187), and that under the rules of suretyship, an agreement between the obligee and the obligor which makes the surety's promise materially more burdensome releases the latter. See 1 A.L.P. 311. However, since the renewal options were contemplated in the original lease, this argument would probably fail, and T would probably be liable for the rent and taxes.

E. Transfer by lessor: Essentially the same rules apply when it is the *lessor*, rather than the lessee, who assigns his interest. That is, the landlord's assignee has the burden of covenants whose burden runs with the land, and has the benefit of covenants whose benefit runs with the land.

> **Example:** L rents premises to T for $300 per month. L then sells his interest in the reversion to P. Since a promise to pay rent is a covenant whose benefit runs with the land (just as the burden does), P may sue T (or T's assignee) for rents falling due after the sale.

1. Express assignment of contract right: The above example, since it refers only to rent defaults occurring after the sale by L to P, is accurate even if L did not expressly assign to P the right to receive rents. This right to receive rents falling due after the sale is an attribute of ownership of the land, i.e., it stems from the *privity of estate* between P and T.

a. Privity of contract impliedly assigned: Furthermore, L loses his right to sue for rents falling due after the sale, because his privity of contract rights is impliedly assigned to T. 2 A.L.P. 354.

b. Right to agree otherwise: But L and P could have agreed otherwise; thus they could have agreed that L would continue to have sole rights to collect rents coming due in the future. Conversely, they could have agreed that P would have the right to sue for rents that came due *before the sale*; in the absence of such an agreement, only L has this right (since P was not in privity of estate with T at the time these rents fell due).

2. **Burdens upon landlord's assignee:** After a sale of the landlord's interest, the new owner is *liable* for *performance of any promises made by the landlord* whose *burden runs* with the land. Thus if L promised T that he would *keep the premises in repair*, P, who buys the land from L, is liable for making the repairs after the sale. (This is true even if the premises were in disrepair at the time of the sale; but P is entitled to a reasonable time to bring the property back into shape. See Rest. 2d, §16.1, Illustration 30.)

   a. **Tort liability of landlord's assignee:** The *tort liability* of the landlord's assignee is a confused area. Certainly the assignee is liable for his own actions. Thus if he negligently performs repairs, or lets the property run down in a jurisdiction which imposes an implied warranty of habitability, he will have tort liability even to a tenant whose lease was signed with the prior landlord.

      i. **Actions of prior owner:** But the assignee will probably *not be liable for actions of his predecessor*, even though the injury does not occur until after the sale; thus if L leases property to T, and L negligently performs a repair, P (who buys property from L) will probably not be liable even if the negligent repair results in injury after P's purchase.

      ii. **Warranty of habitability:** The implied warranty of habitability, however, is an *on-going duty*; thus if the premises are in disrepair when L sells to P, P will probably have tort liability if he fails to correct the dangers within a reasonable time. See Rest. 2d, §17.5, Comment 1.

   b. **Landlord's liability after transfer:** Conversely, the landlord probably does not escape tort liability by the mere act of selling his interest. If he has concealed a defect at the time he enters into a lease, or negligently does a repair, he will be liable even for injuries occurring after a sale. But in the case of an on-going duty, such as the duty to maintain habitable premises or make repairs, he will probably be relieved of liability at approximately the same time that his assignee becomes liable. That is, if L fails to keep the premises habitable, then sells to P, once a reasonable time has passed and P should have corrected the problem, L will probably be relieved of liability for accidents happening thereafter, and P will have sole liability. See Rest. 2d, §17.1, Comment f (on the related issue of landlord's liability for concealed defects after he transfers the property).

3. **Attornment by tenant:** At common law, an assignee from the landlord did not have any enforceable rights against the tenant until the tenant somehow recognized the assignee as his new landlord. This recognition was called *attornment*. Typically, this was done by the first payment of rent from the tenant to the assignee. Today, the concept of attornment is irrelevant, since an assignee automatically has rights against the tenant simply by virtue of the assignment. 1 A.L.P. 309-10.

F. **Agreements by the parties about transfer:** Our entire discussion of transfer thus far assumes that the lease itself contains no provisions restricting transfer. Most leases, however, contain a promise by the *tenant* that he will not *assign or sublease* his interest *without the landlord's consent*.

   1. **Generally enforced:** In most jurisdictions, such a clause is *enforced*, even if the landlord is completely *unreasonable* in refusing to consent to the transfer. See, e.g., *Gruman v. Investors Diversified Services, Inc.*, 78 N.W.2d 377 (Minn. 1956), so holding, principally on the grounds that the landlord has made a personal choice in selecting a particular tenant, and should not be forced to settle for a substitute, however objectively

reasonable.

a. Strictly construed: However, such anti-transfer clauses are ***strictly construed*** against the landlord. Thus if the clause only prohibits assignment, it will not bar a sublease, and vice versa.

b. Waiver: Also, the landlord may, by his words or conduct, ***waive*** the benefit of the anti-transfer clause. For instance, if the new tenant takes possession (either under an assignment or sublease), and the landlord ***knowingly accepts rent directly from him***, this will probably be a waiver of the benefit of the clause.

2. *Dumpor's Case*: Suppose the landlord expressly consents to a particular transfer, or otherwise waives his objection to it; does this bar him from objecting to a ***subsequent*** transfer? In the famous ***Dumpor's Case***, 76 Eng. Rep. 1110 (K.B. 1603), the court held that ***L's consent to one assignment destroyed the anti-assignment clause completely***, because the clause could not be "apportioned". Most American courts continue to follow the rule in *Dumpor's Case*. See, e.g., *Reid v. Wiessner Brewing Co.*, 40 A. 877 (Md. 1898), applying the rule even though the initial consent was to a particular assignee, not to a general assignment by whomever the tenant chose (as had been the situation in *Dumpor's Case*).

a. Criticism and exceptions: Even the courts which apply the rule in *Dumpor's Case* frequently criticize it. Perhaps as a result, the rule is subject to many exceptions, which whittle down its importance. For instance, most courts do not apply it to a consent to a ***sublease***, as opposed to an assignment. Furthermore, the landlord is always free to make his consent to a particular assignment ***expressly conditional*** upon there not being any further assignments; this would certainly seem to be enough to avoid the rule. Also, the landlord can put a clause in the lease itself saying that any assignment shall not be a waiver of the right to object to subsequent ones; this, too, would probably avoid the rule. See 1 A.L.P. 305.

b. Minority reject rule: Some courts (still a minority, but probably increasing in number) ***reject*** the rule in *Dumpor's Case* completely. See Rest. 2d, §16.1, Comment g, rejecting the rule.

Example: L leases a movie theatre to T. L consents to an assignment by T to T1. T1 pays all rents for the period it keeps possession, but never assumes T's promises made in the lease. T1 then assigns to T2, which goes bankrupt after taking possession. L has meanwhile assigned to L1. L1 sues T1 for rents accruing from the time T2 took possession. The original lease contains a clause prohibiting assignment or sublease without L's consent.

Held, for L1. The rule in *Dumpor's Case* should not be applied, particularly where, as in the present case, the lease impliedly provides that the covenant against transfer will be binding upon assignees of the original tenant. Furthermore, when T1 assigned to T2, L1 explicitly stated that it would continue to hold T1 liable, thus manifesting its lack of intent to consent to the second assignment. *Childs v. Warner Bros. Southern Theatres, Inc.*, 156 S.E. 923 (N.C. 1931).

Note: Observe that the court in *Childs* allowed L1 to recover against T1 for rent accruing ***after T2 abandoned possession***. Since T1 did not assume T's obligations under the lease, the liability must have been based upon privity of estate. Yet privity of estate is generally held to terminate when a further assignment is made. (*Supra*, p. 188.) Apparently, the court must have implicitly held that an assignment in violation of an anti-assignment clause does not suffice to terminate privity of estate. This conforms with the view of at least some courts, which hold that a landlord has three choices in the event of an invalid assignment: (1) to declare a forfeiture (so that the landlord regains possession of the premises); (2) to treat the assignment as void, so that the assignor's interest remains; and (3) to consent to the assignment. Thus the court in *Childs* appears to have allowed L1 to elect course (2). But other courts give the landlord only the choice between (1) and (3).)

3. **Consent not to be unreasonably withheld:** A growing majority of states now hold, either by statute or by case law, that even where the lease prohibits assignment or sublease without the landlord's consent, the ***consent may not be unreasonably withheld***. See, e.g., N.Y. Real Prop. L. §226-b, under which L may not unreasonably withhold his consent to a sublease in a multiple dwelling.

> **Example:** L leases aircraft hanger space to T1. The lease provides that written consent by L is required before T1 may assign or sublet his interest. T1 wants to assign the lease to T2. T2 is in all respects a more suitable tenant (e.g., he is in better financial condition than T1), but L refuses to give his consent solely because he wants higher rents than provided in the original L-T1 lease.
>
> *Held*, L is entitled to withhold his consent only if L has a ***commercially reasonable*** objection to the assignment. Allowing a landlord to unreasonably refuse consent violates the public policy of prohibiting unreasonable restraints on alienation. It also violates the principle, increasingly recognized, that there is a duty of good faith and fair dealing inherent in every contract. Therefore, L was entitled to refuse consent based on commercially reasonable considerations (e.g., the financial responsibility of the proposed assignee, the suitability and legality of the proposed use, the need for remodeling, etc.), but L was not entitled to withhold consent merely because property values had increased and the lease was now below-market. (But if the lease had expressly provided that L could withhold his consent even unreasonably, such a clause would have been enforced. Here, however, the lease was silent about whether L could unreasonably withhold his consent, and this ambiguity must be resolved against L.) *Kendall v. Ernest Pestana, Inc.*, 709 P.2d 837 (Cal. 1985).

a. **Restatement:** The Second Restatement follows essentially the same approach as *Kendall, supra*. The Restatement provides that the landlord may not unreasonably withhold his consent to any transfer (whether sublease or assignment, and whether residential or commercial). Rest. 2d, §15.2(2). However, this rule does not apply if a *"freely negotiated provision"* in the lease explicitly gives the landlord an absolute right to withhold consent. Comment i to §15.2 states that a provision is not "freely negotiated" "where the party which must submit to the withholding of consent has no significant bargaining power in relation to the terms of the lease."

b. **Duty to mitigate:** Observe that in those states placing a duty upon the landlord to *mitigate his damages* if the tenant abandons the premises (*supra*, p. 180), this duty amounts to the same thing as a prohibition on unreasonable withholding of consent. That is, if the tenant proposes a subtenant or assignee, and the landlord refuses to consent, the tenant can simply abandon the premises. Then if the landlord still refuses to accept the new tenant (who by hypothesis is a reasonably suitable tenant), the landlord must bear his own damages.

c. **Landlord makes deal directly with proposed assignee:** In a jurisdiction prohibiting the landlord from unreasonably withholding his consent to a transfer, the landlord can attack the problem by obtaining a lease provision giving him the right to *make his own deal* directly with the proposed assignee or subtenant. If he exercised this option, the original lease terminates, and a new lease with the proposed assignee is substituted. Such a clause will probably be enforced in most states, although Rest. 2d, §15.2, Comment i would not permit such a clause unless it were "freely negotiated".

> **i. Advantage:** One advantage to the landlord of this approach is that if the proposed assignee is willing to pay more than the original lease amount, the surplus accrues to the benefit of the landlord, not the original tenant.

> **Example:** L unreasonably refuses consent to a proposed assignment by T to X, all the while intending to make a separate deal, at higher rent, with X. (New York does not prohibit such unreasonable refusal of consent in this type of transaction.) T sues L for deceit. *Held*, T has no cause of action, even in fraud. T received a release (so that L could re-let to X), and therefore sustained no damages, which are necessary in a deceit action. *Dress Shirt Sales, Inc. v. Hotel Martinique Assoc.*, 190 N.E.2d 10 (N.Y. 1963).

4. **Waiver by landlord:** Even in situations where the landlord would have the right to consent to the assignment or sublease, his failure to take prompt action when he learns of the attempted assignment or sublease will constitute a *waiver* by him of his right to block it. See Rest. 2d, §15.2, Comment f. To put it another way, the assignment or sublease that takes place in violation of a provision of the lease is not void, but merely *voidable*.

> **Example:** L leases to T; the lease provides that T may not assign or sublease without L's consent, T assigns to T2. L accepts T2's first rent payment without protest. He then decides that he doesn't really want T2 AS A tenant, and declare the lease terminated. L will probably not be permitted to terminate the lease, since he waived his right to do so by accepting the rent and by failing to take prompt action once he learned of the transfer. See Rest. 2d, §15.2, Illustr. 5.

IX. SOME IMPORTANT LEGISLATION

A. **Introduction:** We now consider briefly three types of legislation which play an important part in present-day landlord-tenant law, particularly in the residential context.

B. **Fair Housing Laws:** Congress has forbidden many forms of *discrimination* in rental housing, by enacting the Civil Rights Act of 1968, Title VIII of which is commonly called the *Fair Housing Act*. 42 U.S.C. §§ 3601-3631. The Act prohibits discrimination on the basis of race, color, religion, sex or national origin, in certain real estate transactions. *Rentals* are covered, except that certain rentals of *owner-occupied* dwellings, and of single-family houses whose owner owns no more than three units, are exempted from the Act. Further discussion of the Act is given *infra*, p. 292.

1. **Unintended effect on minorities:** The Fair Housing Act prohibits only *intentional* discrimination on the basis of race, sex, etc. — it does not prohibit policies which have an unintended disparate *effect* on one race. For instance, a landlord's rule that a prospective tenant's net weekly income must be equal to 90% of a month's rent does not violate the Act, even though it may disqualify a higher proportion of blacks than whites, as long as the policy is not adopted for the *purpose* of discriminating against blacks. See *Boyd v. Lefrak Organization*, 509 F.2d 1110 (2d Cir. 1975).

a. ***Prima facie* case based on effect:** On the other hand, procedural rules may give the plaintiff some help in proving discriminatory motive. most courts hold that the plaintiff has made out a *prima facie* case by showing that the defendant's actions have a discriminatory ***effect***. Then, the **burden shifts to the defendant** to show that his actions were not motivated by racial, sexual or other forbidden considerations. D&K, p. 461. The fact that a landlord rarely if ever rents to a black, and the fact that a landlord's facially neutral eligibility rules are applied more stringently to black applicants than white ones, are examples of how a plaintiff may show a discriminatory effect (thus shifting the burden of explanation to the defendant).

2. **Race-conscious policies to promote integration:** The Fair Housing Act, as noted, prohibits racial discrimination in housing. Does this prohibition mean that the owner of, say, an apartment building may not select tenants on the basis of their race, in order to **promote integration**? The answer seems to be **"yes,"** according to the leading case on the subject, *U.S. v. Starrett City Associates*, 840 F.2d 1096 (2d Cir. 1988).

   a. **Facts:** In *Starrett City*, the Ds, operators of the largest housing development in the nation, wanted to maintain an integrated development. Because there were always many more black applicants than white ones, the Ds realized that the development would become heavily minority if apartments were rented out on a "first come, first served" basis without regard to race. Therefore, the Ds instituted a policy of race-conscious tenant selection, by which they attempted to keep the development at a mix of 64% white, 22% black and 8% Hispanic.

   b. **Practice rejected:** But the Second Circuit held that this scheme (which had been used for years with the knowledge and consent of federal housing officials) **violated the Fair Housing Act,** because it discriminated against black would-be tenants. The Act "does not allow appellants to use rigid racial quotas of indefinite duration to maintain a fixed level of integration . . . by restricting minority access to scarce and desirable rental accommodations otherwise available to them." (A dissent argued that the clear purpose of the Act was to promote integration, and that the Act should be interpreted so as to permit a race-conscious scheme whose purpose and effect were to promote integration.)

3. **State laws:** A number of state have enacted laws similar to the federal Fair Housing Act. In certain situations, a plaintiff is required to use these available state remedies before he may sue under the federal Act.

   a. **Refusal to rent to children:** These state laws have sometimes been interpreted to bar landlords from discriminating against **families with children** (whom landlords often avoid because of noise, mischief and other bother). Thus the California Supreme Court has interpreted that state's anti-discrimination law as barring landlords from instituting a blanket no-children policy. (Instead, landlords in California must make a determination about noise, rowdiness, etc., by considering each child and family case-by-case.) See *Marina Point, Ltd. v. Wolfson*, 640 P.2d 115 (Cal. 1982).

C. **Federally-funded housing:** The federal government plays an important role in the construction and maintenance of **low-income housing**. Under one program, the government makes funds available to local government agencies, to be used directly for construction of publicly-owned housing. In other programs, Congress has attempted to bring private capital into the low-income housing market, by federally insuring mortgages, granting interest subsidies on mortgages, and paying rent supplements to landlords who hold their rents below a certain level.

1. **Eviction:** One important question that arises in the context both of federally owned, and that of federally-funded but privately owned, housing, is how and when a tenant may be *evicted*. Many such tenants have at-will tenancies or month-to-month periodic tenancies. Recall that in a purely private situation, such a tenancy may be terminated without cause (*supra*, p. 138). However, this does not seem to be the case where there is public involvement.

   a. **Publicly-owned housing:** In the case of *publicly-owned* housing, HUD regulations now specify that a tenant has *due-process rights* before he may be evicted, and may only be evicted for *just cause*. It seems probably that these regulations will be binding on all buildings built with federal funds administered through local government agencies. B,C&S, pp. 476-77.

   b. **Privately-owned housing:** Where the housing is *privately-owned*, but *federally assisted*, a similar right not to be evicted without reasonable cause *probably also exists*. See, e.g., *Joy v. Daniels*, 479 F.2d 1236 (4th Cir. 1973) (Where L received subsidized mortgage interest rates and rent supplements from the federal government, L's eviction efforts became "state action," which could not be carried out without due process).

2. **Warranty of habitability:** Does the landlord in publicly-owned or publicly-assisted housing make an *implied warranty of habitability*? In a case involving publicly-owned housing (acquired by HUD in a foreclosure), one court has held that there is *no* judicial implied warranty of habitability, on the grounds that any such warranty should be established by the legislature, which established the federal housing program in the first place. *Alexander v. U.S. Dept. of HUD*, 555 F.2d (7th Cir. 1977). There is virtually no case law on whether there is such a warranty in the case of privately-owned but publicly-assisted housing.

D. **Rent control laws:** Many cities, and a few states, have enacted *rent control statutes*. Usually, these statutes restrict only *residential* rents, not commercial rents.

   1. **How statutes work:** Typically, rent control statutes establish a "base rent" for each unit. Often, this is the market rent prevailing at the time the measure is enacted. Then, the landlord may subsequently raise rents beyond the base rent only to the extent needed to give him a *"fair return"*. What constitutes a "fair return" is usually determined year-by-year, and typically depends on increases in the landlord's costs (e.g., labor, real estate taxes, etc.), changes in the Consumer Price Index, or both. Often, the landlord is allowed an extra increase if he makes capital improvements to the property.

   2. **Constitutionality:** Rent control statutes are generally *constitutional*, so long as they allow the landlord a *reasonable rate of return*. The most important principle relating to fair-rate-of-return is that according to most courts, the landlord must be given the benefit of a *"hardship relief"* provision, whereby he can get an increase above the stated maximum if he can show special facts (e.g., that he paid market value for the building, but that rents in the building at the time he purchased it were way below market). See, e.g., *Cromwell Associates v. Mayor & Council of Newark*, 511 A.2d 1273 (N.J. Super. Ct. 1985) (statute limiting hardship relief to a total of 25% increase per year is unconstitutional, because in rare instances hardships may require an increase of more than this.)

3. **Restrictions on non-renewal of lease:** Often, rent control restrictions limit the landlord's right to refuse to *renew* a tenant's lease. This is especially true of rent control statutes that give the landlord the right to an extra rent hike when a new tenant arrives — without a provision requiring the landlord to offer the existing tenant a new lease, the landlord would simply refuse to renew, and rent to a new tenant at the higher rate. See D&K, p. 554, n. 65.

a. **Anti-demolition rules:** A few rent control statutes have gone even further, and restrict landlords' freedom to remove rental units from the market by *converting* them to condominiums or *demolishing* them. For instance, a Santa Monica, California, ordinance requires approval by the rent control board before any conversion or demolition of a rental unit; the ordinance was upheld in *Nash v. City of Santa Monica*, 688 P.2d 894 (Cal. 1984).

4. **Economic criticism of rent control laws:** Most *economists* criticize rent control laws, on the theory that when rents are kept artificially low, landlords *don't build as much housing* as they would if the market for rents were free, and let the *quality* of the stock they already own *decline*. See D&K, pp. 562-65. Also, some critics of rent control argue that where landlords are deprived of the right to rent to the highest bidder, they often use other factors such as credit-worthiness, or even illegal factors such as race, sex or ethnic origin, in deciding whom to rent to. D&K, p. 563.

a. **Case law:** For a good overview of the arguments made by economists against not only rent control laws but other government regulation of housing markets (including laws letting the tenant make a repair and deduct it from the rent, or allowing the tenant to withhold rent until needed repairs are made), on the grounds that all of these regulations decrease the quantity and quality of the housing stock, see the majority opinion of Judges Posner and Easterbrook in *Chicago Board of Realtors, Inc. v. City of Chicago*, 819 F.2d 732 (7th Cir. 1987).

i. **Rationale:** That opinion argues that the true beneficiaries of such housing-market regulations are not poor people, but middle-class people. For instance, those who own their own home get an advantage, as landlords convert rental property (which is now less attractive) to owner property, thus increasing the supply of owner housing and decreasing its price. Similarly, more affluent tenants benefit, since they are more attractive to landlords because they are less likely to take advantage of devices like rent strikes. The losers are poor tenants, newer tenants, and landlords (frequently out-of-state or out-of-town landlords who can't vote in the local elections where the regulations are adopted), Posner and Easterbrook say.

Chapter Review Questions

(Answers are at back of book)

41. On July 1, 1989, L and T orally agreed that T would lease L's premises for one year, the lease to commence on August 1 of that same year and run until July 31, 1990. T gave a deposit as called for in the oral agreement. On August 1, when T tried to take possession, he discovered that L had rented the premises to someone else. Does T have a valid cause of action against L for breach of the lease?

42. L and T agreed that T would rent an apartment from L for $800 per month. No specific term was set. T took occupancy on July 1, and paid the rent for that month.

(a) What type of tenancy have the parties created?

(b) Suppose that after approximately two years, T wants to terminate the arrangement. If T gives notice of termination on July 15, what is the date on which his termination will be effective, under the common-law view?

43. Leonard leased a store to Terry, for a lease term ending August 30, 1989. In July of 1989, Leonard signed a lease with Tina for the premises, to commence September 1, 1989. Leonard knew that Tina planned to operate a new retail store, and that it would be important to Tina to be selling her Fall clothing inventory starting promptly in September. When Terry's lease term ended, he refused to vacate the premises, and was still there on September 20, at which time he moved out. May Tina sue Leonard for damages for failing to make the premises available to her on September 1?

44. Lester, the owner of an apartment building, rented a first floor apartment to Tess. Shortly thereafter, Lester rented ground-floor space (immediately below Tess's apartment) to the proprietor of Heavy Metal Heaven, a rock and roll club. The lease between Lester and Heavy Metal provided that Heavy Metal would conduct its activities so as not to materially inconvenience any tenants of the apartment building. But Heavy Metal set its loudspeakers to the maximum level, so that every night, Tess was unable to sleep until the club closed at 2:00 a.m. Tess decided that she could no longer tolerate the noise, and moved out. She then delivered to Lester a notice stating, "I consider our lease at an end." Lester relet the premises at a lower rate. May Lester recover from Tess the difference between the rent paid by Tess and the lower rent he is now receiving?

45. Same facts as the prior question. Now, however, assume that it is a tight housing market, and Tess has not been able to find another apartment at the same (relatively affordable) rate she is paying to Lester. Tess has therefore remained a resident in the apartment, but has gone on a rent strike, notifying Lester that she will not pay any rent until he makes the noise stop. Assuming that Tess continues to withhold the rent, may Lester have her evicted?

46. Lila, a notorious slum lord, rented a one-bedroom apartment to Terence for $400 per month. The lease made no explicit warranties regarding condition of the premises. Unbeknownst to Terence at the time the lease was signed, the apartment was (and still is) infested with rats, and the toilet did not and does not work. Terence is quite poor, and cannot pay moving expenses or a security deposit to move to a different apartment. He would like to be able to withhold the rent until the rats are exterminated and the toilet fixed. In a jurisdiction following the unmodified common-law rule on relevant issues, may Terence withhold rent on the grounds that the apartment is not habitable?

47. Same facts as the above question. Now, assume that the jurisdiction takes an approach towards the relevant issues that is fairly typical of the way most states now approach the issues. May Terence withhold rent?

48. Lena is a professional landlord, who owns a number of apartment buildings in the City of Ames. She rented an apartment in one of these buildings to Troy. The lease provided for a one-year term, with no renewal options. After Troy moved in, he discovered that the heat was inadequate, that the locks did not work, and that other things were wrong. He therefore lodged a complaint with the City of Ames Housing Agency, which is in charge of seeing that landlords obey their statutory obligations concerning residential housing. At the Agency's demand, Lena reluctantly fixed the problems. At the end of the one-year lease, Lena notified Troy that she would not renew his lease. Lena customarily renews residential leases, and gave Troy no explanation of why she would not renew his, though he suspects that this is due to his complaint to the Agency. If Troy refuses to move out at the end of the lease term, and Lena sues to evict him, what defense should Troy raise? What is the likely result if he does raise it?

49. Lana, a homeowner, rented her home to Tully in 1989 under a one-year lease, since she was to be abroad on an academic sabbatical for that year. The lease said nothing about the parties' obligations in the event of sudden destruction of the premises. Tully agreed to pay a rent of $500 per month. (The house had a fair market rental value of $1,000 per month, but Lana charged less because she liked Tully and thought he would take good care of the house.) After Tully had occupied the house for four months, the house was struck by lightning, and its upper floor (of two) was destroyed. The house is still "habitable" in the sense that Tully could live there, but only under much less pleasant circumstances (including the lack of a formal bedroom) than he had anticipated.

(a) May Tully terminate the lease and stop paying rent?

(b) May Tully recover damages from Lana for his "loss of bargain"? If so, in what amount?

50. Ludlum rented a suite in an office building he owns to Trotta. As part of the lease, Trotta gave Ludlum a two-month security deposit. The lease was for five years. After three years, Trotta moved out without cause, and stopped paying rent. Because the real estate market was a tight one, Ludlum almost immediately found a new tenant. Ludlum therefore sent Trotta a letter stating, "I am hereby terminating our lease because of your abandonment of the premises. You will be held responsible for all damages I suffer." Ludlum then relet the premises to the new tenant at the same monthly rent, so that his only losses are the loss of one month's rent ($1,000). Ludlum would like to be able to keep the entire security deposit until the expiration of the original five-year Ludlum-Trotta lease term. May he do so?

51. Same facts as the prior question. How could the party to whom your answer was unfavorable have altered the result, either by a drafting change or by subsequent conduct?

52. Lombard leased office space to Toland, for a two-year term. At the end of the lease term, Toland attempted to renew the lease, but Lombard refused. One week after the lease expired, Toland still had his furnishings on the premises. Summary proceedings were available to Lombard to evict Toland, but these would have taken approximately two months, and Lombard had a tenant who wanted to take occupancy immediately. Therefore, over a weekend, Lombard entered Toland's premises, moved his furniture into the hall, and changed the locks. When Toland arrived Monday morning, he found his furniture in good shape, but he was effectively out of business until he could arrange to move into new quarters; this took him two weeks, during which time he lost $10,000 worth of business. If Toland sues Lombard for $10,000 in damages, will Toland recover?

53. Link leased an apartment to Taylor. With two years to go on the lease (which was for $1,000 per month), Taylor moved out and sent Link a letter saying, "I don't want the premises any more." Link allowed the premises to remain vacant, and notified Taylor that he was doing so. Link made no effort to re-let the premises, though he could easily have done so for about the same $1,000 per month that Taylor had been paying. After the term expired (with 24 months of rent unpaid), Link sued Taylor for the cumulative unpaid rent. May Link recover this amount?

54. Lillian, the owner of an apartment building, leased an apartment to Tracey, for two years at $1,000 per month. After one year of the lease had expired, Tracey wanted to travel in Europe for 10 months. She therefore transferred to Stuart the right of occupancy for the next 10 months, reserving to herself the right to occupy the premises for the final two months of her lease with Lillian. Rent payments (at the same $1,000 per month) were to be made by Stuart to Tracey, and Tracey would pass them on to Lillian. Tracey went off on her trip, and failed to make any payments to Lillian. Lillian has now learned that Tracey has become insolvent. Meanwhile, Stuart, after occupying the premises for four months, has moved out, and is apparently not sending rent payments to Tracey. The premises are currently unoccupied. Lillian would like to sue Stuart for both the four payments he owes Tracey covering the time he actually occupied the premises, plus the six payments that became due after he left the premises. Which, if any, portion of this money may Lillian recover from Stuart?

Questions 55 through 61 below relate to the following fact pattern:

Lloyd, the owner of Blackacre, leased the property to Thelma for a five-year term. In this lease, Thelma promised to pay Lloyd rent of $1,000 per month. Three years into the lease, Thelma assigned her remaining interest in the lease to Tim. In the Thelma-Tim transaction, Tim did not expressly promise Thelma to perform Thelma's obligations under the master lease, but merely accepted from Thelma a document stating, "I hereby assign to you all my rights under my lease with Lloyd." Tim then moved onto the property.

55. After Tim moved in, he made the first six monthly $1,000 payments directly to Lloyd, and Lloyd made no objection. Then, Tim did not make any payments for the next three months. If Lloyd sues Thelma for the three months during which Tim did not make payments, may Lloyd recover?

56. Same facts as the prior question. Assume, now, that Lloyd does not sue Thelma for the missed three months, but instead sues Tim for this period. Assume further that Tim was in residence during the three months for which no rent was paid. May Lloyd recover the three months rent from Tim?

57. Same facts as the prior two questions. Now, assume that after missing three months of rent, Tim assigned to Theo any interest that Tim had in the premises. Tim moved out. Theo took possession, and failed to pay the next six months rent. If Lloyd sues Tim for this six-month period, may Lloyd recover?

58. Now, assume that at a time when Tim was in possession (having received an assignment from Thelma of Thelma's rights, but having not made any promises of his own), Lloyd sold the property (and assigned all of his rights in the property) to Leon. In the sale documents, Leon did not make any promises to Lloyd, and merely gave Lloyd the purchase price. Assume further that in the original Lloyd-Thelma lease, Lloyd promised to keep the premises in repair. During Tim's occupancy, Leon has not made required repairs. May Tim sue Leon for damages?

59. At a time when Tim was in possession (having taken an assignment from Thelma but not having made any promises), Lloyd sold the property to Leon, as in the prior question. Tim failed to pay rent for six months while he was in possession. Leon has sued Tim for this rent. May Leon recover from Tim?

60. Assume that the original Lloyd-Thelma lease stated, in a negotiated term, that Thelma would not sublet or assign without Lloyd's written consent. Also, assume that when Thelma assigned to Tim, Thelma (as required under the lease) asked Lloyd's consent, and Lloyd consented because he felt that Tim was at least as responsible a tenant as Thelma. Now, Tim seeks to assign to Theo, but Lloyd objects because he feels (reasonably) that Theo is irresponsible. If Theo takes possession, may Lloyd have Theo evicted?

61. Same facts as the prior question. Now, assume that the anti-assignment clause in the Lloyd-Thelma lease was continued in the fine print "boilerplate" of the standard residential lease prepared by Lloyd, and that at the time that lease was signed, the residential housing market was sufficiently tight that nearly all landlords insisted on imposing similar no-assignment provisions. Thelma now wishes to assign her remaining rights to Tim. Tim is willing to assume all of Thelma's obligations, and is a financially responsible and otherwise good tenant. Lloyd refuses to consent to the assignment, solely because he wishes to raise the rent to $2,000 per month (now the prevailing market rent for such an apartment, because of a rise in real estate prices since the Lloyd-Thelma lease was signed). May Lloyd prevent Tim from taking occupancy?

EASEMENTS AND PROMISES CONCERNING LAND

Introductory note: This chapter considers various rights which one may have in the land of *another*. These fall into two broad classes: (1) *easements* (and the related concept of licenses); and (2) *promises concerning land*, which include both covenants that may be enforced at law, and so-called "equitable servitudes", which are enforceable in equity (usually by injunction).

I. EASEMENTS GENERALLY

A. Definition of easement: An *easement* is a privilege to *use the land of another*. Easements can be of either an affirmative or negative nature.

1. Affirmative easements: An *affirmative* easement is one which entitles its holder to *do a physical act* on the land of another. Most easements are of this variety.

Example: A is the owner of Blackacre. He gives B a *right of way* over Blackacre, so that B can pass from his own property to a highway which adjoins Blackacre. B holds an affirmative easement, since he is permitted to make physical use of A's property (by passing over it).

2. Negative easement: A *negative* easement is one which enables its holder to *prevent* the owner of land from making certain uses of that land. Such easements are comparatively rare, and do not permit the holder of the easement actually to go upon the property.

Example: A owns Whiteacre, which is right next to the ocean. B owns Blackacre, which is separated from the ocean by Whiteacre. A gives B an easement of "light and air", which assures B that A will not build any structure on Whiteacre which will block B's view of the ocean. This is a negative easement, since it does not authorize B to go on A's property, but allows B to restrain A from certain uses of A's property. (The negative easement would probably be enforced by an injunction, but might also be enforced by a suit for damages.)

B. Easements appurtenant vs. easements in gross: A second important distinction is between easements that are *appurtenant* to a particular piece of land, and those that are *"in gross"*.

1. Appurtenant easement: An easement *appurtenant* is one which benefits its holders in the use of a *certain piece of land*.

a. Dominant and servient tenements: The land for whose benefit the appurtenant easement is created is called the *dominant tenement*. The land that is burdened, or used, by the easement is called the *servient tenement*.

Example: Blackacre, owned by S, stands between Whiteacre, owned by D, and the public road. S gives D the right to pass over a defined portion of Blackacre to get from Whiteacre to the road. This right of way is an easement that is appurtenant to Whiteacre. Blackacre is the servient tenement, and Whiteacre is the dominant tenement.

    b. Test for appurtenance: For an easement to be appurtenant, its **benefit** must be intimately **tied to a particular piece of land** (the dominant tenement). It is not enough that the beneficiary of the easement happens to have an interest in a piece of land that is made more valuable by the easement.

        Example: Suppose that A, the owner of Blackacre, gives B the right to come onto it and mine coal. (This is a profit, not an easement, but the two are substantially similar for our purposes; see *infra*, below.) Suppose also that B owns nearby Whiteacre, in which he already has a mine. The fact that the easement makes B's mine on Whiteacre more profitable, because he can now mine two areas rather than one with economies of transportation, labor, etc. is not enough to make the easement appurtenant to Whiteacre. Rest., §453, Illustration 2. But if the terms of the easement were expressly that only the owner of Whiteacre could mine from Blackacre, and that this easement would apply to any subsequent purchaser of Whiteacre from B, this would probably be enough to make the easement an appurtenant one.

2. Easement in gross: An easement **in gross**, by contrast, is one whose benefit is **not tied to any particular parcel of land**. The easement is thus **personal** to its holder.

        Example: O, the owner of Blackacre, gives his friend E the right to come onto Blackacre anytime he wants and use O's swimming pool. O grants this right purely out of his friendship for E, and without respect to E's ownership of any nearby land. This easement is in gross, and is personal to E, even if E happens to owns a nearby parcel.

    a. Benefit tied to parcel: An easement appurtenant and an easement in gross can usually be distinguished by analyzing the benefit which the easement confers. If it is a benefit which can **only** accrue to one who is in possession of a particular parcel (the dominant tenement), the easement must be appurtenant, rather than in gross.

        Example: O owns three lots. Lot 3 is used as a filling station. O conveys Lot 2, but reserves a right of way over Lot 2 to be used as a driveway. When O dies, she devises Lot 3 to her daughter, P. D eventually gains title to Lot 2. P sues for a declaration that she holds a valid easement over Lot 2. *Held*, the easement is appurtenant, since the driveway could only be of use to the possessor of Lot 3. Therefore, the easement was automatically transferred when Lot 3 (the dominant estate) passed by will to P, and P has the full benefits of the easement. *Mitchell v. Castellaw*, 246 S.W.2d 163 (Tex. 1952). (Another aspect of *Mitchell* is discussed *infra*, p. 208.)

    b. Consequence of distinction: The principal consequence of the distinction between easements appurtenant and easements in gross relates to **assignments** and **division**. Whereas an easement appurtenant passes with ownership of the dominant parcel (as in *Mitchell, supra*), an easement in gross is sometimes not assignable at all, and is frequently not divisible for use by several persons independently of each other. These issues are discussed more fully *infra*, p. 218.

3. Profit: A property interest related to the easement is the **profit**, sometimes called the **profit a prendre**. The profit is the right to go onto the land of another and **remove the soil or a product of it**. Thus the right to mine **minerals**, drill for **oil**, or capture wild game or fish, are all traditionally called profits.

a. **Reason for distinction:** Under English law, there is an important distinction between profits and easements: a profit may be in gross, but an easement, generally, may not be. But under American law, an easement in gross may exist, as noted above. Therefore, in virtually all circumstances, the right to enter land and remove materials from it is functionally identical to an easement. Accordingly, all statements made below about easements are applicable to profits, unless the contrary is indicated. See Rest. Special Note to §450, stating that the Restatement does not use the term "profit" at all.

II. CREATION OF EASEMENTS

A. **Four ways to create:** There are four ways in which an easement may be created: (1) by an *express* grant (which generally must be in writing); (2) by *implication*, as part of a land transfer; (3) by strict *necessity*, to prevent a parcel from being landlocked; and (4) by *prescription*, similar to the obtaining of a possessory estate by adverse possession.

B. **Express creation:** The most straightforward way of creating an easement is by a *deed* or *will*. Thus A, the owner of Blackacre, could give B, the owner of Whiteacre, a deed expressly stating that B has the right to use a particular strip of Blackacre as a right of way, for a certain period of time.

1. **Statute of Frauds:** The express grant of an easement must, in all cases, meet the *Statute of Frauds*, as it applies to the creation of interests in land. This means that there must be a *writing*, signed by the owner of the servient estate. Also, any *recording act* (*infra*, p. 360) will apply, so that if the holder of the easement does not record, he may lose the easement as against a subsequent bona fide purchaser of the servient estate.

   a. **Short-term easement:** Recall that, in most states, a lease for less than one year does not have to be in writing. It could be argued that an easement for less than one year should similarly not have to be in writing. However, a lessee takes actual possession of the leasehold estate, whereas the holder of an easement does not take actual, continuous, possession of the servient tenement. For this reason, most courts require even a very short easement to be in writing; see Burby, p. 68.

      i. **Restatement rule:** But Rest. § 467, Comment f, requires a writing only where an estate of the same duration would have to be in writing.

   b. **Failure to satisfy statute:** If the easement is one which must satisfy the Statute of Frauds, and the parties fail to do so, a *license* (similar to an easement except that it is revocable at the will of the licensor) will generally be created. See *infra*, p. 225.

2. **Words creating:** It may sometimes be hard to tell whether the words of a grant create a possessory estate or merely an easement. Generally, if the deed stresses that the interest is being created only for a *specific, relatively narrow purpose*, an easement, not a possessory estate, is created.

   a. **Too broad for enforcement:** The property to be used, and the allowable use, must be set forth with at least reasonable *definiteness*. Thus a grant of rights to make "recreational uses" of a large tract of land will, in some states, be too vague for enforcement.

3. **Reservation in grantor:** The owner of land may convey that land to someone else, and *reserve for himself* an easement in it. Thus A may give B a deed for Blackacre, with a

statement in the deed that "A hereby retains a right of way over the eastern eight feet of the property." This is called an *easement by reservation.*

    a. Statute of Frauds: The Statute of Frauds normally requires a writing signed by the party "to be charged". Since an easement by reservation is enforceable against the grantee, not the grantor, it might be thought that the usual American form of deed (signed only by the grantor) would not be effective as to the reservation. But the courts have held that the grantee, by accepting the deed, and recording it, **binds himself** as to the reservation even without a signature. 2. A.L.P. 253.

4. Creation in stranger to deed: At common law, it was **not** possible for an owner of land to convey that land to one person, and to establish by the same deed an easement in a **third person.** As the rule was sometimes stated, an easement could not be created in a *"stranger to the deed"*. Burby, p. 71.

    a. Modern view: Some modern courts have now abandoned this rule, and permit an easement to be created by a deed in a person who is neither the grantor nor grantee. Even among courts paying lip service to the common-law rule, an exception for a use made upon the property prior to the conveyance is often made. See 2 A.L.P. 254-55, n. 2. Rest. § 472 rejects the common-law rule entirely.

        Example: O sells two lots (Lots 19 and 20) to A. Lot 19 has a building on it; Lot 20 is vacant, and is used by O's church as a parking lot. O's deed of Lot 20 to A is expressly made "subject to an easement for automobile parking during church hours for the benefit of the church. . . ." A records the deed to Lot 20, and then sells both lots to B. The deed received by B does not contain an easement. Several months later, B finds out about the easement clause in the first deed, and brings an action to quiet title against the church (i.e., to gain a declaration that the church has no valid easement.) He relies on the common-law rule that an easement may not be created in a stranger.

        Held, for the church. The common-law rule against easements in a "stranger to the deed" is a product of feudal notions that have no relevance today. It not only frustrates the grantor's intent, but is also inequitable because the grantee has presumably paid a reduced price for title to the encumbered property. Here, for instance, O testified that she discounted the price she charged A by one-third because of the easement. Nor has B relied upon the common-law rule, since he did not even read the deed to A until several months after buying the property. Therefore, the easement is valid. *Willard v. First Church of Christ, Scientist, Pacifica,* 498 P.2d 987 (Cal. 1972).

C. Creation by implication: The situation discussed just previously was that in which the owner of land expressly creates an easement. It may happen, however, that two parties are situated in such a way that an easement could be created, but no express language to that effect is used. If certain requirements are met, the court may nonetheless find that an easement has been created **by implication.**

    1. Exception to Statute of Frauds: Since an easement may normally be created only by compliance with the Statute of Frauds (*supra*, p. 203), creation of an easement by implication is in effect an **exception to the Statute of Frauds.** For this reason, the requirements for creation of an easement by implication are designed to ensure that there is strong circumstantial evidence that the parties **did in fact intend** to create or reserve the easement.

2. Summary of requirements: For an easement by implication to exist, these requirements must be met: (1) land is being *divided up* so that the owner of a parcel is either selling part and retaining part, or is subdividing the property and selling pieces to different grantees; (2) the use for which the implied easement is claimed *existed prior to the severance* referred to in (1), and was apparent and continuous prior to the severance; and (3) the easement is at least *reasonably necessary* to the enjoyment of what is claimed to be the dominant tenement. See Nutshell, pp. 169-77. Each of these requirements is discussed in detail below.

3. Severance from common owner: An easement by implication constitutes an exception to the Statute of Frauds. To limit this exception, and to guard against false claims, an easement will only be implied where the owner of a parcel *sells part and retains part*, or *sells pieces simultaneously* to more than one grantee. (This is called the requirement of *"severance."*) One of the pieces then becomes the dominant tenement, and the other the servient tenement. This means that an *easement in gross cannot be created by implication*.

> **Example:** O owns a two-acre parcel, with a building on each half. The only access from the rear half to the street is by crossing the front half. O sells the rear half to E, and keeps the front half for himself. Provided that the requirements of prior use and necessity (discussed below) are met, E will gain an easement by implication over the front half, even though the deed from O to E is silent about any easement.

> **Example:** A and B are neighboring landowners. A new street is built adjoining B's property, and the only way A can get to it directly is by crossing B's property. He crosses for several years along a particular portion of B's property, and then sells his land to C. No easement against B's property could have been created by implication, since there was no conveyance between A and B. If A, or C (or one after the other) uses the path long enough, an easement by *prescription* may be created (*infra*, p. 210), but this is a completely different matter. Also, if the new road is the only public way, and at one time in the past the parcels owned by A and C were under common ownership, an easement by *necessity* (*infra*, p. 209) may exist. But in the absence of a conveyance between A and B, no easement by implication can exist.

> **Example:** O, the owner of Blackacre, conveys the entire parcel to B, There is a swimming pool on the property, and as part of the transfer B promises O orally that O may use the swimming pool whenever he wants. No easement by implication is created, because O is selling his entire parcel, rather than selling part and retaining part. To put it another way, O's easement, if it existed, would be in gross, and no easement in gross may be created by implication. (Nor does O have an express easement, because the Statute of Frauds is not satisfied). O therefore has merely a license, which may be revoked by B whenever he desires. (See *infra*, p. 225.)

a. Easement may be by reservation: As the first of the three consecutive examples above shows, the implied easement may be in favor of the grantee against property retained by the grantor. But the implied easement may also be *reserved* by the grantor, for his benefit against the property received by the grantee.

i. Stricter standards: However, the courts are somewhat more *reluctant* to find that an easement has been impliedly reserved in favor of the grantor than that it has been impliedly granted to the grantee. This is partly because the deed is almost always drawn up by the grantor, who thus has complete freedom to require that an explicit reservation of easement be put in. This stricter standard for implied reservations is reflected principally in the degree of **necessity** that the easement must have; the requirement of necessity is discussed *infra*, p. 209.

b. Must arise at time of severance: For an implied easement to be created, it must arise **at the time of severance**, not subsequently.

Example: O owns a parcel, with a house on the rear half and a house on the front half. O conveys the rear half to A, but the deed explicitly provides that A may not use an existing driveway through the front parcel, and must instead use a rear exit to a different road adjoining the rear half. A then sells the property to B, and the deed purports to give B an easement over the front half. At the same time, O orally promises B that B may have an easement over the driveway.

No easement exists, however, either by implication or express grant. This is because an implied easement over the front half could only have been created at the moment the front half was severed from the back half, and the deed from O to A explicitly ruled out such an implied easement. Thereafter, it was too late for creation by implication, and not even O's promise (nor the statement in the deed from A to B) could create an easement. (Nor is O's oral statement sufficient to create an express easement, since it does not meet the Statute of Frauds. B might be able to argue that because of the statement, O is **estopped** to deny that any easement exists; however, this argument is unlikely to succeed.)

c. Prevented by express clause: As the above example indicates, an express provision in the deed to the effect that no easement exists will prevent creation of an implied easement, even if the circumstances are such that the easement would otherwise be created. Rest., § 476, Comment d.

4. Prior use: Most courts also required that the use for which the easement is claimed have existed **prior** to the severance of ownership. As the idea is sometimes put, there must have been a **"quasi-easement"**, in favor of one portion of the property and against the other portion, while both were under common ownership. The benefitted portion is called the **quasi-dominant tenement**, and the burdened portion the **quasi-servient tenement**.

Example: O owns two houses side by side on one parcel. To have access to the garage behind house 1 from the street, he builds a driveway which runs between the two houses. To the extent that the driveway runs on the property immediately adjoining house 2, this property is the "quasi-servient tenement", The property on which house 1 (including the garage) is located is the "quasi-dominant tenement." There is thus a "quasi-easement." If O then conveys house 2, including part of the land and the driveway, to A, an implied easement in favor of house 1 will be reserved (assuming all other requirements of implied easements are met). Or, if O conveys house 1, an implied easement in favor of that house will be granted (again, assuming all other requirements are met).

a. Not absolute necessity in some courts: Many courts impose an absolute requirement that there have been a previous use similar to the easement claimed. But other courts seem to consider the existence or non-existence of a prior use as merely **one factor** in determining whether an implied easement has been created.

This is the approach of the Restatement, which lists prior use as one of the eight factors, none of which is absolutely essential; Rest. § 476.

b. Apparent use: To the extent that a prior use is required, the requirement is met only if the use is *apparent*. That is, the use must be one which the grantee either *in fact* knew about when he received his interest, or *could have learned about* with *reasonable inspection*.

    i. Underground sewer: "Apparent" is *not* the same thing as "visible", however. All that is required is that the existence of the use would be disclosed by inspection, even if not physically seen. For instance, where *sewer pipes* ran underground from house 1 under house 2 and into the main sewer system, a court held that the quasi-easement under house 2 was apparent even though not visible. The court reasoned that a plumber could have ascertained that the pipes from house 1 must have run under house 2; therefore, the purchaser of house 1 from the owner of the parcel including both house 1 and 2 received an implied easement for the pipes to run under house 2. *Romanchuk v. Plotkin*, 9 N.W.2d 421 (Minn. 1943).

c. Document showing use: Even if the use does not actually exist before the severance of ownership, the use requirement may be met by *documents* referring to the fact that the use will exist in the future. For instance, in *Krzewinski v. Eaton Homes, Inc*, 161 N.E.2d 88 (Ohio 1958), the Ps were shown a *plat* (i.e., a map of a proposed subdivision; see *infra*, p. 298), on which a proposed road was shown as abutting the property the Ps planned to purchase. The contract of sale then described the property by reference to the plat. The court held that even though the road did not exist prior to the sale, the reference to it on the plat gave the Ps an implied easement for its full length as shown, and the developer was required to construct it in full.

d. Use pursuant to sales contract: If the uses begin when the property is under *contract* to be sold, but before title is actually transferred, this will probably be sufficient to meet the "prior use" requirement.

e. Permanent and continuous: Courts also frequently require that the use prior to severance be *permanent and continuous* rather than merely sporadic. Thus if a driveway were laid out, but not paved, and used only once every six months, this might prevent the prior use requirement from being satisfied. (But if the property has undergone a *permanent physical change*, such as the paving of a driveway, this will probably meet the test of "permanent and continuous", even though the owner does not make actual beneficial use of the change very often. See 2 A.L.P. 262.)

5. Necessity: According to most courts, the easement must be *reasonably necessary* to the enjoyment of what is claimed to be the dominant tenement. It is not clear whether the degree of necessity is to be measured by the use prior to severance, or the use claimed after severance; since, by hypothesis, these must be at least reasonably similar anyway, the issue is usually not important.

    a. Reservation distinguished from grant: Where the implied easement is created by *grant* (i.e., in favor of the grantee), most courts require only *"reasonable"* necessity. Thus the fact that the grantee could use his property to some extent even without the easement will not be fatal to his claim. But where the easement is *reserved* (i.e., in favor of the grantor rather than the grantee), most courts require that it be *"strictly"* or "absolutely" necessary.

Example: O owns a large plot, which can be thought of as three distinct lots. A filling station exists on Lot 3. As part of the filling station operation, a wash shed, with a concrete floor, is laid, which extends onto Lot 1. O conveys Lot 1 to A, with no express reservation of an easement for the shed. Title to Lot 1 eventually passes to P, and title to Lot 3 passes to D. P sues D for the encroachment, and D claims that an implied easement was reserved by the conveyance of Lot 1 to A.

Held, a reservation of an easement will be implied only where the claimed right is "strictly necessary" in order for the grantor to continue using his retained property. Here, there was no showing that O (or her successors, A and D) could not have altered or moved the wash shed so that it fit solely on Lot 3. The burden of showing strict necessity is on D. (A new trial is ordered on the issue of strict necessity.) *Mitchell v. Castellaw*, 246 S.W.2d 163 (Tex. 1952).

   i. Contrary view: But other courts, probably a *minority*, hold that strict necessity does not need to be proved *even for an implied reservation*, although a somewhat greater degree of necessity will be required than in the case of an implied grant. This is the view of Rest. § 476, Comment c. See also *Van Sandt v. Royster*, 83 P.2d 698 (Kan. 1938), in which the owner of two houses sold house 2 with sewer pipes running under it connected to, and for the benefit of, house 1. The court held that, although a separate sewer line could be constructed by the owner of house 1 that would not cross under house 2, this would involve "disproportionate effort and expense", and that an implied easement by reservation existed.

b. Both parcels conveyed at once: As noted, the requisite severance of ownership exists where the quasi-dominant estate is conveyed to one grantee, and the quasi-servient estate is *simultaneously* conveyed to another grantee. In fact, Rest. § 476, Comment f, takes the position that an implied easement is even *more likely* to arise in this situation than in the usual case where one parcel (either the quasi-dominant or quasi-servient tenement) is retained by the grantor. As the Restatement reasons, "it is reasonable to infer that a conveyor who has divided his land among simultaneous conveyees intends that very considerable privileges of use shall exist between them." This is particularly true where the conveyance is among *family members*.

Example: O owns two houses on one parcel. A driveway serving house 2 is located close to house 1. As part of a family settlement, O conveys house 1 to his son A and house 2 to his son B; the driveway ends up on A's parcel. A court will be quite willing to find that an implied easement in favor of house 2 was granted, against house 1, for use of the driveway.

6. Easement of light and air: A right to have one's *view* remain *unobstructed*, commonly called an easement of *"light and air"*, *cannot, in most states, be created by implication*.

Example: O owns a parcel which contains a house on one half and undeveloped land on the other half. O has intentionally refrained from building anything on the other half, so that he can keep the view from the house (which looks out over the vacant half onto the ocean) unobstructed. O then sells the half with the house to A. Most courts will *not* permit A to argue that he has received an implied easement of light and air over the vacant parcel, such that O may not build a structure on it which would block A's view. To allow such an easement to be implied "would seriously hamper land development." Burby, p. 74-75. (But such an easement of light and air may be created by express grant.)

    a. Solar energy: An easement to receive sunlight for the purpose of deriving *solar energy* might more likely be created by implication than an easement merely to "enjoy" sunlight. For instance, if O in the above example had installed solar collectors in the house he sold to A, A might prevail in his claim that O cannot now block the sunlight by building a large structure on the vacant piece. See *Prah v. Maretti*, 321 N.W.2d 182 (Wisc. 1982), discussed *infra*, p. 404, in which the court protected the right of access to solar energy, not by use of implied easements but by the law of private nuisance.

D. Easement of necessity: Two parcels may be so situated that an easement over one is *"strictly necessary"* to the enjoyment of the other. If so, the courts are willing to find an "easement by necessity". Unlike the easement by implication, the easement by necessity does *not require that there have been an actual prior use* before severance. Conversely, however, the necessity must be *"strict"* rather than "reasonable" (the usual standard for implied easements).

    1. Landlocked parcels: The most common example of such an easement is where a parcel is *"landlocked"*, and access to a public road can only be gained via a right of way over adjoining property.

    2. Common grantor: Although the courts do not require a use prior to severance, they do, however, require that *at one time*, both the alleged dominant tenement and the alleged servient tenement have been owned by the same person. But if this requirement is met, it does not matter that no actual use of the claimed right of way occurred until much later.

        Example: O owns a 140-acre parcel. In 1895, he conveys forty acres to X. For the next forty years, X and his successors in title are able to get to the public highway by using a private road belonging to Y, that does not run over any part of what was originally the unified 140-acre tract. In 1937, the forty-acre parcel is bought by P. The remaining 100 acres are inherited by D. Shortly after P buys the small parcel, Y closes his private road. P requests that D grant him a right of way over the 100-acre parcel, since there is now no other way for him to get to the public road.

        Held, for P. Since the entire 140 acres were at one time under the common ownership of O, an easement by necessity in favor of P over the lands now held by D will be found. Because the easement is based upon strict necessity rather than upon implication, it does not matter that the right of way claimed did not exist prior to the conveyance by O, or even for forty years subsequently. The right of way is treated as having lain dormant, and may now be used by P since lands of third parties are no longer available. *Finn v. Williams*, 33 N.E.2d 226 (Ill. 1941).

    3. Duration: But the duration of an easement by necessity will be only for *so long as the necessity exists*. Thus if, in the *Finn* case, Y were once again to make the right of way over his land available, the right of way over D's property would probably cease.

    4. Restatement view: The Restatement does not have a special class for easements by necessity. This is because prior use is not a strict requirement for easements by implication. Thus if, in a particular case, the necessity is sufficiently great, an easement by implication arises under the Restatement view even without prior use. Rest. § 476,

Comment g.

E. Easement by prescription: Recall the a possessory estate in land may be gained by **adverse possession** (*supra*, p. 26). An easement may be created by similar means. Such an easement is called an easement by **prescription**.

1. **Fiction of "lost grant":** At early common law, courts were reluctant to acknowledge that an easement could be gained without there ever having been consent between the parties. Therefore, they employed the fiction of a *"lost grant"*, by which, in the distant past, it was assumed, the holder of the claimed servient estate granted an easement to the holder of the claimed dormant estate. This "lost grant" could be presumed whenever it would be shown that a particular use had been made from "time immemorial".

2. **Use of statute of limitations by analogy:** American courts **decline** to use the "lost grant" fiction. Instead nearly all states refer to the **statute of limitations** applicable to adverse possession actions, and apply it **by analogy** to easements.

   Example: In state X, the statute of limitations on actions to recover possessions of real estate is 21 years. That is, an owner of record loses his rights to sue an adverse possessor after this time and the latter gains title. A, the owner of Lot 1, uses a path over Lot 2, owned by B, for 21 years. Assuming that the nature of the use meets the requirements discussed below, after the 21 years A has gained an easement by prescription, and may use the path as a right of way forever afterwards.

3. **When statute starts to run:** The statutory period does not begin to elapse, according to most American courts, until the owner of the servient tenement **gains a cause of action** against the owner of the dominant tenement. For this reason, an easement of *"light and air" cannot be acquired by prescription*.

   Example: D owns two adjoining lots. He sells one to P, who builds a house on it. D builds a house on the other lot, and leaves enough space between the side of his house and the edge of his property so that light enters that side of P's house, and there is a view. Twenty-four years later, D builds a store in the alley, which takes up only the property retained by D, but which blocks P's light and view. *Held*, P did not obtain an easement of light and air by prescription. The 20-year period of prescription could only begin when D had a cause of action against P for using D's property. Since all P did was to look out over D's property, D never gained a right of action, and the period of prescription never began to run. *Parker & Edgarton v. Foote*, 19 Wend. 309 (N.Y. 1838).

4. **Disabilities:** Recall that in an adverse possession case, the running of the statute of limitations may be **tolled** if the record owner has certain **disabilities**. (*Supra*, p. 36.) Similarly, most courts allow a "tolling" of the prescription period. Thus if the owner of the alleged servient tenement is a minor, the use of his property as a right of way by a next-door neighbor might not count towards the statutory period.

5. **Use must be adverse, not permissive:** Just as possession must be adverse in an adverse possession case, so the **use** must be **adverse** to the rights of the holder of the servient tenement, and not with the latter's **permission**.

   a. **Not in subordination:** For a use to be adverse, it must not be in **subordination** to the servient owner's rights. Thus if the dominant owner acknowledges that his use is only valid because of the servient owner's consent, the use is not adverse.

Example: P and D are next-door neighbors. Because he believes in being a good neighbor, and to help P, D agrees that P may use D's driveway to get to P's garage. P thanks D for this, and gives no indication that he is asserting an actual legal right to use the driveway. P's use is clearly in subordination to D's rights, and is therefore not adverse. Even if the usage continues longer than the statute of limitations period, no easement by prescription will be gained. Instead, the use is merely a *license*, which is revocable at will by D.

i. **Unilateral consent by servient owner:** But a subordination occurs only if *both* parties agree or appear to agree to it. For instance, assume that in the above example, P claims (even completely without merit) that he has a legal right to use D's driveway. The fact that D agrees to tolerate this use does not convert P's use into a subordinate one. P's use is therefore adverse, and at the end of the statutory period an easement by prescription will be created. This will occur even if D expressly reserves the right to terminate his permission, so long as P does not acknowledge that such a revocation of permission would be binding upon him. This makes sense, since D is at all times free to change his mind, revoke his permission, and start a lawsuit against P if he continues to make his use. If D does not do so during the whole statutory period, it is not unfair to burden him with the use that he has tolerated for so long.

b. **"Hostility" not required:** Although the use must be adverse, it does *not* have to be *"hostile"*. If the parties make an arrangement which the dominant owner is justified in regarding as permanent, this may be enough to make his use adverse even though there are no ill feelings between the two owners.

Example: A and B are adjoining homeowners. They agree to build a driveway between the two houses that will rest half on A's property and half on B's. They split the expenses and create a paved, permanent driveway. Both parties use the driveway continuously. Twenty-five years later, after A's house has been bought by P, and B's house by D, P sues to prevent D from using P's portion of the common driveway. *Held*, for D. Concededly, neither A's nor B's conduct in building and using the driveway was "hostile". Yet, because the driveway was expansive, made of concrete, and permanent, the court will presume that each party intended a more permanent arrangement than simply a license revocable at the will of either. Therefore, the use by both A and B was adverse, and ripened into an easement by prescription at the end of the statutory period. (A dissent argued that neither A nor B made any claim of absolute right in the other's property, and that there was merely a revocable oral license, which did not give rise to an easement by prescription.) *Shanks v. Floom*, 124 N.E.2d 416 (Ohio 1955).

Note: In this type of common driveway situation, the courts are split. About half of the courts would probably agree with the position of the dissent in *Shanks*, that only a revocable oral license, not ripening into an easement by prescription, existed. See, e.g., *Lang v. Dupuis*, 46 N.E.2d 21 (Ill. 1943), finding no adverse use on facts nearly identical to those of *Shanks*. If the driveway in *Shanks* had merely been an *unpaved* one requiring no expenditure and not having a permanent character, nearly all courts would probably conclude that the use was not adverse on either side, and thus did not ripen into an easement by prescription. In such a situation, the court would probably treat the uses as being "mutually advantageous" and "mutually permissive".

c. Shift from permissive to adverse: It is possible for a use to begin as a permissive one (i.e., under a license), and then shift to an adverse one. However, for such a shift to occur, the licensee must openly **renounce** the license and bring home to the licensor that the former's use henceforth is not subordinate. Thus in *Lunt v. Kitchens*, 260 P.2d 535 (Utah 1953) the use of a driveway began as a license by D to P. The fact that, over the years, P and his family used the driveway continuously (more often than D used it) and repaired it when it became muddy by throwing ashes on it, was not enough to renounce the license and begin an adverse use. (The tearing down by P of a fence put up by D was sufficient to renounce the license, but this occurred too soon before the lawsuit for the period of prescription to run.)

   i. Change in manner of use: A *change* in the manner of use may be enough to constitute a shift from a permissive use to a new, adverse, one. Thus in *Hester v. Sawyers*, 71 P.2d 646 (N.M. 1937), D used an existing road over P's property under what was clearly a license. When this road became unusable because of a fence built by P, D built a new road on P's property following a slightly different path, but for the same general purpose, and used it for more than the statutory period. The court held that this new road, insofar as it was constructed and maintained by D and followed a different course, constituted a new, adverse, use.

d. Shift from adverse to permissive: Conversely, a use may begin as adverse, and then become permissive if the parties so agree. If the use once again becomes adverse, the statutory period must *elapse all over again*, since the existence of the permissive interval prevents the first and second adverse periods from being "continuous and uninterrupted" (as discussed *infra*).

6. Open and notorious: The use must be *"open and notorious"* throughout the statutory period. That is, the use must be such that the owner of the servient tenement is put on notice that the use is occurring. See the analogous open-and-notorious requirement in the context of adverse possession, *supra*, p. 26.

7. Continuous and uninterrupted: The use must be *continuous and uninterrupted* throughout the statutory period. A similar requirement exists in the context of adverse possession, but since possession is involved there, the would-be adverse possessor must literally maintain possession continuously. An easement, on the other hand, involves only use, rather than possession; therefore, all that is required is that the *attitude* of *non-subordination* on the part of the user must be continuous, and the use itself must at least be reasonably continuous measured by the needs of the user. Thus in the case of a right of way over a driveway, the continuity requirement would not be violated if the user was out of town for a month, so long as he made reasonably frequent use when he was present.

a. Occasional use not sufficient: The continuity requirement serves the same purpose as the "adverse use" requirement, i.e., to prevent a helpful neighbor from unwittingly encumbering his property by tolerating permissive uses or occasional trespasses. Thus if the use is so *infrequent* that *a reasonable landowner would not be likely to protest*, and would view the matter as an occasional minor trespass, the continuity requirement is not satisfied.

b. Use not necessarily exclusive: Since an easement is merely a use, rather than a possession, the use does *not* have to be *exclusive*. Thus if A uses P's driveway frequently and adversely, the requisite continuity is not destroyed by the fact that B also uses the driveway just as often. This stems from the idea that only the attitude of non-subordination, not the physical use, must be continuous. See Rest. § 459(1).

  c. Protest by servient owner: If the servient owner is able to compel the dominant owner to stop the use, either by suit or other means, the requirement of continuity is obviously not satisfied. But if the servient owner merely *protests*, or brings an *unsuccessful lawsuit*, this will *not* be sufficient to interrupt the use. (However, if a lawsuit is brought before the end of the prescriptive period, and the plaintiff ultimately gains a judgment, this will "relate back" to the start of the suit, preventing a prescriptive easement from arising.)

    i. Traditional view: Recall that older cases often engaged in the fiction that a prescriptive easement arose from a theoretical "lost grant". These cases often held, as a consequence of the "lost grant" theory, that a use would ripen into a prescriptive easement only if it was with the *"acquiescence"* of the servient owner; non-acquiescence was viewed as rebutting the presumption that there was an actual lost grant. Consequently, these courts sometimes held that a *protest* by the servient owner, if it did not lead to an actual cessation of use, was sufficient to interrupt the continuity of possession. See, e.g, *Dartnell v. Bidwell*, 98 A. 743 (Me. 1916), holding that a letter of protest from D to P, ordering him to cease his use, was sufficient to interrupt D's acquiescence, and prevent a prescriptive easement from arising. Nearly all modern courts, however, have dispensed with the requirement of "acquiescence", and with the consequent rule that a protest is by itself sufficient to block a prescriptive easement.

8. Tacking: Recall that the statute of limitations in adverse possession cases may be satisfied by combining, or *tacking*, the possession of more than one person, provided that they are in privity with each other. The concept of tacking similarly exists in the context of prescriptive easements. Rest. § 464.

  a. Appurtenant easements: Where the easement is *appurtenant*, the privity required between the users is virtually the same as is required in adverse possession cases; thus grantor and grantee, landlord and tenant, life tenant and remainderman, or testator and legatee, would all be pairs as to whom tacking would apply.

  b. Easements in gross: Where the easement is *in gross* (which is possible though unlikely to occur in practice), it is hard to say what kind of privity is required; a caveat to Rest. § 463 takes no position on this question.

9. Difficulty of ascertaining: How can the lawyer for a purchaser of land tell whether the land his client is about to buy is burdened by any prescriptive easements? There is no easy, sure-fire, way to do this.

  a. Physical inspection: He could have his client check the property physically, to see whether there are any indications of an adverse use (e.g., a path cut across the back yard, leading from a neighbor's house to the street). Also, the client could ask nearby residents whether they knew of any use. But since a prescriptive easement, once it has been created, need no longer be actively used (so long as it is not affirmatively abandoned; see *infra*, p. 224), this will not be foolproof.

      b. Warranty: Another solution is for the buyer's lawyer to attempt to insert into the deed a warranty by the seller that there are no easements, whether prescriptive or otherwise. Then, if a prescriptive easement does exist, at least the buyer can sue.

F. Easement by custom: Normally the adverse use must be by one person, or by two or more persons who are in privity with each other. But the common law also recognized the doctrine of easement *by custom*, according to which use "for time immemorial" by the *public at large* could create an easement in favor of that public.

    1. American view: Most American courts have refused to allow an easement to be impliedly created in the public at large.

        a. Rule against Perpetuities: One argument made against such public easements is that the Rule Against Perpetuities is violated, because no owner of a fee simple could make a conveyance free of the easement (since there is no individual who could release his easement). *Sanchez v. Taylor,* 377 F.2d 733 (10th Cir. 1967).

        b. "Time immemorial": Another argument against public easements is that generally, in America, no custom has existed "from time immemorial" (as required in England). See, e.g., *Gillies v. Orienta Beach Club,* 289 N.Y.S. 733 (1935), rejecting easements by custom, on the grounds that New York has had recording acts since early in its history, and that a fifty-year public use (of a beach) cannot be considered a custom from time immemorial.

    2. Oregon view: But at least one state, Oregon, does permit an easement by custom to arise in favor of the public. In *State ex rel. Thornton v. Hay,* 462 P.2d 671 (Ore. 1969), the court held that the custom of members of the Oregon public to use ocean beaches was sufficiently long-standing and notorious to give rise to an easement for recreational use of these beaches by the public. The court rejected the argument that Oregon has existed as a state for too short a time for there to be a custom from "time immemorial"; the court noted that "the European settlers were not the first people to use the dry-sand areas as public land."

    3. Implied or express dedication: Even in states not recognizing easement by public custom, the owner of land may expressly or impliedly *"dedicate"* it to the public use. This is typically done with respect to roads and highways. For instance, suppose Developer owns a large subdivision, and would like to have the city where the subdivision is located build and maintain streets. He may make an offer of dedication of certain land, either as an outright grant or as an easement, to the city; if the city accepts, the public gains either an easement or a fee simple, and the city then has the burden of maintaining the road. Even without an explicit agreement, the dedication can occur impliedly, as where the public uses the property for a long time, and the public welfare would be seriously inconvenienced if the use were then curtailed. See B,C&S, p. 808. See also *infra,* p. 299.

G. Tidal lands and the "public trust" doctrine: Apart from the methods described above for created a formal easement, the *public as a whole* has something like an easement on the *navigable waterways* and on *seashores*. Under the *"public trust"* doctrine, the state holds title to navigable waterways and *tidelands* in trust for the public, and must safeguard the public's interest in these lands. R&K, p. 635.

    1. Derived from federal law: The public trust doctrine derives from federal law. But it has been left mainly to *state law* to apply the doctrine, so there is variation from state to state.

2. **Access to seashore:** The most important aspect of the public trust doctrine is that it guarantees to members of the public the right to **use** the "tidelands" portion of the **ocean shore** for **swimming**, **bathing**, and other **recreational purposes**. Tidelands are the shore lands between the mean high-tide mark and the mean low-tide mark of the ocean. R&K, p. 635.

   a. **Applies even if property is in public hands:** The state is required to preserve these public-trust rights even if the state has transferred the property to **private hands**. Thus even if a municipality were to transfer a particular stretch of ocean tide lands to a private buyer, the public would have a quasi-easement to continue to use the property for recreational purposes.

   b. **Access through private property to public property:** Furthermore, some courts have held that the public has a quasi-easement, or right of access, **through private property** to get to public ocean-front property. See, e.g., *Matthews v. Bay Head Improvement Assoc.*, 471 A.2d 355 (N.J. 1984), holding that the public must be given "reasonable access" through private property to get to the publicly-owned shore front (though the court did not say in that case how much access should be required, or who should have to give it). The court in *Matthews* also held that the public had the right to sunbathe on privately-owned **dry-sand areas** (the beach area inland of the high-tide mark) as an adjunct to the right to use the tidelands themselves.

III. SCOPE OF EASEMENTS

A. **General rules:** Once it is established that an easement exists, questions arise as to the types of uses to which it may be put by the holder of the easement, and the rights of the owner of the servient tenement. The manner in which the easement was created often has an important bearing on these questions.

   1. **Expressly created easement:** Where the easement is created by an **express** written conveyance, the terms of that conveyance will normally control. Such a grant will usually spell out not only the physical area involved (e.g., "a ten-foot strip along the entire southern border of the property"), but will also generally spell out the allowable use (e.g, as a right of way for the delivering of coal to the coal chute at the back of A's property"). If the conveyance is ambiguous, the court will look at the circumstances surrounding its making to determine the parties' intent.

   2. **Implied easement:** If the easement is created by **implication**, the court will look to the use as it existed prior to the conveyance. That use, and any similar use which the parties might reasonably have expected, will be permitted. Burby, p. 83.

   3. **Prescriptive easement:** When the easement was created by **prescription**, the allowable use is determined by reference to the adverse use that continued during the statutory period and created the easement. The holder of the easement is not restricted to the precise use which occurred during the prescriptive period; he is, however, limited to the same **general pattern** of use. Rest. § 478, Comment a. Another way of putting the test is that the present use must be sufficiently similar to the older use that the court may conclude that the property owner **would not have objected** to this new use (just as he did not object to the old one).

      a. **Increase in burden:** One important factor is whether the new use represents a **greater burden** on the servient tenement than the old use. The bigger the increase in burden, the less likely the court will be to permit the new use.

Example: A right-of-way easement is created by prescription in favor of the sole house then located on a dominant tenement. After the easement is created, two more houses are built on the dominant property. *Held*, the residents of all three houses may use the right of way, since the basic use (as a pedestrian right of way) remains unchanged, and the increased burden is slight or nil. *Baldwin v. Boston & M.R.R.*, 63 N.E. 428 (Mass. 1902).

Example: O owns land adjoining a lake. He puts a twelve-inch pipe five feet below the lake's water level, and for 20 years draws off water for his use on his land. The level of the lake falls so that the twelve-inch pipe is above the water line. O now wishes to replace the pipe so that it will be below the new level of the lake, and plans to keep on drawing the same amount of water per year that he has been drawing in the past. A, who also owns lakeside property, seeks an injunction to stop O from making this replacement. We shall assume that O has been withdrawing more water from the lake over the past 20 years than he is entitled to as a riparian owner.

A is probably entitled to his injunction. In *Kennedy v. Niles Water Supply Co.*, 139 N.W. 241 (Mich. 1913) a court held on similar (though not identical) facts that O gained a prescriptive easement *only for use of the original pipe*. The court reasoned that A and the other riparian owners acquiesced only to the lowering of the water level to the original pipe; O's conduct therefore imposed a greater burden than that to which the others had acquiesced. A contrary ruling, the court said, would mean that O has "the right, as the level of the lake is lowered, to lay successive pipes until it draws off the last drop of water which the lake contains," provided that the rate of withdrawal is not greater than it was before.

4. **Enlargement by prescription:** Regardless of the original use, an easement can always be *enlarged by prescription*. For instance, suppose that a conveyance grants an easement as a right of way "solely for pedestrians". If the path is used by an adjoining landowner as an automobile right of way for longer than the statute of limitations period, the use will have been expanded by prescription to include automobiles. See Burby, p. 86. (But the new use must be sufficiently different from the old one that the owner of the servient tenement is placed on notice that an expanded right is being claimed.)

B. **Development of dominant estate:** It frequently happens that the dominant estate undergoes a general *change in use*. The question then arises whether such a change justifies a corresponding change in the use to which the easement may be put.

1. **Reasonable development contemplated:** Resolution of this question is likely to depend in part upon whether the easement was created expressly, by implication or by prescription.

2. **Normal development:** But regardless of how the easement was created, the court will normally allow a use that arises from the *normal, foreseeable, development* of the dominant estate, where this would *not impose an unreasonable burden* on the servient estate. See Rest. §§ 479 and 484. The *Baldwin* case, *supra*, is an example of this, since it was reasonable foreseeable that the dominant parcel would someday have more than one dwelling on it.

C. Use for benefit of additional property: An easement appurtenant is, by definition, used for the benefit of a particular dominant estate. The holder of that dominant estate will normally ***not*** be allowed to extend his use of the easement so that ***additional*** property owned by him (or by others) is benefitted. This is true even if the use for the benefit of the additional property does ***not*** increase the ***burden*** on the servient estate.

> **Example:** D owns parcel A and P owns parcel B. Parcel A stands between parcel B and the roadway. Parcel C is on the other side of parcel B, even more landlocked. An easement has long existed across parcel A for the benefit of parcel B. (Thus parcel A is the servient tenement and parcel B is the dominant tenement.) P now builds a house that is located partly on parcel B and partly on parcel C. P also builds a driveway leading from the easement across B, then across C, then back to the house:

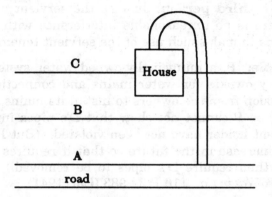

> D asserts that P has no right to use the easement for the benefit of parcel C, and therefore blocks the easement. P sues to have the obstruction removed, and D counterclaims for trespass.
>
> *Held*, for D. "[A]n easement appurtenant to one parcel of land may not be extended by the owner of the dominant estate to other parcels owned by him, whether adjoining or distinct tracts to which the easement is not appurtenant." The express grant of easement from D's predecessor to P's predecessor made it clear that only parcel B, not parcel C, was to be the dominant tenement. Therefore, when P built the house partly on parcel C, and built the driveway so that it crossed parcel C on the way to the house, P was attempting to misuse the easement by extending it to cover another parcel. This amounted to trespass, for which D can recover damages. This is true even though the burden on parcel A was not increased by this scheme (since the easement previously served a house located solely on parcel B, and that house was replaced by a single house straddling the B-C boundary). However, D may not be given an injunction against P's continued use of the easement, because the appellate court will respect the trial court's finding that there was no "actual and substantial injury" to D, one of the requirements for an injunction. (A dissent argues that an injunction should be given to D against trespass, even though the burden to D's property has not been increased by the misuse.) *Brown v. Voss*, 715 P.2d 514 (Wash. 1986).

D. Use of servient estate: To the extent that the holder of the easement gains rights over the servient tenement, the owner of that servient tenement loses the ability to make unrestricted use of his property. However, he may nonetheless make any use of the servient tenement that does ***not unreasonably interfere*** with the easement.

   1. Different location: If the easement is for a particular portion of the servient tenement, the servient owner may ***not*** force the easement holder to use a ***different*** portion.

Example: P holds a right of way over a particular 18-foot strip of D's property. D wishes to put a building on part of its property, and proposes to make a different path for P. (D will also raise its building off the ground so that there are eight feet of headroom over the old path.) P sues to enjoin the structure.

Held, for P. D was entitled to use its property in any way it wished so long as P's easement was not unreasonably interfered with. The eight feet of headroom were not sufficient, since it was not reasonable to prevent P from using vehicles over eight feet high along the right of way. Given this fact, D cannot avoid the problem by forcing P to use a different path; the easement was a grant of a particular parcel of land (the original 18-foot strip) and P is entitled to insist on that strip, whether his insistence is reasonable or not. *Sakansky v. Wein,* 169 A. 1 (N.H. 1933).

2. **Use given to third person:** Just as the servient owner may use his property as he wishes if there is no unreasonable interference with the easement, so he may *permit third persons* to make such use of the servient tenement.

Example: P, a municipally-owned water system, holds easements from various property owners for water mains and connections. D, a private competitor, gets permission from the owners to install its mains in the same five-foot trench. *Held,* insofar as P cannot not show that D's pipes interfere with its own, P's rights as easement holder have not been violated. (But P's rights have *priority,* and if P's needs increase in the future so that it requires the entire five-foot area for itself, it can then require D's pipes to be removed.) *Pasadena v. California-Michigan Land & Water Co.,* 110 P.2d 983 (Cal. 1941).

IV. TRANSFER AND SUBDIVISION OF EASEMENTS

A. **Transfer of burden:** When title to the *servient estate* is transferred, the burden of the easement *remains* with the property. An easement is just like any other encumbrance upon real estate (e.g., a mortgage) in this respect.

Example: O, the owner of Blackacre, gives A, a neighboring landowner, a right of way over Blackacre. O then sells Blackacre to B. Following the sale, the easement remains valid against Blackacre; that is, it runs with the land, rather than being personal to O.

1. **Subdivision:** Similarly, if the servient estate is *subdivided,* the burden of an easement still attaches to the same parts of the land as before. Of course, the easement may only burden a portion of a larger parcel; after the subdivision, only the portion containing the burdened land will be encumbered. Thus in the above example, if O sold half his property (the half containing the right of way) to B, and the other half to C, only B's portion would be subject to the easement.

B. **Transfer of benefit:** Most of the questions regarding transfer and subdivision involve the *benefit side*.

1. **Transfer of easements appurtenant:** An easement *appurtenant* will normally *pass with the transfer of the dominant estate*. The new owner of the dominant estate has full rights to the easement, and the transferor loses his rights to the easement. Rest. §487.

Example: O, a developer, builds a swimming pool in its subdivision. In its deeds to various purchasers of lots, it inserts a provision that "the grantee and his immediate family only, shall enjoy the free use of the swimming pool." A buys a lot under these terms, and subsequently sells it to D. D's attempts to use the pool are resisted by P (a community organization which is the successor in title to O).

Held, for D. The easement in the pool was clearly intended as an easement appurtenant, rather than an easement in gross; the pool was obviously intended to benefit purchasers in their status as landowners in the development. The reference to "the grantee and his immediate family only" means that only the immediately family of a particular landowner may use the pool, not that a landowner's right to use the pool may not be assigned together with an assignment of the lot. *Maranatha Settlement Assn. v. Evans*, 122 A.2d 679 (Pa. 1956).

a. **Exceptions to automatic transfer:** The general rule that an easement appurtenant is automatically transferred together with the dominant estate, applies *unless there is a contrary agreement*. Such a contrary agreement may occur either at the time the easement is created, or at the time the dominant estate is transferred.

Example: O owns two adjoining parcels, Lot 1 and Lot 2. He sells Lot 1 to A, and at the same time grants A the right to use a driveway on Lot 2. The deed expressly provides that this right of way will exist only so long as Lot 1 is owned by A himself. If A sells Lot 1 to B, the easement will be extinguished.

Example: Same facts as the above example, except that O does not impose any restriction on transfer. A transfers his interest in Lot 1 to B, but expressly provides that the right to use the driveway does not pass to B. Assuming (as seems probable) that O intended the easement to belong only to the person who owns Lot 1, the restriction imposed by A will either destroy the easement or be ineffective (in which case B would get the easement). The court would decide which of these two outcomes occurs by trying to figure out what A and B would have done had they realized that the easement could not remain in A. Rest. §487, Comment b.

2. **Sub-division:** Similar rules apply to an easement appurtenant where the dominant estate is *sub-divided* into smaller lots, rather than transferred as a whole. That is, if the physical layout of the dominant estate is such that the owners of two or more of the sub-divided lots can take advantage of the easement, each will normally have the right to do so. But if only one part of the dominant estate can benefit, that portion will become the only dominant estate after the subdivision.

Example: A owns Lot 1, and X owns adjacent Lot 2. A private road runs from a garage on Lot 1 through Lot 2 to a public road. A subdivides Lot 1 into a parcel bought by B and a parcel bought by C. If the parcels bought by B and C are laid out such that each one can have access to the private road without going on the other's land, each will have the right to the easement (and there will thus be two dominant tenements). But if B can get to the private road only by going over A's portion, he will not have a right to the easement, and A's parcel will be the only dominant tenement.

a. **Extreme increase in burden:** Occasionally, subdivision of the dominant tenement would result in such a *large increase* in the *burden* caused to the servient tenement that not all the new subdivision owners will be allowed their easement.

This is done as a matter of **construction**, not law; that is, the court concludes that the creator of the easement did not intend for it to pass to each new owner in the event of a sub-division.

    i. Illustrative case: For instance, in *Bang v. Forman*, 222 N.W.96 (Mich. 1928), O, a developer, sold off 25 lots, each having a 50-foot beach front and an easement over the beach frontage of the other lots. D then bought three of the lots, and subdivided them into 26 much smaller lots, the purchasers of which were purportedly granted the same easement; D also built a cement roadway from the public highway to the beach, to facilitate use of the easement. The court held that O had not intended the easement to be apportionable in the event of a drastic subdivision, such as that here (where 26 families instead of three would now have use of the beach).

    ii. Must be drastic increase: But the increased burden must generally be quite *dramatic* for the court to conclude that apportionment was not intended by the original parties to the easement.

3. Easements in gross: Traditionally, the principal distinction between an easement appurtenant and an easement *in gross* is that whereas the former is assignable, the latter is *not transferable*. Burby, p. 67. The rationale for this distinction is that an easement appurtenant can only be assigned or divided in the same way that the dominant tenement is, a self-limiting feature that is not present in the easement in gross.

    a. Modern view: Modern courts are much more *willing* to allow assignment and transfer of easements in gross. Such courts tend to distinguish between easements that are primarily *commercial*, and those that are primarily *personal*.

        i. Personal easements: In the case of a *personal* easement, the creator probably granted the easement because he was friendly with the beneficiary, or for other social purposes; he probably did not intend that it would be transferable. This would be true, for instance, if A gave his friend B, who lived a few blocks away, the right to swim in A's pool; A probably does not intend B to have the right to transfer this privilege (even assuming that it is an irrevocable easement rather than a revocable license).

        ii. Commercial easements: In the commercial context, by contrast, alienability is much more likely to be intended by the parties. One who gives a telephone company the right to string phone wires over his property, for instance, probably intends that this right should pass to any other company that takes over the telephone operations. See Rest §489, making commercial easement in gross *automatically alienable*.

        iii. Non-commercial easements: Under this modern view, even a *non-commercial* easement in gross may be alienable if the parties *explicitly or impliedly so agree*. Rest. §491. The court will consider the circumstances as well as the parties' words, in determining their intent as to alienability.

    b. Divisibility: The traditional view, insofar as it prevented even transfer of easements in gross, *a fortiori* prohibited the *division* of such an easement into smaller parts.

        i. Restrictions under modern view: Under the modern view, even those easements in gross that would be alienable (i.e., typically, commercial ones) are ***not***

necessarily divisible. Such an easement may be assigned to more than one person, but they may *not generally make separate uses*; instead, they must hold *"as one"*.

Example: O holds the exclusive right to fish and boat on the waters of a particular lake. He conveys to his brother, A, a one-fourth interest in these rights. O and A then set up a partnership, in which they operate boat- and bath-houses, and rent boats to persons wishing to use the lake. After A's death his heirs purport to assign to D (a church group) the right to have its members use the lake. O sues to block D from using the lake.

Held, for O. The easement owned by O was in gross. It was an alienable right (since the conveyance of the rights to O included a reference to his heirs and assigns). But it was not divisible, in the sense that O and A each had the right to make separate uses, and grant separate licenses. Therefore, the license to D issued by A's heirs was not valid without the consent of O. *Miller v. Lutheran Conference & Camp Ass'n*, 200 A. 646 (Pa. 1938).

ii. **Exclusive easement:** If the easement is an *exclusive* one, so that the owner of the *servient* tenement does not have the right to make the same use, the courts are at least somewhat more willing to *allow apportionment*, since multiple users will not be interfering directly with the servient owner's use. But since such multiple uses may interfere with other uses by the servient owner (e.g., the right to fish and boat on a lake might interfere with the servient owner's rights to bathe), the courts are nonetheless somewhat reluctant. If the easement is not only exclusive, but paid for in such a way that the *more use is made*, the *more money the servient owner receives* for it, the court is fairly likely to allow apportionment, since this is in the servient owner's interest. Rest. §493, Comment c. Thus if, in *Miller, supra*, the grant of the easement to O had provided that he would pay the owner of the lake a royalty based on total license revenues, the court might have been willing to let O and A issue separate licenses.

4. **Profits in gross:** Courts have always been *willing to permit the assignment* of most *profits* in gross (i.e., the right to remove timber, water, minerals or other items from the soil). This is perhaps because most profits in gross, unlike most easements in gross, are of a commercial nature, and it is likely to be the parties' intent that they be assignable.

Example: O receives the right to draw water from a lake, which he uses to run a mill. O stops running the mill, and assigns his water-drawing rights to A, who uses the water to run a large hotel at a different location. *Held*, the right is "an absolute right to take profit or produce from the land . . .", not restricted to use with any particular dominant estate. Therefore, it is freely transferable. *Loch Sheldrake Associates v. Evans*, 118 N.E.2d 444 (N.Y. 1954)

a. **Division:** But as with the modern view of easements in gross, courts are more reluctant to permit *division* of a profit in gross. If the profit is non-exclusive, so that the servient owner may also take the products of the land, division of use by the holder of the profit is likely to be much more burdensome to the servient owner.

Example: O conveys an island, but retains a non-exclusive right to remove sand from it. O now tries to assign this right to three independent contractors, engaged in building a huge plant for the U.S. government. *Held*, the assignment/division is not valid. "To permit [O] to apportion his right to sand among three such contractors engaged in such an enterprise would have required quantities of sand never dreamed of by the parties at the time this deed was made." *Stanton v. T.L. Herbert & Sons*, 211 S.W. 353 (Tenn. 1919).

  i. Exclusive profit with royalty: If, by contrast, the profit is *exclusive*, and provides for a *royalty* to the servient owner based upon use, the court is quite likely to allow apportionment, since this is in the servient owner's benefit. The right to mine coal from the servient land, for instance, which is to be paid for on a per ton basis, would probably be apportionable, unless there was a clear intent to the contrary. See Rest. §493, Illustration 1.

V. TERMINATION OF EASEMENTS

  A. Introduction: There are a variety of ways in which an easement may terminate. The more important of these are discussed below.

  B. Natural expiration: Most easements are probably for an *unlimited duration*, i.e., easements in fee simple. But the parties may always agree that an easement is to have a shorter duration. Thus O might give A a 20-year easement to use his driveway as a right of way, or the parties might limit the easement to A's lifetime. At the end of this period, the easement would simply cease to exist, and would no longer be an encumbrance.

  1. Purpose no longer applies: Or, the easement might be for a certain purpose, and will terminate when that purpose is no longer relevant; thus if O gave A an easement to run his sewer line under O's property, this easement would cease if A was subsequently able to make a direct hookup to the street.

  C. Merger: An easement is, by definition, an interest in the land of another. Therefore, if ownership of a servient estate and of the appurtenant dominant estate come into the hands of one person, the easement appurtenant is *destroyed by merger*. This destruction is permanent, even if a severance of the dominant and servient interests subsequently occurs.

  Example: O gives a right-of-way easement to A, his next-door neighbor. O then buys A's property. This will cause a merger between the dominant and servient estate, and the easement will be extinguished. Then, if O re-sells what was formerly A's property to B, the easement will not be revived (although a new easement by implication or by prescription might arise). See Rest. §497.

  1. Easement in gross: Similarly, if the holder of an easement in gross acquires the servient estate, this will cause an extinguishment of the easement by merger. Rest. §499.

  D. Destruction of servient estate: The easement will sometimes involve use not just of the servient land, but of a *structure* on that land. If so, *destruction* of the servient building by fire, other act of God, or the act of a third person, will terminate the easement.

  1. Act by servient owner: One state, Massachusetts, even permits an easement to be destroyed by the *intentional* act of the owner of the servient estate. In *Union National Bank of Lowell v. Nesmith*, 130 N.W. 251 (Mass. 1921), two adjoining buildings had a common entrance and common stairways. The court held that the owner of one could knock down his building and build a new one without providing a common entrance or stairway.

a. Majority rule: In all other states, apparently such an intentional destruction by the servient owner would not extinguish the easement. But if the servient owner lets the property *deteriorate* over a length of time, this may be sufficient to destroy the easement. See *Rothschild v. Wolf*, 123 P.2d 483 (Cal. 1942) (dictum).

E. Prescription: Just as an easement may be created by *prescription*, so it may be extinguished by this means. That is, the servient owner or a third person may use the servient property in a way inconsistent with the easement, for the statute of limitations period.

> **Example:** O gives A a right of way over O's property, and later builds a fence blocking the right of way. The easement will be destroyed by prescription after the fence has been in place for the statute of limitations period.

F. Release: The easement holder may execute a *release* in writing, surrendering the easement.

G. Forfeiture: If the easement is used in such a way that the burden on the servient tenement is materially *increased*, and there is no way to scale the use back to its original level, the easement may be destroyed by *forfeiture*.

1. *Crimmins* case: For instance, in *Crimmins v. Gould*, 308 P.2d 786 (Dist. Ct. App. Cal. 1957), D held a right of way over property owned by P. D subdivided his own land, and built a road on it which connected the right of way to a public highway. The court held that this materially increased the burden on the right of way, and that there was no feasible way of reducing this burden while maintaining the original easement. Therefore, D was held to have forfeited the easement entirely.

H. Tax sale of servient property: If the servient property is sold at a *tax sale*, easements appurtenant to it will generally *not* be extinguished, since such easements increase the value of the dominant tenement (thus increasing the tax valuation of that dominant tenement); it would therefore be unfair to deprive the dominant owner of the benefits for which he is paying taxes. Rest. §509, Comment d.

1. Easement in gross: But an *easement in gross* is generally extinguished by a tax sale of the servient tenement. 2 A.L.P. 309.

I. Estoppel: Even if the holder of the easement does not intend to abandon it (see *infra*, p. 224), his conduct may be such that he is *estopped* from subsequently exercising his easement rights. This will occur if (1) the holder's conduct or words are *reasonably likely to lead the owner of the servient tenement to change his position in reliance*, and (2) the latter in fact does so. See 2 A.L.P. 305.

> **Example:** E holds an easement to use a driveway running over O's land. E then builds his own driveway, and uses it instead of O's driveway for ten years. O, who assumes that E has abandoned his easement of O's driveway, tears up the driveway and plants a lawn. A court will probably find that E should reasonably have foreseen that his building of his own driveway, and his using it instead of O's for ten years, would cause O to think that E was abandoning his easement. Assuming that O's filling in of his own driveway was in direct reliance upon this mistaken impression, the court will hold that E is estopped from demanding his easement rights now.

1. Extent necessary for protection: But the estoppel will only occur to the *extent necessary to protect* the servient owner's reliance interest. Suppose, for instance, that in the above example, O, after filling in and planting his driveway, later decides that he wants to restore the driveway. Once he rebuilds the driveway, E will probably regain his easement rights. 2 A.L.P. 307.

J. Abandonment: Normally, an estate in land cannot be destroyed by *abandonment*; this is certainly true of the possessory estates. But an easement is merely a use rather than a possessory interest. Accordingly, courts permit it to be terminated by abandonment in certain circumstances.

    1. Words alone insufficient: The easement holder's *words alone* will *never* be sufficient to constitute an abandonment. Thus if O gives A a right of way over O's property, no oral or written statements by A that he doesn't want the easement any longer, or that he abandons it, will be sufficient to destroy it. (However, if the writing is signed by A, it may be a valid release, as distinguished from an abandonment.) Rest. §504. Comment c.

    2. Intent plus conduct: For the easement to be abandoned, there must be an *intent* on the part of the easement holder to abandon it, coupled with *actions* manifesting that intent.

        a. Non-use: *Non-use* of the easement for a sustained period of time may furnish sufficient evidence of the intent to abandon. It may also meet the conduct requirement. But this depends on the circumstances. For instance, if A owns a summer cottage, which holds an appurtenant easement to use a driveway on B's next-door property, A would not be held to have abandoned his easement if he failed to use it for three years, if the reason for this was that he didn't use the cottage at all during that period. The test is *whether the non-use justifies the conclusion that the easement holder in fact intends never to use the easement again*. Rest. §504. Comment d.

        b. Mistake as to location of easement: As an illustration of the rule that a clear intent to abandon must be shown, consider *Lindsey v. Clark*, 69 S.E.2d 342 (Va. 1952). There, D held a right of way over the south side of P's property. Because of a mistake by D's predecessors, all easement holders in D's chain of title, and D himself, used a strip on the north side of the property instead. The court held that there was no intent to abandon the south strip; instead, there was an intent to use whatever right of way the user was entitled to, and merely a mistake as to where the strip was. Accordingly, the court held that there was no extinguishment of the south easement. (But the court also used its equitable powers to transfer the easement to the north side, to avoid forcing P to remove an obstruction he had placed on the south strip.)

        c. Inconsistent use: The intent to abandon is often evidenced by an act that is *inconsistent* with continued use of the easement. See, e.g., *Carr v. Bartell*, 9 N.W.2d 556 (Mich. 1943) (P places barn over half of right of way; that portion of the right of way held extinguished by this act.)

    3. Illustrations: The following hypothetical illustrates some factual situations in which the claim may arise that an easement has been abandoned (or that the holder is estopped from asserting it).

        Hypothetical: O is the owner of a parcel of land bounded by the Susquehanna River. In 1922, O grants E, who owns the adjoining parcel, the right to flood O's land at any time. This conveyance of easement is recorded. In 1930, O conveys his land to A, with the deed to A making no mention of the flood rights. In 1969, E wants to build a dam on the river in such a way that the land now owned by A will be flooded to the extent permitted under the 1922 easement. We will examine E's rights under each of the following factual settings: (a) The land over which the flood rights were granted is now in the same condition as it was in 1922, and E has refrained from building the dam until now because he didn't need it. (b) E orally told A in 1935 that he would never exercise the flood rights, and A's land is in the same condition as it was in in 1922. (c) A built a house in 1964 on the land, and the house would be ruined if E now were to exercise the flood rights. (d) E orally told A in 1960 that he would never use the flood rights, and A then built a house on the property, which house would now be ruined if E exercised the flood rights.

(a) Mere non-use, without an intention to abandon, will not be enough to extinguish an easement. Since E can presumably demonstrate that although he didn't need the dam till now, he always thought that someday he might, the court is unlikely to find that he has intended to abandon. This was the result reached, on these facts, by *Graham v. Safe Harbor Water Power Corp.*, 173 A. 311 (Pa. 1934).

(b) An oral statement that one intends to abandon an easement is not effective. It is not effective as a release, since it does not meet the Statute of Frauds. It is not effective as an abandonment, since some conduct evidencing the intent to abandon must also be present. See 2 A.L.P. 302. It is possible that the non-use for a long period of time, accompanied by the oral statement, might be enough to meet the conduct-plus-intent requirement; it would be a question of fact as to whether the non-use manifested an intent to abandon. See Rest. §504, Comment d, and Illustration 4.

(c) The fact that A has built a house has no bearings on whether E has abandoned his easement. The building of the house may, however, contribute to a finding that E is *estopped* from now exercising his rights. But a case justifying estoppel will generally arise only where there is reasonable reliance upon the conduct or words of the easement holder. The finder of fact might conclude that non-use for such a long period would foreseeably cause A to believe that there had been an abandonment, and that A's assumption of abandonment was reasonable. See 2 A.L.P. 306.

(d) Here, there is a good chance that E will be estopped from exercising his flood rights. It was quite foreseeable that E's oral statement would cause A to build some structure on the land, and A's construction was clearly in reliance on E's statement. See 2 A.L.P. 305.

K. Revocation: An easement is a full-fledged interest in property (albeit, a non-possessory, "incorporeal" one). Therefore, it is ***not revocable*** at its grantor's will. What would otherwise be an easement will, if it is revocable, generally be a ***license*** (discussed immediately *infra*).

VI. LICENSES

A. Nature of license: A *license* is a right to use the licensor's land that is ***revocable*** at the will of the licensor. This quality of revocability is the main feature which distinguishes licenses from easements. (But there are two special types of licenses which are not fully revocable; these are discussed *infra*, p. 227.)

B. How license created: A license, since it is revocable, is considered a relatively insignificant interest. Therefore, it is ***not required*** to satisfy the ***Statute of Frauds***, and may be created orally.

Example: O, the owner of Blackacre, orally tells A, his next-door neighbor, that A may use O's pool any time he wishes. O has created a license in A to use the pool; O is the licensor and A is the licensee. If A uses the pool, he is absolved from liability for trespass. But O has the right to revoke the license at any time, and any use of the pool by A after that is a trespass.

1. **Attempt to create easement:** One way in which a license may be created is where a landowner gives another a right to use for former's land, which use would be an ***easement*** if formal requirements (particularly the Statute of Frauds) were satisfied, and these requirements are not.

     Example: O orally tells A that A may use O's driveway as a right of way to get from A's land to the public highway. The parties believe that this oral agreement is sufficient to give rise to an easement, and intend that it be irrevocable. Nonetheless, because the Statute of Frauds, applicable to easements, has not been satisfied, only a license is created. O may revoke the license at any time.

2. **License that could never be easement:** Only certain uses of land are capable of being made easements. Other uses are so transitory, or so different from the common-law notion of an easement, that even if they are created in writing, and involve the use of land, they are not easements. These uses will generally (though not always) be licenses, even if they are in writing.

     a. **Ticket:** A ***ticket*** to a sports event, concert, or other public spectacle, is always considered a license rather than an easement. Thus even if the ticket were considered to be a writing of a type sufficient to meet the Statute of Frauds, and stated that the right to attend was irrevocable, it would still only be a license. See, e.g., *Marrone v. Washington Jockey Club*, 227 U.S. 633 (1912), where P held a racetrack admission ticket, and was prevented from entering by the Ds (the track owners), who accused him of having doped horses. The Supreme Court held that the ticket was only a revocable license, not a conveyance of an interest in property, and that P had no right to force his way into the track, or to sue in trespass for the refusal to let him enter.

     b. **Right to park:** Similarly, the right to use a ***parking lot*** is generally only a license, not an easement or a lease. See, e.g., *South Center Dept. Store, Inc. v. South Pky. Bldg. Corp.*, 153 N.E.2d 241 (App. Ct. Ill. 1958), where P, a lessee of office space from D, had the right to use D's parking lot "so long as said lot is operated by or for [D] for parking purposes." The court held that this created only a license, and that when D leased the lot to X for X to operate a for-profit lot, the license to P was terminated.

     c. **Right to post sign:** Where the owner of land gives another person the right to ***erect a sign*** on the former's premises, this right may be either a lease, license, or easement, depending on the wording and intent of the parties. See, e.g., *Baseball Publishing Co. v. Bruton*, 18 N.E.2d 362 (Mass. 1938), where D gave P the "exclusive right and privilege" to maintain an advertising sign "for a period of one year with the privilege of renewal from year to year for four years more at the same consideration." The court held that this was an easement in gross for one year, and a contract to give such an easement for an additional four years.

3. **Intent to make revocable:** An easement, as noted, can never be revocable at the will of the grantor. Therefore, if the parties create what would otherwise be a valid easement, but they provide that the easement is revocable at the grantor's will, a license

results. See Rest. §514, Comment c and Illustration 2.

C. Remedies for wrongful revocation: The fact that a license is revocable as a matter of property law does not mean that the revoking licensor necessarily escapes liability entirely. If the parties agree, either in writing or orally, that the license will not be revoked, the court may find that revocation is a *breach of contract*, and gives rise to contract damages. This is particularly likely to be the case in the sort of license described in paragraph B(2) above, as to which the Statute of Frauds does not apply; thus the ticket holder in *Marrone* could probably sue for contract damages for being excluded, at least if he could show that there was an express or implied understanding that such a ticket is not revocable.

1. **Licensor's right to self-help:** Suppose the licensor revokes what purports to be an irrevocable license. Since this revocation is effective as a matter of property law, the licensee becomes a trespasser if he does not leave the premises promptly. However, it is not clear that the licensor then has the right to use *self-help* to evict him; Rest. §519, Comment b, states that "the fact that the licensor has broken his contract may deprive him of the remedy by way of self help which a possessor of land ordinarily has as against a trespasser on his land."

D. Exceptions to revocability: As noted, a license is normally revocable at the licensor's wish, even if the parties have agreed otherwise. But there are two special situations where the courts restrict or eliminate the revocability of a license.

1. **License coupled with interest:** If the licensee holds an interest in *personal property* located on the licensor's land, the license is said to be *"coupled with an interest"*. Such a license may only be revoked if this would not unfairly interfere with the licensee's rights in the chattel. For instance, if A sells B furniture on A's land, and tells B that he has two years in which to remove them, A may not revoke this license effective immediately. A court will at least extend the license long enough to give B a reasonable time to get the furniture. See Rest. §519, Illustration 2.

2. **Oral license acted upon:** The most important case where a license may be irrevocable is that in which the use *would have been an easement* except that it did not meet the Statute of Frauds, and the licensee makes *substantial expenditures* on the land in *reliance* on the licensor's promise that the license will be permanent or of long duration. Most (though not all) courts will give the licensee at least limited protection from revocation. See Rest. §519(4).

   Example: P orally gives D the right to build a ditch from the Santa Ana River across P's property, to irrigate D's land. D spends $7,000 building the ditch. A year later, P revokes his permission, but D continues to enter the land to make repairs on the ditch. P sues D for trespass. *Held*, for D. D admittedly received only a license, not an easement, because there was no writing. However, "where a license has entered under a parol license and has expended money, or its equivalent in labor, in the execution of the license, the license becomes irrevocable, the licensee will have a right of entry upon the lands of the licensor for the purpose of maintaining his structures, or, in general, his rights under his license, and the license will continue for so long a time as the nature of it calls for." Here, the license will continue as long as D continues to use the ditch for irrigation purposes. To refuse to give D this right after his substantial expenditures would be unjust. *Stoner v. Zucker*, 83 P. 808 (Cal. 1906). See also *Ricenbaw v. Kraus*, 61 N.W.2d 350 (Neb. 1953), reaching a similar conclusion on similar facts.

a. **Limited extent:** As the decision in *Stoner* indicates, the license will be irrevocable *only to the extent necessary to protect the licensee's reliance interest*, i.e., his investment in the improvements. Suppose, for instance, that O orally gives A, an electric company, the right to build whatever power lines it needs over a strip of O's property. A builds one line, and then O revokes. A court might allow A to keep the existing power line as long as it needs it, but would probably not permit A to build any additional lines, even though the license contemplated these; only maintenance of the original line is necessary to protect A's reliance interest. See Rest. §519, Illustration 3.

b. **Criticism of doctrine:** The irrevocability-by-estoppel doctrine has been criticized on the grounds that it adds greatly to the uncertainty of titles, and that it does not necessarily conform to the licensor's intent. Clark, Covenants and Interests Running With Land 64 (2d Ed. 1947), quoted in C&J, p. 598, note 2.

c. **Rights of subsequent purchaser:** The courts are split as to the rights of a *subsequent purchaser of the licensor's land*. If the subsequent purchaser has notice of the license and of the licensee's reliance upon it, his right to revoke will probably be limited in the same manner as that of the original licensor; see, e.g., *Buckles-Irvine Coal Co. v. Kennedy Coal Corp.*, 114 S.E. 233 (Va. 1922), to this effect.

    i. **Without notice:** But where the subsequent purchaser takes *without notice* of the license, or without notice of the expenditures made in reliance on it, the solution is not clear. *Buckles-Irvine, supra*, indicates that the purchaser may revoke the license. But Rest. §521(4) appears to put the purchaser in the licensor's shoes.

VII. COVENANTS RUNNING WITH LAND — INTRODUCTION

A. **Covenants generally:** As we have just seen, an easement may run with the land, both as to benefit and burden. We now turn to the broad category of covenants, or promises, which may under certain circumstances run with the land. A covenant running with the land is simply a contract between two parties, which, because it meets certain technical requirements, has the additional quality that it is *binding against one who later buys the promisor's land*, and/or *enforceable by one who later buys the promisee's land*.

1. **Distinguished from easements:** Covenants running with the land typically involve a promise to pay for certain benefits received by the promisor's land, or a promise by the promisor that he will or will not do certain things with his land. Particularly in the case of a promisor's promise not to use his land in a certain way, such a covenant could have deemed to fall within the category of easements. But as noted *supra*, p. 201, the English courts recognized only a few distinct types of negative easements (e.g., the easement of light and air, or that of lateral support). Therefore, all other negative land-use promises, if they are to run with the land, must satisfy the requirements of real covenants.

2. **Legal as opposed to equitable relief:** The promises being discussed in this section are those that are *legal*, as opposed to *equitable*, in nature. That is, when they are breached the relief granted is *money damages*, not an injunction or specific performance. However, a promise regarding land may also give rise to what is commonly called an *equitable servitude*, which is enforceable at equity by an injunction or by an order of specific performance; equitable relief is discussed beginning *infra*, p. 238.

     a. Building restrictions: When the promise is that the promisor's land will *not be used in a certain way*, the promisee will generally be interested in gaining an injunction from a court of equity, not in recovering money damages. For instances, if the promisor covenants that he will not build a non-residential structure on his property, the promisee will generally wish to block construction of a commercial building, not merely wait for the building to be built, and recover damages. Therefore, the rules on real covenants are of greatest interest where promise is to *pay money*, or to do an *affirmative act* (e.g., maintain a fence), rather than to refrain from making a particular use of land.

  3. Distinguished from ordinary legal contract: As noted, a covenant running with the land is in some respects no different from an ordinary contract. But there are two principal differences, both relating to transfer.

     a. Assignment of rights: First, *rights* (as opposed to duties) under an ordinary contract can be assigned, but this requires an *express* assignment; rights under a covenant running with the land are *implicitly* assigned by a sale of the promisee's land (*infra*, below).

     b. Delegation of duties: Secondly, *duties* under an ordinary contract can be *delegated* by the promisor to a third person, but that third person is liable to the promisee only if the former expressly *assumes* responsibility for performance. In the case of a covenant running with the land, by contrast, one who purchases the promisor's land *automatically* is required to perform the promise, so long as he owns the land; this is true even if he has no intention of being bound, and even if he didn't know about the promise when he bought the land (assuming that the requirements of the recording act are met; see *infra*, p. 360).

  4. Comparison with landlord-tenant contracts: The general principles of covenants running with the land have already been discussed in the landlord-tenant context. Thus we saw that one who takes an assignment from a tenant automatically gains both the duty to perform promises made by the tenant that run with the land, and the right to enforce certain promises made by the landlord that run with the land. Similarly, one who buys land from the landlord gains both rights and duties. In this chapter, our focus is upon covenants made between *owners in fee*, and on how these covenants are binding upon one who buys from the promisor, and enforceable by one who buys from the promisee.

B. Statute of Frauds: For a covenant to be binding upon the promisor's assignee, it must "touch and concern" the land (see *infra*, p. 234). Therefore, nearly all American states view such a covenant as in effect creating an interest in land. Accordingly, they hold that such a promise is *within the Statute of Frauds*, and must be in writing, at least if an assignee of the promisor is to bound. 2 A.L.P. 364. (It is not clear whether the promisor himself may be bound if the promise is oral.)

     Example: D, a developer, sells a parcel of land to O. As part of the sale transaction, O promises that it will pay D $100 per year for maintenance of a private road and private recreational facilities for the benefit of O's land and other land in the subdivision. If O's promise is to be binding upon X, who later buys O's land, the promise must be in writing (though not necessarily signed by O; see *infra*, p. 230). It is not clear whether the promise is binding on O himself if it is not in writing.

1. **Acceptance of deed poll:** Most property sales are made by a *deed poll*, i.e., a deed signed by the grantor but not by the grantee. Where the covenant is one that is made by the grantee, nearly all courts hold that the grantee's *acceptance of the deed poll* satisfies the Statute of Frauds, with respect to any promise made by the grantee that is recited in the deed. 2 A.L.P. 365.

2. **Exceptions to Statute:** Two exceptions to the Statute of Frauds may apply: the doctrine of *estoppel* and that of *part performance*. These doctrines are more likely to be applicable where the suit is brought at equity rather than at law; see, e.g., the theory of "implied reciprocal easements" discussed *infra*, p. 240.

VIII. COVENANTS — RUNNING OF BURDEN AND BENEFIT

A. **Summary of requirements for running:** There are several technical requirements which must be met before the burden of a covenant will run with the land. There are similar, though not identical, requirements for the benefit to run with the land. Both sets of requirements are discussed extensively below; they may be summarized as follows:

1. **Requirements for running of burden:** For the *burden* to run (i.e., to be binding on the promisor's assignee): (1) the promise must be enforceable between the *original* parties; (2) the original parties must *intend* that the burden will run; (3) the burden must *"touch and concern" the promisor's land*, and (at least according to the Restatement), the benefit must touch the promisee's land; and (4) there must be *privity of estate*, which in most states means a land transfer between promisor and promisee, plus a succession of estate from promisor to the promisor's assignee.

2. **Requirements for running of benefit:** For the *benefit* to run (i.e., to be enforceable by the promisee's assignee): (1) the promise must be enforceable between the *original parties*; (2) the original parties to the covenant must *intend* that it be enforceable by an assignee; (3) the benefit must *"touch and concern" the promisee's land*; and (4) *privity of estate*, in the sense of a land transfer between promisor and promisee, is sometimes but not always required; privity in the sense of an assignee who succeeds to the promisee's entire estate is generally not required.

B. **Enforceable between original parties:** Neither the benefit nor the burden will run unless the promise is *enforceable between the original parties*. The satisfaction of the Statute of Frauds, discussed *supra*, is one aspect of this requirement. Also, the promise might fail to be enforceable between the original parties because of a *lack of consideration*. Or, the covenant might fail to be enforceable because it is racially discriminatory, and therefore will not be judicially enforced under the doctrine of *Shelley v. Kraemer*, discussed *infra*, p. 252.

C. **Intent of parties:** For the burden to run, the original parties (the promisor and the promisee) must *so intend*. Similarly for the benefit to run, the promisor and promisee must have this intention.

1. **Use of word "assigns":** One way in which the necessary intent is often shown is by including the word *"assigns"* in the deed or other writing containing the promise. Thus if Developer wishes to sell a lot to Homeowner by a deed containing a restriction against non-residential buildings, the deed might provide that "this restriction shall bind Homeowner, his heirs, assigns and successors in interest." Developer would also probably provide that the restriction could be enforced by "Developer, its assigns, transferees or successors in interest, including any neighborhood association established for the purpose of enforcing such restrictions."

a. **Word not necessary:** However, most courts hold that the use of the word "assigns" is not absolutely necessary, and that the intent of the parties can be gauged from the entire instrument and surrounding circumstances. 2 A.L.P. 365-66. This modern view is in contrast to an earlier English case, *Spencer's Case*, 77 Eng. Rep. (1583), which held that at least where the covenant relates to a thing that is not in existence at the time of the covenant, the word "assigns" must be expressly mentioned for the assignee to be bound.

D. **Privity between promisor and promisee ("horizontal" privity):** Courts are in dispute about exactly what the relationship between the original *promisor* and *promisee* must be for the covenant to run. This requirement, called the requirement of *"horizontal" privity*, is treated differently by the Restatement depending on whether it is the running of the burden or that of the benefit which is in question; accordingly, we treat these two cases separately here.

1. **Running of burden:** The English common law has traditionally refused to allow the burden of a covenant to run with the land where the original parties to the covenant were *"strangers to title"*. That is, *if promisor and promisee had no property relationship between them at the time of the promise, the burden will not run*. At the least, this view means that two *neighboring landowners* cannot get together and agree that neither would use his property for a certain purpose, and have this restriction be binding upon a subsequent purchaser from either of them.

   Example: O is the proprietor of Beaufort Iron Works, a piece of real estate. O agrees with P, a railroad company (in which O has an interest) that all limestone for the Beaufort Works will be procured from a certain quarry, and transported by O via the P Railroad. O sells his interest in the ironworks to D, giving D full notice of this promise. D refuses to use the quarry or the railroad exclusively, and the P Railroad sues to restrain D.

   Held, the promise is not binding on D. For P to hold D liable, a new type of property interest would have had to have been created by the covenant, so as to bind the land. But parties are not free to create such novel incidents of ownership; if they were, the state of title to property would be impossible to determine. Such a promise might have been binding on D if O and P had each had an interest in the ironworks property at the time the promise was made; but O and P were strangers to title. Therefore, P's only remedy is against O for breach of contract. *Keppell v. Bailey*, 39 Eng. Rep. 1042 (1834).

   a. **Present law:** The vast majority of American states today *maintain* this rule that the burden will not run if the promisor and promisee had no property relationship at the time of the promise. So most court would agree with the decision in *Keppell*, *supra*.

   b. **Tenurial view:** The strictest interpretation of the common-law privity requirement is that the burden of the promise runs with the land only where there is a *continuing tenurial relationship* between promisor and promisee. Under this view, only where the promisor and promisee are *landlord and tenant* will the burden run with the land; if promisor and promisee are owners in fee, the privity requirement is not satisfied, even if the promisor bought his land from the promisee, who has retained other land to which the promise relates. This is the English view. It is doubtful that this strict view is followed anywhere in America today.

c. **Conveyance between promisor and promisee:** In all American jurisdictions except Massachusetts, the horizontal requirement is met so long as the promise is made as part of a transaction in which the promisee is *selling the burdened land* to the promisor, or vice verse. Thus suppose that A sells Blackacre to B, and retains the adjoining Whiteacre. B promises A that B will maintain a hedge along the edge of Blackacre where it adjoins Whiteacre. All states but Massachusetts would make the covenant binding upon C (who buys Blackacre from B), because the hedge promise was made as part of the conveyance from A to B.

  i. **Promise can't be made after conveyance:** But this vendor-purchaser means of satisfying the privity requirement is not met if the promise is made *after* the conveyance.

  Example: A owns a large mill site. He conveys part of the site to B on June 5. On June 11, A and B sign an agreement providing for the construction of a dam that will benefit the property of both, and the splitting of expenses for the building and maintenance of the dam. B then assigns his parcel to D, and A's parcel is acquired by P. The dam is subsequently damaged, and D tells P to take care of the work. P has the work done, and sues D for half of the expense.

  Held, for D. The promise to pay for construction and repair of the dam was made only after the conveyance between A and B; therefore, at the time of the promise, there was no longer privity of estate between the two, and the burden of the promise could not run with the land conveyed to B. (This promise might be enforceable at equity if D took with notice of the promise, but there is no evidence that he did so.) *Wheeler v. Schad*, 7 Nev. 213 (1872).

  ii. **Grant of easement:** As one would expect, the grant of a continuing *easement* will always satisfy the privity requirement, if it is made before or at the same time as the covenant that is to run. See, e.g., *Carlson v. Libby*, 77 A.2d 332 (Conn. 1950), where A gave B an easement to build a railroad siding, in return for a promise that B would grant to A, or to whomever owned the nearby property presently held by A, the right to use the siding. The court held that B's promise to allow A or its successor to use the property was binding upon D, who bought B's easement rights, in favor of P, who bought title to A's property.

d. **Restatement view:** Like all states but Massachusetts, the Restatement, in §534, recognizes either a vendor-purchaser relationship between the original parties, or a continuing property relationship between them as sufficient to meet the horizontal privity requirement. But under the Restatement, as in most states, two neighboring landowners who are strangers to each other's title cannot make a covenant the burden of which will run at law. (But horizontal privity is *not* required, under the Restatement view, for the *benefit* to run; see *infra*, p. 233.)

e. **Argument for abolishing requirement:** At least one well-known commentator, Judge Clark, has argued that the entire requirement of horizontal privity serves no useful purpose, and that, for instance, neighbors who are strangers to each other's title should be able to make covenants the burden of which will run. See Clark, Covenants and Interest Running With Land (1947) 116-37. Four states have apparently agreed, and have *abolished the horizontal privity requirement* (California, Montana, North Dakota and South Dakota); but in each case this appears to be because of statutory provisions rather than judicial decision. Powell, par. 674, p. 716.

2. Running of benefit: The vast majority of jurisdictions apply the same horizontal privity requirement for the running of a **benefit** as they do for the running of a burden, whatever that rule is in the particular jurisdiction. Thus on the facts of *Wheeler v. Schad, supra*, p. 232, a state which would hold that lack of horizontal privity bars recovery against D would also hold that it bars enforcement by P (even against B, the original promisor).

    a. Restatement view: But the Restatement has adopted a nearly unique middle position: although privity between promisor and promisee is required for the running of the burden, it is **not required for the running of the benefit**. Rest. §548. It is certainly true that the need to preserve the alienability of land is much more directly served by a horizontal privity requirement in the case of running benefits. Also, the idea of an assignment of contract rights is well-established (though such an assignment in other contexts requires an intentional, express, transfer of rights, in contrast to the automatic passing of rights pursuant to a land sale). But only a few cases have followed the Restatement distinction; for one, see *City of Reno v. Matley*, 378 P.2d 256 (Nev. 1963).

E. Privity involving litigants ("vertical" privity): Just as the original promisor and promisee must have a certain relationship (horizontal privity, just discussed), so the **promisor and his successor in interest** must have a certain relationship if the burden is to run; this is referred to as **"vertical"** privity. Similarly, the **promisee and his successor** must have a certain relationship (though the rules are more liberal) for the benefit to run; this is also referred to as vertical privity.

    1. Running of burden: For the burden to run, the party against whom it is to be enforced must succeed to the **entire estate** of the original promisor. Only then are the promisor and his successor said to be in vertical privity.

        a. Landlord-tenant: We saw this requirement in the context of landlord-tenant promises, where an assignment by the tenant to an assignee met the vertical privity requirement, but a sublease did not, so that the landlord had no right of direct enforcement of the covenant against the sub-tenant. (See *supra*, p. 184.)

        b. Must be entire estate: Similarly, where the promisor is an owner in fee, he must assign his entire estate, not merely a lesser part. Thus if Covenantor holds a fee simple, and transfers merely a **life estate** to X, X will not be liable for the burden of the covenant since he has not succeeded to Covenantor's entire fee simple.

            i. Geographical portion: But when we say that the assignee must take the "entire" estate, we mean the word entire in a **durational**, not geographical, sense. Thus if Covenantor assigns a **geographical portion** of his holding to X, but gives X a fee simple in that portion, the requirement of privity is met as to that portion.

        c. Breaches before or after ownership: Because the assignee's liability is based solely on privity of estate, he is not liable for breaches of the covenant that occurred **before** he acquired his interest. Similarly, if he re-transfers his interest to another, he is not liable for breaches occurring **after** this re-transfer. Powell, Par. 680, p. 730.

    2. Running of benefit: On the benefit side, the requirement of vertical privity is much more **relaxed**. The benefit may be enforced by anyone who has taken **possession** of the promisee's property and has acquired some portion of the promisee's estate.

a. Life tenant: Thus a *life tenant* may enforce the promise, even though the reversion remains in the original promisee. The reason for this is that the benefit of covenants running with the land is primarily attached to possession of the benefitted estate. 2 A.L.P. 392. Contrast this with the running of the burden, where only one who succeeds to the covenantor's *entire* interest will be burdened with the covenant; see *supra*, p. 230.

b. Must be legal, not equitable: But the benefit probably must be enforced by one who has a *legal, not equitable*, interest.

> **Example:** CE conveys part of his land to CR. The deed to CR contains a promise that CR, his heirs and assigns, will maintain a fence between the land kept by CE and the land transferred to CR. CE then contracts to sell the land kept by him to CE1; payment is to be made in installments over a five-year period, at the end of which CE is to give CE1 a deed. CE1 takes possession of the land. Two years later, CR refuses to repair the fence. CE1 has up to this point performed all his obligations under the contract. CE1 repairs the fence and sues CR for the cost of the repairs.
>
> CR can probably successfully claim that CE1 has no legal estate in the benefitted property, and that such a legal estate is necessary for a suit at law for damages. It is true that CE1 gained *equitable* title by virtue of the contract of sale; but this, even when coupled with possession, was held to be insufficient to allow a suit on the covenant at law in *Haynes v. Buffalo, New York & Philadelphia R.R.*, 38 Hun. 17 (N.Y. 1885). See also 2 A.L.P. 392. Thus, CR can claim, any suit for damages must be brought by CE, since he still holds legal title.

c. Homeowners' association: The privity question arises most often on the benefit side where the plaintiff is a *homeowners' association* or "property improvement association", set up by a developer to collect annual fees from homeowners in a subdivision; the fees are used to maintain any common areas and to enforce building restrictions. If the association does not in its own name hold any of the land in the subdivision, may it sue to collect the annual fees?

> **i. Suit allowed:** Generally, the courts have *permitted* associations to bring such suits. See, e.g., *Neponsit Property Owners' Ass'n v. Emigrant Industrial Sav. Bank*, 15 N.E.2d 793 (N.Y. 1938), where the court held that "in substance, if not in form, there is privity of estate" between the Association (which did not own any of the land in the subdivision) and the individual landowner. The precise basis for the court's holding is unclear, but it should be noted that the covenant expressly provided that the right to collect the annual fee could be assigned to a property owners' association that might thereafter be formed. Such a clause suggests that a *third-party beneficiary* theory might be relied on to permit the association to sue, and a number of courts have used such a theory. (See the discussion of other aspects of the *Neponsit* case *infra*, p. 237.)

d. Adverse possession: An *adverse possessor* probably lacks even the looser vertical privity needed on the benefit side. (Certainly he does not have the privity needed for the *burden* to run.)

F. The "touch and concern the land" requirement: In *Spencer's Case*, 77 Eng. Rep. 72 (1583), it was held that for a covenant to run with land, it must *"touch and concern"* the land. Just as this requirement applies to a covenant made in a lease (*supra*, p. 184), it applies where the covenantor and covenantee are both owners in fee. It is necessary to analyze first where the *burden* of the covenant runs with a promisor's land, and then whether the *benefit* of the promise runs with the promisee's land.

1. **Running of benefit:** For the *benefit* to run, that benefit must *touch and concern the promisee's land*. But once this requirement is met, the benefit will run *even though the burden does not*. That is, *the benefit can run even if the burden is "in gross"*, i.e., personal to the promisor. 2 A.L.P. 374.

2. **Running of burden:** For the *burden* to run, that burden must *"touch and concern" the promisor's land*. Assuming that the burden does touch and concern the promisee's land, an important issue is whether that burden will run if the *benefit* does not touch and concern the promisee's land. That is, may the burden run when the benefit is in gross?

   a. **Some states allow:** Some states, probably about half, allow the burden to run where the benefit is in gross. Powell, Par. 675, p. 718.

      Example: A, the owner of Blackacre, sells it to B. B promises, in return, that he will not operate a liquor store on the property, so as not to compete with a similar store owned by A on different property. The jurisdiction is one which takes the view that a non-competition promise does not touch and concern the promisee's land though it does touch and concern the promisor's land. (See *infra*, this page.) B then sells Blackacre to C. A number of courts would hold that the burden runs with the land (and thus binds C) even though the benefit is in gross, i.e., personal to A.

   b. **Restatement view:** But the remaining courts, and the Restatement do not permit the burden to run if the benefit is in gross. Under this view, for the burden to run, both benefit and burden must touch and concern the relevant parcel. Rest., §537, and Comment c thereto.

      i. **Rationale:** The Restatement position is based upon the idea that the running of burdens *inhibits the alienability of land*, and should therefore not be permitted unless other land is thereby benefitted. (This view is also reflected in the Restatement requirement that the burden bear a "reasonable relation" to the benefit; see Rest., §537.)

3. **What constitutes touching and concerning:** Courts are not in agreement on the precise test for determining when the burden or benefit of a covenant "touches and concerns" land. See the discussion of such covenants in the landlord-tenant context, *supra*, p. 185, for an analysis of the major views.

4. **Doing or refraining from physical act:** Where the promisor has covenanted to do or refrain from doing a *physical act* on his land, in most cases the burden of this promise will touch and concern the land. It does not follow, however, that the benefit will touch and concern the promisee's land (assuming that he has any, which will not necessarily be the case).

5. **Non-competition clause:** Where the grantor retains land of his own, the grantee will frequently promise not to use the land transferred to him so as to *compete* with a business run by the grantor on the retained land. Conversely, the grantor may promise not to compete with the business which the grantee expects to run. Either way, the courts are *split* as to whether the non-competition clause touches and concerns the land.

   a. **Burden:** The ***substantial majority*** of courts agree that such a non-competition clause touches and concerns the land of the ***promisor***, since it restricts his use of the land.

   b. **Benefit of clause:** Historically, there has been a split among courts as to whether the ***benefit*** of a non-competition clause touches and concerns the ***promisee's*** land. Today, however, nearly all courts hold that such a promise ***does*** touch and concern the promisee's land, since by restricting competition it makes that land more valuable. Powell, Par. 678, p. 724. Rest., §543(2)(b), and Comment e thereto, similarly treat the non-competition clause as being sufficiently related to the promisee's land as to permit the benefit to run (even though the ***burden*** does not, as discussed *supra*, run under the Restatement rule).

     Example: Kotseas sells Parcel A to Trust. The deed, in addition to imposing restrictions on Parcel A, includes restrictions on land abutting Parcel A that is retained by Kotseas. In particular, the deed restricts Kotseas from using the abutting land for a "discount store," which would compete with Trust's contemplated use of Parcel A. (The deed allowed Kotseas to use his land for a "drug store.") The deed expressly says that these restrictions shall be considered as restrictions running with the land. Several years later, Trust conveys Parcel A to Plaza. Then, Kotseas leases its abutting land to CVS for use as a "discount department store and pharmacy." Plaza sues Kotseas and CVS to enjoin them from operating the competing discount store. Both argue that Massachusetts law has always prevented the benefit of a non-competition covenant from running with the land.

     Held, for Plaza. The Massachusetts rule preventing the benefit of a non-competition covenant from running with the land (adopted in *Norcross v. James*, 2 N.E. 946 (Mass. 1885), a Holmes opinion), is hereby overruled. It would be unfair to apply that rule, since Kotseas has presumably been paid extra money in return for limiting the uses which he could make of his retained land, and since freedom from discount store competition was part of the inducement for Trust's purchase. However, the only non-compete covenants whose benefit will be held to run with the land are those which are "consistent with a reasonable overall purpose to develop real estate for commercial use." *Whittinsville Plaza Inc. v. Kotseas*, 390 N.E.2d 243 (Mass. 1979).

6. **Exclusive dealing clause:** A similar type of clause provides that the grantee will buy from or sell to only the grantor, or vice versa. Such a clause, called a ***"trade only"*** or ***"exclusive dealing"*** clause, is subject to much the same difference of opinion as the non-competition clause. In general, a state is likely to follow the same position regarding the "touch and concern" requirement as it would in the non-competition case, since the policies involved are similar. See Powell, Par. 678, p. 725.

   a. **Unduly burdensome:** But the court is likely to scrutinize the contract to determine whether the promisor's rights ***as landowner*** (not just as contracting party) are deeply implicated by the clause.

     Example: All deeds issued by Developer include a promise by the grantee that the grantee will pay $35 per year for water which the grantee will take from Developer's well. One of the original grantees, X, sells his parcel, which after several resales comes to be owned by D. P (a successor in title to Developer's remaining interest in the development) sues D to collect for water, which D is not using. P relies on the original promise made by X, and argues that the burden of this promise ran with the land and is thus a covenant enforceable against D as the present owner of the parcel.

Held, for D. The promise to take water from Developer, and pay for it, does not truly "touch and concern" the land, because it "does not substantially affect the ownership interest of the land owners" in the subdivision. There are other sources of water, which D and other landowners are able to (and in fact do) use. Nor is there evidence that the price of water will become prohibitive for other owners if D is allowed to terminate his purchase. Finally, the covenant has no duration, so that it poses an "undue restriction on alienation [and] an onerous burden in perpetuity." Therefore, the promise is a personal one binding only upon X, the original grantee, and not upon D. *Eagle Enterprises, Inc. v. Gross*, 349 N.E.2d 816 (N.Y. 1976).

7. **Payment of money:** Covenants that are sought to be enforced at law (as opposed to equity) often involve the ***payment of money***. (See, e.g., *Eagle Enterprises, supra*.) It is hard to generalize about when such promises to pay money will run with the land of either the promisor or promisee. This depends principally on what the promisor receives in return for his promise of payment.

    a. **Payment to homeowners' association:** The most common such promise is one made by a purchaser of a lot in a subdivision to make payments to a ***homeowners' association*** for maintenance of common areas and enforcement of architectural and use restrictions. Since in return for payment of such dues the homeowner gets the benefit of the common areas and/or the restrictions on development (e.g., maintenance of a strictly residential neighborhood), the burden of the promise is usually held to touch and concern the promisor's land. See, e.g., *Neponsit Property Owner's Ass'n v. Emigrant Industrial Sav. Bank*, 15 N.E.2d 793 (N.Y. 1938), holding that the burden of such a promise to pay dues touched and concerned the lot owner's land, because the dues were necessary to maintain the roads, beaches, parks and other common areas.

        i. **Benefit side:** The ***benefit*** will also generally run, if the association has actual title to the common areas. If it does not, the benefit is in gross and the issue of "touch and concern" does not arise on the benefit side. (However, the benefit may be made ***expressly assignable*** in the instrument between the original parties. Thus the original promisee is often the developer, and the landowner agrees that the developer may assign to a homeowners' association to be organized subsequently.)

        ii. **Dues must be reasonable:** But even though the promise to pay may run on both the benefit and burden side, the court may nonetheless exercise its equitable jurisdiction to assure that the dues provision is interpreted in a ***reasonable manner***. See, e.g., *Kell v. Bella Vista Village Property Owners' Ass'n*, 528 S.W.2d 651 (Ark. 1975) (a provision allowing the homeowners' association to charge a lower common-areas fee to unimproved lots than to ones with homes on them is invalid, since the owners of the vacant lots have the same privilege of using the common facilities.)

    b. **Duty to pay treated as lien:** The covenant to pay money may also provide that if the debt is not paid, there shall be a ***lien*** on the land, so that the land can be sold to satisfy the debt. Such a lien by its nature "runs with the land", so that it is enforceable even if the promise to pay money is one which does not "touch and concern" the land in the jurisdiction in question. In such a situation, the result would be that the assignee is not personally liable for the debt (because by hypothesis the covenant does not run on the burden side at law), but he may nonetheless lose the land to a foreclosure proceeding.

  i. Restatement view: The Restatement goes even further. Rest., §540, Comment c, states that such a lien will be *implied* by *operation of law* if the promise is to pay money in return for benefits received on the land, even if there has been no explicit agreement that a lien will result. The cases do not seem to support this rule; see 2 A.L.P. 388, n. 7.

G. Notice to assignee: A covenant will run at law, on the burden side, only if the assignee receives *notice* of it before he receives his interest in the land. R&K, p. 481. However, a covenant that is to run with the land will almost always be subject to the *recording acts*. Therefore, if it is recorded, the assignee will be deemed to have had "record notice" of it (see *infra*, p. 368), and will be bound.

  1. Failure to record: If the covenant is *not* recorded, it will not be binding on a subsequent *bona fide* purchaser (i.e., one without knowledge of the promise), just as any other unrecorded interest in land that is required to be recorded will not be binding against such a purchaser. (See *infra*, p. 360.)

H. Covenantor's liability after assignment: When the covenantor *transfer* his interest to another, he will of course be liable for any breaches of the covenant that have occurred *prior* to the transfer. But it is not clear whether he is liable for breaches which occur *after* the transfer.

  1. Land use covenant: If the covenant relates to the use of the covenantor's land, the court is likely to hold that there is an implied *release* of the covenantor from future liability once he assigns his interest. The courts have focused upon the fact that there is no longer privity of estate between covenantor and covenantee, and have disregarded the fact that there is still privity of contract; this result seems fair, since by transferring, the covenantor has lost his ability to see that the land use restrictions or affirmative duties are carried out. 2 A.L.P. 389.

  2. Duty to make payment: But where the covenant is a *duty to pay money*, it is not so clear that the covenantor is relieved of future liability by transferring his interest. However, since most such promises are for long durations or without time limits (e.g., a duty to make payment to a homeowners' association for maintenance of common areas), the court will in practice usually relieve the covenantor, since otherwise his liability would be unlimited. 2 A.L.P. 389-90.

    a. Contrast with leases: Observe that this policy of discharging the covenantor is different from that followed in the landlord-tenant context. See *supra*, p. 187.

I. Covenantee's rights after assignment: Conversely, the *covenantee* is only entitle to sue for breaches of the covenant occurring while he owns his interest. Once he transfers his interest to another, he *loses the right to sue for any breaches occurring thereafter*. After the transfer, he is no longer in privity of estate with the covenantor, and the courts deem the privity of contract relationship between the two to have been impliedly terminated by the transfer. Thus only the covenantee's assignee may sue for a new breach. 2 A.L.P. 390.

IX. EQUITABLE SERVITUDES

A. Building restrictions: A suit at law on a covenant running with the land can only culminate in *money damages*, as we have seen. This relief is generally adequate where the covenant is a promise to pay for benefits received on the land (e.g., a promise to pay dues to a homeowners' association) or an affirmative promise to take certain acts on the land (e.g., a promise to maintain a fence). But where the promise is a **negative** one, involving a **restriction on building**, money damages are not usually the desired relief. Rather, an **injunction** against the forbidden construction is the relief generally desired by the promisee.

1. **Technical requirements:** Furthermore, as we have seen, the enforcement of a covenant at law, particularly against an assignee of the original promisor, is fraught with technical difficulties. Privity of estate between the promisor and the promisee (*supra*, p. 231), and between the promisor and the latter's successor (*supra*, p. 233). Furthermore, the covenant must "touch and concern" the land, at least that of the promisor (*supra*, p. 234). These requirements may prevent the obtaining of money damages against the person now in possession of the promisor's estate, even where money damages would be adequate relief.

B. ***Tulk v. Moxhay***: The inadequacy of legal remedies for breach of a building restriction led to the famous English case of ***Tulk v. Moxhay***, 41 Eng. Rep. 1143 (1848).

1. **Facts of *Tulk*:** In *Tulk*, P was the owner of an empty piece of ground in Leicester Square, as well as of several houses surrounding it. He sold the vacant ground to Elms; the deed to Elms contained Elms' promise to maintain the vacant ground as a garden, with no structure on it. Title to the ground eventually passed to D, whose deed contained no such promise, but who conceded that he knew of Elms' original covenant. P sued D for an injunction to prevent him from building on the garden.

2. **No remedy at law available:** Even if P had wished, he could not have waited until D destroyed the garden, and then sued for monetary damages. The reason for this was that under the English interpretation of the requirement of horizontal privity, there must be a continuing property relationship between promisor and promisee, thus making it impossible for a grantor in fee to impose a running covenant on his grantee. (See *supra*, p. 231.)

3. **Equitable relief:** English courts prior to *Tulk* had apparently held that if a covenant was not enforceable at law, it could not be enforced at equity either. But the court in *Tulk granted P an injunction even though the covenant was not enforceable at law*.

   a. **Unjust enrichment:** The court relied principally on a theory of **unjust enrichment**. The court assumed that Elms had paid a lower price for the garden, in view of the restriction on its use. If Elms were allowed to convey to D free of the restriction, "nothing could be more inequitable than that the original purchaser should be able to sell the property the next day for a greater price, in consideration of the assignee being allowed to escape from the liability which he had himself undertaken."

   b. **Interference with contract:** Also, allowing the assignee to take free of the restriction would deprive P of what he had bargained for. The court relied on a theory quite close to what we recognize today as "interference with contract."

4. **Effect of notice:** The court stressed that D had had **actual knowledge** of the promise made in the deed to Elms. It seems probable that the restriction would **not** have been binding on D had he taken without actual or constructive knowledge; later cases have indeed imposed a notice restriction (see *infra*, p. 244).

C. Equitable servitudes: Since *Tulk v. Moxhay*, equity courts in both England and America have been willing to enforce an agreement as an *"equitable servitude"* against the burdened land, as to subsequent purchasers who took with **actual or constructive notice**. They have done so **whether or not** the agreement constituted a valid **covenant running with the land** at law. (See the discussion *infra*, p. 241 as to privity and the "touch and concern" test where equitable relief is at issue.) See 2 A.L.P. 403.

1. **Theory for enforcement:** Courts are not all in agreement on the theory for granting equitable relief (usually an *injunction*). Some cases hold that equity is merely granting specific performance of a contract concerning land (just as a court of equity will order a vendor under a sale contract to complete the conveyance to the vendee; see *infra*, p. 324).

   a. **Majority "property interest" view:** But the majority of courts and authorities hold that the agreement creates an *"equitable property interest"* in the burdened land, similar to an easement. As a consequence of this theory, the promisee may enforce the agreement without showing that appreciable damage or injury to his property will occur from a breach (a showing that must be made in the usual suit for specific performance). See 2 A.L.P. 403-04.

D. Statute of Frauds: At least in those courts following the majority view that an equitable servitude is a property interest, the servitude must **satisfy the Statute of Frauds**. See, e.g., *Sprague v. Kimball*, 100 N.E. 622 (Mass. 1913) (developer's promise to insert restriction in later conveyance by him not enforceable because not in writing.)

1. **Acceptance of deed poll:** As with covenants at law, an equitable servitude will meet the Statute of Frauds requirement if it is contained in a **deed poll** that is accepted by the grantee/promisor (but not signed by him). 2 A.L.P. 407.

2. **Reference to filed plat:** Restrictions on building are frequently contained not in the deed, but in a **plat** of a **subdivision**. (See *infra*, p. 298.) If the plat is recorded, and the deed makes reference to the plat (even if only as a means of identifying the property conveyed), the Statute of Frauds is satisfied as to the restrictions. 2 A.L.P. 408.

   a. **Subsequently-filed plat:** But a plat or series of restrictions that is recorded **after** a grant cannot be binding on the grantee. This is true even where grantor and grantee orally agreed that the grantee would take subject to restrictions which might be subsequently recorded. See, e.g., *Riley v. Bear Creek Planning Committee*, 551 P.2d 1213 (Cal. 1976).

3. **Implied reciprocal servitude:** Suppose that the deed given to a grantee contains a promise by him to obey certain restrictions on use. If the grantor (probably a developer) agrees orally that he will **insert similar restrictions in other deeds** given to subsequent buyers, does this oral promise satisfy (or constitute an exception to) the Statute of Frauds? The courts are **split** on this issue, which is discussed extensively *infra*, p. 246. See particularly *Sanborn v. McLean, infra*, p. 248.

4. **Identification of benefitted land:** Assuming that the servitude is created in writing, courts are in dispute about whether the **benefitted land** (i.e., who may enforce the restriction) must also be **identified** in the writing. This issue is discussed further *infra*, p. 243.

E. Affirmative covenants: Most of the agreements for which equitable enforcement is sought are **negative** in nature; they generally are agreements not to violate certain building restrictions. The English courts have **refused** to allow equitable enforcement of **affirmative promises**, at least against subsequent purchasers from the promisor. 2 A.L.P. 438.

1. **English view illustrated:** Thus if Grantee promised Grantor that Grantee would maintain a hedge at the edge of the property, and Grantee conveyed to X, the English courts might award money damages against X if he failed to maintain the hedge (assuming that all other requirements for the running of a covenant at law were met), but they would **not** issue a "mandatory injunction" requiring him to keep the hedge in force. The New York courts originally followed this English rule; see *Miller v. Clary*, 103 N.E. 1114 (N.Y. 1913).

2. **American view:** But the **vast majority** of **American** courts have been **willing** to grant equitable enforcement of affirmative as well as negative agreements. See, e.g., *Petersen v. Beekmere, Inc.*, 283 A.2d 911 (Super. Ct. N.J. 1971), holding that a homeowner's promise to buy a share of stock in a community association was not rendered unenforceable at equity because it was affirmative. (But the court declined to enforce the promise at equity for other reasons, discussed *infra*, p. 249.) Even New York has apparently now changed its position and is willing to enforce affirmative promises at equity; see *Nicholson v. 300 Broadway Realty Corp.*, 164 N.E.2d 832 (N.Y. 1959) (enforcing at law a covenant to supply heat, but indicating that enforcement at equity would also probably be available where appropriate.)

F. **Requirements for running:** The requirements for the **running** of an equitable servitude (i.e., enforcement by or against someone other than the original parties) are significantly more **liberal** than for the running of a covenant at law: (1) **privity is not generally required**, either of the horizontal or vertical variety; (2) although the burden must usually "touch and concern" the land in order to run, in most courts the burden can run even though the benefit does not "touch and concern" the land; (3) for the benefit to run, the original parties must be fairly specific about who may enforce the promise; and (4) a subsequent purchaser from the promisor will be bound only if he had actual or constructive **notice**. These requirements, which are discussed below, are of course in addition to the requirements that must be satisfied before the agreement may be equitably enforced between the original parties to it (e.g., satisfaction of the Statute of Frauds).

G. **Privity:** The various requirements of **privity**, so important to the enforcement of a covenant at law against and by successors to the original parties, are **not applicable to an equitable servitude**.

1. **Between original parties (horizontal privity):** The lack of a privity requirement is most significant with respect to the **original parties** to the agreement creating the servitude. Whereas a covenant at law will run only if the original parties had some sort of property relationship (though exactly what is required varies; see *supra*, p. 230), the servitude is binding on successors **even if covenantor and covenantee were strangers to each other's title**. Thus **neighboring landowners** who have not had any other property transactions between them may agree that neither will build a commercial structure on his land; this agreement will create an equitable servitude, enforceable against or by a purchaser from either.

2. **Between covenantor and subsequent possessor:** Similarly, anyone who **takes possession** of the burdened property will be bound by the servitude, even though he is **not in privity of estate with the original promisor**. The theory for not having a "**vertical privity**" requirement on the burden side is that the servitude is itself a property interest that burdens the land, and whoever takes possession takes subject to that.

a. Compared to covenant at law: Thus whereas a covenant at law will bind only one who takes the *same estate* as the promisor, the servitude will be binding upon even the holder of a lesser estate. For instance, a *lessee* will be bound, and even a mere *licensee* will also be. One court has even gone so far as to hold that an *adverse possessor* takes subject to the servitude, though the merits of this holding are doubtful. 2 A.L.P. 427-28.

3. Between covenantee and his successor: Similarly, there is virtually no requirement of vertical privity between the original *covenantee* and one who gains possession of the *benefitted* land from him. Here, there is less contrast to the covenant at law, since there is hardly any privity requirement in the latter situation either (see *supra*, p. 233).

   a. Benefit in gross: It may be that the servitude is such that it is not for the benefit of any particular parcel of land, or at least not for the benefit of any land owned by the promisee. This situation, where the benefit is said to be *in gross*, is discussed *infra*, p. 243.

H. The "touch and concern" requirement: Neither the benefit nor the burden of a restrictive covenant will run unless it can be said to *"touch and concern"* the promisor's (in the case of a running burden) or the promisee's (in the case of a running benefit) land. But the courts' interpretation of what constitutes "touching and concerning" is somewhat more liberal than in the case of a covenant at law.

1. Promisor's land: The vast majority of *restrictions* upon the *promisor's* use of his own land will be found to "touch and concern" that land. Since these use-restriction cases are the main situations where equitable relief is sought, the touch and concern requirement will nearly always be met on the burden side.

   a. Non-competition clause: The courts are in dispute as to the status of a *non-competition clause*, just as they are where enforcement of such a clause is sought at law. (See *supra*, p. 235.) However, most courts hold that, in the equitable servitude case, such a clause touches and concerns the promisor's land (i.e., the land where the forbidden business may not be carried on).

      i. Restatement view: The Restatement, in §539, Comment k, similarly takes the position that the burden of such a non-competition clause runs at equity, even though not at law. Thus the beneficiary of such a clause may obtain an injunction against the promisor's successor, but may not (under the Restatement) obtain money damages against him for breach of the clause.

2. Promisee's land: On the *benefit* side, the equity courts are also more liberal. Where the agreement involves a building restriction, or other promise that affects the quality of a neighborhood or area, it will be held to "touch and concern" the land of *any land-owner* in that *neighborhood or area*, not just an immediately adjacent one. 2 A.L.P. 412-13. Thus if a lot owner promises that he will not construct a commercial building on his premises, *any nearby landowner may sue for an injunction*. (But it must also be shown that the original parties *intended* the land of the plaintiff in question to be benefitted; the requirement of intent to benefit specific land is discussed *infra*, p. 244.)

   a. Non-competition clause: A *covenant not to compete* with the promisee's land is generally held to touch and concern that land (just as it is generally held to touch and concern the promisor's land). But a few courts hold that only the value of the promisee's land, not its physical use, is affected, and that therefore the non-competition clause does not touch and concern the promisee's property.

3. Running of burden where benefit is in gross: Recall that where the benefit is *in gross*, there is dispute about whether the burden may run at law (*supra*, p. 235). The courts are similarly in dispute about whether *equity* will enforce a burden where the benefit is in gross.

a. English view: The English courts refuse to grant equitable enforcement of the burden against a successor if the benefit is in gross, i.e., where there is not particular land that is benefitted by the agreement. The principal example of this view is *London County Council v. Allen*, 3 K.B. 642 (Eng. 1914). There, the Council (a kind of government agency) and Allen (a developer) agreed that Allen would not build any structures upon certain portions of his land, which were to be reserved for roads. Allen conveyed to his wife, who build three houses on the restricted area. The Council sued for a mandatory injunction to have the houses removed.

    i. Holding in *London County Council*: The Council conceded that this covenant would not run against Mrs. Allen at law, since it did not "touch and concern" any land held by the Council (which owned no land in the vicinity). The court concluded that the covenant should not run against an assignee in equity either, because there was no benefitted land. (The court conceded that it was "very regrettable that a public body should be prevented from enforcing a restriction on the use of property imposed for the public benefit against persons who bought the property knowing of the restriction, by the apparently immaterial circumstance that the public body does not own any land in the immediate neighborhood." But the court felt itself bound by prior holdings.)

    ii. Rationale: The English refusal to enforce at equity a burden where the benefit is in gross, is logical, given the English refusal to recognize the running of *easements* in gross against a subsequent owner of the servient estate. (See *supra*, p. 220.) However, the English view on equitable servitudes has been criticized because of its assumption that the rules of law (governing easements in gross) should also be binding upon equity. 2 A.L.P. 429.

b. American courts in dispute: Since American courts nearly all now allow an easement in gross to be binding against a succeeding owner of the servient estate (*supra*, p. 220), one would expect that the English prohibition on the equitable running of a burden when the benefit is in gross would not be followed. However, the American courts are in fact *in dispute* on this issue. Probably a majority of courts still follow the English view, and do not let the burden run where the benefit is in gross. See 2 A.L.P. 429-30.

    i. Minority: But a substantial minority (probably growing) allow the burden to run where the benefit is not tied to any particular parcel. Thus these courts would find for the Council in *London County Council, supra*.

    ii. Homeowners' association: The issue of the running of the burden where the benefit is in gross also arises where a *homeowners' association* sues to enforce building restrictions. Since such an association often owns no property in the development, it could be argued that the restriction should not be enforceable at equity against an assignee of the original lot purchaser. But the courts by and large *permit the association to obtain an injunction* in this situation. See, e.g., *Merrionette Manor Homes Improvement Ass'n v. Heda*, 136 N.E.2d 556 (App. Ct. Ill. 1956), allowing an injunction against the violation of restrictions in this situation.

I. Intent to benefit particular land: If the benefit is to run to a particular piece of land (so that its owner may enforce the promise), it is not enough that the agreement "touch and concern" that parcel. It must also be the case that the original parties *intended* to benefit that particular parcel. 2 A.L.P. 415-16.

> **Example:** A and B, next-door neighbors, agree that neither will build an outhouse on his property. B begins to build an outhouse, and C, his neighbor on the other side, sues for an injunction. Since there is no evidence that A and B intended their agreement to benefit other nearby landowners, C will not be able to obtain the injunction.

1. External evidence about intent: All states but California permit a showing of an intent to benefit a particular parcel by evidence *external* to the written agreement. Thus the court will hear evidence about the geographical location of the burdened and allegedly benefitted lands, and the physical location of the buildings on them. But evidence of an oral agreement to benefit the particular land, without any other, more tangible, evidence, will probably not be sufficient to overcome the Statute of Frauds.

2. General development plan: The intent to benefit particular lands may also be shown from the fact that there was a *general development plan*. The effect of such a plan on the intent requirement is discussed *infra*, p. 245.

J. Notice to subsequent purchaser: Equity will not enforce an agreement against a subsequent purchaser unless he had *notice* of the restriction. This rule stems from the doctrine that equitable interests are cut off by a transfer of legal title to an innocent purchaser for value (see *infra*, p. 359).

1. Notice as beneficiary: The subsequent purchaser must not only have notice that there is a restriction, but he also must probably have notice as to *who may enforce* that restriction. See, e.g., *Rodgers v. Reimann*, 361 P.2d 101 (Ore. 1961).

2. Significance of recording: The notice requirement is satisfied not only if the subsequent purchaser has actual knowledge, but also if he has *"constructive"* knowledge. Such notice occurs most often where the restriction is *recorded* before the subsequent purchaser takes. Record notice will bind the subsequent purchaser only where the restriction is one which is *required to be recorded*; but since most recording acts are drafted broadly enough to encompass all equitable restrictions, recordation of the restriction will generally be dispositive on the issue of notice.

> **Example:** P sells a parcel to A and B, by a deed forbidding the sale of groceries or bottled drinks on the land conveyed (to protect P's operation of a grocery store on a different nearby parcel). The deed, including the restriction, is recorded. A and B then convey to D1 (with the deed silent as to the restriction), and D1 leases the premises to D2. P sues for an injunction, barring D1 and D2 from selling groceries on the parcel.
>
> *Held*, for P. The recording statute required the recording of all deeds, and the recordation of the deed containing the restriction was thus constructive notice on both D1 and D2. Therefore, an injunction shall be granted against both D1 and D2 (even though there was no evidence that D2, at least, knew of the restriction when he entered the lease). *Oliver v. Hewitt*, 60 S.E.2d 1 (Va. 1950).

a. Duty to search parallel records: If the restriction appears in the purchaser's direct chain of title, this will, as noted, be sufficient to place him on constructive notice of the restriction. But there may be circumstances where even a restriction recorded *outside of the direct chain of title* will constitute constructive notice.

Example: Developer sells numerous lots in a subdivision, and imposes residential restrictions on some of them. Lot 86 is then sold without restrictions, and title to it passes eventually to D, who begins building a gas station. The Ps (owners of other lots in the subdivision) sue D to stop the building of the gas station. *Held*, for the Ps, because D had constructive notice of the restrictions. It is true that D, by searching title all the way back to Developer, would not find any restrictions in the record. But in view of the exclusively residential nature of the neighborhood, D was under a duty to check the title of *neighboring lots*; if he had done so, he would have found that these were conveyed with restrictions. Since some of these lots were conveyed before Lot 86 was sold by Developer, D would then have realized that a "reciprocal negative easement" attached to all lands retained by Developer (including Lot 86) when the first restricted lot was sold. Therefore, D had constructive notice of the reciprocal negative easement, which is binding upon D so that he will be enjoined from building the gas station. (For a fuller explanation of the "reciprocal negative easement" theory of this case, see *infra*, p. 247.) *Sanborn v. McLean*, 206 N.W. 496 (Mich. 1925).

K. Significance of building plan: A developer will often formulate a *general building plan* or development plan, by which all or most of a subdivision is to be made exclusively residential, with provision for parks, roads, and other common areas. Usually this plan is embodied in a subdivision *plat*, or map, which is recorded, together with the applicable restrictions and covenants. The purpose of such a plan is to assure each prospective purchaser that he will be buying into a planned residential neighborhood. Once the developer has sold off the lots, he typically disappears from the picture, at least as far as enforcing the covenants is concerned. Therefore, it becomes important to know the circumstances under which one lot owner may enforce the restrictions against another. The answer to this question depends upon several factors, particularly the wording of the restrictions, and whether the plaintiff seeking enforcement received his land before or after the party against whom he wishes to enforce the limitation.

1. **Enforcement by developer:** The developer himself, of course, will be able to enforce the restriction so long as he owns some of the remaining property. Enforcement by him does not involve the running of the benefit, so that he will always be able to enforce either against the original buyer (the promisor) or against an assignee from the promisor who takes with actual or constructive notice.

2. **Enforcement by subsequent purchaser from developer:** When enforcement is sought against a purchaser by a *later purchaser* from the developer, the latter will have to show that the earlier purchaser and the developer agreed that the benefit would run to the latter's land. (This is a general requirement for the running of the benefit of a servitude; see *supra*, p. 230.) This showing may be made in one of several ways.

   a. **Express provision in deed:** The deed from the developer to the earlier purchaser may itself *expressly* provide that enforcement may be obtained by any subsequent (or prior) purchaser of a different lot from the developer.

   b. **Existence of building plans:** Even where the deed from the developer to the early purchaser does not say anything about the benefit, the *mere existence of a building plan* will probably be enough to create a presumption that other purchasers whose lots fall within the terms of the plan were intended to be benefitted.

Example: Developer devises a residential development plan for the Happy Acres subdivision. He tells each prospective purchaser about the plan, including the fact that it will keep the community entirely residential. He then sells Lot 1 to A, with all the restrictions of the plan embodied in the deed. But the deed to A does not specifically refer to the plan, and does not indicate who may enforce the restrictions. Developer then sells Lot 2 to B. Since B can show that a general plan existed at the time of the deed to A, and that A knew of this plan, the court will presume that all subsequent lot purchasers were intended to be benefitted by the restriction in A's deed.

   i.   How to prove plan existed: If the defendant/purchaser's deed does not refer to the plan, how can the plaintiff/subsequent purchaser prove the plan's existence? This can be done by *oral testimony* that the developer *displayed the plat* to each prospective purchaser (including, presumably, the defendant), or that the nature of the plan was *advertised* prior to the transaction with the defendant. 2 A.L.P. 419.

   ii.   Evidence that other lots are restricted: A general plan may also be shown by evidence that all *other lots* in the vicinity contain similar restrictions. However, it must be shown that the general plan existed *prior to the sale to the defendant* (or to the defendant's predecessor in title). 2 A.L.P. 418. Therefore, a showing that restrictions were placed in *subsequent* deeds will not be relevant; only restrictions inserted prior to the sale to the defendant will show that a plan existed at the time the defendant bought.

   iii.   California bars external evidence: As noted, courts generally allow a showing that a general plan existed even though the deed does not refer to such a plan. But California requires that the existence of a general plan, or some other expression of intent to benefit particular land, must appear *in the deed itself*, and *may not be proved by extrinsic evidence*. See *Werner v. Graham*, 183 P. 945 (Cal. 1919).

   c.   Knowledge by subsequent purchaser: Courts are in dispute as to whether the subsequent purchaser from the developer must be *aware* (at the time he buys) of his right to enforce restrictions in deeds to prior purchasers. Under the majority view as to the nature of a servitude, i.e., that it is an equitable property right, rather than a contract right, knowledge by the subsequent purchaser is *not required*. 2 A.L.P. 420.

3.   Enforcement by prior grantee: Now consider the converse situation: an early grantee from the developer wishes to enforce a restriction against a *later purchaser* from the developer, or that later purchaser's assignee. Unlike the case of enforcement by a subsequent grantee, this is not a matter of the simple running of a benefit; the problem is that the plaintiff has by hypothesis received his land before the restriction against the defendant even existed. Nonetheless, there are several ways in which enforcement by the prior grantee may be available.

   a.   Express promise of restriction made by developer: The developer may make an *express written promise* that his remaining land is subject to the same restrictions. If so, his retained land becomes immediately burdened, and this burden will simply run with the land when he conveys it to later purchasers. The prior purchaser will thus have no difficulty in enforcing the restrictions against the later buyers.

b. Third-party beneficiary theory: If the developer does not make an express written promise in the deed to restrict his retained land, but he later does insert restrictions in deeds to subsequent purchasers, the prior purchaser may be able to use a ***third-party beneficiary*** theory to enforce the restriction against these later purchasers. Such a theory has been applied in a few cases, but more importantly, it is adopted by the Restatement; see Rest. § 541, Comments c and f.

> **Note:** In the examples which follow, the lots are numbered 1, 2, 3 etc. to indicate the order in which they are conveyed by Developer. Lot 1 in each case will be conveyed to A, lot 2 to B, etc.

> **Example:** Developer owns a large tract. He sells Lot 1 to A, by a deed containing various restrictions on the use to which the Lot may be put. The deed says nothing about the status of the land retained by Developer. Developer then conveys Lot 2 to B, with the same restrictions present. If A can prove that Developer and B intended that prior purchasers of land from Developer would have the right to enforce the restrictions against B, under a third-party beneficiary theory A will be entitled to enforce the restrictions against B. See Rest., §541, Comment f.

c. Implied reciprocal servitude: Again assuming that the developer has not expressly and in writing restricted his remaining land, the second, and better-accepted, theory allowing a prior purchaser to enforce against a later one is that of the *"implied reciprocal servitude"*. This theory holds that if the prior purchaser acquires his land in ***expectation*** that he will be entitled to the benefit of subsequently created servitudes, there is ***immediately*** created an "implied reciprocal servitude" ***against the developer's remaining land***. 2 A.L.P. 426. (Sometimes the phrase "implied reciprocal ***easement***" is used, but it means the same thing.)

> **i. General plan must exist:** Unlike the third-party beneficiary theory, this implied reciprocal servitude theory will usually apply only where it is shown that there was a ***general development plan*** in existence at the time the prior purchaser bought. Otherwise, there will normally be no way for the prior purchaser to show that he reasonably expected to have the benefit of such restrictions placed in subsequent deeds. See *Snow v. Van Dam*, 197 N.E. 224 (Mass. 1935), discussed further *infra*, p. 248.

> **ii. Restrictions not inserted in later deeds:** The implied reciprocal servitude theory is applicable if the developer inserts the promised restrictions in later deeds. But the theory's greatest value to the early purchaser is that some courts may apply it ***even if the restrictions are not inserted in the later deed***.

> **iii. No oral promise:** If the developer has made an oral promise to the early purchaser that later sales will contain the restriction, the implied reciprocal servitude theory will probably be applied by most courts. But some courts have gone so far as to hold that ***even if there is no such oral promise*** made to the early purchaser, if that purchaser can show that a general plan of restrictions exists, the implied reciprocal servitude will arise against the developer's remaining land.

> **Example:** Developer, who owns a large tract, sells numerous lots in it in 1892 and 1893. Each deed limits construction to residences costing more than $2,500. In late 1893, Developer conveys Lot 86 to X, without any restrictions. Part of Lot 86 eventually passes to D, who begins to build a gas station. The Ps, owners of

nearby restricted lots, sue for an injunction. There is no evidence that Developer made any explicit promises to the buyers of the restricted lots that he would impose similar restrictions on later purchasers.

Held, for the Ps. The mere fact that all of the earlier deeds contained identical residential-only restrictions, and that the entire neighborhood was residential, is enough to prove that Developer was following a common plan or scheme. Therefore, when he sold the early lots, his remaining land became subject to a reciprocal negative easement, with the same restrictions as those imposed on the lots already sold. Although D's own chain of title did not disclose this restriction, the nature of the neighborhood put him on notice that a reciprocal negative easement might exist, and he was under the duty to check other deeds from Developer. If he had done so, he would have discovered the restrictions, and therefore the reciprocal negative easement; consequently D had constructive notice of the restriction, and took subject to it. *Sanborn v. McLean*, 206 N.W. 496 (Mich. 1925).

    iv. Statute of Frauds: Observe that the concept of implied reciprocal servitudes is in a sense an exception of the Statute of Frauds, since the theory is that the restriction on the developer's remaining land arises without any reference thereto in the deed. Many states will not permit the reciprocal servitude to arise without an explicit promise by the developer *in the deed* that he will subject his remaining lots to the same restriction; see, e.g., *Sprague v. Kimball*, 100 N.E. 622 (Mass. 1913), where Developer orally promised each purchaser that he would restrict the remaining lots; this promise was held ineffective because it did not satisfy the Statute of Frauds.

    Note on Massachusetts law: Thus *Sanborn v. McLean* would turn out differently in Massachusetts, because of *Sprague v. Kimball*. But if the developer keeps his oral promise, and *does insert the restriction* in the later deeds, the prior purchaser is allowed to enforce the restriction even in Massachusetts, as long as he can show that there was a general building scheme. This was the result, for instance, in *Snow v. Van Dam*, 197 N.E. 224 (Mass. 1935); the court noted that because of *Sprague*, the implied reciprocal easement theory was not strictly applicable. Yet the court allowed enforcement, saying "The rationale of the rule allowing an earlier purchaser to enforce restrictions in a deed to a later one pursuant to a building scheme, is not easy to find. . . . Perhaps it is enough to say that the extension of the doctrine, even if illogical, has been made too often and too consistently to permit withdrawal or retreat."

    v. Plan must be in effect at earlier time: For the implied reciprocal servitude theory to apply, the prior purchaser must show that a general building plan existed *at the time he bought*, since it is at that time that the implied reciprocal easement in the grantor's remaining lands must arise, if at all. Similarly, if the developer exacts *stricter* restrictions in later deeds, an earlier purchaser will probably not be able to enforce these more severe restrictions under the implied reciprocal servitude theory. 2 A.L.P. 426.

4. Re-subdivision by covenantor: Suppose one purchases a lot from a developer, subject to certain restrictions, and then *re-subdivides* the lot without imposing the restrictions on the new purchasers. May the purchaser of one of the new sub-parcels enforce the restrictions against the purchaser of another sub-parcel? In general, the courts have *allowed* such enforcement, but only where there is shown to be a general building plan. 2 A.L.P. 434.

Example: Developer sells Lot 1 to A, with the deed providing that the land will not be used for non-residential purposes. A divides the land in half, selling the west half to B and the east half to C; neither B's nor C's deed contains any restrictions. If B can show that there was a general building plan in existence when A bought the lot from Developer, he will probably be able to enforce the residential-only restriction against C. This is because the existence of the common plan shows that Developer and A intended that both benefit and burden of the restriction would run with Lot 1 (or portions of it). If such a common plan were not shown, the court would presume that the benefit was intended to be either personal to Developer, or solely for the benefit of Developer's remaining land, and not for the benefit of subsequent owners of a portion of Lot 1.

5. Land subsequently acquired by developer: Suppose the developer promises the purchaser of a restricted lot that all lots subsequently sold by the developer will be subjected to a similar restrictions. As we have seen, there are a number of theories by which this early purchaser will be able to enforce the restriction against a later purchaser, perhaps even if the restriction is not inserted in the latter's deed. But suppose that at the time of the earlier sale, the developer does *not yet own* the land that he has promised will be restricted in subsequent deeds; if he later acquires this land, and resells it, can the earlier purchaser nonetheless enforce the restrictions?

    a. Common plan: There is at least one situation where some courts have been willing to grant enforcement. If the developer *records a plat* for a subdivision, and does not yet own all the land shown on the plat, his promise to an early purchaser that he will place similar restrictions in the remaining land when he obtains it, will be enforced. 2 A.L.P. 437.

6. Requirements for valid building plans: For a building plan to have the effects discussed above, it must meet certain requirements.

    a. Writing: The plan itself will usually be in writing, generally in the form of a subdivision map and attached restrictions and covenants, all of which are typically recorded. But as noted (*supra*, p. 245), some courts, permit the existence of a plant to be proven by external evidence (e.g., proof that all lots were subjected to the same restrictions, or that the developer advertised and spoke about a uniform plan).

    b. Inclusion of all lots: All lots that are supposed to be within the plan must *in fact be brought within it*. If the developer omits the restrictions from some lots (and the implied reciprocal easement theory does not apply to burden these lots; see *supra*, p. 247), the court is likely to hold that it would be unfair to enforce the restrictions on the lots that are burdened. See, e.g., *Petersen v. Beekmere, Inc.*, 283 A.2d 911 (Super. Ct. N.J. 1971).

        i. Varying restrictions: It is not required that all lots be subjected to precisely the same restrictions. However, variations in the restrictions must not be *unfair*. Thus all residential lots would probably have to be subjected to the same restrictions, but within a subdivision some lots could be designated as commercial or public, and others as non-commercial.

    c. Definiteness: The restrictions imposed pursuant to the plan must be at least *reasonably definite*. For instance, in *Petersen v. Beekmere, Inc, supra*, certain lot owners were required to covenant that they would join a neighborhood association, for an initial fee of $100 plus unspecified annual assessments. The court held that the lack of a formula by which to calculate the amount of future assessments, the lack of a duration on the duty of membership, and the non-transferability of membership even if the lot owner sold his land, made the covenant too vague and potentially unfair for enforcement.

d. **"Strict construction" not necessarily followed:** Some cases, particularly older decisions, state that restrictive covenants will be "strictly construed" against the draftsman or beneficiary. Under these cases, wherever possible the court will find that the proposed use does not violate the restriction.

   i. **Modern view:** But many modern cases have turned away from this view, and simply attempt to define the intent of the parties, even if this means enforcing a somewhat ambiguous restriction. See, e.g., *Joslin v. Pine River Development Corp.*, 367 A.2d 599 (N.H. 1976), stating that "the modern viewpoint is that the former policy of strictly construing restrictive covenants is no longer operative"; the court held that a series of restrictions on buildings was obviously designed for the more general purpose of keeping the subdivision entirely residential, and that one landowner could not use his lot for public beach and boating purposes, even though this would not explicitly violate the building regulations.

e. **Architectural approval clause:** A building plan will often contemplate the establishment of a *homeowners' association*, which is to enforce the restrictions after the developer is no longer on the scene. Frequently, the restrictions inserted in the deeds provide that no new construction may be made unless the association *approves the plans*. Such *"architectural approval"* clauses are generally *upheld*. See, e.g., *Rhue v. Cheyenne Homes, Inc.*, 449 P.2d 361 (Colo. 1969), where such a clause was enforced even though it contained no details as to the standards by which the "architectural control committee" should make its decisions. The court affirmed the committee's refusal to allow P to move his 30-year-old Spanish-style house into the subdivision, which was composed only of "modern ranch-style or split-level" homes; the court accepted testimony that the house would "devalue the surrounding properties" because it was "not compatible" with the modern house already in place.

   i. **Control must be reasonable and in good faith:** The restrictions must be interpreted by the association or architecture committee in a *reasonable, good faith, manner*. But the courts have been relatively reluctant to overturn an association's restriction where it is not motivated by malice and has some reasonable relation to the goal of maintaining a residential neighborhood.

f. **Right to modify restrictions:** The developer will sometimes seek to retain, on behalf of himself or an anticipated homeowners' association, the right to *waive* or *release* the restrictions as to a particular lot. If this is done in a blanket form, with no indication of the circumstances under which such a release or waiver may occur, the court may find that the entire set of restrictions *does not run with the land* on either the benefit or burden side.

   Example: Developer subdivides a large tract, and imposes various restrictions on each of the lots. Each deed provides that the restrictions may be "altered, or annulled at any time . . . by written agreement by and between [developer], his successors, or assigns, and the owner for the time being of the premises in respect of which it is agreed to alter, or annul, the said . . . restrictions. . . ." Through various conveyances, the Ds end up the owners of a lot, and wish to build a structure in violation of the restrictions. They are sued by the Ps, owners of the adjoining lots.

Held, for the Ds. The general reservation by Developer of the power to waive the restrictions negatived the overall building plan, and destroyed the ability of the burdens and benefits of the restrictions to run with the lots in the subdivision. Even though this right was actually exercised only once in 23 years, the existence of the right meant that no owner could be sure that restrictions on other lots would not be waived without that owner's consent. Thus the reciprocal enforceability required for a building plan did not exist, and the right of enforcement was personal to Developer. *Suttle v. Bailey*, 361 P.2d 325 (N.M. 1961).

i. **Limited right to modify:** But a more limited right to modify, which makes it clear that no modification or release may be made that would conflict with the spirit of the overall plan, will probably not destroy the mutual enforceability between landowners. See, e.g., *Rick v. West*, 228 N.Y.S.2d 195 (Sup. Ct. West Co. 1962), where the developer retained the right to make exceptions to the restrictions in certain "special unforeseen conditions", provided that "the spirit and intent of these covenants and restrictions are adhered to." The court held that this limited reservation did not by itself invalidate the plan, and that such items as minimum lot size and angle of lots could be modified. But the proposed sale of a fifteen-acre tract to a hospital would not preserve the residential nature of the subdivision, and it was not within the developer's power to waive the restriction for this purpose.

L. **Selection of neighbors:** Covenants and restrictions are sometimes used not to control land use, but to facilitate the **selection of neighbors**. For instance, each deed executed by a developer may provide that the purchaser must become a member of the homeowners' association, and that he may not sell his land to anyone who is not a member of that association. If the association has untrammeled power to decide who may become a member, existing members (i.e., existing residents of the development) will have the *de facto* right to select their neighbors. Such arrangements are theoretically enforceable (either by damages for their breach or by an injunction against the forbidden sale), but they are likely to run up against one or both of the following obstacles to enforcement:

1. **Restraint on alienation:** First, the arrangement may be held to be an illegal *restraint on alienation*. See the general discussion of restraints on alienation *supra*, p. 98. For instance, in *Lauderbaugh v. Williams*, 186 A.2d 39 (Pa. 1962), all deeds from a developer provided that any future purchaser must be a member of the Lake Watawga Association. The by-laws of the Association provided that objection by any three association members would suffice to deny entrance to a new member, without the necessity for any statement of reasons for the denial. The court held that this right of blackball, coupled with the lack of admission standards and the lack of any stated time limit on the restriction, made the provision an unenforceable restraint on alienation.

   a. **Right of first refusal:** But if the Association has merely a *right of first refusal*, rather than the outright power to block a transfer, this may save the arrangement from being an illegal restraint on alienation. See, e.g., *Gale v. York Center Community Cooperative, Inc.*, 171 N.E.2d 30 (Ill. 1960).

   b. **Co-ops and condos:** In the case of *cooperative associations* and *condominium* units, share restrictions usually take the form either of a requirement that the owners' association approve any proposed transfer, or a right of first refusal. These restrictions are usually *upheld*. See, e.g., *Penthouse Properties, Inc. v. 1158 Fifth*

Avenue, Inc., 11 N.Y.S.2d 417 (App. Div. 1939), holding that the unrestricted right of a co-op board to approve a transfer was not a restraint on alienation, because of the importance of a new member's financial responsibility, among other factors.

i. Reasonableness: Most courts hold that condo and co-op transfer restrictions will only be upheld if they are **reasonable**.

Example: Every owner of a condominium unit in the Laguna Royale (a 78-unit oceanfront apartment complex) signs an agreement that provides, in part, that no owner will transfer his interest without the consent of the Owners' Association. The Ds, owners of one unit, purport to assign undivided one-fourth interests in the property to themselves and three other couples; the four couples agree that each will use the unit for one thirteen-week period per year. The Owners' Association refuses to consent to this transfer and sues to have it invalidated.

Held, for the Ds. The Owners Association, in approving or rejecting transfers, must exercise its power in a "fair and non-discriminatory manner", and may withhold approval "only for a reason . . . rationally related to the protection, preservation and proper operation of the property. . . ." Here, the Association's refusal to consent was unreasonable. The Association's argument that the proposed use would be unreasonably intense, and interfere with other residents' quiet enjoyment, is rebutted by the Association's own bylaws, which allow any unit to be rented so long as the rental is for at least ninety days. Since the Ds could rent the unit to each of the other three couples for a thirteen-week period, it was unreasonable for the Association to refuse to let the Ds accomplish the same usage by transfer. (A dissent argued that it was not unreasonable for the Association to prevent owners from "embarking on a time-sharing enterprise".) *Laguna Royale Owners Association v. Darger*, 174 Cal. Rptr. 136 (Cal. App. 1981).

ii. New York: But a few states, most notably New York, seem to hold that co-op and condo associations may behave **unreasonably** in refusing to consent to transfers, as long as the refusals do not constitute a violation of federal or state civil rights laws. Thus former President Nixon, as well as a number of actors and rock stars, have been rejected by Manhattan co-ops, because the co-op boards thought that the applicant's celebrity and/or security arrangements would lead to inconvenience. (But a refusal to consent based on the applicant's race or national origin would violate federal civil rights laws, and would thus be struck down even in New York. See *infra*, p. 292.) See also D&K, p. 934.

iii. Preemptive option: Many co-op and condo associations restrict transfers not by keeping the right of approval, but by instead keeping a **right of first refusal**. That is, the association has a stated time in which it can match the proposed selling price and acquire the unit itself. Usually such "preemptive options" are upheld. D&K, pp. 933-34.

2. Discrimination laws: A restriction on transfer may also violate various **anti-discrimination laws**.

a. Enforcement by courts: If the restrictive covenant prohibits ownership by non-Caucasians, for instance, it will be unenforceable as a **constitutional matter**. In *Shelley v. Kraemer*, 334 U.S. 1 (1948), the Supreme Court held that judicial enforcement of such a covenant by the granting of an injunction constituted **state action**, and was therefore violative of the Fourteenth Amendment. And in *Barrows v. Jackson*, 346 U.S. 249 (1953), the Court held that the grant of money damages for the breach of such a covenant was also a breach of the Fourteenth Amendment (even if granted against the white seller, rather than against the non-white buyer).

    b. Statutes: *Shelley* and *Barrows* did not proscribe the mere making of such restrictive covenants, or even their voluntary self-enforcement by the owners making them; only judicial enforcement was prevented. But the Fair Housing portion of the 1968 Civil Rights Act, and the Civil Rights Act of 1866 (42 U.S.C. §1982) may prohibit the mere making of such a restriction; certainly the carrying out of such an agreement, as soon as it results in one party's refusing to sell to a non-white, violates both of these statutes. For a brief discussion of anti-discrimination statutes, see *infra*, p. 292.

M. Restriction to single-family use: Covenants and restrictions often attempt to preserve the residential quality of a development. Most significantly, covenants and restrictions often prohibit the construction of anything but *single-family residences*, and prohibit anything but a single family from using each residence.

    1. Enforceable: Generally, such restrictions are *enforced* by a court. For instance, a restriction limiting properties to single-family uses would generally be enforced to prevent operation of a retail store or a hospital on the premises.

    2. Broadening definition of "family": However, courts in recent years have generally broadened the meaning of "family". For instance, an unmarried heterosexual couple, a homosexual couple, or a married couple caring for a large number of foster children, would all have a good chance of persuading a court that they are living as a "family unit" and thus not violating a single-family restriction. See *City of White Plains v. Ferraioli*, 313 N.E.2d 756 (N.Y. 1974) (married couple, two children and ten foster children are a "family" for purposes of zoning ordinance.)

        a. Group home for the retarded: The most controversial issue is whether a *group home for the mentally retarded* is a single-family residence for purposes of a restriction or covenant. Here, the courts have split, but the modern trend seems to be in favor of regarding such a group home as a single-family residence. See D&K, pp. 910-11. Alternatively, some courts concede that a group home for the retarded may not be a single-family residence, but then simply refuse to enforce the covenant on the grounds that it is void as against public policy. See, e.g., *Crane Neck Association, Inc. v. New York City/Long Island County Services Group*, 460 N.E.2d 1336 (N.Y. 1984). See the further discussion of group homes, in the context of zoning laws, *infra*, p. 293.

N. Restrictions on activities: Covenants and restrictions may affect not only the type of dwelling and who lives there, but also may police more narrowly the *activities* that take place. For instance, homeowners associations and condominium associations (see *infra*, p. 355) often enact *rules and regulations* governing such items as *pets*, *satellite dishes*, the *parking of vehicles*, and other aspects of everyday life.

    1. Must be reasonable: Generally, courts *enforce* such restrictions (assuming that they satisfy the requirements for covenants, listed above), but only to the extent that the restrictions are *reasonable*. Furthermore, many courts insist that the restriction must be reasonable *as applied* to the particular homeowner before the court, so that it is not enough that the restriction is reasonable in a general sense.

        Example: P lives in a condominium association whose by-laws prohibit all cats and dogs. A California statute renders such condominium by-law restrictions enforceable "unless unreasonable." The association fines P repeatedly in order to induce her to get rid of her three cats. P sues for declaratory relief (seeking a holding that the restriction is unreasonable as applied to her), as well as for damages for invasion of privacy, intentional and negligent infliction of emotional distress, etc.

Held, for P on most grounds. The association may not impose a blanket restriction on pets. Each situation must be judged on its own specific facts. Remanded to the trial court to determine whether P's three cats unduly interfere with the rights of other association members. (Also, P, by asserting that the fines and other enforcement activities have caused her distress, has stated a claim for negligent infliction of emotional distress.) *Nahrstedt v. Lakeside Village Condominium Assoc., Inc.*, 11 Cal.Rptr.2d 299 (Cal.App. 1992).

O. Termination of servitudes: There are a number of ways in which a servitude may *terminate*. The most important of these are as follows:

1. Abandonment: A servitude, like an easement, may be extinguished by *abandonment*. Abandonment requires the showing of an *intent* by the beneficiary to abandon it, as manifested by *conduct* (rather than merely words).

a. Developer: For instance, a developer might sell a few lots with building restrictions, and then fail to insert restrictions in subsequent lots. A small number of omissions will not normally be enough to constitute abandonment (though this may be enough to stop the burden from being enforceable by anyone except the developer, on fairness principles; see *supra*, p. 249). But if a substantial number of the lots are not restricted, the court is likely to interpret this as a manifestation of the developer's intent to abandon the general building scheme. 2 A.L.P. 440. Similarly, a *generalized* failure of the various lot owners to enforce the restrictions might constitute an abandonment; but the lack of enforcement must be so general that the objectives of the building plan can no longer be maintained — sporadic violations are not sufficient. *Id.*

2. Merger: If the burdened and benefitted parcels come under *one ownership*, the servitude will be destroyed by *merger*.

3. Equitable defenses: There are several traditional *equitable* defenses which are available, just as in any other type of equity suit:

a. Unclean hands: If the complainant has *violated a similar servitude* that burdens his own lot, he will be subject to the defense of *unclean hands*. This defense will apply even if the complainant's violation is *less serious*, as long as it is substantial rather than trivial. However, the two restrictions must be of the *same general nature* for the defense to apply; thus one who violated a promise to pay dues to a homeowners' association would probably not be subject to the unclean hands defense, if he were suing another lot owner who had violated a servitude prohibiting non-residential structures. 2 A.L.P. 441.

b. Acquiescence: The defense of *acquiescence* arises where the complainant has *failed to enforce similar servitudes against third-parties*, that are of the same type as that complained of. The theory behind this defense is that by acquiescing, the complainant has led the party against whom enforcement is now sought to believe that the restrictions will no longer be enforced.

i. Must be damaging to complainant: However, the acquiescence defense applies only where the prior, tolerated, breach was not only of the same type, but was also ***substantially damaging*** to the complainant's interests. Thus if the prior breach occurred in a part of the subdivision ***distant*** from the complainant, the latter will not be deemed to have acquiesced, and may sue a nearby party. Also, if there are several violations, the complainant is not expected to take action against all at once; as long as he is taking reasonable action one case at a time, he will not be held to have acquiesced. 2 A.L.P. 442.

c. Laches: Whereas acquiescence is the failure of the complainant to sue third persons, ***laches*** is the failure of the complainant to bring suit against the ***defendant himself*** in a timely manner following the violation. Generally, a delay in bringing suit will not by itself be enough to deprive the complainant of his right to enforce the restriction, but it will be a factor to be added to others (including acquiescence, change of neighborhood, etc.).

4. Change of neighborhood: It will frequently happen that a restricted, residential-only area, becomes surrounded by commercial or other non-residential development. An owner of one of the restricted plots adjoining the newly-developed area may then argue that this new development has ***so*** changed the neighborhood that it is unfair to force him to keep his property residential, since it will be worth much more if used for commercial purposes.

a. Few cases allowed: In a few cases, where the individual landowner has been able to show that his property is almost ***valueless*** for residential purposes due to the surrounding commercialization, the courts have granted relief against the residential-only restriction. For instance, in *Downs v. Kroeger*, 254 p. 1101 (Cal. 1927), D sought to avoid enforcement of such a restriction against him by showing that his property bordered newly-built business structures and a new streetcar line, and that is was not fit for residential purposes; the court accepted these arguments, and held that it would be "unjust, oppressive, and inequitable to give effect to the restrictions. . . ."

b. Majority view: But most courts faced with this situation have realized that if they relieve a border lot of the restrictions, there will be a ***"domino" effect***: the restricted owners whose lots are next inside the border will now be able to argue that enforcement of the restrictions is unfair against them, till finally the restrictions will now longer apply even in the center of the once restricted area. See, e.g., *Cowling v. Colligan*, 312 S.W.2d 943 (Tex. 1958), relying on this rationale in refusing to waive a restriction against a border lot, even though the lot was worth $10,000 per acre for residential use versus $35-43,000 per acre for commercial use.

i. Unjust enrichment: Furthermore, the purchaser of the border lot by hypothesis knows or should know that the restriction exists, and that as the owner of a border lot he will have no protection on one side. Therefore, he will probably ***pay a lower price*** for the lot than would someone at the center of the restricted tract. If the court were to relieve him from the restriction because of foreseeable changes outside the tract, he would be gaining an unjust windfall at the expense of the interior lot owners. 2 A.L.P. 447.

ii. All or nothing approach: Therefore, most courts will not relieve the restriction unless the changes outside the tract affect the ***entire tract*** in such a way that the benefits of the restrictions are no longer generally available. See, e.g.,

Osborne v. Hewitt, 335 S.W.2d 922 (Ct. App. Ky. 1960). See also Rest., §564, Illustration 1, making it clear that the restricted area as a whole must be incapable of benefitting from continued enforcement before the court will decline to enforce the restrictions.

c. **Money damages:** If the "change of neighborhood" defense does apply to bar an injunction, may the holder of the benefitted lot nonetheless recover *money damages* for breach of the restriction? The courts are split on this question, though the modern tendency seems to be to hold that where the facts merit a denial of injunctive relief, they should also eliminate a recovery of damages at law. See Powell, Par. 684, pp. 741-42.

d. **Distinguished from abandonment:** The "changed neighborhood" problem, just discussed, should be distinguished from the situation where changes occur *within the restricted area itself*. In this latter situation, the problem is really one of abandonment, discussed *supra*, p. 254.

e. **Not applicable to easements:** The changed neighborhood defense is probably not applicable at all where an *easement*, rather than a restriction, is being enforced. Thus in *Waldrop v. Town of Brevard*, 62 S.E.2d 152 (N.C. 1950), a developer sold D, a township, part of a larger tract, and explicitly gave the town the right to run a garbage dump on the portion conveyed. The court treated this transaction as giving the town an easement over the rest of the tract to the extent necessary to run the dump. Consequently, the court refused to allow lot owners who subsequently built homes near the dump on land they bought from the developer to enjoin the dump on the grounds of "neighborhood change". The court noted that "Changed conditions may . . . justify the non-enforcement of restrictive covenants, but a change . . . will not in any manner affect a duly recorded easement previously granted."

f. **Doctrine of "relative hardship":** The related equitable doctrine of *"relative hardship"* has also sometimes been recognized by the courts. If the damage to the burdened landowner that would result from enforcing the restriction against him is *disproportionately greater* than the benefit which would accrue to the benefitted landowners(s), the court may use its equitable powers to decline enforcement. But the courts are as hostile to this defense as they are to the "change of neighborhood" defense; as a practical matter the relative hardship defense will be allowed only where the restriction is ambiguously worded, or where enforcement will be of no substantial benefit to the plaintiff. The mere fact that the burden to the defendant is greater than the benefit to the plaintiff will generally not suffice. 2 A.L.P. 443-44.

i. **Restatement takes minority view:** But the Restatement takes a minority view, that the relative hardship defense will apply "if the harm done by granting the injunction will be disproportionate to the benefits secured thereby", even if there would nonetheless be a material benefit. Rest., §563.

5. **Government action:** *Government action* may have the effect of terminating a servitude.

a. **Condemnation:** If the property burdened by a servitude is *condemned for public use, the servitude is extinguished* if it is inconsistent with the proposed use.

i. **Benefitted owners' right to compensation:** The courts are in dispute as to whether the owners of the lots benefitted by the servitude may obtain *compensation* for this extinguishment. Some courts have denied compensation, on the grounds that it would be prohibitively expensive, and would give owners who had reason to expect a condemnation an incentive to enter into collusive servitudes to gain awards. See, e.g., *Arkansas State Highway Comm. v. McNeill*, 381 S.W.2d 425 (Ark. 1964). But a majority of courts *permit compensation*, on the grounds that the benefit of a servitude is a property interest, and may not be taken without compensation for the decrease in value of the benefitted land. See Powell, Par. 686, p. 744. Rest., §566 follows the majority view.

b. Statutory limits on duration: The *Rule Against Perpetuities* is generally held to be *not applicable* to covenants restricting land use. C&L, p. 1054. Yet such covenants and restrictions clearly fetter the alienability of land. For this reason, just as a number of states have restricted the duration of possibilities of reverter and rights of entry (see *supra*, p. 49), so some of these states have placed *limits on the duration* of covenants running with the land and equitable restrictions. See, e.g., Minn. Stat. §500.20(2). Some of these statutes apply only to restrictions created after the enactment of the statute, thus limiting the act's utility in clearing old titles.

P. Summary of the effect of equity on law: The willingness of courts to grant equitable enforcement (particularly injunctions) for covenants goes a long way towards making the traditional rules for covenants *at law* irrelevant. There are two principal reasons for this:

1. Applies to affirmative covenants: First, equitable relief is no longer limited to cases of negative, restrictive, covenants. *Affirmative* promises may be enforced by equity in most states (see *supra*, p. 240). This means that nearly any covenant at law is potentially susceptible to equitable enforcement against subsequent purchasers with notice, even if it would not run at law as to the burden. Thus a promise to pay dues to a homeowners' association, or to maintain a hedge, might both be enforced at equity against a subsequent purchaser with notice, even if money damages (the remedy at law) would not be available against that person.

2. Privity not required: Secondly, the requirements of vertical and horizontal privity, applicable to the running of covenants at law, are not applicable to cases where enforcement at equity is sought (*supra*, p. 241). Since injunctions are a satisfactory (though not always ideal) remedy for breach of most covenants, it is a rare case where lack of privity will make a big difference. See B,C&S, p. 653, note 1.

a. Touch and concern: Furthermore, since the "touch and concern" requirement is often more liberally interpreted in equity suits (especially with respect to covenants not to compete), the importance of this requirement is lessened.

Chapter Review Questions
(Answers are at back of book)

62. Orin owned a large country estate, Country Oaks, which contained a trout stream. Orin's friend and neighbor Norman, owner of an adjacent parcel, fished in the stream for several years with Orin's consent. Orin decided to sell Country Oaks to Alfred, but wanted to protect Norman's fishing rights. Therefore, with Alfred's consent, Orin's deed to Alfred contained an easement granting Norman and his successors the right to fish in the stream in perpetuity, as well as the right to get to the stream by a path running through the estate. Five years later, Alfred conveyed Country Oaks to Barbara. The Alfred-to-Barbara deed did not contain any easement for fishing.

(a) If the jurisdiction follows the traditional common-law approach to relevant issues, may Norman continue to fish in the stream?

(b) In a jurisdiction following a contemporary approach to the relevant issues, may Norman continue to fish in the stream?

63. Angela is the owner of Auburnacre. Burt is the owner of Blueacre. The two parcels are adjacent, and have never (at least as far as property records go back, which is 200 years) been under common ownership. A lake, located on public land and open to the public, borders the eastern edge of Auburnacre; the Auburnacre-Blueacre border is on the west side of Auburnacre. For many years, the lake had been useless because it was algae-infested. However, in 1985, the state redredged and reclaimed the lake, so that it is now usable for fishing. Beginning in 1985, Angela allowed Burt to cross Angela's property to get to the lake for boating. (Because the land is out in the country where few roads exist, Burt would have to drive for 25 miles in order to get to the lake if he were not permitted to cross Auburnacre.) No written agreement between Angela and Burt regarding Burt's right to cross Angela's land ever existed.

In 1989, Burt conveyed Blueacre to Carter. Shortly thereafter, Carter attempted to cross Auburnacre to get to the lake. Angela objected, and thereafter put a roadblock across the path, in the middle of Auburnacre, that Burt had formerly used. May Carter compel Angela to remove the roadblock so that Carter can cross over to use the lake?

64. For many years, Daphne owned a 160-acre parcel of waterfront land, known as Lakeview Farms. In 1980, Daphne sold a 10-acre portion of Lakeview Farms (the part farthest away from the water) to Frederika. Frederika then built a fashion mall on her 10-acre portion. Of the 160 original acres of Lakeview Farms, only the 10-acre parcel now owned by Frederika adjoins the public roadway. In 1982, Frederika sold her 10-acre parcel to Gil, who operates the fashion mall today. In 1985, after the fashion mall was built, Daphne built a golf course on her remaining 150 acres. After the course was opened, Daphne instructed all golf patrons to enter via a private road which cuts through Gil's property and thus joins the golf course to the public road. (Otherwise, the patrons wouldn't be able to reach the golf course by car at all.) May Daphne's patrons use this road over Gil's objections?

65. Astrid and Ben were adjacent landowners. Astrid's property was valuable beach front property. Ben's property adjoined Astrid's on the side away from the ocean. From 1970 to 1987, Ben and his family continually (at least once a week in nice weather) got to the beach by walking along a beaten path crossing Astrid's side yard. (They could have driven to a public beach four blocks away, but preferred walking directly to the beach area behind Astrid's house.) Astrid never gave permission to Ben to use this path in this way, but she did not voice any objection either. Then, in 1987, Astrid sold her property to Charles. Charles immediately barred the path so that Ben could no longer use it. The statute of limitations for actions to recover real property in the jurisdiction is 15 years. Does Ben have a right to continue using the path to the beach?

66. From Dunes Development Co., George purchased a house just off the 16th fairway of Sandy Dunes Country Club. The Club was constructed by Dunes Development Co. The deed from Dunes stated that George would have the right to free use of the Sandy Dunes Golf Course indefinitely, but was silent on whether the golf rights received by George were transferable. Two years later, George sold the house to Henry. By then, the course was no longer being operated by Dunes Development Co., but rather, by Ian, who bought it from Dunes. When Henry attempted to use the golf course for free, Ian refused. If Henry brings suit against Ian to enforce the free-golf provision of the deed, will Henry prevail?

67. Quince owned a limestone quarry, and a manufacturing plant in which he worked the limestone into gravestones and monuments. A parcel owned by Pierce lay between the quarry and the manufacturing plant. Therefore, Quince purchased from Pierce an easement to drive his trucks along a 10-foot-wide strip of Pierce's land, so the stone could be taken from the quarry to the manufacturing plant. Quince's business grew over the years, and in 1980, Quince shuttered the plant, and built a newer, larger plant some miles away. At the time the old plant was shuttered, Quince told Pierce by telephone, "I won't be needing the easement across your land anymore." Shortly thereafter, Quince sold the quarry, as well as the shuttered plant and the land it stood on, to Raymond. Raymond immediately started driving his trucks from the quarry to the plant. If Pierce brings suit to stop Raymond from crossing Pierce's property, will Pierce be successful?

68. Abbott and Bingham were adjacent landowners, and fanatic tennis players. Abbott, the richer of the two, built a clay tennis court on his property. At the time of construction, he said to Bingham, "For as long as you own your property, you are free to use the court whenever you wish, so long as I am not playing on it." Bingham immediately sent Abbott a letter, stating, "I want to thank you for your generosity in allowing me to use your tennis court whenever I want (assuming you are not using it, of course) for as long as I stay in the house. I regard this as significantly enhancing the value of my own property." For 10 years, the arrangement worked well. Then, Abbott discovered one day that Bingham was having an affair with Abbott's wife. Abbott angrily wrote to Bingham, "I am hereby revoking your right to use my tennis court. Never set foot on my property again, under pain of prosecution for trespass." Bingham now sues for a declaratory judgment that he is entitled to use Abbott's court. The state where the land is located has a 25-year statute of limitation on adverse possession actions.

(a) What property interest, if any, did Abbott grant to Bingham at the time the court was constructed?

(b) Should the court hold that Bingham has the right to use Abbott's court now?

69. Allison and Bertrand were neighboring land owners who owned fee simples in adjacent parcels of land. The parcels were separated by a fence which lay on Allison's property. Since proper maintenance of the fence was important to Bertrand's property as well as to Allison's, both parties agreed that when the fence needed repairs and painting from time to time, Allison would cause this to be done, and Bertrand would then reimburse Allison for half the cost. The agreement also provided that if Bertrand did not pay a debt that was properly owing, Allison could get a lien on his land for the unpaid debt. The agreement was embodied in a document signed by both parties, and filed in the local real estate records indexed under both Allison's and Bertrand's names. The document did not specifically give Bertrand any right to come upon Allison's land to make the repairs if Allison declined to do so.

Two years after this agreement, Bertrand conveyed his parcel to his daughter, Claire, in fee simple. Claire never explicitly or implicitly promised to pay for repairs to the fence. Five years after this conveyance, Allison spent $1,000 to have the fence extensively repaired and repainted. (There had been intervening repairs which occurred while Bertrand still owned his parcel, and which he paid for. The $1,000 was for work done to repair wear and tear that occurred after Claire took title.) Allison now seeks to recover $500 from either Bertrand or Claire. If both refuse to pay, will Allison's suit be successful against Claire, assuming that there is no special statute in force relevant to this question?

70. Same basic fact pattern as prior question. Now, assume that Bertrand never made the conveyance to Claire. Assume further that Allison, five years after her deal with Bertrand, conveyed her parcel to her brother Doug. If Doug sues Bertrand for enforcement of the promise, may Doug recover?

71. Same basic fact pattern as prior two questions. Now, assume that the original Allison-Bertrand document also contained a promise by Allison that she would not replace the wooden fence with a structure made of any other material (because Bertrand liked the look of natural wood). (This promise was contained in the document that was filed in the land records.) Assume that as in the prior question, Allison conveyed the property to Doug, and further assume that Bertrand conveyed his property to Claire. If Doug begins to replace the wooden fence with a shiny metal one, may Claire get an injunction against Doug?

72. Harry and Isadore were adjacent landowners in a residential area. Each believed that swimming pools were "tacky." They therefore agreed, in a writing signed by both, that neither would ever permit his property to have a swimming pool placed upon it. Three years later, Isadore sold his parcel to James. At the time of purchase, James did not have actual knowledge of the Harry-Isadore agreement. A check by James of the real estate records failed to disclose the Harry-Isadore agreement (because it had never been filed by either party). If James had asked Isadore, Isadore would have told him about the agreement, but James never asked, and Isadore never thought to mention it. James has now begun work to prepare his site to contain a swimming pool. If Harry sues to enjoin the construction by James, should the court grant Harry an injunction?

73. Developer, a residential real estate developer, purchased a farm and set about creating "Happy Farms," a planned residential community. Developer prepared a subdivision map (or "plat") for Happy Farms, which showed that all 36 lots on Happy Farms were to be used for residential purposes, showed where roads and sewers were to run, and contained other details indicating that the property would be a residential community. Developer then sold parcel 1 at Happy Farms to Kathy. In the deed from Developer, Kathy agreed that her parcel would be subject to the restrictions contained in the plat, which was filed in the real estate records. Developer did not state in the deed that other parcels later sold by him would be subject to similar restrictions, though Developer orally told Kathy, "Other buyers will be subject to the same limitations, so you'll be sure that you'll have a purely residential community with high standards."

Developer then sold parcel 2 to Lewis. Due to Developer's administrative negligence, the deed to Lewis omitted the restrictions contained in Kathy's deed. However, there is evidence that Lewis knew that a general residential plan had been prepared by Developer and filed in the real estate records. Several years later, Lewis attempted to open a candy store on part of his property. (This is allowed by local zoning laws, since the area is zoned mixed-use.) If Kathy sues Lewis to enjoin him from using his property for non-residential purposes, will the court grant Kathy's request?

ZONING AND OTHER PUBLIC LAND-USE CONTROLS

Introductory note: This chapter is primarily about the law of zoning. However, we also consider two other types of land-use regulation: (1) regulations on subdivision; and (2) regulations protecting the environment or protecting historical structures. We also consider two problems raised by the U.S. Constitution's "taking" clause: (1) the possibility that a land-use regulation may so interfere with an owner's enjoyment of his property that the regulation is found to be a "taking" for which the government must pay compensation (a topic which we consider at the very start of this chapter); and (2) the laws on "eminent domain", or condemnation (a topic which we consider at the very end of this chapter).

I. THE "TAKING" CLAUSE, AND LAND-USE CONTROLS AS IMPLICIT TAKINGS

A. **Fifth Amendment's "taking" clause:** Governments, both state and federal, have the right to take private property for public use. This power is known as the right of "eminent domain" (discussed *infra*, p. 308). However, the Fifth Amendment to the U.S. Constitution provides that *"private property [shall not] be taken for public use, without just compensation."* This is the so-called *"taking"* clause. This clause is made binding on the states by means of the Fourteenth Amendment.

   1. **Land-use controls as takings:** If the state institutes formal eminent domain (or "condemnation") proceedings, in which it seeks to gain title to private property so that the property can be used for public use, the "taking" clause clearly requires that the government *pay* the fair value of the property it has taken. See *infra*, p. 262. But suppose the government never seeks to obtain formal title to private property, and instead merely imposes extensive *regulations* on how the landowner may use his property. Normally, land-use controls will *not* constitute a taking for which the government must pay compensation. But very occasionally, the regulation may so drastically interfere with the private owner's use of his property, or with the value of that property, that the court will conclude that there has been an *implicit* "taking", and that one or both of the following remedies must therefore be awarded: (1) a striking down by the court of the regulation; or (2) an award of damages to the land owner for his lost use or value.

   2. **Question presented:** In this section, we therefore try to answer the following question: what is the borderline between a "taking" (for which compensation must be paid under the Fifth Amendment's "taking" clause) and a mere "regulation" (for which no compensation is required)?

   3. **State constitutions:** Before we delve extensively into this question, you should aware that the constitutions of *all* states except North Carolina contain similar explicit "takings" clauses. 91 Harv. L. Rev. 1463, n. 3. Many of these state constitutional provisions prohibit not only the uncompensated "taking" of private property, but also the uncompensated *"damaging"* thereof. In general, however, the state clauses are subject to roughly the same interpretations as the federal ones.

B. **Two remedies:** Suppose that a court does determine that a land-use regulation is so extensive that it amounts to a "taking". Most commonly, the court simple strikes down the regulation (perhaps concluding that an uncompensated taking violates the owner's substantive due process rights; see *infra*, p. 271). But, the court may, in addition to striking down the statute, also award the owner *damages* for the temporary taking found to have occurred prior to the court's decision. A suit by a landowner seeking money damages for a land use regulation is usually called a suit for *"inverse condemnation"*. (The remedies that may be ordered once the court finds a taking to have occurred are discussed more extensively *infra*, p. 267.)

C. **The taking-regulation distinction:** If the court finds that private property has been "taken" by the government, compensation must be paid. But if the state merely *regulates* property use in a manner consistent with the state's "police power," then no compensation needs to be paid, even though the owner's use of his property, or even its value, has been substantially diminished. It thus becomes crucial to distinguish between a compensable "taking" and a non-compensable "regulation." Land-use regulations that may require the court to distinguish between taking and regulation include *zoning* regulations, *environmental protection* rules, *landmark preservation* schemes, and other schemes by which the government does not attempt to take title to a landowner's property but does regulate his use of that property.

   1. **General principles:** The fact that a state or a local government labels something a "regulation" does not mean that it will not be found by a court to have amounted to a taking for which compensation must be paid. For a land use regulation to avoid being a taking, it must satisfy two requirements: (1) It must *"substantially advance legitimate state interests"*; and (2) It must not "den[y] an owner *economically viable use* of his land." *Agins v. Tiburon*, 447 U.S. 255 (1980).

   2. **Difficult to apply:** These two requirements have been very difficult to apply in practice. However, we can say the following about them:

   a. **Legitimate interests:** A *broad range* of governmental purposes constitute "legitimate state interests" — maintaining residential zoning, preserving landmarks, and protecting the environment, are among the interests that the Supreme Court has found to be adequate.

   b. **Tight means-end fit:** There must be a relatively *tight fit* between the state interest being promoted and the regulation chosen, as the result of *Nollan v. California Coastal Commission*, discussed *infra*, pp. 266-67. More than a mere "rational relation" between means and end is required where a regulation interferes with land use.

   c. **Deprivation of all use:** Few land use regulations are likely to be found to deny the owner *all economically viable use* of his land. But regulations denying the right to build *any dwelling* on the land would qualify. See *First English Evangelical Lutheran Church*, *infra*, pp. 267-68, where such a denial of all economically viable use was found to have occurred.

   3. **Physical use:** If the government makes or authorizes a *permanent physical occupation* of the property, this will *automatically* be found to constitute a taking, no matter how minor the interference with the owner's use and no matter how important the countervailing governmental interests. In *Loretto v. Teleprompter Manhattan CATV Corp.*, 458 U.S. 419 (1982), the Court formulated this *"per se"* rule, and applied it to invalidate a statute which required landlords to permit cable television companies to install their cable facilities on the landlord's rental property. (The scheme permitted landlords to charge the cable companies what was in most instances a maximum one-time fee of $1.)

a. Rationale: The Court distinguished between cases where the state merely prescribes how the owner may use his property (in which case a balancing test is applied to determine whether there is a taking) and cases of permanent physical occupation. The latter type of invasion is "qualitatively more intrusive than perhaps any other category of property regulation," and therefore requires compensation regardless of whether the government action achieves an important public benefit, and regardless of whether it has more than a minimal economic impact on the owner. (Here, for instance, compensation was required even though, by the majority's admission, only about 1 1/2 cubic feet were involved.)

b. Easement is physical occupation: A post-*Loretto* case shows that the Court will take an expansive view of what kind of regulation constitutes a "physical occupation" of the owner's property. In that case the Court held that a state's refusal to grant a building permit except upon the transfer to the public of a permanent ***easement*** for the public to pass along a strip of the owners' property constituted a "permanent physical occupation" of that property. See *Nollan v. California Coastal Commission*, discussed more extensively *infra*, pp. 266-67. The easement in *Nollan* would simply have permitted members of the public to walk along the owner's sandy strip parallel to the ocean on their way from one public beach to another. Even though this easement would not have permitted any given individual to remain on the owner's land, a physical occupation was found to exist, so that there was a taking of the owners' property.

4. Diminution in value: The more drastic the ***reduction in value*** of the owner's property, the more likely a taking is to be found. The size of the ***"diminution in value"*** produced by the regulation is probably the single most important factor in most courts determination of whether a land-use regulation constitutes a taking.

a. *Mahon* case: The significance of a large diminution in value is shown by the classic case of ***Pennsylvania Coal Co. v. Mahon***, 260 U.S. 393 (1922).

i. Facts: A landowner had bought the surface rights to land, and the house on it, under a chain of title which reserved to a coal company the right to mine coal from under the property. Thereafter, Pennsylvania enacted a statute preventing subsurface mining where a house might be caused to sink. The effect of the statute was to bar the coal company completely from mining under the owner's land.

ii. Holding: The Supreme Court held that the regulation so utterly impaired the right to mine coal that it was nearly the equivalent of an appropriation or destruction of the coal. Therefore, the regulation was a taking, which could not be carried out without compensation to the coal company. The Court, in a majority opinion by Justice Holmes, noted that "while property may be regulated to a certain extent, if regulation goes too far it will be recognized as a taking."

iii. Dissent: But a dissent, by Justice Brandeis, argued that the regulation was merely "the prohibition of a noxious use," and therefore did not require compensation. (The "noxious use" factor is discussed immediately below.)

iii. May no longer be valid: The result in *Pennsylvania Coal* may no longer be valid. In *Keystone Bituminous Coal Ass'n v. DeBenedictis*, 480 U.S. 470 (1987), the Court by a 5-4 vote upheld a modern (1966) Pennsylvania version of the statute struck down in *Pennsylvania Coal*. The 1966 statute required that 50% of the coal beneath existing public buildings and dwellings be left in place to provide surface support. The majority made some efforts to distinguish *Pennsylvania Coal*, but there is so little difference between the two statutes that it seems likely that *Pennsylvania Coal* would turn out the other way if decided today. However, the general principle for which the case is cited — that the more drastic the reduction in value of the owner's property, the more likely a taking is to be found — remains valid. (*Keystone* also illustrates that where the state is acting to prevent **harm to the public**, the courts will be very reluctant to invalidate the regulation as a "taking." See the discussion of the "prevention of harm" rationale, *infra*, p. 265.)

5. Denial of all economically viable use of land: Since (as just noted) the more drastic the reduction in value of the owner's property, the more likely a taking is to be found, it's not surprising that the Court has imposed a flat rule that a taking occurs where an owner has been deprived of **all economically viable use** of his land. See *Agins v. Tiburon*, discussed *supra*, p. 262. Cases in which such an extreme taking deprivation of economically viable use is found are very rare. The fact that the **particular** use made by the plaintiff has been completely foreclosed will not be enough. For instance, suppose a parcel contains an aluminum smelter worth $100 million, and the city where the smelter is located then bans all smelting. The fact that P's *particular* land use — operation of the smelter — has been totally foreclosed will not be enough to make the regulation a "taking"; P is still free to convert the smelter to other uses, or even to raze it and put up some other structure (or sell it to someone who will). On the other hand, a **total ban** on the building of **any structure** on property is likely to be enough to deny the owner "all economically viable use" of his land, and thus to constitute a taking automatically.

> **Example:** South Carolina, in order to protect its coastline from continued erosion, enacts the Beachfront Management Act, which defines certain "critical areas" of erosion danger, and bars any owner of a lot in a critical area from building any permanent habitable structure on the parcel. P is the owner of two parcels which, at the time he bought them for nearly $1 million, were allowed to have houses built upon them; passage of the Act has the effect of preventing P from building any permanent structure on either lot. P contends that this "regulation" deprives him of all economic use of his property, and thus constitutes a taking. A lower state court agrees that P has been deprived of all economically viable use, but the South Carolina Supreme Court reverses on the grounds that even if this is true, the state may regulate to preserve its citizens' health and safety, and that such regulation is not a taking.
>
> if P has truly been deprived of all economically viable use of his property, a "taking" has occurred. It is up to the South Carolina courts to decide whether P has really been deprived of all economically viable use. If he has been, a taking exists even though the state is trying to protect the health and safety of residents. *Lucas v. South Carolina Coastal Council*, 112 S.Ct. 2886 (1992).

a. Ban on hotel demolition: For another illustration of a taking that deprives the owner of all economically viable use of his land, consider a New York City ordinance that put a five-year moratorium on the demolition or conversion of single-room occupancy (SRO) hotels, and required the owners of these buildings to make them habitable and lease them at rent-controlled rates. The highest court of New York State held that such an ordinance, by prescribing the sole purpose for which property may be used (and by, in fact, stating that the property *must* be used for this purpose rather than left vacant) amounted to an uncompensated, and thus unconstitutional, taking. *Seawall Assoc. v. City of New York*, 542 N.E.2d 1059 (N.Y. 1989).

6. **"Prevention of harm" or "noxious use" rationale:** A regulation rather than a taking is likely to be found where the property use being prevented is one that is *harmful* or *"noxious"* to others. For instance, a zoning ordinance may properly prevent the operation of a steel mill in the middle of a residential neighborhood; in general, anything which the common law would recognize as a public or private *nuisance* may be barred by regulation, without the need for compensation.

   a. **Favoring one private interest over another:** Occasionally, a zoning or other public decision that a land use is "noxious" will be the product of a clear decision to *favor one private interest over another*. Nonetheless, the fact that a private interest, rather than the "public interest" as a whole, is being benefited, will not render the regulation a compensable taking.

      Example: Many red cedar trees in the state of Virginia are infected with cedar rust, a disease that is highly dangerous to apple orchards. Virginia passes a law requiring the destruction, as a public nuisance, of all red cedar trees within a prescribed distance from an apple orchard. Cedar owners are paid only the cost of removing their trees, not the value of the trees.

      Held, the ordinance, and the consequent uncompensated destruction of the cedars, were not a compensable taking. The state had the right to conclude that apple orchards were more important to the state economy than cedars, and its decision to sacrifice the latter to save the former did not violate due process. *Miller v. Schoene*, 276 U.S. 272 (1928).

D. **Particular types of land use regulation:** Let's now look at some particular types of land use regulations, to see whether they are valid regulations or compensable takings. (Sometimes, the court strikes down a regulation on the grounds that it is so broad as to violate the owner's *substantive due process* rights, rather than because it is a compensable "taking". But roughly the same criteria seem to apply for a due process attack, as for an attack based on the "taking" clause.)

   1. **Zoning regulation:** In cases where *zoning regulations* impair an owner's use of his property, the Court has been especially reluctant to find a compensable taking. A zoning ordinance will not be stricken as violative of due process unless it is "clearly arbitrary and unreasonable, having no substantial relation to the public health, safety, morals or general welfare." *Moore v. East Cleveland*, 431 U.S. 494 (1977) (also discussed *infra*, p. 271.)

      a. *Moore*: *Moore* itself was an extremely rare invalidation of a zoning ordinance. The ordinance there allowed only members of a "family" to live together, and defined "family" so narrowly that a grandmother was barred from living with her two grandchildren, one by each of two different children.

   2. **Other environmental regulation:** Regulations designed to protect the *environment* are similarly subjected to only mild review, even if the property owner's ability to use his land is substantially circumscribed. See, e.g., *Goldblatt v. Hempstead*, 369 U.S. 590

(1962), upholding a town "safety regulation" preventing a property owner from continuing to mine a sand and gravel pit as he had done for 30 years; the ban was justified as a "reasonable" exercise of the "police power," and the Court contended that the diminution in the value of the property, although relevant, was not conclusive.

3. **Landmark preservation:** *Landmark preservation* schemes, like zoning and environmental regulations, will seldom constitute a taking. For instance, in *Penn Central Transportation Co. v. New York City*, 438 U.S. 104 (1978), the Court found that the New York City Landmarks Preservation Law did not effect a taking of plaintiff's property. The case is discussed further *infra*, pp. 304-05.

E. **Tight means-end fit required:** The above discussion of regulations involving zoning, environmental protection, landmark preservation, etc., suggests that a variety of governmental objectives will be found to satisfy the requirement that the government pursue a "legitimate state interest". However, the Supreme Court requires a *very close fit* between the *means* chosen by the state (i.e., the particular land use regulation selected) and the governmental objective being pursued. Even a compelling state interest will be to no avail if the means chosen by the government are not quite closely tailored to advance that interest. This approach to the means-end fit was announced in *Nollan v. California Coastal Commission*, 107 S. Ct. 3141 (1987).

1. **Facts:** The land use regulation at issue in *Nollan* prevented the Ps from rebuilding their house on their beach front property unless they first gave the public an *easement* across a sandy strip of the property adjacent to the ocean. The California Coastal Commission, which imposed this requirement, was concerned that if the Ps replaced their small bungalow with a much larger three-bedroom house, several types of harm would occur: (1) The view of the ocean would be blocked; (2) Private use of the shore front would be increased; and (3) This construction, coupled with other nearby construction, would make it harder for the public to get to and from public beaches north and south of the Ps' property (beaches which would be connected if the Ps gave the public the required easement).

2. **Holding:** By a 5-4 vote, the Court held that the Commission's refusal to issue the building permit except upon transfer of the easement amounted to a taking, for which compensation must be paid. In arriving at this conclusion, the majority opinion (written by Justice Scalia), reasoned as follows: (1) If the government had simply required the Ps to give the public an easement over their property, this would clearly have been a taking, since it would be a "permanent physical occupation" (even though no particular individual would be permitted to station himself permanently on the property); (2) An outright refusal by the government to grant the permit would not constitute a taking if it *"substantially advanced a legitimate state interest"* and did not *"deny an owner economically viable use of his land"*; and (3) The conditions attached to the permit must be evaluated by the same standard, so that only if those conditions "substantially advanced" the legitimate state interests being pursued would the conditions be valid.

   a. **Loose means-end fit:** Requirement (3) was not satisfied, in the majority's view, because the harms feared by the government would not be cured or even materially lessened by the means chosen (the easement). For instance, there was no reason to believe that the easement would reduce obstacles to viewing the beach created by the new house, since the easement would only help people already on public beaches north or south of the Ps' property. In the majority's view, the building restriction was "not a valid regulation of land use but 'an out-and-out plan of extortion.'"

3. Significance: *Nollan*, when taken together with *First English* (*infra*, p. 266, holding that damages must be paid for even a temporary taking caused by an invalid land use regulation) shows that the Supreme Court gives a **stringent review** to land-use regulations.

F. Remedies for temporary takings: The issue of whether a "taking" has occurred will usually arise in one of two ways: (1) the landowner sues to **enjoin** a regulation, contending that the regulation is violating his due process rights; or (2) the landowner brings an **"inverse condemnation"** suit, claiming that the government has effectively appropriated his property, and must pay for it. In a suit brought under (1), the court will simply **strike the regulation** if it finds that due process has been violated; it will not order "just compensation" to be paid. But in an inverse condemnation suit, if a taking is found to have occurred, the court will order **just compensation**.

    1. Temporary takings: The Supreme Court has held that where a land use regulation is so broad that it constitutes a taking, the landowner may bring an inverse condemnation suit and receive **damages** for the **temporary** taking (temporary because the regulation is struck down by the Court). This key holding occurred in *First English Evangelical Lutheran Church v. Los Angeles County*, 482 U.S. 304 (1987).

        a. Background: Prior to *First English*, state courts had almost always rejected landowner claims that the land use regulation in question constituted a taking for which monetary compensation must be paid. The state courts had held that the proper remedy for an unconstitutional land use regulation was merely to **strike the zoning regulation**, so that the landowner would receive no compensation but would regain the use of his property. (These courts gave the local government the theoretical right to elect to pay the value of the property and maintain the regulation, but, as a practical matter, the local government almost always redrafted its zoning ordinance rather than pay compensation.)

            i. No damages allowed: In other words, in the case of a zoning or other land-use regulation that the owner contended went beyond lawful regulation, the state courts forced the landowner to bring an injunction suit, and did not permit an inverse condemnation suit for damages. The prevailing state court view thus amounted to a holding that the landowner is never entitled to damages for the **temporary** taking of his property that occurs between the time the regulation goes into effect and the time it is struck down by the court. See, e.g., *Agins v. City of Tiburon*, 598 P.2d 25 (Cal. 1979), *aff'd* (without reaching merits), 447 U.S. 255 (1980).

        b. Supreme Court allows suit: But the Supreme Court, in *First English*, held that whenever a landowner successfully demonstrates that his property has been "taken" by a land use regulation, the Takings Clause **requires that compensation be paid** for this period up to the striking of the regulation.

            i. Rationale: In reaching this conclusion, the Court relied heavily on earlier cases holding that the government's appropriation of private property during World War II, though "temporary," nonetheless constituted a taking. Therefore, " 'temporary' takings which, as here, deny a landowner all use of his property, are not different in kind from permanent takings, for which the Constitution clearly requires compensation."

ii. Application to facts: Thus P in *First English* would be entitled to compensation if it could prove what it alleged in its complaint: that an ordinance passed in 1979 forbidding all use of property within a newly-established "interim flood protection area," and not invalidated by the time the suit started in 1985, deprived it of all use of its property during that period.

2. **Scope of decision:** *First English* is probably not as far-reaching as it might at first seem. The case does not establish that any time a land use regulation interferes with an owner's use of his property and is later found to be invalid, compensation must be paid. Instead, the case only holds that where an owner is denied *all use* of his property, and for at least a reasonably *substantial time* (e.g., the six or more years in *First English*), compensation must be paid. The majority expressly noted that it was *not* dealing with the "quite different questions that would arise in the case of *normal delays* in obtaining building permits, changes in zoning ordinances, variances, and the like. . . ." In fact, it seems improbable that a landowner whose right to develop his property is held up by such "normal" delays in getting approval could obtain compensation, even if the zoning approval process in question was eventually held to be invalid.

II. ZONING — GENERALLY

A. **General nature of zoning:** The principal type of public land-use regulation existing in America is *zoning*. Zoning is generally done on the local, municipal, level. The municipality's power to zone comes from the state "police power" (discussed further *infra*, p. 274), which is delegated by state statute to the locality.

B. **Use zoning:** Perhaps the most important kind of zoning is "use zoning", by which the municipality is divided into districts, in each of which *only certain uses* of land are permitted.

1. **Euclid case:** Such a use zoning scheme was approved by the U.S. Supreme Court in *Village of Euclid v. Ambler Realty Co.*, 272 U.S. 365 (1926).

   a. **Facts of Euclid:** P, a realty company, owned vacant land in the Village of Euclid which it wished to develop for industrial purposes. The land lay in a district that the Village had zoned solely for residential uses. P claimed that the value of its land was thereby reduced from $10,000 per acre to $2,500 per acre, and that the ordinance was an unconstitutional violation of P's due process and equal protection rights.

   b. **Holding:** The Supreme Court held that a zoning measure would be struck down as unconstitutional only if it was *"clearly arbitrary* and *unreasonable*, having no substantial relation to the public health, safety, morals, or *general welfare."* The use zoning scheme, insofar as it reduced traffic and noise in residential areas, and facilitated fire prevention (by making it possible to keep fire apparatus suitable for each district's particular use) passed muster under this general standard. The court refused to evaluate the wisdom of each minor provision of the ordinance, since the overall reasonableness of the scheme was clear.

2. **"Euclidean" zoning:** The *Euclid* case, by resolving doubts about the constitutionality of use zoning, gave rise to a rapid spread of similar ordinances across the nation. The division of a municipality into separate use districts is in fact frequently referred to as "Euclidean zoning".

3. **Cumulative use scheme:** The ordinance in *Euclid*, like most of the ordinances adopted in the early days of zoning, was *cumulative* in nature. That is, each successive

district (starting from single-family residential and going through heavy industrial) permitted all the uses allowed in the previous districts, and added some new ones. Thus single-family residential use was allowed in *every district*, even heavy industrial.

    a. Modern trend differs: But recently enacted ordinances have usually departed from this cumulative scheme. In particular, residential use is generally not allowed in a district zoned for industry. Dwellings in industrial areas are undesirable on health and safety grounds; also, the industrial users may be harassed by nuisance suits brought by the residential owners, and the availability of the large tracts often needed by industry may be curtailed by the intermingling of small residences. See 4 Williams §101.13.

C. Density controls: Distinct from restrictions on use are zoning restrictions which regulate, directly or indirectly, the *density* of population or construction. The usual purposes of such regulations are to maintain the community's attractive appearance, to avoid an overburdening of public facilities (e.g., schools, parks, sewers, etc.) and sometimes (though almost never publicly admitted) to exclude undesirable residents (e.g., poor families who will live in apartments). Many of these density regulations are discussed extensively *infra*, p. 287, in the treatment of exclusionary zoning. A few of the more common techniques are:

    1. Minimum lot size: The establishment of a *minimum lot size* for single-family homes;

    2. Setbacks: *"Setback"* requirements, mandating a certain amount of unbuilt land on some or all sides of the structure;

    3. Minimum square footage: Particularly in single-family residential zones, a *minimum square footage* for the dwelling (e.g., no dwelling permitted with fewer than 1,000 square feet of floor space);

    4. Height limits: In the case of office towers and apartment buildings, *height limits*.

III. LEGAL LIMITS ON ZONING

A. Constitutional limits: Both the federal Constitution and those of the individual states may impose limits on zoning. Furthermore, at least three different constitutional clauses (in the federal Constitution, and in the constitutions of most states) may bear on the zoning problem. These are (1) the *due process* clause (which has both procedural and substantive implications); (2) the *equal protection* clause; and (3) the *"takings"* clause. (The "takings" clause is discussed *supra*, p. 261, so here we consider only the due process and equal protection clauses.) In the discussion which follows, references are to the federal Constitution unless otherwise noted.

B. Procedural due process: The Fourteenth Amendment of the U.S. Constitution provides that no state shall "deprive any person of life, liberty, or property, without *due process of law.*" The due process clause has been construed to impose certain *procedural requirements* upon the zoning process; that is, putting aside the substantive content of zoning decisions, there are certain restrictions on the *means* by which zoning actions may be taken.

    1. Administrative action only: Procedural due process requirements apply only to zoning actions that are *administrative*, rather than *legislative*, in nature. See 91 Harv. L. Rev. 1508. Thus where an entire, general, municipal zoning ordinance is adopted (clearly a legislative act), there are no procedural due process requirements at all. In this situation, there is no requirement that a landowner who will be affected by the new ordinance be given a hearing; nor is there any requirement that the legislative body which passes the ordinance (typically the town council or board of supervisors) be "impartial".

a. Distinction between legislative and administrative action: In the zoning context, it is not always simple to determine whether a given action is administrative or legislative. Generally an act by an **elected body**, that concerns broad **policy** issues, is a legislative act; thus the enactment of a city-wide zoning ordinance, or of a "master plan" (see *infra*, p. 276) will almost always be considered legislative. The granting of a **variance** (*infra*, p. 278) or of a permit for a **special use** (*infra*, p. 280), since it is usually given by a non-elected body (e.g., the board of zoning appeals), and concerns only one or a small number of property owners, is generally considered to be administrative.

i. Zoning amendment: Courts are in dispute as to the status of a **zoning amendment** which applies only to a small area. Such an amendment is legislative in the sense that it is enacted by the elected body that promulgated the ordinance in the first place, but it is administrative insofar as it affects the rights of only a limited number of individuals. The modern tendency seems to be to treat such amendments as being **administrative**; see, e.g., *Fasano v. Board of County Comm'rs of Washington Co.*, 507 P.2d 23 (Ore. 1973), holding that the decision to change the zoning classification of a particular parcel of property is an administrative act, conferring upon affected landowners the right to a **hearing**, to an impartial tribunal, to a record of the proceedings and findings of fact, and to relatively strict judicial review.

2. What process is due: Once it is established that the proceeding is administrative rather than legislative, an affected landowner receives several procedural protections:

a. Right to hearing: He has the right to a **hearing**, at which he may present evidence and make arguments.

b. Impartial tribunal: He has the right to a decision-making body that is **impartial**. Thus the officials making the decision must not have any **pecuniary interest** in the outcome and must not be subject to undue nonpecuniary influences (e.g., violent community sentiment). 91 Harv. L. Rev. 1526.

c. Explanation of decision: The body which makes the decision must **explain its reasons** for its decision; this will usually require it to make **findings of fact** (e.g., that the denial of a variance to O would not cause him "unnecessary hardship" because he brought the need for the variance upon himself; see *infra*, p. 278).

3. Which owners have property interests: Even if a decision is administrative, not every property owner who may be affected by it will have the right of procedural due process. Certainly an owner whose own property will be subject to a change in classification has such a right. Probably neighboring landowners whose own property may change substantially in value because of the decision are also protected. Thus if O sought a variance to put a lumberyard in a residential area, neighboring lot owners would certainly have the procedural protections referred to above. See 91 Harv. L. Rev. 1517.

4. Referenda and initiatives: Some states and municipalities provide for deciding certain types of zoning questions by **referenda** or **initiatives**, two forms of popular vote. Since an affected citizen will probably not receive a fair hearing or an "impartial" tribunal (since the entire electorate is the tribunal), and will certainly not receive a statement of reasons for the decision, such zoning by popular vote is permissible only if it is treated as legislative. The Supreme Court has permitted such popular vote techniques in the zoning area; see *City of Eastlake v. Forest City Enterprises, Inc.*, discussed *infra*, p. 290.

C. Substantive due process: At one time (particularly during the New Deal), courts were quick to strike down all sorts of legislative measures on the grounds that they violated the *substantive* property rights of individuals. This was done under the doctrine of "substantive due process". The entire substantive due process concept, which rests largely on courts' willingness to strike down legislation which they believe to be unwise, is seldom applied today. In the zoning area, an ordinance or administrative decision is generally held to be violative of substantive due process only if it fails to bear a *rational relationship* to a *permissible state objective*. To put it another way, the zoning action does not violate substantive due process if it is within the government's *"police power"*, a term discussed further *infra*, p. 274.

1. **Broad objectives:** Since under *Village of Euclid v. Ambler Realty Co.*, discussed *supra*, p. 268, permissible state objectives of zoning include "the public health, safety, morals, or general welfare", it is a relatively rare zoning action that does not have a "rational relationship" to one of these extremely broad objectives. See, e.g., the discussion of "aesthetic zoning", *infra*, p. 274, such zoning for aesthetic purposes is generally permitted today.

2. **Family gets special protection:** One area in zoning law where a substantive due process argument may well succeed is where the ordinance *substantially interferes with family rights*. For instance, in *Moore v. City of East Cleveland*, 431 U.S. 494 (1977), the city of East Cleveland zoned a certain area for single-family occupancy. It defined "family" so as to exclude most extended families; a "family" could include a couple, their parents, and their dependent children, but no more than one child with dependent children. The ordinance thus prohibited P from living with her two sons and her two grandsons, one from each son. The city commenced criminal proceedings against P for the violation, and she was convicted (and sentenced to five days in jail!)

   a. **Holding in *Moore*:** The Supreme Court reversed P's conviction on substantive due process grounds. The majority opinion noted that freedom of choice in matters of family life is one of the liberties protected by the due process clause; the East Cleveland ordinance had the effect of "slicing deeply into the family itself." The Court rejected the idea that only the "nuclear" family is entitled to due process protection: "The tradition of uncles, aunts, cousins, and especially grandparents sharing a household along with parents and children has roots equally venerable and equally deserving of constitutional recognition." In view of the importance of these familial rights, the Court held, the City failed to establish a strong enough connection between the ordinance and its objectives (which the City claimed were to prevent overcrowding, minimize traffic, and avoid a financial burdening of the local schools).

      i. **No "strict scrutiny":** The Court in *Moore* did *not* apply a *"strict scrutiny"* standard (as is generally applied in cases where state action discriminates against a racial minority). But it seemed to require more than a mere "rational relation" between the ordinance and the municipality's objectives.

   b. **Dissent:** Four members of the Court dissented in *Moore*. Justices Stewart and Rehnquist based their dissent on the grounds that although certain family rights are entitled to due process protection, "The interest that the appellant may have in permanently sharing a single kitchen and a suite of contiguous rooms with some of her relatives simply does not rise to that level . . ." (in contrast to, *inter alia*, the right of parents to send their children to private schools or to have their children instructed in foreign languages.)

3. **Compared with *Belle Terre***: But the Supreme Court, in granting family relations substantive due process protection against interference from zoning, has limited the idea of "family" to ***relatives by blood or marriage***. In the pre-*Moore* case of ***Village of Belle Terre v. Boraas***, 416 U.S. 1 (1974), the Village of Belle Terre limited its entire area to single-family dwelling use; the word "family" was defined as "one or more persons related by blood, adoption, or marriage, living and cooking together as a single house-keeping unit. . . ." The ordinance also permitted a household of "a number of persons but ***not exceeding two*** . . . living and cooking together as a single housekeeping unit though not related by blood, adoption, or marriage. . . ."

   a. **Argument in *Belle Terre***: The Ps in *Belle Terre* sought to rent their house to six unrelated college students. The Ps claimed that the ordinance was unconstitutional on a number of grounds, including the fact that it violated the privacy rights of potential newcomers, and interfered with the right to travel.

   b. **Holding**: The Court found the ordinance to be ***constitutional***. It was not troubled by the fact that the ordinance placed no limit on the size of biological families, yet limited households of unrelated persons to two. The Court cited the Village's desire to maintain "A quiet place where yards are wide, people few, and motor vehicles restricted. . . . It is [permissible] to lay out zones where family values, youth values, and the blessings of quiet seclusion and clean air make the area a sanctuary for people." The Village's restrictions were held to be rationally related to these permissible objectives.

      i. **Distinction from *Moore***: Thus *Belle Terre* can be seen as holding that zoning may substantially restrict the rights of people to form households together, whereas *Moore* indicates that the same zoning power will be substantially curtailed if it is used to affect the traditional (biological) family structure. Many recent cases agree that this is how the two cases are to be harmonized; see, e.g., *Elliott v. City of Athens* (discussed more extensively *infra*, p. 293), holding that a city may prohibit more than four unrelated people from living together in a house zoned single-family-residential, even though a biological family could not be limited in this way.

4. **Drastic reduction in value**: A second situation in which a substantive due process attack on a zoning regulation might succeed is where the regulation ***almost completely destroys*** the pre-existing ***economic value*** of the property. (Note that a regulation which almost completely destroys the economic value of property is also likely to be found to constitute a "taking" for which compensation must be paid under the "diminution in value" standard often used by courts. See *supra*, p. 263.)

5. **Application to particular landowner**: In applying the "rational relation to permissible state objective" test for substantive due process, courts tend to give a fairly heavy presumption in favor of the validity of the state action. But if the landowner can show that the measure is clearly ***unreasonable*** and ***irrational as applied to him***, the court may strike it on due process grounds. For instance, in the post-*Euclid* case of *Nectow v. City of Cambridge*, 277 U.S. 183 (1928), P owned a parcel which fell into two zones, so that most of his land was usable for commercial purposes but a small end strip

was not. The Supreme Court accepted a special master's finding that including the strip within the residential-only zone would not advance the general welfare (since the proximity of other commercial uses made the strip unusable for residential purposes). Particularly in view of the substantial injuries suffered by P as a result of the use restriction, the Court found that the necessary "substantial relation" between the ordinance and the permissible objective (general welfare) was not satisfied, and that the zoning of the strip violated P's substantive due process rights.

    a. Modern view: However, after *Nectow* the Supreme Court got out of the business of reviewing zoning ordinances (it did not decide another zoning case until the *Belle Terre* case almost 50 years later). State courts have been much less sympathetic than the *Nectow* case to the argument that a particular boundary line does not advance the general welfare. The modern trend seems to be to hold that boundary lines must be drawn somewhere, and that a complaining landowner must make a clear showing that the particular line has been drawn for discriminatory purposes. The fact that the court itself might have drawn the line in a different, better, place, will generally not be sufficient to establish a violation of due process.

D. Equal protection: The ***Equal Protection*** Clause of the Fourteenth Amendment, preventing any state from depriving a citizen of "equal protection of the laws," may also occasionally come into play in the zoning context. For instance, any zoning ordinance which was adopted for the purpose of ***excluding blacks or other racial minorities*** would violate the equal protection clause. (But a discriminatory intent, rather than merely a discriminatory effect, is required; see the discussion of *Village of Arlington Heights v. Metropolitan Housing Development Corp., infra,* p. 288.)

    1. "Rational relation" test: Normally, a zoning action that differentiates between two classes of people or between two uses does not violate the equal protection clause so long as it bears a *"rational relation"* to a permissible state objective. This is the same test as is used in the substantive due process area (*supra,* p. 271).

    2. "Strict scrutiny": However, there are two types of situations where more than a mere "rational relation" between a zoning measure and its objective will be required.

        a. Suspect classification: *"Strict scrutiny"* will be given to any measure which *discriminates* (and is intended to discriminate) on the basis of race, religion, (possibly) sex, or other *"suspect classification"*.

        b. Fundamental interest: Alternatively, strict scrutiny will be given to any classification which *affects a "fundamental interest"* (e.g., the right to travel interstate, the right to vote, etc.). However, since the right to housing has been held by the Supreme Court not to be a "fundamental interest" (see *Lindsey v. Normet, supra,* p. 176) a zoning ordinance will rarely merit strict scrutiny because of the fundamental interest doctrine; the sole exception is likely to be where the rights of individuals to make intimate *family* decisions are involved, such as in the *Moore* case (*supra,* p. 271).

    3. Significance of "strict scrutiny" standard: Where the existence of a suspect classification or fundamental interest does trigger a "strict scrutiny" standard, the zoning measure will be struck down unless the state meets the burden of showing that it has a *"compelling interest"* in meeting the objective in question, and that this objective cannot be satisfied by less objectionable means. No recent Supreme Court zoning cases have applied the strict scrutiny standard. See, however, the dissent by Justice Marshall in the *Belle Terre* case (*supra,* p. 272), arguing that the choice of household companions involves the fundamental rights both of association and privacy, and that the Belle Terre ordinance did not withstand the consequent strict equal protection scrutiny required.

Note on the "police power": When courts uphold a particular zoning action, they frequently do so by saying that the action is within the *"police power"* of the municipality. The term "police power" is a shorthand phrase which generally means that the goal being furthered by the municipality is a legitimate objective. The dimensions of the police power have been substantially expanded since the Supreme Court decided the *Euclid* case, *supra*, p. 268; *Euclid's* formulation of the police power was limited to measures substantially related to "public health, safety, morals, or general welfare." As is discussed further *infra*, below, most courts today regard the police power as extending to measures reasonably related to *aesthetic objectives*, "family values" (explicitly approved in the *Belle Terre* case), and perhaps even such values as "preserving [the] 'charm' of the New England small town" (see *Steel Hill Dev., Inc. v. Town of Sanbornton*, 469 F.2d 956 (1st Cir. 1972).)

In general, rather than speaking in terms of the "police power," it is probably more accurate to evaluate a zoning measure in terms of the individual constitutional requirements discussed above (procedural and substantive due process, and equal protection) and the one constitutional provision discussed below (the "takings" clause).

E. Burden of proof: Regardless of the grounds upon which a zoning regulation is attacked, the attacker has the *burden of proof*. The municipality's action is presumed to be valid until the challenger comes forward with evidence showing a violation of substantive due process, equal protection, the takings clause, etc. See, e.g., *Goldblatt v. Town of Hempstead*, 369 U.S. 590 (1962).

F. Aesthetic zoning: As the *Euclid* case made clear, the permissible objectives of zoning include protection of the "public health, safety, morals, [and] general welfare." This formulation left unanswered a question that became increasingly important following *Euclid*: may the zoning power be used for the purpose of pursuing *aesthetic* objectives?

1. **Traditional reluctance to allow:** During the early days of zoning (i.e., before 1930), the vast majority of courts refused to allow aesthetic considerations as a basis for zoning regulations. These decisions relied principally on the arguments that: (1) it is unfair to allow the majority to *impose its tastes* upon everyone; and (2) it is impossible to formulate standards that are *sufficiently precise* to avoid discrimination and corruption in enforcement.

2. **Allowable as one (but not sole) objective:** Since the 1930's, most courts have come to hold that aesthetic considerations may constitute *one factor* in the municipality's zoning decision, but that such considerations may not be the *sole factor*. This view, like the earlier complete prohibition on aesthetic considerations, seems founded upon fears of tyranny by the majority and discriminatory application. By requiring non-aesthetic factors (presumably more "objective") to be present, courts will be able to guard against these dangers.

   a. **Architectural review boards:** A number of municipalities have established *architectural review boards*, which have a right or approval over the plans for any proposed building. Such ordinances have generally been upheld.

3. **Allowed as sole objective:** Some states, though not most, now hold that aesthetic considerations may constitute the *sole criterion* for a particular zoning regulation. See, e.g., *People v. Stover*, 191 N.E.2d 272 (N.Y. 1963), upholding a prohibition upon the use of a clothesline in a front or side yard abutting the street!

4. **Exclusionary zoning:** Some recent cases have held that a municipality may not exclude all multi-family or low-income housing. An architectural review ordinance, and perhaps other kinds of aesthetically-based zoning, might run afoul of these cases if they have the effect of barring multi-family or low-income housing. See the discussion of exclusionary zoning beginning *infra*, p. 287.

IV. ZONING — ADMINISTRATION

A. **Zoning administration generally:** Zoning regulations are almost invariably promulgated at the local, municipal, level. The municipality's power to zone is delegated to it by the state, pursuant to a *zoning enabling statute*.

1. **Standard Enabling Act:** Nearly all states have passed a version of the Standard State Zoning Act (referred to henceforth as the Standard Act), which was promulgated in 1923 by the U.S. Department of Commerce.

   a. **Permissible goals:** §1 of the Standard Act provides that zoning may be used "for the purpose of promoting health, safety, morals, or the general welfare of the community. . . ." Since this is the same formula as used by the Supreme Court in *Euclid, supra*, p. 268, in delineating the constitutional bounds of the police power, courts have usually not needed to distinguish between the statutory limits upon a municipality's zoning power and the constitutional limits on that power.

B. **Bodies involved in zoning:** There are a number of different governmental entities involved in the zoning process.

1. **Local legislature:** The zoning code and amendments to it, are enacted by the *local legislature*. At the municipal level, this means the town council, Board of Supervisors, or other popularly elected body.

2. **Buildings department:** Day-to-day enforcement of the zoning scheme is usually handled by a local *administrative* agency, typically the buildings department. This department usually has inspectors who investigate complaints that zoning violations exist. It is also this department that generally issues permits for new construction, and which therefore determines in the first instance whether a proposed structure satisfies the zoning requirements.

3. **Board of adjustment:** A *board of adjustment* or *board of zoning appeals* is usually appointed. This board hears appeals from the denial of building permits, and from the building department's enforcement of zoning laws. However, its primary function is to award or deny *variances* (see *infra*, p. 278) and *special use exceptions* (*infra*, p. 280).

4. **Planning or zoning commission:** The local governing body will generally appoint a *planning commission or zoning commission*. This body is generally composed of local residents who have an interest in land use, including developers, contractors, architects, real estate brokers, etc. See Land Use Nutshell, pp. 62-63. The commission proposes to the local legislature a master plan (if there is to be one; see *infra*), as well as the test of the contemplated zoning ordinance and any amendments. The

commission's role is purely *advisory*; all enactments are made by the local legislature.

C. The master plan and its effect: In the early days of zoning, zoning ordinances were often adopted without a great deal of study, and without much thought about future development of the community. Increasingly, however, communities have adopted a so-called *"master plan"* or "comprehensive plan", which analyzes long-range population and employment prospects for the community, and contains general standards for present and future development. A master plan might, for instance, recommend that a particular undeveloped area on the outskirts of the community be presently zoned for agricultural purposes, with the expectation that in perhaps ten years the town will have developed sufficiently to make this area desirable for residential use.

   1. Who prepares: The plan is generally prepared by the planning commission and its technical staff. It becomes effective when it is adopted by the local legislature.

   2. Conflict between plan and ordinance: Particularly where a community has had a zoning scheme before it has adopted a master plan, the plan and the ordinance may come into conflict.

      a. Prior ordinance: Where the ordinance exists *prior* to the adoption of the master plan, most courts hold that the *master plan controls*. Therefore, the prior inconsistent ordinance must be conformed. See, e.g., *Baker v. City of Milwaukie*, 533 P.2d 772 (Or. 1975), holding that the master plan's efficacy depends on prior ordinances being conformed with it, and that a variance allowing a higher number of units per acre than allowed in the plan is invalid, even though the variance was valid under the pre-existing ordinance.

      b. Post-plan ordinance: Where a zoning ordinance is passed *after* a master plan has been enacted, courts similarly require that the ordinance be at least generally consistent with the plan.

      Example: The Ds (the Board of Commissioners of Washington County) approve an application by X for a change of the zoning of his 32-acre parcel so as to allow a mobile home park to be constructed. The Ps, neighboring homeowners, bring suit to overturn the decision. *Held*, for the Ps. Although the adoption of a broad zoning plan is a legislative decision that will not be overturned by a court unless it is arbitrary or discriminatory, the rezoning of a single parcel is really an administrative act, and the court must review it closely. Therefore, the burden was upon the one seeking change to demonstrate the need for it; in this case, it was X who sought a change in the zoning status of his property, not the Ps. To meet this burden, X was required to show that the proposed change was compatible with the master plan previously adopted by the county; there is no evidence that this burden was met. Therefore, the zoning change is invalid. *Fasano v. Board of County Commissioners of Washington Co.*, 507 P.2d 23 (Or. 1973).

         i. Plan not binding in all details: However a comprehensive plan is necessarily general in nature, and is designed so that it will remain applicable over a substantial period of time, even as conditions change. Accordingly, courts will generally not required that every zoning action taken after adoption of a master plan conform in every precise detail to the plan itself.

   3. Adoption of plan not required: As *Baker* and *Fasano* illustrate, once a master plan is adopted, the zoning ordinances must be in general conformity with the plan. But most states do not have a requirement that a master plan *in fact be adopted*. See American

Law Institute, Model Land Development Code (henceforth referred to as Model Code), Note 2 to §3-101.

   a. **"In accordance with comprehensive plan":** The Standard Act (*supra*, p. 275) which is in force in nearly all states, requires that zoning regulations be made *"in accordance with a comprehensive plan. . . ."* However, this requirement has generally *not* been construed to mean that a separate master plan must be adopted by a municipality. Instead, most courts have held that the **zoning scheme itself** may evidence sufficient uniformity to satisfy the "comprehensive plan" requirement, without the existence of a separate master plan.

   b. **Some states now require:** A few states (e.g., California, Florida, Oregon, Washington) now require municipalities to enact a comprehensive land development plan. See Model Code, Note 1 to §2-101. But the Model Code, although strongly supporting the idea of local comprehensive planning, rejects the imposition of a statutory requirement that such a plan be adopted. *Id.*

4. **Regional and state-wide planning:** Since the early days of zoning, the zoning power, including comprehensive planning of development, has been almost completely in the hands of local municipalities. Not surprisingly, neighboring towns have often failed to coordinate their strategies, so that one town may allow, say, a large industrial development which will adversely impact a residential area in an adjacent town. A few states have therefore attempted to reserve zoning and planning powers at the **state level**. These states include Hawaii, Oregon, and Florida. See B,C&S, pp. 1226-31. In these jurisdictions, the state is given the ability to **override** municipal land use decisions in certain circumstances, typically including large development proposals (for instance, the creation of a "new town," i.e., a large residential community to be created from scratch).

D. **Zoning amendments:** A zoning ordinance may be **amended** only by the body which enacted it, i.e., the local legislature. Depending on the circumstances, the amendment may be either of a large portion of the ordinance, or of a relatively small aspect (e.g., the zoning of a particular parcel).

   1. **Must not be arbitrary or discriminatory:** A zoning amendment, like an original ordinance, must not be **arbitrary** or **discriminatory** This requirement is at the base of the decision involving "spot zoning", discussed *infra*.

   2. **Must conform to plan:** If a master plan has been adopted, zoning amendments must be in conformity with that plan. See, e.g., the *Fasano* case, discussed *supra*, p. 276.

   3. **"Spot zoning" invalid:** Courts have always insisted that a zoning scheme be reasonably uniform, rather than arbitrary and discriminatory. This does not mean of course, that all parcels must be zoned for the same uses; it means that like parcels must be treated in the same way, and that the government must have a valid reason for zoning two similar parcels differently. When courts find that like parcels have been treated differently, they frequently strike down the offending portion of the ordinance as **"spot zoning"**. The issue of "spot zoning" generally arises in the context of an amendment to an existing plan, rather than in the original adoption of the plan.

      a. **Relation to "comprehensive plan" rule:** The "spot zoning" rule is thus really a restatement of the universal requirement (stemming from the Standard Act) that zoning be "in accordance with a comprehensive plan". Where a master plan has been adopted, the court may point to the fact that the zoning amendment deviates from the master plan as one of the reasons why the amendment constitutes "spot zoning". Even in the absence of a master plan, the fact that a particular amendment is not consistent with the rest of the overall ordinance will make it "spot zoning".

b. Tests for "spot zoning": There are three fairly specific factors which must usually be present before an amendment is struck down as "spot zoning":

i. Very different use: First, the use permitted by the rezoning must generally be *very different* from the prevailing uses in the surrounding area. Generally, this will mean a business or industrial use in the middle of a residential area. A less jarring juxtaposition (e.g., multi-family dwellings surrounded by single-family ones) will probably not be sufficient.

ii. Small area: Secondly, the area rezoned must generally be *rather small*. In many cases, it will be *one parcel*, and it will rarely be more than a few.

iii. Benefit of one or few owners: Thirdly, the rezoning will generally be considered "spot zoning" only if it is for the *benefit* of the sole or few owners whose property has been rezoned, rather than for the benefit of the community at large. See, e.g., *Board of Appeals of Hanover v. Housing Appeals Commission*, 294 N.E.2d 393 (Mass. 1973), defining "spot zoning" as "a singling out of one lot for different treatment from that accorded to similar surrounding land indistinguishable from it in character, all for the economic benefit of the owner of that lot."

E. Variances: If a zoning ordinance were inflexibly administered, so that no deviations were ever permitted, great hardship might result to a particular landowner. For instance, if an ordinance prevented the building of a residence on a lot having a street frontage of less than 100 feet, the owner of a irregularly shaped, 98-foot frontage parcel, would have to bear an extreme hardship. Virtually all zoning ordinances therefore have a provision for the granting of *variances*, i.e., relief in a particular case from the enforcement of an ordinance.

1. Standard Act's test: Most states, in their enabling acts, have used the test stated in the Standard Act: variances will be allowed where "owing to special conditions, a literal enforcement of the provisions of the ordinance will result in unnecessary hardship." However, the variance must be such that "the spirit of the ordinance shall be observed and substantial justice done."

2. Summary of requirements: Most states impose three specific requirements for the granting of a variance: (1) denial would result in *"unnecessary hardship"* to the owner; (2) the need for the variance is caused by a problem *unique to the owner's lot*, and not one shared generally by lots in the area; and (3) the variance would not be inconsistent with the *overall purpose* of the ordinance, and would not be inconsistent with the general welfare of the area.

3. "Unnecessary hardship": The landowner must show that literal enforcement of the ordinance would result in *"unnecessary hardship"* to him.

a. No conforming use: Courts vary in the degree of hardship which they require to be shown. Virtually all courts agree that the mere fact that the property would be *worth more* if the variance were allowed is *not* by itself sufficient to meet the "unnecessary hardship" standard.

i. Minority view: Some courts go even further, and hold that the owner must show that there is *no reasonable conforming use* which he can make of that property. See, e.g., *Puritan-Greenfield Improvement Ass'n v. Leo*, 153 N.W.2d 162 (Ct. App. Mich. 1967).

b. **Self-induced hardship:** The hardship may not be *"self-induced"* on the part of the property owner. This means, for instance, that the owner of a parcel may not divide it and sell parts of it in such a way that he is left with an irregularly-shaped parcel which cannot conform to the ordinance. Similarly, if the owner knows of the ordinance and *willfully builds in violation of it*, he will generally not be entitled to a variance if he is later caught, even though redoing the construction work might be extremely expensive and the damage to neighbors trivial. See 5 Williams §146.02.

   i. **Purchase with notice:** But the courts are split as to whether the acquisition of land, with *knowledge* of the zoning restrictions, prevents the purchaser from obtaining a variance because of the self-created hardship rule. Some courts, including those of New York and Pennsylvania, have held that knowledge of the restriction is fatal to the purchaser's claim of unnecessary hardship; see, e.g., *Application of Devereux Foundation, Inc.*, 41 A.2d 744 (Pa. 1945).

   ii. **Contrary view:** But other courts hold that knowledge by the purchaser of the zoning restriction is not by itself enough to defeat his claim of unnecessary hardship. By hypothesis, the original owner of the property could procure the variance himself (otherwise, the issue of whether knowledge by the purchaser was fatal would not arise). Therefore, these courts reason, it is illogical to require that original owner to invest the time and money to obtain a variance merely in order to sell his property.

   iii. **Premium price paid by purchaser:** In a state which does not hold that mere knowledge by the purchaser is fatal to his variance rights, may the purchaser *pay a premium price* for the land in hopes of getting a variance, and then claim that he will suffer extreme financial hardship if the variance is not granted? Most courts will probably not allow him to do so, since this is a relatively clear case of self-inflicted hardship. See, e.g., *Josephson v. Autrey*, 96 So.2d 784 (Fla. 1957).

c. **"Practical hardship":** The enabling statutes of some states differ from the Standard Act, in that they permit a variance not only where there is "unnecessary hardship," but also where there are *"practical difficulties"* (presumably a less rigorous showing than "unnecessary hardship"). Some other states having such statutes have held that a showing of "practical difficulties" will suffice only where an *area variance*, rather than a *use variance*, is sought. See, e.g, *Hoffman v. Harris*, 216 N.E.2d 326 (N.Y. 1966). The distinction between an area variance and a use variance is discussed further *infra*, p. 280.

4. **Unique to particular lot:** Most courts (and in fact most ordinances), permit a variance to be issued only where the hardship complained of is *unique* to the particular lot in question, or at most to a few nearby lots. If the hardship is one that is shared by many similarly-situated lots, the appropriate remedy is a *zoning amendment*, not a variance.

a. **Rationale:** Otherwise, the result will be that only one of numerous similarly-situated landowners will have procured relief, and the uniformity that is a *sine qua non* of every zoning ordinance will be destroyed.

5. **No harm to surrounding neighborhood:** The variance may not be issued if *harm would result* to the *surrounding neighborhood*. For instance, construction of a medical office building in a residential area might increase traffic and harm the residential appearance of the neighborhood; even if the landowner met the "unnecessary hardship" and "unique difficulty" tests, the variance would be denied for this reason.

6. **Distinction between use and area variance:** A number of courts have distinguished between *use* and *area* variances. A use variance is one which permits the property to be put to a use not permitted by the ordinance. An area variance, by contrast, merely relaxes a regulation governing the physical layout of the structure; thus relief might be given from a minimum frontage, minimum floor area, maximum height, or other requirement. Since a use variance is likely to have a greater impact upon the surrounding neighborhood, courts have often been stricter in reviewing such variances than area ones.

   a. **Outright prohibition:** Some other states, including California, Connecticut, North Carolina, Missouri and Texas, have *flatly prohibited use variances*. 5 Williams §132.02. This has been done both by statute and by case-law.

7. **Variances granted too freely:** The almost universal evidence is that zoning boards grant variances *too freely*, with sufficient concern for the statutory requirements. For this reason, courts have become increasingly strict in their scrutiny of variances; some have taken the view that if there is any real doubt about whether a variance was justified, it should not be given.

F. **The "special use" or "special exception":** Most zoning ordinances provide for the issuance of so-called *"special use"* permits, or, as they are sometimes called, *"special exceptions"*. (Here, we use the more descriptive of the two phrases "special use".)

   1. **Nature and purpose:** There are certain uses which are, in the abstract, beneficial to the community. Yet, because they typically serve fairly large numbers of people, and create traffic congestion and other problems, it is not desirable to make these uses available *as of right* in any particular zone. On the other hand, it is not desirable to exclude them entirely. The "special use" concept is an attempt to solve this dilemma; the zoning ordinance provides that a specified use is permissible in some (or all) zones, but *only upon the express approval* of the board of adjustment (or other entity).

      a. **Approval of particular use:** The board of adjustment thus has the opportunity to make sure that the special use is located where it will not cause hardship to surrounding property owners. For instance, the board will often insist that the use be placed so that there is easy access to a major street, thus avoiding traffic tie-ups in otherwise quiet residential neighborhoods.

   2. **Typical uses:** As noted, the special uses are invariably expressly enumerated in the zoning ordinances. Typically, the listed uses include *private schools, clubs, hospitals and churches*, all uses which serve a considerable number of people. Occasionally, certain types of businesses open to the public at large (e.g., gasoline stations) are also included.

   3. **Who makes decisions:** The zoning ordinance, as noted, usually grants the power of deciding on a special use application to the local board of zoning adjustment (or board of zoning appeals, as the board is sometimes called). However, in some states the *local legislature* reserves the power to *itself* to pass on such applications. Finally, in a very few instances, the planning commission is the body which passes upon the application.

4. Distinguished from variance: Some courts have muddled the distinction between a special use permit and a variance. However, the two are fundamentally different. The variance is generally available only in cases of "unnecessary hardship" (see *supra*, p. 278), and is not usually for a use that will serve large numbers of people. The special use, by contrast, is available only for use types specifically listed in the ordinance, which are chosen because of their public benefit function; no showing of hardship on the part of the owner is required.

5. Standards for granting permits: Most litigation on special use permits has centered upon whether the **standards** set forth in the ordinance to guide the administrative agency are **sufficiently definite**. Insufficiently precise standards pose the danger of arbitrary action and favoritism.

    a. No standards: If the ordinance simply says that the administrative agency may issue special permits "as it sees fit" or "within its discretion", with no standards at all, the ordinance will be struck down as an improper delegation of legislative power to an administrative agency. 5 Williams §150.02.

    b. General welfare: Many ordinances merely state that the special use may be granted only where it is in accordance with the **"general welfare"** of the community, or some similarly vague standard. Although a standard this imprecise makes it very difficult for an owner who has been denied a special use permit to challenge the decision judicially, such standards have generally (but not always) been upheld. See 5 Williams §150.05.

G. Two modern discretionary techniques: In traditional Euclidean zoning, control of building **density** is implemented on a lot-by-lot basis. For instance, a Euclidean ordinance may provide that a district shall be used solely for single-family residence purposes, that each lot shall be at least one-fourth of an acre, and that front and side yards shall be of a certain minimum area. Such a scheme has the desired result of preventing overbuilding, and a consequent strain on schools, sewers and other public facilities. However, it often makes for boring architecture and land use, with each house and each block looking almost the same.

1. Solutions: Therefore, community planners have devised a number of modern techniques which help prevent this boring sameness, while maintaining the same overall proportion of unbuilt space as in a comparable straight Euclidean scheme. These devices may also have the virtues of: (1) concentrating dwellings within a narrower area, so that public transportation can be more efficient; (2) making better use of areas not suited for construction of dwellings because of topographical features (e.g., a large rock outcropping which would be better used for recreational space than expensively dynamited away to build a house); and (3) lowering construction costs because streets, sewers, etc. can be concentrated within a narrower area. The two principal devices used today to produce these results are: (1) **cluster zoning**; and (2) **Planned Unit Developments (PUD's)**.

2. Cluster zoning: Under the **"cluster zoning"** concept, the size and width of individual residential lots in a development may be reduced, **provided that the overall density of the whole tract remains constant.** In effect, an area equal to the total of the areas 'saved' from each individual lot is pooled and used as common open spaces (e.g., a private park or swimming complex). 2 Williams §47.01. Cluster zoning may be accomplished not only by building single-family houses on smaller detached lots, but also by building garden apartments or "town houses".

a. **No major legal issues:** Cluster zoning ordinances do not raise any major legal or constitutional issues. Therefore, as long as the ordinance is clearly drawn and does not discriminate against certain owners in an unfair way, it should withstand legal challenge.

3. **Planned Unit Development (PUD's):** A newer and broader device serving similar aims is the ***Planned Unit Development (PUD)***. Whereas cluster zoning ordinances generally allow only residential use, in a PUD, commercial (and occasionally industrial) facilities will frequently be allowed to be intermingled with residential uses.

   a. **How it works:** The idea behind the PUD is that the developer submits a proposal for a development containing both residential (probably a mixture of single-family and multi-family) and commercial uses, designed in such a way that the overall population and building density is no higher than under a comparable single-use district.

      i. **Advantages:** As with cluster zoning, one advantage is that more usable common open space is preserved without increasing population density. Another advantage, not shared by cluster zoning, is that ***stores and other supporting commercial uses*** can be planned so as to be ***convenient to the residences***. The PUD is thus often a small community in its own right, complete with commercial areas, schools, recreational facilities, etc.

   b. **Legal challenge:** Most states that have considered the question have ***upheld*** the legality of the PUD concept. See, e.g., *Cheney v. Village 2 at New Hope, Inc.*, 241 A.2d 81 (Pa. 1968).

   c. **Procedural rules:** Most PUD ordinances set forth fairly strict procedural requirements which must be met by a developer. In one case, the ordinance required that a developer submit ***detailed sketches*** of the buildings which he proposed to put in his PUD. The court held that once the planning commission and the city council approved the sketches and the PUD, the sketches became ***binding*** on the developer. Since the buildings as built deviated substantially from these sketches, neighboring property owners were held to be entitled to removal of the structures or to money damages compensating them for the decline in their property values. *Frankland v. City of Lake Oswego*, 517 P.2d 1042 (Or. 1973).

H. **Other discretionary techniques:** Two other modern techniques, while not directed at the problem of maintaining density controls without monotony or unnecessary expense, are based upon the same desire for flexibility as the cluster zoning and PUD concepts.

   1. **Floating zones:** A *"floating zone"* is a zone which is established by zoning ordinance, with specified uses, but which is ***not mapped in any particular location*** at the time the ordinance is passed. Instead, the scheme contemplates that a developer will later apply to have the floating zone made applicable to his land. The zone is thus said to "float" over the entire land in the community, until it is subsequently ***"anchored"*** on a particular site.

      a. **Advantage:** The key advantage of the floating zone technique is, of course, ***flexibility***. The town can agree that a certain type of use (i.e., a light industrial park) is in theory desirable, and can postpone the question of exactly where this use should be permitted until a particular proposal is put forward. The danger of permitting the use as of right over a large area (which might lead to too many such uses, e.g., too many industrial parks) is avoided.

b. Criticism of floating zones: Floating zones are criticized for the same reasons as are PUDs. Since the initiative is left with the developer (usually without very precise standards as to when an application should be granted), there is great opportunity for arbitrariness and *"backroom" deals.*

2. Conditional or "contract" zoning: Another device used to preserve flexibility is often called *"conditional"* zoning (if it is upheld) or sometimes *"contract"* zoning (usually when it is struck down). By this device, the rezoning of a particular parcel is made *subject to the developer's promise to comply with certain conditions,* which will presumably better protect neighbors. For instance, a parcel in a residential area might be rezoned for light industry, but only if the developer agreed to large set-backs and a low floor-space-to-land-area ratio.

    a. Some courts allow: About half of the present-day courts apparently *allow* some form of conditional zoning. 1 Williams §29.01. These courts have generally looked to whether the conditions imposed are for the benefit of nearby property owners; if so, the scheme is valid, even though it represents a private "deal" applicable to one parcel only.

    Example: Landowner, the owner of Blackacre, applies for a rezoning that would allow Blackacre to be used for business. D, the village where Blackacre is located, grants the application subject to a number of conditions. One of the conditions is that no structure presently on the land may be altered without the consent of D. (The conditions do not prevent D from withholding its consent unreasonably.) Landowner sells Blackacre to P. P then applies to D for approval to enlarge and extend the building currently located on Blackacre. D denies the application without giving any reasons. P sues to compel D to either approve his application or give a rational reason for denying it. P claims that the conditional rezoning was illegal, and that the conditions should therefore be reinterpreted to bar D from unreasonably refusing to consent.

    Held, for D. The New York courts will permit conditional zoning, provided that it is reasonable. Therefore, the court will construe, exactly as written, the conditions agreed to between D and Landowner. *Collard v. Incorporated Village of Flower Hill,* 421 N.E.2d 818 (N.Y. 1981).

    c. "Contract" and "conditional" zoning distinguished: Many courts distinguish between "contract" zoning and "conditional" zoning; according to these courts, only the latter is permissible. See, e.g., *Cross v. Hall County,* 235 S.E.2d 379 (Ga. 1977). The phrase "contract zoning" is now used mainly to refer to an arrangement whereby the municipality enters into a *binding commitment* with the landowner. Such binding commitments will usually be *struck down* by the courts. (However, even a conditional zoning arrangement that purports to reserve to the municipality the right to change its mind may amount to a binding commitment, because it may be held to give the owner vested rights if he makes changes in reliance.)

I. Official map statutes: A community with a large segment of undeveloped land may contemplate that some day the land will be developed for residential or commercial purposes. When that development occurs, streets and parks will, of course, be necessary. Yet, if early construction is carried out by individual landowners, without any government supervision, it is likely to turn out to be very difficult to place the parks and build the streets after the fact; the municipality may have to use very costly eminent domain procedures to gain the necessary land. Subdivision controls (discussed *infra,* p. 298) are one attempt to combat this difficulty. *Official map statutes* are another.

1. **How the statute works:** Such official map statutes are generally part of the state enabling act. The enabling act provides that a municipality may *adopt an official map*, which shows not only present, but *planned* streets (and sometimes parks). The effect of the adoption on an official map by a municipality is that, *even though the land shown on the map as reserved for future streets or parks remains private*, private construction on this land is *prohibited*.

   a. **Effect of construction:** If the landowner goes ahead and builds on property (owned by him) reserved for future street use, the municipality is relieved from having to pay the value of the improvement when it finally takes the street under its eminent domain powers. Thus the municipality is assured of only having to pay the value of unimproved land when it ultimately uses its eminent domain proceeding; also it is not put to the expense of acquiring the property now (perhaps many years before it will wish to build the street or park).

2. **Hardship owner:** Obviously, this sort of prohibition may cause extreme hardship to a particular landowner. The owner of a relatively small parcel might, for instance, find that the official map shows a proposed road running right through his property; if he can't build anything useful on the land without going onto the reserved area, his ability to use the property may be delayed indefinitely. Therefore, virtually all official map statutes provide that the municipality must grant such *exceptions* as are necessary to permit a reasonable return on the property. Thus a landowner might be permitted to build a small house but not a 40-story office building, so that the ultimate costs of acquiring the property through eminent domain will be held to the minimum compatible with a reasonable return for the owner. See, e.g., *State ex rel. Miller v. Manders*, 86 N.W.2d 469 (Wisc. 1957), interpreting the state enabling statute to contain such an exception procedure for hardship cases, and holding the statute constitutional on that ground.

J. **Non-conforming uses:** When a zoning scheme is adopted for the first time, or when an existing zone is changed to a stricter use, there are likely to be existing uses that are not in conformity with the new rules. These are called *non-conforming uses*.

   1. **Constitutional issue:** An ordinance could theoretically be drafted in such a way as to outlaw all non-conforming uses immediately upon the enactment of the ordinance. However, such an ordinance would almost certainly be invalid as an unconstitutional violation of due process. Therefore, virtually all ordinances either (1) grant a non-conforming user a *substantial period within which he may continue his use* (see discussion of the amortization technique *infra*, p. 286); or else (2) let him continue that use indefinitely.

      a. **Significant problem:** When the first zoning ordinances were enacted, it was thought that non-conforming uses would fade from the scene rather quickly. However, this has not turned out to be the case. Particularly where the non-conforming use is a commercial one in what has now been zoned as a residential area, the use will probably have a *monopoly* on that kind of business in the neighborhood, and this will tend to increase the value and prolong the existence of the use. (Thus one who had a neighborhood grocery store in what is now a residential-only zone might well have an incentive to continue that use indefinitely.) For this reason, there is a substantial body of litigation concerning exactly what constitutes a non-conforming use, and what terminates that use.

   2. **Degree of use necessary:** The relevant date for determining the existence of a non-conforming use is the *effective date of the ordinance*. By this date, the use must be a

reasonably substantial one. Mere *preparation* for the use is generally *not* enough. Thus suppose one wished to run a commercial laundry in a residential area; the mere fact that one had quit one's job and borrowed money from a bank in order to set up a laundry on a particular site would not be sufficient; actual operation of the laundry would have to be commenced prior to enactment of the ordinance.

    a. Construction of building: Where the use involves the construction of a special building, however, certain kinds of preparation may be enough. For instance, if one actually *began construction* of a building specially designed as a laundry, a rezoning becoming effective after the building was half-completed might not stop the project. In part, this would depend on the developer's state of mind; if he knew that the rezoning was likely, and rushed to get his building started before the ordinance could be passed, the court is not likely to by sympathetic to him. By contrast, if he began the building with no reason to expect a rezoning, and local opposition induced the city council to pass the ordinance when the building was half-completed, this would probably be enough to establish a non-conforming use. See 4 Williams §111.02 (and 1985 Supplement thereto).

3. Change of use: A non-conforming user may wish to *change* the particular use to a different, but also non-conforming, one. Most courts have not allowed him to make a significant change in the non-conforming use. Thus in most jurisdictions a non-confirming laundry could not be changed to a non-conforming grocery store. (But a few states have permitted a change in the use where it constituted an *"upgrading"*, i.e., where the new use was more desirable than the old.) See generally 4 Williams §112.01-112.10 (and 1985 Supplement thereto).

    a. Change of ownership: But a *change of ownership* is not considered a change in use. The non-conforming use thus had the opportunity to *transfer his interest at will*. *Id.*, §112.13 This factor has contributed greatly to the tendency of non-conforming uses to continue for long periods of time.

4. Expansion of use: A similar issue is present where the non-conforming user wishes to *expand* his present operation, without changing to a different use.

    a. Change of building or lot size: Where he sought to do this by *enlarging his building or lot size*, the courts have generally *not* allowed him to do so. *Id.*, at §113.03 (and 1985 Supplement thereto).

    b. Increase in volume: But if the expansion takes the form only of an *increased volume of activity* without an enlargement of the physical facilities, it will generally be allowed. Thus an expansion, even a dramatic one, in the number of customers patronizing a beauty parlor would not prevent the beauty parlor from continuing to be a valid non-confirming use. *Id.*, at §113.06 (and 1985 Supplement thereto).

5. Termination of use: If the use ceases to exist for some reason, may it be *resumed*? The issue arises in two principal situations: destruction and abandonment.

    a. Destruction: If a building which houses a non-conforming use is *destroyed* by fire, flood or other outside force, many ordinances do *not* permit it to be *reconstructed*. Most modern decisions have held that such a ban on reconstruction is constitutionally permissible. *Id.* at §114.03. The theory behind most of these decisions is that construction of new building is a new use, rather than a continuation of the old, and is therefore an unreasonable prolongation of the non-conforming use.

b. **Abandonment:** If the use is *abandoned*, it may not then be recommenced. However, the mere cessation of the use, even for a substantial period of time, will not necessarily constitute abandonment. As with easements (*supra*, p. 222), abandonment will generally be deemed to occur only where there is both an *overt act* of cessation plus an *intent* to abandon. *Id.*, at §115.03. Thus if the owner can show that he had no intent permanently to cease the use, he will probably not be held to have lost the right to recommence.

6. **Amortization:** As noted, non-conforming uses have not tended to disappear by themselves. Many municipalities have responded to this problem by so-called *amortization* provisions, by which the non-conforming use may continue *only for a certain length of time* following enactment of the zoning restriction. The theory behind such provisions is that the owner will have had time to recover (i.e., amortize) his investment, and to make plans to continue the use somewhere else if he wishes.

a. **Generally upheld:** Early cases generally disallowed the amortization technique on constitutional due process grounds. But since about 1960, the substantial majority of cases that have considered the issue have *upheld* such provisions, provided that the amortization period is indeed sufficiently long for the owner to recover his costs and to arrange an alternative location.

Example: D runs a wholesale/retail plumbing supply business in a residential building, and uses the outdoor portion of the lot for storage. An ordinance requires these uses to be terminated within *five years*. *Held*, the ordinance is valid. There is no distinction between requiring discontinuance of a non-conforming use within a reasonable period, and prohibiting the enlargement of a non-conforming building, or the resumption of a non-conforming use after a period of non-use, both of which are clearly valid exercises of the police power. Nor is there a taking of D's property without compensation, since he has been given a reasonable time (in this case, actually eight years between enactment of the ordinance and bringing of this suit) in which to recover his investment and move his business. The moving costs would be less than one-half of one percent of D's gross sales for the five-year period, and the property is usable for residential purposes. *City of Los Angeles v. Gage*, 274 P.2d 34 (Dist. Ct. App. Cal. 1954).

b. **Minority view:** But a minority of states (including Pennsylvania, Missouri, Arkansas, Idaho, Indiana, Ohio and Delaware) hold that amortization amounts to an *improper taking of private property*. Often, these minority states have concluded that the federal or state *Constitution* prohibits the amortization technique, because it amounts to a taking without due process of law.

Example: The Moon Township zoning ordinance provides that any pre-existing use which would be a violation of a newly-enacted zoning restriction has 90 days from enactment of the restriction to come into compliance. This amortization rule would force P, the owner of an adult bookstore, to close the bookstore and relocate it to a small area elsewhere in the town which allows adult bookstores. P asserts that this constitutes a taking of his property without compensation.

Held, for P. The Pennsylvania Constitution guarantees the "inherent and indefeasible" right of its citizens to possess and protect property, and to be paid compensation if their private property is taken. Any amortization and discontinuance of a lawful pre-existing non-conforming use is *per se* confiscatory and violative of the Pennsylvania Constitution. Also, if municipalities were free to amortize non-conforming uses out of existence, future economic development would be seriously compromised, because the possibility that the municipality could enact zoning changes to force a cessation of business might deter investors. (A concurrence argues that a reasonably long amortization period should be found valid, but agrees that 90 days is in any case much too short to be reasonable.) *P.A. Northwestern Distributors, Inc. v. Zoning Hearing Board*, 584 A.2d 1372 (Pa. 1991).

V. EXCLUSIONARY ZONING

A. Meaning of "exclusionary" zoning: Euclidean zoning, when it first began to be practiced, was in theory designed principally to separate the various potential land uses within a particular community, so that industry would not interfere with residential use, etc. It soon became apparent, however, that zoning could furnish a means of keeping certain groups and uses *completely out of the community*. The use of zoning laws to exclude certain types of persons and uses, particularly *racial and ethnic minorities*, and *low-income persons*, is now generally referred to as *"exclusionary zoning"*. Another term sometimes used is *"snob zoning"*.

1. **Examples of exclusion:** A town could theoretically enact an ordinance completely barring, say, all blacks from residing within the town. Such an ordinance, however, would be instantly struck down as unconstitutional. Therefore, exclusionary zoning techniques are generally much more subtle and indirect. Most exclusion takes the form of restrictions on the *types of allowable residential uses*, so that those uses likely to be of interest to racial minorities or low-income groups are either not permitted at all or severely circumscribed.

   a. **Minimum acre single-family zoning:** For instance, a municipality could reserve all of its residential land for single-family detached homes on one-half acre minimum lots. Since this would render impossible the construction of conventional apartments, garden apartments, town houses or even inexpensive small single-family houses, virtually no low-income families, and probably relatively few Blacks or Hispanics, would be able to move into the town.

   b. **Other devices:** Other devices which might be used to exclude racial and ethnic minorities and the poor, include:

      i. A *ban on multiple dwellings*;

      ii. If apartment buildings are allowed, a *minimum floor area* for each living unit;

      iii. A prohibition on *publicly-subsidized housing*;

      iv. If apartments are allowed, a *maximum on the number of bedrooms allowed* per living unit (to prevent large families from burdening the school system); and

      v. A ban on *mobile homes*.

2. **Federal versus state case law:** Substantial litigation on exclusionary zoning has taken place in both the federal and state court systems. For a number of reasons which are discussed below, federal courts have been relatively reluctant to strike down zoning schemes that have an exclusionary purpose, or effect, or both. State-court decisions, by

contrast, which are frequently reached on the basis of the interpretation of the state constitution rather than the federal one, have been much quicker to limit municipalities' right to exclude particular racial, ethnic and economic groups. Because the federal and state patterns have diverged so sharply, each is considered separately.

B. Federal case-law: Where a zoning scheme is attacked in *federal court* as being exclusionary, the attack may be based upon either constitutional or statutory principles.

   1. **Constitutional argument:** A constitutional attack on a zoning scheme alleged to be exclusionary would probably have to be based upon the *equal protection clause* of the Fourteenth Amendment. (See *supra*, p. 273, for a brief discussion of this clause.) Recall that where government action discriminates either on the basis of a "suspect classification" or with respect to a "fundamental interest", the action is subjected to "strict judicial scrutiny", and the state must show a *compelling interest* in the scheme. By contrast, where neither a suspect classification nor a fundamental interest is involved, the government action will violate the equal protection clause only if it bears *no rational relation* to a permissible state objective.

      a. **Suspect classification:** In the zoning context, virtually any scheme has a rational relation to the permissible state objective of protection the "general welfare". Therefore, as a practical matter, unless the plaintiff can invoke strict scrutiny by showing either that the zoning action involves a suspect classification, or that it affects a fundamental interest, the constitutional attack is almost certain to fail. To make matters even more difficult for a federal plaintiff, the Supreme Court has held that the right to housing is not a "fundamental interest". (See *Lindsay v. Normet*, discussed *supra*, p. 176.) Consequently, an equal protection attack in the zoning area will generally be based upon a theory that a *"suspect classification"* is at issue.

   2. **"Effect" versus "purpose":** The best chance for showing that an ordinance is based upon a suspect classification is to demonstrate that it has *racial* implications. Originally, it was not clear whether a racially discriminatory *effect* was all that had to be shown, or whether a racially discriminatory *purpose* on the part of the government had to be demonstrated. Then, in *Village of Arlington Heights v. Metropolitan Housing Development Corp.*, 429 U.S. 252 (1977), the U.S. Supreme Court explicitly held that a racially discriminatory *purpose*, not merely effect, needed to be shown before an ordinance would be subject to strict equal protection scrutiny.

      a. **Facts of *Arlington Heights*:** In *Arlington Heights*, a non-profit corporation, MHDC, tried to build a federally subsidized low-income housing project in an affluent nearly-all-white Chicago suburb. The town refused to rezone the site of the proposed project from single-family residential to multi-family, largely on the grounds that property values near the project would drop sharply. The Seventh Circuit Court of Appeals held that this refusal had a discriminatory impact, and that this impact was enough to require a showing of compelling state interest (which the court found to be absent). The court relied on the fact that the refusal would have a disproportionate impact on blacks, since blacks constituted 40% of the Chicago-area low-income residents who would be eligible to become tenants of the project (although they constituted a much lower percentage of the overall Chicago-area population). The court also relied on the fact that Arlington Heights, despite its rapidly growing population, had remained almost all white.

      b. **Supreme Court holding:** The Supreme Court reversed, holding that a showing of discriminatory *purpose* on the part of the town in rejecting the zoning change was *required* before the strict scrutiny/compelling state interest test could be triggered. A discriminatory *impact*, *no matter how substantial*, could *not* by itself be enough.

c. Not necessarily sole purpose: The Court did not require that a discriminatory purpose be the *sole* purpose of the town action, merely that it be *one* motivating factor.

d. Ways to prove: The Court suggested several ways in which the plaintiff might prove that a racially discriminatory intent was a factor in the decision:

    i. Historical background: The *historical background* of the decision might shed light. For instance, if municipal officials had behaved with a discriminatory purpose on prior occasions, this would at least suggest that a similar purpose was at work in the present case.

    ii. Nature of present case: The specific sequence of events leading up to the challenged decision might also give evidence of discriminatory purpose. For instance, if the land in question in *Arlington Heights* had been previously zoned for multi-family use, and the town had changed its classification when it found out that a low-income project was contemplated, this would have been strong evidence of discriminatory purpose.

    iii. Administrative history: Minutes of the town council meeting, reports by the city planning commission, or other *documents* of administrative or legislative history, may provide evidence. Occasionally, a *member* of the legislative or administrative body might be called on to testify as to his and others' motives.

    iv. Discriminatory effect: Even the discriminatory *effect* itself, though not dispositive, may be considered as *evidence* of a possible discriminatory purpose, particularly if there were no other rational explanation of the decision.

e. Evidence of "same result": The Court also indicated that if the plaintiff were able to show a discriminatory purpose, the municipality could defend by showing that "the same decision would have resulted even had the impermissible purpose not been considered." Presumably some objective proof in support of such a defense would be required, e.g., a showing that in similar situations in the past, the municipality had indeed reached the same result without racial considerations.

3. Economic discrimination: Where the zoning scheme has a discriminatory effect of intent with respect to the *poor*, a successful equal protection attack is even more difficult. Even if the plaintiff can show that the *intent* (not just the effect) is to discriminate against the poor, strict scrutiny will probably not be triggered; the Supreme Court has shown no sign that it is willing to treat wealth classifications as inherently suspect. See 91 Harv. L. Rev. 1678. Where a discriminatory effect is all that is shown, the plaintiff virtually never prevails.

4. Impact on family: If the challenged ordinance has a sharp impact upon the *family*, an equal protection attack, or a due process one, may have a reasonable chance of success. The Supreme Court has repeatedly held that the right to make decisions in the raising of one's family is a fundamental right, and that government action infringing upon that right must be subjected to strict scrutiny both from an equal protection and due process standpoint. See, e.g., *Moore v. City of East Cleveland*, discussed *supra*, p. 271, where the Court held that an ordinance restricting the rights of certain relatives to live together was a violation of due process. (But cf. *Village of Belle Terre v. Boraas*, discussed *supra*, pp. 272-73, holding that this right did not extend to unrelated persons desiring to share a household.)

5. **Effect on mentally retarded:** If a zoning ordinance affects the *mentally retarded*, a successful equal protection attack is difficult, because mental retardation has been held not to be a suspect, or even quasi-suspect, classification. *City of Cleburne, Texas v. Cleburne Living Center*, 473 U.S. 432 (1985).

  a. **Successful suit:** However, even though zoning ordinances directly affecting the mentally retarded are judged under the very forgiving rational-relation standard, an attack on such an ordinance can nonetheless be occasionally sustained. In *City of Cleburne, supra*, for instance, a city ordinance required that any group home for the mentally retarded obtain a special use permit, and the city declined to issue the permit to the plaintiffs. The Supreme Court, although it left the ordinance on the books, invalidated it as it applied to the group home. The Court concluded that "requiring the permit . . . appears to rest on an irrational prejudice against the mentally retarded," since no special use permit was required for similar uses (e.g., nursing homes, apartment houses, etc.). (See the discussion of special uses, *supra*, p. 280. See also Emanuel on *Constitutional Law* for a more extensive discussion of *Cleburne*.)

6. **Referenda and initiatives:** There has been a recent tendency to subject many land-use decisions to popular vote, through the use of *initiatives* and *referenda*. (In an initiative, the electorate votes on an issue upon which the legislature has not yet passed; in a referendum, the electorate approves or disapproves of the decision already made by the legislature.) The extent to which initiatives and referenda may be used to pass exclusionary legislation is at present unclear.

  a. **Invalid delegation argument fails:** There are at least some sorts of land use decisions which may constitutionally be submitted to the electorate, as the result of *City of Eastlake v. Forest City Enterprises, Inc.*, 426 U.S. 668 (1976). In *Eastlake*, voters passed an initiative amending the city charter to require that all planned use changes approved by the City Council must further be approved by a 55% referendum vote. The plaintiff, a developer, received from the City Council a rezoning of its land for multi-family high-rise purposes, but was unable to build because it did not procure the requisite referendum approval. The plaintiff claimed that the mandatory referendum requirement was an unconstitutional delegation of legislative power to the people, violative of the plaintiff's due process rights.

    i. **Supreme Court holding:** The Supreme Court *rejected* the delegation of powers argument. That argument was based on the idea that delegation by the legislature must be accompanied by *clear standards*, so that the resulting actions can be judicially reviewed. Here, however, the legislative power was not delegated to an administrative body or a narrow segment of the community, but instead was *reserved* by the electorate as a whole. Therefore, the requirement of discernible standards did not apply.

  b. **Conscious bias:** The fact that a zoning decision is made by the electorate, rather than by a legislature or agency, does not insulate it from substantive due process or equal protection attack. For instance, if the purpose of the referendum in *Eastlake* had been, say, to establish a zone in which only white families could reside, it would clearly be a violation of both due process and equal protection. See, e.g.,

James v. Valtierra, 402 U.S. 137 (1971), upholding a referendum requirement for public housing projects, but only because it was not enacted principally for the purpose of discriminating against the poor.

7. **Standing:** The Supreme Court has placed an additional, huge, stumbling block in the path of those who would challenge exclusionary zoning on constitutional grounds: the federal-court **standing** requirements.

   a. **Warth case:** In *Warth v. Seldin*, 422 U.S. 490 (1975), a number of plaintiffs claimed that the zoning policies of the town of Penfield, New York, were exclusionary; the suit was a broad-based attack on the zoning policies in general, not a litigation over whether a particular site should be zoned for, say, multi-family use. The Court held that each of the classes of plaintiffs lacked standing.

      i. **Standing denied:** Most importantly, the Court denied standing to minority group members who were not residents of Penfield (but who lived instead in nearby Rochester, of which Penfield is a suburb); the Court held that a non-resident plaintiff must allege "specific, concrete facts demonstrating that the challenged practices harm *him*", and must also demonstrate how the remedial action sought in the complaint will redress this harm. Since the non-resident plaintiffs merely made the general argument that if Penfield's zoning were less exclusionary, they might be able to live in the town, they failed to meet these tests.

      ii. **Other classes denied:** Similarly, a group of Rochester's taxpayers (who argued that they bore increased taxes because Penfield's failure to zone for low-income housing caused Rochester to build more of it), and a civil rights group representing various Rochester residents, were also held to lack standing.

   b. **Result of Warth:** The net result of *Warth* is that standing in federal cases will be present only where **site-specific relief** is sought, i.e., where the rezoning of a **particular parcel** for, say, low-income use is at issue. Furthermore, even in a site-specific case, there are probably only two classes of persons who have standing: (1) an individual who can show that his low income and proximity to the proposed housing are such that he has a **substantial probability of becoming a resident** of that housing; and (2) the developer seeking to build the housing. (Indeed, these two classes of persons were explicitly found to have standing in *Village of Arlington Heights v. Metropolitan Housing Development Corp.*, 429 U.S. 252 (1977), discussed more extensively *supra*, p. 288.) Civil rights groups, residents of nearby towns claiming that they have been forced to bear more than their "fair share" of low-income or integrated housing, and even residents of the defendant town who claim that they are being deprived of the ability to have an integrated community, probably lack federal court standing under *Warth*.

   c. **Standing to assert rights of third parties:** Still another obstacle to federal court standing in zoning cases is that a plaintiff may generally assert **only his own rights**, not the rights of **third parties** who are injured by the zoning action under attack. This limitation is likely to prove particularly crucial in suits brought by **developers**.

      i. **Petaluma case:** For instance, in *Construction Industry Ass'n of Sonoma County v. City of Petaluma*, 522 F.2d 897 (9th Cir. 1975), the plaintiff was an association of builders, which attacked Petaluma's municipal ordinance limiting construction of new housing. The Association itself had standing, since it could show that its members suffered direct economic hardship from the growth limits. The builders were thus able to attack the ordinance on substantive due process grounds (unsuccessfully, as it turned out; see *infra*, p. 294). But they were *not* entitled to make a constitutional *"right to travel"* argument on behalf of residents of nearby towns who were unable to move to Petaluma because of the construction controls; the court stressed that only if the plaintiff and the third party had a close, on-going relationship, could the former assert the rights of the latter. Here, there was merely the prospect of a future purchase-sale contract between the builders and these non-residents.

8. **Federal statutory (Fair Housing Act) suits:** Because of the Supreme Court's hostility to constitutionally-based attacks on exclusionary zoning, most federal court plaintiffs have relied on federal *statutory* law in support of their anti-exclusionary zoning battles. In particular, plaintiffs have invoked the *Fair Housing* Title of the Civil Rights Act of 1968, 42 U.S.C. §§3601-3619 (also discussed *supra*, p. 194).

   a. **Operative language:** Plaintiffs have generally relied on a provision of the Fair Housing Act which makes it unlawful to "make unavailable or deny, a dwelling to any person because of race, color, religion, sex or national origin." 42 U.S.C. §3604(a). Nearly all federal courts which have considered the matter concede at least that zoning enacted for the purpose of limiting access by racial or ethnic minorities would violate §3604(a).

      i. **Discrimination against the handicapped:** Congress amended the Fair Housing Act in 1988 to prohibit discrimination against the *handicapped*. So zoning restrictions enacted for the purpose of limiting access by, say, developmentally delayed or physically disabled persons would violate the Act.

   b. **Standing:** Standing requirements in Fair Housing Act suits have been much more liberally interpreted than in suits, such as *Warth*, brought on constitutional grounds. In *Trafficante v. Metropolitan Life Insurance Co.*, 409 U.S. 205 (1972), the Supreme Court found a "congressional intention [in the Fair Housing Act] to define standing as broadly as is permitted by Article III of the Constitution." Therefore, a non-resident who alleges that racially motivated exclusionary zoning by the defendant municipality prevents him from living there will probably not have to show that a change in the zoning would produce suitable housing for him. Also, assertion of the rights of *third parties* may be allowed; a developer might, for instance, be permitted to argue that the Fair Housing Act rights of black non-residents not participating in the suit have been violated. See 91 Harv. L. Rev. 1686, n. 286.

   c. **Discriminatory effect versus purpose:** Recall that a discriminatory *purpose*, not just effect, is required for a *constitutional* attack on exclusionary zoning under the Supreme Court's *Arlington Heights* decision. (See *supra*, p. 288.) But the Supreme Court has never decided whether a discriminatory purpose must also be shown for a Fair Housing Act violation. Most lower federal courts, however, have held that the plaintiff in a Fair Housing Act suit need *not* show that the defendant had a discriminatory intent. See, e.g., *Huntington Branch NAACP v. Town of Huntington*, 844 F.2d 926 (2d Cir. 1988).

      i. *Prima facie* case: Instead, most federal courts hold that the plaintiff merely has to prove that the defendant's land-use controls merely have a *disparate effect* upon blacks or other racial minorities. Once the plaintiff makes the showing, the *burden* then *shifts* to the defendant municipality to show that it was acting in pursuit of a legitimate governmental interest, and that there was no less-discriminatory way of achieving that same interest.

ii. **Application:** The facts of *Huntington Branch, supra,* illustrate how this "disparate effect" test can be applied to strike down a city's zoning policies on Fair Housing Act grounds. Huntington's zoning ordinance allowed multi-family housing projects to be built only in a particular urban renewal area, where 52% of the residents were minorities. The town refused to rezone to allow an integrated low-income housing project to be built in a residential neighborhood where 98% of the residents were white. The court held that this was enough to establish a disparate impact on racial minorities, thus making a *prima facie* violation of the Fair Housing Act. The town's assertion that it was limiting projects to the urban renewal area in order to preserve that area was not enough to rebut this *prima facie* case, since the town could have pursued the less-discriminatory alternative of allowing multi-family projects to be built in *both* the urban renewal and the heavily-white residential area. See Cribbet, p. 455.

d. **Group homes and anti-rooming-house ordinances:** Non-profit organizations frequently seek to set up **"group homes,"** that is, "small, decentralized treatment facilities housing foster children, the mentally ill, the developmentally disabled, juvenile offenders, ex-drug addicts, alcoholics, and so on." D&K, p. 1102. Since the residents of a proposed group home would generally be handicapped persons, and since the Fair Housing Act now prohibits discrimination against the handicapped (see *supra,* p. 292), the home's proponents often try to show that a zoning regulation has a disparate effect on the handicapped.

i. **Occupancy limits:** Most commonly, a city places a limit on the **maximum number** of unrelated persons that may live together, and this number is low enough to make a proposed group home infeasible. However, the Fair Housing Act expressly allows the use of **"reasonable** local, state, or federal restrictions regarding the maximum number of occupants permitted to occupy a dwelling." Often, towns have been able to keep out group homes by showing that their maximum-occupant regulation was "reasonable." See, e.g., *Elliott v. City of Athens,* 960 F.2d 975 (11th Cir. 1992), holding that it was not unreasonable for the City of Athens, Georgia to allow no more than four unrelated persons to live together in a single dwelling in a single-family-zoned area, even though this would have the effect of making a proposed group home for recovering alcoholics infeasible.

ii. **State statutes:** But about half the states have **state statutes** dealing with the group-home problem, typically by **preempting** the application of local zoning ordinances to group homes and setting state-wide rules on such homes instead. D&K, p. 1104, note 3.

C. **State case-law:** The highest courts of at least four states (New Jersey, New York, Pennsylvania and Michigan) have taken a radically different view of the legality of exclusionary zoning from that taken by the federal court cases discussed above. Whereas even zoning having a distinct racially discriminatory effect is difficult to attack in federal courts, these states have invalidated ordinances which exclude primarily on the basis of *economic status*.

1. **Traditional views:** Traditionally, state courts were reluctant to invalidate exclusionary zoning devices, and granted municipalities a great deal of latitude in furthering the *"general welfare"*.

2. **New cases:** The recent group of state court cases invalidating zoning ordinances as exclusionary still typically focus on the "general welfare". Now, however, it is not merely the general welfare of the ***present residents*** of the ***particular community*** that is at issue; instead, the welfare of the ***entire region*** is the relevant criterion. A municipality whose zoning practices fail to advance the general welfare of the region may violate both the ***state constitution*** and the ***state enabling act***.

    a. **Standing:** At least some state courts have also imposed more relaxed ***standing*** requirements than have the federal courts. For instance, in *Southern Burlington County NAACP v. Township of Mt. Laurel*, 336 A.2d 713 (N.J. 1975), discussed more extensively *infra*, the court held that the non-residents plaintiffs, who lived in nearby towns and who "desire[d] to secure decent housing . . . within their means elsewhere" had standing; the court did not require a showing that a favorable decision would probably lead to construction of low-cost housing, and that these particular plaintiffs would move into it.

        i. **More limited view:** Other state courts, however, have imposed stricter standing requirements. In most states, it is probably necessary for the plaintiff to show injury to a property interest; therefore, a non-resident, since he does not own land in the community, must rely on a land developer to represent his interest in the litigation. See Land Use Nutshell, pp. 203-04. Also, although a developer will be entitled to show that his own rights have been violated by the exclusionary scheme, he may not be entitled to assert the rights of the absent non-residents. *Id.* Therefore in many state courts the standing obstacles are as severe as they are in federal courts (see *supra*, p. 291).

3. ***Mt. Laurel* case:** The landmark state-court exclusionary zoning case is ***Southern Burlington County NAACP v. Township of Mt. Laurel***, 336 A.2d 713 (N.J. 1975) (probably along with *Javins v. First Nat. Realty Corp.*, *supra*, p. 151, one of the two most important property cases of the last 30 years).

    a. **Facts of *Mt. Laurel*:** The Ps represented Black and Hispanic persons living in or near Mt. Laurel, who claimed that the town's zoning policies prevented them from finding low- or moderate-income housing. (The court treated the case as one involving principally economic, rather than racial, exclusions.) The Mt. Laurel zoning scheme contained two principal exclusionary features: (1) all areas zoned for residential use required ***single-family detached dwellings*** with substantial minimum lot-size and floor-area restrictions; and (2) nearly 30% of the town's land area was zoned for industrial use, even though less than 1% of this area was actually used by industry (the rest remaining vacant). (Several PUD's had been built, but these were designed to contain upper-income apartments, principally one-bedroom ones so that families with school-aged children would not be attracted.)

    b. **State constitution and statute violated:** The court concluded that the Mt. Laurel zoning scheme violated the substantive due process and equal protection rights guaranteed by the ***state constitution*** (the requirements of which, the court noted, "may be more demanding than those of the federal Constitution"). Also, the court held, the scheme failed to serve the ***general welfare of the region as a whole***, and thus violated the state enabling statute.

    c. **"Fair share" requirement:** The key element of the court's holding was that a municipality ***may not foreclose opportunities for low- and moderate-income housing***, and must offer an opportunity for such housing "at least to the extent of the municipality's *fair share* of the present and prospective *regional need* therefor." Here, there was evidence that a substantial number of residents of Camden (a decaying older city) and other nearby towns would have moved to Mt. Laurel if low- and moderate-income housing had been available.

i. **Defining relevant region:** For purposes of determining a municipality's fair share of regional housing needs the court declined to give a fixed test for ascertaining the relevant region. It noted that confinement to a certain *county* "appears not to be realistic", but that restriction within the boundaries of a *state* seems "practical and advisable". (But the court noted that a *developing* municipality could not ignore a demand for housing within its boundaries on the part of people who commute to work in another state.) With respect to Mt. Laurel in particular, the court defined the relevant region as "those portions of Camden, Burlington and Gloucester Counties within a semicircle having a radius of twenty miles or so from the heart of Camden City."

d. **Property tax rationale unacceptable:** There was no evidence that the Mt. Laurel City Council had desired to discriminate against low- and middle-income families as such. Instead, the town claimed (and the court accepted) that the town simply desired to make sure that any new housing would "pay its own governmental way". Thus families with school-aged children were discouraged, since schooling of such children placed a large fiscal burden on the town. Similarly, a large portion of the undeveloped land was allocated for industrial and commercial purposes because such use produce attractive tax ratables. The court flatly *rejected* (apparently for all circumstances) *fiscal considerations* as a defense for exclusionary zoning; "municipalities must zone primarily for the living welfare of people and not for the benefit of the local tax rate."

e. **Intent not necessary:** The court stated (in footnote 8) that its holding was not dependent upon whether Mt. Laurel *intended* to limit low- and moderate-income housing. So long as Mt. Laurel's zoning policies had this *effect*, the presence or absence of intent was irrelevant. (This is in sharp distinction to the Supreme Court's *Arlington Heights* decision, *supra*, p. 288, where the equal protection clause was held to proscribe only those action taken with racially discriminatory intent.)

f. **Remedy:** The court declined to strike down the entire Mt. Laurel zoning scheme as invalid. Instead, the town was ordered to redraft those portions of its zoning scheme which served as barriers to low- and middle-income housing. The court indicated that at a minimum this would require:

i. **Multi-family housing:** The permitting of *multi-family housing*, without restrictions on the number of bedrooms;

ii. **Small dwellings:** The allowing of *small dwellings* on *very small lots*;

iii. **PUD's:** If PUD's are to be used, a "reasonable amount of low- and moderate-income housing" in each PUD, unless opportunity for such housing had already realistically have been provided for elsewhere in the town;

iv. **Industrial land:** A reservation of land for industrial of land for industrial and commercial purposes not exceeding the amount "reasonably related to the present and future potential" for such uses (clearly not the present 4,121 acres, of which only 100 had been actually used); and

v. High density zoning: In general, *high density zoning*, "without artificial and unjustifiable minimum requirements as to lot size, building size, and the like. . . ."

4. **Cases from other states:** Cases in several other states have followed at least some aspects of the *Mt. Laurel* decision.

    a. **New York and Pennsylvania:** For instance, in *Berenson v. Town of New Castle*, 341 N.E.2d 236 (N.Y. 1975), the New York Court of Appeals adopted a modified version of the *Mt. Laurel* doctrine. And in Pennsylvania, the state supreme court has followed the *Mt. Laurel* approach even more closely. See, e.g., *Surrick v. Zoning Board*, 382 A.2d 105 (Pa. 1977), where an ordinance barring nearly all multi-family developments was struck down as violative of substantive due process; the court explicitly adopted the "fair share" principle.

    b. **Statutes in other states:** Other states have enacted *statutes* which may serve to reduce exclusionary zoning.

        i. **California:** For instance, an amendment to the California Planning Enabling Act, Cal. Gov't Code §65302(c), requires every municipal master plan to contain a "housing element", which "shall make adequate provision for the housing needs of *all economic segments of the community.*" (However, it is not clear whether regional, as opposed to merely municipal, needs must be considered. But see *Associated Home Builders of Greater Eastbay, Inc. v. City of Livermore*, 557 P.2d 473 (Cal. 1976), discussed *infra*, p. 301, indicating that California now follows the *Mt. Laurel* "regional fair share" approach.)

        ii. **Massachusetts:** In Massachusetts, a statute, Mass. Gen. Laws Ann. 40B, §§20-23, establishes a local board of appeals which may issue permits for low- and moderate-income housing upon application by any public or non-profit agency; the appeals board has the power to supersede local zoning restrictions.

5. ***Mt. Laurel II*:** Back in New Jersey, the *Mt. Laurel* decision did not produce the result the court expected: eight years later, Mt. Laurel still had an exclusionary zoning code, and no low- or middle-income housing had been built in the town. The New Jersey Supreme Court then decided *Southern Burlington NAACP v. Township of Mt. Laurel*, 456 A.2d 390 (N.J. 1983), popularly known as *"Mt. Laurel II"*. Here are some of the important aspects of that decision, in which the court tried to put some muscle behind its prior pronouncement that communities may not zone so as to keep out their fair share of the region's poor and middle-income families:

    a. **Mature towns:** *Every* community, not just those that are still "developing", must bear its fair share of the region's low- and middle-income housing needs. The fact that a community is *"mature"* will not prevent it from having a "fair share" obligation, so long as the community has at least *some* undeveloped land.

    b. **Affirmative devices:** A community will not meet its "fair share" obligation merely by removing exclusionary provisions from its zoning code. Each town has an *affirmative obligation* to do everything in its power to cause a fair share of low- and middle-income housing to be built. If because of high land prices, political pressure, or other reasons, removing the exclusionary provisions is not enough to bring about actual construction, then the community must do more. Possible affirmative steps a city could take include: (1) granting *"density bonuses"* (i.e., the right to build extra housing beyond what would normally be allowed by the zoning ordinance) if the builder promises to make some of the units be low-income ones; (2) cooperating with the developer in obtaining **federal subsidies** for low-income housing; and (3) eliminating bans on **mobile homes**.

c. **Builder's remedy:** The courts should be free to impose a so-called **"builder's remedy"** where appropriate. If the plaintiff who brings a *Mt. Laurel*-type suit is a builder who wants permission to build low- or middle-income housing on property he owns, and the court concludes that the defendant town has not met its fair share obligation, then the trial court is free to **allow the builder to build his project** even though the town has never given a permit for it. This will give the builder an inducement to bear the legal expense and wait of lengthy litigation. (Without a builder's remedy, a builder might fight a long lawsuit, have the ordinance struck down, but then watch the town rezone in a way that complies with the court's order, yet not have his own property be part of the new rezoned area. This possibility would discourage builders from bringing *Mt. Laurel*-type suits.)

d. **Legislature reacts:** But the New Jersey legislature has subsequently **undermined** much of what the Supreme Court was trying to do in the two *Mt. Laurel* cases. The New Jersey Fair Housing Act of 1985, for instance: (1) puts a moratorium on the builder's remedy; and (2) allows suburban towns (with the approval of a state Council on Affordable Housing) to get out of up to half of their fair share obligation by compensating **cities** (including, presumably, depressed inner cities like Camden and Newark) to rehabilitate *their* housing stock. This "transfer option" has been criticized as turning *Mt. Laurel* upside down, by keeping the poor in the inner cities instead of letting them move into the richer suburbs. See D&K, p. 1127.

6. **Some defenses:** At this point, it is worthwhile to examine some of the possible **defenses** that a municipality might raise to a *Mt. Laurel*-type attack on its zoning practices.

a. **Benign intent:** An argument that the township did not **intend** to discriminate against low- and moderate-income housing will almost certainly not be successful. Such a defense was expressly forestalled in *Mt. Laurel*, and appears not to be recognized in the other states applying some version of *Mt. Laurel*.

b. **Preservation of property values:** Similarly, the argument that the zoning practice is an attempt to "preserve property values" is likely to prevail.

c. **Fiscal justifications:** The desire to **maximize property tax revenues** and to avoid having to furnish new **municipal services** (e.g., new schools and parks) was expressly rejected as a defense in *Mt. Laurel*, as well as in an earlier Pennsylvania case, *In re Girsh*, 263 A.2d 395 (Pa. 1970).

d. **Other towns better-suited:** The argument that other towns are **"better suited"** for low- and moderate-cost housing (e.g., because land values are lower there) would probably not be successful in New Jersey, but might prevail in New York under the *Berenson* decision. (Of course, even in New Jersey a town would have no fair share obligation if it could show that the **entire** regional demand for low-cost housing had already been met.)

e. **Ecological grounds:** A showing that the town's present zoning policies are justified on **ecological grounds** would probably be a successful defense. However, the *Mt. Laurel* court cautioned that ecological difficulties must be "substantial and very real . . . [and] not simply a makeweight. . . ." Thus the fact that adequate water and sewage facilities did not yet exist in the undeveloped area of Mt. Laurel was no defense, since these facilities could be built.

   f. **Orderly growth:** The town might argue that its policies represent an attempt to *control its growth* in an orderly manner rather than an attempt to keep out low- and moderate-income families. At least if the town can show that its growth-control restrictions do not have a disproportionate impact on low- and moderate-income construction, the plan will probably be upheld. If, however, the growth-control scheme is such that the land prices of developable sites skyrocket, and builders of luxury units are the only ones who can afford these sites, this might constitute an exclusionary practice. See 91 Harv. L. Rev. 1658. Other aspects of growth-control regulations are discussed *infra*, p. 300.

7. **Remedies:** *Mt. Laurel I* and *II* suggest some of the remedies which a court may decree once it has found that a municipality has practiced exclusionary zoning. The general types of possible relief include the following:

   a. **Builder's remedy:** In a suit brought by a developer, the court might conclude that the project sought to be built by the developer is *suitable for that specific site* the court could therefore order the municipality to rezone to allow that particular project. This is the so-called *"builder's remedy"*, approved by the New Jersey Supreme Court in *Mt. Laurel II*. See *supra*, p. 297.

   b. **Invalidation of ordinance:** The court can simply strike down all or part of the ordinance, without stating how the ordinance should be rewritten. This has the virtue of leaving actual land-use decisions to the local legislature in the first instance (preventing the court from becoming a "super zoning authority"), but it encourages delay and minimal redrafting on the part of recalcitrant towns.

   c. **Redrafting of ordinance:** Finally, the court can issue specific instructions as to the re-drafting of the ordinance. For instance, the court might direct the defendant town to: (1) permit multi-family housing without *bedroom restrictions* (as in *Mt. Laurel I*); (2) grant *"density bonuses"* to reward any developer willing to put up low- or middle-housing; and (3) eliminate a zoning ban on *mobile homes*.

VI. REGULATION OF SUBDIVISION AND GROWTH

   A. **Subdivision generally:** The principal process by which vacant land is developed for residential purposes is known as *subdivision*. Subdivision is usually defined as the dividing of a parcel into two or more *smaller* ones, for resale to different purchasers.

   B. **Mechanics of subdivision:** Generally, subdivision is performed by a professional developer, who buys a large parcel for the purpose of building *single-family residences* on the subdivided parcels.

   1. **Filing of plat:** To begin the subdivision process, the developer usually records a *subdivision map*, or *plat*. The plat shows the entire parcel, and indicates the boundaries of each lot that the developer proposes to carve out and sell. Once the plat has been recorded and approved by the municipality, the developer can sell lots simply by reference to the lot number as shown on the plat, rather than by a complex "metes and bounds" description. (Also, the municipality can collect taxes based on these lots as shown on the plat.)

C. Municipal regulation: It is not surprising that most municipalities have exercised their power to regulate the subdivision process rather closely. It is at the moment of subdivision that the layout of streets, availability of parks, suitability of water mains and sewers, etc., are all likely to be determined for better or worse. Therefore, most municipalities require a developer to gain municipal approval of his subdivision plans before the plat may be recorded (and before sales of lots, or construction of dwellings on them, may be made).

    1. Distinguished from zoning: Subdivision control is thus distinct from zoning. The latter generally regulates the types of buildings that may be constructed, and the uses to which these may be put. Subdivision control, by contrast, regulates such items as the layout of streets, the setting-aside of park land, the construction of sewers, etc. There is, however, no fundamental reason why zoning and subdivision control cannot be administered in a single process by a single local agency (though this is in fact almost never the case). The ALI Model Code integrates zoning and subdivision controls; see §2-101(4).

    2. Enabling act: Because of the historical distinction between subdivision controls and zoning controls, the former are usually authorized by a separate state *enabling statute*. The Standard Act, referred to repeatedly *supra* in the zoning context, contains a separate title authorizing subdivision controls; a version of this title is in force in most jurisdictions.

D. Types of local regulation: Following are some of the types of regulations which municipalities often impose on subdividers:

    1. Street design: *Street design* is often a critical force of the subdivision controls. For instance, the proposed streets must generally be in conformity with the town's master plan, must be of a certain width, and must perhaps be made out of a certain type or types of material.

    2. Sewers and water mains: Detailed specifications for *water mains, sewers, gutters* and other drainage facilities are often prescribed.

    3. Dedication of land: The developer will almost always be required to *dedicate*, i.e., *donate* to the municipality, the land allocated on his plat for streets.

        a. Installation of facilities: Furthermore, the subdivider will generally be required to *perform the work* for various facilities himself. He will thus generally be required to *pave the streets, install sidewalks*, and install water mains, sewers, and other drainage facilities at his own expense, according to the town's specifications. See B,C&S, p. 1318.

        b. Acceptance by city: Once these developer-installed facilities are complete, however, and meet with the city's approval, *maintenance* of them becomes the city's responsibility (to be financed out of property taxes).

        c. Upheld by courts: Subdividers have sometimes attacked the required dedication of streets and construction of improvements as being a *"taking"* of private property without compensation. However, the courts have generally sustained such requirements as a *reasonable exercise of the police power*. *Id.* The cases have reasoned that the municipality has an obligation to make sure that future residents of the subdivision will have adequate facilities, and that these facilities will not have to be paid for by the town. Also, the subdivider himself gets financial benefits by being allowed to subdivide (e.g., the value of his land increases substantially, and he is able to sell by reference to lot numbers on the filed plat); therefore it is not unfair to ask him to undertake certain of the costs associated with the subdivision.

    4. Park- and school-sites: Land for *parks* and *school-sites* is often required to be dedicated.

E. Growth control: Consider a community which is not yet substantially or fully developed. Ordinary zoning or subdivision controls will normally not by themselves permit the community to regulate either its *rate* of growth, or the *sequence* in which the various parcels of developable land are developed. Consequently, the town might find that it is growing so fast that its population is doubling, or even quadrupling, every decade. Also, the sequence of development will be determined principally by what large vacant parcels happen to come on the market at any particular time. Thus at a time when the town is built up principally around a "downtown" core, a major subdivision may be constructed at the outer edge of town, with nothing in between. Such a haphazard development process is likely to strain the schools and other municipal facilities (e.g., one school running on double session, and another underutilized or usable only by extensive busing; insufficient fire protection; costly road construction across areas that do not yet need roads, etc.).

    1. Municipal growth control plans: Accordingly, a number of municipalities have attempted to control their growth, both as to rate and as to the sequence by which individual parcels are developed. Typically, such growth control plans attempt to: (1) limit the overall increase in population to an amount substantially less than that which would occur if there were no growth regulation; and (2) insure that each major parcel is developed only when appropriate school, sewage and other facilities either exist or are presently sensible investments.

    2. Legal problems: Any such growth control plan necessarily means that some developers will not be permitted to develop their land at the moment they choose to do so (or, at the least, that they will have to sustain large additional costs to build the necessary public facilities themselves). Therefore, such plans are subject to at least two kinds of potential legal challenges: (1) that by limiting an owner's right to develop his property at a particular time, the regulations exceed the police power and are therefore a "taking" without compensation; and (2) that the regulations are *exclusionary* vis-a-vis prospective new residents. Nonetheless, several cases make it clear that a well thought-out plan for orderly growth can survive legal challenge.

    3. The *Ramapo* case: The best-known case on the validity of growth-control regulations is *Golden v. Planning board of Town of Ramapo*, 285 N.E.2d 291 (N.Y. 1972). In *Golden*, the New York Court of Appeals upheld a growth-control scheme that barred any residential construction (except construction of a single home by the owner of a parcel) except where there were adequate sewers, public schools, parks, roads and fire houses.

    4. Explicit quota system approved: The Ramapo growth-control plan upheld in *Golden*, *supra*, did not set a fixed limit on the number of new units which might be constructed during any one year. But such fixed limits have sometimes been upheld. For instance, a scheme expressly limiting the number of new subdivision units to 500 per year was upheld in *Construction Industry Ass'n of Sonoma County v. City of Petaluma*, 522 F.2d 897 (9th Cir. 1975).

    5. Relevance of welfare of entire region: Both the *Golden* and *Petaluma* cases, although making reference to the regional impact of municipal growth-control decisions, essentially held that each municipality has the right to regulate its own growth regardless of the impact on the surrounding region. A California Supreme Court case, by contrast, has expressly held that *regional impact* is a factor to be considered in determining whether a growth-control scheme is a valid exercise of police power. In *Associated Home Builders v. City of Livermore*, 557 P.2d 473 (Cal. 1976), the city of Livermore prohibited issuance of residential building permits until local educational, sewage disposal, and water supply facilities met certain standards. (The plan was thus similar to the Ramapo plan construed in *Golden*.) The court was unable to decide the constitutionality of this plan, because of the limited factual record before it. However, it laid down several important propositions to be used by the trial court in evaluating the plan on remand:

    a. No right to travel infringed: The ordinance did not penalize travel and resettlement, but merely made it more difficult for a non-resident to establish his residence within the city of Livermore. Therefore, the ordinance did not substantially infringe upon the right to travel, and it would not be subject to *strict constitutional scrutiny* on right-to-travel grounds. Consequently, the city did not have to show a compelling interest in the ordinance. Rather, the ordinance must be upheld if it was "fairly debatable that [it] is reasonably related to the public welfare. . . ."

    b. Exclusionary ordinance distinguished: The court distinguished the present ordinance from one which excludes non-residents on the basis of *race* or *poverty*; the Livermore ordinance "impartially bans all residential construction, expensive or inexpensive." The court implied, but did not expressly hold, that such an exclusionary statute would be subject to strict scrutiny, and would be upheld only if there were a compelling state interest supporting it.

    c. Regional impact: In determining whether the ordinance was reasonably related to the public welfare, the trial court must first determine whether the ordinance had an impact upon an area outside the city's own boundaries. If so, the *impact on this region* must be considered. If the ordinance did not benefit the welfare of the region as a whole (e.g., because it exacerbated a regional housing shortage), this regional impact might outweigh the benefit to the city; if so, the ordinance would be invalid.

        i. Similarity to Mt. Laurel view: In ordering the trial court to consider the regional, not just city-wide, impact, the court was thus in effect adopting the *Mt. Laurel* "regional fair share" approach. See *supra*, pp. 294-95.

    d. Dissent: A dissent argued that the Livermore ordinance was in reality not a temporary moratorium, but a total and perhaps permanent prohibition. The dissent noted that the ordinance provided no timetable for the provision of the public facilities in question, and that there was no incentive for the present residents to spend municipal funds to prepare these facilities for newcomers. The moratorium was therefore "likely to continue for decades . . . ; procrastination produces its own reward: continued exclusion of new residents."

6. Use of minimum acreage zoning: The use of a large *minimum lot-size* requirement is a traditional means for controlling population growth, since it guarantees low population density. In any jurisdiction following the *Mt. Laurel* anti-exclusionary zoning approach, the use of large minimum lot sizes on a permanent basis will almost certainly be invalid. But the use of such minimums to create a *temporary "holding zone"* may be upheld.

7. **Exclusion of racial minorities or the poor:** Most of the cases which have construed growth-control regulations have carefully scrutinized them for evidence of an intent to discriminate against *racial minorities* or the *poor*. Certainly an *intent* to discriminate against these groups is likely to be struck down by a state court, and perhaps by a federal court interpreting the Fourteenth Amendment (in the case of racial discrimination) or the Fair Housing Act (in the case of either racial or poverty classifications).

   a. **Mere effect:** Where the growth-control plan will have merely an exclusionary *effect* on these groups, it is less clear how the court will react; this is likely to turn on its general attitude towards exclusionary zoning. One commentator suggests that a growth-control plan may avoid being exclusionary only if it: (1) requires that a percentage equal to the regional "fair share" be set aside expressly for low-cost housing (so that developers of luxury units will not preempt the limited number of building permits because of their ability to pay higher prices for the land); and (2) is uniformly applied to all types of development (so that multi-family housing, say, is not the only category whose growth is limited). See 91 Harv. L. Rev. 1658-59.

VII. HISTORICAL AND ENVIRONMENTAL PRESERVATION

A. **Historical preservation:** Certain buildings, or an entire district, may be of great *historical* or *architectural* interest. A number of municipalities have therefore sought to protect such buildings from demolition or radical alteration, or such districts from an incompatible mixing of old and modern styles.

B. **Historic districts:** A *historic district* is a group of buildings or a neighborhood exhibiting a *common style* of historical or architectural interest. It may be the case that none of the buildings in the district, taken individually, would have great historical or architectural interest; but taken as a whole, the area is worth maintaining because it reflects the life style or architecture of a given period.

   1. **No alterations allowed without permit:** It is generally impractical for a city to acquire every building within a historic district and make them all museums. Therefore, the usual method of preserving historic districts is to designate the district, and then provide that *no alterations, demolition* or *new construction* may take place within it without the approval of a special district board. Such historic district ordinances have been passed (and upheld) in Massachusetts (the Beacon Hill area of Boston), New Mexico (the "Old Santa Fe Style" architecture in that city); and Louisiana (the "Vieux Carre" area of New Orleans). See Land Use Nutshell, pp. 219-21.

   2. **Legal challenges:** These historic district ordinances have been subjected to two main types of legal attack: (1) that they are *arbitrary* and *discriminatory* (either in general or as applied in a particular case) because they lack sufficiently precise standards to guide the board in issuing construction permits; and (2) that they constitute a "taking" without compensation, because they prevent the owner from making a profitable use of his property. In general, the courts have leaned over backwards to find the ordinances *valid* against these types of attacks. See, e.g., *Maher v. City of New Orleans*, 516 F.2d 1051 (5th Cir. 1975), upholding the New Orleans "Vieux Carre" ordinance, which provided that no construction, alteration, or demolition work within the geographic boundaries of the district could be done without a permit from the Vieux Carre Commission.

C. **Individual landmarks:** Alternatively, a municipality may designate *individual buildings* as *landmarks*, because of their unusually historical or architectural importance. The legal issues involved in landmark preservation are similar to those raised in the historic district context. However, the owner of property within a historic district has at least a certain measure of protection against arbitrariness by virtue of the fact that the restrictions apply to his entire geographical neighborhood. The owner of an individual building, by contrast, has less protection against arbitrary or discriminatory action, since the standards by which individual buildings are selected for landmark status are inevitably somewhat vague and subjective. Nonetheless, the courts have gone out of their way, as in the case of historic district laws, to uphold such landmark preservation laws both in general and as applied in specific cases.

1. **How the laws work:** The typical landmark preservation ordinance, like most historic district laws, prevents the alteration or destruction of a designated landmark without approval of a specifically-appointed board or commission.

2. **The *Penn Central* case:** The general acceptability of landmark preservation ordinances, at least for federal constitutional purposes, is assured by the U.S. Supreme Court's decision in the ***Penn Central*** case.

   a. **Facts of *Penn Central* case:** The Ps, the owners of Grand Central Terminal, sought to build a large modern office building on top of the Terminal. The New York City Landmarks Preservation Commission, relying on the Terminal's status as a landmark, refused to approve any of the Ps' proposals. One of the proposed schemes would have destroyed the southern facade of the terminal (the Beaux Arts facade which resulted in the landmark designation), and the other would have rested a fifty story office building on the roof of the terminal (a result which the Landmarks Commission referred to as "an aesthetic joke").

      i. **Theory of suit:** The Ps sued to invalidate the landmark preservation provisions, on the grounds that they prevented the Ps from obtaining a reasonable return on their investment in the terminal, and therefore amounted to a taking without compensation.

   b. **New York court's decision:** The New York Court of Appeals, in *Penn Central Transportation Co. v. City of New York*, 366 N.E.2d 1271 (N.Y. 1977), upheld the regulations. This decision made several major points:

      i. **"Socially created value" does not count:** The landmark designation is not an unconstitutional taking of the Ps' property unless it deprives them of a ***reasonable return*** on the property. However, in measuring the reasonableness of the return, the value of the property should only be measured by looking to the privately-created, investment-backed, value of the Terminal and the land under it. The portion of the Terminal's value that is due to the contribution of ***society*** (e.g., the selection of the Terminal as a connecting point for much of New York City's transit system, the large federal investment in railroads in years past, the provision of fine civil services, etc.) may not be counted.

      ii. **Ps' other properties:** In measuring the return which the property is capable of producing, the fact that the Terminal may be currently operating at a loss is not dispositive; the issue is whether the Terminal ***could*** produce a reasonable return if it were operated efficiently.

      iii. **Transferable development rights:** Under the landmark preservation law, the Ps had the ability to ***transfer*** their development rights above the terminal to ***other parcels of land in the vicinity***. Particularly since the Ps themselves own eight such parcels (including four hotels), the value of these ***transferable development rights*** (TDRs) is significant, and is to be counted in determining whether a reasonable return is possible. The Ps failed to carry their burden of demonstrating that even when the value of these TDRs is counted, a reasonable return is not possible.

c. Supreme Court affirms: The *Penn Central* decision was affirmed by the U.S. Supreme Court, in ***Penn Central Transportation Co. v. City of New York***, 438 U.S. 104 (1978). Apart from some general observations on the tests to be used in determining whether a taking has occurred, the Court stated the following major propositions:

i. Landmark preservation valid state objective: The preservation of buildings and areas with special historic, architectural, or cultural significance is an ***"entirely permissible governmental goal."***

ii. Not arbitrary or discriminatory: The Ps argued that landmark designation statutes are fundamentally different from zoning or historic-district legislation, because they allow the municipality to single out owners of particular buildings to bear the entire burden of the program, and that this selection is potentially arbitrary and highly subjective. The Court noted that zoning and historic-district legislation also frequently places an uneven burden. Also, the New York City landmarks law is part of a "comprehensive plan" of preservation, and over 400 landmarks have been designated, a strong indication that arbitrariness is lacking. Finally, there was no evidence that the Landmark Commission's action in this particular case was arbitrary or inappropriate (the Ps did not even claim that it was), and the courts will be able to detect such arbitrariness should it occur in specific cases in the future.

iii. Reasonable return present: Apart from their "arbitrary and discriminatory" argument, the Ps also claimed that their ability to use the property was so diminished that a ***taking*** had occurred. The Court ***rejected*** this claim. First, it noted that the landmarks law did not interfere in any way with the present uses of the Terminal (as a railroad terminal containing office space); this present use must, the Court said, be regarded as the Ps' "primary expectation concerning the use of the parcel." Also, there was no evidence that ***all*** development of the air space would be prohibited, merely that a structure in excess of fifty stories would be, thus a much smaller building might be permitted, and would contribute to a reasonable rate of return on the parcel.

iv. Value of TDRs counted: Finally, the Court noted, the TDRs had a value, which must be counted in measuring a reasonable return. The Court conceded that these TDRs "may well not have constituted 'just compensation' if a 'taking' had occurred." Nonetheless, these TDRs had some value, and this must be computed in determining the threshold question of whether a reasonable return was permitted; since a reasonable return was possible, no taking has occurred.

Note: Observe that, by the Supreme Court's theory, a municipality interested in gaining the use of a parcel could avoid having to pay the full market value of the property (which is required in eminent domain proceedings) by merely awarding enough compensation to ensure a reasonable return; that way, no taking would occur. This would in effect change the meaning of "just compensation" from "compensation for all loss of value" to "compensation only up to the level of reasonable return". See 92 Harv. L. Rev. 226-27.

v. "Socially created value" not reviewed: The Supreme Court explicitly avoided evaluating the New York Court of Appeals' refusal to count "socially created value" in determining the overall value upon which a reasonable return must be permitted. This "socially created value" exclusion thus remains the law in New York.

d. Rehnquist dissent: A dissent by Justice Rehnquist contended that a taking had occurred. According to the dissent, any substantial interference with property rights constitutes a taking unless: (1) the use being prohibited is a nuisance; or (2) the prohibition applies over a broad cross-section of land and thereby "secures an average reciprocity of advantage," whereby each owner whose use is restricted gains substantial advantages in return. Factor (1) was clearly not present; nor was factor (2), since the loss of revenue suffered by the Ps was infinitely greater than any advantage which they obtained from the landmark preservation scheme. Since neither of these two factors was present, the dissent said, there was a taking even though a reasonable return on investment may be available to the Ps.

e. TDRs sold: The New York Court of Appeals and the Supreme Court appear to have been correct in their belief that the TDRs in *Penn Central* were of substantial market value. Following the decision, Penn Central sold off a portion of the air rights to Phillip Morris, which was building a new corporate headquarters across the street from Grand Central Terminal; Phillip Morris paid $2,000,000 for the right to build 75,000 square feet of additional floor space. *New York Times*, Dec. 14, 1978, p. D1, col. 3-5.

E. Preservation of open areas: The preservation of *open areas* is sometimes a worthwhile governmental goal. As in the case of preserving historical districts and landmarks, court have in general sustained fairly significant restrictions on the development of open spaces.

1. Urban park land: The preservation of *urban park land* may be a legitimate governmental objective, if the landowner is left a means of obtaining a reasonable return from his property.

2. Wetlands and coastland: The legality of open-space preservation has arisen most frequently in the context of preservation of *wetlands* and coastland. "Coastland", as the term implies, is the area along the seacoast; "wetland" areas are defined as areas that are transitional between dry land and open water, and include inland swampy areas. Preservation of both kinds of area serves several important issues; protection of marine life (particularly shellfish) and the safeguarding of water supplies are probably the two most important.

a. Drastic measures: Protection of these areas requires the imposition of extremely far-reaching restrictions; in the typical wetlands preservation ordinance, no filling, dredging, or construction is permitted (so that hunting, fishing, shellfish nurture and tourism may be the only allowable uses). Not surprisingly, owners of wetland and coastland areas have attached such ordinances as being takings made without compensation, and therefore violative of substantive due process.

b. Schemes generally upheld: By and large, most courts which have recently considered the issue have *upheld* such wetland and coastland preservation schemes, on the grounds that preservation of these areas is a goal of overriding social importance, out-weighing the landowner's interest in land development.

    c. Recent Supreme Court decisions: But several recent Supreme Court decisions may make it somewhat harder for wetland and coastland preservation schemes to pass constitutional muster.

        i. Substantial promotion of legitimate government interest: First, the Court has held that a quite tight ***means-end fit*** is required for land-use regulations that substantially interfere with an owner's use of his property. Any substantial interference will be a compensable "taking" unless it ***"substantially advances a legitimate state interest."*** See *Nollan v. California Coastal Commission, supra,* p. 266. Thus in *Nollan,* a regulation that prevented the Ps from rebuilding their beach house unless they first gave the public an easement across a sandy strip of property adjacent to the ocean was ruled a compensable "taking," because the means chosen by the government (the easement) was not sufficiently well-suited to achieving the government's goal (maintaining public access to the beach). So as the result of *Nollan,* state and local governments will have to show that they're not regulating wetland and coastland areas more tightly than is reasonably required to achieve the government's admittedly important preservation interest.

        ii. No economically viable use allowed: Second, the Court has held that if the wetland or coastland regulation deprives the user of ***all economically viable use*** of his land, it will automatically constitute a taking. For instance, a ***total ban*** on the building of ***any structure*** is probably enough to deny the owner "all economically viable use" of his land. See *Lucas v. South Carolina Coastal Council,* 112 S.Ct. 2886 (1992) (also discussed *supra,* p. 264). Since wetland and coastland regulations often do contain such a blanket prohibition on building, a taking will frequently be found.

        iii. Damages for temporary taking: Finally, if the wetland or coastland regulation is found to constitute a taking, probably the court will have to award ***damages*** to the owner, not just strike down the regulation. This result probably follows from *First English Evangelical Lutheran Church v. Los Angeles County, supra,* p. 267.

  3. Floodplain restrictions: Similar statutes prevent all or certain development in ***floodplains,*** i.e., land whose low elevation or other topographical character subjects it to substantial danger of flooding. Here, too, if the statute prevented an owner from making any economically viable use of his property, the statute would probably constitute a taking for which compensation would have to be paid by the government.

F. Constitutional provision without statute: Several states have amended their ***constitutions*** to provide certain environmental rights.

  1. Pennsylvania: The Pennsylvania Constitution, for instance, contains a provision granting the people of that state "a right to clean air, pure water, and to the preservation of the natural, scenic, historic and aesthetic values of the environment." (The Constitution also states the "the Commonwealth shall conserve and maintain [these resources] for the benefit of all the people.") In *Commonwealth of Pennsylvania v. National Gettysburg Battlefield Tower,* 311 A.2d 588 (Pa. 1973), the Pennsylvania Supreme Court had not passed a ***statute*** setting forth the means of protecting these environmental resources, the court held, the executive branch should not have the power to enjoin the construction of a 307-foot tower (a private tourist attraction) near the Gettysburg Battlefield.

G. Federal and state environmental policy statues: Apart from land use regulations that are motivated by a concern for the environment, there is now a separate body of federal and statute statutory law directed at broader environmental concerns; these statutes may affect not only land-use, but also use of automobiles, operation of factories, and other activities outside the traditional scope of property law. A detailed consideration of environmental law is beyond the scope of this outline; however, the following is a brief description of some of the highlights of this area:

1. **National Environmental Policy Act (NEPA):** The *National Environmental Policy Act of 1969 (NEPA)*, 42 U.S.C. §4321 *et seq.*, attempts to make all federal policies, regulations and laws compatible with preservation of the environment. Probably the most significant faces of NEPA is its requirement that every **federal agency**, whenever it makes a report or recommendation on proposed legislation or other federal actions, must file an **environmental impact statement** (EIS). The EIS must discuss, *inter alia*, the environmental impact of the proposed action, and alternatives to the proposed action.

   a. **Relevance of local zoning laws:** An EIS needs to be filed only where the proposed federal action is **major"**, and its effect on the human environment is **significant"**. The extent to which the proposed use deviates from the uses permitted under local zoning laws will be relevant in determining whether the environmental impact will be "significant".

   b. **Injunction may issue:** If an agency does not file an EIS in a situation where it is required to do so a court may issue an **injunction** against the proposed action until the EIS is filed.

2. **State NEPA-like statutes:** A number of **states** have adopted their own environmental policy acts modeled on NEPA. These include California, North Carolina, Massachusetts and Washington. See Land Use Nutshell, p. 244.

   a. **California requires EIS for private projects:** The California Environmental Quality Act (CEQA) requires filing of an EIS when local governments take actions having a substantial environmental impact. This requirements has been interpreted by the California Supreme Court to include situations where local government issues a **permit** for a project to be built by a **private developer**. *Friends of Mammoth v. Board of Supervisors*, 502 P.2d 1049 (Cal. 1972).

      i. **"Discretionary" requirement:** A subsequent amendment to CEQA requires an EIS only when the issuance of the permit is a "discretionary" rather than a "ministerial" action, i.e., an action requiring judgment and deliberation rather than merely a determination of whether there has been conformity with applicable statutes or ordinances. Thus the issuance of a variance to allow a large housing development would probably require an EIS to be filed by the local government, whereas the certification by a local building inspector that a proposed subdivision conforms to existing zoning ordinances would probably not require an EIS, since the latter would be found to be a ministerial, not discretionary, action.

3. **Federal pollution legislation:** Other federal statutes apply solely to certain types of **pollution**. In contrast to the primarily procedural requirements of NEPA, these pollution acts give federal agencies (primarily the Environmental Protection Agency) the substantive ability to prevent pollution by private industry. See, e.g., the Clean Air Act, 42 U.S.C. §1857 *et seq.*; the Federal Water Pollution Control Act, 33 U.S.C. §1251 *et seq.*; and the Noise Control Act of 1972, 42 U.S.C. §4901 *et seq.*

VIII.   EMINENT DOMAIN

A. Eminent domain generally: The power of *eminent domain* is the power of government (either federal or state) to take private property for public use. The confines of the power of eminent domain are set by the Fifth Amendment to the U.S. Constitution, which provides: "[N]or shall private property be taken for public use without just compensation."

   1. **Condemnation proceedings:** Generally, the power of eminent domain is invoked through *condemnation proceedings*. The government decides that a certain parcel is necessary for public use, and (assuming that private negotiations with the owner do not lead to a sale) brings a judicial proceeding to obtain title to the land. As part of this proceeding, the court decides upon the "just compensation" due to the owner.

   2. **Inverse condemnation:** Occasionally, however, the government will simply make *use* of a landowner's property, without bringing formal commencement proceedings. In this situation, the landowner may bring a so-called *"inverse condemnation"* action, in which he seeks a judicial declaration that his property has been taken by the government. In an inverse condemnation action, the landowner seeks, in effect, a *forced sale*, not merely damages.

      a. **Relation to a tax on land-use regulation:** We have encountered the concept of inverse condemnation before — remember that a landowner who feels that land use regulations have deprived him of an unreasonably large portion of the value of his property may bring an inverse condemnation suit against the government, and may recover damages if he convinces the court that the regulation amounts to a compensable "taking". (See *supra*, p. 261.) But an inverse condemnation suit may also be brought by an owner against a government body that is truly *"using"* the owner's property, not just regulating it. For instance, suppose that D, a city, builds an airport right next to P's property, and planes using the airport fly so low (or make so much noise) that P's property is rendered unusable. P may well succeed with an inverse condemnation suit that argues: "D is using my property in a way that amounts to a 'taking' of it, so D must pay the property's fair market value."

B. What constitutes "public use": The takings clause of the Fifth Amendment has been interpreted to prohibit the taking of private property for *private use, even if just compensation is made*. Thus the government cannot simply take private property from one person, and give it to another, without any public purpose. Accordingly, there has been substantial litigation about what constitutes a *"public use"*, as distinguished from a private one. Most of this litigation has been in the context of *urban renewal*.

   1. **"Public use" construed broadly:** The Supreme Court has construed the requirement of a "public use" quite broadly. So long as the state's use of its eminent domain power is *"rationally related* to a *conceivable public purpose,"* the public use requirement is satisfied. *Hawaii Housing Authority v. Midkiff*, 467 U.S. 229 (1984).

      a. **Transfer to private owner:** Thus in *Hawaii Housing Authority*, the Court upheld a scheme whereby Hawaii used its eminent domain power to acquire lots owned by large landowners, and transferred them to the tenants living on them or to other non-landowners. Because there was tremendous inequity in land ownership (on Oahu, the most urbanized island, twenty-two landowners owned 75.5% of the privately-owned land), and because thousands of homeowners had been forced to lease rather than to buy the land under their homes, the state's scheme was a rational attempt to remedy a social and economic evil. As with any other state conduct sought to be justified as an exercise of the police power, all that was required was that the legislature "rationally could have believed" that the act would promote a legitimate objective; the scheme here easily passed this test.

b. Never publicly used: The *Hawaii Housing Authority* case also makes it clear that for an exercise of eminent domain to constitute the requisite "public use", it is *not* necessary that the government actually *possess* and *use* the property at any point during the taking. Thus, the Hawaiian land distribution scheme was not invalidated by the fact that each lessee kept possession of the land throughout the condemnation proceedings.

2. Urban renewal: In the context of *urban renewal*, it is similarly clear that the taking is for a "public use" (and therefore legal) even though the resulting renewal project is operated by private agencies for private use, and even though the building being condemned is not a slum. See *Blum v. Parker*, 348 U.S. 26 (1954), to this effect.

a. General Motors plant: An even more dramatic example of the fact that there may be a "public use" even where one person's private property is taken and given to another is *Poletown Neighborhood Council v. City of Detroit*, 304 N.W.2d 455 (Mich. 1981). There, the court held that private property could be taken and transferred to General Motors for an auto plant even though the sole public benefit would be a "bolstering of the economy."

3. Property taken need not be slum: Also, most courts have held that an urban renewal program is valid, and the taking is for a public use, even if particular parcels which are condemned are *not* themselves *blighted*.

C. Measuring "just compensation": The most frequently litigated issue in eminent domain proceedings is the *value of the property*. The Constitution requires that *"just compensation"* be paid, but this is of course an ambiguous term. The courts have generally held that the *fair market value at the time of taking* is what must be paid.

1. Measuring "market value": The fair market value, in turn, is based upon the *"highest and best use"* that may be made of the property (at least under current zoning regulations). Thus if a vacant parcel is zoned for subdivision, the value that must be paid is the value the land would have to a subdivider (even though the owner himself may never have contemplated subdividing the property). Land Use Nutshell, pp. 287-89.

2. "Substitution cost" not required: Suppose that because of the unusual needs of the property owner, the cost to *replace* the condemned parcel is greater than the market value of that parcel. The condemnee is entitled to receive only the market value, not the higher "substitution value" of the land in this situation. *United States v. 50 Acres of Land*, 469 U.S. 24 (1984). This is true even where the condemnee is a state or city that has a legal obligation to procure a replacement facility (e.g., the city that had to procure a substitute sanitary landfill in *50 Acres*). However, the "substitute parcel" measure may be allowed where market value is too difficult to determine, or where use of that standard would "result in manifest injustice to owner or public." *Id.*

Chapter Review Questions

(Answers are at back of book)

74. For 20 years, Dexter has operated a private dump in the town of Hampshire. The dump now receives approximately 500 tons of garbage per year, about the same annual amount that it has always received. The only negative environmental effect from operation of the dump is odor, and the odors are no more serious than they have always been, i.e., a mildly disturbing garbage smell that depending on wind condition can be perceived as far as one-half mile away from the dump. As the town has become more affluent, the citizens have become increasingly unhappy about the dump. Finally, the Hampshire Town Council recently passed a zoning ordinance providing that no dump may be operated within the town, and further providing that any existing dump must be discontinued within two years following passage of the ordinance. Because Dexter's property now has a huge pile of unsightly garbage on it, its value has declined to $200,000 (versus an approximately $1 million value as an operating dump). Dexter has brought an inverse condemnation suit against Hampshire, arguing that the ordinance amounts to a "taking" of his property and that he must therefore be compensated for the $1 million value it has (though he is willing to give the town a credit for the $200,000 that the property will be worth after it is no longer a dump). Should the court award Dexter the $800,000 relief he seeks?

75. Jones operates a car dealership along a highway located in the town of Nordstom. For 20 years, Jones has had a billboard on the edge of his property extolling his dealership's virtues to passersby on the highway. Then, the Nordstrom Town Council enacted a comprehensive zoning ordinance, which among other things bars all billboards anywhere in the town. The "pre-existing uses" section of the ordinance provides that any non-conforming use must be phased out within five years of the ordinance. Jones has sued to overturn the ordinance as applied to him, arguing that while Nordstrom has the right to ban billboards prospectively, it may not require him to remove an existing billboard because this constitutes a taking of his property without due process. Will Jones prevail?

76. The town of Twin Peaks is a long-established wealthy community whose residents include almost no blacks or other minorities, and almost no poor people. Twin Peaks never had a comprehensive zoning ordinance until 1980. That year, it enacted an ordinance which, among other aspects, provided that no home may be built on a parcel of land containing less than two acres. Prosser, a local developer, acquired a 10-acre parcel on a quiet street in Twin Peaks. He proposed to build 20 single-family residences on the parcel. Prosser realized, of course, that he would not be permitted to build the development unless he could either have the two-acre minimum removed from the ordinance, or obtain a variance for his development. The Town Council refused to do either. Prosser is reluctant to sue the town, because he does not want to alienate it.

However, Twin Peaks has been sued by Prince, a black resident of nearby Glendale, who argues that if the two-acre minimum were lifted, he would be able to afford, and would choose, to live on Prosser's development. Prince contends that Twin Peaks' refusal to lift the minimum violates his equal protection rights. At trial, Prince has been able to prove that the two-acre minimum has the effect of dramatically reducing the number of black residents in Twin Peaks, since most nearby blacks are insufficiently wealthy to afford the two acre parcels. However, neither side has produced any evidence as to whether the Town Council of Twin Peaks was motivated by a desire to keep out blacks, either at the time the ordinance was originally enacted or at the more recent time when the Council refused to lift the two-acre minimum. On these facts, should the court find that Twin Peaks has violated Prince's equal protection rights?

77. Same facts as prior question.

   (a) What statutory action, if any, could Prince bring that would have a good probability of success?

   (b) Will Prince succeed with such an action?

78. Same facts as prior two questions. Now, however, assume that there is convincing evidence that the Town Council of Twin Peaks was *not* motivated by any racially-discriminatory intent, and that the two-acre minimum zoning rule was enacted for the purpose of maintaining the "uncrowded" and "pastoral" nature of the town. Assume that Twin Peaks is located in the state of New Jersey. No relevant statutes have been enacted.

    (a) What theory might Prosser (the developer, see Question 76) use to attack the two-acre rule?

    (b) If the court agreed with Prosser's suit, what remedy would the court be likely to award?

LAND SALE CONTRACTS, MORTGAGES AND DEEDS

Introductory note: This chapter examines the various steps in the process of transferring (or "conveyancing") land.

I. LAND SALE CONTRACTS

A. Function of a contract: It is theoretically possible for the parties to a commercial land transfer to accomplish the entire transfer in one step. The seller could simply tender his deed, and the buyer could simultaneously hand over the purchase price. If the transaction were handled this way, no *contract* to sell land would be necessary.

1. The gap: However, in practice, it is almost always desirable for there to be a *gap* (usually several months) between the time when the parties agree on a deal, and the time when the title actually passes. During this gap, the buyer typically: (1) arranges financing; and (2) checks the seller's title. For the parties to be bound during this gap, there must be an enforceable agreement between them; this is the purpose of a land sale contract.

B. Statute of Frauds: The *Statute of Frauds* is applicable in all states to any contract for the sale of land, or for the sale of any interest in land. Therefore, either the contract itself, or a memorandum of it, must be *in writing*.

1. Memorandum satisfying: Normally, the contract itself will be in writing, so that the entire agreement of the parties is documented. However, a *memorandum* of the parties' agreement, specifying some terms but not the entire oral agreement, may also satisfy the Statute.

a. Elements of memorandum: Generally, the memorandum must state with reasonable certainty the following elements: (1) the name of each party to the contract; (2) the land to be conveyed; and (3) the essential terms and conditions. 3 A.L.P. 16.

i. Price: Usually, the memorandum must list the *purchase price*. However, if the party seeking to enforce the contract can show that the parties did not set a price, and instead agreed that a "reasonable price" would be paid, no statement about the purchase price need appear in the memorandum. 3 A.L.P. 20.

ii. Signature: The *signature* of the *party to be charged* (i.e., the party against whom enforcement is sought) must appear on the contract. Thus if Seller writes a letter to Buyer, confirming the provisions of their oral contract, this letter can constitute a sufficient memorandum if Buyer seeks to enforce the contract against Seller, but not if Seller seeks to enforce it against Buyer.

b. Intent to make subsequent writing: The parties may sometimes prepare a *preliminary, informal*, document, while intending to execute a more complete and formal document later on. The fact that the parties intend to execute a later writing does not make the first writing insufficient as a memorandum. However, the intent to make a later writing may constitute *evidence* that the parties did *not intend to be bound* until they had done so.

Example: D1 and D2 are tenants in common in Blackacre, subject to a life estate in D3 (their mother). All of the Ds tentatively decide to sell the property, and D1 signs a preliminary, handwritten, agreement with P listing the basic terms of the transaction. D1 and P agree that they will meet later on with P's lawyer to sign a more formal contract. They have the meeting, but no formal contact is ever signed because the Ds object to P's proposed draft. P sues all the Ds for specific performance.

Held, for the Ds. "[T]he mere intention to reduce an informal agreement to a formal writing is not of itself sufficient to show that the parties intended that until the formal writing was executed the informal agreement should be without binding force. . . . However, the fact that the parties contemplate the execution of a formal document is some evidence, not in itself conclusive, that they intend not be bound until it is executed." Here, where the transaction was reasonably complex, and where only one of the three co-owners signed (although she purported to sign for D2 as well as for herself), the requisite intent to be bound was not present. *King v. Wenger*, 549 P.2d 986 (Kan. 1976).

c. Broker's contract as memorandum: A document may satisfy the memorandum requirement even if it was prepared for an entirely different purpose. For instance, a contract between the seller and a *real estate broker*, authorizing the broker to sell the property on certain terms, was held sufficient to bind the seller in *Ward v. Mattuscheck*, 330 P.2d 971 (Mont. 1958). The court noted that the listing contract contained all the essential terms on which the seller was willing to sell; when the buyer gave the broker a signed statement agreeing to buy in accord with these terms, the court found a valid contract between seller and buyer.

2. Contract for brokerage commission: In many states, a contract between an owner and a *real estate broker* is brought within the Statute of Frauds. Thus the broker cannot collect his commission unless he has a written agreement. See Burby, pp. 287-88; see also Boyer, p. 366.

3. The part performance exception: There is one major exception to the Statute of Frauds for land sale contracts. Under the doctrine of *part performance*, a party (either the buyer or seller) who has taken action in *reliance* on the contract may be able to gain at least limited enforcement of it at *equity*.

a. Acts by vendor: If the vendor *makes a conveyance* under the contract, he will then be able to sue for the agreed-upon price, even if the agreement to pay that price was only oral. 3 A.L.P. 26. This can be thought of as use of the part performance doctrine, though technically what has happened is that once the conveyance is made, the promise to pay is no longer within the Statute.

i. Price is land interest: However, this exception does not apply if the price is *itself* an interest in land (i.e., the deal is an exchange of one parcel for another). 3 A.L.P. 26.

b. Acts by purchaser: The courts are in sharp dispute as to what acts *by the purchaser* constitute part performance entitling him to specific performance. Here are some of the acts that some courts have deemed to be sufficient part performance:

i. Possession alone: In a number of states, it is sufficient that the purchaser has *taken possession* of the property, even if the purchaser has done nothing else.

ii. Possession and payments: In some states, possession alone is not enough, but possession coupled with *payment by the purchaser* is enough.

iii. Possession and improvements: In some states, possession accompanied by the making of valuable and lasting *improvements* (e.g., construction of a house or garage) is sufficient. This is true in some of the states which also recognize possession-with-payment as sufficient.

iv. Change of position: In some states, the fact that the purchaser has *changed his position* in *reliance* on the agreement is a factor. In some of these states, this change of position must be accompanied by the taking of possession. In other states, a change in position alone (without taking of possession) suffices, at least where the seller agrees that the oral agreement was in fact made.

Example: Seller and Purchaser orally agree on the sale of Blackacre for $15,000. Purchaser gives Seller a deposit check for $500, but Seller merely keeps the check, without ever endorsing it or depositing it. Neither party contemplates a subsequent written agreement. Purchaser immediately enters into a binding contract to sell his existing house. Seller then reneges, after receiving a higher offer from someone else. Purchaser sues for specific performance. Seller defends on the ground of Statute of Frauds, but agrees that the oral agreement was in fact made.

Held, Purchaser wins, and specific performance is ordered. Under Rest. 2d of Contracts, §129, "a contract for the transfer of an interest in land may be specifically enforced notwithstanding failure to comply with the Statute of Frauds if it is established that the party seeking enforcement, in *reasonable reliance* on the contract and on the continuing assent of the party against whom enforcement is sought, has *so changed his position* that injustice can be avoided only by specific enforcement." The facts here satisfy this standard, which the court accepts. *Hickey v. Green*, 442 N.E.2d 37 (Mass. App. 1982).

v. No act suffices: In a few states, there is *no act of part performance* that is sufficient to make the oral contract enforceable.

See C&J, p. 989, note 3.

c. "Unequivocally referable" requirement: Courts generally require that the part performance be *"unequivocally referable"* to the alleged contract. That is, the person seeking enforcement must show that the part performance was clearly *in response* to the oral contract, and not explainable by some other facet of the parties' relationship. This is usually so even though great hardship may result from the court's decision not to enforce the contract.

Example: D, an elderly widower, tells the Ps that if they will give up their business and home, and move in with him to care for him during his life, he will leave his house and land to them when he dies. The Ps do as D requests, and not only live with and care for him, but pay his food bills. P dies without a will or any other writing to confirm the promise. The Ps sue D's estate for specific performance (i.e., for a judicial decree that the land be conveyed to them).

Held, for D's estate. The Ps' conduct was not unequivocally referable to a contract for the sale of land. The Ps were not truly in possession of the land while they cared for D (since D retained possession, and merely shared it with them). Nor were their care for him, and their expenditures on his food bills, clearly referable to the alleged contract of sale, since the Ps might have been doing this out of "a vague anticipation that the affection and gratitude . . . would, in the long run, ensure some indefinite reward." (This was particularly likely since one of the Ps was distantly related to D.) The Ps' appropriate remedy is a suit at law for the value of services rendered; the loss sustained by the Ps when they sold their business (a loss which probably will not be compensable in a damage action) is a hardship, but the existence of a hardship does not displace the requirement of unequivocal reference to the alleged contract. *Burns v. McCormick*, 135 N.E. 273 (N.Y. 1922) (a Cardozo opinion).

    i. Some flexibility: Actually, although courts generally recite the "unequivocal referability" requirement, they usually don't enforce it stringently. After all, virtually every act or combination of acts by the person seeking enforcement could be explained by some reason other than an oral contract of sale (e.g., an oral lease). What courts really require is that the acts *"point with reasonable clarity* to the presence of a contract." C,S&W, p. 666.

    ii. Defendant admits contract: Furthermore, if the defendant *admits* that the oral agreement took place, but nonetheless tries to plead the Statute of Frauds, courts will not generally apply the "unequivocally referable" requirement at all. See, e.g., Rest. 2d, Contracts, §129, Comment d: "It is commonly said that the action taken by the purchaser must be unequivocally referable to the oral agreement. But this requirement is not insisted on if the making of the promise is admitted or is clearly proved." Thus in *Hickey v. Green, supra*, the court ordered specific performance even though the plaintiff's act (sale of his house) could have been very plausibly explained by any of a number of other possible reasons apart from the oral deal — the court was heavily influenced by the fact that the seller admitted that the oral agreement had been reached.

  d. Use of other party's part performance: In most cases, the part performance will be that of the party seeking to have the contract enforced. But most courts hold that a party may also gain specific enforcement of a land sale contract based upon *the other party's part performance*. See, e.g., *Pearson v. Gardner*, 168 N.W. 485 (Mich. 1918) (seller granted specific enforcement of oral contract where buyer moved into premises and made physical changes which lowered the value of the property; seller is thus entitled to unpaid portion of sale price in return for deed.)

4. Oral modification and rescission: Where an enforceable land sale contract exists, the courts are split as to whether it may be orally *rescinded* or *modified*.

  a. Rescission: A slight majority of jurisdictions hold that a land sale contract may be *orally rescinded*. C&J, p. 1018, n. 1. See, e.g., *Niernberg v. Feld*, 283 P.2d 640 (Colo. 1955) ("[A]n executory contract involving title to, or an interest in, lands may be rescinded by an agreement resting in parol. The Statute of Frauds concerns the making of contracts only, and does not apply to the matter of their evocation.")

    i. Minority view: But a substantial minority holds that the rescission must be in writing. This is particularly likely to be the case where, as in usually the situation, the original contract creates an *equitable interest* in the land on the part of the buyer (see *infra*, p. 325); in such a case, a number of courts have reasoned that the rescission effects a re-transfer of this equitable interest back to the legal owner, and therefore is itself a contract for the transfer of a land interest within the scope of the Statute of Frauds. See 3 A.L.P. 13.

b. Modification: The courts are less willing to permit an oral *modification* (as opposed to rescission) of a contract. Most courts reason that a contract is the sum of its terms, and that enforcement of a land sale contract some of whose terms are oral (the modified terms) contravenes the policy of the Statute of Frauds. See Rest., Contracts, §223; A.L.P., 1976 Supp. at 455. Some courts, however, have permitted a modification to be oral where the modification is slight, or where the modification is deemed to be of the "performance" rather than of the "contract". Most courts reject this distinction.

    i. Estoppel or waiver: Even where the oral agreement to modify is held unenforceable, the *action* of one or both parties may constitute an *estoppel* or *waiver*. If a party's oral promise of a modification leads the other party to *change his position in reliance*, the former likely to be estopped from denying the enforceability of the modification (or, what amounts to the same thing, held to have waived the term of the original contract claimed to have been modified).

    Note: One important difference between a binding modification and an estoppel or waiver, is that the estoppel or waiver can be *retracted*, so long as the other party has not yet changed his position in reliance.

C. Time for performance: The sale contract will normally provide a *"settlement date"*, i.e., a date upon which the closing, or passing of title, is to occur. If one party fails to complete the closing on the appointed day, the question arises whether he is liable for breach of contract, and whether he has lost his rights under the contract.

    1. Suit for damages: In a suite for *damages* (i.e., a suit brought at law rather than in equity), the time stated in the contract will be deemed to be *of the essence*, unless a contrary intention appears. 3 A.L.P. 118. Thus if Seller refuses to close on the appointed day, Buyer may bring a suit for damages for the delay, even if it is only a few days. Conversely, Seller may sue Buyer if the latter delays; in this case, the recovery would presumably be for the interest which Seller could have gotten on Buyer's money had the closing taken place as scheduled.

    2. Suit at equity: But in a suit *in equity* (i.e., a suit for specific performance), the general rule is that *time is not of the essence*, unless either: (1) there is an express provision in the contract making time of the essence; or (2) such a provision is to be implied from the nature of the property or the surrounding circumstances. 3 A.L.P. 118.

        a. Right to close late: This means that generally, even though the contract specifies a particular date for the closing, either party may obtain specific performance although he is unable to close on the appointed day. (However, the defaulting party must be ready to perform within a *reasonable time* after the scheduled date.) Thus a buyer who is unable to procure the necessary financing until several days after the scheduled date may obtain a court decree ordering a sale to him; conversely a seller who is unable to clear his title until several days late may gain a decree ordering the purchaser to go through with the transaction.

        Example: Buyer (a contracting company) contracts to buy several finished lots from Seller. The contract provides the Seller is to convey "finished" lots, i.e., with utilities, curbs and gutters. The contract states a date for closing, but does not indicate that time is of the essence. Buyer has trouble lining up its financing, and requests an extension of time to close; Seller grants a shorter extension than that desired by Buyer. Seller proceeds (but in a lackadaisical and dilatory manner) to do some of the "finishing" work. On the new settlement date, neither party makes a demand on the other. Five days later, Buyer tells Seller that it has applied for a title examination which will require about three weeks to complete. Seller states that the sale contract, and the extension, have expired, and that the contract is now void. Buyer sues for specific performance.

Held, Buyer is entitled to specific performance. In a case involving specific performance, time is not of the essence unless the contract or surrounding circumstances explicitly so state. The fact that the original contract contained a stated settlement date is not sufficient to make time of the essence. Nor does the fact that Seller agreed only to a short extension mean that it then regarded time as being of the essence. That being the case, Buyer is entitled to specific performance as long as its delay was not unreasonable; in view of Seller's failure to finish the required work promptly, this delay was reasonable. *Kasten Construction Co. v. Maple Ridge Construction Co.*, 226 A.2d 341 (Md. 1967).

b. Specific contractual provision: As noted, however, the parties may *explicitly provide* in the contract that time is to be of the essence. Where a provision in the contract states that if the buyer fails to tender the payment on the settlement date, the contract will become void and all moneys previously advanced will be forfeited, courts will usually interpret such a clause as making time of the essence. See, e.g., *Doctorman v. Schroeder*, 114 A. 810 (N.J. 1921), where a forfeiture clause was enforced, even though the buyer was only about one-half hour late with the tender, and the seller refused to go through with the contract (or refund the deposit) apparently out of dislike for the buyer and the availability of a different purchaser.

c. Surrounding circumstances: The *surrounding circumstances* may indicated that the parties intend time to be of the essence. For instance, in a period when prices are fluctuating widely, a court may conclude that, although the contract is absent on the issue, the parties intended time to be of the essence. Such intent may also be found when one party is very concerned about a prompt closing and the other party knows of this concern. C,S&W, p. 704.

d. Unilateral action: Some courts hold that where the contract does not explicitly make time of the essence, *either party*, by a *unilateral notification* to the other that it will insist upon strict adherence to the contracted-for settlement date, may make time of the essence. See, e.g., *Schmidt v. Reed*, 30 N.E. 373 (N.Y. 1892). However, the notification must be given at least a reasonable time before the scheduled closing date.

e. Waiver: Even where time would otherwise be of the essence, a party may *waive* his right to assert that fact. For instance, if a party agrees (even orally) to adjourn the closing, he will not be allowed to claim, after the original settlement date, that the other party has defaulted. But such a waiver may be *retracted* as long as the other party has not yet relied to his detriment. See 3 A.L.P. 122-23.

D. Marketable title: In the vast majority of cases, the contract will require the vendor to convey a *marketable*, or *merchantable, title*. However, the courts are not in agreement as to the circumstances in which this obligation arises, or on what exactly a marketable title *is*.

1. Implied in contract: If the contract is *silent* on the issue of the kind of title to be conveyed by the vendor, an obligation to convey a marketable title will be *implied*.

a. Quitclaim deed: The parties, are, of course, free to provide that something less than a marketable title will suffice. However, the courts will not be quick to interpret language in the contract as calling for less than a marketable title. For instance, in *Wallach v. Riverside Bank*, 100 N.E. 50 (N.Y. 1912), the contract called for Seller to deliver a *"quitclaim deed"* to described property. (A quitclaim deed, described more fully *infra*, p. 337, is one which does not purport to do anything more than convey whatever interest the grantor has, if any.) The court held that there was nonetheless an implied obligation to furnish marketable title, and that this obligation was not met by a deed signed by the grantor but not by the grantor's wife (since this left the property subject to the wife's inchoate right of dower). The court reasoned that the fact that the buyer may have been willing to take a quitclaim *deed* (and thus be deprived of any remedies against the vendor if the title should prove bad following the closing) did not mean that the *contract* called for anything less than good title.

2. General definition of "marketable title": Although courts may disagree as to whether a title is marketable on a particular set of facts, most courts agree on the general *standard* for determining marketability: as one court put it, a marketable title is one which is "free from *reasonable doubt* both as to matters of law and fact, a title which a reasonable purchaser, well informed as to the facts and their legal bearings and willing and ready to perform his contract, would, in the exercise of that prudence which businessmen ordinarily bring to bear upon such transactions, be willing to accept and ought to accept." *Robinson v. Bressler*, 240 N.W. 564 (Nev. 1932).

a. Reasonable man standard: Thus it is *not* sufficient that a court would probably hold the title good in a *litigation*. The title must be *free from reasonable doubt* so that the buyer will be able to resell in the future. If, in the particular community, title examiners have set certain informal standards (e.g., that no title is good so long as there is a recorded mortgage without a recorded discharge), a court is likely to hold that a title failing to meet these informal standards is not marketable, even though the court might well decide in the vendor's favor if he brought a quiet title action effective against the whole world. As the idea is often put, the purchaser should not be required to *"buy a lawsuit"*.

Example: In the seller's claim of title, the record shows that a prior grantor took as grantee on a deed dated December 29, 1927, and conveyed via a deed dated December 28, 1927. *Held*, the seller's title is unmerchantable. It is possible that the December 28 deed was not delivered until after the December 29 deed (which would have made the December 29 deed effective to convey title). However, the title must be treated as unmarketable "if a reasonably careful and prudent man, familiar with the facts, would refuse to accept the title in the ordinary course of business. It is not necessary that the title be actually bad in order to render it unmarketable. It is sufficient if there is such a doubt or uncertainty as may reasonable form the basis of litigation." There was such a doubt here. *Bartos v. Czerwinski*, 34 N.W.2d 566 (Mich. 1948).

3. Deducible of record: In most courts, the validity of the title must be apparent *from the record*, without resort to unrecorded documents or other external evidence. Again, the rationale for this is that when the purchaser wants to resell, he should not have to present documents, or procure testimony, to show that what appears on the record to be bad title is in fact good title. Thus the vendor may not establish marketability by an unrecorded deed, or by showing that title vested in a predecessor by adverse possession.

(But a minority of courts permit such external evidence if it is clear and convincing. See 3 A.L.P. 129.)

    a. Abstract of title: Often, the question of whether merchantability of record is required is obviated by the fact that the contract calls for the vendor to submit an "abstract of title" to the purchaser. Since an abstract is merely a summary of what is on the record, courts invariably interpret the requirement of an abstract to mean that the record title as shown in the abstract must meet the requirements of the contract. See, e.g., *Douglass v. Ransom*, 237 N.W. 260 (Wis. 1931).

4. Insurability: The fact that a title company is willing to *insure* the title is *not* by itself sufficient to make the title marketable. See, e.g., *Hebb v. Severson*, 201 P.2d 156 (Wash. 1948), to this effect. (For one thing, a title company will insure almost any title so long as the policy excepts listed defects as found in the title company's search.) However, the parties are free to specify in their contract that all that is required is a title which is insurable by a designated company with designated exceptions.

5. Defects making title unmarketable: There are a large number of different defects which might make a title unmarketable, and it is not feasible to list them all here. However, some of the more important types of defects may be summarized. These can be divided into broad classes: (1) defects in the record chain of title; and (2) encumbrances.

    a. Defects in the record chain of title: Anything in the prior chain of title indicating that the vendor does not have the *full interest* which he purports to convey, may be a defect.

        i. Variation of names: Thus a substantial variation between the *name* of the grantee of record in one link and the name of the grantor in the following link is a defect.

        ii. Misdescription: A substantial variation in the *description of the land* between one deed and the next may be a defect.

        iii. Not suitable for recordation: If one of the deeds was *defectively executed*, so that it was not eligible for recording (even though it was in fact recorded), this will be a defect. Thus an *unnotarized or unwitnessed deed*, in many states, renders title unmerchantable. (But so-called "curative acts" in many states make such technical defects irrelevant after a short number of years following filing; see *infra*, p. 369.)

        iv. Lack of capacity: If there is evidence that the grantor in some link was an infant, insane, or otherwise *incompetent* at the time he conveyed, this will be a defect. (Although, merchantability usually may not be proved by evidence outside the record, *lack* of merchantability may be.)

        v. Adverse possession: Where the title is required to be marketable of record, the title will be insufficient if it is based on *adverse possession*. Even where external evidence may be shown in support of the title, the vendor will bear the burden of showing beyond a reasonable doubt that all elements of adverse possession (see *supra*, p. 26) were met.

    b. Encumbrances: Even though the vendor may have valid title to the property, it may be subject to *encumbrances*, a class which includes such things as mortgages, liens, easements, equitable restrictions and encroachments.

i. Mortgage: An outstanding mortgage, of course, constitutes an encumbrance making the title unmarketable. However, the vendor has the right to **pay off the mortgage at the closing**, out of the sale proceeds (though the purchaser has the right to insist that this be done simultaneously with the closing, rather than subsequently).

ii. No discharge of record: It will often be the case that an **old mortgage**, granted by a prior owner, is not shown on the record as being discharged. Nonetheless, this will not be fatal defect if either: (1) the vendor has an unrecorded satisfaction of mortgage in his possession; or (2) so much time has passed that the statute of limitations has almost certainly barred any attempt to foreclose the mortgage. 3 A.L.P. 134. (But the mere fact that more than the statute of limitations period has passed since the mortgage was issued is not sufficient; the running of the statute may have been tolled by agreement or by payments, and only when so much time has run that even a tolling is highly unlikely to keep the mortgage presently enforceable, will the defect be treated as trivial.)

iii. Liens: *Liens* against the property are likely to constitute an encumbrance. For instance, **unpaid taxes**, judgments obtained by creditors, or mechanic's liens filed by persons who have done work on the property, may all constitute defects. (Again, however, the vendor has the right to pay these off at the closing.)

iv. Easement: An **easement** will be a defect, if it reduces the **"full enjoyment"** of the premises. (But if the easement was notorious and visible, the purchaser will probably be deemed to have seen it, and to have agreed to take subject to it, when he signed the contract. See 3 A.L.P. 137.)

v. Use restrictions: Privately-negotiated **use restrictions** (e.g., on the type of structures which may be built, or their locations) are defects; this is true even if they are also imposed upon neighboring property, and the net result is beneficial. Thus where such restrictions exist, the contract should provide that title will pass "subject to restrictions of record" or some similar formula. (But a restriction that is clearly **obsolete** or unenforceable is not a defect. Similarly, a restriction that merely **matches existing law** does not render title unmerchantable.)

vi. Encroachments: An **encroachment** by a neighboring landowner (e.g., a driveway or part of a building running onto the vendor's own land) will constitute a defect, if it interferes seriously with the use and enjoyment of the premises. 3 A.L.P. 140. Conversely, if one of the structures on the vendor's land seriously encroaches onto a neighbor's property, title will also be unmarketable. *Id.*

vii. Land-use and zoning violations: A violation of land-use restrictions that are imposed by **law** (as opposed to restrictions privately-agreed upon) may or may not be treated as encumbrances. Most courts hold that violations of **building codes** are **not** encumbrances on title. C,S&W, p. 729. But a violation of a **zoning ordinance** usually **is** treated as an encumbrance. C,S&W, p. 730. (Most courts distinguish between executory contracts on the one hand, and covenants and deeds on the other — the buyer may refuse to close on the executory contract if there is a zoning violation, but may not recover for breach of the covenant against encumbrances for a zoning violation once the transaction has been closed. See, e.g., *Frimberger v. Anzellotti*, 594 A.2d 1029 (Conn.App. 1991), holding that the sale of property containing illegally-filled wetlands did not breach the covenant against encumbrances. See also C,S&W, p. 865. For a discussion of post-closing suits on the covenant against encumbrances, see *infra*, p. 350.)

6. **Time when title must be marketable:** Unless the contract specifies otherwise, the vendor's title is not required to be marketable *until the date set for the closing*. Thus the vendor may sign a contract to sell property which he does not yet own, and the purchaser cannot cancel the contract prior to the closing date because of this fact. 3 A.L.P. 141.

   a. **Installment contracts:** But suppose that the contract is an *installment agreement*, by which the vendor is required to convey title only after each installment of the purchase price has been paid. The courts are in dispute as to whether the purchaser is required to continue paying installments if it develops that the vendor's title is not presently merchantable.

      i. *Luette* **case:** One case refusing to let the purchaser stop his payments in this situation is *Luette v. Bank of Italy Nat. Trust & Savings Ass'n.*, 42 F.2d 9 (9th Cir. 1930). In *Luette*, the Ps signed an installment sales contract calling for them to make payments from 1926 through 1933, after which D would convey the property. In 1930, the Ps became aware that a third person has asserted homestead rights in the land; this homestead claim was denied by a federal administrative judge, but was on appeal at the time the Ps sued D for the right to cancel the contract. The court held that "there can be no rescission by a vendee of an executory contract of sale merely because of lack of title in the vendor prior to the date when performance is due" and that an installment contract was no different than any other kind of contract. (But if the unmerchantability of title had been indisputable, it is not clear that the court in *Luette* would have reached the same result.)

E. **The "gap" between contract and closing:** Between the contract and the closing is what lawyers commonly call the *"gap"*. During the gap, the parties are particularly concerned with two things: (1) the state of the title; and (2) the buyer's financing.

   1. **Checking title:** As soon as the contract is signed, the buyer's lawyer will begin to have the seller's title checked. In some parts of the country, it is the custom for the seller to obtain an "abstract of title", which is then presented to the buyer. In other areas, the buyer's lawyer conducts his own examination of title, or hires a title company to do this. In any event, sometime prior to the scheduled closing date, the buyer's lawyer reports to the seller's lawyer any objections which he has to the state of title. This gives the seller the opportunity to correct the defects (which may be easy, in the case of, say, tax liens, or difficult, in the case of a substantial adverse claim to the fee simple).

      a. **Waiver:** The buyer's lawyer must be careful not to commit a *waiver* when reporting his title objections to the seller's lawyer. If he cites certain defects, and fails to mention others, he is likely to be held to have waived the latter even before the settlement date arrives. See 3 A.L.P. 146. Even in the best case, he will have to give the seller an adjournment of the closing date to give him a chance to remedy the omitted defects.

2. **Checking the survey:** The buyer's lawyer will also want to obtain and examine a *survey* of the premises. (Often, this is available from the seller, who had it done before he purchased the property.) Assuming that the surveyor has used the correct metes and bounds description (this must be compared with the metes and bounds description, if any, on the contract and the abstract of title), examination of the survey will show whether the lot the buyer is getting corresponds to what he thinks he is getting. The survey might disclose, for instance, that part of what the buyer thinks is going to be his backyard belongs to the next-door neighbor. Or, even worse, the survey might disclose that part of the house itself encroaches onto a neighbor's land. Violations of municipal setback ordinances and encroachments by neighbors onto the seller's land may also be revealed.

3. **Physical inspection:** The buyer's lawyer should encourage his client to conduct a close *physical inspection* of the property prior to closing. The buyer should look for signs of *easements* (e.g., a beaten path across the yard), or signs of *adverse possession*. He should try to gain at least an approximate sense of whether any building restrictions or zoning regulations are being violated. Also, inspection of the physical systems of the structure (heating, plumbing, air conditioning), as well as the soundness of any appliances which may be part of the transaction, should be made, perhaps with the aid of an expert.

4. **Procuring financing:** The buyer is rarely able to pay the entire purchase amount out of his own funds. Therefore, the contract usually contains a provision making the buyer's duty to close *contingent* upon his obtaining a *mortgage* for a certain amount. If such a clause exists, the buyer must, during the gap, make a *good-faith attempt* to procure the mortgage financing.

   a. **Contents of mortgage clause:** The mortgage clause in the contract will usually state not only the amount of the mortgage which the purchaser wishes to obtain, but the maximum interest rate he wishes to pay, and the minimum length. Then, if the purchaser is unable to get a mortgage satisfying all three of these terms, he is relieved from the contract. One court has gone so far as to hold that a clause stating that the contract was "contingent upon the purchaser obtaining the proper amount of financing" was so vague that the entire contract was void for *indefiniteness*; *Gerruth Realty Co. v. Pire*, 115 N.W.2d 557 (Wis. 1962).

F. **The closing:** At the closing, the seller tenders his deed, and any other documents required by the contract or by local custom (e.g., a bill of sale for any personal property involved in the transaction, a satisfaction of mortgage indicating that the mortgage has just been paid off, etc.). The buyer checks each of the proffered documents, and when he is satisfied that everything is in order, tenders payment.

1. **Mortgage lender:** In any transaction where part of the sale price is being furnished by a mortgage lender, the lender's attorney will also have to approve each document.

2. **Adjustments:** It is rare that the exact purchase price is the amount that changes hands at the closing. Instead, the parties make *"closing adjustments"*. Thus the amount due from the buyer may be *decreased* by the amount of the deposit paid on signing of the contract, the pro-rated portion of taxes for the current year (if the seller has not already paid these), etc. Conversely, the amount may be *increased* by the value of fuel on hand, and any items paid by the seller in advance (e.g., prepayment on taxes).

3. Tender: In the usual transaction, the seller's duty to deliver the deed and the buyer's duty to pay the money are **concurrent**. Therefore, if one party is expected to default, the other party must be sure to **tender his own performance**, in order to be able to hold the other party in default, and sue for damages and/or specific performance. The party who tenders must also make a formal **demand** that the other party **perform**.

> **Example:** Seller contracts to sell a house to Buyer, the closing to occur on November 15. Ten percent of the purchase price is deposited as earnest money. The closing is adjourned to December 15. On November 30, Buyer informs Seller that Seller's title is unmarketable, and demands a return of the down payment. Seller refuses. On December 15, Buyer's lawyer comes to Seller's lawyer's office and demands return of the down payment, but neither party tenders his own performance, nor demands the other's performance. Buyer sues Seller for return of the down payment, and shows that there were indeed defects in the title as of December 15 (e.g., lack of a certificate of occupancy for a swimming pool). Seller counterclaims for damages for Buyer's repudiation of the contract.
>
> *Held*, for Seller, who does not have to give back the down payment and who may recover damages. It is true that title was unmarketable as of the closing date, but the defects were minor. Buyer was entitled to recover his deposit only if Seller was in default on the closing day; since Buyer did not tender the full purchase price and demand a conveyance of marketable title, Seller was never placed into default. Conversely, Seller would normally be required to show that he made a tender and demand before he would be entitled to recover damages from Buyer; here, however, Seller's failure to make a tender of marketable title was largely induced by Buyer's advance notice that he would not perform, and the lack of tender is therefore excused. *Cohen v. Kranz*, 189 N.E.2d 473 (N.Y. 1963).

a. Effect of other party's repudiation: As *Cohen* makes clear, a tender is necessary only where there is some chance that it would be effective. Thus if the other party has **repudiated** (as the buyer in *Cohen* had done), or if the other party's inability to perform is **incurable** (as would have been the case in *Cohen* if the defect in title were severe and out of the seller's control), no tender and demand for performance is necessary. See 3 A.L.P. 148.

G. Remedies for failure to perform: Where one party fails to perform a land sale contract, there are two distinct remedies which may be available to the other party: (1) a suit for damages; and (2) a suit for specific performance. (Both of these types of relief may generally be sought in the same proceeding, although sometimes an actual award of one will preclude the other.)

1. Damages: In nearly all situations, when one party breaches a land sale contract, the other may sue for **money damages**.

a. Measure for damages: In most American jurisdictions, the **measure of damages** for breach of a land sale contract is the **difference between the market price and the contract price** (sometimes called the **"benefit of the bargain"** rule). Thus if the seller breaches, the buyer can recover the amount by which the market value exceeded the contract price; conversely, the seller can recover from a defaulting buyer the amount by which the contract price exceeded the market value. See 3 A.L.P. 170-72. See, e.g., *Smith v. Warr*, 564 P.2d 771 (Utah 1977).

i. Exception for unmarketable title: But a number of states (not a majority) although they follow the general rule just stated, impose an exception where suit is brought against the seller for *failing to convey a marketable title*; if the seller has *acted in good faith*, these jurisdictions allow the plaintiff to recover only his *out-of-pocket* expenses. See, e.g., *Kramer v. Mobley*, 216 S.W.2d 930 (Ky. 1949), holding that the buyer in such a case was entitled to a return of his down payment with interest, and any expenses reasonably incurred in connection with the contract (e.g., fees for title examination), but nothing more.

b. Liquidated damages: The parties are always free to agree, in the contract, upon *liquidated damages* in the event of a breach. The most common example of such a clause is one providing that if the buyer defaults, the seller may *keep the buyer's deposit*, or earnest money.

2. Specific performance: In the vast majority of cases, an action for *specific performance* may be brought against the defaulting party, whether she be vendor or purchaser. A decree of specific performance is a court order requiring the defendant to go through with the transaction (to convey the land, if the defendant is the vendor, or to pay the purchase price, if the defendant is the purchaser).

     a. Equitable remedy: Specific performance is an *equitable remedy*. However, whereas equitable remedies (especially injunction) in other contexts are allowed only where a damage action would be inadequate, a less strict rule is followed in real estate specific performance cases. Courts reason that the buyer should not be relegated to a damage claim because each piece of land is "unique"; conversely, the seller should not be limited to a damage action because this leaves him with the burdens of owning and maintaining the land (e.g., paying taxes). 3 A.L.P. 173.

     b. Where not allowed: However, there are a few circumstances in which all or some courts *refuse to allow specific performance*.

         i. Hardship on one party: Since specific performance is an equitable doctrine, it will not be granted where this would result in *undue hardship* or unfairness to one party. This might be the case, for instance, if the *circumstances changed* substantially between the time the contract was signed and the closing date. For instance, in *Clay v. Landreth*, 45 S.E.2d 875 (Va. 1948), both buyer and seller contemplated that buyer would use the property for purposes of building a storage plant, but between the signing of the contract and the closing date the lot was rezoned for residential purposes. The court rejected the seller's request for specific performance, on the grounds that this would be unfair to the buyer.

         ii. Unmerchantable title: If the seller's title is unmarketable (and the defect cannot be cured by a simple application of the sale proceeds), the court will not, of course, grant the seller a specific performance decree against the buyer for the entire purchase price. (The court may, if the defect is not too grave, grant such a decree with a deduction for the defect. 3 A.L.P. 178.)

         iii. Suit by buyer: If the seller's title is defective, and it is the *buyer* who brings the suit for specific performance, it will generally be granted to him (probably with an abatement of the purchase price to reflect the defect). If the defect is one which could easily be cleared up, the court may, as part of its decree, order the seller to do this. But the court will rarely order the seller to engage in a costly quiet title suit to clear the title. See, e.g., *Bartos v. Czerwinski*, 34 N.W.2d 566 (Mich. 1948), refusing to require the seller to rectify a defect in a prior link in the title chain by bringing a quiet title action, and relegating the buyer to an action for damages.

3. **Two measures not always inconsistent:** Obviously a party to a breached contract is not entitled to be made more than whole. This means that he may obtain specific performance or damages for the difference between market price and contract price, but not both. However, a party who obtains specific performance may nonetheless be entitle to *incidental* damages (e.g., losses directly resulting from the delay in obtaining possession). 3 A.L.P. 182.

4. **Purchaser's rights to recover deposit:** Suppose the purchaser has paid an earnest money deposit; may he recover this sum? Obviously if the seller is in default, the buyer can get his money back as part of his damage or specific performance action. But if the seller is not in default, time is of the essence, and the buyer fails to pay the balance on time, most courts *do not allow him to recover his deposit*; see 3 A.L.P. 196. Similarly, if time is not of the essence, but the purchaser delays for more than a reasonable period following the scheduled closing date, he will generally lost his deposit.

   a. **Special rules for installment sales:** But where the seller has made substantial payments under an *installment contract*, the courts are much more inclined to give him back some or all of his money if he defaults. Installment contracts are discussed further *infra*, p. 335.

H. **The equitable conversion doctrine:** During the gap between the signing of the contract and the delivery of the deed, important questions about the rights of the parties may arise. For instance, the property may be *destroyed* during the gap, one of the parties may die, or either party's assets may be subject to collection attempts by creditors. Issues raised by these situations have traditionally been dealt with by reference to the doctrine of *equitable conversion*.

   1. **General meaning of doctrine:** As noted previously, courts of equity will grant either party to most land sale contracts the relief of *specific performance* of the contract. Since the purchaser will be entitled to specific performance, the courts treat the *signing of the contract as vesting in the purchaser equitable ownership* of the land. Conversely, since the vendor will be entitled to a specific performance decree (for the purchase price), he is treated as becoming *equitable owner of the purchase price*. Legal title remains in the vendor, but he holds the land as trustee for the vendee's benefit; the vendor, however, obtains a *lien* (an equitable interest) on the land to secure payment of the purchase price. For some purposes, (e.g., devolution on death), the vendor is treated as holding personal property and the vendee as holding real property. See Cribbet, pp. 190-91.

      a. **Must be specifically performable:** Because of the close links between the doctrines of specific performance and equitable conversion, equitable conversion will apply *only where the contract is one that may be specifically enforced*. Thus if the contract is one where the circumstances would make it unjust for specific performance to be decreed (e.g., *Clay v. Landrath, supra*, p. 324), the court will probably also refuse to apply the equitable conversion doctrine.

      b. **Effect of option to purchase:** American courts have generally held that an *option to purchase* real estate does *not* give rise to an equitable conversion *until the option is exercised*.

Example: Testator gives Purchaser a 60-day option to buy real property. Before the 60 days have elapsed (and before the option is exercised), Testator dies. Before the option expires, Purchaser exercises it, and pays the purchase price into court. Because Testator's will leaves part of the real property to his sister, she argues that she is entitled to part of the purchase price in lieu of the property. But Testator's sons argue that exercise of the option should "relate back" to the day the option was created, thus invoking the equitable conversion doctrine; then, since the purchase price would be personal property, the sons as distributees of Testator's personal property would take. *Held*, for the sister. No equitable conversion took place until the option was exercised, and by the time it was exercised, the real estate already belonged to the sister. *Eddington v. Turner*, 38 A.2d 738 (Del. 1944)

2. **Effect of party's death:** The equitable conversion doctrine is often applied to resolve questions of *devolution of property* upon the death of either the vendor or vendee.

   a. **Death of vendor intestate:** In earlier times, if a person died intestate, his real property went to his heirs, and his personal property to his "next of kin". Often, these were two different classes of people. If the vendor under a land sale contract died while the contract was still executory, application of the equitable conversion doctrine meant that: (1) the next of kin, not the heirs, collected the purchase price; and (2) the heirs had to execute the deed (since they were still the holders of the bare legal title). Statutes in most states have obliterated the difference between heirs and next of kin; in these states, application of the equitable conversion doctrine will rarely make a difference in cases of intestacy.

      i. **No abolition:** But in a state which has not yet abolished the difference between heirs and next of kin, equitable conversion can still be important. See, e.g., *Shay v. Penrose*, 185 N.E.2d 218 (Ill. 1962), where the doctrine was applied to a long-term installment contract, thus giving the unpaid balance of the purchase price to the decedent's next of kin, not to the heirs. (The next of kin was also given the right to declare the contract in default, and to consent to an assignment of it.)

   b. **Vendor dies testate:** If the vendor dies *with a will*, and leaves his real property to one person and his personal property to another, the equitable conversion doctrine is likely to have an important effect. If the will was drawn *prior to the making of the contract*, and the contract was still executory at the moment of the vendor's death, then the equitable conversion doctrine applies so that: (1) *the purchase price goes to the person to whom the personal property was bequeathed*; and (2) *the person to whom the real estate was bequeathed gets nothing*.

      i. **Will drafted after sale contract:** If the will devising the real estate is drafted *after* the contract has been signed, and the will makes *specific reference* to the parcel which is under contract, the courts generally give the devisee of the real property the purchase proceeds. In this situation, the bequest is construed as having been intended, in effect, as a bequest of the purchase price. 3 A.L.P. 71.

   c. **Death of purchaser:** If the *purchaser* dies while the contract is still executory, the equitable conversion doctrine applies so that: (1) the person entitled to receive the decedent's real estate (either under the will or under the intestacy statute) is entitled to the land; and (2) the recipients of the personal property not only do not receive the land, but must pay any remaining portion of the purchase price out of their shares of the estate. See Cribbet, p. 191.

3. **Risk of loss:** The most important, and difficult, issue regarding equitable conversion involves the *risk of loss*, i.e., the risk that the property will be injured or destroyed between the signing of the contract and the delivery of the deed. Courts have followed three main approaches to this problem:

a. **Loss always on vendee:** A majority of states have adopted the traditional English view that, since the vendee acquires equitable ownership of the land as soon as the contract is signed, *the risk of loss immediately shifts to him*. This is true even though the vendee *never takes possession* prior to the casualty.

Example: D contracts to sell land to P. Prior to the delivery of the deed, and while D is still in possession, an ice storm damages all the pecan trees on the property, reducing its market value by $32,000. *Held*, the loss falls on P (who does not get back his earnest money, and who has to pay damages for refusing to go through with the contract). In Georgia, as in most states, the doctrine of equitable conversion means that the risk of loss passes to the vendee as soon as the contract is signed; no exception is made merely because the vendee has not yet taken possession. *Bleckley v. Langston*, 143 S.E.2d 671 (Ga. 1965).

i. **Exception:** But courts applying this majority rule recognize an exception to it: the vendor will bear any loss which results from his *neglect*, default, or unreasonable delay in carrying out the contract.

ii. **Unmerchantable title:** Also, the vendor must bear the loss if, at the time it occurred, he was not in a position to convey the title which he had contracted to convey (e.g., because his title was *unmerchantable* due to, say, tax liens). In such a situation, the purchaser is not regarded as the "equitable owner" of the property, since he could not be forced in a specific performance suit to pay full price for the defective title; see B,C&S, p. 978-79, note 2. See, e.g., *Sanford v. Breidenback*, 173 N.E.2d 702 (Ct. App. Ohio 1960), where at the time of the destruction the vendor had not yet complied with certain requirements of the contract (e.g., presentation of an easement for a septic tank); the court held that since this would have prevented a specific performance decree at the moment of the destruction, no equitable conversion had taken place. Therefore, the risk of loss remained on the vendor.

b. **"Massachusetts" view:** A minority of courts adhere to the so-called *"Massachusetts" rule* (based on an early Massachusetts decision): the burden of loss remains on the vendor *until legal title is conveyed*, and *even though the purchaser is in possession*. These courts more or less ignore the equitable conversion doctrine, and rely upon the idea that continued existence of the subject matter is an implied condition of the contract.

i. **Insubstantial damage:** Courts applying the "Massachusetts" rule, however, relieve the purchaser from the contract only if the damage is *substantial*. If the damage is not substantial, the purchaser may not rescind and recover his payments, but he will be entitled to an abatement of the purchase price to compensate for the damage.

c. Risk on party in possession: A third view holds that the risk of loss is on the vendor so long as he remains in possession and has title, but that it then *shifts to the purchaser if the purchaser takes possession or title*. This is the approach taken by the Uniform Vendor and Purchaser Risk Act, in force with some variation in eight states (including California, Illinois, Michigan and New York).

> **Note:** Regardless of which of these approaches a particular jurisdiction follows, the parties are always free to make an *explicit agreement* resolving the issue in any way they wish. The Uniform Act, for instance, provides that the Act applies "unless the contract expressly provides otherwise."

4. **Effect of insurance on risk of loss:** Our discussion of the risk of loss thus far has ignored any effect which might flow from the fact that one party had *insurance* on the premises. The courts are in dispute on this issue, just as they are on the risk of loss question where no insurance is present.

   a. Vendor takes out insurance: The issue arises most frequently where insurance is carried *by the vendor* in his own name. In a situation where the risk of loss is on the purchaser, most courts *give the purchaser the benefit of the vendor's insurance*.

      i. Rationale: The rationale for this majority rule is that otherwise, the vendor will receive a large *windfall*: he will receive the full purchase price, plus the insurance proceeds. Therefore, the vendor is deemed to hold the insurance proceeds in a *"constructive trust"* for the vendee. Instead of receiving the proceeds, the vendee is simply given an abatement of the purchase price equal to the amount of the insurance.

   b. Minority view: But a *minority* of American courts follow the traditional English common-law rule that insurance is a *personal contract*, payable only to the insured. These courts thus reject the idea that the vendor holds the insurance proceeds in trust for the vendee; the vendee therefore gets no abatement of the purchase price. See, e.g., *Brownell v. Board of Education*, 146 N.E. 630 (N.Y. 1925).

      i. Exceptions to the minority rule: However, even in states following this minority rule that the purchaser normally does not get the benefit of the vendor's insurance, two exceptions are commonly recognized: (1) if the vendor is *required by the contract* to keep the premises insured for the benefit of the purchaser, the latter gets credit for the insurance proceeds; and (2) if the *purchaser* is required by the contract to *pay* the insurance *premiums* (even though the policy remains in the vendor's name), the purchaser gets the benefit of the proceeds. As an example of exception (2), see *Raplee v. Piper*, 143 N.E.2d 919 (N.Y. 1957).

   c. No duty to insure: Keep in mind that, even in courts following the majority rule, the vendor is *not under any duty* to keep insurance in force on the property. Thus it makes sense for the purchaser to insist on a clause in the contract requiring such insurance to be maintained on the premises for the purchaser's benefit.

   d. Insurance procured by purchaser: Where insurance is procured *by the purchaser* in his *own name*, and there is no contractual requirement on him to do so, the courts have *not* given the *vendor* the benefit of this insurance. Thus if the risk of loss happens to be on the vendor, he will be compelled to convey the property with an abatement equal to the amount of the damage, and the purchaser will get the full benefit of the insurance. Although this approach is not symmetrical with the majority view regarding insurance carried by the vendor, the two situations are not really parallel; in this situation, the parties commonly understand that the purchaser is carrying the insurance solely for protection of his own interest. See Cribbet, p. 195.

I. Assignment of contract rights: Unless the contract provides otherwise, *either party may assign his rights* under it. In this respect, a contract for the sale of land is no different from any other contract. Thus the seller may, prior to the closing, sell the property subject to the outstanding contract rights. Conversely (and more commonly) the purchaser may assign to a third person the right to pay the purchase price and receive the deed.

  1. Prohibition on assignment: However, the parties to the sale contract sometimes insert a clause purporting to *prohibit assignment*. Such clauses are effective in some, but not all, situations. Such a clause brings into play two conflicting policies: (1) the policy in favor of the free alienation of land; and (2) the policy of allowing each party to a contract the right to assure that the other party will fully perform.

  a. Enforcement at law: Generally speaking, the clause will be *enforced by a court of law*. Thus if the contract provides that any assignment will be of no effect, the seller may sue the buyer who has tried to assign, and recover legal damages.

  b. Equitable relief: But if the vendor refuses to go through with the closing because the vendee has assigned, *equity* may give relief. Since the only valid purpose of an anti-assignment clause will generally be to protect the seller's right to receive full payment, the *assignee* may come into court with a tender of the full purchase price, in which case he will usually be awarded specific performance against the vendor. Rest. §416, Comment e. Similarly, if the contract is an *installment* sale, and the original vendee or the assignee (or both) have made substantial payments, the court will often *prevent a forfeiture*. See, e.g., *Handzel v. Bassi*, 99 N.E.2d 23 (App. Ct. Ill. 1951), where the vendee had paid $8,500 of a $21,500 purchase price; the contract provided for issuance of a deed when half the purchase price had been paid. The court enjoined the seller from cancelling the contract until a default by the vendee or its assignee should occur.

J. Real estate broker's role: Most sales of real estate involve a real estate broker. Detailed coverage of the law of real estate brokerage is beyond the scope of this outline. However, we can discuss briefly a few of the common issues in this area.

  1. What the broker does: Normally, the broker makes his money by receiving a commission after the buyer and the seller he has brought together consummate a sale. In most instances, it is the *seller who pays the commission*. Also in most instances, the broker does his work pursuant to an exclusive listing arrangement between him and the seller; generally, this agreement entitles him to be paid even if another broker, or the seller himself, finds the eventual buyer. (Note that the seller's liability for the broker's commission can be limited in the brokerage contract by agreement between the broker and the seller.)

  2. "Ready, willing and able": If the broker finds a buyer who in fact goes through with the transaction, the seller will clearly be liable. However, the law in nearly all states has traditionally been that the broker is also entitled to his commission merely by finding a buyer who is *"ready, willing and able"* to consummate the transaction — in other words, the broker who finds such a buyer can collect his commission *even if the transaction never goes through*. (All this assumes, of course, that the prospective buyer produced by the broker is willing and able to do the transaction *at the price*, and *on the terms*, that the seller has set.)

3. **Seller's default:** If the transaction ultimately fails to go through because the seller has changed his mind prior to a contract, or has defaulted after entering into a contract, all courts continue to hold that the broker may collect his commission. After all, in this instance consummation of the deal was within the seller's own control, so he should clearly not be able to escape his brokerage obligation.

4. **Buyer's default:** On the other hand, where the *buyer defaults* on a sale contract, the courts are split. The traditional view has been that even in this situation, the seller must pay the commission because the broker has produced the "ready, willing and able buyer," regardless of what later happens. But a strongly increasing minority of courts now holds that the seller incurs *no liability* to the broker where the buyer defaults.

   a. **New minority rule:** This growing minority viewpoint is exemplified by *Tristram's Landing, Inc. v. Wait*, 327 N.E.2d 727 (Mass. 1975), in which the plaintiff-broker produced a buyer who signed a purchase contract but then defaulted at the closing. The court held that the would-be seller owed no commission, because a commission would be due only where the broker not only produced a purchaser ready, willing and able to buy on the seller's terms, but also completed the transaction. The court reasoned that an owner who makes a brokerage agreement is not merely seeking a purchaser who will enter into a contract, but rather one who will *buy and pay*.

      i. *Quantum meruit* **claim:** Suppose that the broker produces a prospective purchaser who enters into a contract, puts down a deposit, defaults, and forfeits the deposit. In this situation, even a court following the *Tristram's Landing* approach might well hold that the broker has a *restitution* claim to some part of this forfeiture, on the theory that it is the broker's efforts that have given the owner this "windfall." The *Tristram's Landing* court itself expressly declined to decide whether the broker should be entitled to part of the forfeited deposit in this circumstance.

II. MORTGAGES AND INSTALLMENT CONTRACTS

A. **Two devices to secure repayment:** Normally, the purchaser is not sufficiently liquid to be able to pay the entire purchase price at once. Therefore, it is necessary for him to find some device by which to pay the purchase price over a period of time. Beyond the portion of the money which the purchaser is able to pay right away, the remainder of the price must in effect be lent either by the vendor or by some third party; in either case, the lender will want *security* for repayment. There are two basic approaches to securing repayment: (1) the *mortgage*; and (2) the *installment sale contract*.

B. **Nature of a mortgage:** If the buyer does his financing via a *mortgage*, he receives a deed to the property immediately. At the same time, he executes the mortgage. In a conventional third-party-mortgage, the buyer gives the mortgage to a commercial or savings bank, and the loan proceeds are paid to the seller at the closing; the seller is thus out of the picture. In the case of a *purchase money mortgage*, by contrast, the financing is being done by the seller; that is, the buyer pays the seller a down payment, and gives him back a mortgage for the remaining price. Regardless of the type of mortgage, the essence of the transaction is that if the buyer fails to make the payments, the lender may *foreclose* on the property itself (and thus is not required to depend on the personal credit of the buyer). Foreclosure is discussed further *infra*, p. 333.

1. **Key terms:** As a matter of nomenclature, the following are some key terms: (1) the borrower, who gives the mortgage, is called the *"mortgagor"*; (2) the lender, who has the benefit of the mortgage, is the *"mortgagee"*; and (3) the mortgagor is said to retain *"equity"* in the property (an abbreviation for the "equity of redemption", discussed further *infra*, p. 333).

2. **Two documents:** There are two documents associated with nearly every mortgage: (1) the *note* (or "bond"); and (2) the *mortgage* itself.

    a. **The note:** The *note* is the buyer's personal promise to make the repayments. Since the note is not an interest in land, it is not recorded. But it serves an important function: if there is a foreclosure against the property, and the foreclosure sale does not yield at least an amount equal to the outstanding mortgage debt (including accrued interest), the note will serve as the basis for a *deficiency judgment* against the borrower. This is because the note represents a personal obligation of the borrower, not merely an obligation to be repaid out of the land.

    b. **Mortgage:** The *mortgage itself* is a document which gives the lender a claim against the land for the repayment of the amount loaned. All right of foreclosure comes from this document, not from the note. Since the mortgage in effect gives the mortgagee an interest in the land, the mortgage is *recorded*.

3. **Deed of mortgaged premises:** Usually when mortgaged property is sold, the mortgage is *paid off* at the closing. One reason for this is that if the mortgage has previously been partially paid off, or the land has appreciated in value since the mortgage, the mortgage will probably not meet the financial requirements of the new buyer (since it will be for too small an amount relative to the purchase price). The second reason is that the mortgage may contain a "due on sale", or "acceleration" clause (discussed further *infra*, p. 335). Nonetheless, there are times when the property is sold without paying off the mortgage; this can be done either by: (1) having the purchaser take "subject to" the mortgage; or (2) having the purchaser actually "assume" the mortgage.

    a. **Sale "subject to" mortgage:** If the purchaser merely takes *"subject to"* the mortgage, he is *not personally liable* for payment of the mortgage debt. Of course, if he wishes to keep his equity in the property, he will have to make the payments, since otherwise the mortgagee will foreclose. But if the mortgagee does foreclose, and the property does not bring enough in the foreclosure sale to pay off the outstanding mortgage debt, the mortgagee may *not sue the purchaser for the balance*. (The mortgagee may, however, sue the original mortgagor for this balance, since the sale of the mortgaged premises does nothing to the mortgagor's personal liability.)

    b. **Assumption of mortgage:** It is usually in the original mortgagor's interest to persuade the new purchaser to *assume* payment of the mortgage. This has the effect of making the purchaser *liable* for payment of the mortgage, both to the original mortgagor, and to the mortgagee (probably as a third-party beneficiary). The advantage to the mortgagor is that the foreclosure mortgagee is likely to seek a deficiency judgment against the assuming purchaser before coming after the mortgagor; also, if the mortgagee does get a deficiency judgment against the original mortgagor, the latter can in turn sue the assuming purchaser.

    c. **Novation:** Occasionally, the mortgagor may get the mortgagee to *substitute* the new purchaser for the original mortgagor's own personal liability. This means that not only is the new purchaser personally liable for the mortgage, but the original mortgagor is completely *off the hook*. Such a substitution is called a *novation*. (Needless to say, mortgage lenders are generally not overly enthusiastic about such transactions.)

4. **Assignment of mortgage:** The mortgagee will often wish to liquidate his interest by *selling the mortgage* to someone else. Indeed, government-sponsored corporations like "Fannie Mae" (Federal National Mortgage Assoc.) exist for the sole purpose of enabling banks to write mortgages and immediately sell them to the corporation.

   a. **Transfer of mortgage and note:** Normally, the purchaser of the mortgage will insist on receiving an assignment of both the mortgage instrument and the note.

   b. **Transfer of mortgage only:** As noted earlier, the mortgage exists only as security for the debt. Therefore, a mortgage *cannot be transferred independently of the debt*. Any transaction which purports to transfer the mortgage without the note is void.

   c. **Transfer of note alone:** But a transfer of the *note without the mortgage* is not void. Instead, the mortgage is deemed to pass with the note. Thus even if the buyer receives only the note, he will be able to foreclose on the mortgage if the payments are not made. (However, it is desirable for the purchaser to obtain the mortgage, so that he may record it; otherwise there is a chance that subsequent *bona fide* purchasers or mortgagees may cut off his interest.)

5. **Nature of mortgagee's interest:** The mortgage is generally in the form of an *outright conveyance*, together with a "defeasance" clause which provides that if the mortgagor pays the principal and meets all other obligations of the note, the conveyance to the mortgagee will become void. C&L, p. 744. Thus the mortgage appears to give the mortgagee legal title, subject to a condition subsequent.

   a. **"Title" theory:** Because the mortgage generally looks like a conveyance of the legal title, many states purport to treat the mortgagee as indeed holding legal title. These states are known as *"title theory"* states.

   b. **"Lien theory" states:** But other states have stressed that a mortgage merely gives the mortgagee *security for repayment*, i.e., a lien. These states are thus called *"lien theory"* states. C&L, p. 747.

   c. **Significance of distinction:** In earlier years, there were important practical differences between the way certain problems were handled in lien theory and title theory states. However, today nearly all states *treat the mortgage as a lien* for the vast majority of purposes. For instance: (1) if the mortgagee takes possession before foreclosure, he must apply any rents to his claim against the mortgagor; and (2) as noted, the mortgage follows the debt, so that sale of the note results in an automatic transfer of the mortgage (which would not be the case if the mortgage were really treated as legal title to the property). See C&L, pp. 746-47.

6. **No right to prepay:** The mortgagee has the right to have his money earning interest for the entire term of the mortgage, unless the parties agree otherwise. Thus the mortgagor does not automatically have the right to *prepay* the full principal before the maturity date.

   a. **Prepayment clause:** Therefore, the mortgagor should attempt to insert a clause in the mortgage giving him a *right of prepayment*. In many states, the mortgagor is required to be given this right as a matter of law after a certain period (e.g., after the first two years). The matter is frequently handled by charging the mortgagor a prepayment **penalty** (e.g., six-months interest); the penalty often declines the longer the mortgage has been in force.

7. **Foreclosure:** *Foreclosure* is the process by which the mortgagee may reach the land to satisfy the mortgage debt, if the mortgagor defaults. In order to understand modern-day foreclosure practices, it is necessary to understand a bit about the history of foreclosure.

   a. **History of foreclosure:** Recall that the mortgage is generally in the form of a deed subject to a condition subsequent (that the mortgage be satisfied as of the "law day"). If the mortgagor had not paid the full sum by the law day, the courts of law regarded the mortgagor's interest as being completely extinguished, since the condition subsequent to the mortgagee's deed could now no longer occur.

      i. **Equity of redemption:** But the courts of equity began to give some relief to mortgagors who lost their property in this way. At first, only in special hardship situations (e.g., the mortgagor was robbed on his way to pay off the debt), but then routinely, the courts of equity issued decrees ordering the mortgagee to accept payment by the mortgagor even after default. This right became known as the mortgagor's *equity of redemption*. See Nutshell, p. 319; C&L, pp. 744-45; C&J, pp. 1037-38. This equity of redemption was in accord with the well-established principle that equity abhors a forfeiture.

      ii. **Equitable bill of foreclosure:** This situation made life difficult for the mortgagee, since even after default, and theoretical extinguishment of the legal title, the mortgagor continued indefinitely to have the right to pay his debt and get back the property. This made the property unsalable by the mortgagee, and defeated the purpose of security for repayment. therefore, the equity courts gave relief to mortgagees in the form of a *"bill to foreclose"*. The mortgagee would petition the court to cut off the mortgagor's right of redemption. The court could order that this occur in two different ways: (1) *a strict foreclosure* of the right of redemption, which would bar the mortgagor from redeeming unless he paid up within a specified period (e.g., three months); and (2) a *foreclosure by sale*, in which the property would be sold by an officer of the court, with the proceeds of the sale used first to pay off the mortgagee's claims and the balance paid to the mortgagor.

      iii. **Clauses waiving right of redemption:** Mortgagees have sometimes tried to accomplish the same result as a bill to foreclose by inserting a *clause* into the mortgage itself by which the mortgagor purported to *waive his equity of redemption*. However, the courts have universally refused to enforce such clauses. As the idea is sometimes put, *"Once a mortgage, always a mortgage"*; a mortgage cannot be converted into an outright deed by the mere default of the mortgagor. C&J, p. 1038-39.

   b. **Modern-day foreclosure:** Foreclosure *by sale* has become the standard means of foreclosing mortgages in America. Since it will frequently be the case that the property is worth more than the outstanding mortgage debt (i.e., that the mortgagor has some "equity" in the property), foreclosure by a public sale preserves the mortgagor's right to receive the excess. Also, it safeguards him from being unfairly held for a deficiency judgment.

i. **Judicial foreclosure sale:** In many jurisdictions, a foreclosure sale must be conducted under *judicial supervision*, and is handled by a public official such as a *sheriff*. The court supervises the advertising done to publicize the sale, and supervises the time and place. Such a "judicial foreclosure sale" requires a *costly* and *time-consuming lawsuit* by the mortgagee. On the other hand, the mortgagee usually cannot attack the foreclosure sale after the fact (e.g., on the grounds that it fetched an unfairly low price, and deprived him of his equity) if the judicially-supervised procedure is used.

ii. **Private foreclosure sale:** Some but not all jurisdictions give the lender a second way to foreclose: he may conduct a *private foreclosure sale*, without the need for a formal lawsuit or judicial supervision. In states that allow this method, the lender must usually bargain for it in advance by getting his security in the form of a *"deed of trust"* (rather than a "mortgage"). Under the deed of trust, the borrower conveys title to the property to the lender or to a third party, who holds the title in trust; if the borrower defaults, the trustee can sell the land without going to court. But to prevent the lender from conducting a sale that fetches an *unfairly low price* (so that the borrower either has to pay a deficiency or loses some or all of his equity in the property), statutes and courts require the lender to use *good faith* and *due diligence* to get the highest possible price at the sale. If the lender does not do this, he may lose his right to a deficiency judgment, and may even have to pay the borrower damages equal to the amount of equity that the borrower would have realized from a properly-conducted sale.

Example: The Ps borrow money from D, and give D as security a "power of sale mortgage" (analogous to a deed of trust) on their house. The Ps fall behind in their payments, and D schedules a private foreclosure sale. D takes out the statutorily-required advertisement of sale, but no prospective bidders show up for the sale. The Ps ask for an adjournment, but D refuses. D's representative makes the only bid at the sale. This bid is for $27,000, roughly the amount owed on the mortgage. D thereby takes title. D immediately offers to sell the property for $40,000, and within two days sells it to X (an unaffiliated third party) for $38,000. The only prior appraisal of the property that D had showed it to have been worth $46,000 less than 18 months previously. The Ps bring a lawsuit for damages for the equity that they did not receive but would have received from a properly-conducted sale.

Held, for the Ps. A mortgagee owns the mortgagor a "duty of good faith" and a duty of "due diligence". The mortgagee must therefore "exert every reasonable effort to obtain a fair and reasonable price under the circumstances." Inadequacy of the price received does not alone show a lack of good faith or due diligence. But here, the low price (compared with the prior appraisal), when coupled with the fact that D knew or should have known that the price was low (as demonstrated by the fact that D immediately listed the property for 50% more than the foreclosure-sale price), meant that D lacked due diligence when it refused to either set a minimum bid or postpone the sale until more bidders could be found. The Ps should receive damages equal to "the difference between a fair price for the property and the price obtained at the foreclosure sale." *Murphy v. Financial Development Corp.*, 495 A.2d 1245 (N.H. 1985).

c. **Strict foreclosure:** *Strict foreclosure* is still available as an alternative in a few states (e.g., Connecticut and Vermont). In a strict foreclosure, the creditor takes the property in exchange for cancelling the debt — the mortgagee gives up the right to a deficiency judgment, and the mortgagor gives up the right to any equity. Strict foreclosure is usually employed *in addition to*, rather than in lieu of, foreclosure by sale. The advantage of this approach is that if, for some reason, the foreclosure sale is technically invalid, after the passage of a sufficient time for strict foreclosure to take effect the mortgagor's right of redemption is certain to be cut off. See C&L, p. 748.

    d. Acceleration clauses: A mortgage usually provides that in case of a default, the *entire principal sum* shall become immediately due and payable. Such a provision is known as an *acceleration clause*. If the mortgage did not contain such a clause, the mortgagee would have to start a new foreclosure suit upon each default (and have that proceeding rendered moot by payment of just that outstanding installment).

        i. Waivable: Most acceleration clauses are drafted so that they may be *waived* by the mortgagee. If a waiver provision is omitted, the clause in effect allows full prepayment without a penalty if the mortgagor defaults; the mortgagor might therefore intentionally default, pre-pay in full, and refinance elsewhere at lower rates.

C. Installment contracts: Land, like personal property, can be bought under an *installment contract*. Such a contract provides for a down payment, with the balance of the purchase price to be paid in installments (usually monthly). What makes such an arrangement different from a purchase money mortgage (the other principal means of seller-financing) is that the buyer does *not receive his deed* until *after* he has paid all, or a substantial portion, of the purchase price.

    1. Why used: A buyer almost never uses an installment contract when there is some other financing solution. Such contracts, like their counterparts in the personal property area, are typically used by buyers who have poor credit and no ability to make more than a small down payment; for such buyers an installment arrangement is the only hope of someday gaining title to real estate.

    2. Forfeiture: The most important practical difference between mortgages and installment contracts is the consequences of a *default*. If the mortgagor fails to make his payments, the mortgage must be foreclosed, pursuant to a whole array of statutory and judicial safeguards (involving substantial expense to the mortgagee). Where the installment buyer defaults, on the other hand, the seller generally just exercised his contractual right to declare the contract *forfeited*; no judicial proceedings are necessary, and the buyer ends up forfeiting both the property and any payments he has already made.

        a. Modern treatment of forfeiture: Until the last few decades, courts tended to enforce installment contract forfeiture clauses as written (unless the court could find that the seller has *waived* his right to insist on strict performance, e.g., by accepting last payments in the past). But modern courts have frequently refused to enforce such clauses literally, and have given several types of relief:

            i. Right to foreclosure safeguards: Many courts have held that where the buyer has paid a *substantial portion* of the purchase price, and the seller would be unjustly enriched by a complete forfeiture, *statutory foreclosure proceedings applicable to mortgages* must be used. Thus in *Skendzel v. Marshall*, 301 N.E.2d 641 (Ind. 1973), the buyer had paid $21,000 of a $36,000 purchase price. The court concluded that a $21,000 forfeiture (which would be the consequence of enforcing the contract's forfeiture clause as written) would be unjust, and a violation of the rules against penalty damage clauses. Therefore, the court treated the contract as being a security interest, and required judicial foreclosure proceedings (so that any equity from a foreclosure sale would go to the buyer). See also *Bean v. Walker*, 464 N.Y.S.2d 895 (N.Y.App.Div. 1983), similarly holding that the seller must use foreclosure proceedings where the buyer had made **substantial improvements** to the property, and had paid almost half ($7,100 of $15,000) of the purchase price.

ii. Right to continue contract: An alternative approach is for the court to give the buyer the right to **make the payments on which he has been in default**, and then continue with the contract. That is, he is given, in effect, an "equity of redemption" similar to that of a mortgagor. See, e.g., *Union Bond & Trust Co. v. Blue Creek Redwood Co.*, 128 F.Supp. 709 (N.D., Cal. 1955), giving buyer the right to complete the contract if he paid the entire purchase price plus damages for his delay in performance.

Note: Before the court grants either of the two remedies discussed just previously, it will want to satisfy itself that termination of the contract would indeed amount to an unfair forfeiture. Regardless of the percentage of the contract price paid, if the amount of each payment corresponds roughly to the **fair rental value** of the property, the court is much less likely to award these remedies, on the theory that the buyer has merely been paying a rent-substitute for the fair use he has had of the land.

b. Defenses to summary proceeding: Where an installment seller declares the contract forfeited, his next step is to seek to **evict** the buyer. To do this, he may usually employ **summary proceedings** of the same sort used to evict a tenant (see *supra*, p. 176).

III. DEEDS

A. Nature of a deed: The deed is the document which acts to **pass title** from the grantor to a grantee.

1. Doctrine of merger: The deed typically **replaces the contract** as the embodiment of the parties' relationship. Under the doctrine of **merger**, most obligations imposed by the contract of sale are **discharged** unless they are repeated in the deed. See Cribbet, p. 202. Thus if the contract calls for a merchantable title, as embodied in a warranty deed, but the purchaser carelessly accepts a quitclaim deed, the buyer will not be able to sue on the contractual provisions if the title turns to be defective; he is limited to the provisions of his deed. Thus the contract is relevant only during the gap between its signing and the delivery of the deed.

a. Collateral promise: However, the merger doctrine will not apply where the covenant is **collateral** to the promise to convey land. For instance, if the sale contract contained a promise to do certain construction in accordance with particular plans or specifications, the court might hold that this promise was not merged into a deed for the real estate, since it was collateral to the issue of title to the land.

b. Uniform Act: The Uniform Land Transactions Act would **abolish** the doctrine of merger entirely: "Acceptance by a buyer or a secured party of a deed or other instrument of conveyance is not of itself a waiver or renunciation of any of his rights under the contract under which the deed or other instrument of conveyance is given and does not of itself relieve any party of the duty to perform all his obligations under the contract." §1-309, ULTA.

2. **The modern deed generally:** There are two basic types of deeds: (1) the *quitclaim* deed, in which the grantor makes no covenant that his title is good; and (2) the *warranty* deed, in which the grantor makes one or more promises about the state of the title. (The various covenants for title which might be made in a warranty deed are discussed *infra*, p. 347.)

B. **Description of the property:** An accurate *description of the property* is clearly one of the most important aspects of the deed. Not only must the description correspond to what the parties actually intend to convey, but it should be worded in such a way that the grantee's title will be merchantable for purposes of a future sale.

1. **Types of description:** There are three principal ways of describing land. Their use varies both according to the part of the country, and according to whether the land is urban/suburban or rural.

    a. **Metes and bounds:** A *metes and bounds description* is one which begins by establishing a starting point (usually based on a *"monument"*, i.e., a visible landmark, whether artificial or natural). Then, a series of *calls and distances"* is given, each of which represents a line going in a certain direction for a certain distance. Thus a metes and bounds description might, after specifying a beginning point (e.g., the intersection of two particular streets), state "running thence North 50 degrees 26 minutes 36 seconds West for 273 feet, thence North 59 degrees 30 minutes 8 seconds East for 76 and 37/100th feet," etc.

        i. **Used in east coast:** The metes and bounds description is found most often east of the Mississippi River.

        ii. **Must close:** The metes and bounds description must *"close"*. That is, by following each of the courses and distances, one must eventually be brought back to the starting point. (However, if the failure to enclose is clearly attributable to a particular clerical error, the court may order the deed reformed or interpreted in such a way that the error is rectified. See, e.g., *Hoban v. Cable*, discussed *infra*, p. 338.)

    b. **Government Survey:** In the last part of the eighteenth century, the U.S. Government began surveying the public lands. Nearly all land in states west of the Mississippi (except Texas), and much agricultural land east of the Mississippi but north of the Ohio River, came within the survey. When these lands passed into private use, they were described in terms of this *U.S. Government Survey*. Today, this is the standard method of describing rural lands in vast portions of the country.

        i. **How it works:** The Survey divided the public lands into rectangular tracts by running parallel lines north and south and by crossing them at right angles with other parallel lines so as to form rectangles six miles square. Each of these six-mile-tracts is called a *"township"*. Each township is divided into thirty-six one-mile-square tracts, called *sections*; each section contains 640 acres. The sections are numbered consecutively, beginning with Section One at the northeast corner, and running back and forth one row at a time so that Section Thirty-six is reached in the southeast corner. By dividing each section into smaller segments, one may conveniently describe quite small segments of land.

For instance, a two-and-one-half acre parcel might be described as "the southeast one-quarter of the southeast one-quarter of the southeast one-quarter of the southeast one-quarter of Section 12 in Township O." See C&J, p. 1182.

ii. Not suitable for urban land: But the Government Survey method is not suitable for urban or even suburban land, where the typical lot size is less than one acre.

c. **The plat method:** Recall that a developer who wishes to subdivide his property may record a map, or *plat*, of that property, which shows the location of individual lots. A recorded plat furnishes a convenient means of describing land; the deed merely refers to, e.g., "Lot 2 in Block 5 in Highwood, a subdivision platted on a map filed in the Officer of the Registrar of the County of Westchester on June 13, 1910." Anyone reading this description in the records would then look at the recorded map to see exactly where the boundaries of the lot are located.

2. **Interpreting the description:** In interpreting the description of the land conveyed, the court will attempt to *ascertain the intent of the parties*, particularly that of the grantor. If the language used in the deed is clear and unambiguous, evidence extrinsic to this deed will generally not be considered.

Example: O conveys real property to P's predecessor in title, the deed reciting that it includes "the west 50 feet of Lot 13. . . ." D then conveys adjoining land to D's predecessor in title. D claims that P's deed means that P's lot runs for 50 feet along Oak Street (a street which runs southwest to northeast), rather than for 50 feet east to west; if D is correct, P's lot is only 42 feet wide. D brings a quiet title action. *Held* (on appeal), for P. The deed is unambiguous on its face, and gives P a lot 50 feet wide. Since the deed is unambiguous, the trial judge erred in admitting testimony showing that O had really intended to convey only that portion of the lot which had a frontage of 50 feet along Oak Street. If D sought *reformation* of P's deed, extrinsic evidence might be admissible (the court did not decide whether it would be); but the suit here involved only construction, nor reformation. *Walters v. Tucker*, 281 S.W.2d 843 (Mo. 1955).

a. **Ambiguity:** But if there is some *ambiguity* in the deed, evidence outside of the deed (e.g., the language of the contract, testimony about the purpose of the conveyance, evidence as to the land owned by the grantor prior to the deed, etc.) will be considered. 3 A.L.P. 384.

b. **Reformation for fraud or mistake:** As the *Walters* court suggested in dictum, a deed may be *reformed* by a court of equity when its terms are the result of a mutual mistake or fraud. Evidence extrinsic to the deed is generally admissible for showing fraud or mistake, even if the deed itself is unambiguous. See, B,C&S, p. 773. Reformation for mistake is often used in correcting minor boundary errors.

c. **Insufficient description:** A description may be so hopelessly confused that the court is unable to ascertain at all what land is conveyed. If so, then the entire conveyance may be held to be *void*. But courts will go out of their way to avoid such a result, even if it means correcting what appear to be major error in the parties' language. For instance, in *Hoban v. Cable*, 60 N.W. 466 (Mich. 1894), the deed gave a metes and bounds description which, when followed literally, failed to come even close to returning to the starting point. By making reference to a map of the area, and other language in the deed, the court redrew *two* of the four lines of the deed so that a completely enclosed rectangle was formed.

d. Applicable to two parcels: A description may be so poorly drafted that it *applies to more than one parcel*. If so, the court will accept evidence about which of these parcels was owned by the grantor; if only one parcel meeting the description was owned by the grantor, the court will of course presume that this is the parcel that was intended to be conveyed (rather than presuming that the grantor intended to convey a parcel which he did not own).

Example: O grants a mortgage to P. The mortgage document states that the land is in McDonough County, and that it is "one acre and a half in the northwest corner of Section 5, together with a brewery . . . thereon. . . ." O then grants a second mortgage to D. When P sues to foreclose upon his mortgage, D argues that P's mortgage is fatally indefinite because there happens to be more than one Section 5 in McDonough County. *Held*, for P. The ambiguity is a "latent" one, and may thus be resolved by resort to extrinsic evidence. Evidence was properly accepted that O owned only one brewery in McDonough County, which happened to be in the northwest corner of one of the two Section 5's. This was sufficient to establish the tract intended to be mortgaged. Also, the description of "one acre and a half in the northwest corner" is not fatally uncertain; although the mortgage does not state the shape of this parcel, the court will presume that a square parcel was referred to (since the parcel is described by reference to the U.S. Government Survey method, which is itself based upon rectangular tracts). *Bybee v. Hageman*, 66 Ill. 519 (1873).

i. "Latent" vs. "patent" ambiguities: As the opinion in *Bybee* suggests, some courts have distinguished between *"latent"* and *"patent"* ambiguities. A patent ambiguity is one which appears from examination of the deed itself; a latent one appears only when facts external to the deed are shown (e.g., that there happened to be two Section 5's in McDonough County, in *Bybee*). Courts formerly held that a patent ambiguity must be resolved within the four corners of the document, without resort to external evidence. (The rationale for this rule is that the parties must have been aware of the ambiguity, and attempted to resolve it within the words of the deed itself.) A latent ambiguity, by contrast, could be proved by resort to extrinsic evidence. Today, the rule is rarely followed, and evidence extrinsic to the deed is generally accepted regardless of whether the ambiguity is latent or patent. Cribbet, p. 210.

e. Subsequent actions of parties: In resolving ambiguities, the courts will also look to the *subsequent actions of the parties*. For instance, if either or both have *physically marked the boundaries* in a particular way, the court will treat this as some evidence of their intent (particularly if both have agreed on the marking).

i. Restrictions: However, if the concept of fixing the boundary by post-deed oral agreement is interpreted too loosely, the Statute of Frauds may be swallowed up — parties could convey property with virtually no description, and then orally fix its boundaries, in a way that would wreak havoc on land records and leave third parties in a state of irreversible doubt. Therefore, courts have imposed varying requirements before orally-agreed-upon boundaries will be enforced. See, e.g., *Loverkamp v. Loverkamp*, 45 N.E.2d 871 (Ill. 1943), where the court required that the parties be either in dispute or in doubt about the proper location of the boundary, before their oral agreement fixing it would be enforced.

f. Construction in grantee's favor: One often-cited canon of construction is that the deed will be interpreted in the way which is *most favorable to the grantee*. See Cribbet, p. 210. Since the deed is almost always drafted by the grantor, this amounts to the traditional contract rule that a document will be construed against the draftsman.

> **Example:** Townsend conveys property to Miller. One portion of the deed says that Townsend "[d]oes hereby grant and convey . . . the said tract of land. . . ." But another paragraph gives Miller "The right to enter upon said land, cut and remove trees, mine and remove minerals, and make such alteration . . . as may be required in the removal of said trees or the mining of said ores or minerals." Townsend dies without heirs, and the State of Oregon claims that there escheats to it everything except the raw mineral rights. Millers claims that the entire fee simple was transferred to him.
>
> *Held*, the deed is hopelessly ambiguous as to whether mere mineral rights, or the entire fee simple, were intended to be transferred. Nor is there any extrinsic evidence which sheds light on the controversy. Therefore, the canon of construction that doubts should be resolved in favor of the grantee, and that the greater estate should pass, will be applied. Miller gets the fee simple. *First Nat. Bank of Oregon v. Townsend*, 555 P.2d 477 (Or. 1976).

3. Conflicting terms: A frequent cause of ambiguity is that two parts of the description *conflict* with each other. Apart from the general rules of interpretation discussed above, courts have developed a *hierarchy* for resolving such conflicts. These are not hard-and-fast rules, but simple canons of construction based upon the usual reliability of various types of descriptions; therefore, these rules will yield to clear evidence of the parties' intent. Following are the various types of descriptions, in descending order of presumed reliability.

a. Monuments: *Monuments* (i.e., landmarks which are unlikely to be moved or misidentified, such as streets, rivers, houses, etc.) are considered *most reliable*. As between a natural monument and an artificial one, the natural one is usually preferred.

i. Surveyor's markers: When a *survey* is taken of property, the surveyor usually marks important points on the property with stakes. These are considered artificial monuments, and will generally have priority over most other factors. See, e.g., *Arnold v. Hanson*, 204 P.2d 97 (Dist. Ct. App. Cal. 1949), holding that such stakes controlled over a filed subdivision plat.

b. Neighbor's boundary: Next, if the description refers to a *neighbor's boundary*, this boundary will have preference. However, this preference is usually given only where the boundary is relatively *clearly marked* on the land.

c. Map or plat of survey: Next in preference is the *map* or *plat* derived from a *survey*. 3 A.L.P. 446.

d. Courses and distances: Then, *courses and distances* (e.g., "thence north thirty-six degrees fifty-two minutes sixteen seconds west for 56.7 feet . . . ") are considered.

i. Course vs. distance: When the course conflicts with the distance (i.e., the other aspects of the deed are such that the course and distance cannot both be correct), courts generally give preference to the course (i.e., the angle) rather than the length. This is based on the fact that surveyors are more likely to make errors in measuring distance than in reading the angle from their instruments; see 3 A.L.P. 447. However, the *intent* of the parties will always be the guiding consideration.

 e. Area: A reference to the *area* covered by a tract gets the least preference if it conflicts with anything else. Thus a statement that the tract covers 37,492 square feet will generally not control if it is in conflict with an angle, distance, monument, map or anything else. See 3 A.L.P. 448.

C. Various formalities: We consider now several formalities required for the valid *execution* of a deed.

 1. Identification of parties: The deed must *name* or otherwise *identify* the parties. 3 A.L.P. 281.

  a. Use of blank: If a *blank* is left for the grantee's name to be filled in after delivery, most courts hold that the deed is not effective (though the person to whom delivery is made may bring an action for reformation). Some courts, however, hold that this gives authority to the grantee to fill in his own name, and that when the latter does so, the deed becomes effective. *Id.* at 285.

  b. Reservation of title to stranger: Some courts still adhere to the common-law rule that if a person is not named as a grantee, an interest in him may not be reserved by the grantor. As the rule is sometimes put, "An interest may not be reserved in a stranger to the deed." See, e.g., *Willard v. First Church of Christ Scientist, Pacifica*, 498 P.2d 987 (Cal. 1972), stating that rule but rejecting it.

 2. Signatures: The grantor must place his *signature* on the deed. However, any mark intended to authenticate the document will suffice (e.g, an "X" mark if the grantor is illiterate). The signature of the *grantee* is *not necessary*.

 3. Seal: At one time, a deed had to have a private *seal* affixed to it to be valid. But today, nearly all states have *abolished* the seal requirement.

 4. Attestation: Statutes in some states require a deed to be *attested* to, i.e., *witnessed* by one or more persons not parties to the transaction.

  a. Survival of non-statutory forms: Keep in mind that a statute which imposes the requirement of witnessing or any other formality may be held to apply only to *certain types* of deeds. Other common-law types of deeds may survive in their original form. For instance, in *French v. French*, 3 N.H. 234 (1825), a statute provided that a deed would be valid if it was, *inter alia*, signed by two or more witnesses. The court held that the intent of the statute was to dispense with the requirement of livery of seisin for a common-law feoffment, and that the statute did not apply at all to a *bargain and sale deed*. Therefore, a bargain and sale deed would be judged by its non-statutory common-law requisites, which did not include the requirement of witnessing.

 5. Acknowledgment: Statutes sometimes require that the deed must be *acknowledged*, i.e., *notarized*. It is only the grantor's signature which must be notarized in such cases. (However, many statutes require acknowledgment and/or attestation only as a prerequisite to *recording*, not as a prerequisite to the validity of the deed between the grantor and grantee.)

6. **Consideration:** The presence of *consideration* is not necessary for the deed to be valid. 3 A.L.P. 287-88.

D. Delivery of the deed: For a deed to be valid, it must not only be executed (as described immediately above), but also *"delivered"*. However, the requirement of "delivery" does not mean that the deed must necessarily be manually given to the grantee. Instead, the delivery requirement is satisfied by "words or conduct of the grantor which evidence his *intention* to make his deed *presently operative* . . . so as to vest title in the grantee and to surrender his own control over the title. . . ." 3 A.L.P. 312. See generally, Nutshell, pp. 247-59.

1. **Matter of intent:** Thus the requirement is not physical at all, but rather, an *intent that the deed shall operate at once.* See, e.g., *McMahon v. Dorsey*, 91 N.W.2d 893 (Mich. 1958) (manual transfer not necessary; delivery may be proved by evidence of the grantor's intent, such as statements to neighbors.)

   a. **Presumptions from transfer of possession:** However, the presence or absence of a manual transfer may give rise to a *presumption* of delivery or non-delivery. If the grantor *retains possession*, there will be a presumption that delivery was not intended; but this may be rebutted by a showing of intent to the contrary (as in *McMahon, supra*). Conversely, if possession is *transferred to the grantee*, a presumption arises that delivery was intended (but may be rebutted by a showing that the deed was not intended to become effective until a later date). Where possession is given to a *third party* who is not the agent of either the grantor or the grantee, no presumption generally arises. (See discussion of escrow, *infra* p. 343.)

2. **Subsequent attempt to revoke:** If the delivery is valid, title passes immediately to the grantee. Thereafter, return of the deed to the grantor has no effect either to *cancel* the prior delivery or to *reconvey* the title to him. 3 A.L.P. 314-15. The only way the title can get back to the grantor is if a new, formally satisfactory, conveyance takes place.

3. **Effective on grantor's death:** The text of the deed, or surrounding circumstances, may show an intent on the part of the grantor that the deed not become effective until his *death*. If so, delivery will not be deemed to occur until death. Furthermore, the court may then treat the document as testamentary, and if it does not satisfy the formal requirements of a will, it will be ineffective.

   a. **Estate to become possessory on death:** But nothing prevents the grantor from delivering a deed which is *effective now*, but which contains a clause making the estate conveyed by the deed *possessory* only at the grantor's death. Thus O might today hand A a deed to Blackacre, with a clause in the deed stating that "the right to possession under this deed shall accrue after the death of O." This would be construed as the *present* grant of a *future interest* in the property, and would be valid. See 3 A.L.P. 315. (One reason for allowing such a present grant of a future estate is that the future estate *vests* at the time the deed is delivered; O loses his absolute control over the property.)

4. **Imposition of condition:** So long as there is the requisite intent that the deed take effect at present, there will not be a lack of delivery merely because, by the terms of the deed, certain events may cause it, or the estate contained in it, to become void.

   a. **Right to revoke:** A similar distinction is generally made between a right to *revoke* the *deed*, and a right to revoke the *estate* conveyed by a deed. The reservation by the grantor of a right to revoke the deed indicates that he has not parted with control of that deed, and that there was therefore no intent to create an estate. But if the deed itself is intended to take immediate effect, the fact that the grantor has a right to revoke the *estate* granted in that deed will not prevent the delivery from being valid, at least if the reservation of the power to revoke is *contained in the deed itself.*

Example: O deeds his residence to D, the deed expressly reserving "a life estate in [the] property [to O] with power to sell, rent, lease or otherwise dispose of said property during his natural lifetime." *Held,* this instrument clearly vested a remainder in fee simple in D, and all that was reserved was a power to revoke the remainder, not a power to revoke the deed itself. Therefore, the deed was not an invalid testamentary transfer. *St. Louis County Nat. Bank v. Fielder,* 260 S.W.2d 483 (Mo. 1953).

Note: Most courts appear to agree with *St. Louis County Nat. Bank v. Fielder,* that reservation in the deed itself of a right to revoke the estate granted is not inconsistent with delivery. But some courts hold such conveyances void on the grounds that they are testamentary. Others hold the conveyance good, but the power of revocation void. See B,C&S, p. 788, note 4.

b. Conditions and reservations not stated in the deed: Where the deed is transferred to the grantee subject to conditions or reservations *not expressed in the deed* (e.g., an oral understanding that the deed will not be effective until the grantor's death), courts generally hold that there is a *valid delivery,* and the conditions and/or reservations are of *no effect.* Burby, p. 304. The rationale for this rule is that it lends stability to record titles, since no examination of any fact not stated in the recorded deed is required. *Id.*

   i. Right to revoke: However, if what is reserved outside the deed is the grantor's right to *revoke the deed itself,* this will probably be convincing proof that no present transfer of title (i.e., no delivery) was intended. Thus transfer to the grantee with the oral statement "I reserve the right to cancel this deed" would show that there was no delivery; transfer to the grantee with the words "I reserve the right to sell the property during my lifetime" would constitute an effective delivery, and the oral reservation would not be enforced at all.

   ii. Difficult distinction: Obviously, the distinction between reservation of control over the deed, and reservation of control of the property or the estate granted, is often extremely hard to perceive. But the philosophical difference is clear; in the one case, an interest in land (albeit a contingent one) is intended to pass immediately, and in the other it is not. 3 A.L.P. 316-17.

5. Delivery to a third party (escrows): A new set of problems arises when physical transfer of the deed is made not to the grantee himself, but to a *third party* to be re-transferred to the grantee if certain conditions are met. Assuming that the third party is not an agent of either the grantor or grantee, the transaction is referred to as an *escrow.*

   a. Why escrows are used: Escrows have become quite common in commercial real estate closings, since they serve a useful function. Their principal purpose is to safeguard the interests of both the buyer and seller while some event is being awaited or verified.

   Example: S contracts to sell Blackacre to P. The land is located in a metropolitan area where the recording office is so overworked that it is impossible to tell on the closing date what the state of the title is at that moment. (Only the state of the title as it stood one week ago is available.) Therefore, S deposits his deed in escrow with Title Company. P deposits in escrow with Title Company both his check for the purchase price and a quitclaim deed back to S. The escrow instructions to Title Company order it to: (1) record S's deed immediately; and (2) as soon as the information is available, check the state of the title up to the date when this deed was recorded.

If title is satisfactory, Title Co. then delivers S's deed to P, tears up the quitclaim deed, and gives S P's check. This way, there is no risk that just prior to the closing, S will defraud P by selling the property to someone else, or mortgaging it. (If title turns out not to be good, the quitclaim deed is recorded and returned to S, and P's check is refunded to him.) See Cribbet, p. 214.

   i. Installment sale contract: Another common use for escrows is in *installment sales contracts*. S, the installment seller, puts the deed in escrow with, say, a bank. P makes his periodic payments (either to the bank or to S directly). After an agreed-upon portion of the payments have been made, the escrow agent delivers the deed to P. P is thus assured that S will not fail to perform as agreed upon, and is also assured that in the event of S's death, no judicial proceedings will be necessary. (See the discussion of grantor's death and the "relation back" doctrine, *infra*, p. 346.)

  b. Terminology: The third party with whom the deed (or any other instrument) is deposited is usually called the *"escrow agent"* or *"escrowee"*. The instruments to him are generally called the "escrow agreement".

  c. Must be to stranger: The essence of the escrow is that it is held by a party who is a *stranger to the transaction*. Thus a transfer of the deed to the grantee himself cannot be an escrow; since it cannot be an escrow, in nearly all states conditions upon the effectiveness of the delivery will not be respected.

    Example: D, a homeowner, arranges to sell his property to P (the State of Hawaii), in lieu of a condemnation proceeding. The parties agree that payment will be made at the same time the deed is tendered to the state. D executes the deed and hands it to the state, but no check is issued by the state until almost eleven months later. Ten months following the transfer of the deed to the state, D purports to cancel the transaction, on the grounds of P's untimeliness in making payment.

    Held, for P. Even though D may not have intended his deed to take effect until payment was made, such a conditional delivery may be accomplished only by use of an escrow. Delivery of a deed to a grantee cannot be an escrow, since a third party who is not a party to the transaction must be used as the depositary. Therefore, the condition did not take effect, the deed was delivered when manual transfer was made, and D cannot rescind the transaction. *State, By Pai v. Thom*, 563 P.2d 982 (Hawaii, 1977).

  d. Reservation of control by grantor: The purpose of the escrow transaction is to ensure that the deed is *removed from the grantor's control*, and that so long as the condition upon which the escrow is constructed occurs, the re-delivery to the grantee will occur. Therefore, if the grantor *reserves dominion and control* over the property, or the right to revoke the escrow, the escrow will *not be valid*, and no delivery to the escrow agent will be deem to have occurred. 3 A.L.P. 319-20.

Example: O gives his brother a deed to Blackacre with instructions to hold it till O's death and to give it to their mother if she survives O. O continues in possession of the property, and treats it as his own (e.g., by farming it, and granting rights of way over it). *Held*, this constituted a reservation of dominion and ownership by O, and no delivery into escrow occurred. Therefore, the transaction was testamentary in character, and was invalid since it did not meet the formal requisites of a will. *Atchison v. Atchison*, 175 P.2d 309 (Ok. 1946)

i. Estate may be contingent: But just as in the case of a delivery directly to the grantee, courts have distinguished between reservation of the right to revoke the *deed* or the *escrow*, and reservation of a *present interest* or of the right to terminate *the estate granted by the deed*. See, e.g., *Smith v. Fay*, 293 N.W. 497 (Iowa 1940), where instructions to the escrow agent that the deed was not to be delivered to the grantee unless the grantee survived the grantor, did not constitute a reservation of the right to revoke the deed, but simply the valid reservation of a life estate in the grantor.

e. Right to remove deed from escrow: Suppose the grantor deposits the deed in escrow, and then attempts to revoke the escrow itself. If the escrow is a *commercial* one, most courts hold that the grantor may do this (and thus that there is not really a valid escrow at all) unless there is an *enforceable contract of sale* between the buyer and seller. See, e.g., *Campbell v. Thomas*, 42 Wis. 437 (1877), where the parties made an oral land sale contract, and the grantor gave the deed to a third person with instructions to deliver it to the grantee if the latter paid a portion of a purchase price. The court held that the escrow was not valid because there was no enforceable contract of sale (due to the failure to comply with the Statute of Frauds), and that the grantor could revoke the escrow and get back his deed.

i. Written escrow instructions: It is *not* usually required, however, that the *escrow instructions themselves* be in writing (though this is obviously a better practice).

ii. Deed as memorandum: If the situation is one in which an enforceable sale contract is required, may the *deed itself* serve as a memorandum of the transaction? Most courts say that it may not. C&J, p. 1169-70, note 4.

iii. Condition certain to occur: If the condition upon which the escrow is based is *certain to occur*, most courts hold that no enforceable contract between grantor and grantee is required. They view the deposit with the escrow agent as being sufficient to transfer the title, since the grantor has lost all control. Thus a deed given to the escrow agent with instructions to deliver it upon the grantor's death is valid even though there is no enforceable contract between grantor and grantee.

f. When title passes: The deposit of the deed with the escrow agent usually *does not act to transfer legal title*. Thus legal title remains in the grantor until the performance of the stated *conditions* or the happening of the stated *event*. Burby, pp. 301-02. Once the event or condition occurs, title *automatically vests in the grantee*; re-delivery of the deed by the escrow agent to the grantee is not necessary (though this re-delivery, sometimes called the *"second delivery"* is customary).

i. Unauthorized delivery: Thus if the escrow agency delivers the deed to the grantee before the condition or event has occurred, this delivery is *ineffective to pass title*.

    ii. Bona fide purchaser: What if the grantee in such a case *records the deed*, and then sells to an innocent third person who buys in good faith and for value (i.e., a *bona fide purchaser*)? The courts are split on this question, with most of them holding that the original grantor keeps title, and that the *bona fide* purchaser is out of luck. See, e.g., *Clevenger v. Moore*, 259 P. 219 (Ok. 1927), to this effect. However, a substantial minority of courts prefer the *bona fide* purchaser, on the grounds that otherwise, the reliability of land records will be damaged (since the *bona fide* purchaser, when he inspects the record, finds a deed to the grantee recorded, with no evidence that there was an escrow at all, let alone whether it was satisfied). See Cribbet, p. 228. See also C,S&W, pp. 790-91.

    iii. Possession yielded to grantee: *All* courts seem to agree that if the grantee not only receives the deed without satisfying the condition, but is also given *possession* of the land by the grantor, a *bona fide* purchaser from the grantee will have priority over the grantor. In this situation, there is no way the *bona fide* purchaser could have learned of the escrow. Boyer, pp. 428-29.

g. The "relation back" doctrine: There is an important exception to the general rule that title remains in the grantor until the escrow condition is satisfied. In a few situations, once the condition occurs, the delivery of the deed *"relates back"* to the moment when the deed was first put in escrow.

    i. Death or incapacity of grantor: The relation back doctrine is most important where the grantor *dies* or becomes incapacitated (e.g., insane) before the condition occurs. Without the relation back doctrine, this death or incapacity would terminate the grantor's ability to complete the transaction. By use of the relation back doctrine, the transaction is completed by the escrow agent once the doctrine occurs. See, e.g., *First Nat. Bank & Trust Co. v. Scott*, 156 A. 836 (N.J. 1931).

    ii. Dower rights of grantor's spouse: Similarly, if the grantor gets married after placing the deed in escrow, the relation back doctrine will be used to defeat any right of dower in the spouse.

    iii. Grantee's death: The *death of the grantee* will also trigger use of the relation back doctrine.

    iv. Conveyance by grantor to third party: If the *grantor*, after depositing the deed in escrow, conveys to a *third-party purchaser*, the relation back doctrine will be used if that third-party purchaser took *with notice* (so that the grantee under the escrow agreement will be protected). But if the grantor conveys to a *bona fide purchaser* (i.e., one without notice of the prior escrowed deed), relation back will not generally be used. See Cribbet, p. 227.

    v. Not used in all situations: It is vital to remember that the relation back doctrine will not be applied in any but the above situations. For instance, if the escrow agent absconds with the buyer's money before the terms of the escrow have been satisfied, this loss falls on the buyer, not the seller, because title to the land has remained in the seller and title to the money has remained in the buyer. Nutshell, pp. 256-57.

    vi. Must be enforceable contract between grantor and grantee: Also, the relation-back doctrine will not apply unless there was an *enforceable contract* between the grantor and the grantee prior to the time the doctrine was triggered.

Example: Grantor and Grantee are negotiating for the sale of Grantor's land to Grantee. Grantor executes a deed to Grantee, and gives it to her lawyers, so that they can deliver it if Grantee accepts Grantor's written offer. On April 1, Grantor dies. Shortly thereafter, without knowing that Grantor has died, Grantee accepts Grantor's offer. On April 28, Grantee pays the purchase price to Grantor's lawyers, and they hand over the deed. The executors of Grantor's estate then sue to cancel the deed.

Held, for Grantor's estate. The relation-back doctrine will normally apply so that the grantor's death during the escrow period will not invalidate the delivery of the deed. But relation-back only applies where, prior to the grantor's death, there was an enforceable contract between the grantor and the grantee. Here, this never happened, and Grantor's offer was terminated by her death. Therefore, the delivery of the deed was of no legal effect. *Merry v. County Board of Ed.*, 87 So.2d 821 (Ala. 1956).

E. Acceptance: Most courts hold that a deed will not transfer title until it is not only delivered, but **accepted** by the grantee. However, such acceptance will be **presumed** if (as is usually the case) the conveyance is beneficial to the grantee.

1. **Rights of third party:** The only situation in which an acceptance issue is likely to arise is where the grantee does not immediately **learn** of the conveyance, and in the meantime, a third party has obtained rights. For instance, suppose that O executes a deed to A, and that O then puts the deed in a safe deposit box. He does not tell A about the conveyance, and then dies. In a suit between O's heirs and A, the heirs might prevail on the grounds that A could not have accepted the deed prior to O's death, because he did not know about it. 3 A.L.P. 333.

F. Covenants for title: Recall that there are two basic classes of deeds: (1) quitclaim deeds, in which the grantor does not make any representations as to the state of his title, but simply passes on whatever interest he has; and (2) warranty deeds, which contain various representations regarding the state of the grantor's title. In this section, we examine the various representations regarding title which are customarily made in a warranty deed; these representations are referred to as **covenants for title**. See generally Nutshell, pp. 259-72.

1. **Covenants in "warranty deed":** There are six covenants (individually discussed below) which are commonly used. Thus where the contract calls for "a general warranty deed" without specifying the covenants to be included in the deed, or where the contract calls for a deed "with the usual covenants", the court is likely to hold that the contract requires a deed with all six of these (although some American courts may not require one, the covenant for further assurance).

   a. **Contract which does not call for covenants:** If the contract does not call for covenants, the contract itself is usually interpreted to contain an implicit representation that the grantor has marketable title. (*Supra*, p. 317.) Then, if the title turns out, prior to the closing, to be unmarketable, the buyer may cancel the deed. But if the buyer **accepts a deed** without some or all of the covenants of title (whether these covenants were called for in the contract or not), any implied or express statements about the title made in the contract are in effect **waived**. Thus the buyer must be careful that the deed itself contains all the covenants of title that he has bargained for.

2. Six covenants: The six commonly used covenants for title are as follows:

a. **Covenant of seisin:** The *covenant of seisin* usually means today that the grantor has an indefeasible estate in the quality and quantity which he purports to convey. (The intricacies of common-law seisin may usually be ignored.) The covenant might be breached, for instance, if a third person had an **outstanding remainder**. Or, it would be breached if a third person had an **adverse possession** of the property, even if this adverse possession had not yet ripened into title; the reason for this is that seisin requires both legal ownership and possession. See 3 A.L.P. 461. Finally, of course, the covenant will be breached if legal title is in someone other than the grantor.

   i. **Pertains to title only:** The covenant of seisin *pertains to the title only, not to encumbrances*. Thus if there is an outstanding mortgage, the covenant of seisin is not breached (though, as discussed below, the covenant against encumbrances is).

b. **Covenant of right to convey:** The covenant of *right to convey* is considered by most courts to be the **exact equivalent** of the covenant of seisin. 3 A.L.P. 460. However, a few courts hold that the covenant of right to convey is not breached where some third party is in adverse possession that has not yet ripened into title, whereas the covenant of seisin is breached by such adverse possession. (According to these courts, both ownership and possession are necessary to satisfy a covenant of seisin, while mere ownership will satisfy a covenant of right to convey.) Burby, p. 314.

c. **Covenant against encumbrances:** The covenant *against encumbrances* is exactly what the name implies, i.e., a representation that there are no encumbrances against the property. Encumbrances are those impediments to title which do not affect the fee simple, but which diminish the value of the land. The various sorts of encumbrances are discussed more extensively *supra*, p. 321, in connection with the definition of marketable title.

d. **Covenants of quiet enjoyment and warranty:** The covenants of *quiet enjoyment* and *warranty* are virtually identical today. They do not promise that title is perfect (this is the role of the three covenants already discussed); instead, they constitute a **continuing contract** by the covenantor that the grantee's **possession** of the land will be defended against claims by third parties in existence on the date of the conveyance. Since they are in effect covenants for continued possession, they will run to future grantees, as is discussed more fully below. See 3 A.L.P. 467.

   i. **General vs. special covenant:** The covenant of warranty may be either *"general"* or *"special"*. A general covenant of warranty is one in which the grantor warrants that no person whatsoever will assert a paramount title. A special covenant of warranty is one which applies only to persons claiming **under the grantor**. Thus if the covenant were a special one, and the grantee were ousted by someone whose title derived from a point prior to the time the grantor gained any interest in the property, the grantee would not be able to sue on the warranty.

e. **Further assurance:** The covenant for *further assurance* is not widely used in the U.S. The covenant is a promise by the grantor that he will, in the future, make **any conveyance necessary** to give the grantee the full title that was intended to be conveyed. Cribbet, p. 295.

3. When and how breached: The six above covenants can be divided into two broad classes: (1) *present* covenants; and (2) *future* covenants.

   a. Present covenants: The covenants of seisin, right to convey and against encumbrances are *present covenants*. That is, they are breached, if at all, at the *moment the conveyance is made*. Therefore, a breach can occur *even though there is no eviction*. All the grantee needs to do to recover on the claim is to show that, in fact, title was defective on the date of the conveyance.

   b. Future covenants: The covenants of quiet enjoyment, warranty and further assurance, by contrast, are *future covenants*. They are breached *only when an eviction occurs*.

   Example: In 1957, P purchases land from D, and receives a warranty deed. In 1974, P grants an option on the land's coal-mining rights to X. Thereafter, P discovers that a prior grantor reserved to himself two-thirds of the land's coal rights in a recorded transaction, so P only owns one-third of the land's coal rights. In 1976, P sues D for breach of the covenant of quiet enjoyment.

   Held, for D. To recover for breach of the covenant of quiet enjoyment, P must show actual or constructive eviction. Here, there was neither, since no one holding a paramount title interfered with P's right to possess the coal (e.g, by beginning to mine it). Nor is constructive eviction shown by the fact that P has been required to renegotiate his contract with X for a lesser amount. If the mere existence of a paramount title were enough to constitute constructive eviction, the warranty of quiet enjoyment would be indistinguishable from that of seisin. *Brown v. Lober*, 389 N.E.2d 1188 (Ill. 1979).

   i. Constructive eviction: However, *constructive* eviction will suffice for the future covenants. Thus if a third party actively asserts a paramount claim, the grantee is not required to litigate the matter and wait to be forcibly evicted; instead, he may *purchase the third party's title* or satisfy the encumbrance in order to avoid eviction.

   ii. Notification to grantor: But the grantee will, if he is wise, give *notice* to the grantor when a third person asserts superior title or an encumbrance. If the grantor is given the chance to contest the claim, and he fails to do so, any settlement reached by the grantee will be binding on the grantor. If, by contrast, notice to the grantor is not given, and the grantee goes ahead and buys the superior title or otherwise settles the dispute, the grantor will have the opportunity, in a subsequent suit between grantee and grantor on the title, to argue that his title was not really defective. Burby, p. 316.

   c. Statute of Limitations: A key consequence of the distinction between present and future covenants involves the *statute of limitations*. The statute starts to run on a *present* covenant *at the time the conveyance is made*; the statute starts to run on a *future* covenant *only when an eviction occurs*. Therefore, when a purchaser only discovers a difficulty with title many years after the purchase, she is likely to find that her only hope of relief lies with the future covenants. For instance, in *Brown v. Lober, supra*, P tried desperately to establish a breach of the warranty of quiet enjoyment (a future covenant) because that claim was not time-barred; there clearly had been a breach of warranty of seisin, but that claim had become time-barred long before P discovered the title problem.

4. Prior knowledge of defect: Suppose that the grantee, before he takes his deed, is *aware* of a defect. Does he thereby waive the protection of the various covenants with respect to this defect? The issue arises most frequently in the case of the covenant against encumbrances.

    a. Ordinary rule: Ordinarily, the rule is that such knowledge does *not* nullify the various covenants. As the court stated in *Jones v. Grow Investment & Mortgage Co.*, 358 P.2d 909 (Utah 1961), a case involving an easement, "The very purpose of the covenant [against encumbrances] is to protect a grantee against defects and to hold that one can be protected only against unknown defects would be to rob the covenant of most of its value." (The court noted that the grantor is always free to restrict any or all of the covenants to those defects not known to the grantee at the time of conveyance.)

5. Enforcement by future grantee (running of covenants): The distinction between the present and future covenants is critical to the issue of whether the covenant *runs with the land*, i.e., whether it is *enforceable by subsequent grantees*.

    a. Present covenants: The present covenants (seisin, right to convey and against encumbrances) are generally held *not to run with the land*. Since these covenants are broken at the moment of the conveyance, they immediately become *choses in action* (i.e., a present right to sue). At common law, such choses in action were not assignable, and the rule against the running of present covenants derives from this fact (even though the prohibition on general assignment of choses has itself been abolished). See, e.g., *Mitchell v. Warner*, 5 Conn. 498 (1825), relying on the chose-in-action rationale.

        i. Minority view: However, a substantial minority of courts now holds that a breach of one of the present covenants *does run with the land*. Some of these courts have relied upon the fact that the prohibition on the assignment of choses in action no longer exists; see e.g., *Schofield v. Iowa Homestead Co.*, 32 Iowa 317 (1871), relying upon this rationale. Other courts have held that the original grantee gains a cause of action, but that this is implicitly assigned to any subsequent grantee, who may then sue the covenantor. (However, this approach often raises problems of the statute of limitations, since the statute presumably starts to run as soon as the initial claim arises.) Still other states have enacted statutes explicitly making such covenants run with the land; see e.g., Colorado Rev. Stat. c. 118, art. 1-21.

    b. Future covenants: The *future* covenants (warranty, quiet enjoyment and further assurance) are universally held to *run with the land*. Since these covenants are not breached until there is an actual or constructive eviction, they would be rendered almost useless if a subsequent transfer of the land cut them off.

    c. Intermediate quitclaim deed: Suppose that an *intermediate deed* in the chain of title is a *quitclaim* deed, or a sheriff's deed (which is generally without warranties), or some other type of transfer without warranties. Is the remote grantee nonetheless entitled to sue the original covenantor? Most courts hold that, assuming the original covenant is one which would otherwise run with the land, the presence of an intermediate deed without covenants does *not prevent the remote grantee from suing* the original covenantor. C&J, p. 1313.

6. Measure of damages: A defect in the title is likely not to be discovered for a substantial period of time following the original conveyance. If the land has increased in value, what *measure of damages* may be recovered by the covenantee (or by a subsequent grantee in a case where the covenant runs with the land)?

   a. Majority view: A substantial majority of courts hold that, if the title proves completely defective, the covenantee may recover the *purchase price paid*, plus interest. He may *not* recover for any *appreciation* in the value of the land (or even for the value of the land as it was at the time of the conveyance, if this is greater than the purchase price). As the court pointed out in *Davis v. Smith*, 5 Ga. 274 (1848), a contrary rule would mean that the covenantor's liability is virtually unlimited, a result that is not the intent of the parties. Also, the court noted, if the covenantor were held liable for an increase in value if title were bad, he should be entitled to participate in an increase in value if title proves good, something which obviously does not happen,.

   i. Minority view: A few courts, all in New England, do give the grantee damages in the amount of the present actual value of the land. See Cribbet, p. 302.

   b. Intermediate transaction: Where the party suing is not the original covenantee, but a *remote grantee*, a number of courts have held that this grantee's damages are *limited to the amount he paid to his own grantor*, if this is less than the amount paid by this intermediate grantor to the covenantor. Thus if O sells to A for $10,000, and A sells to B for $5,000, under this view B would be limited to $5,000 damages in a warranty suit against O.

   i. Contrary view: Other courts, however, do not impose such a limit, and would let B recover the full $10,000 which O received at the time he made the warranty. In support of this latter conclusion, it can be argued that the covenantor knew that he would be liable to the original covenantee for the full amount of the purchase price if title proved bad, and it does not seem fair to let him off the hook merely because a subsequent transaction has taken place, especially if this transaction is for a lower price because of the new purchaser's careful pursuit of a good bargain. See C&J, pp. 1325-26, note 1.

   c. Improvements: It will often be the case that the grantee of a defective title will place *improvements* on the land. If the rightful owner then appears and ousts him, must the owner pay *compensation* for these improvements? At common law, the unfortunate grantee of the defective title was viewed as a trespasser to whom no compensation was due. But cases and statutes in most states now provide for at least some compensation. See, e.g., *Madrid v. Spears*, 250 F.2d 51 (10th Cir. 1957), compelling the rightful owner to pay over the amount by which he was "unjustly enriched" from the improvements, but limiting the compensation to the lesser of the cost of the improvements or the amount which they have added to the land's market value.

7. Estoppel by deed: Suppose that A conveys Blackacre to B by warranty deed, at a time when A does not own Blackacre. If A *later* acquires Blackacre, many courts hold that title to Blackacre *immediately passes to B* by the doctrine of *estoppel by deed* (also called the doctrine of after-acquired title). Thus in a sense, the estoppel-by-deed doctrine furnishes B with an additional protection growing out of his warranty deed. The subject of estoppel by deed is discussed more extensively in the treatment of recording acts, *infra*, p. 374.

G. Warranty of habitability: Recall that in the landlord-tenant context, the original rule that the landlord makes no implied warranties of **habitability** is now widely giving way to the opposite rule. (*Supra*, p. 151.) A similar reversal is occurring in the area of outright sales of residences.

1. **Common law rule:** At common law, there were no implied warranties of title, let alone of habitability. A home buyer, like any other purchaser of real property, had only the benefit of those covenants which he could induce the seller to place into the deed.

2. **Modern trend:** But beginning in the 1960's, courts began to feel that the old rule of *caveat emptor* was no more appropriate in home-sale cases than in cases involving the sale of personal property (e.g., a car). Today, most states (and nearly all the states that have considered the matter recently) hold that a **builder/vendor** makes a warranty of **quality** or **skillful construction** when it sells a house. D&K, pp. 624-25.

   > **Example:** D, a land developer and builder, sells a lot to the Ps, containing a house that D has just built. Less than a year later, the septic tank system installed by D backs a large amount of sewage into the Ps' basement. D refuses to repair the system. It develops that D negligently designed the system so that water from the ground around the house would drain into the septic tank, preventing it from dealing with the sewage.
   >
   > *Held*, the Ps may recover against D on an implied warranty of habitability. The ordinary home buyer does not have the skill to discover defects in plumbing, electrical wiring, construction, etc., and he ought to be able to rely upon the professional builder or developer who sells him a new house. This is particularly so in view of the fact that a home is usually the largest single purchase a family makes in a lifetime. Therefore, a warranty of habitability will be implied in every sale of a new house; also, suit may be brought based upon negligence in the design and construction. The duration of warranty and negligence liability shall be determined by the "standard of reasonableness"; here the liability certainly has not expired, since less than a year elapsed between the sale and the discovery of the defect. *Tavares v. Horstman*, 542 P.2d 1275 (Wyo. 1975).

3. **Use of independent contractors:** Frequently, the developer/builder will not use his own employees to do much of the work, but will instead engage **independent contractors**. Several courts have held that the builder/developer has the same implied warranty liability for the acts of independent contractors done within the scope of their engagement as he would if his own employees had done the work. See, e.g., *Humber v. Morton*, 426 S.W.2d 554 (Tex. 1968) ("It is . . . highly irrational to make a distinction between the liability of a vendor-builder who employs servants and one who uses independent contractors.")

4. **Lender's liability:** Frequently, a developer/builder who sells shoddy homes will go quickly bankrupt. If so, a suit on an implied warranty or on any other theory against him is not likely to be much good. In a leading case, the California Supreme Court has held that a **lender** which participates closely with a builder may be subject to negligence or implied warranty liability for failing to see that the houses so produced are merchantable. In *Connor v. Great Western Savings & Loan Ass'n*, 447 P.2d 609 (Cal. 1968), the defendant Savings & Loan Association not only gave the developer construction loans, but also scrutinized the building plans, selling prices, and other business aspects of the developer's venture, to assure itself that the homes would be sold and the loan repaid. The Bank also wrote a large percentage of the mortgages on the homes that were eventually constructed. Severe defects in the foundations of many of the homes

developed due to the developer's lack of special precautions for building on adobe soil.

a. Holding: The court held that no joint ventures existed between the Bank and the developer. However, the Bank was found to have had a **duty of care** to its shareholders to "exercise its powers of control over the enterprise to prevent the construction of defective homes", and to have negligently failed to discharge that duty. The home buyers, as **third-party beneficiaries**, were entitled to recover for this negligence because: (1) the transaction was **intended** to affect the homeowners; (2) the harm to them was quite foreseeable; (3) it was certain that the owners indeed suffered injury; (4) there was a close link between the defendant's conduct and the resulting defect; (5) the Bank's conduct was morally culpable; and (6) the policy of preventing future harm would be advanced by imposing liability on the Bank. (But other lenders who held mortgages on the homes, and who claimed that their security had been impaired by the Bank's negligence, were not allowed to recover, because the enumerated factors applied less strongly to them.)

b. Dissent: A dissent in *Connor* argued that even if the bank was negligent to its shareholders, this should not serve as the basis for liability to third parties; as the dissent noted, if the Bank were instead an individual financier, "could it be said that the individual's failure to exercise prudence and care in protecting **himself** gives rise to a duty of care to others?"

c. Statutory change: The year after the *Connor* decision, the California legislature passed a statute absolving a real estate lender of all liability for defects in the real estate, unless the loss or damage "is a result of an act of the lender outside the scope of the activities of a lender of money or unless the lender had been a party to misrepresentations with respect to such real or personal property." Cal. Civ. Code, §343. It is quite clear that this statute was intended to, and does, change the result in the *Connor* case.

5. Used homes: The courts have thus far almost always refused to allow an implied warranty claim against one who is **not in the business** of building or selling homes. As a practical matter, this means that an implied warranty suit generally cannot be brought by the buyer of a **used home** against the **person who sold it to him**.

a. Implied warranty suit against builder: But most courts now allow a purchaser of a used home to sue the **original builder** for breach of the implied warranty of habitability, if a defect is latent when the purchaser buys, and appears within a reasonable time after construction. In other words, **privity of contract** seems no longer to be generally required for implied warranty of habitability suits. See, e.g., *Lempke v. Dagenais*, 547 A.2d 290 (N.H. 1988), allowing the purchaser of a used home to recover against the builder for pure economic loss, provided that: (1) the defects were **latent** at the time the plaintiff purchased, so that they could not have been discovered by a reasonable inspection; and (2) the defect manifested itself within a **reasonable time** after construction.

b. Concealment: Also, even a *non*-builder who re-sells a house that he owns may be liable for **concealing** a material defect of which he is aware. See *infra*, p. 354.

6. Commercial buildings: Courts have thus far almost always declined to allow recovery based on implied warranty for sales of **commercial** structures. See *Dawson Industries, Inc. v. Godley Construction Co., Inc.*, 224 S.E.2d 266 (Ct. App. N.C. 1976). But the Uniform Land Transactions Act would permit an implied warranty suit even in the case of a commercial building, so long as the seller is "in the business of selling real estate."

§2-309.

7. **Waiver:** It is not clear to what extent the buyer may *waive* his right to bring an implied warranty or other suit. The courts are likely to be quite strict in construing such waivers, and to require that they be precisely stated, and perhaps separately bargained for.

H. **Misrepresentation and concealment:** A seller of property who *misrepresents* the condition of the property will normally be liable to the buyer for damages, under the common-law doctrine of *deceit* or "fraudulent misrepresentation". Normally, the buyer will have to show: (1) a *false statement* concerning a *material* fact; (2) *knowledge* by the seller that the representation is false; (3) an intent by the seller that the buyer *rely*; and (4) injury to the buyer (e.g., that the house is worth less than it would be had the facts been as represented). See *Johnson v. Davis*, discussed *infra*.

1. **Non-disclosure:** The common law traditionally has *not* made the seller liable for merely *failing to disclose* material defects of which he is aware. But this seems to be changing: Many if not most states that have recently considered the question now hold that the seller has an *affirmative duty* to disclose material defects that he is aware of, and that he will be liable in damages if he does not do so. California, Illinois, Florida and New Jersey are among the states so holding. See, e.g, *Johnson v. Davis*, 480 So.2d 625 (Fl. 1985) ("Where the seller of a home knows of facts materially affecting the value of the property which are not readily observable and are not known to the buyer, the seller is under a duty to disclose them to the buyer. This duty is equally applicable to all forms of real property, new and used." Buyer who put down a deposit without being told of material defects was therefore entitled to have the deposit returned and the contract cancelled.)

   a. **Defect could have been found:** Even these modern cases imposing an affirmative duty on the seller to disclose material defects of which he is aware generally find the seller liable only where *the buyer could not reasonably have discovered* the defect by reasonable diligence.

   b. **Seller caused the condition:** Courts are especially likely to find the seller liable for mere nondisclosure where the seller has *brought about the defect or condition.* For instance, in perhaps the only case in which a court has held that a seller owes the buyer the duty of disclosing the presence of *ghosts*, the court relied on the fact that the seller had previously encouraged the house's reputation of being haunted (by reporting the ghosts' presence to *Readers' Digest* and to the local press). Therefore, the court concluded, "Defendant is estopped to deny [the ghosts'] existence and, as a matter of law, the house is haunted." The court then allowed the buyer to rescind the purchase contract. *Stambovsky v. Ackley*, 572 N.Y.S.2d 672 (N.Y.App.Div. 1991).

   c. **Disclosure statement required:** Some states have enacted *statutes* requiring the seller to give the prospective buyer a *written statement* disclosing facts about the property, including defects.

      i. **California statute:** For instance, Cal. Civ. Code §1102.6 requires disclosure of dozens of facts, including the existence of structural defects, presence of asbestos, radon gas, lead-based paint or other toxics, flooding or drainage problems, and even "neighborhood noise problems or other nuisances." See *Alexander v. McKnight*, 9 Cal.Rptr.2d 453 (Cal.App. 1992), holding that this statute imposes on the seller a duty to warn any buyer about *"problem neighbors,"* such as ones who hold lots of late-night parties, park too many cars on the property, or retaliate against any neighbor who complains.

2. **Doctrine of merger:** Traditionally, sellers were often insulated from liability by the doctrine of *"merger"*. Under the merger doctrine, a contract of sale merges into the deed, and the deed becomes the final expression of the parties' deal. Therefore, even if the seller made representations or gave warranties in the contract, these would be **extinguished** when the buyer closed on the deal and took the deed. (See the fuller discussion of merger *supra*, p. 336.) The merger doctrine would seem to prevent recovery under either an implied warranty of habitability theory or deceit theory. But the merger doctrine has fallen into great disfavor, so that few if any courts would use it to prevent such an implied warranty or deceit recovery. See D&K, p. 616.

I. Cooperatives and condominiums: A few words should be said about two forms of real property ownership which are becoming increasingly common, particularly in or near major cities. These are the *cooperative* and the *condominium*.

1. **Cooperative:** The term *"cooperative"* is usually used to refer to a means of owning a multi-unit dwelling (ordinarily a traditional apartment house). Typically, the building is owned by a cooperative *corporation*. Each resident of the building must be a **shareholder** in the corporation.

   a. **Proprietary lease:** Ownership of the corporate shares does not directly confer the right to occupy a unit, but each shareholder is entitled to enter into a *"proprietary lease"*, in which the corporation is the lessor and the shareholder is lessee. The lease almost always provide that its continuance depends upon the lessee's continuing to be the holder of the same shares in the corporation.

      i. **Charges:** The lease will also require the lessee to pay various charges. Typically, these include: (1) a fixed monthly amount to pay off the lessee's fair portion of the building's **mortgage** interest and principal, if any; and (2) an amount adjusted annually by the board of directors to defray the maintenance and operating costs of the building (the so-called *"carrying charges"*).

   b. **Board's right of approval:** A key feature of the cooperative form of ownership is that the board of directors, or the entire body of shareholders, has the right to **approve or reject** any proposed **sale** of shares in the corporation. Since ownership of shares is a prerequisite to obtaining the proprietary lease, this right of approval gives existing residents of the cooperatives the right to **select their neighbors**. See *Penthouse Properties, Inc. v. 1158 Fifth Avenue, Inc.*, 11 N.Y.S.2d 417 (App. Div. 1939), holding that this right of approval is not an unreasonable restraint upon alienation.

2. **Condominium:** The *condominium*, by contrast, is a form of ownership in which each individual resident holds a fee simple in a certain physical space or parcel, but all the residents collectively own certain *"common areas"*.

   a. **High-rise apartment:** If the property is a conventional high-rise apartment building, the individual resident might own a fee simple only in a defined vertical space, and would not own any part of the ground surface area. The condominium association (which is really just the individual owners acting as tenants in common) then would own the fee simple to the soil and to the stairways, recreational areas and other common areas.

b. "Horizontal" management: In a more *"horizontal"* structure (e.g., two-story *townhouses* spread over a large parcel), each individual resident might own the soil upon which his townhouse stands, but he would not own the surrounding lawns, swimming pool, etc.; these would be held by the condominium association.

c. Charges: In either event, the association sets charges to defray the cost of maintaining the common areas. But maintenance of the interior living unit (probably including plumbing and heating systems, in a townhouse arrangement) is the responsibility of the individual resident.

Chapter Review Questions

(Answers are at back of book)

79. By telephone, Simon agreed to sell, and Bryant agreed to buy, Blackacre for a price of $200,000, the closing to take place on April 1. On March 15, the day after this conversation, Simon sent Bryant a letter confirming all of the relevant terms of the agreement. The letter stated, "I will assume that this letter accurately states our arrangement, and will bind us both, unless I hear from you to the contrary by March 20." Bryant received the letter, but sent no response. On April 1, Simon arrived with a marketable deed at the time and place that his letter specified for closing. Bryant did not show up at all. If Simon sues Bryant for breach of contract, may he recover damages?

80. Tycoon, a wealthy industrialist, has for many years owned a 100 acre parcel of undeveloped, heavily-wooded land, called Twin Oaks, in the state of Bates. Grandson, Tycoon's daughter's oldest son, wished desperately to become a farmer. Tycoon therefore orally proposed to Grandson the following arrangement: if Grandson would move onto the property, construct a permanent dwelling, and clear at least 50 of the acres, he could keep whatever crops (or their proceeds) he could grow on the property. Furthermore, if Grandson did all this and then continued to farm for at least five years, Tycoon would leave the property to Grandson in Tycoon's will. Grandson moved onto the property, built a small cabin, cleared 75 acres, and farmed them for the next seven years, keeping all proceeds as agreed. Tycoon then died, and his will made no mention of the arrangement. (Instead, the will left Twin Oaks to Tycoon's niece, Edna.) If Grandson sues Tycoon's estate for an order of specific performance directing the estate to convey Twin Oaks to Grandson, will Grandson prevail? Assume that Bates follows the majority approach to all relevant matters.

81. Shelby, the owner of Blackacre, contracted to sell the property to Bennett. The contract document, dated March 1, provided that the closing was to take place on April 1. The contract did not contain a "time is of the essence" clause, and did not specify the consequences if either party was unable or unwilling to close on the appointed day. On March 25, Bennett said by telephone to Shelby, "My bank loan hasn't gone through yet. I won't be able to close on April 1, but I will be ready on April 10." Shelby replied, "Either close on April 1, or the contract is off." On April 1, Shelby showed up at the appointed place with a deed, but Bennett did not appear. Bennett tendered a check for the purchase price on April 10, but Shelby refused to take it. There is evidence that Shelby was trying to get out of the contract not because the delay was material in light of the surrounding circumstances, but because someone had unexpectedly come along and offered Shelby a higher price. If Bennett sues Shelby for a decree ordering Shelby to convey the property to Bennett for the contract price, will a court grant Bennett's request?

82. Squires contracted to sell Whiteacre to Brady, the closing to take place on June 1. The purchase price was to be $200,000, in the form of a cashier's or certified check. The contract required Squires to convey a marketable title. On June 1, both Squires and Brady turned up at the appointed place for the closing. Squires tendered a deed, together with an abstract of title showing that Squires had good title. The contract also required Squires to have a Certificate of Occupancy for a newly-constructed deck attached to the house. Brady demanded the Certificate of Occupancy, and Squires said, "I don't have it." Brady responded, "Well, I refuse to close." Squires asked Brady to show him the certified check for the purchase price. Brady said, "I don't have it. I didn't bother going through with my bank loan, because I knew you didn't have the Certificate of Occupancy." (This assertion is true.) Squires refused to return Brady's 10% deposit, paid to Squires at the time the contract was signed. (The deposit is returnable, according to the contract, only if seller is in default and buyer is not, on the closing date.) If Brady sues Squires for the return of his deposit, will Brady win?

83. Same basic fact pattern as prior question. Now, however, assume that the abstract of title proffered by Squires on June 1 showed that the house on the property (an important part of the overall value of the property) encroached 10 feet onto the property of Squires' easterly neighbor. If Brady sues Squires for return of his deposit, and Squires asserts the defense that Brady did not tender his own performance (because Brady did not bring a check to the closing), may Brady recover the deposit?

84. Sherman contracted to sell Greenacre to Bruce. The contract was signed on June 1, 1989, and called for a closing to occur on August 1, 1989. On July 1, 1989, Sherman died. His will (executed in 1988) left all of Sherman's personal property to his daughter Deirdre, and all of his real estate to his niece Nell. The closing took place as scheduled on August 1, with the sale proceeds paid to Sherman's estate. Who should receive the sale proceeds, Deirdre or Nell?

85. Spratt contracted to sell a house to Booth. After the contract was signed, but before the scheduled closing date, the house burned down. Spratt was not at fault. Neither Spratt nor Booth had any insurance in force on the property. On the closing date, is Booth obligated to pay the purchase price to Spratt, in return for a deed to the now-much-less-valuable property?

86. Spence sold a house and lot to Bagley under an installment sales contract. The contract provided for the $200,000 purchase price to be paid at the rate of $5,000 per month for 40 consecutive months (with interest on the unpaid balance also being payable each month). The contract further provided that if Bagley ever became more than 30 days in arrears on any payment, Spence could at his sole option declare the contract forfeited, and reclaim the property. Bagley moved in, and made the first 20 payments without incident. He then lost his job, and fell 90 days behind in the payments. The fair rental value of the property is $2,000 per month. Spence sent Bagley a letter stating, "Because you have violated the terms of our agreement, I am hereby exercising my right to declare the agreement terminated. Please vacate immediately." If Spence seeks an order declaring the contract terminated and decreeing that Bagley leave the premises, will Spence succeed?

87. Steel contracted to sell Greenacre to Boswell. The contract stated that Steel would convey marketable title to Boswell, and that the deed would be a warranty deed free of all easements and other encumbrances. On the appointed closing date, Steel tendered to Boswell a warranty deed which stated that the property is "subject to an easement on behalf of a parcel located to the northwest of the subject parcel, enabling the beneficiary of the easement to use the subject parcel's driveway." Boswell and Boswell's lawyer did not carefully read the deed. Instead, they accepted it, and paid the purchase price, without realizing that the deed was subject to the easement. Several days later, when Boswell's neighbor used Boswell's driveway, Boswell realized that he had been given a deed which did not conform to the contract. Boswell now sues to recover damages under the contract for breach of the representation concerning lack of easements. Assuming that Boswell shows that the property is less valuable because the easement exists, may Boswell recover under the contract?

88. Fred was the owner of Greyacre, located in the state of Cabot. Cabot law requires all deeds for the transfer of real property to be witnessed by two people. Fred, who was getting on in years, decided to make a gift of Greyacre to his son, Stewart. He therefore prepared a deed giving Stewart the property, signed it, and had it witnessed by two people (thus fulfilling all of the requirements for a deed in Cabot). He handed the deed to Stewart, saying, "You are now the owner of Greyacre." The next day, Fred had a change of heart, realizing that he might live another 15 years and wanting the satisfaction of knowing that he was still the owner of Greyacre. He therefore asked Stewart to return or rip up the deed. Stewart was upset, but he was also a dutiful son. He therefore ripped up the deed (first making a photocopy, however), and told Fred that he had done so. Shortly thereafter, Fred died, leaving all of his personal and real property to his daughter, Denise. Who owns Greyacre, Stewart or Denise?

89. In 1970, Spitzer conveyed Blackacre to Butler, under a standard warranty deed. In 1990, as Butler was preparing to resell the property, he discovered that Spitzer's predecessor in title had lost his title through adverse possession before ever conveying to Spitzer. The present holder of title by adverse possession is Adolf, who is not in possession of the property (Butler is), and who has never actively asserted rights to the property. Butler realizes that he will not be able to convey a marketable title to any subsequent purchaser because of Adolf's superior title. Butler therefore wishes to sue Spitzer for breach of some or all of the covenants of title. The statutes of limitation on actions for breach of the covenants of seisin, right to convey and against encumbrances are all five years in the jurisdiction. The statutes of limitation on the covenants of quiet enjoyment and warranty are both three years. If Butler brings suit in 1990 against Spitzer for breach of all of these covenants, on which, if any, may he recover? For each covenant on which he may not recover, state the reason.

90. Same facts as prior question. Now, assume that Butler, without disclosing the fact that Adolf has a superior title, conveys the property by warranty deed to Capshaw in 1990. In 1992, while Capshaw is still the record owner of the property and in possession of it, Adolf brings an action for a declaration that he is the legal owner of the property. If Capshaw immediately brings suit against Spitzer for violation by Spitzer of the covenant of quiet enjoyment, may Capshaw recover? (Assume that nothing in the Butler-to-Capshaw deed refers to any covenants made by Butler's predecessor(s) in title.)

91. Schneider conveyed a house and lot to Block, under a general warranty deed. The deed did not list any encumbrances or encroachments. At the time Block received (and paid for) the deed, he was aware that a garage built and belonging to Schneider's eastern neighbor, Jones, was located half on Jones' property and half on Schneider's property. (Block closed the transaction anyway, because he thought he was getting a price that was good enough to overlook this problem.) Several years later, Block decided that he had made a mistake in tolerating this state of events. He therefore instituted a suit against Schneider for breach of covenant.

(a) For breach of which covenant should Block sue?

(b) Will Block be found to have waived the benefit of that covenant by agreeing to close with knowledge of the problem?

92. Developer was in the business of buying large parcels, subdividing them, and building new houses on each. Developer sold a newly built house and the lot on which it stood to Benjamin, a would-be homeowner. The transaction was done by warranty deed. Both the sale contract and the deed contained the following statement in capital letters: "DEVELOPER MAKES NO OTHER WARRANTIES, EXPRESS OR IMPLIED, REGARDING THE STATE OF THE LAND OR STRUCTURES BEING TRANSFERRED." Unbeknownst to either Developer or Benjamin, Developer's employees, because of their ignorance, had failed to use the proper mix of sand and gravel in the cement employed for the building's foundation. Hairline cracks began to appear shortly after the closing, and within one year the house was structurally unsafe and unsalable.

(a) What action, if any, should Benjamin bring against Developer?

(b) What is the probable result of the action you advised bringing in (a)?

93. Same facts as prior question. Assume that during his first and only year of ownership, Benjamin did not become aware of the cracks in the foundation. At the end of a year, he sold the house to Carter, and Carter moved in. If Carter sues Benjamin on the same theory as you gave in your answer to part (a) of the prior question, will Carter succeed against Developer?

THE RECORDING SYSTEM
AND TITLE ASSURANCE

Introductory note: In this chapter, we examine the various statutory schemes, called recording acts, which govern most priority disputes in real estate. Then we treat various ways in which the buyer of property may be assured that his title is valid; the most significant among these is the title insurance policy.

I. COMMON-LAW PRIORITIES

A. Conflicts in real estate: The vast majority of situations in which there are two or more conflicting claims to a particular piece of real estate are resolved by use of recording acts, discussed below. However, occasionally the recording act will not govern a particular situation, and it becomes important to understand the *common-law* system of priorities. In this common-law scheme, a critical fact is whether the claim is legal or equitable.

1. **Two legal claims:** If two conflicting claims to a parcel are *both legal, the first in time prevails*, unless the earlier claimant is *estopped*, by virtue of his actions, from asserting his interest. C&L, p. 801.

2. **Two equitable claims:** If the two conflicting claims to a parcel are *both equitable*, the *earlier one prevails* unless either: (1) the earlier claimant is estopped, because of his actions, from asserting his interest; or (2) the later claimant then acquires the *legal title* in good faith (i.e., without notice of the prior equitable interest) and for a valuable consideration. *Id.*

   > **Example:** O contracts to sell Blackacre to A on January 1. He contracts to sell Blackacre to B on February 1. Assuming that A has done nothing to estop himself from asserting his claim over B (e.g., by denying to B that he, A, has a contract to purchase the land), A has priority, and if A and B both sue for specific performance, only A will be granted it. But if B, before learning of A's interest, also acquires the legal title for value (by closing the sale transaction), B will then have priority both as to his equitable and his legal claim.

3. **Legal claim vs. equitable one:** If the conflict is between the holder of a *legal* interest and the holder of an *equitable* one, the *legal* interest: (1) *always prevails* if his claim is the *earlier* in time; and (2) prevails even if his claim is later in time, if he acquired the legal title in *good faith* and for a *valuable consideration*.

   a. **Legal cuts off equitable:** To put case (2) in another way, a *legal interest will always cut off an earlier equitable interest* if the legal interest is obtained for *value*, and *without knowledge* of the equitable one. Thus if O contracts to sell Blackacre to A, and then actually deeds it to B for a valuable consideration, B will have complete ownership rights if he was not aware of the contract to A. (But if B was aware of the contract with A, a court will order him to specifically perform, i.e., to sell the property to A.)

II.   RECORDING STATUTES

A.   General function of recording acts: The weaknesses of the common-law scheme in dealing with conflicting claims are readily apparent. Since that scheme operates (with just one exception) in favor of the earlier interest, a prospective buyer has no assurance that he is getting a valid title. He can, of course, make inquiries about whether there has been a prior transaction, but if the seller falsely denies that there has been such a transaction, the later purchaser is out of luck (though he may be able to sue the seller for fraud). The principal function of *recording acts*, in force in every jurisdiction, is to give this second purchaser a way to *check* whether there has been an earlier transaction. If the earlier transaction is not recorded, the later purchaser will gain priority (though, depending on the state, he may have to take without actual knowledge of the earlier transaction, and he may have to record before the earlier transaction is recorded.).

    1.   Relations between original parties: The recording acts only govern the relationship between a grantee and a subsequent purchaser of the same property, *not the relation between the grantor and grantee under a particular conveyance*.

        Example: D conveys the timber located on a particular tract to P. Then, he sells the same timber to X, who promptly records his deed before P has recorded his. Because of the recording act, X's deed takes priority over P's. P sues D for his double-dealing. *Held*, for P. The recording act has no effect upon the relations between both parties to a particular deed, i.e., P and D. Therefore, P may recover in quasi-contract for the amount by which D was unjustly enriched from his double-dealing (since D should not be allowed to keep the purchase price from P and the purchase price from X for the same property). *Patterson v. Bryant*, 5 S.E.2d 849 (N.D. 1939).

B.   Different types of acts: There are three basic types of recording acts, the so-called *"pure race"* statues, the *"pure notice"* statues, and the *"race-notice"* statutes. To these three may be added a fourth which is a variant of either the race-notice or pure notice types: the *"period of grace"* statute.

    1.   Pure race statutes: A *race* statute places a premium on the *race to the recorder's office*. The subsequent purchaser must *record before the earlier purchaser*, but he is protected *whether or not he has actual notice* of the earlier conveyance. Although most of the earliest recording acts were of this nature, few pure race statutes remain on the books.

    2.   Pure notice statute: A pure *notice* statute provides that an unrecorded instrument is invalid as against *any* subsequent purchaser without notice, whether or not the subsequent purchaser records prior to the first purchaser.

    3.   Race-notice statute: A *race-notice* statute protects the subsequent purchaser only if he meets *two* requirements: (1) he records *before* the earlier purchaser records; and (2) he takes *without actual notice* of the earlier conveyance.

        a.   Judicial interpretation: Occasionally, the statutory language appears to establish a pure notice scheme, but the *judicial interpretation* of it makes it into a race-notice statute. See, e.g., *Simmons v. Stum*, 101 Ill. 454 (1882).

    4.   Grace period statutes: A *"period-of-grace"* statute protects the first grantee for a *set period* of time *whether or not he records*. If he still has not recorded at the end of the period, he loses this special protection. The period of grace is combined with one of the other types of statutes, usually notice or race-notice. Period of grace provisions were common in earlier days, when it might take days or weeks to get to the recorder's office. Most such statutes have now been repealed.

Example: The Delaware recording act, Del. Code Ann. Tit. 25, §153, provides that any deed not recorded within fifteen days after delivery shall not be good against a subsequent purchaser or creditor for valuable consideration unless the latter creditor or purchaser had notice of the deed. This means that if the prior grantee records within fifteen days after getting his deed, his interest is good against *any* subsequent purchaser. If he does not record during this time, the situation is governed by notice rules, and a purchaser or creditor who takes without notice prevails (whether or not he records first). See C&L, p. 814.

5. **Representing the buyer:** The actions which a buyer has to take to ensure good title will vary, depending on the type of statute in force.

Example: Suppose a lawyer is representing the purchaser in a real estate transaction. What should he do before paying over the purchase price to the grantor to assure that his client will prevail over prior deeds or other instruments that have been executed by the grantor and not recorded? We will examine this issue for: (a) a notice jurisdiction; (b) a race-notice jurisdiction; (c) a period-of-grace jurisdiction; and (d) a race jurisdiction.

(a) In a *notice* jurisdiction, the lawyer should check the record at the last second, just before paying over the money, to make sure that no one has recently recorded (which would give constructive notice). Also, he should ask his client whether he has actual notice of any such transaction. There is no special hurry to record the deed.

(b) In a *race-notice* jurisdiction he should do both of the things stated in (a). Also, however, there is the danger that after he pays over the money, the holder of a prior conveyance will record before he has a chance to. The best way to protect his client is to have the sale money put in *escrow* until the new deed is recorded.

(c) In a *period of grace* jurisdiction, all of the above protections may be necessary (especially if the period of grace provision is in conjunction with a race-notice or pure race provision). However, the escrow should last even longer, until a time equal to the grace-period has elapsed since the closing; this is the only way to be sure that a conveyance was not made just prior to the one received by the buyer, which could be recorded within the grace period and thus get automatic priority.

(d) In a *race* state, the transaction should be handled the same way as the race-notice situation, except that the lawyer does not have to ask his client whether he has actual notice of any prior conveyance.

6. **Grantees from different grantors:** Where the grantees who have conflicting claims to property received their grants from the same grantor, operation of the various types of recording statutes is relatively straightforward. But where the conflict is between *grantees from different grantors*, matters become more difficult, as shown in the following two examples.

Example 1: O executes and delivers to A a deed conveying Blackacre, owned by O. A does not record the deed. O then executes and delivers to B a deed to Blackacre, which B purchases in good faith and for valuable consideration. B does not record his deed. A then records his deed, and after recording it, he deeds Blackacre to C, which C purchases in good faith for valuable consideration. In a contest between B and C, we will examine who prevails in a jurisdiction having: (a) a notice statute; (b) a race-notice statute; (c) a grace period statute, if A's recording is after the grace period has expired; and (d) a race statute.

No matter what type of statute is involved, C is going to have to win if reliance on the record is to be encouraged. When C goes to check title, all he finds is a recorded conveyance from O to A, so he rightfully assumes that A has valid title. In case (a) (notice statute), B's title is admittedly better than A's. But C, since he is buying without notice of B's unrecorded conveyance, has a better title than B (and a better title than held by his own grantor, A!) In case (b) (race-notice), A's title is better than B's, since B has failed to record before A; therefore C will prevail (though if B were then to record before C did, a court might award priority to B). In case (c) (period-of-grace), when A records after the grace period, the statute will probably be treated as applying either notice or race-notice principles; in either event, C wins for the reasons stated in (a) and (b). In case (d) (race), A has beaten B in the race to record, so C takes A's superior title. (But again, if C fails to record before B does, a court might award priority to B, though this seems unlikely for the reasons stated in the example which follows.)

Example 2: O delivers to A a deed to Blackacre, owned by O. A does not record. O then deeds Blackacre to B; B purchases *with knowledge* of A's prior unrecorded deed. B records his deed and then deeds the property to C; C purchases without knowledge of A's prior unrecorded deed. A then records. C then records. In a contest between A and C, we will examine who prevails in a state having: (a) a notice statute; (b) a race-notice statute; (c) a period-of-grace statute, if A recorded after the period of grace; and (d) a race statute. We will also look at whether the answer changes if C reconveys to B, and the contest is between B and A.

As with the previous example, encouragement of reliance on the recording acts dictates that C should win, since there was no way he could tell about the deed from O to A by inspecting the record prior to making his purchase. In (a) (notice), C will win because he took without notice of A's deed. In (b) (race-notice), the answer is less clear. C has lost the race to record to A. However, most statutes requiring a race require it only where the contest is *between grantees from a common grantor*. See 4 A.L.P. 538. Since C and A are claiming under different grantors, C's failure to record will probably not be fatal. In case (c) (period of grace), the period of grace will have no effect since A recorded after its expiration, and the case will be resolved on either notice or race-notice principles (either of which should produce a victory for C). In case (d) (race), the same issue arises as in the race-notice case; again, C will probably not be required to race with A, since they did not take from the same grantor, and C should win.

If B now repurchases the land from C, a different result will probably occur in cases (a), (b) and (c). The general rule is that if a person takes without notice (here, C), his resale market will be protected; even a person with knowledge of the earlier deed will take free and clear of that deed. But the exception to this is in the case of repurchase by the prior grantor himself (here, B); the prior grantor is bound by his own knowledge. Thus since B could not have prevailed under any statute requiring lack of knowledge (i.e., notice, race-notice or period of grace tied to either notice or race-notice) he must lose. See *infra*, p. 381. But B would win in a pure race jurisdiction, since notice is completely irrelevant.

C. Mechanics of recording: It is worth understanding a little bit about the mechanics of recording.

1. **Deposit with recorder:** The grantee (or the grantee's title insurance company) brings the deed to the recording office (which is generally located in the county where the land lies). The recorder stamps the date and time of deposit, and usually photographs the deed; then, the original deed is returned to the grantee. The copy is then placed in a chronological book containing all recorded deeds. (A separate book may be kept for each of the various types of land interests, e.g., a book for mortgages, a book for tax-sale deeds, a book for ordinary private deeds, etc.; or, all may be consolidated into one book.)

2. **Indexing:** Then, the deeds are *indexed*. A grantor index is almost always prepared, which enables a searcher to find all conveyances made by a given grantor. A grantee index is also almost always made, which permits the searcher to find all conveyances made *to* a particular grantee. In some localities, a *tract* index is prepared; this is extremely valuable, because it enables a searcher to find all transactions involving the particular tract of land in question. How a title searcher uses each of these indexes is discussed extensively *infra*, p. 369.

D. **What instruments must be recorded:** The recording acts generally apply to nearly every instrument by which an interest in land, *whether legal or equitable*, is created or modified. Thus not only fee simple conveyances, but also mortgages, restrictive covenants, tax liens, etc., are brought within the recording act. Furthermore, any instrument *modifying* any of these (e.g., a satisfaction of mortgage) is brought with the act. Thus all of these documents must be recorded, or their holder runs the risk of having his interest subordinated to that of a later purchaser.

1. **Unrecordable interests:** However, there are a few sorts of interests which do not have to be recorded. In any priority dispute involving such an interest, the recording acts become *irrelevant*, and the conflict is governed by common-law principles.

   a. **Adverse possession:** The most important category of interests which do not have to be recorded (and which in fact are not recordable) are *titles based upon adverse possession*. Adverse possession, of course, does not give rise to an instrument at all; therefore, the adverse possessor does not have to record.

      i. **Adverse possessor has priority:** In a priority dispute between an adverse possessor and the grantee of a conveyance executed after the adverse possessor's claim ripened, the adverse possessor will prevail based upon the common-law rule that the earlier in time of two legal interests takes priority. (See *supra*, p. 359.) See *Mugaas v. Smith*, 206 P.2d 332 (Wash. 1949), favoring the adverse possessor over a subsequent *bona fide* purchaser, on the grounds that "titles matured under the statute of limitations are not within the recording acts." Also, the court noted, since a title gained by adverse possession cannot be recorded, a contrary holding would mean that the adverse possessor "must keep his flag flying forever, and the statute ceases to be a statute of *limitations*"; that is, the possession would have to remain continuous, open and notorious forever.

      ii. **Abandonment:** The adverse possessor's common-law priority remains even if, after his title ripens, he *abandons* the premises. Recall that a title obtained by adverse possession is like any other title, and cannot be extinguished through abandonment (*supra*, p. 40). Thus if A adversely possesses Blackacre for the statutory period and then abandons it, and the record owner conveys to B, B will lose in a suit against A even though there was no way B could have known, from inspection either of the record or of the physical premises, that the adverse claim existed!

b. Easements: A similar question arises in connection with *easements* created by *implication* or *necessity* (neither of which gives rise to a recordable document). The courts are *split* as to whether an easement created by *necessity* is extinguished by a subsequent *bona fide* purchaser of the servient estate. An easement created by implication (based on a prior "apparent" use; see *supra*, p. 207) will generally be *cut off* by a subsequent *bona fide* purchaser without notice.

i. Inquiry notice: But both an easement by necessity and an easement by implication are likely to place the subsequent purchaser on "inquiry notice" (see *infra*, p. 376), since the existence of the easement itself will probably leave physical clues on the servient estate. See 4 A.L.P. 602-03.

2. Written but unrecordable interests: In addition to the above non-documentary interests, there are a few types on interests which are represented by instruments, but which are nonetheless treated as *non-recordable* by the particular recording act.

a. Short leases: For instance, in many states, a *short-term lease* (e.g., less than three years), may not be recorded. If so, that lease will be valid against a subsequent *bona fide* purchaser. 4 A.L.P. 551.

b. Executory contract: Similarly, some states do not permit executory *contracts of sale* to be recorded. If so, the buyer suffers no statutory penalty by failing to record (but even under common-law principles, his equitable interest will be subordinate to that of a subsequent legal claimant who takes without notice).

E. Parties protected: If a grantee fails to record, what groups of persons may claim the benefit of the recording act? We put aside the possible requirement that the subsequent grantee record (a requirement imposed by race and race-notice jurisdictions). Also, we defer for later discussion (beginning *infra*, p. 368), the issue of what constitutes "notice" in a notice or race-notice jurisdiction. The issue we focus on here is the requirement that the subsequent grantee either be a "purchaser for value" or a creditor meeting certain standards.

1. Purchaser for value: In the substantial majority of states, a grantee receives the benefit of the recording act (i.e., he may take priority over an earlier unrecorded conveyance) only if he *gives value* for his interest. As the idea is usually put in these statutes, the earlier unrecorded conveyance is "void as against any subsequent purchaser in good faith and *for a valuable consideration*."

2. From whom purchased: One who purchases for valuable consideration *from the record owner* will of course be protected. But also, one who buys from the *heirs or devisees* of the record owner will also be protected.

> **Example:** Nancy Fiske, the owner of Blackacre, conveys the property to her daughter Mary by a deed dated 1864 (though Mary's interest is made subject to a life estate in Mary's brother Benjamin and sister-in-law Elizabeth). This deed to Mary is not recorded until 1867. In 1865, Nancy dies, leaving Benjamin, her son, as her sole heir. In 1866, he conveys a fee simple interest in Blackacre to P, which is recorded immediately. P discovers Mary's remainder and Elizabeth's one-half life estate, and sues to have their interests declared void. They defend by claiming that after the deed from Nancy to Mary, Nancy had no more seisin, and thus nothing descended to Benjamin at Nancy's death; therefore, they claim, Benjamin had no title to convey to P.

Held, for P. Although following the conveyance by Nancy, Nancy had no title, she still had the ability to *convey* to a *bona fide* purchaser for value a title which would be superior to the earlier unrecorded deed. This power to convey a good title *passed to Benjamin* on Nancy's death. Thus although Benjamin himself did not have a good title as against Nancy (and Elizabeth), he had the ability to convey a good title to a subsequent good-faith purchaser for value, such as P. P was entitled to rely on the record, which showed that Nancy died seised of the property, and that it then passed to Benjamin. *Earle v. Fiske*, 103 Mass. 491 (1870).

3. **Donee:** If the statute requires that the subsequent grantee have paid consideration, a *donee* will *not be protected* by the act. Furthermore, many statutes which do not expressly require payment of consideration by the subsequent grantee have been *judicially interpreted* to include such a requirement.

   a. *Eastwood* **case:** See, however, *Eastwood v. Shedd*, 442 P.2d 423 (Colo. 1968), where the statute was amended by removing a reference to *bona fide* purchasers, and making an unrecorded conveyance void "as against any class of persons with any kind of rights." The court held that this gave protection to a subsequent donee, though the court conceded that this interpretation made Colorado the only state which accords such broad protection to a subsequent grantee.

4. **Less than market value:** Though consideration is required, it does *not* have to be an amount *equal to the market value of the property*. 4 A.L.P. 557.

   a. **Nominal consideration:** On the other hand, most courts hold that it is not enough that the grantee paid merely *nominal* consideration, or that the deed recites payment of value when in fact no value was paid. About the farthest any court has gone toward approving nominal consideration is *Strong v. Whybark*, 102 S.W. 968 (Mo. 1907), where the deed recited a consideration of "natural love and affection and five dollars. . . ." The court held that "A valuable consideration is defined to be money or something that is worth money. . . . It is not necessary that the consideration should be adequate in point of value." Here, the consideration was small or even nominal, but was nonetheless adequate, the court held. But 4 A.L.P. 558, n. 9, states that *Strong v. Whybark* "*must be considered to have been erroneously decided.*"

5. **Pre-existing debt:** Where the grantee receives a conveyance or mortgage on account of a *pre-existing debt*, whether he is protected by the recording act will depend on how the debt is disposed of.

   a. **Debt cancelled:** If all or part of the debt is *cancelled* in return for the conveyance, the grantee is generally (but not always) deemed to have given consideration.

   b. **Mortgage as security:** Where a *mortgage* is given as security for the antecedent debt, the mortgage is not a purchaser for value if he maintains exactly the *same* rights of collection he had before. If, on the other hand, he makes a legally enforceable contract to *extend the time for payment*, or otherwise bindingly modifies the debt to the debtor's advantage, this will constitute the giving of value for the mortgage.

      i. **Must be binding:** But the modification must be *specific* and *enforceable*. Thus in *Gabel v. Drewrys Ltd., U.S.A., Inc.*, 68 So.2d 372 (Fla. 1953), O was in debt to D. D promised to forebear from suing O for the moment, in return for which O gave D a mortgage of his assets. In a contest between D and P, the holder of a prior unrecorded mortgage, P prevailed because D had not given a definite extension of time, and had kept the freedom to sue whenever it wanted, thus not giving up anything of value. (But the general rule, as exemplified by *Gabel*, conflicts with the Uniform Simplification of Land Transfers Act, §1-201, which provides that a person gives "value" for rights if he acquires them as security for, or in total or partial satisfaction of, a pre-existing claim.)

6. **Promise to pay:** A *promise to pay*, even if legally binding, is usually *not* considered to constitute the giving of value. B,C&S, pp. 819-20. This rule has been criticized, on the grounds that the grantee who has legally bound himself to pay may also have changed his position in reliance on the record. 4 A.L.P. 558. In any event, if the grantee's promise takes the form of a *negotiable instrument*, and the instrument is in fact negotiated to a third party, the promisor will then be deemed to have given value. *Id.* at 559.

7. **Partial payment:** Suppose that, at the time the subsequent grantee discovers the prior conveyance, he has paid *only a portion* of the purchase price. In this situation, the subsequent grantee is protected *"pro tanto"*, i.e., to the extent of his payments.

   a. **Three methods:** This is accomplished by courts in at least three different ways, depending on the equities of the particular case: (1) if the land can be conveniently *divided*, the innocent purchaser is allowed to keep a portion equal to the proportion of payments made; (2) the innocent purchaser is given a *lien* on the land for the amount of the money paid by him, and legal title to the land is given to the earlier grantee; and (3) the innocent purchaser gets *title* to all of the land, but the earlier grantee may *recover* from him the *unpaid portion* of the purchase price. See *Durst v. Daugherty*, 17 S.W. 388 (Tex. 1891), summarizing the equities of the various approaches.

8. **Burden of proof:** The cases are in utter confusion and dispute as to the party on whom the *burden of proof* lies on the issue of consideration (or, for that matter, on the issue of notice, discussed *infra*, p. 368). See C&J, pp. 1259-60, notes 1, 2.

F. **Creditors:** *Creditors* of a landowner may also come within the protection of the recording acts. If the creditor receives a *mortgage* from the landowner, he is treated as a "purchaser", and must generally meet the consideration requirement discussed above. We concentrate here on creditors to whom the landowner does not voluntarily give a lien against the property.

   1. **Unsecured creditors:** An *unsecured*, general, creditor gains *no protection at all* from the recording acts. The theory behind this rule is that a creditor who has not in some way acted to protect himself is in no better position than the careless prior purchaser who has failed to record. 4 A.L.P. 610.

   2. **Judgment and attachment creditors:** In most states, a creditor may in some circumstances *attach* his debtor's property at the beginning of a lawsuit. And in all states, a creditor who *obtains a judgment* may *record* it. Since both the attachment and the judgment become *liens* against the real estate, the lien holder will be protected under the recording act against a prior unrecorded purchase or encumbrance, *if* the statute explicitly protects lien creditors, or uses general words broad enough to include them (see, e.g., the Colorado statute interpreted in *Eastwood v. Shedd, supra*, p. 365).

a. **Limited statute:** But if the statute only protects "purchasers", the courts generally do *not* give the lien creditor protection; this is usually on the grounds that he has *not relied on the record* either in creating the original obligation or in obtaining the lien. See C&J, p. 1249, note 1.

b. **Unrecordable prior interest:** Keep in mind that the rights of a subsequent judgment creditor, like those of a subsequent grantee, will be governed by the recording act only where the prior unrecorded interest was *recordable*. (See *supra*, p. 363.)

> **Example:** P sells property to D on credit. D promises to execute and deliver to P a purchase money mortgage on the property. D fails to keep this promise, and gives mortgages on the property to X and Y. Later, Z obtains a judgment lien against the property. P then sues D, X, Y and Z in an attempt to establish that D's promise to grant a mortgage created a constructive trust for P's benefit against the property.
>
> *Held*, a constructive trust may not cut off the rights of X and Y, since they lent in reliance on the record. But if a constructive trust is shown to exist, it will be *superior to Z's judgment lien*. It is true that the D.C. statute in question gives the protection of the recording acts to judgment creditors, but this protection is good only against interests *capable of being recorded*. Since P's constructive trust was not capable of being recorded, under general equitable principles Z should not take priority (because it did not gain its lien in reliance on the record). *Osin v. Johnson*, 243 F.2d 653 (D.C. Cir. 1957).

3. **Purchaser at execution sale:** If the state protects judgment creditors, one who *purchases at the execution sale* will of course be protected. Even if the state does not give judgment creditors protection, one who purchases at the sale *without notice* of the prior unrecorded interest will be protected (since he is giving new value in good faith).

a. **Purchase by creditor:** If the judgment creditor himself purchases at the execution sale, and is not aware of the prior unrecorded interest, the courts are *split*. Most courts do not let him purchase, on the grounds that he is "bidding in" the amount of his debt, and is therefore not giving new value. But other courts protect him, noting that he has usually advanced legal fees in bringing about the execution sale, and is also giving up his judgment in return for the purchase, both of which factors constitute new value. See 4 A.L.P. 614.

G. **Circularity of liens:** Occasionally, a situation may result in which there are *three* liens, with the first being prior to the second, the second prior to the third, and the third prior to the first. This problem is known as the *circularity of liens*.

> **Example:** O owns Blackacre, valued at $20,000. O borrows $5,000 from A, and gives A a mortgage on Blackacre to secure the loan. A does not record the mortgage. O then borrows $7,000 from B, giving B a mortgage on the land. B has actual knowledge of the prior unrecorded mortgage to A. B records his mortgage the day it is given to him. O then borrows $3,000 from C, giving C a mortgage on the land. C has no knowledge of A's prior unrecorded mortgage, but is aware of B's prior recorded mortgage. C records the mortgage when it is given to him. Blackacre is sold in a foreclosure proceeding, and the sum of $10,000 is netted. Assuming the jurisdiction is a race-notice state, a circularity of lien will result. A's mortgage is superior to B's, since B has knowledge of A's. B's mortgage is superior to C's, since it was recorded first, and C knew about it. C's mortgage is superior to A's, since A's was not recorded and C had no notice of it.

1. **Various approaches:** Courts have evolved several different approaches to deal with the circularity of liens problem. Most courts apply some sort of *"fault"* approach, since usually one party may be seen to be somewhat *more at fault* than the others. For instance, in the above example, A seems to be the most at fault, since it was his failure to record that gave rise to the difficulty. (It is true that B could have insisted that his mortgage refer to the fact that there was a prior mortgage to A, which would have given notice to C; but nothing in the recording system requires him to do this.) Therefore, the fairest situation seems to be to satisfy the reasonable expectations of B and C, and give the balance to A.

   a. **How this works:** This means: C gets the amount of the fund less the amount of the mortgage to which he knew he was subordinate (B's), or $10,000—$7,000 $3,000 (which satisfies C in full, as it happens, in this particular case). B expects to be subordinate to A's interest, so it is fair to give him $10,000—$5,000 $5,000 (and to disregard C's interest). A then gets the remaining $2,000 (since there is no reason why, as between him and B, A should get the benefit of C's priority over B). See 4 A.L.P. 626-29, for a summary of this and other approaches.

H. Formal requirements for recording: In a race or race-notice jurisdiction, the subsequent purchaser will of course be protected only if he records his deed. Furthermore, the instrument must be one which is in fact *eligible to be recorded*. If it is not, the purchaser will not be protected even if the recording clerk makes a mistake and accepts the document.

   Example: O conveys to P, who does not record. O then conveys to X, but the deed is improperly acknowledged (because O does not appear before the notary). Since the improper acknowledgment is not apparent from the face of the deed, the recorder accepts it for recording. X then conveys to D, who records. Only after that does P record his deed. *Held*, D is not entitled to the benefit of the recording act as against P, because a deed in D's chain of title (the deed to D's grantor) was not capable of being recorded even though it was in fact recorded. *Messersmith v. Smith*, 60 N.W.2d 276 (N.D. 1953).

   1. **Must record whole chain of title:** The *Messersmith* case also illustrates that in a race or race-notice jurisdiction, the subsequent grantee must see to it that his *entire chain of title* is recorded, not just his own conveyance. (This requirement is discussed further *infra*, p. 372.) Normally, this is not an unreasonable requirement to place on the subsequent grantee. But in a case like *Messersmith*, where there was no way D could have known that the earlier deed in his chain was not properly recordable even though it was recorded, the result seems harsh and unfair; certainly P who had failed to record his deed, was not in any way prejudiced by the "unrecordability" of the deed to X.

I. Notice to subsequent claimants: In all jurisdictions except those having pure race statutes, the most important question is likely to be: was the subsequent purchaser put on *notice* of the earlier deed? (Even in a pure race jurisdiction, the existence of notice via filing will be relevant.) There are generally considered to be three types of notice: (1) *actual* notice; (2) *record* notice; and (3) *"inquiry"* notice. Each of these is discussed in a separate section below.

J. Actual notice: If the subsequent purchaser is shown to have had *actual notice* of the existence of the prior unrecorded interest, he will not gain the protection of the recording act in a notice or a race-notice jurisdiction.

K. Record notice: One function of the recording acts is to assure the holder of an interest that if he records it, he will not be vulnerable as against any subsequent interest. Therefore, **adequate recording** will always constitute notice (called **"record notice"**) to subsequent claimants. However, the mere fact that a deed is recorded somewhere in the public records does not mean that the recording is adequate.

1. Defective document: A document which is **not entitled to be recorded** will not give record notice, even if the document is in fact mistakenly accepted for recording. Thus a document which is **not acknowledged**, in a jurisdiction which requires acknowledgement, will not give record notice. Nor, of course, will a deed which is **void** for some reason give record notice; see, e.g., *Stone v. French*, 14 P. 530 (Kan. 1887) (lack of delivery prior to grantor's death).

a. Curative acts: However, most states have adopted **"curative"** acts. These provide that after the expiration of a certain period of time following recording, the failure to conform to certain formal requirements for recording ceases to be material. Typically, these acts apply to defective acknowledgement, lack of signature, irregularity in a probate proceeding, or infirmity in a tax sale or judicial sale of the property. Such acts have two results: (1) documents which have been recorded for more than the period mentioned in the curative act (often only one year) are record notice to subsequent takers; and (2) a potential purchaser who finds deeds, probate proceedings, etc. in his grantor's chain of title may **rely** on the technical adequacy of these documents.

b. Actual knowledge: Even though a document is not entitled to be recorded, many courts hold that if the subsequent purchaser **actually** sees it in the record, he is placed on **"inquiry"** notice (see *infra*, p. 376); if further inquiry would show that the deed itself was valid between the parties to it (even though not recordable), he will not be protected by the recording act. 4 A.L.P. 607-09. However, other courts hold that a document not entitled to be recorded will not even give inquiry notice to one who becomes aware of it. *Id.* at 608.

2. Mechanics of title examination: Proper recording places subsequent purchasers on notice even if they **never actually see** the document that has been filed. That is, the court imputes to the subsequent purchaser that knowledge which he **would have obtained** had he conducted a **diligent title search**. To know what documents a diligent title searcher would find, it is necessary to have a fairly detailed understanding of the mechanics of title examination.

a. Two indexes: All recording offices maintain two vital sets of indexes. One of these is the **grantor** index, which lists in alphabetical order all persons who have become grantors, the date upon which they did so, the grantee, perhaps a brief description of the property, and a reference to the book in which the full instrument is recorded. The other major index is the **grantee** index, which is similar to the grantor index except that it is organized by alphabetical order of grantees. Thus if one were interested in a deed from John Smith to William Doe, one could locate it by looking in the grantor index under "Smith" or by looking in the grantee index under "Doe"; either of these indexes would point to the same bound volume and page number where the deed itself was recorded.

b. Tracing back to root: The first step in searching title is to establish a **"root"** from which the title can be traced back down to the present. One begins by deciding upon a **time limit** for the search. Typically, only the **most recent 50 or 60**

years of ownership of the property are searched, since it is unlikely that a defect in the chain of title from before that time will have present implications. C&L, pp. 878-80. Then, it is necessary to find out **who owned the property, say 50 years ago**. This person, once he can be found, is the "root".

  i. **Use of grantee index:** The way the "root" is located is by use of the grantee index. The title searcher of course knows the name of the present potential seller. Let us assume that his name is David Drew. At some point, obviously, David Drew should have become a grantee of the property, so his name will be listed in the grantee index. Searching the grantee index, we find that the property was conveyed to Drew by Charles Crow. Now checking Crow in the grantee index, we find that he took from Bernard Bird, and checking Bird, we find that he took from Abner Ax. If we find that Abner Ax had record title to the property 50 years ago, he will be our "root".

  ii. **Breaks in chain:** In this checking backward process, there are likely to be breaks in the chain. The grantee index included only those who took by *inter vivos* conveyance. Thus one who has obtained his title by **will** or **intestacy** will not be shown; instead, the local **probate records** will have to be checked. (This may be difficult, since we don't know the name of the decedent; all we can do is to hope that it is the same surname as that of the person we believe took by the will or intestacy.) Similarly, a **tax sale** might break the chain, so the registry of tax deeds would have to be checked on the chance that there was such a sale.

c. **Tracing forward to present:** Once the "root" has been located, the title searcher starts the really important part of his task. It is now necessary to trace the title **back down through the present**, making sure that **each grantee did not dispose of the property except via the chain of title that leads to present prospective seller**.

   Example: Assume that by the tracing-backwards-through-the-grantee-index procedure, we have established that Abner Ax is our root, and that he took the property in 1912. Using the **grantor** index, we check to see if Ax made any conveyances of the property at any time after 1912. If we are in luck, we will find that he made no conveyances of the property before conveying to Bernard Bird (who, it will be recalled, was part of our backwards chain of title) in 1928. The deed from Ax to Bird will be scrutinized, to see whether it indicated any defect in title (e.g., that the property is subject to a restrictive covenant in favor of Ax).

   Then, Bernard Bird's name will be searched in the grantor index for the period from 1928 until his first conveyance of the property (which, we hope, will be to Charles Crow). Suppose that the conveyance to Crow is indeed the first, and that it is in 1943. Then Crow will be searched in the grantor index from 1943 until the conveyance to David Drew (the prospective seller). If Drew took in 1960, his name will have to be searched in the grantor index from 1960 down to the present, to make sure that he has not already disposed of the property.

d. **Overlapping search periods:** Generally, the searcher will search each grantor in the grantor index only for the period **after the grantor took title**. (The consequence of this is discussed *infra*, p. 374.) It would usually be safe to stop the search for that grantor on the day he conveyed to someone else. But in many states there is a possibility that the grantor may have failed to pay taxes, and by statute the property could have been foreclosed upon for a short time (e.g., three years in Massachusetts) following the failure to pay taxes, even if the taxpayer transferred the property to another.

> **Example:** Assume the record contains the following conveyances (a) deed from A to B, dated July 1, 1915, acknowledged September 15, 1916 and recorded December 1, 1931; (b) deed from B to C, dated June 1, 1950, acknowledged on the same day and recorded two days later. The client is purchasing from C. What names should be checked in the Grantor Index, and for what period of time?
>
> We would run A's name from the time he took the property until at least the end of 1931 (since a second conveyance by A made any time before recording of the A-to-B deed could have priority over that deed, if it were recorded before the A-to-B deed was recorded). Also, we would probably check another two or three years after 1931 to make sure that there was no tax foreclosure against A's interest that would be good against B. We would run B's name from the day he got title (which would either be the date of execution and delivery or the date of acknowledgment, depending on what local law requires for the effectiveness of a conveyance as between the parties to it). We would run this until at least 1950 (when he deeded the property to C), and perhaps a couple of years beyond for the reason given in connection with A. We would run C's name from the time he took title until the present.

e. **Mortgages:** During the search, it may develop that the property was *mortgaged* at various times. There ought to be a *satisfaction of mortgage* recorded for each of these mortgages except for the one held by the present seller. But if there is a lack of a mortgage satisfaction, it may not be fatal if the mortgage itself dates back more than a certain period; the period is usually related to the statute of limitations, and is established by local title-searching custom.

f. **Probate proceedings:** If one of the links in the chain is a *probate proceeding*, the will will have to be examined to see who was entitled to the property.

g. **Other encumbrances:** Numerous other possible defects may appear, e.g., federal tax liens. Discussion of these is beyond the scope of this outline. See C&L, p. 889.

h. **Tract indexes:** In a few jurisdictions, the recorder's office maintains a *tract index*, i.e., an index showing all transactions in connection with a particular tract of land (e.g, a city block). This renders the title searcher's job much easier, since: (1) there is less chance of confusion from similar grantor or grantee names, or from the fact that a grantor has had interests in several parcels in the same county; and (2) one can go further back, and trace the title of each grantee all the way down to the present without undue effort, so that many of the "chain of title" problems, discussed *infra*, are eliminated. Even where the recorder's office does not maintain a tract index, the title companies maintain a "plant", or abstract, for each parcel, which amounts to the same thing (see *infra*, p. 386).

3. **"Chain of title" problems:** As the above discussion of the mechanics of title searching makes clear, the searcher is heavily dependent upon the grantor and grantee indexes, and upon the need to search these indexes only for the time that a grantor appears on the record to have title. Since any search is conducted only within these limits, it is quite possible that the search will not find a deed which in fact affects the title, but which is "lost" within the vastness of the recorder's office. In general, the recording of an instrument gives record notice to a subsequent searcher only if that searcher *would have found the document* using the generally-accepted searching principles discussed above. A recorded instrument which would not be found by these principles is said to be

outside of the searcher's "chain of title". There are five major ways in which a recorded instrument can be outside the chain of title.

a. Unrecorded links: Recall that once the searcher has established a "root" of title, he then traces title by using the grantor index, checking that index for each person known to have been a grantee. If there is an *unrecorded deed* from a known grantee to a third person, then even if the deed from that third person to someone else, and all subsequent deeds, are recorded, the searcher will have no way of finding them, and these deeds will not be of record notice to him.

Example: Stephen Adams, the owner of Blackacre, conveys to Kanouse in 1847; this deed is never recorded. Kanouse mortgages the property to Estell, also in 1847, and the mortgage is recorded. In 1849, S. Adams conveys the same property to Simpson; Simpson immediately gives a mortgage on the property to Pamela Adams; both deed and mortgage are promptly recorded. This mortgage is ultimately assigned to P. P sues Estell's estate to determine the priority of their mortgages.

Held, for P. It is true that Estell's mortgage was both executed and recorded before either the Adams-Simpson deed or the Simpson-Pam Adams mortgage (under which P claims). However, at the time the Simpson-Pam Adams mortgage was issued, the deed from S. Adams to Kanouse was not of record (and in fact has never been recorded). Therefore, Pam Adams had no way of finding out about the Kanouse-to-Estell mortgage, since searching Adam's name in the grantor index would not have led her to Kanouse, and Kanouse's name would never have been searched to find the deed to Estell. Accordingly, Pam Adams was not on notice of the Kanouse-to-Estell mortgage, and the Pam Adams mortgage is thus protected by the recording act. A purchaser will not "be bound to take notice of the record of a deed executed by a prior grantee whose own deed has not been recorded. . . . And where the deed of a vendor is not recorded, then the record of a mortgage given by the vendee for the purchase money will not be notice to a subsequent purchaser. . . . For in any such case the purchaser is without a clue to guide him in searching the record." *Losey v. Simpson*, 11 N.J. Eq. 246 (1856).

i. "Wild" or "fugitive" deed: An instrument issued by a grantor whose own source of title is not recorded (e.g., the Kanouse-to-Estell mortgage in *Losey*) is commonly referred to as a *"wild"* or "fugitive" instrument.

ii. B.F.P. must record whole chain: In *Losey*, it was the holder of the *prior* instrument (Estell) who ran afoul of the rule that the entire chain of title must be recorded. But the requirement that the whole chain be recorded must also be observed by a *subsequent bona fide purchaser* who wishes to gain the recording act's protection against prior unrecorded instruments. That is, the *bona fide* purchaser must see that his entire chain of title is recorded, if he is to prevail against a prior unrecorded document. (This can be thought of as an illustration of the general rule that the subsequent *bona fide* purchaser gains the protection of the recording act only if the deed was both recorded and properly recordable; see *supra*, p. 368.)

Example: McCann conveys to Raab in 1928. The deed is not recorded at that time. Raab conveys to the Ds in 1932, and the deed is not recorded. In 1933, McCann conveys the same property to Gage, and also in 1933 Gage conveys to the Ps. This latter deed is recorded as soon as it is executed, but the McCann-to-Gage deed is not. In 1936, the Ds record the McCann-to-Gage deed and the Raab-Ds deed. Shortly thereafter, P records the deed from McCann to Gage. P and the Ds each assert superior title.

Held, for the Ds. It is true that the deed from Gage to P was recorded before either the McCann-Raab deed or the Raab-Ds deed. However, the McCann-Gage deed was not recorded until after the McCann-Raab and Raab-Ds deeds. P's sole claim is that she is protected by the recording act as a subsequent purchaser in good faith and for valuable consideration; since the jurisdiction has a "race-notice" statute, P was required to make a valid recording before the Ds. For a recording to be valid, the **entire chain** of title back to the common grantor (McCann) must have been recorded before the Ds recorded their deed. The rationale for this is that the recording act is designed to protect only those who purchase in reliance on the record title; since P purchased from a stranger to the record title (at the time she purchased, there was no recorded deed from McCann to Gage), she should not gain the benefits of the recording act. *Zimmer v. Sundell*, 296 N.W. 589 (Wis. 1941).

Note: However, in a **pure notice** jurisdiction, the subsequent *bona fide* purchaser probably does **not** have to see that the entire chain of title is recorded (though this is not absolutely clear). Thus P, in *Zimmer, supra*, might have been saved had Wisconsin had a notice rather than a race-notice statute.

iii. Effect of tract index: Observe that if the recorder's office maintained a **tract** index, the "missing link" problem would be much less likely to arise. For instance, in *Losey v. Simpson, supra*, p. 372, either Pamela Adams or P would have looked at the tract index for the particular parcel involved, and would have seen the mortgage from Kanouse to Estell, even though no link from S. Adams to Kanouse would have been present. This would have been sufficient to put Pam Adams and/or P on "inquiry notice" to find out more about the missing Adams-to-Kanouse link (though on the actual facts of *Losey*, inquiries were indeed made to Kanouse, who denied the existence of the deed to him). See the discussion of inquiry notice *infra*, p. 376.

iv. Suit against title insurance company: Normally, chain of title questions will arise in a suit between rival claimants to the property. However, such questions may also be relevant in a suit against a **title insurance company**. For instance, in *Ryczkowski v. Chelsea Title & Guaranty Co.*, 449 P.2d 261 (Nev. 1969), a title insurance policy excluded from coverage "easements, claims of easements, or encumbrances which are not shown by the public records." Because an easement, although recorded, was outside of the insured's chain of title, the insurance company was held not liable.

b. Misindexing: The theory behind the "chain of title" rules is that a searcher will rely heavily upon the grantor and grantee indexes. This being the case, one would think that if the recorder's office **misindexed** a deed, this would place the deed outside the chain of title. However, in the substantial majority of states, the grantor and grantee indexes are **not always required by statute**. In these states, the courts have almost always held that a **mistake in indexing** does **not** remove the deed itself from the chain of title. 4 A.L.P. 603-05.

i. Statutorily required: But in those five or six states where indexes are required by statute to be kept, the courts have held that a record is not effective to give notice if it is not indexed or is materially incorrectly indexed. See, e.g., *Mortensen v. Lingo*, 99 F.Supp. 585 (D. Ala. 1951): "Not only does it seem unreasonable to require each person interested in ascertaining the status of the title to any piece of property to examine every page of a great number of volumes, but to hold that the index, notwithstanding that it is required to be kept by statute, is no part of the record is to deny any effect to the provision requiring the maintenance of an index."

c. Late-recorded documents: In searching title, the custom is to examine a record owner's name in the grantor index only *up until the time he is shown as having made a conveyance*. While in the vast majority of cases one can indeed assume that no effective conveyance could take place after this date, there is one situation where this is not true.

> **Example:** In 1960, A conveys to B, who does not record. In 1965, A conveys to C, who records but has notice of the deed to B. In 1967, B records the deed from A. In 1970, C conveys to D, a purchaser for value who has no actual notice of the deed from A to B. D immediately records his deed from C. Observe that when D is checking the records, he will not check A's name in the grantor index for any period later than the time when the deed from A to C appears (1965). Thus he will never find the deed from A to B. Yet in a pure notice jurisdiction, he will win if the deed from A to B is deemed to be outside of the chain of title, and he will lose if that deed is held to be within the chain of title.

> **i. Better view:** The better view, apparently followed by about half of the courts in pure notice states that have considered the question, is that *D wins* in the above example, because his chain of title comprises *only those instruments executed by grantors during the time when* (according to the record) they were *owners* of the property. 4 A.L.P. 599. A contrary rule, these courts point out, would require the searcher to search the name of each owner of the property from the day he got title *all the way to the present*; in the case of a parcel which has changed hands many times, this would be prohibitively expensive.

> **ii. Other view:** Nonetheless, a number of other courts have held that *D loses*, i.e., that the deed from A to B is within D's chain of title even though it was recorded after the deed from A to C. *Id.*

> **iii. Does not arise in race-notice state:** Observe that this question probably cannot arise in a race-notice or pure race jurisdiction. Thus on the fact of the above example, D will probably lose because he failed to record his deed prior to the recording of the A-to-B deed; the issue of whether D was on record notice of the A-to-B deed is thus irrelevant, since D has failed to win the race to record. 4 A.L.P. 597-98.

d. Early-recorded documents: The converse problem is more likely to arise. The title searcher will always begin checking the grantor index under a particular owner *only from the date that owner gained title*. Normally this will be adequate, but there is one situation (in some states) where a conveyance made by a grantor *before* he became owner of the property may have an effect upon the title.

> **i. Estoppel by deed:** Before we can understand the situation, however, it is necessary to consider the common-law doctrine of *estoppel by deed*. This doctrine holds that where a person (call him O) makes a conveyance of property to another (call him A) before he has ever obtained title, and then subsequently the grantor (O) does obtain title, this title *passes immediately* to the grantee

(A). The name "estoppel by deed" arises from the fact that the grantor is "estopped" from denying the validity of his earlier deed. See, e.g., *Robben v. Obering*, 279 F.2d 381 (7th Cir. 1960), applying the doctrine.

   ii. Effect on title searcher: If the estoppel by deed doctrine is applied, and the estoppel is held to be binding upon a subsequent *bona fide* purchaser, then that purchaser's failure to check the records prior to the date the owner of record obtained title will be ruinous.

      Example: Meirink executes an oil and gas lease on a tract to Obering as lessee in 1953. This deed contains a covenant of warranty, and is apparently promptly recorded by Obering. In 1956, an oil well is found in an adjacent tract. Meirink at that point discovers that he owns only a one-fourth interest in the tract, and that three of his relatives (including his brother Arthur) each own another one-fourth. Meirink obtains a quitclaim deed from Arthur on July 20, 1956, and then conveys that interest back to Arthur the same day (this quitclaim deed being recorded promptly). Arthur then executes an oil and gas lease of his interest to Robben. Robben, asserting his status as a good-faith purchaser, sues Obering to establish Robben's entitlement to one-fourth of the minerals found on the tract.

      Held, for Obering. Under the doctrine of estoppel by deed (or "after-acquired title"), when Arthur quitclaimed his interest to Meirink, the mineral rights to the interest immediately passed to Obering because of the prior lease to him. Thus Meirink's quitclaim deed back to Arthur was ineffective to assign any mineral rights to Arthur, and Arthur's mineral deed to Robben was also ineffective. The estoppel resulted from the fact that Meirink made a warranty of title. *Robben v. Obering, supra.*

   iii. Criticism: The court in *Robben* held that the estoppel-by-deed operated against Robben even though, assuming that Robben restricted his title search on Meirink from the time he took the one-fourth interest from Arthur, there was no way Robben would have found the lease to Obering. The court did not explain why the lease to Obering was not regarded as being outside of Robben's chain of title; nor have the other courts (probably a minority) reaching similar results given a satisfactory explanation of this.

   iv. Majority view: The *majority* of courts hold that even though the estoppel by deed doctrine may apply as between the original grantor and grantee (e.g., as between Meirink and Obering), the doctrine is *not binding against a subsequent good-faith purchaser*. This seems to be a much better rule, since it means that a title searcher does not have to check the grantor index under a particular owner's name until the date on which that person is shown to have become the owner of record. See, e.g., *Sabo v. Horvath*, 559 P.2d 1038 (Alaska 1976), reaching this result on the grounds that "requiring title checks beyond the chain of title could add a significant burden as well as uncertainty to real estate purchases. . . . The records as to each grantor in the chain of title would theoretically have to be checked back to the later of the grantor's date of birth or the date when records were first retained." (But the court recognized that its holding means that the grantee who discovers that he received his grant before the grantor actually owned the property must *re-record* his deed.)

  e. Easements and servitudes prior to subdivision: The owner of a parcel may sell part of it, and in so doing give the grantee rights against the grantor's remaining property (e.g., an *easement* or the benefit of an *equitable servitude*). When the grantor then sells his remaining land, the purchaser will not necessarily discover the existence of these interests.

i. One view: The courts are about evenly split as to whether the purchaser of the land retained by the grantor is on record notice of these interests. The courts that hold that he is **not on notice** use "chain of title" reasoning.

Example: O is the owner of both Blackacre and Whiteacre. He conveys Whiteacre to Marsh, the deed providing that Marsh (and those taking under him) will obey certain building restrictions. The deed also provides that O will not sell Blackacre without inserting in the deed a similar set of restrictions. Blackacre passes to O's heirs, who sell it to P without inserting the restrictions. P finds out about the restrictions, and sues the heirs for breach of title covenants, on the grounds that he is bound by the restrictions.

Held, for the heirs. There was a breach of the title covenants only if P was bound by the restrictions in the deed from O to Marsh, and P would be bound only if the O-to-Marsh deed were part of P's chain of title. P was not under an obligation to examine every deed ever executed by any person in the chain of title, but only those deeds *for the land in question* (i.e., Blackacre). "[I]t would impose an intolerable burden to compel [a title searcher] to examine all conveyances made by everyone in his chain of title." *Glorieux v. Lighthipe*, 96 A. 94 (N.J. 1915).

ii. Other view: But an equal number of courts hold that the title searcher must indeed examine *every deed issued by one who is in the chain of title,* to verify whether that deed affects the property title to which is being searched. See, e.g., *Finley v. Glenn*, 154 A. 299 (Pa. 1931), so holding on facts very similar to those of *Glorieux*. See also 4 A.L.P. 602, holding that the *Finley* rationale is the correct one, and suggesting that in a situation like than in *Glorieux*, the deed to Whiteacre should have been indexed as affecting both Whiteacre **and** Blackacre. See also *Guillette v. Daly Dry Wall, Inc.* 325 N.E.2d 572 (Mass. 1975), agreeing with the *Finley* rationale.

f. Effect of actual or inquiry notice: Keep in mind that even though an instrument may be outside the title searcher's chain of title, either **actual** or **"inquiry"** notice may exist as to that instrument. For instance, in the *Glorieux* case, if the deed to P stated that the title was "subject to any restrictions imposed by a deed to Marsh," this would be enough to put P upon inquiry notice of the equitable restriction, and the fact that the deed to Marsh was not in his chain of title would be irrelevant. Inquiry notice is discussed immediately below.

L. Inquiry notice: Even if the purchaser has neither record nor actual notice of a prior unrecorded conveyance, he may be found to have been on *"inquiry" notice* of it. Inquiry notice exists where the circumstances are such that a purchaser is in *possession of facts which would lead a reasonable person in his position* to make an *investigation*, which would in turn advise him of the existence of the prior unrecorded right. Just as a purchaser is on record notice even though he never sees the prior recorded instrument, so a purchaser is on inquiry notice *even if he does not in fact make the investigation*.

1. Only what search would have disclosed: However, even where there are facts which would lead the purchaser to make an investigation, he will be responsible for *only those facts which the investigation would have disclosed*. 4 A.L.P. 566-67.

2. **References in record:** An instrument which is definitely within the purchaser's chain of title may contain a *reference to another document*, one which might be either outside of the chain of title or not recorded at all. The traditional rule has been that while such a recital does not place the purchaser on record notice of the referred-to instrument, he is placed upon *inquiry* notice of it. If he fails to make the inquiries, and these inquires would have yielded him reasonably definite knowledge of the instrument, he will lose his status as a *bona fide* purchaser.

> **Example:** O, owner of Blackacre, gives Campbell a mineral lease on the property. The lease is not recorded. O then gives Rock an option to purchase her land, but the option is expressly made subject to the lease to Campbell. The option is promptly recorded. The lease is assigned to D, and the assignment is recorded. Then, O conveys the fee to P. When D asserts its right to the minerals found on the land, P sues to establish its status as a *bona fide* purchaser taking free of the unrecorded lease.
>
> *Held,* P was charged with all references made in any document in her chain of title. She was thus charged with knowledge of the reference in Rock's recorded option to the unrecorded Campbell lease. This placed her under the duty to inquire of Campbell about his rights under the lease, and such inquiry would have shown that there was indeed a valid lease. P was not entitled to rely on O's representation that there was no outstanding leases on the property. *Guerin v. Sunburst Oil & Gas Co.,* 218 P. 949 (Mont. 1923).

   a. **Criticism:** The majority rule, exemplified by *Guerin*, that one is on inquiry notice of any recital contained in an instrument in one's chain of title, has been *criticized*. As one authority has put it, "That this places an unreasonable burden upon the title searcher can scarcely be denied. Indeed, it is entirely inconsistent with the spirit and purpose of the recording acts in that it compels the title searcher to investigate the existence of unrecorded instruments." Simes & Taylor, Improvement of Conveyancing By Legislation 101-02 (1960).

   b. **Actual knowledge of recital not needed:** Observe that the inquiry notice rule will come into play even if the purchaser does *not* have *actual* notice of the *recital* (let alone of the unrecorded document to which the recital refers). Thus in *Guerin*, P could not raise the defense that she never saw the option contract which contained the reference; this option contract was in her chain of title, and she was responsible for reading everything in it.

   c. **Statutory relief:** Because of the burdens which the majority rule places on title searchers, a number of states have enacted *statutes* which abolish or limit the effect of recorded recitals to unrecorded instruments. See, e.g., §3-207 of the Uniform Simplification of Land Transfers Act, which makes a recorded reference to another instrument ineffective unless the latter is referred to *by its record location* (thus automatically making ineffective all references to unrecorded documents).

3. **Quitclaim deed in chain:** Recall that a *quitclaim deed* is a deed in which the grantor makes no warranties or representations about the state of his title. A few jurisdictions hold that the existence of a quitclaim deed anywhere in the chain of title puts the purchaser upon inquiry notice as to the possible inadequacy of the title held by the grantor under that quitclaim deed. An additional small minority holds that a purchaser is on such inquiry notice if the deed under which he himself takes in a quitclaim deed, but not if the quitclaim deed occurs earlier in the chain of title. 4 A.L.P. 585-86.

a. Majority rule: But the *majority* of courts hold that a quitclaim deed is to be treated *exactly the same* as a warranty deed for inquiry notice purposes, i.e., that existence of a quitclaim deed does *not* put the purchaser on notice of anything. See, e.g., *Strong v. Whybark*, 102 S.W. 968 (Mo. 1907), where the court stated that "A purchaser for value by quitclaim deed is as much within the protection of the registry act as one who becomes a purchaser by a warranty deed." (Other aspects of *Strong v. Whybark* are discussed *supra*, p. 365.)

4. Recorded but defective deeds: Recall that a deed which is recorded but which was *not entitled to recordation* (e.g., a *defectively acknowledged* deed) does not constitute record notice to subsequent purchasers. However, a number of states provide (either by statute or case-law) that existence of such an erroneously-recorded deed puts purchasers upon inquiry notice of the interest represented by the deed. 4 A.L.P. 606-07.

5. Notice based on possession of property: Probably the most important source of inquiry notice is *possession* of the parcel in question by a person who is *not the record owner*. The purchaser is generally held to have a duty to: (1) *view* the property, to see whether it is in the possession of someone other than the record owner; and (2) if there is such a possessor, to inquire as to the source of his rights in the property. If the possessor has rights under an unrecorded document, and the court is satisfied that the possessor would have informed any inquirers about these rights, the subsequent purchaser will be deemed to be on notice of these rights even though he never in fact learned about the possession at all.

Example: Barker conveys an 880-acre timberland tract to P in 1948. P does not record his deed. He does, however, take possession of the property (by posting a no-trespassing sign with his name and address on it, locking the gates, and letting his friends live in residential dwellings on the property, though P himself does not live there). This "possession" by P goes on through 1951. In 1951, Barker conveys the property again, to D; this deed is promptly recorded. Then, P records his deed. P brings a quiet title action against D and several other defendants.

Held, for P. D was under a duty to ascertain who was in possession of the tract when he bought it. Although P was not physically living on the tract, there were ample signs of his possession of it. Had D looked closely at the property (rather than just looking at an aerial map or flying over it), he would have been led to make inquiries of P, who would have revealed his claim. Therefore, D is not a good-faith purchaser and is not protected by the recording act. *Wineberg v. Moore*, 194 F.Supp. 12 (N.D. Cal. 1961).

a. Combined with equitable claim under contract: The doctrine that possession constitutes inquiry notice can be combined with the doctrine that a vendee under a land-sale *contract* has equitable rights to the property that can take precedence over the rights of the vendor's creditors (see *supra*, p. 327). By putting these two doctrines together, it can happen that a person who has an *unrecorded contract to buy property* from a vendor, and who then takes possession, will have priority over a later deed or mortgage issued by that same vendor and recorded. Furthermore, if the vendee in possession then pays off the contract (even after the competing mortgage or deed has been recorded), the vendee will usually take title free and clear.

Example: Waldorff contracts in writing to buy condominium Unit 111 from Chocktaw (the developer) on April 4, 1973. Waldorff pays $1,000 as a deposit at this time, against a total purchase of $23,550. That same month, Waldorff begins

1 1/2 years of continual occupancy of the unit, and pays all carrying fees. On October 10, 1973, Chocktaw executes a note and mortgage for the entire development (including Unit 111) in favor of Bank. Bank promptly records. In 1974, Waldorff agrees to write off a $35,000 debt owed to it by Chocktaw, and in return Chocktaw executes a quitclaim deed (*supra*, p. 377) to Unit 111 in favor of Waldorff; this deed is recorded in 1975. In 1976, Bank tries to foreclose against Waldorff's interest in Unit 111.

Held, for Waldorff. The 1973 contract between Chocktaw and Waldorff created an equitable interest on Waldorff's part. Since Waldorff was in possession, this should have put Bank on notice that Waldorff might be asserting some interest to the property. Therefore, Waldorff's equitable claim was superior to the later, but recorded, mortgage by Chocktaw in favor of Bank. When Waldorff in effect "paid" the remaining price due under its purchase contract (by cancelling the debt owed to it by Chocktaw), this had the effect of freeing Waldorff of Bank's lien. (The fact that other people occupied other units in 1973, as part of Chocktaw's marketing campaign, but had no legal or equitable interest to those units, did not prevent Waldorff's occupancy from putting Chocktaw on notice — Chocktaw had the burden of making individual inquiries to each possessor.) *Waldorff Insurance and Bonding, Inc. v. Eglin National Bank*, 453 So.2d 1383 (Fl. D.C. App. 1984).

b. Possession consistent with record title: However, if the possession of property is **consistent with the record title**, the purchaser is generally entitled to assume that the possessor has no additional, unrecorded, rights.

Example: The record shows that title to Blackacre is held by A and B as tenants in common. B conveys his undivided one-half interest to A, but the deed is not recorded. A is in sole possession. B then purports to convey his one-half interest to C, who does not have actual knowledge of B's unrecorded conveyance to A. Despite A's sole possession of the property, C was not put on inquiry notice; he was entitled to ignore A's possession, since that possession was consistent with the record title (because either tenant in common has the right to full possession and use of the property; see *supra*, p. 125). 4 A.L.P. 580.

i. Exception for tenant: However, an exception to the "possession consistent with record title" rule is usually made where the possessor is shown by the record to be a **tenant**. The reason for this is that informal unrecorded modifications of lease rights (e.g., an extension to the term of the lease, or an option to purchase the leased premises) are so common that the usual assumption that the possessor has no rights not shown in the record is unwarranted. See generally 4 A.L.P. 577.

c. Inquiry futile: Keep in mind that in situations involving possession by one other than the record owner (as in any other case involving inquiry notice), the purchaser will be held to a duty to inquire only where **inquiry would not have been fruitless**. For instance, in *Losey v. Simpson*, 11 N.J. Eq. 246 (1856) (discussed *supra*, p. 372), Kanouse, although shown on the record as merely a mortgagee, was in actual possession of the property. The court noted that the holder of the subsequent interest had in fact made inquiry of Kanouse, and that he had denied any title to the property; this was sufficient to nullify any duty of further inquiry.

d. Statutory modification: Also, keep in mind that the whole subject of inquiry notice is likely to be affected by **statute**. For instance, by statute in a number of states, the purchaser is required to make inquiry of a possessor who is not the holder of record only where the purchaser is *aware* of the possession. In such states, the purchaser thus has no duty to visit the property.

M. Timing of notice: All of the above discussion relates to the issue of what constitutes "notice" to a purchaser who is asserting that he is a bona fide purchaser. A related question is, "*At what time* must the purchaser be a b.f.p.?" If the purchaser pays money and receives a deed simultaneously, there is no problem: the purchaser receives the protection of the recording act only if she is without knowledge of the prior conveyance at the moment she exchanges money for the deed. But often, the buying of land is a *process* that takes time. The purchaser might pay money today, and receive the deed next month. Or, she might receive the deed today, and pay for the land next month. If the purchaser receives notice of the transaction in between the two steps, is she protected?

1. **Must have made substantial payment:** Nearly all courts hold that the buyer must have made *substantial payment* before being put on notice of the prior conveyance — the fact that she has received the deed, or even recorded it, is not enough. Thus if Buyer receives the deed on April 1, records it on April 15, receives notice of a prior conveyance on June 1, and pays the purchase price on June 15, Buyer will almost certainly not be protected by the recording act — she had the opportunity to decline to pay the purchase price on the grounds of the prior conveyance, so the recording act should not protect her.

2. **Payment is sufficient:** Conversely, most courts hold that the buyer *is* protected if she paid all or a substantial part of the purchase price before receiving notice of the prior conveyance, even if she had not received the deed or recorded it. C,S&W, pp. 845-46.

3. **Installment contract:** The greatest problems occur where the second purchaser is buying under an *installment contract*, and has made some, but not all, payments at the time she discovers the prior conveyance. How the case comes out depends in part on whether the installment buyer receives actual or inquiry notice on the one hand, or mere record notice on the other.

   a. **Mere record notice:** Most cases hold that where the subsequent purchaser, after making some payments, merely receives *record notice* of the earlier conveyance, this does *not* count as notice, so the later purchaser is protected by the recording act as she continues to make installment payments.

      Example: O conveys to A, who does not record. O conveys to B under an installment contract, calling for 15 years' worth of monthly payments, against a total purchase price of $100,000. After B has paid six months of installments, A records, but B does not learn of this fact. B continues making payments for another six years. A now brings an action to quiet title in himself.

      Most courts would rule that B is a bona fide purchaser who gets protection from the recording act. To hold otherwise would mean that B had the extreme burden of checking the records anew before making each payment. C,S&W, p. 846. (There is one case holding that B is not protected in this situation, *Alexander v. Andrews*, 64 S.E.2d 487 (W.Va. 1951), but almost no other courts or commentators have agreed with it.)

   b. **Actual notice:** On the other hand, once the installment purchaser receives *actual* notice of the prior conveyance, nearly all courts agree that she is *not protected* as to any *further payments* she makes. What, then, happens if she has paid, say, half the purchase price and then receives actual notice of the prior interest? Most often, courts give the prior holder (A in the above example) title to the land, but give the installment buyer (B) the right to **get back her payments** plus interest. C,S&W, p. 847. Other courts give the land to B, provided that she continues to make the installment payments — this protects B's benefit of her bargain. Finally, still other courts treat the two claimants as tenants in common, with the installment buyer getting a fractional interest equal to the portion of the purchase price paid (so that if B has paid one-third the purchase price, she would get a one-third undivided interest as tenant in common). C,S&W, p. 847.

N. Purchaser from one without notice: Assume that a purchaser takes without notice of a prior unrecorded instrument. When he **resells** the property, what is the effect of knowledge either by him, or by the new purchaser, of the unrecorded document?

    1. Protection of seller's market: In order to protect the innocent purchaser's market for the property, the courts uniformly hold that the new purchaser is to be treated as a *bona fide* purchaser who may claim the benefit of the recording act, **even if he buys with actual notice**, 4 A.L.P. 567-58. That is, once an interest is purged by its acquisition by one without notice of the prior unrecorded document, the interest remains "clean".

    2. Exception: The sole exception to this is that if the subsequent interest is **reacquired** by a **prior grantee who had notice**, the title again becomes subject to those claims with which it was charged previously. *Id.* at 568.

        Example: O conveys to A, who does not record. O conveys to B, who takes with notice of A's unrecorded interest. Because the jurisdiction has a notice or a race-notice statute, B's interest is not good against A's. B now conveys to C, who takes without notice. If C were to convey to D, D would take free and clear of A's interest, even if D had actual notice of A's interest. But if C **reconveys to B**, the property in B's hands is once again subject to A's claim. This prevents B from "laundering" his title by conveying to an unsuspecting third person and reacquiring it.

III. TITLE REGISTRATION (THE TORRENS SYSTEM)

A. Nature of registration: In the recording systems which we have examined thus far, the record merely furnishes *evidence* of title. In parts of the U.S., by contrast, a quite different optional system is available, in which *the title itself* is registered. This system, called the *title registration* system or *Torrens* System, enables the owner of a parcel to obtain a *certificate of title*, similar to an automobile certificate of title. When the holder of the certificate wishes to sell the property, his prospective purchaser merely has to inspect the certificate itself (on which nearly all encumbrances must be noted), and a lengthy title examination is unnecessary.

B. Historical background: The Torrens System was the brainchild of Sir Robert Torrens, who thought of it while he was collector of customs in Australia. Torrens saw the ease by which title to **ships** was transferred, because of the system of registration of ownership. He succeeded in getting a similar system established for land titles in Australia, and the system was ultimately established in England as well.

    1. American use: In the U.S., the Torrens System has never really caught on, for reasons discussed below. Today, there are only five states that have a substantial amount of land registered under the Torrens System: Hawaii, Illinois (Cook County),

Massachusetts, Minnesota (Hennepin and Ramsey Counties) and Ohio (Hamilton County). See D&K, p. 764.

> **a. Never required:** In no place is the owner of land *required* to register under the Torrens System (though once an owner does so, subsequent owners must continue under the System).

C. How the System works: Because the Torrens System is entirely optional, the registration process begins with an *application* by a person claiming ownership of a parcel to have it registered.

> **1. Notice to all record interests:** The registration clerk, after receiving the registration application, inspects the ordinary land records to ascertain the names of all persons who appear to have an interest in the property. *Notice* is given to them, and is also usually published.

> **2. Judicial proceeding:** Then, a court hears the claim of any person asserting an interest in the property. If the court is satisfied that the applicant indeed has good title, it orders a *certificate of title* to be issued to him. Also noted on the certificate are any encumbrances which the court has concluded to be valid. A *duplicate copy* of the certificate of title is *kept in the registration clerk's office*.

> **3. Subsequent conveyances:** When the holder of the first certificate of title (or the holder of a subsequent certificate) wishes to sell the property, he shows the certificate to the prospective purchaser, who can quickly see the state of the title by a simple examination. (Because of the possibility that there have been *involuntary* encumbrances against the property, the purchaser should probably also check with the registration clerk's office; see *infra*.)

>> **a. Transfer of title:** Execution and delivery of a *deed* by the registration holder to the purchaser is *not sufficient* to transfer title. Rather, the transfer occurs when the parties go to the registration clerk, tender the original certificate, and receive a new one from the clerk. At the same time, of course, the clerk's copy of the old certificate is marked void, and a copy of the new certificate is entered in the clerk's records. Any encumbrances noted on the old certificate, if they are still in effect, are carried over onto the new certificate.

> **4. Involuntary liens or transfers:** Tax liens, judgment liens, and mortgage foreclosure sales are examples of interests created *without the consent* of the owner of the property. If the owner's title is embodied by his certificate, how is the holder of the lien or the purchaser at the foreclosure sale to obtain this certificate and get the new interest noted on it? The answer is that an application must be submitted to the *registration clerk* to have the involuntary interest noted on the registrar's copy of the certificate. Once the notation is made, the fact that it is not necessarily embodied upon the owner's copy becomes irrelevant (which is why the purchaser must be sure to check the registrar's copy before parting with his money).

>> **a. Federal tax lien:** See *U.S. v. Ryan*, 124 F.Supp. 1 (D. Minn. 1954), holding that even a federal tax lien did not become effective until notice of it (including an accurate description of the parcel) was filed with the registration clerk; the effect was that a subsequent purchaser took free of the lien (even though the lien was filed in the regular land records, and would have been good had the tract not been under the Torrens System). This case illustrates that a lawyer practicing in a jurisdiction where Torrens Registration is allowed but not mandatory must always take care to

discover whether the particular tract he is interested in has been registered, since even such matters as the filing of a lien may have to be done differently.

D. Conclusiveness of certificate: The certificate of title is substantially more *conclusive* than are ordinary land records. For instance, the certificate has *priority over any adverse possessor* (assuming that the adverse possession did not begin until after the title had been registered). Nonetheless, there are at least four situations where a purchaser who relies on a clean certificate of title may end up not getting a good and unencumbered title.

    1. Failure of original proceeding: First, an *inadequacy* in the *original proceeding* to register the title may mean that a prior interest is not wiped out. For instance, in *Follette v. Pacific Light & Power Corp.*, 208 P.295 (Cal. 1922), O, the owner of a tract, gave a utility easement to D, a power company. The easement was duly recorded. O then filed an application to have his land registered, and did not mention D's easement in the application. D did not receive notice of the registration proceeding, which culminated in the issuance of a certificate of title to O with no mention of the easement. O then sold the property to X, who resold it to P (neither of whom had any actual knowledge of the easement).

        a. Holding: The court in *Follette* held that D's easement was valid as against P, because of D's failure to receive notice of the registration proceeding. To the extent that the California registration statute purported to make D's interest void as against P, the statute was held unconstitutional, since this would have amounted to a deprivation of D's property (i.e., the easement) without due process of law.

    2. Fraud or forgery: Secondly, a certificate obtained by *fraud* or *forgery* may in some cases fail to be valid against the holder of a prior interest.

        a. Owner entrusts certificate: But if the owner *entrusts* another with the certificate of title, the owner will *not be protected* if the trustee conveys without permission to a third person. See *Eliason v. Wilborn*, 281 U.S. 457 (1930), in which the Supreme Court so held, noting that "As between innocent persons one of whom must suffer the consequence of a breach of trust the one who made it possible by his act of confidence must bear the loss."

    3. Short-term lease: A *Short-term lease* (usually defined as being three years or less) is often excluded from operation of the registration system. Therefore, one who relies on the certificate will not have priority over such a short-term lessor (so that the purchaser should check to see whether a tenant is in possession of the land).

    4. Tax liens: Under federal law, notice of a *federal tax lien* is not required to be deposited with the registrar's office unless a state statute so requires. Therefore, if the state has not enacted such a statute, a purchaser cannot rely even upon the registrar's copy to establish that there are no federal tax liens, and this must be independently verified by looking at the regular county land records.

E. Insurance funds: Most Torrens Systems have established an *insurance fund*, whereby one who has suffered damages due to reliance either upon a certificate of title or upon the functioning of the registrar's office may be made whole. The insurance pool is funded by a small tax upon all registrations.

    1. California experience: Observe that such a fund will not be very adequate in the first years following enactment of a Torrens System. One early judgment for $48,000 more than wiped out California's Torrens insurance fund, and led directly to the state legislature's decision to abolish the entire Torrens System shortly thereafter. Powell, Par. 921, pp. 1063-64.

F. **Possession by stranger to title:** Once the land has been validly registered, the entry of an adverse possessor or the creation of an unrecorded interest will, as noted, not be binding upon a subsequent purchaser who relies upon the certificate of title (which, of course, does not show the adverse possession or other unrecorded claim). But if the subsequent purchaser has *actual knowledge* of the stranger's possession, at least one court has held that he loses his right to rely upon the certificate. See *Killam v. March*, 55 N.E.2d 945 (Mass. 1944) (involving an unregistered lease).

G. **Future of the Torrens System:** The Torrens System has never really caught on in the U.S. As noted *supra*, pp. 381-82, in only five states is there a significant amount of land covered by the System.

    1. **Reason for lack of acceptance:** There are at least three important reasons why the System has not been used more widely:

        a. **Lack of conclusiveness:** Even though the certificate of title is reasonably conclusive, there remain a number of things that still have to be checked in most states (see *supra*, p. 383). Thus if one has to check the non-Torrens land records to see whether there is, for instance, a federal tax lien, much of the advantage of the certificate is lost.

        b. **Expense of initial registration:** The cost of an *initial registration* of a parcel is quite substantial, since a judicial proceeding similar to a quiet title suit is required. Concededly, the cost of checking title in future transactions will be minimized, but the original owner is likely to be unwilling to pay a substantial sum so that future owners may transfer the property more cheaply. Powell, Par. 922, pp. 1067-68.

        c. **Resistance by title companies and bar:** Lastly, the System is obviously detrimental to the interests of *title insurance companies*. The title insurers would be almost entirely supplanted by a mandatory registration system, at least if it included a government-sponsored insurance fund as most option Torrens systems now do. Similarly, in areas of the country where title insurance has not become the standard method of operation, *lawyers* who search title or give opinions from abstracts (see *infra*, p. 385) have opposed the Torrens System.

    2. **Future prospects:** It seems unlikely that the Torrens System will ever become much more widely used in America than it is today. The three factors listed above are likely to be of continued importance. In fact, the writing of title insurance is likely to increase in volume, making the political realities alone probably fatal to the implementation of registration schemes where they do not already exist. All this is unfortunate, since most observers agree that were we starting from scratch, a registration scheme would be much superior to the recording-act system.

IV. METHODS OF TITLE ASSURANCE

A. **Various methods:** Apart from examination of the land records themselves, there are various means by which the purchaser of land can attempt to assure himself of a valid title.

B. **Covenants for title:** One method, of course, is by having the seller give *covenants for title*. However, as we saw *supra*, p. 347, covenants for title, as a method of title assurance, have at least two very severe drawbacks: (1) they rely upon the personal solvency of the seller; and

(2) the measure of damages applied by the courts is often woefully inadequate to compensate for the real loss caused by a breach.

C. Examination by a lawyer: A prospective purchaser of land could conceivably examine the land records himself. But apart from the large amount of time this would take, he would not know how to interpret the documents. Therefore, in many areas of the country, title examination is performed by the ***buyer's lawyer***. Occasionally, the lawyer himself does the examination of the title records. More commonly, however, the lawyer obtains an ***abstract*** of title from an abstract company. (Usually, the sale contract requires the seller to buy the abstract and supply it to the buyer's lawyer.)

   1. Nature of abstract: The abstract is a summary of the salient date on each conveyance in the chain of title, and each encumbrance of record. The abstract is compiled by the abstract company not via a *de novo* search of the records, but rather, from a ***private tract index*** kept by the abstract company. The lawyer then reviews the abstract, and gives the client a written ***opinion*** as to the state of the title.

   2. Lawyer's liability: The lawyer is not liable for any misstatement contained in the abstract itself. (This is the abstract company's responsibility, and it may be liable for negligence to the buyer.) The lawyer is, however, liable for his own negligence in rendering an opinion on the title as it is presented in the abstract. Thus if the abstract exposes a major defect (e.g., an unpaid tax lien), and the lawyer does not warn his client about it, he is likely to be held liable on a negligence theory for any loss sustained by the client. Cribbet, pp. 323-25, n. 58.

     a. Lack of privity: If the abstract company or the buyer's lawyer has been negligent, the liability of each will of course extend to the party with whom the contract (to provide the abstract or render the opinion) was made. But ***third parties*** not in contractual privity with the abstractor or lawyer may also be able to recover.

      Example: A contract for the sale of land provides that Seller will supply Buyer with an abstract of title. Seller contracts with D, an abstract company, to provide the abstract. Buyer relies on the abstract, which negligently omits a utility easement.

      Held, Buyer may recover in negligence from the abstract company, even though there was no contract between the two. This result is justified by the theory of ***third-party beneficiary contracts***, since D knew that the abstract was intended to be used by this particular buyer. (An earlier case in which no cause of action was allowed in favor of a buyer who relied upon an abstract done for a seller ***several links earlier in the chain of title*** is distinguishable; only the party whose identity and intent to use the abstract is known to the abstractor will be protected.) *Slate v. Boone County Abstract Co.,* 432 S.W.2d 305 (Mo. 1968).

      i. Lenders protected: Similarly, other courts have held that a ***lender*** who relies upon an abstract or opinion prepared for one of the parties to the sale may sue; see, e.g., *Chun v. Park,* 426 P.2d 905 (Haw. 1969).

D. Title insurance: At present, the leading means by which a buyer of property can assure himself of a good title is ***title insurance***. Whereas a lawyer's opinion based upon an abstract of title gives rise to only negligence liability, the title insurer's liability is absolute (apart from the exceptions noted in the policy).

   1. Practical importance: This means that the insured will be able to recover from a title insurer (but not from a lawyer or abstract company) if the title is bad for any of the following illustrative reasons: ***disability*** of a grantor in the chain of title; ***forgery*** of an instrument in the chain; fraudulent representation of ***marital status*** by a grantor (so that the spouse's inchoate right of dower perseveres); undisclosed heirs of an owner/decedent; and defects in the conveyances in the chain of title due to ***lack of delivery***. See Cribbet, p. 327. All of these are defects which could affect the validity of the buyer's title, but which would not be found even by the most careful title searcher.

   a.   Litigation costs: The policy will also cover the insured's ***litigation costs*** in defending his title, even if the defense is successful.

   b.   Liability for subsequent warranties: The policy typically also covers any loss which the insured may sustain if he gives ***covenants of title*** when he re-sells the property. Thus when the insured sells the property, his policy is transformed from an owner's policy to a ***warrantor's policy***. (But the new purchaser of the property is not covered by the policy, unless he pays the company a supplementary fee.)

2.   The "title plant": When the title company receives (usually from the buyer's lawyer) an application for a title policy, the company does not conduct a *de novo* search of the public land records. Instead, the company has built over the years a ***"title plant"***. The title plant is, in effect, a ***tract index***; every parcel has its own index entry, and all conveyances or encumbrances affecting that parcel are noted on the index. The company also keeps photocopies of the recorded documents themselves, so that these can be examined without the need to return to the public records. The system is maintained by a "take-off" person, who photocopies the newly-filed documents at the recording office each day. See C,S&W, pp. 854, 874.

3.   Scope of coverage: As noted, title insurance covers risks which would not be disclosed even by a competent examination of the public records, and also the risk of errors made by the company in its title examination. Nonetheless, most title policies do contain a number of ***exceptions***. In fact, one of the buyer's lawyer's major functions is to evaluate the exceptions demanded by the title company and to be sure that these do not swallow up the bulk of the protection being sought.

   a.   Facts which survey would show: Nearly all policies exclude facts ***which an accurate survey of the property would disclose***. Thus ***encroachments*** (either by the insured onto adjacent property or vice versa) and violations of ***setback*** rules are not generally covered.

      i.   What is "correct" survey: However, a survey is considered ***"correct"*** so long as it ***corresponds to the description of the property as it appears in the deed*** from the seller to the insured. The fact that the description recited in the seller's deed to the insured and relied on by the surveyor is itself wrong will not prevent the survey from being "correct".

      Example: O is the owner of Blackacre, a 10-acre parcel. O conveys two of the acres to X. O then conveys Blackacre to P, keeping the metes and bounds description as if the two-acre conveyance to X had never been made. At the time of the O-P conveyance, P gives D (P's title company) a survey that corresponds to the metes and bounds shown on the proposed O-P deed. P buys Blackacre. After X shows that X owns the two acres, and that P owns only eight, not 10, acres, P sues D under the title policy.

      If D defends on the grounds that a "correct" survey would have shown that the two acres belong to X rather than P, D will lose with this assertion — so long as the survey matches the description in P's deed (which it does), the survey will be deemed "correct," and the standard title policy exclusion for facts "which an accurate survey of the property would disclose" does not come into play.

b. Possession: Also, rights of *parties in possession* not shown by the public records are usually excluded. Thus the title policy *does not protect against a claim of adverse possession*, at least if the physical possession still exists at the time the policy is written. Accordingly, the buyer must still inspect the property.

c. Charges not shown as liens: The policy also usually excludes taxes or special assignments which, at the time the policy is issued, do *not yet appear as liens* on the public record. See, e.g., *Mayers v. Van Schaick*, 197 N.E.296 (N.Y. 1935), where a special assessment to establish a village park had been enacted prior to issuance of the policy, but became a lien only thereafter; the policyholder was found to be without protection even though the assessment had to be paid off by him in forty annual installments!

4. **Effect on value:** Title insurance generally protects the insured only from defects clouding *title*; it does not usually insure against defects that merely reduce the property's *value*. For instance, a title policy will usually be held not to protect the insured against the existence of a *restrictive covenant* (or against a violation of that restrictive covenant), even though the existence or violation of the restrictive covenant diminishes the value of the property. Similarly, a title policy will almost never be held to protect the insured against the presence of *hazardous waste* on the site.

> **Example:** P buys 30 acres of land from X. In connection with the purchase, P buys a title insurance policy from D. Before issuing the policy, D causes a survey and inspection to be made; the inspector notices various tanks, pumps, pipes and other improvements, but does not suspect a hazardous waste problem. After closing, P discovers hazardous waste on the property, and is forced to spend large sums to clean it up, both to protect the property's value and to avoid the state's right to put a lien on the property to guarantee payment of cleanup costs. P asserts that D should have to pay for the cleanup, under the title policy.
>
> *Held*, for D. No clause in the policy obligates D to pay for cleanup costs. The clause guaranteeing that P's title would be "marketable" is not breached by the pollution, because P's *title* is perfectly marketable, even though the land itself is not marketable due to the waste on it. Similarly, the clause protecting against "encumbrances on title" is not violated, because although such a clause protects against existing liens, it does not protect against the possibility that the state might in the future get a lien to cover cleanup costs. *Lick Mill Creek Apartments v. Chicago Title Insurance Co.*, 283 Cal.Rptr. 231 (Cal.Ct.App. 1991).

5. **Zoning and building code violations:** Most title policies exclude coverage for violations of *zoning ordinances*, *building codes*, and the like. So it is up to the insured and his lawyer, not the title company, to guard against the possibility that, say, the property is an office building located in an area that is zoned residential.

a. Exception for litigation: But some courts have held that where a zoning or building code violation has already led to *litigation* by the date the policy is issued, the exclusion for code violations does not apply. Thus in *Radovanov v. Land Title Co. of America, Inc.*, 545 N.E.2d 351 (Ill.App. 1989), the policy excluded "the effect of violations of building ordinances." But the court held that while exclusion might protect the insurer against having to cover losses from the mere fact that the building violated the ordinance, it did not protect it from having to pay for the consequences of a lawsuit commenced by the city before the policy date, in which the city alleged numerous code violations and sought to have the building demolished or a receiver appointed for it.

6. Duty to make reasonable search: Apart from the insurance company's liability on the policy itself, it has potential liability for the *way in which it prepares the title report*. The title report, which is submitted to the buyer's lawyer before the policy itself is issued, is essentially a summary of the state of the title. As a practical matter, this title report is often as important to the buyer's lawyer as the eventual policy. Some recent cases have held that the insurer has an implied duty to make a *reasonable search* and to *disclose to the customer* the findings that would result from a reasonable search. Under these cases, if the insurer fails to make the reasonable search and disclosure, it may be liable for *negligence, even as to an item which has been excluded from coverage by the policy*. C,S&W, p. 875. See, e.g., *Shotwell v. Transamerica Title Ins. Co.*, 558 P.2d 1359 (Ct. App. Wash. 1976).

   a. Majority does not find tort liability: But *most* cases do *not* impose an implied duty of reasonable care as to the title search, and hold that only if the title company *expressly agrees* to perform a search and disclose its results to the insured will there be liability in tort.

   Example: P contracts to buy a tract of land from X. The contract describes the land by reference to a previously-conducted survey (the "Price Walker" survey), and states that the tract consists of 19 acres. The purchase price is computed on a per-acre basis. P asks D, a title company, to supply a title report and a title policy. The policy excludes any damage from any "matter which could be disclosed by an accurate survey. . . ." The title report prepared by D makes no mention of the fact that the deed by which X originally acquired the property recited the size as being 12.5 acres, as shown on a different survey. This deed and the survey on which it was based were present in D's title "plant" at the time it prepared the title report and policy for P. P now attempts to recover from D for the tort of negligence for failing to disclose that the prior survey showed 12.5 rather than 19 acres.

   Held, for D. In New Jersey, "a title company's liability is limited to the policy and . . . the company is not liable in tort for negligence in searching records." Here, if D had expressly agreed to conduct the search and disclose the results to P, D could be liable for breach of this express duty, but the mere issuance of a policy does not constitute such a commitment. Nor does the fact that D charged P a separate $75 fee for "title examination" amount to such an express agreement to inspect and disclose, since the charge was merely to cover D's internal procedures in deciding whether to issue the policy. Case remanded to determine whether anything else D did constituted an express commitment to make a reasonable inspection and disclosure, in which case D would be liable for failing to report the acreage discrepancy. *Walker Rogge, Inc. v. Chelsea Title & Guaranty Co.*, 562 A.2d 208 (N.J. 1989).

7. Lawyers' insurance funds: In areas of the country where examination of title by lawyers has served an important function, the inroads of title insurance have not made lawyers happy. In a number of states, bar association groups have gotten together to form *lawyer-owned* and -administered title insurance companies.

   a. How it works: A lawyer must pay a fee to join the plan (or "fund", as it is usually called). By doing so, he becomes authorized to examine the record or an abstract in the usual way. He then issues a policy for the fund on the title which he has examined, and collects an insurance fee (in addition to his professional service fee). Part of this fee is then paid over to the fund to be used to defray claims. See B,C&S, pp. 887-90.

8. **Damages:** If the insured does sustain loss as the result of a covered title defect, his claim is limited to the *face amount* stated in the policy, usually the *purchase price*. This means that if the defect does not come to light until after the property has greatly appreciated in value, the insured may not be made whole.

    a. **Difference in value:** But the courts do, however, generally give the insured the difference between the value the property would have had upon the date of the policy had it been free of defects, and its actual value, including the defects, on that date (up to the amount of the face value, of course). See *Beaullieu v. Atlanta Title & Trust Co.*, 4 S.E.2d 78 (Ct. App. Ga. 1939), awarding the insured this measure of damages, and rejecting the title company's contention that the measure of damages should be the difference between the purchase price of the land and the market value of the land with the defect (a measure which would have stripped the plaintiff of the benefit of his bargain).

    b. **Clause in policy:** However, if the policy itself contain a clause prescribing a different method of calculating damages, the courts will generally enforce it (assuming that it is not grossly unreasonable). See, e.g., *Lawyers' Title Insurance v. McKee*, 354 S.W.2d 401 (Civ. App. Tex. 1962), enforcing a special clause governing liability for a partial defect.

E. Proposals for reform: The present American recording system, while it is workable, is often cumbersome and expensive for the buyer. Following are some of the reforms which have been suggested:

1. **Compulsory tract indexes:** Recall that many of the ambiguities of a recording system, particularly "chain of title" problems, would be cured if the recorder's office maintained a complete *tract index*. (*Supra*, p. 373.) Accordingly, many commentators have called for state legislatures to *require* the maintenance of such a tract index in each recording office.

2. **Torrens System:** The Torrens System (*supra*, p. 381) would make the whole land transfer process as easy as the transfer of automobiles or stock shares. However, for the reasons discussed above, it is unlikely that the Torrens System will ever be widely utilized.

3. **Marketable title acts:** One "reform" which has been adopted in a number of states is so-called *"marketable title"* legislation. Such legislation *shortens the period of time* for which the land records must be examined. For instance, the marketable-title portion of the Uniform Simplification of Land Transfers Act (the Model Act) provides that one who has an unbroken chain of title going back thirty years or more has a marketable title except as to matters stated in that chain. U.S.L.T.A. §3-302.

    a. **"Root of title" a forgery:** A key feature of the Model Act is that once one has located a document that has been of record for more than 30 years (the "root of title") the chain of title stemming from it will be valid *even if the root is itself a forgery*.

b. **Rights of possessor:** The marketable title acts usually do not bar the rights of any person who is *in actual possession* of the property at the time the person asserting the benefit of the act takes his interest. See Model Act, §3-306(2). Thus the purchaser must still make a physical inspection of the property.

c. **Right to re-record:** The holder of any interest in the property is always given the right to *re-record his interest*; if he does this less than 30 years prior to the time the person claiming the benefit of the marketable title act takes his interest, the prior interest will not be cut off (since a search back 30 years will uncover the re-recorded interest).

   i. **Consequence:** However, this means that a person who, when he gets his interest, immediately records, is *not indefeasibly vested* as he would be under a conventional recording act. Furthermore, the rightful owner will not necessarily even receive any notice that someone else is claiming an interest, and will have no reason to consider the necessity of re-recording. This danger is all the more devastating in view of the fact that a completely forged deed by a person who has *never had any connection with the property* may nonetheless be filed and form a root of title which, 30 years later, will cut off the prior interest. See B,C&S, pp. 962-63.

d. **Dangerous to rely on 30-year search:** Proponents of marketable title acts say that such acts make title searching easier, by allowing the searcher to go back only for the statutory period (e.g., 30 years under the Model Act). But because the holder of an adverse interest may re-record (as described in paragraph c above), or keep the interest alive by conveying it during the statutory period, relying on a 30-year search can be dangerous. This is true even apart from the danger of forgery. The problem is that there may be a *separate chain of title*, begun *more than 30 years ago*, that derives from the same grantor as the one who is the original grantor of the chain you are now looking for; if you go back only 30 years, you may never discover this other chain, and it may have priority. The problem is especially acute where (as is usually the case) the only index is a grantor/grantee index, not a parcel index.

   Example: In 1916, Sprague conveys a fee simple interest in Blackacre to Waters. However, the deed reserves to Sprague the oil and gas rights in the land. The transaction is immediately recorded. Sprague dies in 1931; she bequeaths the oil and gas rights to her daughters. The daughters eventually leave these interests to their children. Instruments reflecting the present ownership of the oil and gas interests by Sprague's grandchildren are recorded in the appropriate county in 1957.

   Meanwhile, in 1936, Waters, without mentioning the reservation of oil and gas rights, conveys Blackacre by warranty deed to his children; this conveyance is immediately recorded. After some transfers among the Waters children (recorded in 1980), William and Shirley Waters now hold the surface interests. William and Shirley Waters now claim, in 1983, that the Ohio Marketable Title Act (which says, generally, that possession of an unbroken chain of title for 40 years wipes out any earlier interest) gives them clear title to the oil and gas interests.

   Held, the Sprague grandchildren, not the Waters, own the oil and gas rights. A claimant gets the benefit of the Ohio Marketable Title Act only when the claimant and his predecessors have an *unbroken* chain of title going back 40 years. The chain will be deemed broken if there has been a recording of a different claim to the property, even if this opposing claim is *outside the chain of title* of the person claiming the benefit of the Act. Here, when the bequests from Sprague to her children and from those children to the grandchildren were recorded in 1957, this recording served to break the Waters' chain, even though a searcher in the position of the Waters children as of the date of the conveyance to them (1980) would not have discovered the Sprague 1957 recording by tracing the Waters' title back 40 years. "A 'marketable title' . . . is subject to an interest arising out of a 'title transaction' . . . which may be part of an independent chain of title." It is true that this construction of the Ohio Act means that searchers may have to search more than 40 years to be safe, but the purpose of the Act is not merely to limit the period of searching. *Heifner v. Bradford*, 446 N.E.2d 440 (Ohio 1983).

Note: On the facts of *Heifner*, one does not feel too sorry for the Waters children, since they apparently received the property by gift, and their donor was the one who failed to disclose to them that he didn't have the oil and gas rights. But suppose that, in 1980, the Waters children had sold to a completely innocent bona fide purchaser for value, X. If X had merely traced title back 40 years, he would never have discovered that the property was owned prior to 1916 by Sprague, and would thus never have discovered the 1957 recording of the bequest from Sprague to her children and grandchildren. Consequently, if X had said to himself, "I've traced the title back 40 years and haven't discovered any conflicting claim in my chain, so I must have a clear title under the Marketable Title Act," X would simply have been wrong.

  e. Constitutionality: Because of the possibility that a rightful owner will be cut off, it might be thought that marketable title acts would be held unconstitutional. However, the acts have generally been *upheld* against attacks that they operate retroactively, that they deprive persons of property without due process of law, and that they impair contract rights. *Id.* at 961.

   i. Illustrative case: See, e.g., *Presbytery of Southeast Iowa v. Harris*, 226 N.W.2d 232 (Iowa 1975), upholding a statute which makes a possibility of reverter void 21 years after it is recorded, unless it is re-recorded every 21 years; the court held that the re-recording privilege saved the act from being a violation of landowners' due process rights.

4. Role of the lawyer: A good part of the expense of land transfers is for legal fees. It has seemed to many observers that all or most of the work typically done by lawyers in residential real estate transactions could just as well by done by non-lawyers (e.g., title insurance companies or real estate brokers). In fact, in California it is rare for a residential transaction to be handled by a lawyer.

  a. Non-lawyer drafting: The drafting of documents and closing of transactions by laymen has often been held to be *unauthorized practice of law*, and therefore prohibited by statute. See, e.g., *State v. Buyers Service Co.*, 357 S.E.2d 15 (S.C. 1987), holding that D, a title company, engaged in the unauthorized practice of law by preparing deeds and mortgages, by preparing title abstracts on which buyers relied, and by conducting real estate and mortgage loan closings without a lawyer present.

   i. Some courts loosen the reins: But in recent years, many courts have interpreted their unauthorized practice of law statutes so as to allow at least some simple drafting and counselling in the residential real estate context to be done by non-lawyers. See, e.g., *State ex rel Indiana State Bar Ass'n v. Indiana Real Estate Ass'n, Inc.*, 191 N.E.2d 711 (Ind. 1963), holding that real estate brokers may use and fill in bar-association-approved forms for brokerage listing agreements, sale contracts, options and leases (but holding that a *deed* should be drafted only by lawyers, in view of the large amount at stake).

Chapter Review Questions

(Answers are at back of book)

94. Oliver conveyed Whiteacre to Arkin in 1980; Arkin did not record at the time. Oliver then conveyed to Beacon in 1982. Beacon did not know about the deed to Arkin at the time he took. In 1983, Arkin recorded, without knowledge of the conveyance by Oliver to Beacon. In 1984, Beacon discovered the conveyance to Arkin by doing a title search, and immediately recorded. If the jurisdiction has a "race notice" statute, who has title as between Arkin and Beacon, and why?

95. Oliver conveyed Whiteacre to Arkin, for value, in 1980. Through negligence, Arkin did not record at the time. Oliver, who was aware of Arkin's failure to record, sold the property to Beacon in 1982. Just before the conveyance to Beacon, Oliver told Beacon, "I conveyed to Arkin in 1980, but Arkin has not recorded. As long as you record before Arkin can, you'll be safe." Beacon paid almost full value for the property, and immediately recorded (still in 1982). In 1983, Arkin suddenly realized, with panic in his heart, that he had failed to record, and that Beacon had recorded. Arkin immediately recorded. In a race-notice jurisdiction, who has priority, Arkin or Beacon, and why?

96. Oliver conveyed Whiteacre to Arkin in 1980. At the time, Arkin did not record. Oliver then conveyed Whiteacre to Beacon in 1982. Beacon did not record. Beacon, at the time he took, did not have actual knowledge of the conveyance to Arkin. In 1983, Arkin recorded. Beacon has never recorded. In a "pure notice" jurisdiction, who has priority, Arkin or Beacon, and why?

97. In 1960, Odell conveyed Blackacre to Arias. Arias did not record at the time. In 1970, Odell conveyed to Beck. At the time of the conveyance, Beck had actual notice of the earlier conveyance to Arias. Beck recorded immediately after receiving his deed. In 1980, Beck conveyed to Cabbott. Cabbott had neither actual nor constructive notice of the conveyance by Odell to Arias, and Cabbott paid Beck fair value. In 1985, Arias finally recorded. In 1987, Cabbott recorded. The jurisdiction has a race-notice statute. As between Arias and Cabbott, who has title?

98. In 1950, Osborn gave a gift of Whiteacre to Abrams. At the time, Abrams did not record the deed. In 1960, Osborn purported to give Whiteacre as a gift to Boone. At the time Boone received his deed, he had no knowledge of the earlier gift to Abrams. Boone immediately recorded. In 1965, Abrams recorded. The jurisdiction has a race-notice statute. As between Abrams and Boone, who has title?

99. In 1960, Orcini conveyed Blackacre to Arlen for value. Arlen never recorded his deed. In 1970, Arlen conveyed to Bishop. Bishop paid fair value, and promptly recorded. In 1980, Orcini conveyed Blackacre to Chavez. Chavez had no knowledge of the earlier Orcini-Arlen conveyance, or of the Arlen-Bishop conveyance. Chavez paid fair value, and immediately recorded. The jurisdiction has a race-notice statute. In a dispute between Bishop and Chavez, who has superior title to Blackacre?

100. In 1950, O'Neill conveyed Blackacre to Arens. At the time, this deed was not recorded. In 1960, Arens conveyed to Burrows. This deed was not recorded at the time. In 1970, O'Neill conveyed to Craft. This deed was never recorded. In 1980, Craft conveyed to Dempsey. Dempsey promptly recorded his deed from Craft. Neither Craft nor Dempsey, at the time each took his conveyance, had any actual knowledge of the O'Neill-to-Arens-to-Burrows line of conveyances. In 1985, the O'Neill-to-Arens and the Arens-to-Burrows deeds were recorded by Burrows. The jurisdiction has a race-notice statute. In a contest between Burrows and Dempsey, who has priority?

101. In 1975, Oakley conveyed Blackacre to Andrews for value. Andrews never recorded the deed. In 1985, Oakley conveyed the same property to Burns for value. Burns promptly recorded. At the time Burns took, Andrews was in possession of the property (as, indeed, he had been since 1975), and the property (a farm) contained a mailbox with Andrews' name prominently displayed on it. Burns lived far away from the property, and never visited it before he took. If he had visited it, he would have seen signs of Andrews' possession. If he had spoken to Andrews, Andrews would have explained that he was the owner. The jurisdiction has a pure notice statute. In a contest between Andrews and Burns, who has superior title?

102. In 1960, Olivia conveyed Blackacre to Albright. At the time, Albright did not record his deed. In 1970, Olivia conveyed Blackacre to Brown. Brown took without any notice (actual or record) of the earlier conveyance to Albright. Brown promptly recorded. In 1975, Albright belatedly recorded. In 1985, Brown conveyed to Crystal. Crystal bought for value. Brown, being an honest sort, disclosed to Crystal before the sale that there was an earlier conveyance by Olivia to Albright, and that that conveyance had been subsequently recorded. (Crystal paid a somewhat lower price to reflect the possible uncertainty about title.) Crystal promptly recorded her deed. The jurisdiction has a race-notice statute. In a contest between Albright and Crystal, who wins?

103. Barnes contracted to purchase Blackacre from Selish. As part of the contract, Selish provided Barnes with a metes-and-bounds survey of the property, which was in fact an accurate description of the property which Selish intended to sell and Barnes intended to buy. The survey did not disclose that the garage located principally on the property encroached three feet onto the neighboring property; in fact, the survey did not show the garage structure at all. However, if Barnes (or his lawyer) had measured the distance from the house to the garage, and compared this with the distance from the house to the rear property line, they would have seen by looking at the survey that the garage must encroach on the neighbor's property. In any event, Barnes bought the property without being aware of the encroachment. At the time of the closing, Barnes purchased from Title Co. a standard title insurance policy on the property. The policy excluded any "any facts which an accurate survey of the property would disclose." The title report that accompanied the policy did not refer in any way to the fact that the garage encroached or might encroach on the neighbor's property. Three years after the purchase, Barnes was sued by the neighbor, who obtained a court order compelling Barnes to remove the encroaching garage, at a cost of $40,000. If Barnes sues Title Co. for $40,000, will Barnes recover?

RIGHTS INCIDENT TO LAND

Introductory note: In this chapter, we consider several rights which one holds by virtue of being a landowner: (1) the right not to have one's *use and enjoyment of the land* unreasonably interfered with (*nuisance*); (2) the right to have lateral and subjacent *support* for one's property; (3) the right to control "diffused surface water" (*drainage*); (4) the right to *water* flowing through or near one's property; and (5) the right to the *air space* above one's property.

I. NUISANCE

A. Nuisance generally: The subject of *nuisance* is usually covered more closely in the course on Torts. See Emanuel on *Torts*. Therefore, we examine it here only in a cursory fashion.

   1. Public vs. private nuisance: The term "nuisance" is used to cover two quite different types of harms, one called "public" nuisance and the other usually called "private" nuisance. Public nuisance is an interference with a right common to the general public. Our primary interest here is in *private* nuisance, i.e., an interference with a private landowner's *use and enjoyment of his land*.

   2. Distinguished from trespass: Whereas *trespass* is an interference with the plaintiff's right to *exclusive possession* of his property, nuisance is an interference with his right to *use and enjoy* it.

B. Interference with use: The interference with the plaintiff's use and enjoyment must be *substantial*.

   1. Inconvenience: If the plaintiff is personally injured, or his property is physically damaged, the interference will always be *"substantial"*. But if the plaintiff's damage consists in his being *inconvenienced* or subjected to unpleasant smells, noises, etc., this will be substantial damage only if a person in the community of *normal sensitivity* would be seriously bothered.

C. Defendant's conduct: There is *no* general rule of *"strict liability"* in nuisance. In other words, the plaintiff must show that the defendant's conduct was *negligent*, *intentional*, or *abnormally dangerous*.

   1. Intentional: Most nuisance claims arise out of conduct by the defendant that can be called *"intentional"*. This does not mean that the defendant has *desired* to interfere with the plaintiff's use and enjoyment of his land, but simply that he *knows with substantial certainty* that such interference will occur. For instance, a factory owner whose plant spews pollutants and smoke into the air over plaintiff's property will be held to have intended this interference, at least if the plaintiff can show that he put the defendant on notice of what was happening by making a complaint.

   2. Unreasonableness: Even if the defendant's conduct is intentional, the plaintiff may not maintain his nuisance suit unless he shows that the defendant's actions were also *unreasonable*.

      a. Significance: This means that even if the defendant intentionally interferes with the plaintiff's rights, he will have a kind of "privilege" to do so, as long as the interference is not unreasonable. Thus in *Bove v. Donner-Hanna Coke Corp.*, 258

N.Y.S. 229 (App. Civ. 1932), D ran a coke factory which sent steam, gas, pollutants and odors onto P's nearby private residential premises. The court held that the area was well suited for industrial use (mainly because of its proximity to cheap transportation), and that D's operation was therefore not unreasonable. (The court also relied on the fact that the area had been industrial before P moved in, and that the area had been zoned for industry; these aspects of the case are discussed *infra*, p. 396, and below, respectively.)

b. Nature of neighborhood: In determining what is reasonable, the ***nature of the neighborhood*** is likely to be quite significant. A steel mill located in an otherwise completely residential area is obviously much more likely to be found to be an unreasonable interference with the rights of surrounding landowners than is a steel mill in the middle of an industrial park.

> **i. Zoning:** The ***zoning*** of the area will be important to the court's determination of the nature of the neighborhood. Indeed, some courts have given almost complete deference to the local municipality's decision to zone for certain uses. Thus in *Bove, supra*, p. 394, the court noted that the Buffalo City Council had explicitly zoned the area in question to allow a coke plant. The court noted that "It is not for [this] court to step in and override such a decision, and condemn as a nuisance a business which is being conducted in an approved and expert manner, at the very spot where the council said that it might be located."

D. Defenses: The defendant may raise a number of ***affirmative defenses*** to a private nuisance claim.

1. Assumption of risk: The most significant of these, for our purposes, is the defense of ***assumption of risk***. Most frequently, the defense applies in zoning cases where the plaintiff has purchased his property with ***advance knowledge*** that the nuisance exists. In such a case, he is said to have ***"come to the nuisance"***.

> **a. Not absolute defense:** Older cases sometimes treated the fact that the plaintiff "came to the nuisance" as an ***absolute*** defense. The modern tendency, however, is to treat this as merely ***one factor*** in evaluating the reasonableness of the defendant's conduct. See Restatement (Second) of Torts, §840D.

> **b. Locality:** The court is much more likely to hold that "coming to the nuisance is a defense if the defendant's activity is ***suitable*** for the area where it occurs, and the plaintiff's own use is out of step with that area. (See *Bove v. Donner-Hanna Coke Corp., supra*, pp. 394-95, where the court found the defendant's coke plant reasonable, since the area was generally industrial, and has had that character before plaintiff moved her residence there.)

> **Example:** D has operated a cattle feed lot (producing "over a million pounds of wet manure per day") for many years, in a completely rural area outside Phoenix. P, a developer, builds a development called "Sun City", one portion of which adjoins the feed lot. The flies and odor make this portion of the development unhealthy and almost unusable for residential purposes.
>
> *Held*, P has "come to the nuisance", and if its interests were the only ones at stake, it would not be entitled to an injunction. But since the rights of innocent third parties (the inhabitants of Sun City) are also involved, D will be enjoined from operating the feed lot, and forced to move. However, again because it has come to the nuisance, P will have to ***indemnify*** D for its costs in moving. *Spur Industries, Inc. v. Del E. Webb Development Co.*, 494 P.2d 700 (Ariz. 1972).

E. Remedies: The plaintiff may have one or more of three possible *remedies* for private nuisance.

1. **Damages:** If the harm has already occurred, he can recover *compensatory damages*. If it is not clear whether the harm will continue in the future, he can usually recover only for the damages sustained up till the time of suit, and he must bring successive actions for subsequent harm. But if it appears that the nuisance will probably be a permanent one (e.g., a polluting factory that is likely to stay in business), he can and must recover all damages, past and *prospective*, in one action.

2. **Injunction:** If the plaintiff can show that damages would not be a sufficient remedy, he may be entitled to an *injunction* against continuation of the nuisance. (Since courts typically regard every parcel of land as having a unique use, the plaintiff will frequently be able to make the showing that compensatory damages are not an adequate remedy.)

   a. **Balancing test:** To get an injunction, the plaintiff must show that the harm to him actually *outweighs* the utility of the defendant's conduct. (He probably does not have to make such a showing for damages, so long as the defendant's conduct is unreasonable.)

      Example: D operates a large cement plant, which employs over 300 people and which cost more than $45,000,000. The Ps, neighboring landowners, sue for nuisance, because of dirt, smoke and vibrations from the plant. *Held*, an absolute injunction against D should not issue, in view of the great disparity between the economic consequences to D and its employees (as well as the local economy) in closing down the plant, and the consequences to the plaintiffs in allowing it to continue. However, it is fair to require D to pay for the harm it causes, regardless of the utility of the plant. Therefore, a temporary injunction will be issued, to be suspended if D makes payment of permanent damages to the Ps.

      A dissent argued that the majority's holding "is the same as saying to the cement company, you may continue to do harm to your neighbors for so long as you pay a fee for it." Also, the dissent noted, once such permanent damages are paid, the incentive to alleviate the wrong would be eliminated, thereby continuing air pollution of the area. *Boomer v. Atlantic Cement Co., Inc.,* 257 N.E.2d 870 (N.Y. 1970).

3. **Self-help abatement:** In some situations, the plaintiff may have the right to use the *"self-help"* remedy of *"abatement"*. That is, he may have the right to enter the defendant's land to remove the nuisance. But he may use only reasonable force to do this, and must ordinarily first complain to the defendant and wait for the latter to refuse to remedy the condition himself.

II. LATERAL AND SUBJACENT SUPPORT

A. Nature of interest: Every landowner is entitled to have his land receive the necessary *physical support* from adjacent and underlying soil. The right to support from adjoining soil is called the right of *"lateral* support"; the right to support from underneath the surface (applicable only where there has been a severance of the surface and sub-surface rights) is known as the right to *"subjacent* support". Our focus here is principally upon lateral support, with a few words *infra*, p. 397, as to subjacent support.

   Example: A and B are adjoining landowners. A constructs a large excavation extending almost to the edge of his property. This causes B's soil to run into A's excavation, impairing the surface of B's property. B's right to lateral support has been violated, and he may recover damages.

B. Ground for liability: The right to lateral support is **absolute**. That is, once support has been withdrawn and injury occurs, the responsible person is liable **even if he used utmost care** in his operation. 6-A A.L.P. 100.

    1. Building on land: However, the absolute right to lateral support exists only with respect to land in its **natural state**. If the owner has constructed a **building**, and the soil under the building subsides in part due to the adjacent owner's acts, but also in part **because of the weight of the building itself**, the adjacent owner is **not liable** (in the absence of negligence).

        a. Weight of building not factor: Suppose, however, that the soil caves in and the building is damaged, but the owner is able to show that the cave-in would have occurred **even had the building not been present**. The adjacent landowner is obviously liable for damage to the soil, but is he liable for damage to the building? A substantial number of American courts (perhaps even a majority) hold that the excavator is **not** liable for damage to the building. *Id*, at 117. But English courts, and the remaining American courts, hold that he **is** liable for the damage to the building, just as he is for the harm to the land. See, e.g., *Prete v. Cray*, 141 A. 609 (R.I. 1928), reasoning that damage to the building is a **direct consequence** of the damage to the land, and that the general tort rule that one is liable for the direct consequences of one's actions should apply.

    2. Withdrawal of water: Suppose the adjacent landowner, pursuant to his excavation, causes **water** to flow from beneath P's land, thereby weakening the surface of P's property. The courts are in dispute about whether P's right to lateral support has been violated in this situation. A number of courts which follow English Rule allowing absolute privilege to withdraw groundwaters (see *infra*, p. 401) hold that the right to lateral support is not violated. But Rest. 2, Torts §818 provides that even though one may be privileged to withdraw water or other substances from underneath another's land, this does not give rise to a privilege to cause subsidence of the other's surface.

    3. Statutory modifications: Statutes have been enacted in a number of states, and ordinances in many municipalities, contracting or expanding the common-law right of lateral support. A frequent type of provision grants the owner of a building limited protection from damage, even if the building's weight contributes to the subsidence of his land. For instance, a California statute provides that an excavator is strictly liable for damages to a neighbor's structure, but only if the foundation of the neighbor's structure exceeds the "standard depth" of nine feet. Cal. Civ. Code §832.

        a. Public excavation: But if the excavation is done by the **government**, the California statutory limit on liability may not apply. See, e.g., *Holtz v. Superior Court of City and County of San Francisco*, 475 P.2d 441 (Cal. 1970).

    4. Contractual arrangements: Adjoining landowners are always free to make **private contractual arrangements** expanding or contracting the common-law right of lateral support. For instance, the owners of adjacent buildings often make a **party wall agreement**, whereby each agrees not to do anything to disturb a wall that is common to the two structures.

C. Subjacent support: The right to **subjacent** support arises only where sub-surface rights (i.e., mineral rights) are **severed** from the surface rights. When such a severance has taken place, the owner of the surface interest has the right not to have the surface subside or otherwise be damaged by the carrying out of the mining. 6-A A.L.P. 127. This right is similar to the right of lateral support; the principal difference is that the surface owner has a right to support not only of unimproved land, but of **all structures existing on the date when the severance took place**. *Id*. at 128-29.

III. WATER RIGHTS (INCLUDING DRAINAGE)

A. Drainage (diffused surface waters): *"Diffused surface waters"* are waters that are spread over the surface of the ground without observable channels or banks, and which have no predictable flow. Thus they are distinguished from water in watercourses (e.g., streams and lakes), discussed *infra*, p. 399. Diffused surface waters may come from rainfall, melting snows, springs, etc. Although there are rules as to the landowner's right to make use of surface waters on his property, the principal body of law concerning these waters relates to the owner's right to **drain** them from his property.

    1. Three theories: Three distinct theories governing drainage rights have been recognized:

        a. "Common enemy" rule: The common-law view, recognized in almost half of the states, is that diffused surface waters are the *"common enemy"* of man. Therefore, an owner is privileged to **dam** against them, throw them back upon the land they came from, or deflect them onto adjoining lands. 6-A A.L.P. 189.

        b. Civil-law doctrine: By a doctrine adopted from the civil-law countries, and applied in a substantial minority of states, exactly the opposite rule obtains. That is, an owner may **not** channel the drainage, or otherwise change its **natural flow** in any way. *Id*, at 190-91.

        c. "Reasonable use" doctrine: Neither of the two above views is economically efficient, since the "common enemy" rule may result in a landowner having his land ruined by other owner's dumping excessive water on it, and the "natural flow" view prevents an owner from adjusting the drainage so as to render his own land usable. Therefore, courts adhering to both of the above doctrines have (usually *sub silentio*) moved from these extremes to a common middle ground, whereby the owner may make only *"reasonable"* changes in the natural drainage pattern. Another group of courts have explicitly rejected both of the above rules, and state that in **all instances the test shall be whether the owner's handling of the surface waters is reasonable**. See, e.g., *Pendergast v. Aiken*, 236 S.E.2d 787 (N.C. 1977).

        Example: D owns a large tract of land which is upland from P's property. The natural drainage of D's property is such that surface water runs into a small stream which passes through P's property. D clears his tract, builds a large development, and changes the drainage so that a hugely increased volume of surface water passes into the stream. This stream thereafter erodes P's property, and floods every time there is a hard rain (damaging P's basement).

        Held, the prior rule in New Jersey, that a landowner may increase the volume of the drainage as much as he wants so long as it flows to the same place it otherwise would have, is rejected. Instead, the "reasonable use" rule will be followed. In the present case, it is not reasonable that D should be entitled to increase the drainage flow so substantially without paying for a means of protecting P's property. Therefore, the trial judge correctly ordered that D pay for installation of piping to transport the water across P's property. (This is true even though the creation of the development, and the consequent drainage, is itself a social good; the drainage should be permitted, but the person profiting from it, not an innocent adjoining landowner, should pay.) *Armstrong v. Francis Corp.*, 120 A.2d 4 (N.J. 1956).

B. **Water in watercourses (streams and lakes):** Whereas diffused surface water is seldom desired or appropriated by landowners, the opposite is true of water in *watercourses* (i.e., *streams and lakes*). As to these, disputes between landowners will center on who has the right to *use* the water. There are two fundamentally distinct and incompatible approaches to this conflict: (1) the common-law *"riparian rights"* theory; and (2) the statutory *"prior appropriation"* theory.

   1. Nomenclature: First, as a matter of nomenclature, the word "riparian" is formally used only to refer to land abutting a *stream*. The word *"littoral"* is used to describe land abutting a *lake*. However, since the rights of riparian and littoral owners are virtually indistinguishable, the term "riparian" is used exclusively in the following discussion.

   2. Common-law riparian rights: In all parts of the country except for about 17 western states, the common-law *"riparian rights"* theory is in force. The key to this theory is that *no advantage is gained by priority of use*. 6-A A.L.P. 159. The fact that a riparian owner has used stream- or lake-water for a certain purpose for many years (e.g., to run a mill) does not give him any greater rights than if he were making this use for the first time.

      a. "Natural flow" vs. "reasonable use": Within courts following the common-law approach, there is a split as to what use the owner may make, comparable to the split among courts on the drainage problem. Some courts purport to apply a *"natural flow"* approach, by which each waterfront owner is entitled to the flow of streams and level lakes in their *natural condition*, without material reduction in quantity or quality as the result of other riparian or non-riparian owners. *Id.* at 162.

      b. "Reasonable use": But most courts follow the *"reasonable use"* approach to riparian rights. A riparian owner, under this view, is entitled to only so much of the water as he can put to *beneficial use* upon his land, with due regard for the equal and correlative rights of other riparian owners. Thus whereas an owner under the "natural flow" theory may sue at least for nominal damages if the flow of water to him is materially interfered with (even if the owner would not have had a use for the water anyway), the owner in a "reasonable use" state may sue only if he has a beneficial use for the water with which the actions of another person (either another riparian owner or a non-riparian person) have interfered. *Id.* at 163-64. Since the "reasonable use" theory is more frequently applied, our remaining discussion of riparian rights assumes that this approach is in force.

      c. "Natural" vs. "artificial" uses: In determining what constitutes a reasonable use, the courts distinguish between so-called *"natural"* and *"artificial"* uses. Each riparian owner has an *absolute right* to all or any part of the water for *"natural"* uses, without regard to the effect which his use has upon other (usually downstream) owners. Thus as to natural uses, the upstream owner has *preferred status*.

i. Artificial uses: But with respect to *"artificial"* uses, each owner must follow two rules: (1) he may not take *any* water for such uses, until the "natural" needs of *all* other riparian owners (upstream and down-stream) have been satisfied; and (2) if water is available after satisfaction of everyone's "natural" uses, each owner's rights to take for artificial uses is *equal*. *Id*. at 165.

Example: P and D each operate a steam mill on the same stream; D's mill is upstream from P's. Normally there is enough water for both mills, but a drought strikes. D makes a dam across the stream right below his mill, thereby diverting all of the water to his own mill and leaving none for P. P sues.

    Held, for P. Had D's use been for his "natural" wants, he would have been entitled to all of the water. However, use for running a steam mill is not a "natural use", but is rather an "artificial" one. A riparian owner may use water for artificial purposes only by sharing equally with others who wish to make artificial uses. Whether an owner has shared equally (and thus made "reasonable use") in a particular situation is a question of fact for the jury. Here, the jury properly concluded that D's use was unequal and unreasonable, since nothing was left for P. *Evans v. Merriweather*, 4 Ill. 492 (1842).

d. What is "natural" use: Water for drinking and bathing, and for the raising of farm animals, is always considered *"natural"*. Most courts hold that use of small quantities for *irrigation* of small areas of farmland is also "natural", but that large-scale irrigation is an artificial or "commercial" use. 6-A A.L.P. 165. (However, in relatively arid areas, even large-scale irrigation may be given a preference over other types of commercial uses. *Id*. at 166.)

i. Pollution: An owner's use will generally not be considered reasonable (regardless of whether it is "natural" or "commercial") if it results in a material *pollution* of the water source. *Id*. at 168.

e. Who is "riparian owner": *Only riparian owners* are entitled to make use of the water, under the riparian rights doctrine. A "riparian owner" is one whose land *abuts* the stream or lake, at least in part. Thus one whose land is not contiguous with the water at any point may not carry the water by pipe or ditch to his property. (Furthermore, courts have imposed a number of other limitations; for instance, if a person owns a large tract of land, part of which abuts the water and part of which is beyond the watershed, only the part within the watershed may benefit from the water use. *Id*. at 160.)

3. Prior appropriation doctrine: Seventeen *arid* states (all of them west of the Mississippi) have adopted a completely different theory, called the *prior appropriation* doctrine. In about half of these states, this doctrine is the only source for water rights; in the remainder, rights may derive either from the common-law riparian doctrine or from the prior appropriation theory.

a. History: The prior appropriation theory dates from the mid-nineteenth century, when gold miners (who were trespassers on the land they worked anyway) adopted the custom of diverting streams without regard to the needs of those working downstream. Miners' groups, to preserve the peace, instituted a system of "first come first served"; that is, damming and diversion of streams was protected in order of priority of use. In 1866, Congress enacted a mineral law formalizing this system, and most of the western states enacted similar statutes of their own.

b. **How the system works:** In some of the prior appropriation states, an application for a *permit* must be made; if the application is accepted by the governing agency, the user's priority dates from the time of application. See, e.g., Cal. Water Code, § 1450-51. In other states, the right to appropriate is *absolute* (i.e., no permit is required) and the priority of the right dates from the time the appropriator begin construction of the necessary works to take the water. 6-A A.L.P. 174.

c. **Riparian ownership not required:** A key feature of the prior appropriation system is that water may be appropriated by a *non-riparian owner*. (However, he will have to procure an easement across the property of at least one riparian owner in order to transport the water to his own property.) See e.g., *Coffin v. Left Hand Ditch Co.*, 6 Colo. 443 (1882), holding that a landowner may transport water from a stream to a point outside the stream's watershed, in order to irrigate his property; once he does so, his use gains priority over the subsequent use by one who abuts the stream.

d. **Scenic uses:** At least one state has held that there are circumstances where appropriation can occur *without the taking of physical possession*. See *State of Idaho, Dept. of Parks v. Idaho Dept. of Water Administration*, 530 P.2d 924 (Idaho 1974), holding that the legislature may constitutionally provide that certain waters are deemed "appropriated" for the preservation of scenic beauty and recreational uses (even though no physical appropriation takes place.)

e. **Rationale for prior appropriation theory:** In the arid states where it applies, the prior appropriation theory works much better than the riparian-rights theory. In these states, water is an extremely valuable commodity; there are many worthwhile water-related projects which require large amounts of capital, and which will not be carried out unless the investors know that their right to the necessary water is assured.

f. **Coexistence of two theories:** In California, Texas and seven other states, the doctrine of prior appropriation exists *side by side* with the riparian-rights doctrine. These states have evolved a complicated system for adjusting conflicts between those persons having rights by appropriation and those having rights by virtue of their status as riparian owners; in general, riparian rights are limited, because of the greater suitability of the prior appropriation system. 6-A A.L.P. 172-73.

C. **Groundwater:** Still another series of doctrines have been developed to deal with *groundwater*, i.e., water below the surface. Underground streams or springs that are clearly attached to surface streams or lakes are treated the same way the surface water would be treated (i.e., either by the riparian rights doctrine or by prior appropriation, as the case may be). Where the subsurface water is not connected to any surface watercourse, there are three principal approaches:

1. **"English" rule:** In England, and in some American states, a landowner is given an *absolute interest* in all the water which he can draw to the surface of his own land. Even though the water may come from a larger pool that is partially *below the surface of other owners' property*, the owner is free to draw as much as he wishes, even the entire pool. This is true even if this injures the neighboring landowner, and even if the water is then transported to serve other, distant, lands held by the same owner. The sole limitation is that the owner may not extract the water "maliciously" (or, as the idea is sometimes put, he may not wantonly *"waste"* the water).

2. American "reasonable use": In most American states, an owner may make only *"reasonable use"* of groundwater drawn from under his property. It is deemed "reasonable" for use to use as much of the water as he wishes for applications on the parcel which sits on top of the pool; but he may *not divert* the water to other property which he may own. 6-A A.L.P. 196.

3. Appropriation rights: In about half of the states which follow the doctrine of *prior appropriation* for surface waters, the prior appropriation theory is followed as to groundwater as well. B.C&S, p. 212.

4. Subsidence of neighboring lands: Suppose that A, by removing large quantities of water from his land, not only dries up the aquifer beneath B's property (the most common kind of injury) but also causes the *surface* of B's property to *fall*. Most courts have held that this subsidence does not change the applicable rule. Thus, the courts following the "English" rule hold that as long as there is no malice, A can remove so much water that B's land subsides, even if this leads to flooding or erosion; those following the American "reasonable use" rule generally hold that there is no liability so long as the amount of water taken is not unreasonably great (though the determination of "reasonableness" may be influenced by the fact that the land has subsided).

> **Example:** D, a development company, drills many wells on its Texas property, and extracts hugh quantities of subsurface water, which it sells to industrial users. The Ps, nearby landowners, claim that these withdrawals have caused their own lands to subside severely, causing erosion and flooding.
>
> *Held*, for D. For the time period in which D's actions occurred, Texas followed the "English" rule; therefore, the Ps may not recover even though D may have placed its wells too close together or otherwise negligently and foreseeably caused the subsidence to Ps' lands. However, in the future, Texas will hold that a landowner who negligently withdraws water from his own land in a way that proximately causes another person's land to subside will be liable for damages. This prospective-only ruling will safeguard D's reasonable reliance on the state of property law as it existed at the time of D's acts. *Friendswood Development Co. v. Smith-Southwest Industries*, 576 S.W.2d 21 (Texas 1978).

IV. AIR RIGHTS

A. Airplane flights: The old English common law purported to follow the dictum *"cujus est solum, ejus usque ad coelum,"* literally, "he who owns the soil owns upward into Heaven". With the age of aviation, it quickly became obvious that even if this saying applied to some uses of airspace, it could not apply to airplane flights. Landowners have seldom brought suit against the operators of individual airplanes; rather, most litigation on the consequence of airplane flights has been against the operators of *airports*, which are usually government-owned facilities. These suits have generally been in "inverse condemnation" (*supra*, p. 308).

1. Direct overflights: When the airport permits flights to occur *directly over* a landowner's property, and within the *"immediate reaches"* of his land, the landowner may sue in *trespass*. If sovereign immunity prevents a trespass action, the landowner may nonetheless claim that the direct overflights constitute a *taking* of his property, which under the federal Constitution cannot be done without compensation. In *U.S. v. Causby*, 328 U.S. 256 (1946), the Supreme Court agreed that direct overflights within the immediate reaches of an owner's property would constitute a compensable taking, provided that there was interference with the owner's actual (not just potential) use of the property.

2. **Flights in adjacent areas:** In the *Causby* case, the Supreme Court also indicated that airspace *outside* the "immediate reaches" of the surface has been transformed by federal statutes and regulations into a ***public highway***. The effect of this statement is that such flights (usually construed to be those which do not violate FAA ***minimum altitude*** regulations) do ***not*** constitute a trespass. However, the courts are not in agreement about whether the lack of a formal trespass prevents the overflights from being a taking for which compensation must be made.

   a. **Recovery allowed:** The Restatement of Torts takes the position that if flights outside the immediate reaches of an owner's property nonetheless result in an ***unreasonable interference*** with the owner's ***use and enjoyment*** of his land, this will constitute a ***nuisance*** (not trespass). Rest. 2d of Torts, § 159, Comment m. A number of state courts have followed this theory further, and have held that the existence of a nuisance means that (in the case of a publicly-operated airport) a ***taking has also occurred***. See, e.g., *Thornburg v. Port of Portland*, 376 P.2d 100 (Or. 1962), arguing that if one accepts the fact that direct overflights can so interfere with the use of property that they constitute a taking, "logically the same kind and degree of interference with the use and enjoyment of one's land can also be a taking even though the noise vector may come from some director other than the perpendicular."

      i. **State constitution prohibits "damaging":** Furthermore, a number of state constitutions (in contrast to the federal one) provide that a landowner must be compensated for any ***"damaging"*** of his property, not just for a "taking" of it. Where such a clause exists, the state courts have been even more willing to allow landowners to recover upon a showing that their use and enjoyment of their property has been substantially impaired. See, e.g., *Martin v. Port of Seattle*, 391 P.2d 540 (Wash. 1964).

   b. **Federal court view:** But most ***federal courts*** have held that in the absence of a direct overflight, an owner may not claim that there has been a taking of his property, even though the interference with his use and enjoyment of his land is substantial. See, e.g., *Batten v. U.S.*, 306 F.2d 580 (10th Cir. 1962).

B. **Other air-rights issues:** The courts have recently faced several other issues concerning air rights.

   1. **Right to build tall building:** An owner generally has the right to build as ***high a building as he wishes*** (assuming, of course, that it satisfies all applicable zoning requirements and building restrictions.) Thus in *People ex rel. Hoogasian v. Sears, Roebuck & Co.*, 287 N.E.2d 677 (Ill. 1972), the court held that the residents in the vicinity of the Sears Tower (110-stories tall) could not enjoin the building's completion on account of the fact that the quality of radio and television signals was impaired by the building's height; the court noted that "absent legislation to the contrary, defendant has a proprietary right to construct a building to its desired height and . . . completion of the project would not constitute a nuisance. . . ."

   2. **Cloud seeding:** Does a landowner have a right to the ***weather conditions*** which would naturally obtain over his property? The issue usually arises in connection with ***cloud seeding***. Where the cloud seeding flights do not directly cross over the owner's property, the courts that have faced the issue have almost always held that he has no cause of action (even though the seeding may result in less rain falling on his land.) But

where the flight itself crosses the plaintiff's property, some courts have allowed recovery.

3. **Solar cases:** In these days of burgeoning interest in solar energy, landowners are bound to assert a property interest in the *sunlight* which would naturally strike their property. Generally, American courts have been hostile to the assertion of rights to sunlight. For instance, they have seldom permitted a landowner to acquire an easement of "light and air" by implication or even by necessity. See, e.g., *Maioriello v. Arlotta*, 73 A.2d 374 (Pa. 1950), rejecting P's claim to an easement of light and air by necessity, on the grounds that (*inter alia*) P's sunlight was only partially (though substantially) blocked by D's wall, and that P could obtain more light by placing a skylight in his roof.

   a. **Solar energy:** Where a landowner uses sunlight as a source of *energy*, courts will probably be more willing to hold that he has a protectable property interest. It is too soon to know much about how disputes between A's solar collector and B's sunlight-blocking building will be resolved. But as the following example shows, at least one court has concluded that the law of *private nuisance* (*supra*, p. 394) may furnish a means by which the sunlight-collecting owner may gain relief.

      Example: P has built a residence that makes extensive use of solar collectors for energy. D buys the vacant lot next door, and proposes to construct a building which would substantially block the sunlight from reaching P's collectors. D's proposed home satisfies all current zoning requirements.

      Held, the private nuisance doctrine should be applied to this controversy. Therefore, if P can show that D's building would "unreasonably interfere" with P's use or enjoyment of his property, P will be entitled to enjoin the construction. In determining the "reasonableness" of D's proposed conduct, the lower court should consider such matters as the extent of the harm to P, the suitability of solar heat in this particular neighborhood, the availability of alternatives for P, and the cost to D of avoiding the harm (e.g., by building the house on a different part of his lot.) The fact that D's plans comply with zoning law does not automatically bar a nuisance claim (nor does the fact that P could have avoided the harm by building on a different part of his property). *Prah v. Maretti*, 321 N.W.2d 182 (Wisc. 1982).

      A dissent in *Prah* made several arguments against treating D's use as a nuisance, including: (1) a nuisance is a non-trespassory "invasion" of another's use or enjoyment of land, and D's act of blocking the sunlight would not be an "invasion," especially since the building would satisfy all zoning ordinances; and (2) the solar heating system is an "unusually sensitive use," and such uses cannot be protected by the law of nuisance.

Chapter Review Questions

(Answers are at back of book)

104. Plotnick and Duffy were adjacent property owners. Plotnick's land had a six-story building on it, built in conformity with applicable building codes (including ones governing the depth and strength of the foundation). Duffy's property was undeveloped. Duffy decided to build his own building. He was a very conservative sort. Therefore, he dug an unusually deep foundation (15 feet). Duffy dug only up to his property line. He proceeded without negligence, and in conformity with all codes dictating how to excavate and build a foundation. However, because of the geography of the land, and the unusual nature of Plotnick's foundation, Plotnick's foundation cracked and his building was severely damaged once there was no longer supporting soil on the Plotnick-Duffy border. Plotnick sued Duffy for the damage. Duffy proved at trial that if there had been no building on Plotnick's property, Plotnick's land would not have caved in. May Plotnick recover?

105. Phillips and Decker each own a parcel that abuts on the Bountiful River in the state of Ames. Decker is upstream from Phillips. Since 1986, Decker has operated a private hydro-electric plant. To maintain the necessary pressure, Decker has built a dam on the river, which has the effect of diverting the water through the hydro-electric plant's turbines, and then out onto a pond at the rear of Decker's property. Beginning in 1975, Phillips, a farmer, had been irrigating a five-acre parcel of his property. This worked well until Decker built his dam in 1986; since then so little water has been present in the Bountiful River by the time it reaches Phillips' property, that the pressure needed to perform useful irrigation is not present. Assuming that Ames follows the common-law approach to relevant matters, if Phillips sues Decker for improperly using the water, will Phillips prevail?

106. Same facts as prior question. Now, assume that Decker's use (for hydro-electric) commenced in 1986, and that Phillips did not begin trying to use his property for irrigation until 1989. Ames follows the common-law approach to relevant matters. May Phillips recover against Decker for improper use of water?

107. Same facts as prior question. Assume, however, that Ames is one of the 17 states that have abolished the common-law riparian rights doctrine, and that Ames has replaced that doctrine with the most common alternative. Would Phillips win in a suit against Decker for improper water use?

108. Pringle and Delaney are adjacent landowners. At the time Pringle bought his property in 1970, a six-story office building was already present on that lot. This building goes up nearly to the eastern property line (and does not violate any zoning rules). Delaney has owned his lot (which is to the east of Pringle's property) since 1980. The land has been vacant. Now, Delaney proposes to build a 12-story office building on the western side of his property. This building would conform with all applicable zoning laws. However, the effect of this building will be to deprive Pringle's tenants (at least those in the eastern side of the building) of nearly all of the sunlight and view which they have always had, since the two buildings will only be three feet apart. If Pringle sues Delaney to enjoin Delaney from placing the building so close to the property line that Pringle's tenants' light and view will be cut off, will the court grant Pringle's request?

ANSWERS TO CHAPTER REVIEW QUESTIONS

Here are the answers to the various end-of-chapter Review Questions. The questions are taken from *"First Year Questions and Answers"*, a book of 1144 short-answer questions covering the basic first-year subjects (*Contracts, Torts, Property, Civil Procedure,* and *Criminal Law & Procedure*), each with an extensive answer. (186 of the book's Questions are on *Property*.) I personally prepared all of the questions and answers. This book is available from your bookstore or from Emanuel Law Outlines, Inc. directly.

SLE

1. **No.** To begin with, anyone whose chain of title includes a thief cannot prevail over the "true" owner. But the true owner's right to recover the property can become time-barred. The modern rule on the running of the statute of limitations is sometimes called the *"discovery"* rule; by that rule, the statute of limitations on an action to recover stolen property normally does not begin to run against the record owner until the owner knows, or should know, the identity of the possessor. But the rule assumes that the owner has made prompt *reasonable efforts* to find the possessor or to put the world on notice of the stolen property. Here, Oscar did not do this; for instance, he failed to list the painting in the information bank, a step that a reasonably diligent owner would normally take. Therefore, a court will probably hold that the statute began to run against him immediately. In that event, Anita became the owner by adverse possession in 1980.

2. **Yes.** As a general rule, *a seller cannot convey better title than that which he holds*. This is true of the unknown thief. Therefore, Dealer never got good title (regardless of whether he thought he did), and could not in turn give good title to Arnold. Consequently, even though Arnold paid full value and was completely innocent, he will lose the car. (Statutes in most states set up a certificate of title program, which would have protected Arnold in this situation.)

3. **Denise.** There are three requirements for the making of a valid gift: (1) delivery; (2) intent to make a gift; and (3) acceptance by the donee. Here, the delivery requirement was not satisfied, since Sidney did not give Norman either physical possession of the painting or possession of any symbolic or written instrument representing the gift.

4. **All, probably.** The account here is a "Totten Trust" (the name commonly used to describe an account of the form "A in trust for B"). Most courts, and the Uniform Probate Code, hold that where the trustee of a Totten Trust (here, Albert) dies before the beneficiary (here, Bertha), the beneficiary is *presumed* to be entitled to all funds left in the account. This presumption is rebuttable by a showing that the trustee intended a different result, but there is no such evidence here.

5. **No, probably.** Beck obtained title to the 30 yard strip by the doctrine of **adverse possession**, 20 years after he first fenced in the property (i.e., in 1981). One of the requirements for adverse possession is that the possession be **"hostile."** But most courts hold that one who possesses an adjoining landowner's land, under the mistaken belief that he has only possessed up to the boundary of his own land, meets the requirement of hostile possession. (But a minority of courts would disagree with the result, and would hold that Warren may recover possession because Beck's possession was not hostile.)

6. **Yes.** Steve and Deborah held the property as co-tenants. As a general rule, co-tenants each have equal access to the premises. If Steve had refused Deborah's attempt to live on the premises, then Steve's occupancy for the statutory period would have been "hostile," and Steve would have taken Deborah's half interest by adverse possession. But since Deborah never asked to live on the premises, and Steve never said that she couldn't, Steve's occupancy was not hostile, so he does not take her interest by adverse possession even though he was in sole occupancy for more than the statutory period. Consequently, Deborah still owned her one-half interest at the time of her death, and that interest passed to Frank.

7. **Stokes.** In 1980, Alice became the owner of the strip by adverse possession. Once she gained title by adverse possession, her title was of the same quality, and subject to the same rules, as if she had gotten title by deed. Therefore, she could not convey that title to anyone else except by compliance with the Statute of Frauds. Her oral "grant" to Orlando was ineffective because it was not in writing as required by the Statute of Frauds. Therefore, Alice owned the strip at her death, and it passed to Stokes.

8. **Barbara.** The gift "to Abel and his heirs" does not mean "to Abel for life then to his heirs." Instead, "to Abel and his heirs" means "to Abel in **fee simple**." Therefore, Abel had the right to do whatever he wished with the property, and his deed of it to Barbara was effective. Thus when Abel died, he had no interest in Blackacre to leave to his son and heir.

9. **Yes.** The original grant from O to A was a **fee simple determinable**. We know this because of the phrase "so long as. . . ," and the word "revert." Therefore, after the conveyance, O was left with a **possibility of reverter**. When O died, his possibility of reverter passed to his son S. When A purported to convey a fee simple absolute to B, he really conveyed only a fee simple determinable subject to S's possibility of reverter. When B began using the premises for the forbidden purpose in 1970, title **automatically** reverted to S, without S taking any formal action. Therefore, S remained the owner of the property in 1980, and is entitled to a judicial decree to that effect. (If more than 50 years passed after O's original creation of the fee simple determinable, then S or his successors would lose their right to this decree, since they would be barred by the 50-year statute of limitations on possibilities of reverter.)

10. **No.** Now, the O-to-A conveyance established a **fee simple subject to a condition subsequent**. (The words "upon condition that" or "provided that," when taken with a clause providing for re-entry, establish that a fee simple subject to condition subsequent, rather than a fee simple determinable, was created.) This left O (and, after his death, S) with a right of entry, not a possibility of reverter. By the statute of limitations, S was required to bring his suit for re-entry within one year of B's

commencement of the illegal use, i.e., by 1971. When S did not do so, his right of entry was extinguished. So by comparing this question with the prior one, you can see the importance of distinguishing between a fee simple determinable and a fee simple subject to a condition subsequent.

11. **Life estate *per autre vie* in C, remainder in fee simple in B.** After the initial conveyance by O, A was a life tenant. In all states, a life tenant may convey the interest which he holds, or a lesser one (but not a greater one). Therefore, A was capable of conveying his life estate to C; once that conveyance took place, C had a life estate *per autre vie* (life estate measured by another person's life), since C's interest would end when A died, not when C died. B continued to hold the fee simple remainder that he got when O made the initial conveyance.

12. **A reversion.** When the holder of a vested estate transfers to another a smaller estate, we call the interest which remains in the grantor a "reversion." Since the estate created by O is smaller than the one he held (i.e., a life estate is smaller than a fee simple absolute), what O was left with was a reversion.

13. **Indefeasibly vested remainder.** A remainder is a future interest which can become possessory only upon the expiration of a prior possessory interest created by the same instrument. Since B's interest was created by the same instrument that created A's life estate, and since B's interest will become possessory when that prior life interest expires, B has a remainder. This remainder is a vested remainder, because it is not subject to any condition precedent, and an identified already-born person (B) holds the remainder. The remainder is "indefeasibly" vested because it is certain to become possessory at some future time (even if B dies before A does, the remainder will pass by will or intestacy to B's heirs, and there is certain to be somebody who will be there to take possession when A dies).

14. **Vested remainder subject to open.** For an explanation of why C's interest is some sort of vested remainder, see the answer to the prior question. The vested remainder is "subject to open" because if another child (let's call him D) is born to B, C's remainder "opens up" to give D a half interest in it. The remainder will stay open until either A dies (in which case only the then-living children of B will take anything), or B dies, in which case he can have no further children.

15. **Vested remainder subject to divestment.** B has a remainder vested subject to divestment. If A died immediately, B's interest would become possessory. But if B died without issue (either before or after A's death), B's interest would be completely defeated or "divested". (C's interest, which cuts short B's vested interest, is called an executory interest.)

16. **Contingent remainder.** A remainder is contingent rather than vested if it is either subject to a condition precedent, or created in favor of a person who is unborn or unascertained. Here, the remainder to B is subject to a condition precedent (the condition that B survive A in order for his remainder to become possessory). If B does survive A, his remainder will become vested at the same time it becomes possessory.

17. **Vested remainder subject to divestment.** Notice that the grant here is functionally indistinguishable from that in the prior question, yet the remainder here is vested (subject to divestment), whereas the one in the prior question is contingent. This relates solely to the words: here the clause creating the remainder in B does not contain any limit, and the limit is introduced by a separate clause containing the phrase, "but if." As a matter of interpretation, the separate clause beginning with "but if" indicates that the remainder is being "taken away," and this indicates a condition subsequent rather than a condition precedent (thus a remainder subject to divestment rather than a contingent remainder).

18. **Fee simple in O.** After the initial conveyance by O, D had a contingent remainder. But at the time A died, D did not meet the contingency (having had a child while being married). By the common law doctrine of *destructibility of contingent remainders*, a contingent remainder was deemed "destroyed" unless it vested at or before the termination of the preceding freehold estates. Since D had not met the contingency by the time the prior estate (A's life estate) expired, D's contingent remainder was destroyed. Therefore, O's reversion became possessory, giving him a fee simple absolute. (Today, most states have, by case law or statute, abolished the doctrine of destructibility of contingent remainders.)

19. **Fee simple in B.** By the doctrine of *"merger,"* whenever *successive vested estates are owned by the same person*, the smaller of the two estates is absorbed by the larger. When A conveyed his life estate to B, B then had two successive vested estates (the life estate and the previously-received vested remainder in fee simple). Consequently, the smaller estate (A's life estate) was merged into the fee simple, and disappeared. Then, by the doctrine of destructibility of contingent remainders (see prior question), the destruction-by-merger of A's life estate caused D's contingent remainder dependent upon it to also be destroyed, since that contingent remainder did not vest at or before the termination of the preceding freehold estates.

20. **Fee simple absolute in B.** Under the *Rule in Shelley's Case*, if a will or conveyance creates a freehold in A, and purports to create a remainder in A's heirs, and the estates are both legal or both equitable, the remainder becomes a fee simple in A. Thus by operation of the Rule, A received both a life estate and a remainder in fee simple. Then, by the doctrine of merger, A's life estate merged into his remainder in fee simple, and A simply held a present fee simple. A's quitclaim deed to B transferred this fee simple to B. A had nothing left at the time of his death, therefore, so S took nothing.

21. **Fee simple absolute in B.** The *Doctrine of Worthier Title* provides that if the owner of a fee simple attempts to create a life estate (or fee tail estate), followed by a remainder to his own heirs, the remainder is void. The grantor thus keeps a reversion. So after the initial conveyance by O, A had a life estate and O had a reversion (with the remainder to O's heirs being void). Therefore, O's quitclaim deed to B was effective to pass O's reversion to B. Once A died, the reversion held by B became a possessory fee simple absolute. Since the initial remainder to O's heirs never took effect, S (O's heir) took nothing.

22. **Fee simple absolute in S.** Today, most states make the Doctrine of Worthier Title a rule of construction, rather than an absolute rule of law as it was at common law. In other words, the Doctrine applies only where the grantor's language and surrounding circumstances indicate that he intended to keep a reversion. Here, O's statement that he wants the gift to take effect exactly as written rebuts the presumption that a reversion rather than remainder was intended. Consequently, the gift will take effect as written, which means that O's quitclaim deed to B was of no effect. Consequently, O's heirs held a contingent remainder before O's death, and that remainder vested in S when O died. When A died, S's remainder became possessory.

23. **Fee simple in A subject to an executory limitation, and a shifting executory interest in fee simple in B.** The bargain and sale raises a use in A in fee simple subject to condition subsequent, and a use in B. The Statute of Uses executes both of these uses. The net result is that if A or his heirs serves liquor on the property, then the gift over to B will take effect.

24. (a) **Yes.** A life tenant may not normally remove earth or minerals from the property. (There are two exceptions: (1) if the property was used for mining prior to the commencement of the life estate, the tenant may continue this use; and (2) the tenant may mine if this is the only way of accomplishing the purpose of the life estate. But neither of these exceptions applies here.)

    (b) **Sue for waste.** If the holder of the present interest substantially reduces the value of the future interest, and acts unreasonably under the circumstances, the holder of the future interest has a cause of action for waste. Here, by removing valuable oil, A has reduced the value of O's reversion. The court will certainly award damages, and might also award an injunction against future pumping.

25. **Yes.** The remainder to B is a vested remainder, which vested in interest (though not in possession) on the day of the original conveyance by O. Therefore, the remainder to B vested less than 21 years after some life in being at the creation of the interest (e.g., A's life).

26. **No.** We always analyze the Rule Against Perpetuities as of the date of the conveyance, not by reference to how things actually work out. Viewing the matter from the date of the conveyance, it is possible to imagine a situation in which B would die, an additional son — call him C — would be born to A after the conveyance, A would die, and C would marry and have a child more than 21 years after the death of A and B. Under this scenario, however unlikely it is, the remainder would vest in C more than 21 years after all named lives in being at the creation of the interest.

Because of this possibility, the gift to B (which is a contingent remainder) will fail, *even if it actually turns out that B marries and has a child*. Observe that the key difference between this question and the prior question is that here, the remainder to B is contingent (we don't know at the time of the conveyance which child, if any, of A will marry and have a child), whereas in the prior question, the gift to B and his heirs was a vested remainder. Since the contingent remainder won't vest until it becomes possessory, and this might (however unlikely) be more than 21 years after lives in being at the time of the conveyance, the gift to B fails (whereas the gift to B in the prior question succeeds because it is a vested remainder, which vests at the moment of creation).

27. **No.** What A Corp. has purchased here is an option "in gross." (That is, the option is not granted in connection with a present lease of the property.) An option in gross is subject to the Rule Against Perpetuities — it will be unenforceable if it could be exercised beyond the end of the Perpetuities period, even if the optionee paid real money for it in the belief that it would be exercisable. Since there is no measuring life in being at the time of the option's creation (A Corp. is a corporation, not an individual), the option violated the Rule by being scheduled to last more than 21 years. (But a judge might order B to refund A Corp.'s $20,000 option purchase price.)

28. **No.** As of 1980, it was possible that A would live a long time more, would marry someone born after 1980, and would then die after 2001. That person would thus be a life not yet in being at the time of O's bequest and would be taking more than "lives in being plus 21 years" after 1980. Thus the bequest to "the widow" is invalid. This is true (at least at common law) even though the person who actually takes (here, B) was someone who was in fact born by 1980. This is the *"unborn widow"* rule. (But again, a modern "wait and see statute" would cause the gift to be valid, since the recipient, B, turns out to be someone born before the date of the original conveyance.)

29. **No.** It was possible, viewed as of 1960, that another child (let's call him hypothetically C) would be born to A after 1960. It was also possible that A and B might also die prior to C's ninth birthday. If both of these events happened, C's interest would then vest too remotely (more than 21 years after the deaths of the measuring lives, i.e., A and B). Because of this theoretical possibility, not only was the gift invalid as to children born after 1960, but it was also invalid as to the rest of the *class* of children, i.e., B. (If O had not included the remark about specifically covering later-born children of A, then the court might have saved the bequest by viewing the class as closing at the time of O's death, or by viewing the class as referring only to those members who could take without violating the Rule Against Perpetuities. But with the bequest as written, the common-law approach would be that since there might be a member of the class who could not take without violating the Rule, no member of the class may take.)

30. **Yes.** The most common statutory modification today is the *"wait and see"* approach, by which if the interest *actually* vests within lives in being at the time of creation plus 21 years, the fact that things might have worked out differently is irrelevant. Since here, B was a life in being at the time of O's bequest, the gift to him is valid even though it might have turned out that the later-born C took later than lives in being plus 21 years.

31. **Fee simple in A for 600 acres; life estate in W for 300 acres, with remainder in A.** The common-law estate of *dower* entitles a widow, on her husband's death, to a life estate in one-third of the lands of which he was seised at any time during their marriage, provided that the husband's interest was inheritable by the issue of the marriage (if any). Since H was seised of Blueacre at some point during the marriage (from 1965 through 1970), W held the estate of dower inchoate. On H's death, this became the estate of dower consummate. The husband cannot, by conveying his property during his life, defeat the right of dower. If he purports to make such a conveyance, his widow may subsequently make her claim for dower against the present holder of the property. So W is entitled to have 300 acres set aside for her for life by A; after her death, A can once again take possession of them. (Observe that A's lawyer should have had W join in the deed from H before allowing A pay money for

the property.)

32. **(d), (e) and (f) are all community property.** They are all either H's earnings during the marriage, or things purchased from those earnings. (a), (b), and (c) are separate property, because property received by a spouse before marriage, and property received by gift, inheritance or bequest after marriage, are separate, and income from separate property is separate property.

33. **B and S hold as tenants in common.** Today, all states establish a presumption that an ambiguous conveyance creates a tenancy in common rather than a joint tenancy. Therefore, O's ambiguous conveyance made A and B hold as tenants in common. Consequently, when A died, there was no right of survivorship on the part of B. Instead, A's undivided one-half interest in Blackacre passed to S. S and B now hold as tenants in common.

34. **S and C as tenants in common.** When B conveyed to C, this had the effect of *severing* the joint tenancy between A and B. Therefore, A and C held as tenants in common, not joint tenants, immediately after the conveyance by B to C. Therefore, when A died, C had no right of survivorship. S inherited A's share of the tenancy in common.

35. **Yes.** Each tenant in common is entitled to *possession of the whole property*, subject to the same rights in the other tenants. It does not make any difference that one of the tenants in common has a larger undivided interest than the other — the relative size of the interests matters only when the property is sold and the proceeds are allocated.

36. **Fee simple absolute in Georgia.** Oscar's original conveyance to Henry and Wanda created a tenancy by the entirety in them, since at common law any conveyance to two persons who are in fact husband and wife necessarily results in such a tenancy. (In fact, in the 22 states that retain tenancy by the entirety, there remains a presumption that a husband and wife who take property take it by the entirety.) When Henry conveyed his interest to Georgia, this did not have the effect of destroying the tenancy by the entirety, since such a tenancy is *indestructible* while both parties are alive and remain husband and wife. But the conveyance did have the effect of passing to Georgia whatever Henry's rights were. When Wanda died before Henry, her interest was extinguished, and there was nothing for her to pass to Denise. Since Henry would have taken the entire property had he kept his interest, Georgia steps into his shoes, and takes the entire property.

37. **Wendy and Stan each have an undivided one-half interest as tenants in common.** Where husband and wife are divorced, the tenancy by the entirety automatically ends. In most states, the property is then deemed to be held as tenants in common (i.e., without right of survivorship). Thus when Herb died, his undivided one-half interest as tenant in common passed to Stan.

38. **Yes.** Although a co-tenant is normally entitled to occupy the premises himself without accounting for their reasonable rental value, the same is not true if he leases the premises to a third person. Once he does this, and collects rents, he is required to share these rents with his co-tenant.

39. **No.** Each co-tenant is entitled to occupy the entire premises, subject only to the same right on the part of the other tenant. But the occupying tenant has, in general, no duty to account for the value of his exclusive possession. If Carol refused to let Dan live in the property, then Carol would be liable to pay Dan one-half of the rental value of the premises. But as long as Carol holds the premises open to Dan, she does not have to pay Dan any part of the imputed value of her own occupancy.

40. **She should bring an action for partition.** Any tenant in common or joint tenant (but not a tenant by the entirety) may bring an equitable action for partition. By this means, the court will either divide the property, or order it sold and the proceeds distributed. Normally, each tenant has an absolute right to partition, even over the objection of the other. Here, since the property probably cannot be readily divided, the court will order it sold. Felicia will get half of the sale proceeds.

41. **Yes.** The issue, of course, is whether the L-T lease must satisfy the *Statute of Frauds.* In most states, the Statute of Frauds does not cover a one-year lease, even if the lease is to commence in the future (and thus even if more than one year is to elapse between the date the lease contract is made, and the date on which the lease itself would terminate). So even though more than one year elapsed between July 1, 1989 (the date the lease was orally agreed to) and July 31, 1990 (the last day of the lease), the contract here did not need to be in writing, according to the majority view.

42. (a) **Periodic tenancy.** A periodic tenancy is a tenancy which continues from one period to the next automatically, unless either party terminates it at the end of a period by notice. One way a periodic tenancy is created is where the parties make a lease without setting a duration; in this situation, the period stated for rental payments is usually the period for other purposes. Since L and T stated the rent on a monthly basis, the tenancy will be a month-to-month tenancy.

   (b) **August 30.** When a month-to-month tenancy is terminated, the last date of the lease is generally the end of a period, but not less than one period later than the notice date. Thus T was required to give L 30 days notice, and the lease terminated at the end of the period that was in progress on the 30th day (i.e., the end of the calendar month in which the 30th day after notice occurred).

43. **Split of authority.** Under the so-called "American" view, the landlord has a duty to deliver only "legal" possession, not actual possession. Under the so-called "English" rule, the landlord does have a duty to deliver actual possession. American jurisdictions are approximately split between the two rules. In a court following the "American" view, Tina would not be able to sue for damages (and probably would not be able to cancel the lease either). In a state following the English rule, Tina would be able to recover damages from Leonard, and would probably also be allowed to cancel the lease. (But Tina's damages would probably be limited to the difference between the amount specified in her lease and the fair market value of the space; she would probably not be able to recover profits she would have made during the holdover period, since she is establishing a new venture whose profits are speculative.)

44. **Probably not.** Older cases hold that the landlord generally has no duty to control the conduct of other tenants. But the modern trend is to impute the acts of other tenants to L where these acts are in violation of the relevant leases, and L could have prevented the conduct by eviction or otherwise. See Rest. 2d, §6.1, Comment d.

Especially where, as here, Lester had reason to know before he made the lease with Heavy Metal that a significant chance of inconvenience to others existed, the court will probably hold against Lester.

45. **Yes.** Here, Tess can only claim to have been *"constructively,"* rather than "actually," evicted. Where the eviction is merely constructive, the tenant is not entitled to terminate the lease, or to stop paying rent, unless she abandons the premises. If she stays on the premises, her only remedy is to sue for damages (i.e., the amount by which the premises are worth less to her because of the breach). So even assuming that Lester had a contractual duty to prevent Heavy Metal from making excessive noise, Tess did not have the right to remain on the premises without paying rent.

46. **No.** At common law, the landlord was not deemed to have made any implied warranty that the premises were habitable, even in the case of residential property.

47. **Yes.** Over 40 states now impose some sort of implied warranty of habitability on residential dwellings. In most or all of these, infestation of rats and/or non-working toilets would render the premises uninhabitable, and in nearly all, the tenant would be justified in not paying the rent (or at least in depositing the rent into a court-administered escrow fund pending the repairs).

48. **The defense of retaliatory eviction, which will probably succeed.** Many courts and statutes (probably a majority) hold that even where the lease term is at an end, the landlord may not refuse to renew the lease when this is done for the purpose of retaliating against a tenant who has asserted his right to habitable premises. The doctrine of retaliatory eviction is most likely to be applied where the landlord attempts to terminate the tenancy in retaliation for complaints made to a housing authority about building code violations. See Rest. 2d, §14.9, recognizing the defense on the facts of this question. See also *Edwards v. Habib*, 397 F.2d 687 (D.C.Cir. 1968). The retaliatory eviction doctrine is more likely to be applied where the landlord is a "professional" (i.e., one in the business of renting residential space) than where the landlord is an "amateur" (e.g., one who rents the second floor of his house). See Rest. 2d, §14.8(2).

49. (a) **Yes.** In most states, either by statute or case law, the common law rule that required the tenant to keep paying rent for premises that were no longer usable, has been reversed. Thus the tenant normally may terminate the lease and stop paying rent, if the damage to the premises is substantial.

    (b) **No.** In most courts, termination and abatement of rent is the *sole* remedy available to the tenant where the premises are destroyed. See Rest. 2d, §5.4, Comment f.

50. **No.** By terminating the lease, and re-letting for his own account, Ludlum also effectively terminated his right to keep the security deposit. Therefore, he must return that deposit to Trotta (less his $1,000 damages).

51. **Ludlum could have re-let for Trotta's account rather than his own.** The event that caused Ludlum to have to return the security deposit was not Trotta's abandonment, but Ludlum's letter of termination and his re-letting of the premises for his own account. Instead, Ludlum should have sent a letter to Trotta stating, "I have no obligation to do so, but I will try to re-let the premises for your account, not mine. I will hold you responsible for any shortfall between what I am able to get on the re-letting and the monthly rent you will owe." By this technique, the Trotta-Ludlum lease would have remained in force, and Ludlum would remain entitled to the security deposit until the expiration of the five years.

52. **Split of authority.** The modern trend is to entirely prohibit a landlord from using self-help, so that the landlord must use judicial proceedings. But other courts, probably still a slight majority, permit the landlord to use at least some degree of self-help to regain the premises (e.g., changing of locks or peaceable removal of furniture, but no touching of another human being). Lombard's conduct was probably acceptable in states following the latter approach.

53. **Yes, probably.** The traditional view is that a landlord has *no "duty to mitigate"*, i.e., no duty to try to find a new tenant, and that he may simply let the property stay vacant, and recover rent from the tenant who has abandoned. But a growing minority of courts hold that the landlord does have a duty to mitigate (especially in residential leases).

54. **None.** Since Tracey transferred to Stuart only the right to occupy the premises for *part* of the time remaining on Tracey's lease with Lillian, the Tracey-Stuart transaction was a *sublease*, not an assignment. A sublease by a tenant does not establish privity of estate between the sublessee (Stuart) and the lessor (Lillian). Consequently, the sublessee here is not liable to the lessor even on covenants running with the land. Thus Stuart is liable only to Tracey, not to Lillian, and Lillian cannot recover anything from Stuart.

55. **Yes.** Thelma, as the original tenant, had both privity of estate and privity of contract with Lloyd. When Thelma assigned to Tim, her privity of estate ended. But her privity of contract remained. Therefore, she was still liable on the original lease. The fact that Lloyd accepted rent payments directly from Tim, without objection, was not sufficient to release Thelma from her contractual liability (even though this acceptance of rent may have constituted an acceptance by Lloyd of the validity of the assignment from Thelma to Tim).

56. **Yes.** Since Tim never promised either Thelma or Lloyd that he would perform Thelma's obligations, he had no contractual liability to pay rent. But by taking possession of the premises Tim entered into *privity of estate* with Lloyd. He was therefore liable for performances under the lease whose burden runs with the land. Since the promise to pay rent is such a "running with the land" promise, Tim was liable.

57. **No.** Since Tim never assumed contractual liability for Thelma's promises (see answer to prior question), his obligation was based only on privity of estate. When Tim assigned to Theo, and left the premises, that privity of estate ended. Therefore, there was no basis on which Lloyd could hold Tim liable for the period in which Theo, not Tim, was the occupant.

58. **Yes.** A promise to make repairs runs with the land both as to benefit and burden. Therefore, Tim gets the benefit of that promise, and Leon gets the burden of that promise (even though Leon never promised Lloyd that he would perform Lloyd's repair obligations, and even though Tim had no privity of contract with Thelma).

59. **Yes.** Thelma's original promise to Lloyd to pay rent touched and concerned the land, and therefore ran with the land both as to benefit and burden. Tim, by taking the assignment and moving in, became in privity of estate with Lloyd, and therefore had a non-contractual duty to pay rent for the time of his occupancy (see answer to Question 56 above). Since the benefit of Thelma's promise to pay rent ran with the land, just as the burden did, Leon got the benefit of this running. Therefore, he can recover not just against Thelma, but against Tim.

60. **No, probably.** Most American courts follow the rule in *Dumpor's Case*, by which a landlord's consent to one assignment destroys an anti-assignment clause completely, even though the initial consent was to a particular assignee. (Lloyd could have avoided this problem by making his consent to the original Thelma-Tim assignment "expressly conditional upon there being no further assignments.") A substantial minority of American courts have rejected the rule in *Dumpor's* case; such courts would allow Lloyd to have Theo evicted here.

61. **No, probably.** Most states now hold, either by statute or case law, that even where the lease prohibits assignment or sublease without landlord's consent, the consent *may not be unreasonably withheld*. This is especially likely to be the case where the anti-assignment provision is a boilerplate clause imposed on a tenant who has little or no bargaining power (as was the case here).

62. (a) **No.** At common law, it was not possible for an owner of land (Orin) to convey that land to one person, and to establish by the same deed an easement in a third person. This was the rule against creating an easement in a *"stranger to the deed."*

    (b) **Yes, probably.** Most modern courts have abandoned the common-law "stranger to the deed" rule, and allow an easement to be created by a deed in a person who is neither the grantor nor the grantee. This is especially likely where the easement relates to a use that existed prior to the conveyance. Since Norman fished in the stream prior to the Orin-to-Alfred conveyance, a modern court would probably uphold the easement in the deed to Alfred. Once that easement is recognized as valid, *it burdened the land*, and therefore is still in force even though it was omitted from the Alfred-to-Barbara deed.

63. **No, probably.** Normally, an easement may be created only by compliance with the Statute of Frauds, which did not happen here. Therefore, the only kind of easement that might have come into existence is an easement "by implication." But an easement by implication will only come into existence if (among other requirements) the owner of a parcel sells part and retains part, or sells pieces simultaneously to multiple grantees (the requirement of *"severance"*). Here, neither Angela nor her predecessors ever owned what is today Blueacre and thus never sold any part of it; consequently, the requirement of "severance" is not satisfied. (Nor does an easement "by necessity" exist, because the two parcels, Auburnacre and Blueacre, were never under common ownership.) So Carter has no easement at all.

64. **Yes.** Normally an easement must be express and in writing in order to be valid. However, there are several exceptions to this rule. One of these exceptions is applicable here: an *"easement of necessity"* will be found where two parcels were at one time under common ownership, and an easement over one parcel is "strictly necessary" to the enjoyment of the other. Here, these two requirements are satisfied, since Daphne at one time owned both the area on which the golf course is located and the 10 acres on which the mall is now located, and access to the public road in favor of a "land locked" parcel is the most common example of a "strictly necessary" easement. The fact that the proposed use (access for a golf course) did not exist prior to the severance (i.e., prior to Daphne's transfer of the 10 acres to Frederika) is irrelevant in the case of an easement by necessity. (However, this lack of a use prior to the severance would probably be fatal to an "easement by implication.")

65. **Yes.** Ben has obtained an easement by *prescription*. When one property owner uses another's property for more than the statute of limitations period applicable to adverse possession actions, and does so in an adverse manner (see answer to prior question), an easement by prescription results. The requirement of "adverse" use is satisfied here by the fact that Ben never asked Astrid's permission, and Astrid never expressly consented, merely tolerated the use. The use must be reasonably continuous, which was the case here. The use need not be exclusive, since it is only an easement by prescription, not formal title, that is being granted by adverse possession. This easement by prescription, once it came into existence in 1985, became a burden on Astrid's land, so that Charles is bound even though he was not the owner while the easement was ripening.

66. **Yes.** The original deed from Dunes to George created an easement appurtenant, since the free-golf rights were clearly intended to benefit a purchaser of the house in his capacity as owner of a house adjacent to the course. Both the benefit and burden of an easement appurtenant pass with transfer of the property. Thus the benefit passed when George sold the dominant parcel to Henry, and the burden passed when Dunes Development sold the servient parcel to Ian. (This rule that both benefit and burden pass with the land is always subject to a contrary agreement; thus if the original deed from Dunes to George had said that George's rights were not transferable to a subsequent purchaser of a house, Henry would be out of luck. But here, no such provision was present in the deed.)

67. **No.** An easement is like any other estate in land, in the sense that any extinguishment of it must normally satisfy the Statute of Frauds. Therefore, Quince's oral statement, taken by itself, did not extinguish the easement, and that easement passed to Raymond when the dominant tenement (the quarry and manufacturing plant) were sold to Raymond.

68. (a) **A license.** A license is a right to use the licensor's land that is revocable at the will of the licensor. A license is not required to satisfy the Statute of Frauds, and thus may be created orally. This is what happened here: Abbott did not sign any writing, and Bingham's confirmatory letter did not satisfy the Statute of Frauds as is normally required for an easement (since it was not signed by Abbott, the only person who could create the easement); nonetheless, a license was created.

(b) **No.** The feature that distinguishes a license from an easement is that the license is *revocable at the will of the licensor*. Therefore, Abbott had the right at any time to revoke the license, regardless of his motive.

69. **No.** Since Claire never promised to pay for repairs, the only way Bertrand's promise could be binding on Claire is if that promise was a "covenant running with the land." In particular, Claire will only be bound if the burden of the covenant runs with the land. There are several requirements in order for the burden to run. One is that the burden "touch and concern" the land. Here, this requirement is satisfied, since non-payment would result in a lien which would touch and concern the land. But a second requirement in nearly all states is that there must be *"horizontal privity"* between promisor and promisee. In particular, it remains the rule everywhere (except in four states that have modified it by statute) that the *burden of the covenant may not run with the land where the original parties to the covenant were "strangers to title,"* i.e., had no property relationship between them at the time of the promise. Here, this rule is not satisfied: Allison and Bertrand were strangers to title, and thus could not create a covenant the burden of which would run with the land (unless Allison gave Bertrand an easement to come onto Allison's land to make repairs if she did not do so herself; the facts say that this did not happen).

70. **No, probably.** The vast majority of jurisdictions apply the same horizontal privity requirement for the running of a benefit as they do for the running of a burden, whatever that rule is in the particular jurisdiction. Since the burden of the promise here would not run (see the answer to the prior question) nearly all states would refuse to allow the benefit to run either, so that Doug would not be permitted to recover.

71. **Yes.** Since Allison's promise not to change fences is a negative promise, and the relief sought by Claire is an injunction, the question is whether we have a valid *"equitable servitude"* (not a "covenant at law," as we had in the two prior questions). An equitable servitude is a promise (usually negative in nature) relating to land, that will be enforced by courts against an assignee of the promisor.

The promise here satisfies the requirements for equitable servitudes, which are less stringent than for covenants at law. The promise must "touch and concern" both the promisor's land and the promisee's land; that requirement is satisfied here, since Allison (the promisor) has bound herself with respect to a structure on her property, and the appearance of Bertrand's property is directly affected by the promise. Horizontal privity (privity between Allison and Bertrand, the original promisor and promisee) is *not* required for an equitable servitude; therefore, the fact that Allison and Bertrand had no pre-existing property relationship and were thus "strangers to title" does not prevent Allison's promise from being an enforceable equitable servitude, even though it prevented Bertrand's counter-promise to pay for repairs from being enforceable at law as to Bertrand's successor (see Question 69). Nor is there any vertical privity requirement for equitable servitudes, so Claire could enforce the servitude against Doug even if she only held, say, a lease on the property owned by Bertrand. Courts will not enforce an equitable servitude against an assignee of the promisor unless the assignee was on actual or constructive notice of the servitude at the time he took possession. But the fact that the Allison-Bertrand agreement was filed in the land records put Doug on such constructive notice.

72. **No.** Harry is trying to enforce an equitable servitude against Isadore's property. But equity will not enforce an agreement against a subsequent purchaser unless the purchaser had *notice* of the restriction at the time he took. This notice can be either actual or "constructive." But the facts make it clear that James did not have actual

notice at the time he purchased, and the absence of any valid recordation of the agreement means that James did not have constructive notice either. Therefore, the restriction is not binding against him, and he can build the pool.

73. **Yes, probably.** Most courts will apply the doctrine of *"implied reciprocal servitude"* in this circumstance. This theory holds that if the earlier of two purchasers (here, Kathy) acquires her land in expectation that she will be entitled to the benefit of subsequently created equitable servitudes, there is immediately created an "implied reciprocal servitude" against the developer's remaining land. For this reciprocality doctrine to apply, a general development plan must be in existence at the time of the first sale, a requirement satisfied here. Courts frequently apply the doctrine even where the restrictions are not inserted in the later deed (here, the one to Lewis).

74. **No, probably.** Occasionally, a land-use control is sufficiently draconian that a court will conclude that it amounts to a "taking" for Fourteenth Amendment purposes, for which compensation must be given. But this is extremely rare, especially in the environmental regulation area. A land-use regulation is valid as long as the means chosen "substantially advance" a legitimate state interest, and do not "deny an owner economically viable use of his land." *Nollan v. California Coastal Commission*, 483 U.S. 825 (1987). Here, the town is certainly advancing its legitimate interest in not suffering the noxious odors associated with a dump. Furthermore, Dexter is not being deprived of all economically viable use of his property, but merely the most "valuable" use. So a court is extremely unlikely to hold that the ordinance constitutes a taking. See, e.g., *Goldblatt v. Hempstead*, 369 U.S. 590 (1962) (regulation preventing continued operation of a sand and gravel pit is a valid safety regulation rather than a taking).

75. **No, probably.** The vast majority of states hold that such an "amortization" provision does not violate due process or constitute a taking, as long as the amortization period is sufficiently long for the owner to recover most of his costs and to arrange an alternative use or location. Here, Jones has already had the billboard for 20 years (plus the five-year phase-out), so he has had plenty of time to recoup its costs. Also, he can continue to run his business without the billboard, so the injury to him is not extreme. (But about five states hold, either as a matter of state statutory law or federal constitutional law, that non-conforming uses must be permitted indefinitely, rather than being "amortized.")

76. **No.** Prince probably has standing to assert his claim, since he has been directly affected by the allegedly illegal zoning. However, the Supreme Court has held that a racially discriminatory *purpose*, not merely effect, needs to be shown before an ordinance will be subjected to strict equal protection scrutiny. Without strict scrutiny, the ordinance here merely has to be rationally related to a legitimate state purpose, which is almost certainly the case. So unless Prince is able to bear the burden of showing that the town's ordinance was enacted (or maintained) for racially discriminatory purposes, the fact that the ordinance has a disparate negative effect on minorities is irrelevant to the equal protection claim. See *Arlington Heights v. Metropolitan Housing Development Corp.*, 429 U.S. 252 (1977).

77. (a) **A federal Fair Housing Act suit.** The Fair Housing title of the 1968 Civil Rights Act makes it unlawful to "make unavailable, or deny, a dwelling to any person because of race, color, religion, sex or national origin."

   (b) **Yes, probably.** If Prince had been able to show that Twin Peaks intentionally tried to limit access by blacks, this would be a clear violation of the Housing Act. The Supreme Court has never decided whether a discriminatory purpose (rather than mere disparate effect) must be shown for a violation of the act, but most lower federal courts have held that the plaintiff in such a suit does **not** need to show that the defendant had a discriminatory intent. Instead, plaintiff merely has to prove that the defendant's land-use controls had a disparate effect on blacks or other racial minorities. The burden then shifts to the defendant town to show that it was acting in pursuit of a legitimate governmental interest, and that there was no less-discriminatory way of achieving that same interest. Probably Twin Peaks could not meet this burden, so probably Prince would win his suit on this theory. See, e.g., *Huntington Branch NAACP v. Town of Huntington*, 844 F.2d 926 (2d Cir. 1988).

78. (a) **A *Mount Laurel* "fair share" suit.** In *Southern Burlington County NAACP v. Township of Mount Laurel*, 336 A.2d 713 (N.J. 1975), the New Jersey Supreme Court held that exclusionary zoning practices that fail to serve the general welfare of the region as a whole violate statutory law and the state constitution. The court held that a municipality may not foreclose opportunities for low- and moderate-income housing, and must allow at least that town's "fair share" of the present and prospective regional need for such housing. Since the two-acre minimum prevents even middle-class housing, let alone lower-class housing, from being constructed, the scheme would almost certainly be a *Mount Laurel* violation.

   (b) **Grant a re-zoning of the parcel.** *Mount Laurel* (and a successor case, *"Mount Laurel II"*) hold that where the trial court concludes that the project sought to be built by the developer is suitable for that specific site, the court may order the municipality to rezone the particular project. This is the so-called "builder's remedy." This would permit Prosser to go ahead with his project immediately, rather than merely watch as the town meets its "fair share" obligation by other means, such as allowing an apartment complex to be built in some other part of town. (But the New Jersey legislature has subsequently put a moratorium on the builder's remedy.)

79. **No.** The *Statute of Frauds* is applicable in all states to any contract for the sale of land, or for the sale of any interest in land. Therefore, either the contract itself, or a memorandum of it, must be in writing. Furthermore, the contract or memorandum must be signed by the "party to be charged." On the facts here, the party to be charged is Bryant, and the contract is not enforceable against him because of the lack of signature.

80. **Yes, probably.** Most (but certainly not all) states recognize the *"part performance"* exception to the Statute of Frauds for land-sale contracts. Under this doctrine, a party (either buyer or seller) who has taken action in reliance on the contract may be able to gain enforcement of it at equity. In most states, if the "purchaser" (here, Grandson, in the sense that he was "purchasing" the farm in exchange for his

services) takes possession, makes improvements and changes his position in reliance, this will be the sort of part performance required. Courts generally require that the part performance be "unequivocally referable" to the alleged contract, i.e., that the part performance be clearly in response to the oral contract, and not explainable by some other facet of the parties' relationship. This requirement seems to be met here, since Grandson has made permanent improvements to the property, by building the cabin and cutting down the trees, and these improvements are not readily explainable by the mere Grandfather-Grandson relationship.

81. **Yes, probably.** In a suit for specific performance of a land sale contract, the general rule is that time is *not of the essence* unless the contract expressly so provides or the surrounding circumstances indicate that it is. Thus generally, even though the contract specifies a particular closing date, either party may obtain specific performance although he is unable to close on the appointed day (as long as the defaulting party is able to perform within a reasonable time after the scheduled date). Since the surrounding circumstances do not suggest that time was of the essence from Shelby's perspective, and since Bennett was able to perform within what a court would probably find was a reasonable time of the scheduled closing date (10-day delay), the court will probably grant Bennett a decree of specific performance. (But a few courts, most notably the New York courts, hold that where the contract does not explicitly make time of the essence, either party, by a unilateral notification to the other that it will insist upon strict adherence to the contracted-for settlement date, may make time of the essence. In such a state, Shelby would win.)

82. **No, probably.** The key to solving this question is that where the seller's duty to deliver the deed and the buyer's duty to pay the money are *concurrent*, then each party must be sure to *tender his own performance*, in order to be able to hold the other party in default. Therefore, Brady could hold Squires in default (and get a return of his deposit) only if Brady tendered his own performance. Since Brady did not have the certified check with him, or even have the funds readily available, Brady did not tender his own performance. Consequently, Squires' own "breach" is irrelevant, and Squires will probably be allowed to keep the deposit. (The result might have been different if Squires' failure to comply with the contract stemmed from an incurable problem, such as complete lack of title in Squires; it also would have been different if Squires had repudiated the contract ahead of time. But neither of these events happened here.)

83. **Yes, probably.** The usual rule that each party must tender his own performance in order to hold the other in breach (see prior question) does not generally apply where a defendant's inability to perform is *incurable*. On these facts, Squires' lack of marketable title (due to the encroachment) was so severe, and so impossible to cure, that Brady's failure to tender his own performance would probably be overlooked by the court, and Brady would get his money back.

84. **Deirdre.** "Common sense" would suggest that the answer should be Nell, since Sherman died while still the technical owner of the real estate, so it would seem fair to give Nell the proceeds from the post-death sale of an asset that was earmarked for her. But instead, courts apply the doctrine of *"equitable conversion."* By this doctrine, the signing of the contract is deemed to vest in the purchaser equitable ownership of the land, and the vendor is treated as becoming the equitable owner of the purchase price at that time. As a result of the equitable conversion doctrine, the

purchase price goes to the person to whom the personal property was bequeathed, and the person to whom the real estate was devised gets nothing.

85. **Yes, probably.** Most courts adopt the rule that since the vendee acquires equitable ownership of the land as soon as the contract is signed (see answer to prior question), the risk of loss immediately shifts to him. This is true even though the vendee never takes possession prior to the casualty. There is an exception if the vendor caused the loss negligently, but the facts indicate that this was not the case.

86. **No, probably.** When the purchaser under an installment sales contract has paid a substantial percentage of the purchase price, most courts try hard to avoid allowing the seller to make the buyer "forfeit" his rights under the contract. The court might order Spence to use statutory foreclosure proceedings before evicting Bagley. In that event, Spence would have to put the property up for sale, and would have to pay to Bagley any amount that the property sold for less the $100,000 that Bagley still owes Spence. (In other words, the installment contract would be treated as if it had been a mortgage.) Or, the court might give Bagley the right to make the payments on which he had been in arrears ($15,000), and then continue with the contract. If the $5,000 monthly payments due from Bagley were no more than a fair rental price for the property, the court would probably not use either of these methods, since the situation would be analogous to a tenant who falls behind in his rent. But here, the monthly payments are much more than fair rental value, so the court would, as stated, take steps to avoid forfeiture.

87. **No, probably.** Under the doctrine of *merger*, obligations imposed by the contract of sale are generally discharged unless they are repeated in the deed. There is an exception where the contract covenant is "collateral" to (i.e., not directly related to) the promise to convey land. But here, the representation in the contract that there were no easements related directly to the transfer of title, and most courts would hold that that representation was merged out of existence when Boswell accepted the deed that did not repeat the obligation. (But the Uniform Land Transactions Act, if in force in the jurisdiction, would prevent merger from happening.)

88. **Stewart.** If a deed is validly executed and delivered, title passes immediately to the grantee. Thereafter, return of the deed to the grantor, or even destruction of the deed, has no effect either to cancel the prior delivery or to reconvey the title to the original grantor. The only way the title can get back to the grantor is if a new, formally satisfactory, conveyance takes place. Since Stewart never executed and delivered a valid deed to Fred, title remains in him.

89. **None.** The covenants of seisin, right to convey and against encumbrances are all "present" covenants. That is, they are breached at the moment the conveyance is made. Therefore, a breach of these can occur even though there was no eviction. Consequently, these were violated by Spitzer at the time of the original conveyance (at least the covenants of seisin and right to convey were breached, though the covenant against encumbrances may not have been). However, Butler's problem is that these covenants are time-barred: the five year statute of limitations on each began to run at the time of conveyance, and the actions became time barred in 1975. The covenants of quiet enjoyment and warranty, by contrast, are "future" covenants. That is, they are breached only when an eviction occurs. The covenants both promise that the grantee's possession will not be challenged. An action on either of these future covenants is not

time barred, since they have not yet started to run. However, there is no cause of action on these, either: until Adolf starts eviction proceedings or otherwise actively asserts that his title is superior, Butler has not even been constructively, let alone actually, evicted. Therefore, Butler will have to wait until Adolf actively asserts his title before he may sue Spitzer. To the extent that the uncertainty renders Butler unable to convey a valid title, Butler is simply out of luck.

90. **Yes.** The future covenants (warranty, quiet enjoyment and further assurance) are universally held to ***run with the land***. Since these covenants are not breached until there is an actual or constructive eviction, they would be rendered almost useless if a subsequent transfer of the land cut them off. Therefore, Capshaw can sue Spitzer even though he had no privity of contract with Spitzer.

91. (a) **Covenant against encumbrances.** The covenant against encumbrances is a representation that there are no encumbrances against the property. The encroachment by Jones was such an encumbrance, so this covenant was violated.

(b) **No, probably.** Most courts hold that even where the grantee is aware of a defect, his knowledge does not nullify the relevant covenant. See, e.g., *Jones v. Grow Investment & Mortgage Co.*, 358 P.2d 909 (Utah 1961).

92. (a) **Suit for breach of the implied warranty of habitability.** Many courts today allow a home purchaser to sue a professional developer for the breach of this warranty, in a way that is analogous to the landlord-tenant implied warranty recognized in nearly all jurisdictions.

(b) **Split of authority.** The strong emerging trend is to recognize an action for implied warranty of habitability in sales by professional developers of new homes.

93. **No.** Courts have nearly always refused to allow an implied warranty claim against one who is not in the business of building or selling homes. The consequence is that the buyer of a used home, such as Carter, cannot sue the person who sold it to him (Benjamin).

94. **Arkin, because he recorded first.** Under a race-notice statute, the second grantee (Beacon) will prevail over the earlier grantee (Arkin) only if the second satisfies two requirements: (1) he records before the earlier purchaser records; and (2) he took without notice of the earlier conveyance. Here, Beacon flunked the first of these requirements. (The fact that Beacon had notice at the time he recorded is irrelevant; what counts is whether Beacon had notice at the time he received his deed, which he did not on the facts here.)

95. **Arkin.** A race-notice statute requires that the subsequent purchaser record before the earlier purchaser, and take without notice of the earlier conveyance. (See answer to prior question.) Here, Beacon failed the second of these requirements, since he knew of the conveyance to Arkin at the time he, Beacon, took. Therefore, Beacon's having recorded first does not save him. (The fact that Oliver lied about the way the recording statute works should not insulate Beacon from his own failure to comply with the statute.)

96. **Beacon.** Under a "pure notice" statute, the sole issue is whether the subsequent grantee had actual or constructive notice of the prior grant at the time the subsequent grantee took. At the time Beacon took in 1982, he had neither actual nor constructive notice of the grant to Arkin (the facts tell you he did not have actual notice, and the lack of recordation means that he did not have constructive notice). Therefore, the fact that Arkin later recorded, and that Beacon never recorded, is irrelevant.

97. **Cabbott, probably.** Ordinarily, the second grantee under a race-notice statute must fulfill two requirements to take priority over a prior grantee: (1) he must record before the earlier grantee records; and (2) he must have taken without notice of the earlier grant. Here, Cabbott has not fulfilled the first of these requirements, since Arias recorded before he (Cabbott) did. However, most statutes requiring a race require it only where the contest is *between grantees from a common grantor*. Since Arias and Cabbott are claiming under different grantors, Cabbott's failure to record before Arias probably will not be fatal. Allowing Cabbott to win fulfills the goal of encouraging reliance on the public record: at the time Cabbott took from Beck, paying full value, Cabbott had no practical way to know of the earlier conveyance to Arias, so there is a strong interest in protecting him even though he was negligent by waiting to record. (Obviously, Cabbott could have protected himself fully by recording immediately, so that he would have won the race-to-record with Arias, even though he never knew of Arias' existence.) So the court will probably find for Cabbott.

98. **Abrams.** Boone appears to have fulfilled the two requirements for taking priority over a prior grantee under a race-notice statute: he took without notice of the prior grant, and he recorded before the prior grantee recorded. However, in the vast majority of states, a grantee receives the benefit of the recording act (i.e., he gets to take priority over an earlier unrecorded conveyance) only if he *gives value* for his interest. Here, Boone did not give value, but rather received a gift. Therefore, he gets no benefit from the recording act, and the usual principle of "first in time, first in right" applies. This is true even though Abrams similarly received a gift and thus did not give value.

99. **Chavez.** At first, Chavez appears to violate one of the two requirements for taking ahead of a prior grantee: Chavez failed to win the "race" to record before Bishop did. But in reality, Bishop will be deemed never to have recorded at all. A grantee records only when he *adequately* records. The mere fact that a deed is recorded somewhere in the public records does not mean that the recording is "adequate" — the document must be recorded *in such a way that a reasonable searcher would find it*. Here, only if a searcher would have found the document using the grantor and grantee indexes would Bishop's deed be adequately recorded.

A searcher in Chavez's position would have started with a "root" of Orcini (or one of Orcini's predecessors in recorded title); Chevez would then never have found the Orcini-to-Arlen deed because that deed was never recorded. Thus he would not have known to look in the grantor index to find that Arlen later conveyed to Bishop, and he consequently would never have found the deed to Bishop. In other words, Bishop would be deemed to have adequately recorded only if Bishop made sure that not only was his own deed recorded, but also *the deed by which his grantor took* (the Orcini-to-Arlen deed), and so forth back in the chain at least 50 or 60 years. Since Bishop is in a position equivalent to not having recorded at all, Chavez is the first to "adequately" record, and he is thus the first grantee; it is Bishop who is the second grantee, and he loses because he did not adequately record first. See *Losey v.*

Simpson, 11 N.J.Eq. 246 (1856), holding for the party in Chavez's position on similar facts.

100. **Burrows.** Dempsey's fatal mistake was that although he made sure that his own conveyance (Craft-to-Dempsey) was promptly recorded, he did not make sure that his whole chain of title was recorded. That is, he failed to make sure that the O'Neill-to-Craft deed was recorded. The entire line running from O'Neill through Arens through Burrows was then recorded (in 1985) at a time when Dempsey had still not "adequately" recorded. Therefore, Dempsey, as the second grantee, has not fulfilled one of the two requirements for a subsequent grantee to take under a race-notice statute: he did not win the race to record, because one wins that race only by "adequately" recording, which Dempsey has never done. So just as Question 99 illustrates that the earlier grantee may lose the protection of the recording acts by not seeing to it that his entire chain of title is recorded, so the subsequent grantee may lose the protection of the recording acts by failing to see to it that *his* entire chain of title is recorded.

101. **Andrews.** Under normal principles, Burns would get the benefit of the recording act because he took without actual or record notice of the prior grant (the unrecorded deed to Andrews). But Burns loses because of the doctrine of *"inquiry"* notice. Even if the subsequent purchaser has neither record nor actual notice of a prior unrecorded conveyance, he will be found to have been on inquiry notice of it if at the time he took he was in possession of facts which would have led a reasonable person in his position to make an investigation, which would in turn have advised him of the existence of the prior unrecorded right.

Most courts hold that the subsequent grantee has a duty to *view the property*, and if it is in possession of someone other than the record owner, he must inquire as to the source of the latter's rights in the property. Here, the facts tell us that if Burns had viewed the property, he would have discovered Andrews, and that if he had discovered Andrews, Andrews would have told him that he, Andrews, had an unrecorded deed. Therefore, Burns is charged with inquiry notice of Andrews' deed, and Burns is thus a grantee "with knowledge" of that deed (thereby removing him from the protection of the notice statute).

102. **Crystal.** Brown, at the time he took, met the two requirements for a subsequent grantee to take priority in a race-notice jurisdiction: he won the race to record ahead of Albright, and he took without notice of Albright's deed. That being the case, not only Brown's own "ownership," but his ability to *resell* his property, is protected by courts construing the recording acts. That is, once an interest is purged by its acquisition by one without notice of the prior unrecorded document, the interest remains "clean" when resold, *even if the new purchaser has actual or record notice*.

103. **Yes, probably.** Title Co. will probably argue that it is exculpated by the clause in the title policy excluding facts which an accurate survey of the property would disclose. But even if Title Co. persuades the court that this exclusion covers the garage, Title Co. will probably be liable for *negligence* for not having called Barnes' attention to the encroachment. See, e.g., *Shotwell v. Transamerica Title Ins. Co.*, 558 P.2d 1359 (Ct.App.Wash. 1976), holding that the title insurer could be liable for negligence in the search even as to an item (an easement) which was excluded from coverage by the policy.

104. **No, probably.** Plotnick had an absolute right to *"lateral support."* However, this absolute right exists only with respect to land in its *natural state*. If the owner has constructed a building, and the soil under the building subsides in part due to the adjacent owner's acts, but also in part because of the weight of the building itself, the adjacent owner is not liable in the absence of negligence. Therefore, since Duffy's acts would not have caused Plotnick's land to cave in had the land been vacant, and Duffy behaved non-negligently, Duffy does not have to pay for damage accruing to Plotnick's structure.

105. **Yes, probably.** In a common-law jurisdiction, each riparian owner has an absolute right to all or any part of the water for "natural" uses (regardless of the effect on downstream owners), but an owner may take for *"artificial"* uses only after all natural uses have been satisfied, and then only in parity with other artificial users. Irrigation of small areas of farmland is generally considered "natural," whereas use for hydro-electric power is almost certainly artificial. Therefore, Phillips has priority over Decker; Phillips can recover damages, obtain an injunction, or both. (The fact that Phillips was using the water first does not matter to the result.)

106. **Yes, probably.** Courts following the common-law approach do not grant any advantage based on priority of use. So the fact that a riparian owner has used stream water for a certain purpose for many years does not give him any greater rights than if he were making this use for the first time. Thus the problem is solved the way it is in the prior answer (with Phillips winning because his use is "natural" and Decker's is "artificial").

107. **No, probably.** The 17 arid states that have abolished the common-law riparian rights doctrine have generally adopted the *"prior appropriation"* doctrine instead. In some of these states, a water user must apply for a permit in order to get priority; in these states, the issue would be decided based on who got a permit first (which the facts don't disclose). But in the remaining "prior appropriation" states, the right to appropriate is absolute (i.e., no permit is required) and the priority of the right dates from the time the appropriator began construction of the necessary works to take the water. In such a state, Decker, as the first user, would prevail.

108. **No.** Generally, courts hold that an owner may build as tall as he wants, and as close to his property line as he wants, so long as he does not violate zoning rules. In particular, courts almost never recognize an owner's right to sunlight or view. For instance, courts almost never recognize that a landowner has acquired an easement of "light and air" by implication or even by necessity. So Pringle is almost certainly out of luck. (His remedy was to build his own building far enough in from his property line that even a neighboring building later built right up to that property line would not block his own light completely.)

ESSAY EXAM
QUESTIONS AND ANSWERS

The following Essay Questions are taken from the *Real Property* volume of *Siegel's Essay & Multiple Choice*, a series written by Brian Siegel and now published by Emanuel Law Outlines, Inc. The full volume contains 25 essays (with model answers), as well as 96 multiple choice questions. (The essay questions were originally asked on the California Bar Exam, and are copyright the California Board of Bar Examiners, reprinted by permission.)

QUESTION 1

Landlord rented a furnished apartment in his building to Tenant, a law student, for two years, beginning June 1. When Tenant arrived at the apartment on June 1, Ralph (the prior tenant) was still there. Tenant complained to Landlord and Landlord was able to evict Ralph on June 15. Tenant went into possession of the apartment on June 16. During early July, some children playing baseball broke a windowpane in Tenant's apartment. Tenant demanded that Landlord replace the windowpane, but Landlord refused. Rain, which subsequently came through the broken pane, caused damage to the living room floor, which began to warp.

The apartment above Tenant's was occupied by Charlie, a member of a famous rock group (The Charles River). The daily rehearsals (typically 2:00-6:00 p.m.) of this group interfered with Tenant's law studies so much that he complained repeatedly to Landlord. On July 15, three of Charlie's friends (the other members of Charlie's band) were arrested at Charlie's apartment and charged with possession of narcotics. The noise stopped immediately thereafter.

On August 30, Tenant discovered that the stove in his apartment was no longer functioning. On August 31, Tenant, disgusted with all these events, knocked on Landlord's door, tendered the key to Landlord, and said, "This place is a zoo; I wouldn't live here if you paid me!" Landlord took the key without saying a word. Landlord now comes to you wanting to sue Tenant for the accrued (Tenant has yet to pay any rent) and prospective rent. What would you advise Landlord? Discuss.

QUESTION 2

Alice has just shown you a deed which was recorded 40 years ago. This document reads as follows:

In consideration of love and affection, I hereby grant Sweetholm to my friend Josiah and the heirs of his body, this conveyance to take effect 10 years from the date hereof, provided that if Josiah dies without issue the estate is to go to my brother Ludwig and his heirs, and further provided that if animals, birds or children are ever kept on the property, the estate is to cease and determine.

/Signed/Vladimir

You ascertain from Alicia that her house, with its surrounding grounds of about 10 acres, is known as Sweetholm. Alicia tells you that she bought Sweetholm from Josiah's niece, Jennifer, 11 years ago. The deed transferred to Alicia "all my right, title and interest in Sweetholm." Alicia also tells you that when she bought the property the guest house near the southwest boundary of the estate was occupied by Danny, her cousin. Danny had visited Jennifer 12 years ago and decided to stay to work on a novel. Jennifer had asked Alicia to let Danny stay there for awhile, "since he was finding himself." Alicia said it would probably be "all right, if Danny did not get in my way." Alicia thought it might be a good idea to have a male on the property to frighten away prospective thieves. Soon after Jennifer vacated Sweetholm, Danny built a separate mailbox outside the guest house and placed a doormat in front of the entrance, which read "Welcome to Danny's."

It seems that the estate bordering Sweetholm on the west, Laurel Hill, had been purchased 14 years ago by Wilson, a scientist doing research on the territorial habits of wild dogs, coyotes and wolves. Wilson had captured several wolves and brought them to Laurel Hill. When Alicia took over the property from Jennifer, Wilson talked to her about the wolves. Alicia promised him, in a valid writing, that she would allow the wolves to wander freely over Sweetholm. The wolves soon manifested their territorial behavior and took up residence on the southwest corner of Sweetholm.

Unfortunately, when Danny saw one of the animals wandering around near the guest house about 2 months ago, he suddenly took it into his head that it would make a nice pet. He enticed it into his enclosed patio and kept it there, even when it resisted his first efforts to make friends and bit his hand when he tried to feed it.

About a week ago Alicia received an unpleasant visit from Trivers, Wilson's co-experimenter, who had purchased Laurel Hill from Wilson last summer. Trivers threatened to sue Alicia because Danny had tampered with a subject involved in his experiment. Alicia became upset with the whole thing and evicted both Danny and the wolves from Sweetholm that very evening. Alicia hastily had a chicken wire fence constructed on the western boundary of Sweetholm so that the wolves could not get back in. Last night, (1) Danny called and claimed that he owned the guest house, and (2) Trivers called and threatened to obtain an injunction requiring Alicia to remove the chicken wire fence.

Alicia asks you whether Trivers and Danny really have any viable claims against her. She also wants to know whether there are any other people who might show up to claim an interest in Sweetholm.

In response to initial questioning from you, Alicia tells you that Vladimir is dead and Josef is his sole heir; that Ludwig is dead and Richard is his sole heir; and that Josiah is also dead, but Jennifer, his niece and only heir, is still alive. You have also learned that the Statute of Limitations for actions to recover real property is 10 years. Please evaluate the possible claims of Danny, Trivers, and any other person(s) you think might have a plausible claim to some interest in Sweetholm.

QUESTION 3

Art was the record owner of Greenacre, a vacant tract of land. Art and Bob discussed the sale of this land to Bob, and they orally agreed on a purchase price of $5,000 in cash. Art then typed up a statement setting forth all the terms that had been agreed upon, including the fact that Art would deliver to Carl, a real estate broker, a warranty deed conveying Greenacre to Bob and that Carl would hand deliver the deed to Bob if Bob gave Carl the purchase price within one month.

Art placed one copy of this statement, unsigned, unwitnessed and undated, in an envelope and mailed it to Bob. Upon receiving it, Bob telephoned Art and told him that the statement accurately reflected his understanding and that he would deliver $5,000 in cash to Carl within the month in accordance with their agreement.

Art then executed the warranty deed, complete in all respects, and gave it to Carl with a copy of his statement.

One week later, Art learned that a highway was to be built near Greenacre, greatly increasing its value. Art immediately wrote to Carl, telling Carl he had changed his mind and wanted the deed returned to him.

One day later and before Carl had received Art's last letter, Bob called Carl and said he had to show the deed to his bank to obtain a loan for the $5,000. Carl sent the deed to Bob, who promptly recorded it and immediately executed and delivered a warranty deed for Greenacre to Dale.

Bob has disappeared and has not paid the $5,000 to Art or Carl.

(1) In an action to quiet title between Art and Dale, who prevails? Discuss.

(2) What are the rights of Art and Dale against Carl? Discuss.

ESSAY ANSWERS

ANSWER TO QUESTION 1

Assumptions: The lease was written and signed by Tenant (and so there is no Statute of Frauds (p. 134) problem even though the lease in question exceeded one year).

To advise Landlord ("LL") of his rights against Tenant ("T") it is initially necessary to determine if T can successfully assert any defenses against LL.

Duty to Deliver Possession: Under the English rule (p. 141), a landlord has the obligation to assure his/her tenant that no other party will be in possession of the premises when the lease term commences. T might assert that LL breached his duty, since Ralph was in the apartment when T's lease term began. However, even assuming this jurisdiction adheres to this rule that the landlord must evict holdover tenants, T has probably waived (voluntarily relinquished a known right) this breach by going into possession of premises after Ralph moved out. At most, T can probably deduct the rent attributable to the period from June 1 through June 15. If the American view (p. 141) is followed, LL has the duty only to deliver *legal* possession, not actual possession, so the holdover (Ralph) would be T's problem.

Constructive Eviction ("CE"): A CE occurs where there is a substantial interference with a tenant's right of quiet enjoyment by reason of some cause for which the landlord is responsible, and the tenant vacates within a reasonable time thereafter (p. 150). T might argue that a CE occurred by reason of (i) the noise caused by Charlie's friends, (ii) the broken window pane and warped floor, and (iii) the stove's malfunction.

In response, however, LL could assert the following arguments. With respect to the noises caused by Charlie's band, LL is not responsible for the activities of other tenants (p. 144). In some states, where the lease contains a provision permitting the landlord to evict lessees who are disturbing other tenants, the landlord has been deemed responsible for the former. However, there is nothing in the given facts to indicate such a clause exists. Additionally, even assuming the band noise persisted from June 15th through July 15th (when 3 persons in the band were arrested), this probably did not constitute a substantial deprivation of T's right to the beneficial enjoyment of the premises since it occurred during daylight hours (rather than in the evening), when other tenants would be trying to sleep. Finally, LL could probably successfully argue that T waived the right to assert a CE by waiting 45 days after the noise had ceased to vacate the premises (pp. 144, 150).

As to the broken window pane and consequent warped floor, LL could argue that, at common law, it is T's duty to make repairs (pp. 171) and so T cannot complain about being deprived of the beneficial enjoyment of the premises when the condition which made them unsuitable was T's fault. As to the malfunctioning stove, LL could argue (1) again, this was T's responsibility, and (2) T apparently never even advised LL about this problem (p. 158), and so he did not have the requisite opportunity to remedy this situation.

The Implied Warranty of Habitability: Many states recognize an implied warranty of habitability that leased premises will not become uninhabitable by reason of the landlord's failure to make repairs attributable to the natural deterioration of the premises. (A few jurisdictions limit this doctrine to situations involving housing code violations.) T might argue that defects vital to the use of the premises existed by reason of (i) the broken pane and consequent warping, and (ii) the malfunctioning stove.

The warping was the result of the failure to repair the window; so whoever had the responsibility for repairing would be liable for the warped floor. LL can argue that the widows should have been repaired by T since (1) the pane was broken by other persons (the children playing ball) (p. 153), as opposed to the natural deterioration of the premises, and (2) a broken window is not a defect which causes premises to become uninhabitable. As to the non-functioning stove, LL can argue that the stove would not cause premises to fall below the bar living requirements. Finally, LL was (apparently) never even informed of this event.

LL should prevail against T on this issue too.

Surrender: T will also probably argue that LL's acceptance of the keys to the apartment constituted a surrender (pp. 179); and therefore T is not liable for any rent accruing after August 31. However, the fact that LL merely permitted T to hand the keys to him probably does not, without more, demonstrate a willingness to permit T to avoid his prospective obligations under the lease.

Advice/Extent of LL's Recovery: (We'll assume that rent was payable monthly, and that the lease did *not* have an accelerated rent or liquidated damage clause.)

LL should be able to recover T's unpaid rent, and for the additional rentals as they become due. However, LL should probably attempt to locate a new tenant for the premises since (1) many states require a landlord to mitigate a tenant's liability (p. 181), and (2) it may be difficult for LL to recover any judgment against T (even if one were obtained). Finally, LL should be advised to notify T that any subletting is being done for T's account. This precaution would preclude T from contending that a surrender of the premises had occurred via the subletting (p. 179-80).

ANSWER TO QUESTION 2

Adverse Possession ("AP"): One obtains title to real property by AP where he/she, under a claim of right, enters upon and exclusively occupies another's land in an open, notorious and hostile manner throughout the requisite statutory period. Danny ("D") could claim that by remaining at Sweetholm after the sale to Alicia ("A") without the latter's explicit permission, the "claim of right" and "hostile" elements are satisfied. Additionally, creating a separate mailbox and putting out a welcome sign which bore his name met the "open" and "notorious" requisites (p. 27). Finally, D's occupation of the guest house continued for a period of time in excess of the applicable Statute of Limitations. Thus, D could assert ownership to the guest house (along with an easement hereto and therefrom) under AP.

In some jurisdictions, the claim of right requirement is not satisfied unless the adverse claimant went upon the land with the belief that he/she was entitled to possess it. If this were such a jurisdiction, D's claim of AP would fail. In most states, however, the claim of right element is satisfied merely by the adverse possessor being aware that his/her habitation of the land in question was without the owner's permission (p. 30). If this jurisdiction adhered to the latter view, A could contend that Jennifer ("J") had presumably advised D of her statement that it would be "all right" for D to remain on Sweetholm. If it could be shown that J had so informed D, A should prevail on this issue.

A could alternatively claim that D's occupation of the guest house was *not* "hostile." While this element is usually satisfied by the claimant's use of the land in an "open and notorious" manner, an exception to this rule exists where the rightful owner would not necessarily recognize that the adverse possessor's occupation of the land is hostile to his/her ownership interest (even though aware of it). In such situations the adverse claimant must communicate (via clear words or actions) that the land is being held in derogation of the legal owner's rights thereto. Holdover tenancies often constitute such a situation, since a holdover tenant is usually deemed to be occupying the premises with the landlord's implicit permission.

A could contend that D should be viewed as either having been her guest (i.e., a continuation of the relationship which D enjoyed with J) or a tenant at sufferance. In either event, D would have been obliged to either (1) inform A that his occupation of the guest house was hostile to A's claim of ownership thereto, or (2) have done acts which clearly communicated this view (i.e., prevented A from entering the structure, built a fence around it, etc.). The mailbox would not suffice, since A could have presumed that while D had felt comfortable in permitting J (his cousin) to receive his mail, he would not have the same trust in a stranger. Finally, A would assert that the doormat was not adequate to inform her that D was claiming superior title to the guest house.

A would probably prevail upon the "hostile" issue, and therefore it is unlikely that D would prevail upon his claim of AP.

If, however, D's claim of AP were successful, he would have a right of action against A for evicting him. D would probably be entitled to recover the reasonable rental value of the land during his eviction, as well as any other costs and expenses attendant upon the interference with his right to possession.

Injunction sought by Trivers ("T"): T might initially contend that A had granted an express easement (p. 203) to Wilson ("W") to permit animals involved in the experiment to roam throughout Sweetholm, and easements will automatically run with the benefitted estate.

A would initially argue that the right given to W was a license (p. 225). An easement is ordinarily described as the right of one person to make a particular use of another's land. A license, however, is usually defined as the right to do a particular thing on another's land. A could assert that no right was granted to W to *use* her land. Rather, A merely indicated that W's wolves could randomly traverse Sweetholm. Thus, A would contend that the grant made to W was a license, and such interests are (1) ordinarily *not* assignable, and (2) revocable at any time by the licensor (subject to the licensee's right to recover for monetary damages resulting from the revocation). However, T could argue in rebuttal that since he was engaged in an experiment whereby the wolves wandered onto A's land, W (and now T) was actually *using* the land for a particular purpose (i.e., to record the results of an experiment).

Even assuming the grant to W was an easement, A could contend that it was an easement in gross (rather than an appurtenant easement (pp. 201-02)). Such easements are ordinarily *non-assignable*. Easements in gross are those which *personally* benefit the holder thereof (as opposed to easements appurtenant, which primarily benefit the latter's *land*). The grant in question appears to have been made for the purpose of facilitating W's experiment (rather than enhancing the use or accessibility of Laurel Hill). While T could argue that the use of Laurel Hill is enhanced by having the right to permit animals involved in experimentation to cross into adjoining land, A's grant would probably be characterized as an easement in gross.

T might contend, however, that even assuming the grant to W was deemed to be an easement in gross, it should be viewed as being "commercial" in nature (p. 220). Such interests have been deemed to be assignable where, for example, a severe disruption to a utility (i.e., telephone and sewer lines) would occur if assignment were not allowed. Although T could contend that maintenance of the fence by A would disrupt an experiment which has been carried on for a 14-year period, it is unlikely that T's easement in gross would be considered "commercial." Thus, A would probably prevail on this question.

Finally, T might argue that A's written statement to W, whereby A had agreed that she would take no action to prevent W's animals from coming upon Sweetholm, constituted a covenant which ran with the benefitted land (p. 228). Since T is seeking an injunction, the covenant must be analyzed as an equitable servitude ("ES") (p. 238-39). For the benefit of an ES to run against the covenantor: (1) the original parties must have intended it to run (p. 244), and (2) it must touch and concern (affect the value or use) of the burdened land (p. 242). Although there was no "successors, heirs and assigns" language, some courts take the view that where the promise touches and concerns the burdened parcel, the original parties probably intended for the covenantor's promise to run with the benefitted land. The value and use of Sweetholm is arguably diminished by the fact that wild animals could roam free on a portion of the land. However, A could probably successfully contend in rebuttal that there was no intent that the promise run with the land since it was given specifically to W for the purpose of permitting the latter to complete *his* experimentation.

Thus, T probably *cannot* obtain an injunction against A.

Ownership of Sweetholm: Richard (Ludwig's sole heir) could contend that the conveyance by Vladimir to Josiah was a fee tail (since the grant to Josiah is followed by the words "and the heirs of his body") (pp. 53). Therefore, when Josiah died without issue (J was merely his niece, rather than a lineal descendant), Sweetholm became the property of Ludwig (and his heirs).

A could argue in rebuttal that in many states the fee tail has been abolished entirely, and it is viewed as a fee simple absolute (p. 54). In such case, Josiah would have been entitled to transfer the property to J. In other jurisdictions, however, the failure to have issue results in the estate terminating upon the death of the originally designated party (p. 54). Under the latter view, Ludwig's heirs (Richard) would obtain title to Sweetholm upon Josiah's death. However, in such instance A could probably claim superior title to Sweetholm through AP. While it is not clear when Josiah died and J succeeded to possession of Sweetholm, the facts do indicate that A has apparently occupied the realty for 11 years and paid taxes on it (p. 29). Having purchased the land from J, A presumably went into possession of Sweetholm under color of title (p. 31). It therefore appears that A could defeat any claim of Richard to the property. Richard's remainder is vested, so it is not subject to the Rule Against Perpetuities (pp. 93).

Josef could, however, contend that J had a fee simple determinable (pp. 48-49) or fee simple subject to a condition subsequent (p. 50) with respect to the provision pertaining to animals, and that the triggering event occurred when D retained one of the animals for a two-week period. However, A could contend in rebuttal that whichever future interest was held by Josef is unenforceable because implicit in the grant was that the *grantee* (rather than some other person who undertook such conduct without the owner's knowledge or consent) would not "keep" animals on Sweetholm. A should prevail on this argument, and therefore it is unlikely that Josef could presently claim paramount title to Sweetholm.

ANSWER TO QUESTION 3

(1) *Dale v. Art (quiet title action):* In an action by Dale ("D") to quiet title to Greenacre ("G/A") against Art ("A"), A can be expected to contend that Bob ("B") could not have conveyed G/A to D because no conveyance of G/A was made to B; and thus B had nothing to transfer to D. A transfer of land does not occur until there is delivery (completion of a valid deed by the grantor, with the intention that it be immediately operative) and acceptance of the deed by the grantee (pp. 342, 347). Where an escrow has been established, there is usually a presumption that the grantor intended that the deed *not* be immediately operative until the conditions of the escrow are satisfied. Since the condition precedent to the deed being operative (the payment of $5,000 by B) never occurred, B never acquired title to G/A to transfer to D.

D, however, could contend that A should be ***equitably estopped*** from denying that the transfer to D was invalid. Some states have adopted the rule that where a grantee wrongfully acquires a deed from an escrow holder chosen by the grantor and then conveys the land to a bona fide purchaser ("BFP"), the grantor is estopped from denying the validity of the transfer against the latter (p. 346). Assuming D parted with present consideration to acquire G/A (the facts are silent on this point), D would seem to be a BFP (since the land was vacant, a visit to G/A would not have put D upon inquiry notice of A's ownership interest). Also, since A had given B a warranty deed (as opposed to a quitclaim deed), D would have no reason to investigate B's title beyond a search of the grantor-grantee index.

Assuming D were a BFP, D would additionally contend that there is a maxim in the law that where one of two innocent parties must suffer, the loss should fall upon the more blameworthy person; and that such person is A since (1) A chose Carl, who incorrectly parted with possession of the deed, and (2) by giving Carl a "clean" deed (one with no conditions upon the face of it), A should have realized that it would be possible for B, if he ever obtained the deed from Carl, to "sell" G/A. While A might contend in rebuttal that escrows are a common device for transferring ownership of land and that Carl, as a real estate broker, should have been well aware of the potential for harm if the deed left his possession, D should prevail in his quiet title action against A (even though no actual conveyance took place).

(2a.) *Art v. Carl ("C")*: A would probably sue C for breach of contract and negligence. With respect to the former, C could contend that he has no liability because (1) no contract ever arose between him and A, since C (apparently) received no consideration, and (2) in any event, the Statute of Frauds (which pertains to the sale of land (pp. 312)) was never satisfied, since C never signed the statement prepared by A. However, it would probably be implied into the A-C arrangement that the latter would receive a reasonable compensation for this efforts on behalf of A and B. Additionally, equitable estoppel could probably be successfully asserted to overcome these contentions, since A detrimentally relied upon C to act as escrow agent.

While C might next assert that A's damages are limited to $5,000 (the amount he would have received if the escrow had closed), rather than the enhanced value of the land, A should be able to successfully argue in rebuttal that since the conditions for the close of the escrow were never satisfied, he would have been able to recover the deed back (p. 345). Therefore, he should be able to recover the present fair market value of G/A from C.

A would also contend that C, by agreeing to act as escrow agent, assumed a duty to A that he would not leave A in a worsened position; and so when C did, he became liable to A in negligence. While C might contend that he could only foresee damages of $5,000, A could probably successfully argue in rebuttal that C should have foreseen that (1) misdelivery of the deed could result in greater damages to A since A would have obtained the deed back at the conclusion of the escrow period, and (2) G/A might appreciate in value. Thus A's damages would again be the reasonable value of G/A.

(2b.) *D v. C:* If D paid consideration for the deed received from B and lost his quiet title action against A, he would probably sue C in negligence for permitting B to obtain control of A's deed; and thereby defraud D of whatever consideration he paid to B. While C might argue that he had no duty to D (who did not rely upon C) and that B's fraudulent actions were the actual cause of D's loss, D should be able to recover from C the consideration which was given to B (C should have reasonably foreseen that B might misuse A's deed, especially since it was absolute on its face).

MULTISTATE-STYLE QUESTIONS

Here are 26 multiple-choice questions, in a Multistate-Bar-Exam style. These questions are taken from *"The Finz Multistate Method"*, a compendium of 1100 questions in the Multistate subjects (*Contracts*, *Torts*, *Property*, *Evidence*, *Criminal Law* and *Constitutional Law*) written by Professor Steven Finz of National University School of Law, San Diego, CA, and published by us. This book is available at your bookstore or from Emanuel Law Outlines, Inc. directly.

Questions 1-2 are based on the following fact situation.

Givers executed a deed to his realty known as Givacre, which contained the following clause:

"To Senior Center, for so long as the realty shall be used as a home for the elderly, but if racial discrimination is practiced in the admission of residents to said home, to Senior Life for so long as the realty shall be sued as a home for the elderly."

Senior Center and Senior Life were both charitable institutions devoted to the needs of indigent elderly persons.

1. On the day after the deed was executed, Givers' interest in Givacre is best described as

   (A) a valid reversion.

   (B) a valid possibility of reverter.

   (C) a valid right of re-entry.

   (D) void under the Rule Against Perpetuities.

2. On the day after the deed was executed, Senior Life's interest in Givacre is best described as a

   (A) valid contingent remainder.

   (B) valid executory interest.

   (C) void contingent remainder.

   (D) void executory interest.

Questions 3-4 are based on the following fact situation.

On March 1, Marcel conveyed a tract of realty to her daughters Andrea and Bessie as joint tenants. On April 1, Marcel purported to sell the same tract of realty to Parton by general warranty deed. Parton paid cash for the property, and was unaware of the prior conveyance to Marcel's daughters. Andrea and Bessie recorded their deed on April 3. Parton recorded his deed on April 5. Andrea died on April 7.

3. Assume for the purpose of this question only that the jurisdiction has ONE of the following statutes:

   I. "No conveyance of real property is effective against a subsequent purchaser for value and without notice unless the same be recorded."

   II. "Every conveyance of real estate is void as against any subsequent purchaser in good faith and for value whose conveyance is first duly recorded."

   Is Bessie's right superior to Parton's on April 8?

   (A) Yes, only if the jurisdiction has Statute I.

   (B) Yes, only if the jurisdiction has Statute II.

   (C) Yes, if the jurisdiction has Statute I or Statute II.

   (D) No.

4. Assume for the purpose of this question only that the jurisdiction has a statute which provides, "In determining the priority of conflicting interests in land, the first such interest to have been recorded shall have priority." Who has priority on April 8?

(A) Bessie, because the conveyance to Andrea and Bessie was recorded before the conveyance to Parton was recorded.

(B) Bessie, because the realty was conveyed to Andrea and Bessie before the conveyance to Parton was recorded.

(C) Parton, because Bessie's interest was recorded.

(D) Parton, because Marcel conveyed to him by general warranty deed.

5. After working twenty years for the People's Trust Company, Singer was promoted from assistant manager of the Twin Oaks branch located in another state. When he learned that Bryant was moving to Twin Oaks to replace him as assistant manager, he offered to sell Bryant his home in Twin Oaks for $60,000. After inspecting the premises, Bryant accepted the offer. They entered into a written contract of sale calling for closing of title six weeks after the signing of the contract. Because their employer was eager to have them both start at their new positions as soon as possible, the contract contained a clause permitting Bryant to move into the house immediately. Bryant did so a few days after signing the contract of sale. Singer kept the fire insurance policy on the house in effect, planning to cancel it upon conveying title to Bryant. In addition, Bryant purchased a policy of fire insurance on the house immediately after contracting for purchase of the house. Two weeks after Bryant moved in, a fire of unknown origin partially destroyed a portion of the roof, the entire kitchen, and parts of the exterior of the house. Bryant immediately notified Singer that he was unwilling to complete the transaction at the price originally agreed upon, but that he would be willing to renegotiate to determine a new price based on the diminished value of the real estate as the result of the fire.

If Singer sues for damages based upon Bryant's anticipatory repudiation of the contract of sale, the court should find for

(A) Singer, since the risk of loss passed to Bryant when he took possession of the premises pursuant to the contract.

(B) Singer, since Bryant purchased a policy of fire insurance covering the premises prior to the contract.

(C) Bryant, since Singer had a policy of insurance insuring him against fire damage to the house.

(D) Bryant, since the risk of loss never passed to Bryant.

Questions 6-8 are based on the following fact situation.

Several years ago, the Johnson Chemical Company developed a plan to use underground pipes for the purpose of transporting non-poisonous chemical wastes to a waste storage center located several miles away from its plant. At that time, it began negotiating for the right to lay an underground pipeline for that purpose across several tracts of realty. In return for a cash payment, the owner of Westacre executed a right-of-way deed for the installation and maintenance of the pipeline across his land. The right-of-way deed to Johnson Chemical Company was properly recorded. Westacre passed through several intermediate conveyances until it was conveyed to Sofield about fifteen years after the recording of the right-of-way deed. All of the intermediate deeds were recorded, but none mentioned the right-of-way.

Two years later, Sofield agreed to sell Westacre to Belden, by a written contract in which, among other things, Sofield agreed to furnish Belden with an abstract company, to prepare the abstract. Titleco prepared an abstract and delivered it to Sofield. The abstract omitted any mention of the right-of-way deed. Sofield delivered the abstract of title to Belden. After examining the abstract, Beldon paid the full purchase price to Sofield who conveyed Westacre to Belden by a deed which included covenants of general warranty and against encumbrances. At the time of closing, Sofield, Belden, and Titleco were all unaware of the existence of the right-of-way deed. After possessing Westacre for nearly a year, Belden was notified by the Johnson Chemical Company that it planned to begin installation of an underground pipeline on its right-of-way across Westacre.

6. Assume for the purpose of this question only that Belden subsequently asserted a claim against Titleco for damages which Belden sustained as a result of the existence of the right-of-way. The court should find for

(A) Titleco, because it was unaware of the existence of the right-of-way deed.

(B) Titleco, because the right-of-way deed was outside the chain of title.

(C) Belden, because Belden was a third party beneficiary of the contract between Sofield and Titleco.

(D) Belden, because the deed executed by Sofield contained a covenant against encumbrances.

7. If Belden sues Sofield because of the presence of the right-of-way, the most likely result will be a decision for

(A) Sofield, because Belden relied on the abstract of title prepared by Titleco in purchasing Westacre.

(B) Sofield, because Sofield was without knowledge of any defects in the title to Westacre.

(C) Belden, because the covenants in Sofield's deed to Belden were breached.

(D) Belden, because Sofield negligently misrepresented the condition of title to Westacre.

8. Assume for the purpose of this question only that Belden sued for an injunction prohibiting the installation of the underground pipeline across Westacre. Which one of the following additional facts or inferences, if it was the only one true, which would be most likely to lead the court to issue the injunction?

(A) The Johnson Chemical Company sold its entire business to another company which was planning to continue operating the business exactly as Johnson had operated it, and it was the new company which was attempting to install the underground pipeline.

(B) The Johnson Chemical Company's operation had changed since the conveyance of the right-of-way, and it was now

planning to use the pipeline for the transportation of poisonous wastes.

(C) No use of the right-of-way has been made since the conveyance eighteen years ago, and the law of the jurisdiction sets a ten year period for acquiring title by adverse possession or acquiring an easement by prescription.

(D) In purchasing Westacre Belden detrimentally relied on the absence of any visible encumbrances, and the installation of an underground pipeline will result in substantial reduction in the value of the realty.

9. Lance Industries completed construction of a new office building and rented the entire ground floor to Tollup, an attorney, under a three year lease which fixed rent at six hundred dollars per month. Lance was unable to obtain a tenant to rent any other space in the building. Six months later, Tollup vacated the premises. In a claim by Lance against Tollup for rent for the balance of the term, which one of the following additional facts if it were the only one true, would be most likely to result in a judgment for Tollup?

(A) The day after Tollup vacated, Lance rented the ground floor to another attorney on a month-to-month basis at a rent of five hundred dollars per month.

(B) The day after Tollup vacated, Lance began using the ground floor as a management office for the building.

(C) The reason Tollup vacated was that the building was located in a part of town not easily accessible by public transportation, and as a result many of Tollup's client refused to travel to see him there.

(D) The reason Tollup vacated was that he had been disbarred and was disqualified from the practice of law.

10. Lardner rented a warehouse to Torrelson pursuant to a lease which fixed the rent at five hundred dollars payable at the beginning of each month. The lease contained a provision stating that in the event Torrelson failed to pay rent as agreed, Lardner had the right to terminate the tenancy and re-enter the premises. After Torrelson missed two rent

payments, Lardner threatened to institute an eviction proceeding unless the unpaid rent was paid immediately. The following day, Torrelson moved out, sending Lardner a check for one thousand dollars in payment of rent already owing. Also enclosed was a letter which stated that it was Torrelson's intention to surrender the premises immediately, and an additional check for five hundred dollars in payment of the following month's rent. Lardner made no attempt to re-rent the warehouse, and it remained vacant for the balance of the term of Torrelson's lease. Upon its expiration, Lardner asserted a claim against Torrelson for unpaid rent from the date Torrelson vacated until the end of the lease term.

In deciding Lardner's claim against Torrelson, the court should find for

(A) Lardner, since Torrelson failed to pay the rent as agreed.

(B) Lardner, since the lease reserved a right of re-entry.

(C) Torrelson, since the lease reserved Lardner's right of re-entry.

(D) Torrelson, since, in effect, he gave Lardner a month's notice of his intention to vacate.

11. The City of Hampshire owned land known as Hampshire Heights which was located outside the city limits, east of the city itself. Because the Hampshire River ran along the western edge of Hampshire Heights, the City of Hampshire built a bridge across the river more than fifty years ago. The eastern part of Hampshire Heights had once been used as a storage yard for city maintenance equipment, and was surrounded by an eight foot chain link fence. The part of Hampshire Heights between the fenced yard and the bridge had been used primarily as a dirt road connecting the bridge to the storage yard.

Due to periodic flooding of the Hampshire River, the City of Hampshire stopped using the Hampshire Heights storage yard and bridge thirty years ago. At that time, Adpo built a wooden shack on that portion of Hampshire Heights which had formerly been used as a dirt road between the storage yard and the bridge. Since then, Adpo has been living in the shack, and has been raising donkeys on the land formerly used as a dirt road. In addition, he planted a vegetable garden which produced food for himself and his donkeys.

Earlier this year, the City of Hampshire decided to begin using the Hampshire Heights storage yard again, and demanded that Adpo remove himself and his possessions. Adpo refused, asserting that by adverse possession he had become the owner of the land which he occupied. A statute in the jurisdiction conditions ownership by adverse possession on twenty years' continuous, hostile, open and notorious possession.

If the City of Hampshire institutes a proceeding to eject Adpo from Hampshire Heights, the outcome is most likely to turn on whether

(A) the City of Hampshire had knowledge that Adpo was in possession of part of Hampshire Heights.

(B) the jurisdiction permits the acquisition of city property by adverse possession.

(C) Adpo paid taxes on the land which he occupied.

(D) Adpo occupied Hampshire Heights under color of title.

12. Soon after Harold and Wilhemina married, they became interested in the purchase of a home with a price of $75,000. Because neither of them had been employed for very long, they were unable to find a bank to lend them money for the purchase. The seller indicated that he would be willing to accept a note for part of the purchase price if Harold and Wilhemina could obtain an acceptable co-signor.

Wilhemina's mother Marion said that she would give them the money for the down payment and co-sign the note if Wilhemina and Harold promised to make all payments on the note as they came due, and if the three of them took title to the property as joint tenants. All agreed. On the day title closed, Marion paid $25,000 cash to the seller, and she, Harold, and Wilhemina all signed a note promising to pay the balance, secured by a mortgage on the realty which they all executed. The seller executed a deed conveying the realty to Harold, Wilhemina, and Marion as joint tenants.

Harold and Wilhemina moved into the house, but Marion never did. The following year Marion died, leaving a will purporting to devise her interest in the realty to her husband Allan. The year after that, Wilhemina and Harold were divorced. Wilhemina subsequently executed a deed purporting to convey her interest in the realty to Bernard. Harold subsequently executed a deed purporting to convey his interest in the realty to Charles.

Which of the following best describes the interests of Allan, Bernard, and Charles in the realty?

(A) Allan, Bernard, and Charles are tenants in common, each holding a one-third interest.

(B) Bernard and Charles are tenants in common, each holding a one-half interest.

(C) Bernard and Charles are joint tenants as to a two-thirds interest, and tenants in common as to a one-third interest.

(D) Allan, Bernard and Charles are joint tenants, each holding a one-third interest.

13. In 1970, Altman moved onto Odette's realty and constructed a dwelling without Odette's permission. Since then, she has lived there continuously, openly, and notoriously. In 1977, Odette died, leaving the realty to his 2-year-old son Stephen. At that time Grayson was appointed as Stephen's legal guardian. In 1980, Grayson became aware that Altman was in possession of the realty which Stephen had inherited from Odette. In 1986, after Altman had been in possession of the realty for 16 years, Grayson sued on Stephen's behalf to eject Altman. In her defense, Altman asserted that she had become the owner of the realty by adverse possession.

Has Altman become the owner of the realty by adverse possession?

(A) No, because the statutory period will not begin to run against Stephen until he achieves majority at the age of 18 years.

(B) No, because the statutory period began to run against Stephen when he inherited the realty in 1977.

(C) No, because the statutory period began to run against Stephen when Grayson became aware that Altman was in possession of the realty in 1980.

(D) Yes.

14. Larrick executed a document purporting to lease a parcel of real estate to Teeter for fifty years at an annual rent of $1,000. Twenty years before the scheduled expiration of the lease, the entire parcel was taken by the state for the construction of a reservoir. At a condemnation proceeding, the trier of the facts found that the balance of Teeter's leasehold was valued at $30,000. Of the total condemnation award, Teeter should receive

(A) $30,000, but Teeter will be required to pay Larrick a sum equivalent to the rent for the balance of the lease term.

(B) nothing, because Teeter's interest violates the Rule Against Perpetuities.

(C) $30,000, and Teeter will have no further obligation to Larrick.

(D) $30,000 minus a sum equivalent to the rent for the balance of the lease term, and Teeter will have no further obligation to Larrick.

Questions 15-16 are based on the following fact situation.

Upton is the owner of a hillside parcel of realty known as Slopeacre, on which he grows apples for sale to a company which makes juice from them. For several years, Upton has been irrigating his apple trees with water from a stream which flows across Slopeacre. After flowing across Slopeacre, the stream flows through Flatacre, a parcel of realty located in the valley below Slopeacre. Downey, who owns Flatacre, lives there with his family. Downey's family uses water from the stream for household purposes. This year, Upton informed Downey that he was planning to build a small dam across the stream so that he would be able to pump water out of it more easily for irrigating his apple trees. Downey immediately instituted a proceeding to prevent Upton from constructing the dam.

The jurisdiction determines water rights by

applying the common law.

15. If it were the only one true, which of the following additional facts or inferences would be most likely to cause a court to grant the relief requested by Downey?

(A) Construction of a dam will increase Upton's consumption of water from the stream.

(B) Construction of a dam will change the natural flow of the stream.

(C) Construction of a dam will cause Upton to consume more water from the stream than is reasonably necessary for the enjoyment of Slopeacre.

(D) Upton can continue to pump water from the stream without constructing a dam.

16. Assume for the purpose of this question only that because of a drought there is enough water in the stream to satisfy the needs of either Flatacre or Slopeacre, but not both, and that there are no other riparian owners. Who is entitled to use the water?

(A) Upton, because he is the upstream owner.

(B) Upton, because he needs the water for agricultural use.

(C) Downey, because he needs the water for household use.

(D) Downey, because he is the downstream owner.

17. When Fletcher died he left his farm to his son Sam for life with remainder to Unity Church. Because Fletcher had been a farmer, Sam tried farming the land for a while, but found the work unpleasant. Although gravel had never before been mined or removed from the land, Sam learned that he could derive a substantial income by doing so. He therefore dug a deep and extensive pit on the land from which he began removing gravel for sale to builders and other commercial purchasers.

If Unity Church asserts a claim against Sam because of his removal of gravel the court should

(A) grant Unity Church a proportionate share of any profits derived from the sale of gravel removed from the land.

(B) issue an injunction against further removal of gravel and order Sam to account to Unity Church for profits already derived from the sale of gravel removed from the land.

(C) deny relief to Unity Church, because no right of action will accrue until Unity Church's interest becomes possessory at the termination of Sam's estate.

(D) deny relief to Unity Church, because a life tenant is entitled to remove minerals from an open pit.

18. Oscar, the owner of a summer beach cabin, conveyed it to his daughter Debra as a gift for her sixteenth birthday. Two years later, on her eighteenth birthday, Debra went to the cabin for the first time and found Adamo in possession of it. When she asked what he was doing there, Adamo said, "Anyone who lives around here can tell you that I've been coming here every summer." In fact, Adamo had occupied the beach cabin every summer for the past ten years, but had not occupied the cabin during other seasons. Debra instituted a proceeding to evict Adamo. In defense, Adamo claimed that he had acquired title to the cabin by adverse possession. Statutes in the jurisdiction fix the period for acquiring title to realty by adverse possession at 10 years and the age of majority at 18 years.

Has Adamo acquired title by adverse possession.

(A) No, because computation of the period of adverse possession begins anew each time there is a change in ownership of the realty.

(B) No, because for the past two years the owner of the cabin was under a legal disability.

(C) Yes, if occupancy only during the summer was consistent with the appropriate use of the cabin.

(D) Yes, if Adamo had Oscar's permission to occupy the cabin during the summers.

19. Lenox was the owner of a commercial building which he leased to Ashdown for use as a retail shoe store for a period of five years. In the lease, Ashdown covenanted not to assign the premises without Lenox's written consent. A clause of the lease reserved Lenox's right to terminate the lease in the event of a breach of this covenant. Two years after Ashdown began occupancy, he sold the business to Boyer, his store manager. After obtaining Lenox's written consent, Ashdown assigned the balance of the lease to Boyer. Boyer operated the shoe store for several months and then sold it to Cole. As part of the sale, Boyer executed a document purporting to transfer to Cole all remaining rights under the lease. Boyer did not obtain Lenox's permission for this transfer. When Lenox learned of this transfer to Cole, he instituted a proceeding in which he sought Cole's eviction on the ground that the covenant not to assign had been violated.

(A) The covenant against assignment is void as a restraint against alienation.

(B) Lenox's only remedy is an action against Boyer for damages resulting from breach of the covenant.

(C) Lenox waived his rights under the covenant by consenting to the assignment by Ashdown to Boyerl.

(D) The transfer by Boyer to Cole was not an assignment but a sublease.

Questions 20-21 are based on the following fact situation.

Owsley was the owner of a large tract of realty with its southernmost boundary fronting on a public road. Owsley divided the tract into two parcels, one to the north of the other. Owsley named the southernmost parcel, which fronted on the public road, Southacre. He named the northernmost parcel Northacre, and sold it to Archer. Northacre did not have road frontage, and was accessible only by a visible dirt road which crossed Southacre. The deed by which Owsley conveyed Northacre to Archer contained language granting a right-of-way easement over the dirt road. Several years after purchasing Northacre, Archer purchased Southacre from Owsley. Archer never occupied Northacre and never used the dirt road which crossed Southacre.

20. Assume for the purposes of this question only that Archer subsequently sold Northacre to Barnhart by a deed which made no mention of a right-of-way easement across Southacre. If Barnhart claims that he received a right-of-way easement over Southacre, which of the following would be Barnhart's best argument in support of that claim?

(A) The visible dirt road across Southacre which provided access to Northacre was a quasi-easement.

(B) Since there was no other access to Northacre, Barnhart received an easement by implied reservation.

(C) Since there was no other access to Northacre, Barnhart received an easement by necessity.

(D) The grant of a right-of-way easement across Southacre contained in the deed by which Owsley conveyed Northacre to Archer benefits all subsequent purchasers of Northacre.

21. Assume for the purpose of this question only that Coates subsequently contracted to purchase Southacre from Archer, that Coates inspected Southacre and saw the dirt road which crossed it prior to contracting, and that the purchase contract made no mention of an easement or of the quality of title to be conveyed. Assume further that prior to closing of title, Coates refused to go through with the transaction on the ground that the existence of an easement across Southacre made Archer's title unmarketable. If Archer asserts a claim against Coates for breach of contract, which of the following would be Archer's most effective argument in support of his claim?

(A) A contract to purchase real property merges with the deed by which the title is conveyed.

(B) Coates had notice of the easement at the time he entered into the contract to purchase Southacre.

(C) The existence of an easement does not make title unmarketable.

(D) The purchase contract did not specify the quality of title to be conveyed.

Questions 22-24 are based on the following fact situation.

Zoning laws in Green City provided that all land on the north side of Main Street was restricted to residential use, and that commercial use was permitted on all land on the south side of Main Street. The zoning laws also provided that up two horses could be kept on any land zoned for residential use, but that no business could be operated on land zoned for residential use. Although all the other realty on the south side of Main Street was being put to commercial use, Homer owned and resided in a one story house located on the south side of Main Street.

Green Hills was a housing development located on the north side of Main Street. All deeds to realty in Green Hills contained language prohibiting the keeping of horses anywhere within the subdivision. The subdivision plan which had been filed when Green Hills was created provided that persons occupying realty in Green Hills were permitted to operate small businesses in their homes so long as such operation did not interfere with or annoy other residents in the subdivision.

22. Assume for the purposes of this question only that Typer operated a typing service from an office in her home in Green Hills, and that Foley entered into a contract to buy Typer's typing service and home. After entering into the contract of sale, however, Foley learned of the zoning law which prohibited the operation of any business in a residential zone. He immediately informed Typer that he would not go through with the purchase of Typer's home because of the zoning violation. If Typer asserts a claim against Foley for breach of contract, the court should find for

(A) Foley, because the purchaser of realty cannot be forced to buy a potential litigation.

(B) Foley, but only if he could not have discovered the zoning violation by reasonable inquiry prior to entering into the contract of sale.

(C) Typer, because the zoning law which prohibited the operation of Typer's business existed before the contract of sale was formed.

(D) Typer, because her business was

permitted by provisions of the Green Hills subdivision plan.

23. Assume for the purpose of this question only that Graves purchased the land owned by Homer, tore down the existing house, and began construction of a three story office building. Kaham, who operated a business known as a water slide on the adjacent realty, objected on the ground that the building which Graves was constructing would block off Kaham's air and light, thus diminishing the value of his realty. If Kaham commences an appropriate proceeding against Graves seeking an order which would prohibit construction of the building, the court should find for

(A) Graves if the construction of a three story office building is permitted by the zoning law.

(B) Graves because commercial use of the realty is the highest and best use.

(C) Kaham, because previous use by Homer created an implied easement for air, light, and view.

(D) Kaham, if residential use by Homer was a continuing non-conforming use.

24. Assume for the purpose of this question only that Equis, a resident of Green Hills, began keeping horses in his yard. If his neighbor, Ralph, commences a proceeding in which he seeks an order preventing Equis from keeping horses, the court should find for

(A) Equis because the zoning law permits the keeping of horses.

(B) Equis only if keeping horses is part of ordinary residential use.

(C) Ralph because of the language in Equis's deed which prohibits the keeping of horses.

(D) Ralph only if keeping horses is a nuisance.

Questions 25-26 are based on the following fact situation.

Olsen conveyed a parcel of realty "to Geller so long as liquor is not sold on the premises, but if liquor is

sold on the premises, to the Foundation for Hereditary Diseases." Two years later, Geller began selling liquor on the premises.

25. Which of the following best describes Geller's
    interest in the realty on the day before he
    began selling liquor on the premises?

    (A) void, since the interest of the Foundation
        for Hereditary Diseases could have
        vested more than 21 years after the
        death of all persons who were in being
        at the time of the conveyance.

    (B) fee simple absolute.

    (C) fee simple determinable on special limita-
        tion, since Geller's interest will ter-
        minate if liquor is ever sold on the prem-
        ises.

    (D) fee simple subject to a condition subse-
        quent, which will ripen into a fee simple
        absolute if liquor is not sold during a
        period measured by a life or lives in
        being plus twenty-one years.

26. Which of the following best describes the
    interest of the Foundation for Hereditary
    Diseases in the realty on the day after Geller
    began selling liquor on the premises?

    (A) fee simple absolute if the Foundation for
        Hereditary Diseases is a charity.

    (B) right of re-entry.

    (C) no interest, since at the time of the con-
        veyance it was possible that the interest
        which the deed purported to grant to the
        Foundation for Hereditary Diseases
        would not vest within a period measured
        by a life or lives in being plus twenty-
        one years.

    (D) shifting executory interest which will not
        become possessory until the Foundation
        for Hereditary Diseases takes some step
        to exercise its right.

ANSWERS
TO MULTISTATE-STYLE QUESTIONS

1. **B** A reversion is a future interest of the grantor which will automatically follow a prior estate which will inevitably terminate (e.g., a life estate; a leasehold). A possibility of reverter is a future interest of the grantor which will automatically follow a prior estate which will not inevitably terminate (e.g., fee simple determinable). A right of re-entry is a future interest of the grantor which does not revert automatically, but which requires some act by the grantor in order for him/her to re-acquire a possessory right, and which follows an estate which will not inevitably terminate. Since the property was conveyed only for so long as it is used as a home for the elderly, it will automatically revert to the grantor if that use is ever discontinued. It is, thus, either a reversion or a possibility of reverter. Since it is not certain that it ever will cease to be used as a home for the elderly, however, the prior estate is not one which will inevitably terminate. For this reason, the grantor's interest is a possibility of reverter. **B** is, therefore, correct, and **A** is, therefore, incorrect. **C** is incorrect because if the property ever ceases to be used as a home for the elderly, no act of the grantor is necessary to make his interest possessory. **D** is incorrect because the Rule against Perpetuities does not apply to a grantor's interest.

2. **B** A remainder is a future interest in a grantee which will automatically become possessory following a prior estate which will terminate inevitably (e.g., a life estate). An executory interest is a future interest in a grantee which will not automatically become possessory and which follows a prior estate which will not terminate inevitably. Since the interest of Senior Life will only become possessory if racial discrimination is practiced by Senior Center, and since this may never happen, the interest of Senior Life is best classified as a executory interest. **A** and **C** are, therefore, incorrect. Under the Rule Against Perpetuities, no interest is good unless it must vest, if at all, during a period measured by a life or lives in being plus 21 years. Since Senior Center might begin practicing racial discrimination after the period proscribed by the Rule, the interest of Senior Life seems to violate the Rule. Because of an exception, however, the Rule Against Perpetuities does not apply to the interest of a charity which follows the interest of a charity. Since Senior Center and Senior Life are both charitable institutions, the Rule Against Perpetuities does not apply, and the interest of Senior Life is valid. **B** is, therefore, correct, and **D** is, therefore, incorrect.

3. **B** Under Statute I (a pure notice type statute), Parton's interest would be superior to Bessie's because while Bessie's interest was unrecorded, he purchased for value and without notice of the prior conveyance. Under Statute II (a race-notice type statute) Bessie's interest would be superior even though Parton purchased for value and in good faith (i.e., without notice of the prior conveyance), because Parton's interest was not recorded before Bessie's.

4. **A** Under this recording statute (a pure race type statute), the first interest recorded is superior. Bessie's interest derives from the deed which was recorded on April 3. Since Parton's deed was not recorded until April 5, Bessie's interest had priority.

   B is incorrect because under a race type statute, all that matters is the order in which the interests were recorded. **C** is incorrect because Bessie's interest derives from the deed which was recorded on April 3. The general warranty deed by which Marcel conveyed to Parton will determine Parton's rights against Marcel. But **D** is incorrect because the recording statute determines the rights of Marcel and Bessie as against each other.

5.   A   Whether they apply the doctrine of equitable conversion, the Uniform Vendor and Purchaser Risk Act, or some other system for apportioning the risk of loss under a real estate sales contract, all jurisdictions agree that the risk of loss from causes other than the fault of the vendor passes to the vendee when he takes possession of the realty prior to closing.

             B and C are incorrect because passage of the risk of loss does not depend on the purchase of fire insurance by either party. D is incorrect because the risk of loss passed to Bryant when he took possession of the realty.

6.   C   Some jurisdictions hold that an abstractor of title impliedly warrants the abstract to be accurate; all jurisdictions agree that there is at least an implied warranty that the service will be performed in a reasonable manner. Since the right-of-way deed was properly recorded, Titleco's failure to include it in the abstract which it furnished was a breach of either the promise to perform reasonably or the implied warranty of accuracy. In either event, since Belden was an intended creditor beneficiary of the contract between Sofield and Titleco, Belden can enforce it.

             If there was an implied warranty of accuracy A is incorrect because liability is imposed without fault for its breach. If there was no implied warranty of accuracy, A is incorrect because liability may be imposed if Titleco's lack of awareness of the right-of-way resulted from its failure to act reasonably. Since the right-of-way deed from the owner of Westacre to Johnson Chemical Company was properly recorded before any of the grants of Westacre took place, it was not outside the chain of title, and B is incorrect. D is incorrect because the liability of Titleco does not depend on covenants made by Sofield.

7.   C   The covenant against encumbrances is a representation that there are no easements or liens burdening the realty. If the realty is, in fact, burdened by such an encumbrance, the covenant is breached and liability is imposed on the covenantor.

             This is so even though the purchaser relied on assurances in addition to the covenant, and even though the grantor was unaware of the existence of the encumbrance at the time he executed the covenant. A and B are, therefore, incorrect. D is incorrect because there is no indication that Sofield failed to act reasonably (i.e., was "negligent").

8.   B   The holder of an easement may not unreasonably burden the servient estate by using it in a way not contemplated when the easement was created. Since the dangers incident to the possible leakage of poisonous materials are much greater than those incident to the possible leakage of non-poisonous materials, the change in Johnson's intended use would unreasonably burden the estate of Belden.

             Since most jurisdictions agree that commercial easements in gross may be freely alienated, A is incorrect. Non-use of an easement created by express grant is not sufficient to terminate it unless the holder of the easement was created by deed which was properly recorded, Belden had constructive notice of it when he purchased, and would not have been justified in relying on the absence of visible encumbrances. D is, therefore, incorrect.

9.   B   Ordinarily, a tenant who abandons the premises before the expiration of the lease is liable for rent for the balance of the term. If, however, the landlord *surrenders* its rights under the lease, the tenant will be free from liability for the balance of the term. A surrender generally takes place when the landlord occupies the premises for its own purposes.

             Reletting the premises for the balance of the term might also result in a surrender, but this depends on the intent of the landlord. Here, there was much other vacant space in the building, and the landlord has relet the premises for rent lower than provided in the lease, and on a month-to-month basis. Therefore, it is not likely that Lance's intent was to surrender its rights, but rather, to relet for Tollup's account (as a mitigation of damages). **A** is, therefore, incorrect. The agreement between Lance and Tollup did not restrict use of the premises to any particular activity. For this reason, the fact that the premises are not well suited to the activity which Tollup had in mind, or that Tollup is no longer licensed in the practice for which he planned to use them, is irrelevant to his liability under the lease. **C** and **D** are, therefore, incorrect.

10. **A**   Ordinarily, a tenant who abandons the premises before the expiration of the lease is liable for rent for the balance of the term.

The lease may reserve to the landlord the right to terminate the tenancy and re-enter in the event of non-payment, but **B** is incorrect because this is alternative to the right to collect rent, not the source of it. A landlord who elects to terminate the tenancy, will not be entitled to collect rent for the balance of the term. **C** is incorrect, however, because a landlord may elect not to terminate, as did Lardner, and hold the tenant for rent. **D** is incorrect because neither party to a lease may avoid obligations under it merely by giving notice, unless the lease so provides.

11. **B**   Adpo has been in continuous possession for twenty years. His possession was hostile, because it was contrary to the rights of the City of Hampshire, the land's true owner. It was open and notorious because it was not hidden, and knowledge of his possession could have been obtained by anyone who looked. Having fulfilled all the statutory requirements, he would ordinarily be correct in his assertion that he has acquired title by adverse possession. Most jurisdictions, however, prohibit the acquisition of city or state property by adverse possession. This being the only legal obstacle to Adpo's assertion, the outcome will most likely depend on whether the jurisdiction permits the acquisition of city property by adverse possession.

A is incorrect because if the possession was open and notorious as described above, it does not matter whether the actual owner ever really knew of it. Some adverse possession statutes establish a condition that the adverse possessor pay taxes on the realty during the period of his adverse possession. **C** is incorrect, however, because this statute did not contain such a requirement. An adverse possessor who occupies land under color of title may become the owner of all the land which he believed he owned, including that which he did not actually occupy. Since Adpo asserts ownership only of the land which he occupied, however, color of title is irrelevant, and **D** is incorrect.

12. **B**   Joint tenancy is a form of co-ownership in which the joint tenants have the right of survival. This means that upon the death of one joint tenant, the others receive equal shares in her interest. When Marion died, Harold and Wilhemina received equal shares of her interest. The joint tenancy of Harold and Wilhemina continued, but each held a one-half interest in the whole instead of a one-third interest. Joint tenants may convey their interests inter vivos without each other's consent, but a joint tenant's grantee takes as a tenant in common with the remaining owners. Thus, upon Wilhemina's conveyance to Bernard, Bernard became a tenant in common with a one-half interest; and upon Harold's conveyance to Charles, Charles became a tenant in common with a one-half interest.

A is incorrect because as a joint tenant, Marion could not effectively pass her interest by will. Since a conveyance by a joint tenant makes the grantee a tenant in common, neither Bernard nor Charles received a joint tenancy in any part of the estate. **C** is, therefore, incorrect. **D** is incorrect for this reason, and because Allan received no interest at all under Marion's will.

13. **D** A person may acquire title to realty by adverse possession if she occupies it without its owner's permission openly, notoriously, and continuously for the statutory period of time. This occurs because the running of a statute of limitations then makes it impossible for the adverse possessor to be judicially ejected. Since a new owner acquires the old owner's right to eject an unlawful possessor, the statutory period of limitations continues to run in spite of changes in ownership. For this reason, the fact that Stephen became the owner in 1977 did not restart the period. If the owner of the realty is under a legal disability (e.g., infancy) at the time the adverse possession begins, commencement of the statutory period is delayed until the legal disability has terminated. If the owner is not under a legal disability at the time the possession begins, however, the fact that he subsequently suffers a legal disability, or the fact that title subsequently passes to a person who is under a legal disability will have no effect on the running of the statutory period. Since there is no fact indicating that Odette was under any legal disability in 1970 when Altman began her possession of the realty, the running of the statutory period commenced at that time, and continued without interruption upon the passage of title to Stephen. **D** is, therefore, correct and **A** is, therefore, incorrect. Since only a person with a right of possession can sue to eject an unlawful possessor, the statute of limitations cannot work against the holder of a future interest. Thus, an adverse possessor acquires only the possessory interest which existed at the time of her possession. If, for example, Odette had been the holder of a life estate with a remainder in Stephen, Altman's adverse possession during Odette's life could have led only to Altman's acquisition of a life estate by adverse possession. Then, upon Odette's death in 1977, a new period of possession would have begun against Stephen's fee interest. The will by which Stephen received title spoke only upon Odette's death, however. This means that when Altman began possession in 1970, Stephen had no future interest at all. Since there is no fact to the contrary, Odette's interest must have been a fee when Altman moved on, and it was this fee which Altman acquired by adverse possession. For this reason, **B** is incorrect. **C** is incorrect for the reasons given above, because at the time Altman's adverse possession began, the holder of the fee interest (Odette) was under no disability.

14. **D** If leased realty is taken by eminent domain, the leasehold and the reversion merge in the taker, the leasehold is terminated, and the obligation to pay rent ceases. Since both the lessor and the lessee have had something of value taken for public use, each is entitled to receive just compensation for what s/he has lost. The lessor is entitled to receive the value of the leased premises (including the value of rent to be received) minus the value of the leasehold interest which he has already conveyed. The lessee is entitled to receive the value of the leasehold. If not for the condemnation, however, the lessee would have been required to pay rent in order to enjoy the benefits of her leasehold. Since the condemnation terminates that obligation, the rent which the lessee otherwise would have been required to pay should be deducted from the value of her leasehold.

A is incorrect because the taking terminates the leasehold, and with it, the obligation to pay rent. The Rule Against Perpetuities provides that no interest is good unless it must vest if at all within a period of time measured by a life or lives in being plus twenty-one years. Since a lessee's interest in leased premises vests at the moment the lease is executed, the Rule Against Perpetuities is inapplicable to it. **B** is, therefore, incorrect. Since the condemnation terminates Teeter's obligation to pay rent for the balance of the lease term, allowing her to keep the entire $30,000 would result in her receiving more than she has actually lost. For this reason, **C** is incorrect.

15. **C** Those who own land adjacent to a flowing body of water (i.e., riparian owners) have some rights to use that water. Under modern common law, each riparian owner has the right to make reasonable use of the water. If construction of a dam would result in the consumption of more water than is reasonably necessary, a court might hold that Upton has no

right to build the dam.

A is incorrect because Upton's increased use
of the water might still be reasonable. At one time it was said that no riparian owner was permitted a use which altered the natural flow of the stream. If "natural flow" is given a literal meaning, this would make it virtually impossible for anyone but the furthest downstream owner to use the water. For this reason, the natural flow rule has given way to a rule which bases riparian rights on reasonable use. Thus, even if the dam altered the natural flow, Upton would have a right to construct it so long as his use was reasonable. **B** is, therefore, incorrect. Under the reasonable use test, Upton may dam the stream so long as doing so would not make his water use unreasonable. **D** is incorrect because this would be so even if he could accomplish the same without damming the stream.

16. **C** Under the existing reasonable use doctrine, when it is necessary to determine which riparian owner is entitled to water which is in limited supply, the courts consider many factors. Most important, however, is the use to which each owner puts the water. Although agricultural use is considered "higher" than most other uses, domestic or household use is universally acknowledged to be the "highest" use of all, entitling it to priority over all other uses. Since the choice to be made is between Upton's agricultural use and Downey's household use, Downey's rights will prevail.

A is incorrect because upstream owners do not ordinarily have greater rights than downstream owners. **B** is incorrect because household use is a higher use than agricultural use. **D** is incorrect because with the retreat from the natural flow doctrine, downstream owners do not have greater rights than upstream owners.

17. **B** Voluntary waste consists of some act by a possessory tenant which diminishes the value of the realty or otherwise "injures the inheritance." One of the ways in which it is committed is by removing minerals from the land. Ordinarily, when a life tenant commits voluntary waste, the holder of a vested remainder is entitled to bring an immediate action at law for damages. In the alternative, the remainderman may be entitled to the equitable remedies of injunction and an accounting for profits already derived from the sale of such minerals.

Although it is understood that a possessory tenant may remove minerals from realty which is good for no other purpose, or may continue removing minerals from a mine which was open when his tenancy began, neither of these exceptions applies under the facts in this case. **B** is, therefore, correct. A possessory tenant who commits voluntary waste is not entitled to retain any of the profits from his activity. For this reason, Unity Church is entitled to all profits derived from the sale of gravel, rather than merely to a proportionate share. **A** is, therefore, incorrect. It is sometimes held that the holder of a contingent remainder or a remainder subject to defeasance has no right to sue for waste until its interest vests indefeasibly. Since the remainder interest held by Unity Church is already vested, however, **C** is incorrect. The rule which permits a possessory tenant to continue removing minerals from a mine which was open when he began his tenancy is sometimes known as the "open pit" doctrine. **D** is incorrect, however, because the facts indicate that gravel had never before been mined or removed from the land.

18. **C** Title to property may be acquired by adverse possession if the person claiming such title occupies the realty openly, notoriously, hostilely, and continuously for the statutory period. Possession is "open and notorious" if the possessor has, in general, behaved as an owner. Since Adamo occupied the premises every summer, his possession was open and notorious. Possession is "hostile" if it is contrary to the rights of the owner. Since the facts do not indicate that Adamo had the owner's permission to occupy the cabin, his occupancy was hostile. Although possession must be "continuous," it is not necessary that it be without

interruptions, so long as the interruptions are consistent with the appropriate use of the realty. Since this was a summer cabin, occupancy only during the summers might have been consistent with its appropriate use. If it was, Adamo has acquired title by adverse possession. **C** is, therefore, correct. Once the period of possession has begun, it continues to run in spite of conveyances or other changes in ownership. Thus, **A** is an inaccurate statement and is, therefore, incorrect. If the owner of realty is under a legal disability at the time adverse possession begins, computation of the period of possession does not start until the disability ends. If, however, the owner is not under a legal disability at the time adverse possession begins, subsequent legal disability or legal disability of a subsequent owner does not interrupt the running of the period. **B** is, therefore, incorrect. Because of the requirement that adverse possession be hostile to the rights of the owner, one who occupies with permission of the owner cannot acquire title by adverse possession. **D** is, therefore, incorrect.

19.   C   Under the "Rule in Dumpor's Case," many jurisdictions hold that if a landlord consents to an assignment by the tenant, the covenant against assignment is thereafter waived and the assignee may in turn assign to another without being bound by the covenant. Although it is not certain that the court in this jurisdiction would apply the rule, **C** is the only option listed which could possibly be effective in Cole's defense, and is, therefore, correct. Courts strictly construe restraints against the alienation of leasehold interests. This means that a covenant against assignments does not prevent subleases, and vice versa. **A** is incorrect, however, because although such covenants are strictly construed, they are not void. Ordinarily, an assignment made in violation of a covenant not to assign is valid, and the landlord has no remedy other than an action for damages resulting from the breach. Where, as here, however, the landlord reserves the right to terminate the lease in the event of a violation of the covenant, the assignment is voidable at the landlord's election. **B** is, therefore, incorrect. An assignment is a transfer of all remaining rights under a lease; a sublease is a transfer of less than all remaining rights. Since Boyer transferred all remaining rights to Cole, the transfer was an assignment, and **D** is incorrect.

20.   C   An easement is a right to use the land of another. If the right benefits a parcel of realty, that parcel is known as the dominant estate. The parcel which is burdened by the easement is known as the servient estate. If the dominant estate and the servient estate were owned by the same person. and if a right-of-way easement across the servient estate is necessary to provide access to the dominant estate, the sale of either parcel results in an implied easement by necessity. Since Northacre and Southacre were both owned by Archer, and since the only access to Northacre was over the dirt road which crossed Southacre, Barnhart received an implied easement by necessity over Southacre when he purchased it. **C** is, therefore, correct. When the common owner of two parcels uses one of them for the benefit of the other, and when signs of that use are visible, a quasi-easement may exist which passes by implication to the buyer of the parcel which received the benefit of such use. **A** is incorrect, however, because Archer never actually used Northacre or the dirt road which crossed Southacre. A grantor of realty may reserve for himself an easement to use it, and under some circumstances (e.g., strict necessity), such a reservation may be implied. **B** is incorrect, however, because only a grantor can receive an easement by reservation. Ordinarily, an easement of record benefits subsequent owners of the dominant estate even if it is not mentioned in the deeds by which the dominant estate was conveyed to them. When the dominant estate and the servient estate merge (i.e., are owned by the same person), however, all existing easements terminate. **D** is, therefore, incorrect.

21. **B**   Although the existence of an easement may make title to realty unmarketable, most courts hold that this is not so where the buyer was aware of the easement at the time he contracted to purchase the realty. Since Coates saw the dirt road prior to contracting, it is likely that a court would hold that its existence does not prevent the title from being marketable. While it is not certain that a court would come to this conclusion, the argument in **B** is the only one listed which could possibly provide support for Archer's claim. **B** is, therefore, correct. If a buyer accepts a deed which does not conform to the requirements of the purchases contract, he has waived his rights under the contract because the contract is said to merge with the deed. **A** is incorrect, however, because Coates did not accept the deed and so is still protected by the terms of the contract. Marketable title means title that is reasonably secure against attack. Since the existence of an easement would provide the holder of a dominant estate with a ground to attack the rights of the holder of the servient estate, an undisclosed easement is usually sufficient to render title to the servient estate unmarketable. **C** is, therefore, incorrect. A covenant to deliver marketable title is implied in a contract for the sale of realty unless some other quality of title is specified. Since the contract between Archer and Coates did not specify the quality of title to be conveyed, Archer is required to convey marketable title. **D** is, therefore, incorrect.

22. **A**   Every contract for the sale of realty contains an implied covenant by the seller that he will deliver marketable title. Marketable title means title which is reasonably secure against attack. It is generally understood that title to property which is being used in violation of a zoning law is not marketable. If a seller is unable to deliver marketable title, the buyer is not required to complete the transaction because no person should be required to purchase potential litigation. Since Foley's agreement to purchase the house was connected with his purchase of the business, it is likely that a court would find that the zoning violation constitutes a defect which excuses Foley from going through with the purchase. Although it is not certain that a court would come to this conclusion, **A** is the only option which could possibly be correct. **B** and **C** are incorrect because the courts usually hold that an existing zoning violation makes title unmarketable. **D** is incorrect because a public law which prohibits a particular activity takes precedence over a private rule which permits it.

23. **A**   Ordinarily zoning laws determine the use to which land may be put. Thus, if the zoning law permits the construction of a three story office building, Graves may construct it. **A** is, therefore, correct. **B** is incorrect because there is no rule which requires a court to permit the highest and best use of realty. Although an easement for air, light, and view may be created by express grant, **C** is incorrect because courts do not recognize an implied easement for air, light, or view. If land was being used in a way which violates a zoning law passed after the use began, the non-conforming use is permitted to continue. **D** is incorrect, however, because the non-conforming use is never *required* to continue.

24. **C**   Developers are permitted to create conditions on the use of land in their subdivisions which are more restrictive than public laws. Thus, even where zoning law permits a particular activity, deed restrictions may validly prohibit it. Since restrictions contained in all the deeds to land in Green Hills prohibit the keeping of horses, a court will enforce these restrictions, and Ralph should receive the relief which he seeks. **C** is, therefore, correct, and **A** is, therefore, incorrect. Where a zoning law restricts land to residential use but does not define that use, the resolution of a dispute about whether that activity can be conducted there will depend on whether that activity is part of ordinary residential use. **B** is incorrect, however, because the deed restrictions in Green Hills clearly prohibit the keeping of horses. Although a court may enjoin a nuisance, **D** is incorrect because a court may enforce the deed restrictions without regard to whether keeping horses is a nuisance.

25. C   A fee simple determinable on special limitation is a fee interest which will terminate automatically upon the happening of a specified event. Courts almost always hold that a grant to a particular grantee "so long as" something does not happen creates this interest. C is, therefore, correct. Although an interest which might vest after a period measured by a life or lives in being plus twenty one years is void under the rule against perpetuities, this does not affect the validity of any prior estate. For this reason, even if the interest of the Foundation for Hereditary Diseases violates this rule against perpetuities, that has no effect on the validity of Geller's interest. A is, therefore, incorrect. A fee simple absolute is complete ownership which is not subject to defeasance. B is incorrect because of the special limitation created by the phrase "so long as." A fee simple subject to a condition subsequent is an interest which is subject to defeasance on the happening of a specified event, but which does not terminate until the holder of the future interest takes some step to make his/her interest possessory. D is incorrect because the phrase "so long as" results in an automatic termination upon the happening of the specified event and because the period described by the rule against perpetuities has no effect on an interest which is already possessory.

26. C   Under the rule against perpetuities, no interest is good unless it must vest, if at all, during a period measured by a life or lives in being plus twenty one years. Since liquor might be sold on the premises after the expiration of this period, it is possible that the interest of the Foundation for Hereditary diseases would vest beyond the period of perpetuities. For this reason, its interest is void. C is, therefore, correct. The future interest of a charity is not subject to the rule against perpetuities if it follows the estate of another charity. Otherwise, the rule against perpetuities applies as it would to any other grantee. A is incorrect because there is no indication that Geller is a charity. B is incorrect because only a grantor can hold a right of re-entry. An executory interest is a future interest which follows an estate which is not certain to terminate. If it follows the estate of a grantor, it is a springing executory interest. D is incorrect, however, because the interest of the Foundation for Hereditary Diseases is void as explained above.

TABLE OF CASES

REFERENCES TO
RESTATEMENT OF PROPERTY

SUBJECT-MATTER INDEX

Products for 1999-00 Academic Year

Law In A Flash Flashcards

Flashcards

Civil Procedure 1 ◆	$17.95
Civil Procedure 2 ◆	17.95
Constitutional Law ▲	18.95
Contracts ◆▲	17.95
Corporations	18.95
Criminal Law ◆▲	17.95
Criminal Procedure ▲	17.95
Evidence ▲	17.95
Federal Income Tax*	
Future Interests ▲	17.95
Professional Responsibility (952 cards)	34.95
Real Property ◆▲	18.95
Sales (UCC Article 2) ▲	17.95
Torts ◆▲	18.95
Wills & Trusts	17.95

*Delivery date to be announced

Flashcard Sets

First Year Law Set	99.95

(includes all sets marked ◆ *plus* the book
Strategies & Tactics for First Year Law.)

Multistate Bar Review Set	175.00

(includes all sets marked ▲ *plus* the book
Strategies & Tactics for MBE)

Professional Responsibility Special

Professional Responsibility Flashcards + Strategies & Tactics for the MPRE	$49.95

Law In A Flash Software

Every *Law In A Flash* title and set is available as software.

Requirements: 386, 486, or Pentium-based computer running Windows® 3.1, Windows® 95, or Windows® 98; 16 megabytes RAM; 3.5" high-density floppy drive; 3MB free space per title

- Contains the complete text of the corresponding *Law In A Flash* printed flashcards
- Side-by-side comparison of your own answer to the card's preformulated answer
- Fully customizable, savable sessions — pick which topics to review and in what order
- Mark cards for further review or printing

Individual titles	$19.95
Professional Responsibility (covers 953 cards)	35.95
First Year Law Set*	115.00
Multistate Bar Review Set*	195.00

* These software sets contain the same titles as printed card sets *plus* the corresponding *Strategies & Tactics* books (see below).

Law In A Flash Combo Packs

Flashcards + software, together at a substantial saving.

Individual titles in combo packs	$30.95
Professional Responsibility combo pack	48.95

(Sorry, LIAF Combo packs are not available in sets.)

Strategies & Tactics Series

Strategies & Tactics for the MBE

Packed with the most valuable advice you can find on how to successfully attack the MBE. Each MBE subject is covered, including Criminal Procedure (part of Criminal Law), Future Interests (part of Real Property), and Sales (part of Contracts). The book contains 350 actual past MBE questions broken down by subject, plus a full-length 200-question practice MBE. Each question has a ***fully-detailed answer*** which describes in detail not only why the correct answer is correct, but why each of the wrong answer choices is wrong. Covers the MBE specifications tested on and after July, 1997.

$34.95

Strategies & Tactics for the First Year Law Student

A complete guide to your first year of law school, from the first day of class to studying for exams. Packed with the inside information that will help you survive what most consider the worst year of law school and come out on top.

$12.95

Strategies & Tactics for the MPRE

Packed with exam tactics that help lead you to the right answers and expert advice on spotting and avoiding the traps set by the Bar Examiners. Contains actual questions from past MPRE's, with detailed answers.

$19.95

(This page intentionally left blank)

SAMPLE BRIEFING SHEET

Briefing cases helps you learn an important skill — the ability to extract the important and relevant elements from a case. We have designed a briefing sheet to help you get the most information possible from each case you read. This sheet is designed to help you see the "big picture" (i.e., how this case fits into the subject as a whole), and to give you practice applying the *I-R-A-C* format of exam question analysis (**I**ssue, **R**ule, **A**pplication of Rule to facts, **C**onclusion) in your everyday studies.

Please feel free to make as many copies of this sheet as you need, or visit our website at **http://www.emanuel.com** to download additional copies.

(This page intentionally left blank)

Case Brief

Brief Number: _____ **Date:** _____

Course: _____

Case Information

Case name: _____
_____

Court: _____

Plaintiff: _____

Defendant: _____

Other parties: _____
_____

Case Type
(Select all that apply)

❏ Landmark case   ❏ Statement of majority rule   ❏ Statement of minority rule
❏ Historical case   ❏ Important dissenting opinion   ❏ Statement of older, superseded rule
❏ Bad decision   ❏ Other: _____

Fact Pattern

Facts: _____
_____
_____
_____
_____
_____
_____

Keywords: _____

Procedural History

Prior procedural history: _____
_____
_____
_____

Lower court decision: _____

This court's ruling: _____

Concise Rule of Law

Rule of case: _____
_____
_____
_____
_____

Emanuel Publishing Corp. / 1865 Palmer Avenue / Larchmont, NY 10538 / (800) EMANUEL / Internet: http://www.emanuel.com

Issue #1 **Issue:** _____

_____

_____

Rule of law: _____

_____

Rationale (Application of law to facts): _____

_____

_____

_____

_____

_____

Issue #2
(if applicable) **Issue:** _____

_____

_____

Rule of law: _____

_____

Rationale (Application of law to facts): _____

_____

_____

_____

_____

_____

Issue #3
(if applicable) **Issue:** _____

_____

_____

Rule of law: _____

_____

Rationale (Application of law to facts): _____

_____

_____

_____

_____

_____

Emanuel Publishing Corp. / 1865 Palmer Avenue / Larchmont, NY 10538 / (800) EMANUEL / Internet: http://www.emanuel.com

(This page intentionally left blank)

You can only SHEPARDIZE® using SHEPARD'S®

No other citations service gives you the quality, reliability, and currentness of next generation SHEPARD'S.
SHEPARD'S® Citations Service exclusively on the LEXIS®-NEXIS® services.
You won't find it online anywhere else.

Shepard's®

The Next Generation

Exclusively from

LEXIS Publishing™

LEXIS-NEXIS • MARTINDALE-HUBBELL
MATTHEW BENDER • MICHIE • SHEPARD'S

www.lexis.com™/*lawschool*

We'd like to know . . . .
Emanuel on *Property* (4th Ed.)

We value your opinions on our study aids. After all, we design them for *your* use, and if you think we could do something better, we want to know about it. Please take a moment to fill out this survey and feedback form and return it to us.

We'll enter you in our monthly drawing where 5 people will win the study aid of their choice! If you don't want to identify yourself, that's OK, but you'll be ineligible for the drawing.

Name: _____ Address: _____

City: _____ State: _____ Zip: _____ E-mail: _____

Law school attended: _____ Graduation year: _____

Please rate this product on a scale of 1 to 5:

General readability (style, format, etc.)................................*Poor*	① ② ③ ④ ⑤	*Excellent*		
Length of outline (number of pages).............................*Too short*	① ② ③ ④ ⑤	*Too long*		
Casebook Correlation Chart ....*Not useful*	① ② ③ ④ ⑤	*Useful*		
Capsule Summary: Length...................................*Too short*	① ② ③ ④ ⑤	*Too long*		
Usefulness...............................*Not useful*	① ② ③ ④ ⑤	*Useful*		
Chapter Review and essay questions.........................*Not useful*	① ② ③ ④ ⑤	*Useful*		
Tables and subject-matter index ....*Not useful*	① ② ③ ④ ⑤	*Useful*		
Outline's coverage of material presented in class..............*Incomplete*	① ② ③ ④ ⑤	*Complete*		
OVERALL RATING...*Poor*	① ② ③ ④ ⑤	***Excellent***		

Suggestions for improvement: _____

_____

_____

☞ **What other study aids did you use in this course?** _____

_____

☞ **If you liked any features of these other study aids, describe them:** _____

_____

_____

☞ **What casebook(s) did you use in this course?** _____

☞ **For other subjects, what study aids other than Emanuel do you use, and what features do you like about them?** ____

_____

_____

☞ **Please list the items you would like us to add to our product line:**

Outline subjects: _____

Flashcard subjects: _____

Other products (e.g., software, multimedia, etc.): _____

☞ **If you win our drawing, what one study aid would you like?** _____

Send to: *Emanuel Law* **Survey**   OR   Fax to: *(914) 834-5186*
            1865 Palmer Avenue, Suite 202
            Larchmont, NY 10538

Cut here

**Please
complete & return
the Survey Form
on the other side**